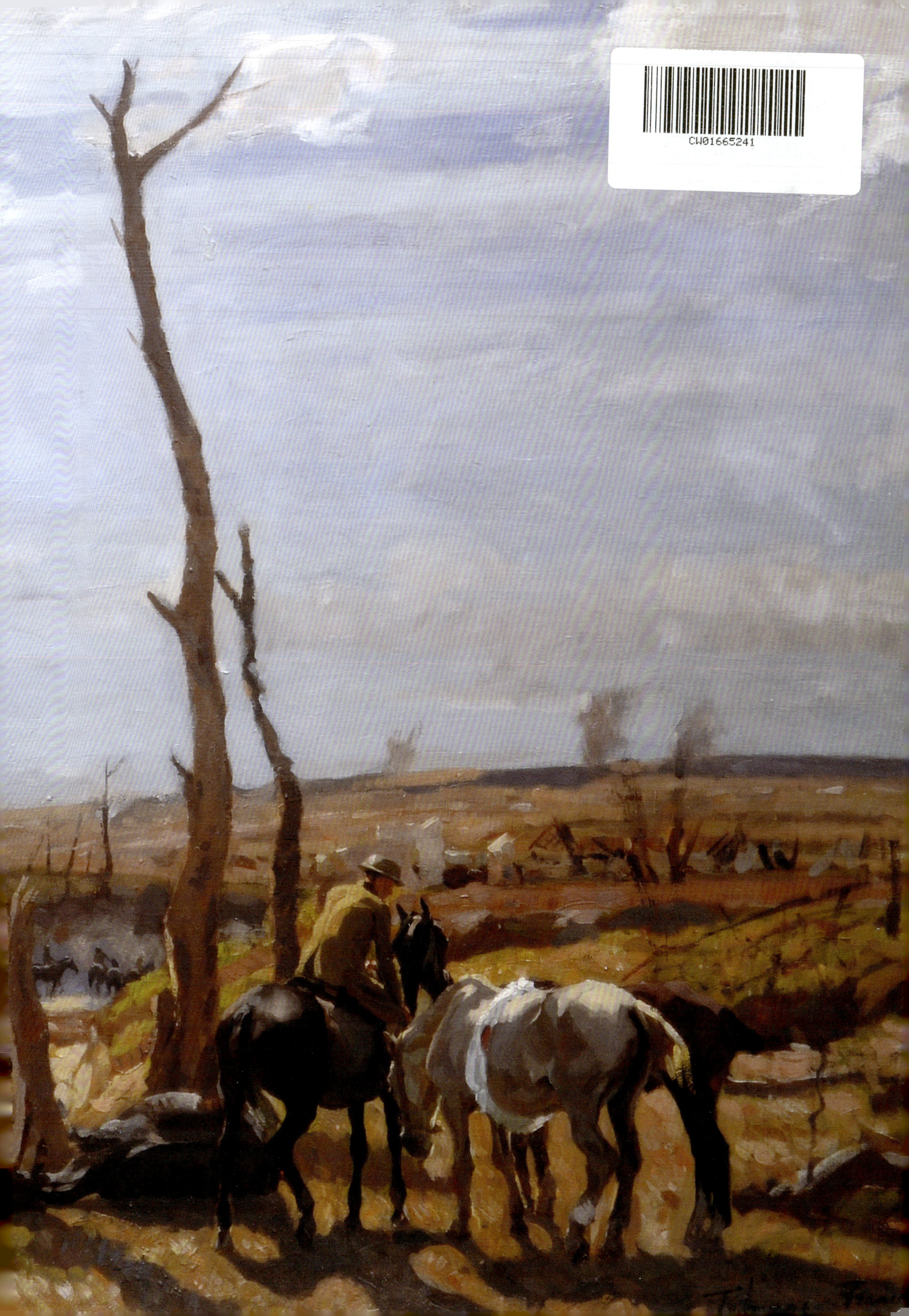

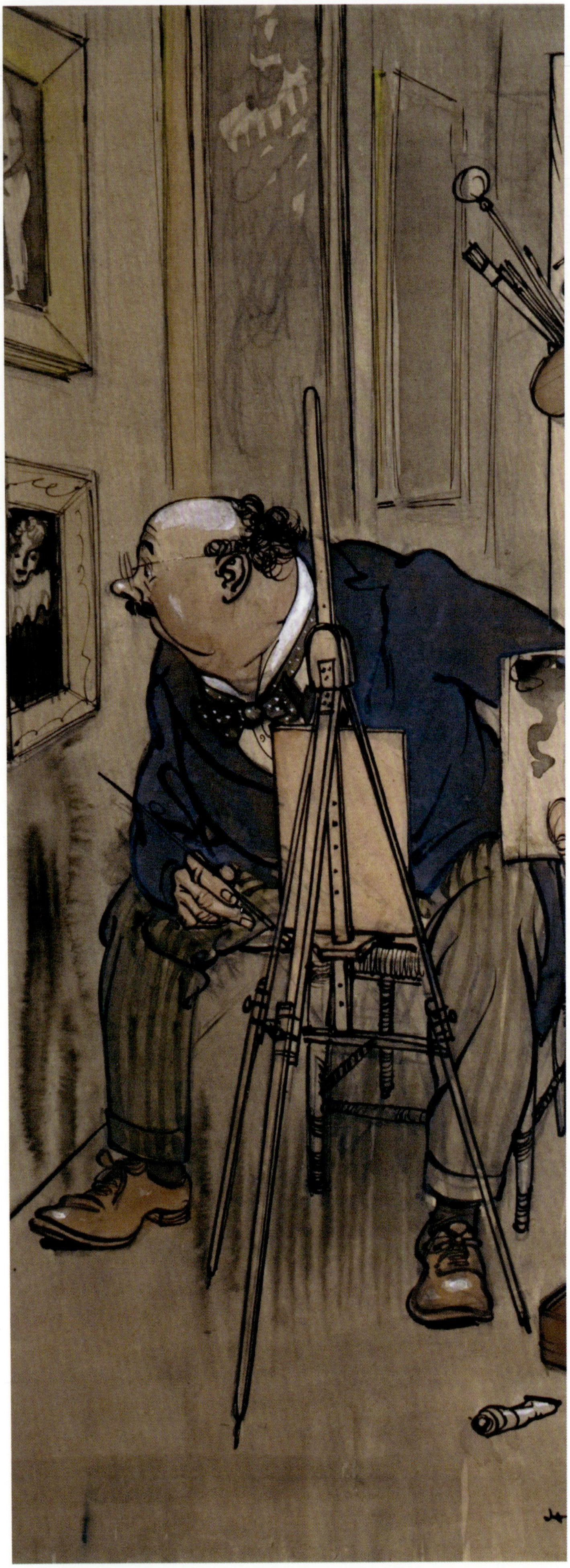

8 & 10 Ryder Street
St James's
London SW1Y 6QB
020 7839 7551
gallery@chrisbeetles.com
www.chrisbeetles.com

ISBN 978-1-914906-00-8

Cataloguing in publication data is available
from the British Library

A Chris Beetles Ltd Publication

General Editor: Chris Beetles

Researched and written by David Wootton,
with contributions from Alexander Beetles,
Kenneth McConkey & Fiona Nickerson

Edited by Pascale Oakley and David Wootton

Design by Pascale Oakley

Photography by Julian Huxley-Parlour
Reproduction by www.cast2create.com
Colour separation and printing by Geoff Neal Litho Limited

Front cover: George Clausen, *The Budding Tree* [**4**]

Front endpaper: Algernon Talmage,
Wounded Horses Returning from the Front, France [**41**]

This page: H M Bateman,
Student Day at the National Gallery [detail of **30**]

Title page: S R Badmin, *Cliff Path, Richmond, Yorks* [**158**]

Page 5: William Orpen, *The Woman in White* [detail of **27**]

Page 175: S R Badmin, *Preparing London for the Summer*
[detail of **129**]

Back endpaper: S R Badmin,
The Season Commences – Richmond [**132**]

Back cover: Frank Archer, *Refugees* [**181**]

A CENTURY OF BRITISH ART

VOLUME ONE

1900–1945

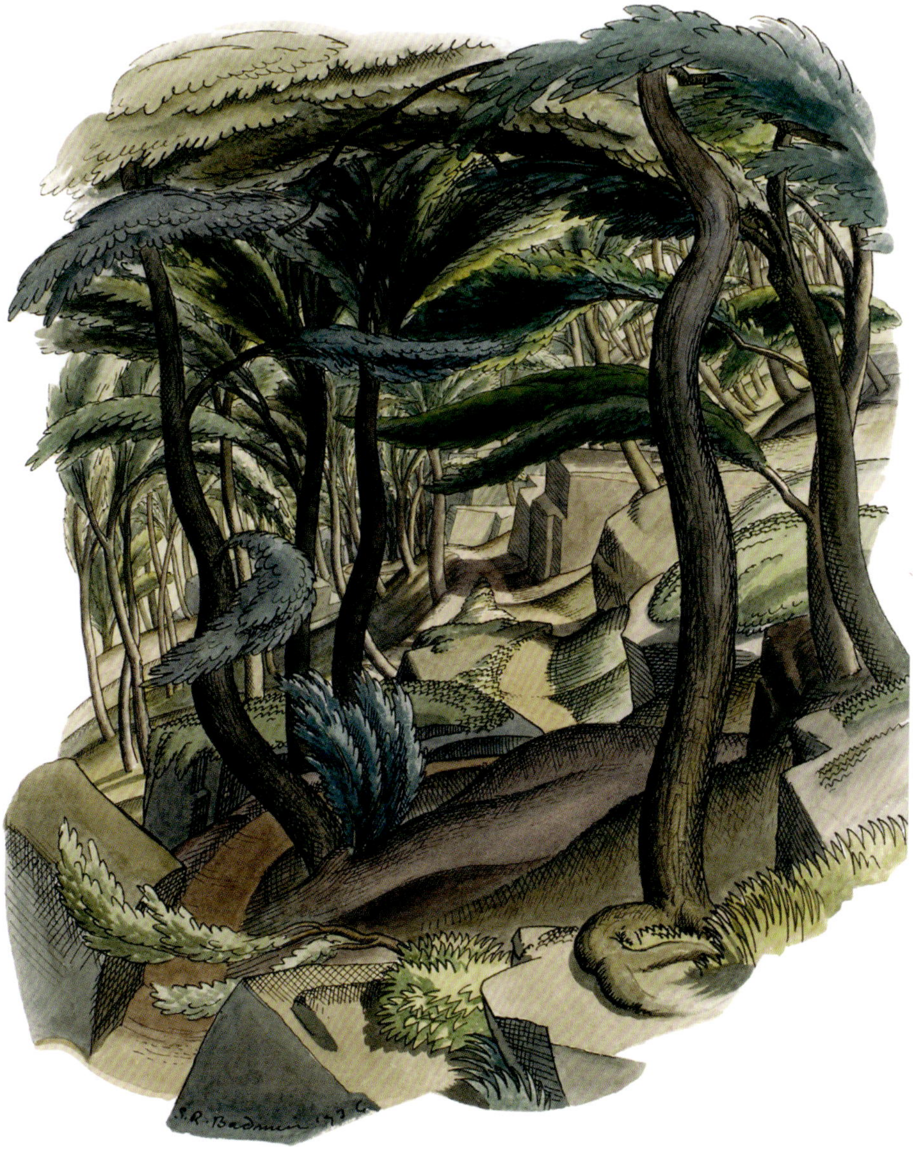

CHRIS BEETLES GALLERY

CONTENTS

CATALOGUE

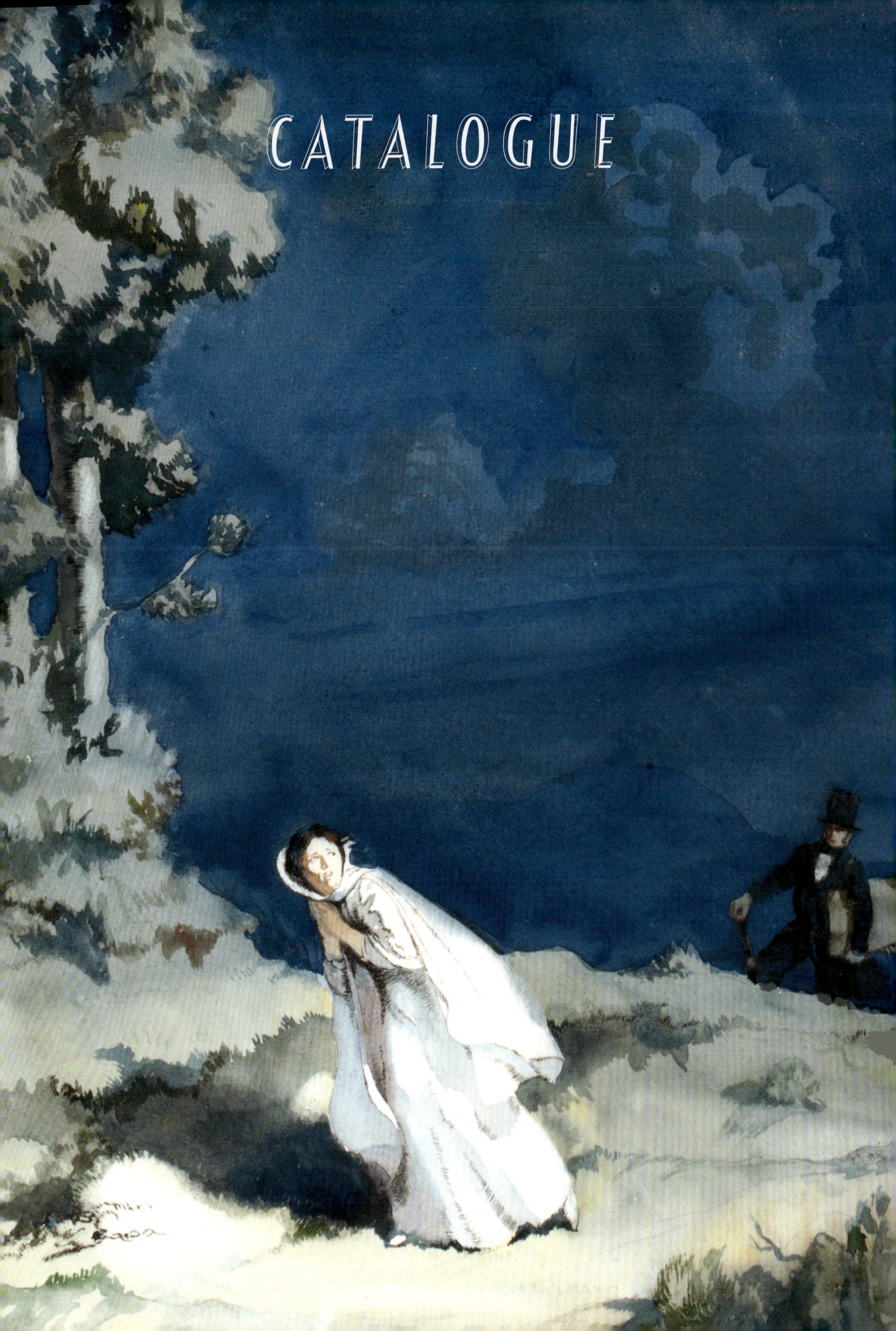

1: EDWARDIAN IMPRESSIONISM

The character of British art in the period between the death of Queen Victoria in 1901 and the outbreak of the First World War in 1914 may, like that of many others, be considered rich and complex. However, from among the many and competing artistic approaches, a new norm – which might be conveniently termed *Edwardian Impressionism* – could be seen to emerge. This new norm was the result of the gradual and protracted acceptance of the principles of French Impressionism, and of an understanding of how to integrate it, both conceptually and practically, into the native tradition.

During the last quarter of the nineteenth century, many British artists were drawn to Paris in order to experience a less rigid system of art education. In so doing, they were also directly exposed to both the artistic tradition and the landscape of France. Few were immediately affected by the techniques of those painters who, from 1874, exhibited as the Impressionists. Rather they were influenced by the Naturalism of the Impressionists' antecedents and contemporaries, and especially by that of Jules Bastien-Lepage. He advocated the practice of painting studies in the open air (*en plein air*) as a way of informing, even enlivening, the canvases produced in the studio. The recurrent subject matter of his canvases – the harsh yet heroic lives of rural workers – was also highly inspiring. Soon numerous groups of Naturalist artists established themselves across Britain, of which the Newlyn School in Cornwall is exemplary.

If Bastien-Lepage provided one way of absorbing French developments, the American expatriate, James McNeill Whistler, offered another. While he was studying in Paris, he became acquainted with key figures of the avant-garde, including Edgar Degas, who even invited him to exhibit with the Impressionists in 1874. While he declined that offer, he accepted some of the group's principles and helped import their visual economy and their modernity into Britain. Notably, he encouraged his disciples to attend to the qualities of oriental art, and to depict the beauty and vitality of urban life.

Though he was too individualistic, even argumentative, to remain a member, Whistler was instrumental in the foundation, in 1886, of the New English Art Club. This society was intended to promote Impressionism and other progressive tendencies and so provide an alternative to the artistic establishment represented by the Royal Academy of Arts. Nevertheless, as the NEAC consolidated its position, many of its members evolved an art that demonstrated the correlations between the French Impressionists and such totemic exponents of the British tradition as Anthony Van Dyck and Thomas Gainsborough in portraiture (see, for instance, the work of John Singer Sargent) and J M W Turner and John Constable in landscape (see Philip Wilson Steer).

The trajectory of Impressionism in Britain can be better understood by focussing on the development of one founder member of the New English Art Club: George Clausen. During his early career, he filtered his experiences of Dutch and French Naturalism in order to create his own distinctive strain of – sometimes stark – ruralist imagery. When some of his paintings were attacked by critics, whose aesthetics had been honed by regular engagement with the Royal Academy's exhibits, he ceased to submit work to that institution for a period of six years. Instead, he advanced his art and raised his profile through his membership of the NEAC. By the time that he returned to exhibiting at the RA in 1891, he had aligned himself more closely to French Impressionism, by brightening his palette, applying paint swiftly in separated strokes, and emphasising effects of light. Though more technically radical than his earlier approach, this new one proved more acceptable to both the critics and the public, especially when it involved more 'English' colours and gentler motifs. Clausen was also accepted by the Academicians, who elected him an associate in 1895, and appointed him Professor of Painting at its Schools in 1903. In that position, he urged students to scrutinise the Old Masters, so acknowledging the importance of tradition to his own art, and the assimilation of Impressionism into the academy.

Owen Baxter Morgan was two decades younger than Clausen, and a student at the RA Schools in the 1890s. His work demonstrates how dominant an artistic language Impressionism became in early twentieth-century London [12]. In fact, it was accepted across Britain, as is exemplified by the Whistlerian tonality employed by the Liverpudlian, James Hamilton Hay [8-9], or the delicate *Japoniste* approach to composition applied by the Scot, Edwin Alexander [13-14]. In many ways, the British brand of Impressionism chimed with the optimism of the Edwardian age, presenting an idealised image of the heart of the Empire and 'the green and pleasant land' evoked by Sir Hubert Parry in his 1916 setting of William Blake's *Jerusalem*. As such, it would also provide an idea of what Britain was fighting for as it entered the First World War.

In its adoption by the British, Impressionism shed its radical status. Indeed, it seemed almost comforting in comparison to the plethora of subsequent avant-garde '-isms' developed in the wake of the two Post-Impressionist exhibitions mounted by Roger Fry at the Grafton Galleries in 1910 and 1912. Nevertheless, it introduced a new freedom of expression into British art, and one that has lasted to this day.

GEORGE CLAUSEN

Sir George Clausen, RA RSW RWS HRBA RI ROI NEAC
(1852-1944)

George Clausen absorbed a range of Continental influences to become a significant *plein-air* artist of scenes of rural life in oil, watercolour and pastel. The striking, sometime stark naturalism that he learned from Bastien-Lepage and Millet gave way to a light-filled, atmospheric Impressionism. While promoting new developments in painting as a leading member of the New English Art Club, he was eventually accepted by more established societies of artists, including the Royal Academy, becoming a notable Professor of Painting at the Royal Academy Schools.

In addition to his distinctive landscapes – both with and without figures – he essayed portraits, nudes, interiors and still life compositions, and produced occasional, but significant murals, one of which was recognised with a knighthood.

For a biography of George Clausen, please refer to pages 176-177.

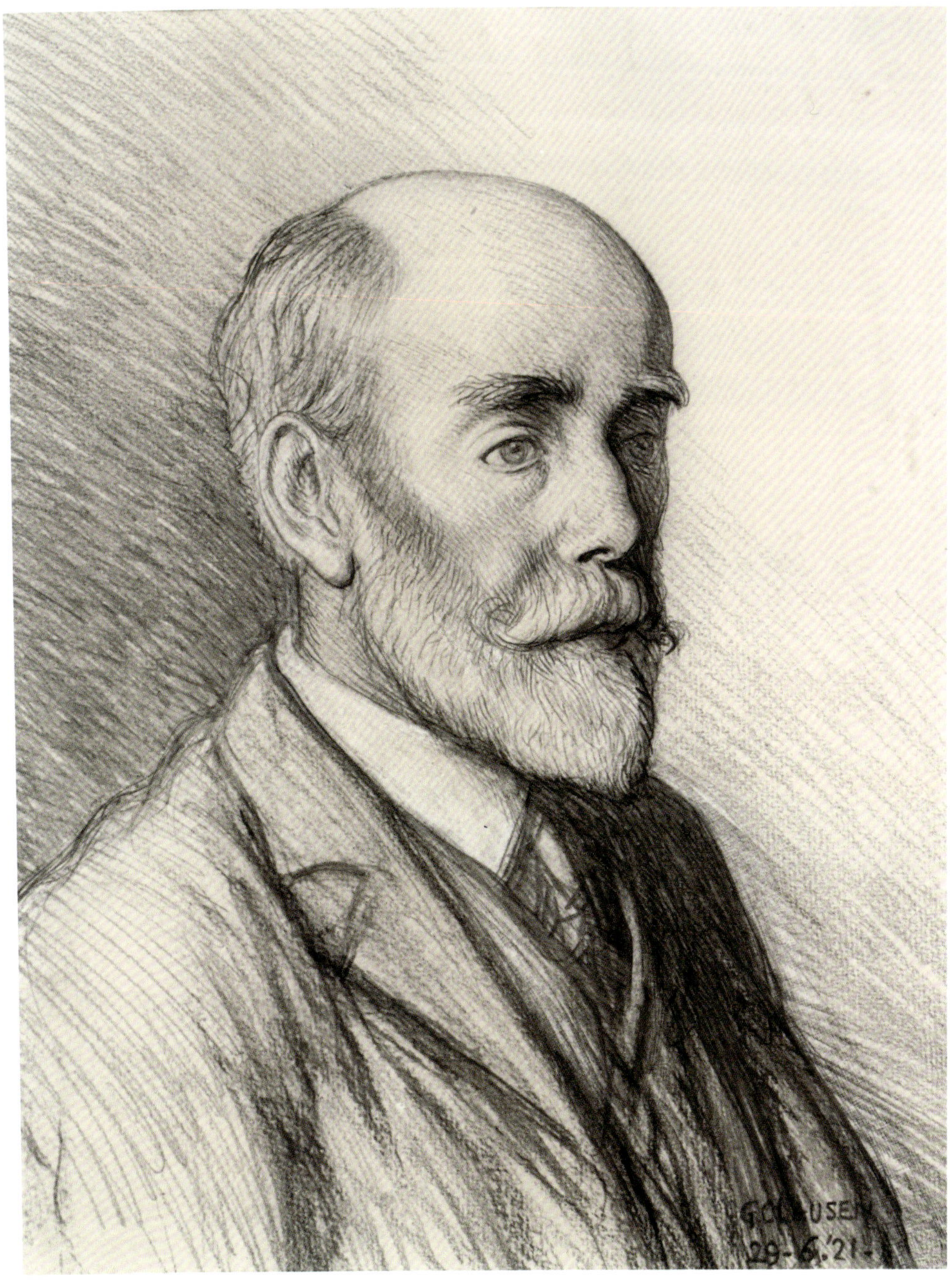

Self-Portrait

George Clausen produced self-portraits across his career – variously in oil, pen, pencil and etching – in which he often showed himself with a brush in his hand, scrutinising his own image, latterly through spectacles. One such is the painted self-portrait of 1920 used as the frontispiece to Dyneley Hussey's monograph of 1923. By contrast, the present drawing of June 1921 suggests a moment of contemplation. He produced it at the time that magazines were beginning to cover his major mural project for the entrance hall of High Royd, Honley, near Huddersfield, Yorkshire, the home of the accountant, G P Norton.

1 **Self-Portrait**
Signed and dated 29.6.'21
Pencil
12 x 9 inches
Provenance: Private Collection of Dr Chris Beetles

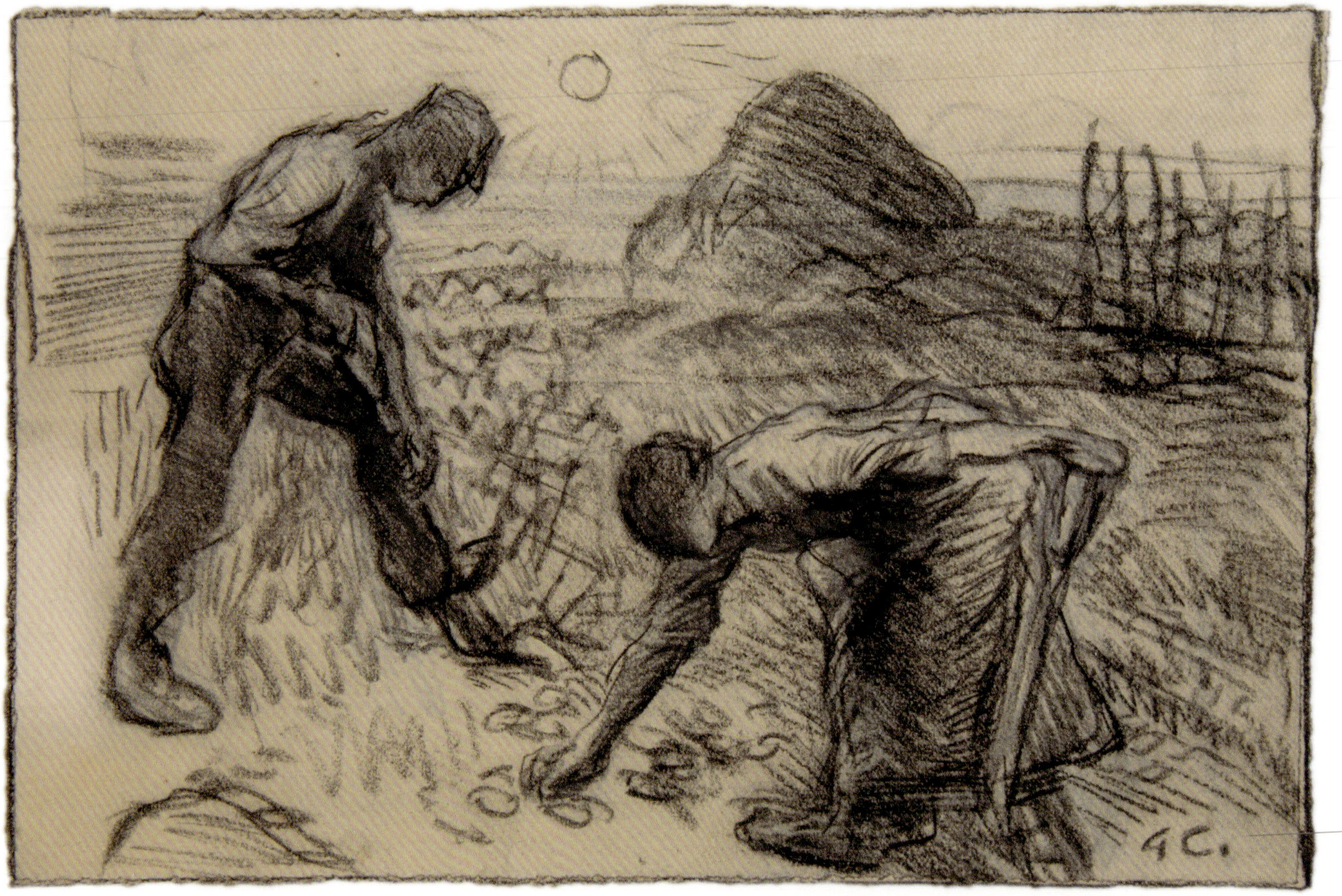

3 **Hay Barn** (opposite)
Signed
Also signed with initials on stone
Lithograph
12 x 9 inches
Provenance: Sir Frederick Wedmore
Literature: Frank Gibson, 'The Etchings and Lithographs of George Clausen, RA', *The Print Collector's Quarterly*, July 1921, Vol 8, No 2: No 2
Exhibited: 'The Society of XII', Messrs Obach & Co, 168 New Bond Street, London, 1905

2 **Allotment Gardens**
Signed with initials
Charcoal on tinted paper
5 ¼ x 7 ¾ inches

Allotment Gardens

The present drawing by George Clausen is a study for his oil on canvas, *Allotment Gardens* (private collection). It is one of at least six studies for the painting, five others being in the collections of the Royal Academy of Arts. Clausen produced the drawings and painting while living at Widdington, in Essex, and based them on the view from his cottage. The finished composition depicts tied labourers digging potatoes on their own plot of land at the end of a full day's work. When exhibited at the Royal Academy of Arts in 1899, as No 115, it suggested to a number of critics the strong influence of the French Realist, Jean-François Millet, and especially one of his most famous paintings, *The Angelus* (1857-59, Musée d'Orsay), which the artist had originally titled 'Prayer for the Potato Crop'. Nevertheless, others commented on its own particular naturalism and immediacy, a writer for *The Graphic* calling the male figure 'a very true type of English rustic character', and one for *The Magazine of Art* stating, in 1900, that the whole 'breathes the very life of the fields'.

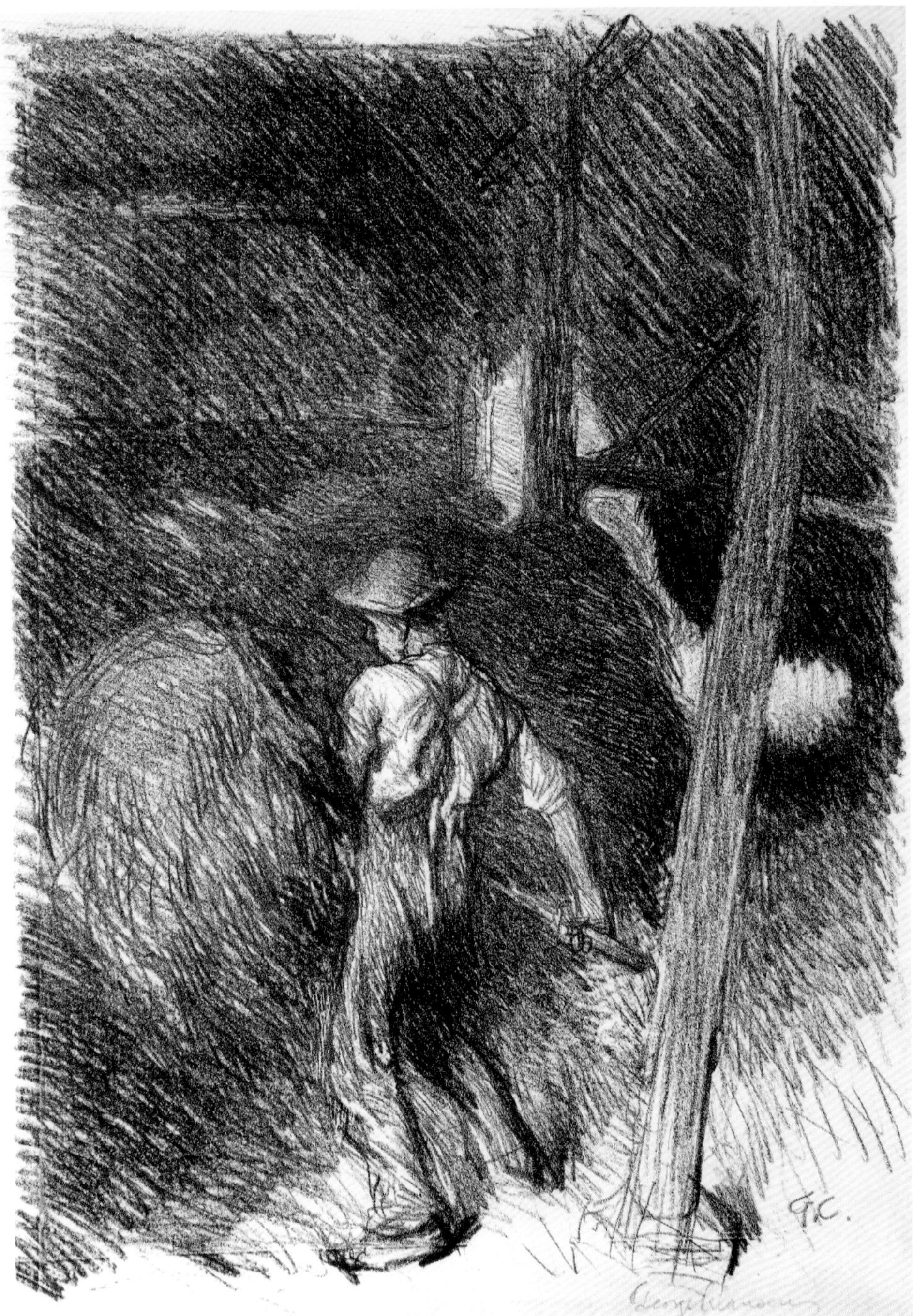

Hay Barn

George Clausen made a small number of lithographs during the period 1895 to 1907, and then abandoned the medium for nearly a decade. The early group rehearses favourite rural motifs, including labourers at work inside a barn, as is represented by the work included here. This lithograph probably relates to a painting of the same title that Clausen exhibited at the Royal Academy of Arts in 1896 (No 838). When he returned to lithography, in 1917, it was in order to create a series of images showing aspects of the production of guns, as one of the limited edition publications issued by the government during the First World War.

An impression of the present work was included in the second exhibition of the Society of XII, held at Messrs Obach & Co, 168 New Bond Street, in 1905. This society was founded in 1903 by Muirhead Bone to raise the status of printmaking, and he acted as its Secretary. In addition to Bone and Clausen, the original members were David Young Cameron, Charles Conder (died 1909), Edward Gordon Craig, Augustus John, Thomas Sturge Moore, William Nicholson, Charles Ricketts, William Rothenstein, Charles Shannon and William Strang. In addition, Alphonse Legros (died 1911) was made an honorary member. In 1907, the society was strengthened by the election of Francis Dodd (Bone's brother-in-law), William Orpen and James Havard Thomas; in 1909, by the election of Ernest Cole; and, in 1910, by the election of Henry Lamb, Walter Sickert and Ian Strang (William's son). The society's final exhibition was held in 1915, by which time Messrs Obach had joined forces with P & D Colnaghi. Clausen contributed drawings to all eight of its exhibitions, and prints to three of them.

KENNETH MCCONKEY

George Clausen's *The Budding Tree*

In 1904 George Clausen stood before an audience of critics, *cognoscenti* and Royal Academy students to deliver the first of a highly successful series of lectures.[1] After 23 years of country living, the artist was returning to the London of his childhood as the Academy's newly appointed Professor of Painting. A permanent move from his old stamping ground in rural Essex in the summer of the following year would become necessary and the new abode – a spacious villa in St John's Wood – saw a complete change in his and his family's way of life. As a painter, Clausen had been known as the champion of the work patterns of the English countryside, and had you been let loose to explore his studio in that year you would find many studies of field workers – shepherds, woodmen, harvesters – who derived their living from the land. Sketchbooks were filled with notes on farmyards, fields and trees; there were even delightful small studies of orchards, hayricks and sheepfolds, but there were very few larger oil paintings that did not primarily address the human figure in such settings. Looking at current works on the easel at the time of his appointment, such as *Gleaners Coming Home* (1904, oil on canvas, Tate), would confirm these observations. Women and children are returning from the fields, heavily laden with bundles of wheat, under a canopy of trees that fringe a country lane. Sunlight filters through the foliage picking out their forms in the dappled shade. This, it would seem, marked the apex of the new professor's career.

But what had those former years working on the rich farmlands of Hertfordshire, Berkshire and Essex taught him, and what experience did he have to impart to his students? As a young artist, his first impetus had been to sweep away the old stereotypical inhabitants of the countryside – the swains and shepherdesses who peopled the counterfeit landscapes that delighted the Victorian *bourgeoisie*. His sights were elsewhere on the realistic truth of 'Courbet, Millet, Manet, and Bastien-Lepage ...' from whose 'Naturalism' he hoped to create a new 'National Art'.[2] In time this had been modified by Impressionism, by the study of light and colour, that brought the group of gleaners vividly before visitors to the Royal Academy exhibition in 1904. The rebel had conquered the establishment. Its walls were tumbling down.

But had these same observers checked their catalogues they would have found that changes were also afoot. Elsewhere in the exhibition there was an unusual painting of *Willow Trees at Sunset* in which no figures were present (1904, oil on canvas, Private Collection). Clausen had painted a picture in which the trees by a pond or country stream, had no particular distinction, and, ostensibly, the subject was missing. There were no proud elms or 'hearts of oak' here; just a well-felt evening light crossing a field and softening the contours of the wayward stumps on the bank in the foreground.

In the next ten years the character of Clausen's work developed in new directions. His duties in the Academy Schools meant that visits to his favourite haunts were restricted, but not completely lost, and while he continued to remain in contact with the farms around his former Essex home, the terrain, once so familiar as a backdrop, was now being viewed more objectively for its unique properties. He would stand on Duton Hill, survey the neighbouring villages and cycle the miles north from here to Widdington and Tilty, and west to Rickling and Clavering. Observing labourers' cottages and ancient barns dating from the Domesday Book, he pedalled towards the squat Tudor tower of the church of St Mary and St Clement, seen in *Clavering Church* (circa 1909, oil on canvas, National Museum of Wales, Cardiff).[3]

On one of these forays, perhaps on a bank of the little river Stort, encircling the parish on its western side, Clausen noted a tree coming into bud. It was early spring, and while the other trees on the opposite bank had been pollarded, this specific specimen stood tall against the twilight glow. Beyond the gate and across the field was human habitation – a thatched cottage with the sun striking its white gable wall. As in *Willow Trees at Sunset*, light was the unifying factor, yet here the tree, regular in shape, was not merely a framing motif, but was in itself, the focus of attention and the subject of the present picture.

Things he had said in his lectures now came vividly to mind. Having expressed his admiration for Constable's trees in *The Valley Farm* (circa 1835, oil on canvas, Tate), he had remarked that 'one of the most difficult things in painting is to paint a tree' and how easy it is to become 'confused ... with the infinity of detail'. 'One often sees,' he continued,

> ... trees painted that look all cut out at the edges, like trees on the stage, and when we look at the edges of a tree against the sky, we see that they look cut out too; but if we look at the tree as a whole – as a great green dome, spreading up and rounding into the sky, with the light showing on it and through it – if we realize this, we can get a little nearer to our tree.[4]

He had, of course, been objecting to the Victorian landscapist's trees that are shaped to become decorative motifs. At the same time 'infinity of detail' needed to be avoided and in support of his arguments Clausen referred his audience to Joshua Reynolds's *Discourses* where Reynolds describes a landscape painter he met in Rome, who was known for representing every individual leaf on a tree. The artist, by contrast, who

> looked at the general character of the species, the order of the branches, and the masses of the foliage, would in a few minutes produce a more true resemblance of trees, than this painter in many months.[5]

Within this prophetic utterance the battle between leaf-after-leaf Pre-Raphaelite detail and the generality of Impressionism was accurately predicted. Truth, for Clausen, as is evident in the newly rediscovered *The Budding Tree*, lay in the authenticity of the encounter, just as the truth of Bastien-Lepage's peasants of the 1880s had been in representing them 'as they lived'.[6] So also the tree, no matter how ignoble, must be presented as it exists, inhabiting space and filtering light through its branches. Trees were not the ornamentation of landscape as they were for some, nor were they freighted with jingoism. The decorative appendage was not what Clausen saw – any more than Samuel Palmer's blossoming Kentish apple tree was a mere colourful embellishment. Reasoning of this sort had made *The Budding Tree* a creative possibility.

Continues on page 12 ☞

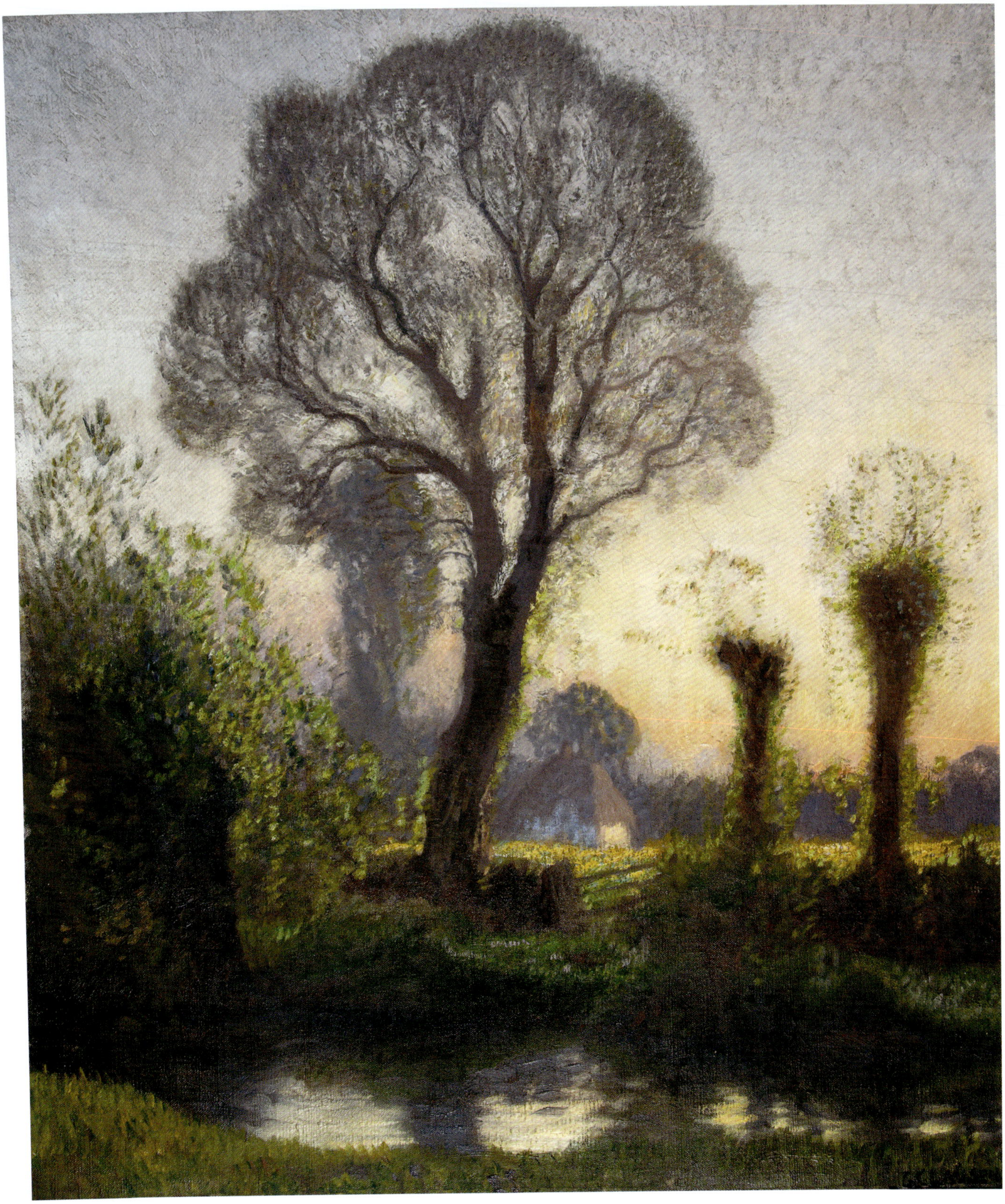

4 **The Budding Tree**
Signed
Inscribed with title on reverse
Oil on canvas
30 x 25 inches
Provenance: The artist until January 1915;
Mr & Mrs RW Sturge, Pendell House, Bletchingley, Surrey, circa 1930s; thence by descent
Literature: *Pall Mall Magazine 'Extra', The Pictures of 1914*, London: Pall Mall Magazine, 1914, Page 97 (illus);
'D H' [Dyneley Hussey], *George Clausen*, London: Ernest Benn, 1923, plate 14;
The Artist, March 1933, Page 24;
Kenneth McConkey, *George Clausen and the picture of English rural life*, Edinburgh: Atelier Books, 2012, Page 162 (Note 121, Page 229)
Exhibited: Royal Academy, Summer Exhibition, 1914, No 383;
Royal Birmingham Society of Artists, January 1915

☞ Yet if after 1905, when the centre of his working life had moved to the St John's Wood studio, there were undoubted moments of frustration. 'Lots of things I see in town I'd like to paint', he wrote to his old friend, Havard Thomas,

> ... in the country one could look at a tree day after day without disturbance and get to understand it, but I've been drawing a little down by the river at St Paul's Cathedral and getting there – through town knocks everything out of my head – then, there one is in the midst of agitations ...[7]

Slow looking, getting to 'understand it', conveys the ambition of *The Budding Tree.* When he quoted Clausen's *Lectures* on the subject, Rex Vicat Cole felt compelled to add, 'familiarity will not in this pursuit breed contempt, but reverence; and casual representation will be replaced in time by free handling, acquired by appreciative knowledge and self-confidence'.[8] In those still moments of the exile's reverie, a contemplative vision emerged.

The picture stood out when shown at the Royal Academy in 1914 as one of four very different submissions.[9] Accompanying *The Budding Tree* was Clausen's portrait of Thomas Okey (Art Workers Guild), author, friend and fellow Guild member, a second was *Primavera,* a studio-based nude, and the third, *In the Fields in June* (National Museum of Wales, Cardiff).[10] Of the four, *Primavera,* dominated the press reports, especially when attacked by a suffragette.[11] Its instant notoriety left *The Budding Tree* under-appreciated at the time, and although war news dominated the papers when it was re-exhibited in Birmingham in January 1915, it was nonetheless acquired by a discerning collector. On this, rather than on the vague classical allusion of *Primavera,* Clausen's path was set for the works of the 1920s. In 1917 he would purchase his own labourer's cottage on Duton Hill and construct a country studio in its garden, so that from here the patient study of light and air in the slow sequences of rebirth in nature could continue.[12] The artist was no romantic pantheist, but he nevertheless addressed the 'sentiment of nature' which, in the great scheme of things, mirrored mankind's rise and fall. For this he was applauded, as a 'true impressionist' who 'does his best when he is entirely possessed by some real scene ... and loses himself as soon as he loses contact with reality'.[13]

The Budding Tree leads us directly to *Sunrise on the Road* (1920, oil on canvas, Ulster Museum, Belfast) and the many landscapes of the inter-war period in which light is only truly perceived as it dissolves into and through the branches of a tree. The 1914 picture contained all the wisdom he had found in studying the work of Claude Lorrain.

'The subject is not the marriage', he declared, when describing Claude's *The Marriage of Isaac and Rebecca* (National Gallery, London),

> ... but the beautiful peep of sunlit country seen through trees. In this picture we may mark how the dark trees accent the sky and the river, and how they have to be painted to express the lightness of the sky. Their colour is sacrificed to their tone. Claude did not wish us to look really at anything but the stretch of open country. We notice the trees, but our eye goes through to the distance ... [14]

The understanding expressed in the landscapes of the 1920s is thus prefigured in *The Budding Tree.* It was the lodestar that carried Clausen through war and pandemic, and its promise of rebirth, became an article of faith. And while recording it demanded serious scrutiny, the wonder remained and was forever.

Notes to George Clausen's *The Budding Tree*

[1] George Clausen, *Royal Academy Lectures on Painting,* London: Methuen & Co, 1913; for reports on the lectures and reviews of their publication, see Kenneth McConkey, *George Clausen and the picture of English rural life,* Edinburgh: Atelier Books, 2012, pages 137-139.

[2] Letter to Robert Macaulay Stevenson, dated 2 March 1886, Private Collection.

[3] These fields are of course now cut by the M11, the main arterial London to Cambridge road.

[4] Clausen 1913, page 101. In quoting this important passage, the conservative Rex Vicat Cole felt compelled to add, 'however, I believe amateurs are not aware of the necessity at all of looking for decorative forms; so, this description of trees seen against the sky should suffice as the basis for closer observation'; Rex Vicat Cole, *The Artistic Anatomy of Trees,* London: Seeley, Service and Co, 1916, page 81.

[5] 'Discourse XI' on 'Genius'; see Robert R Wark (ed), Sir Joshua Reynolds, *Discourses on Art,* New Haven: Yale University Press, 1975, page 199.

[6] George Clausen, 'Bastien-Lepage and Modern Realism', *Scottish Art Review,* vol 1, no 5, October 1888, page 115.

[7] Letter to James Havard Thomas, 21 August 1909, Hyman Kreitman Archive, Tate; quoted in McConkey 2012, page 156.

[8] Vicat Cole, 1916, page 81; Cole quotes Clausen 1913, page 101, as in note 4.

[9] Clausen's account book notes on 28 April 1914 that *The Budding Tree* had been sent to the Academy. After the exhibition it was returned to the artist unsold. It was then dispatched to the Royal Birmingham Society of Arts exhibition for the beginning of the new year. On 12 January 1915 Clausen received a letter from the society conveying an offer of £100 which he accepted and 9 February he received £90 for the picture (less 10% commission).

[10] *In the Fields in June,* a scene representing field workers, was intended to replace a mural that was mooted, but never commissioned for the new museum; see McConkey, 2012, page 164.

[11] Between the closure of the Academy exhibitions and the opening of the Birmingham exhibition, war broke out in August 1914 and these circumstances may well have persuaded the artist to accept a much lower price for the painting than that he had hoped to achieve six months earlier.

[12] McConkey, 2012, pages 162-165. Clausen was broadly in agreement with Alfred East who stressed the importance of the study of trees in his treatise, *The Art of Landscape Painting in Oil Colour,* London: Cassell & Co, 1906, pages 51-63, emphasising the difficulty and subtlety they present, and their change with the seasons.

[13] 'Mr Clausen's Pictures', *The Times,* 12 October 1912, page 8; *The Manchester Guardian,* 21 October 1912, page 6.

[14] Clausen, 1913, pages 98-99.

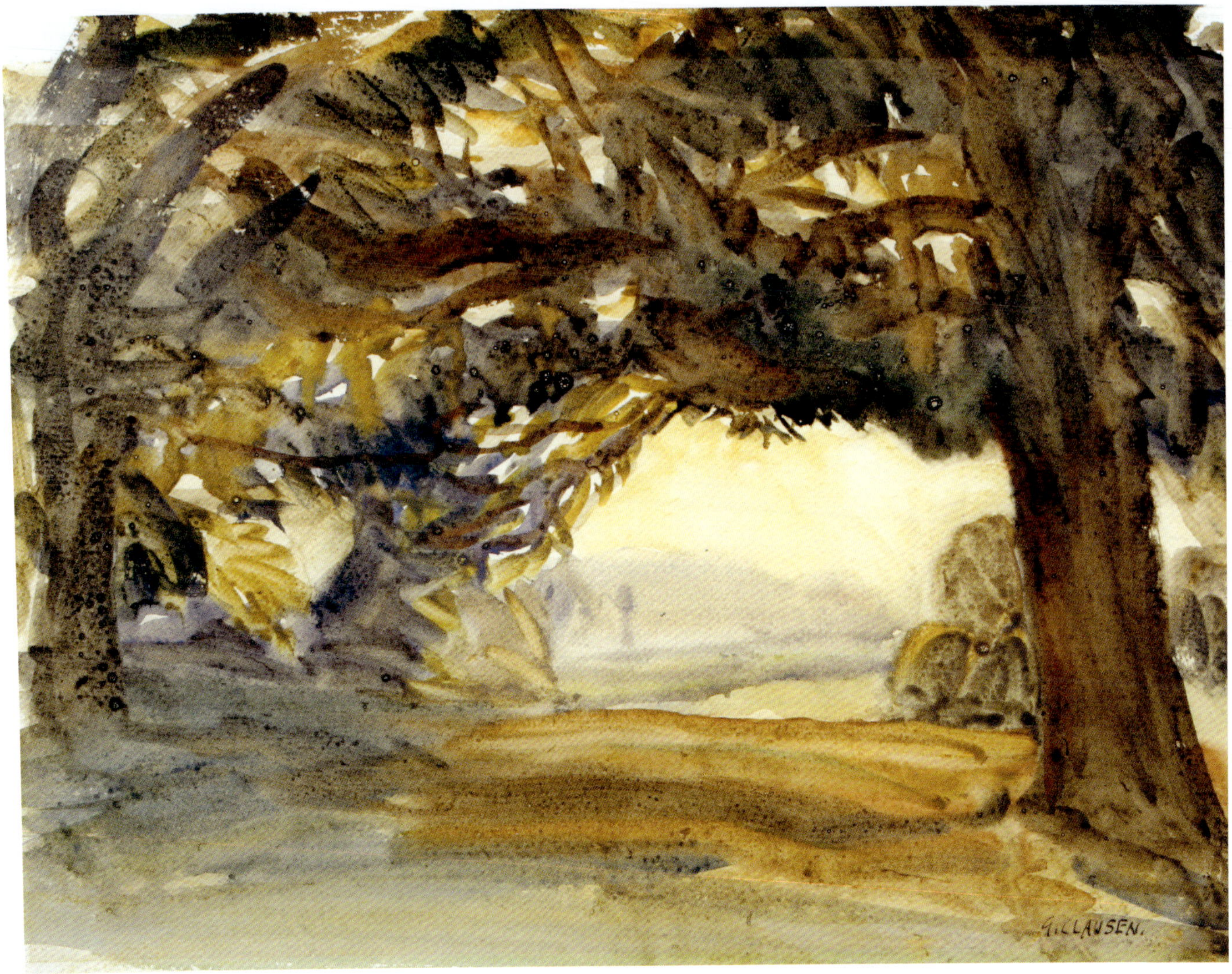

5 **Under the Trees – Evening**
Signed
Watercolour
9 ½ x 11 ¾ inches

Kenneth McConkey *is Emeritus Professor of Art History at the University of Northumbria. He is a leading authority on British, Irish and French painting of the late nineteenth and early twentieth centuries, and especially British Impressionism and the New English Art Club, and the figures of George Clausen and John Lavery. His work on Clausen has spanned his career, and includes, most notably,* Sir George Clausen, RA, 1852-1944 *(the catalogue to the exhibition mounted by Bradford Art Galleries and Museums in 1980) and* George Clausen and the picture of English rural life *(Edinburgh: Atelier Books, 2012).*

McConkey has published extensively on British art since the late 1970s. He is currently an Emeritus Research Fellow in Art History at the Leverhulme Trust and his study of late nineteenth century artistic travel, Towards the Sun: World Pictures by British Artist-Travellers at the turn of the Twentieth Century, *will be published by Paul Holberton Publishing in the autumn of 2021.*

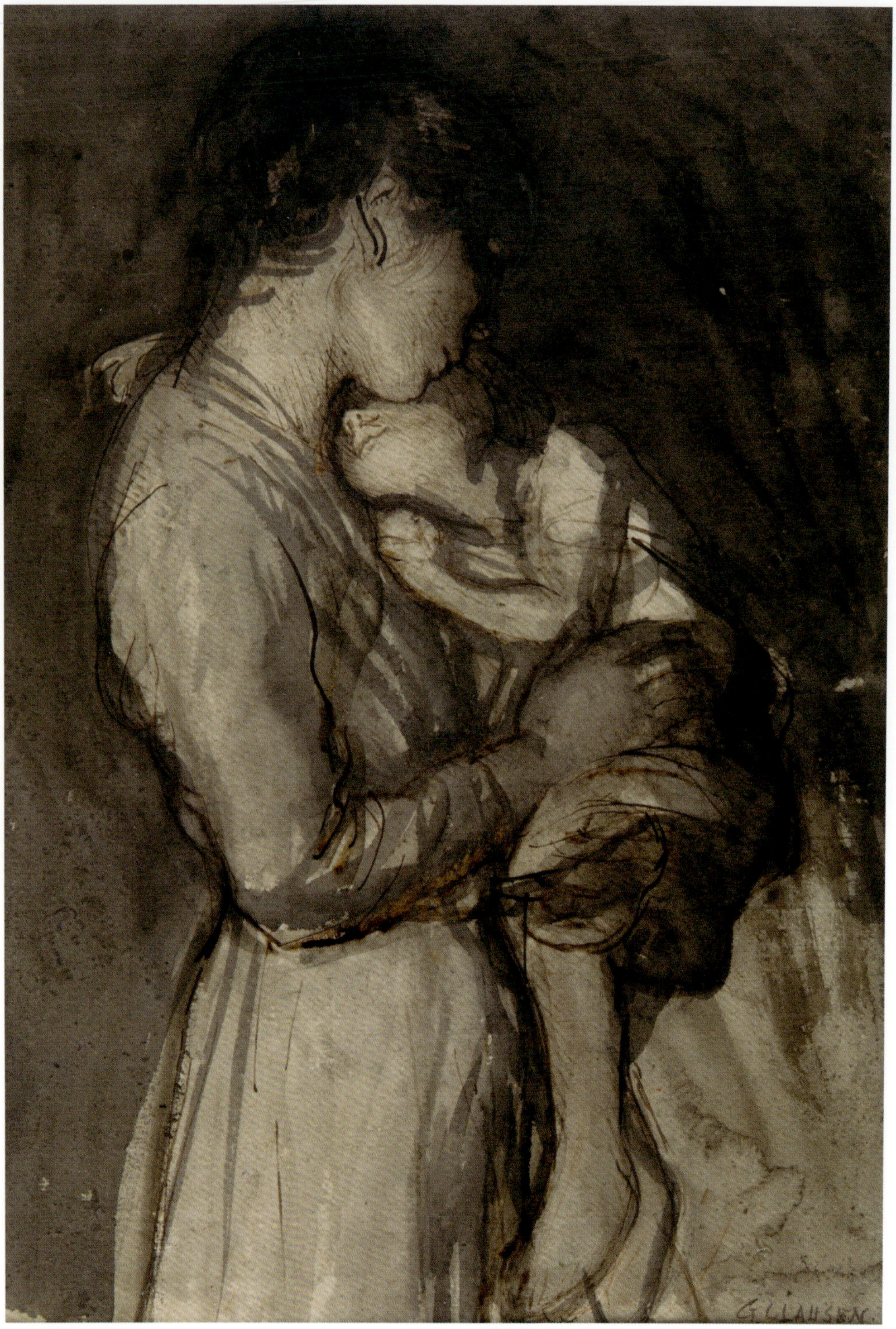

6 **Mother and Child**
Signed
Pen ink and watercolour
12 ½ x 8 ¼ inches

Mother and Child

The present watercolour by George Clausen relates to two of his drawings that are now in the collections of Bristol Museum & Art Gallery. All three were made in the years 1896-97 as studies for the painting, *The Mother*, which was exhibited at the Royal Academy in 1898, as No 582 (and, though unlocated, is illustrated in *RA Pictures*, 1898, page 108). The theme may have been prompted by H H La Thangue's *Man with the Scythe* (1896, Tate) and by contemporary concern in the press about infant mortality among the rural poor.

With thanks to Kenneth McConkey for his help in the compilation of this note.

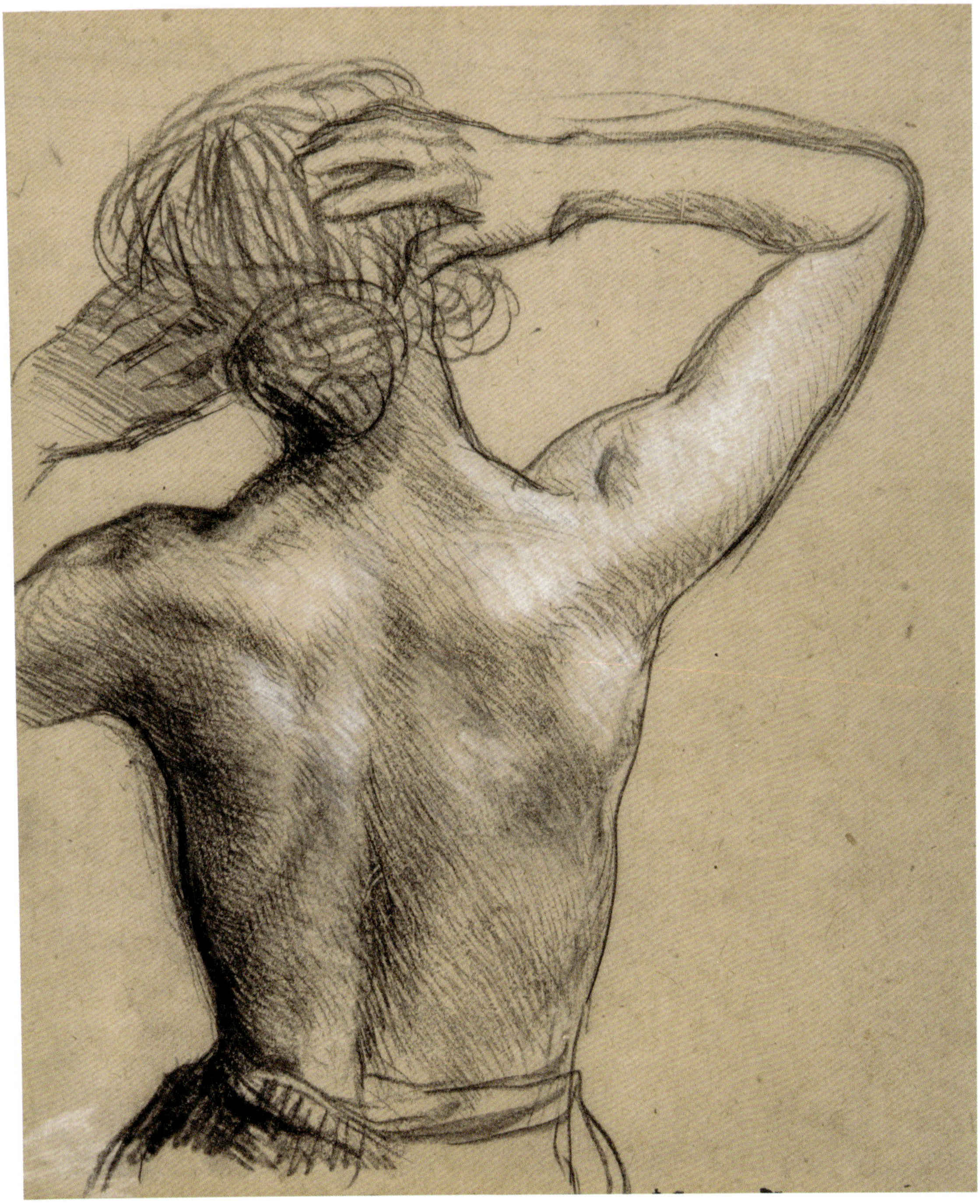

7 **Putting Up Her Hair**
Chalk on tinted paper
11 ¾ x 9 ½ inches

Putting Up Her Hair

The present chalk drawing by George Clausen of a woman putting up her hair seems to relate to *Study of a Female Nude*, dated to about 1918, and now in the collections of The Holburne Museum, Bath. That drawing, in chalk and conté, shows the front view of a woman holding a very similar position. These two studies are among several works by the artist to show nudes arranging their hair, the most well-known and finished of which are probably the oils, *Primavera* (1914) and *Girl Braiding Her Hair* (circa 1917).

JAMES HAMILTON HAY

James Hamiton Hay, LG (1874-1916)

The painter and printmaker, James Hamilton Hay, applied his sophisticated tonal approach to a range of subjects that included landscapes, seascapes, town-scapes and portraits. While absorbing the influences of James McNeill Whistler, Japanese printmakers and various teachers and friends, he made an original contribution to art – and cultural life – at the turn of the century, in the Liverpool area and more widely.

For a biography of James Hamilton Hay, please refer to page 178.

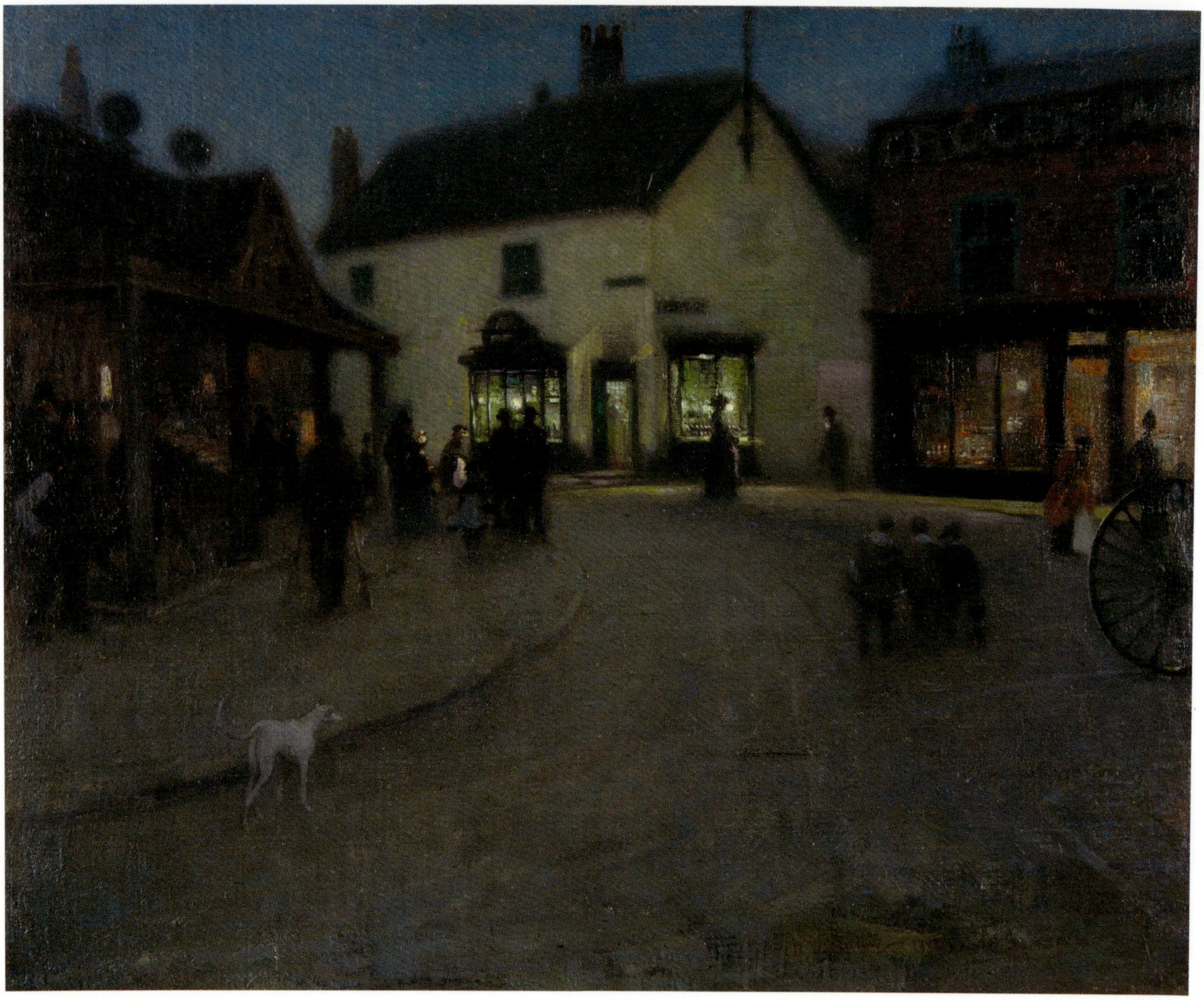

8 **Evening Light, Village Street**
Signed and dated 1908
Oil on canvas board
19 x 23 inches

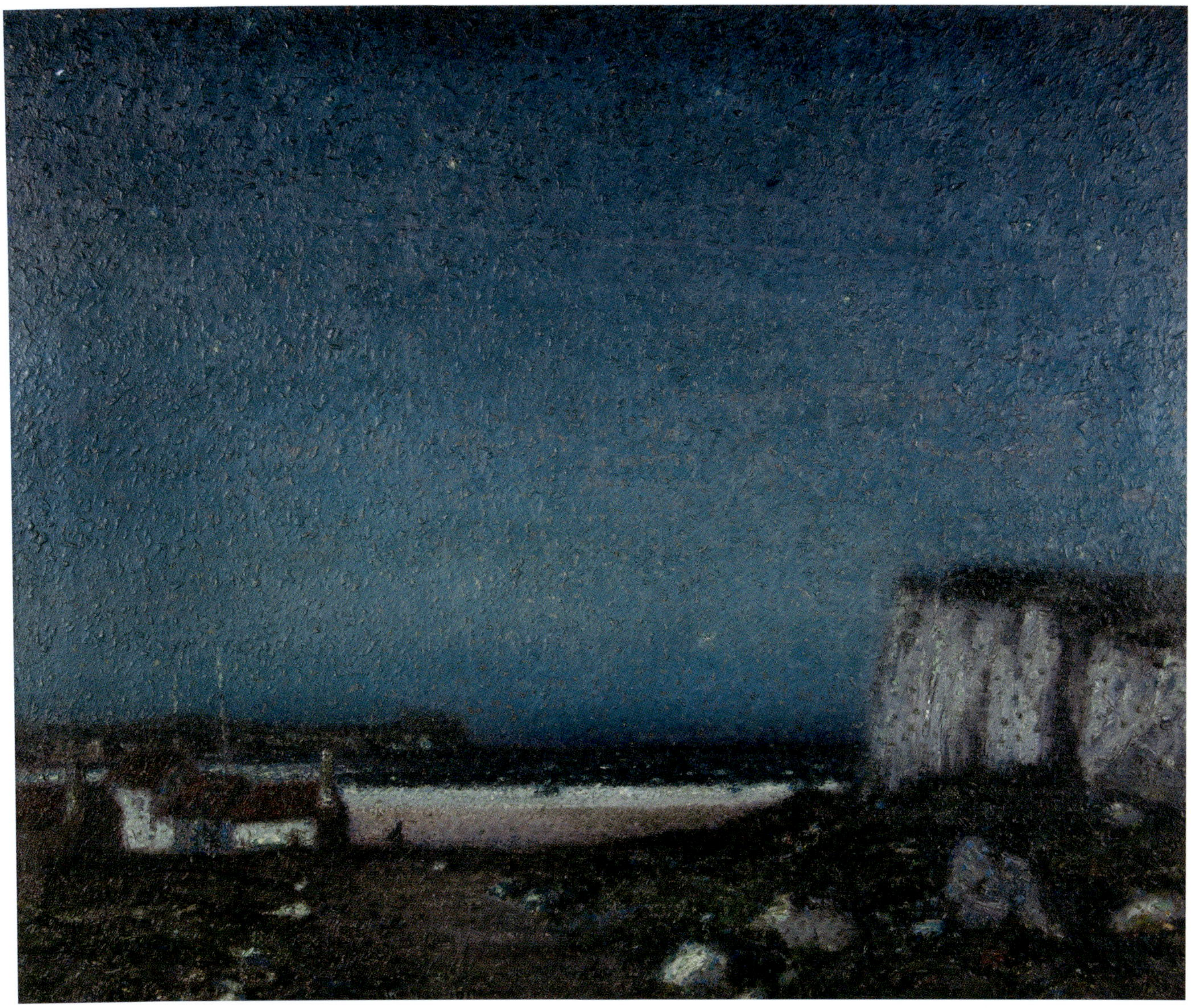

9 **Moonlit Coast**
Signed and dated 1911
Oil on canvas
24 ½ x 29 ¼ inches

FRANCIS E JAMES

Francis Edward James, RWS RBA NEAC (1849-1920)

'Perhaps the revelation of the season to the public ... are the watercolours of Mr Francis E James ... I am deliberately convinced that watercolour has never been used more brilliantly and to more purely artistic effect by any master, living or dead.'
(Walter Sickert, 'The New English Art Club', *New York Herald*, 14 June 1889)

Francis James was a watercolourist of exceptional delicacy and freedom, and contemporaries likened his landscapes and flower subjects to the work of the Japanese. He developed his art in the orbit of both James McNeill Whistler and Hercules Brabazon Brabazon, and joined the New English Art Club as an associate of the Impressionist nucleus, becoming one of the club's most regular exhibitors.

For a biography of Francis E James, please refer to page 179.

10 The Devon Coast
Signed
Watercolour and bodycolour
9 ¾ x 12 ¾ inches
Exhibited: 'Impressionism in Britain', Barbican Art Gallery, London, January-May 1995, No 103;
'British Impressionism', Daimaru Museum, Tokyo, May 1997, No 32

'With complete economy of means he notes the lone ship against a coastline of trees at sunset.'
(Kenneth McConkey, *British Impressionism*, London: Yale University Press/Barbican Art Gallery, 1995, Page 141)

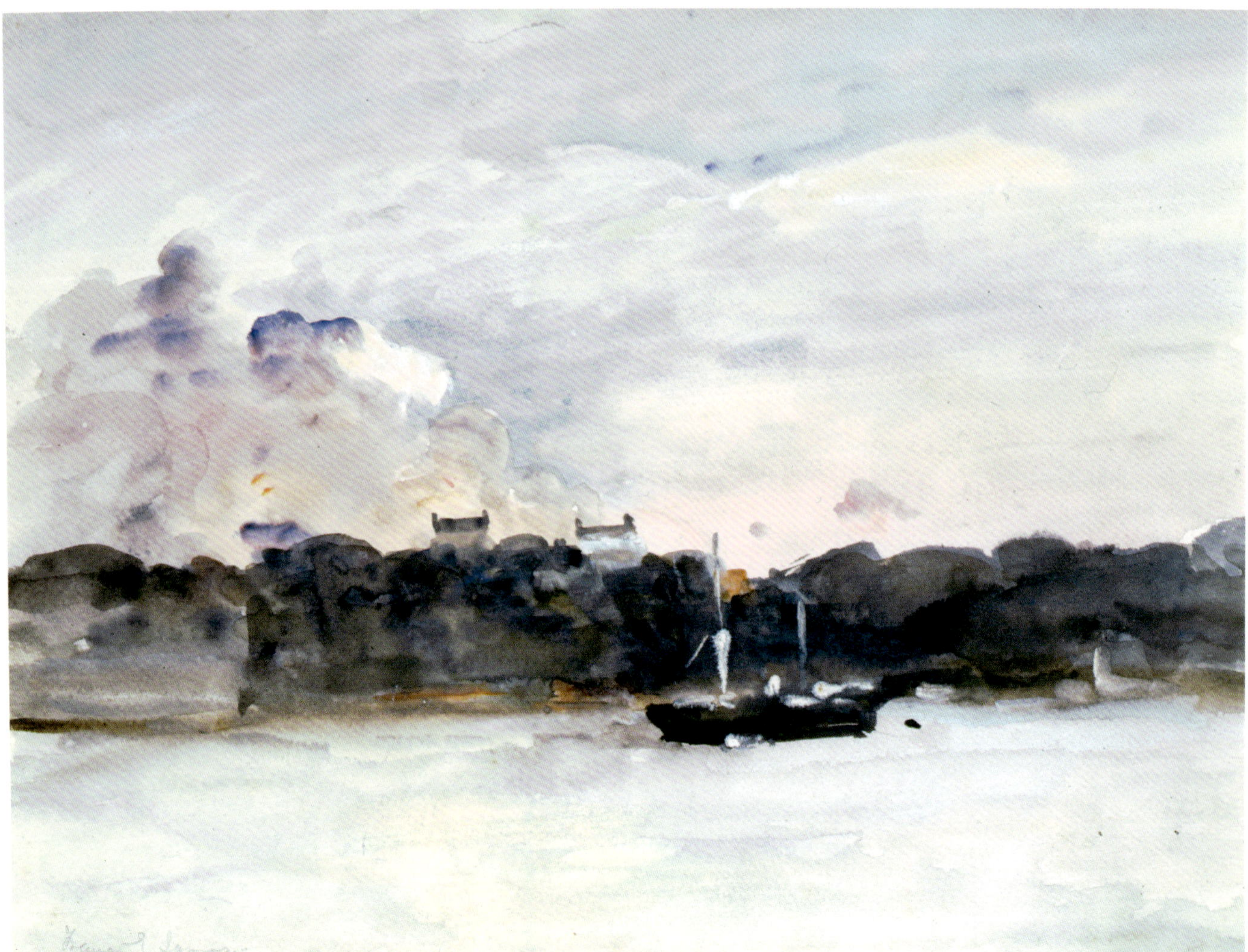

11 **Coastal Scene**
Watercolour with bodycolour
7 x 10 inches

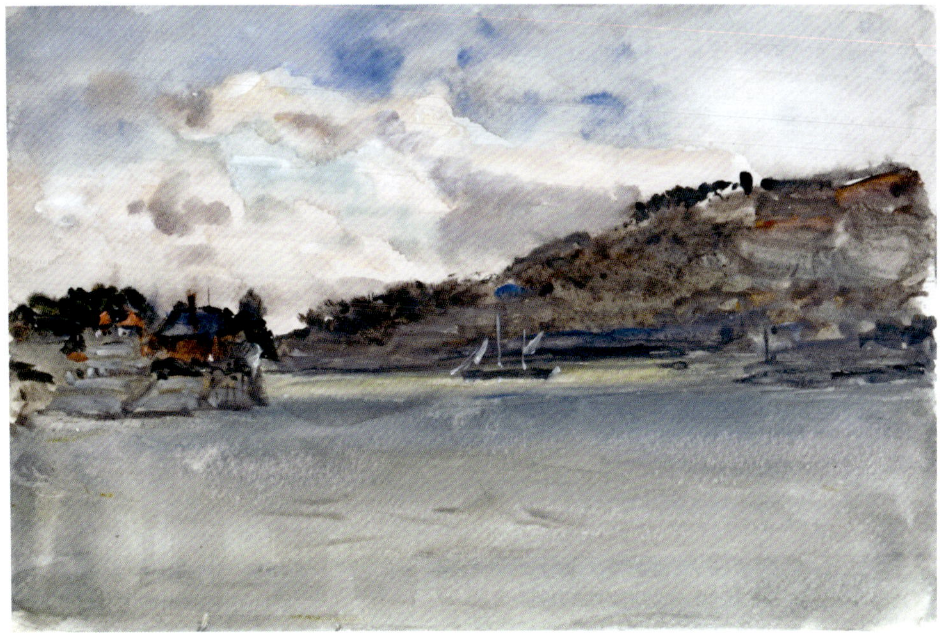

OWEN BAXTER MORGAN

Owen Baxter Morgan (1873-1920)

Owen Baxter Morgan was a painter, in oil and watercolour, of gently impressionistic poetic pastoral landscapes, including sunsets and nocturnes. Sometimes they incorporated figures of farmworkers, involved in such activities as guiding animals and making hay.

For a biography of Owen Baxter Morgan, please refer to page 177.

12 **English Landscape**
Signed
Oil on board
11 ½ x 17 ½ inches

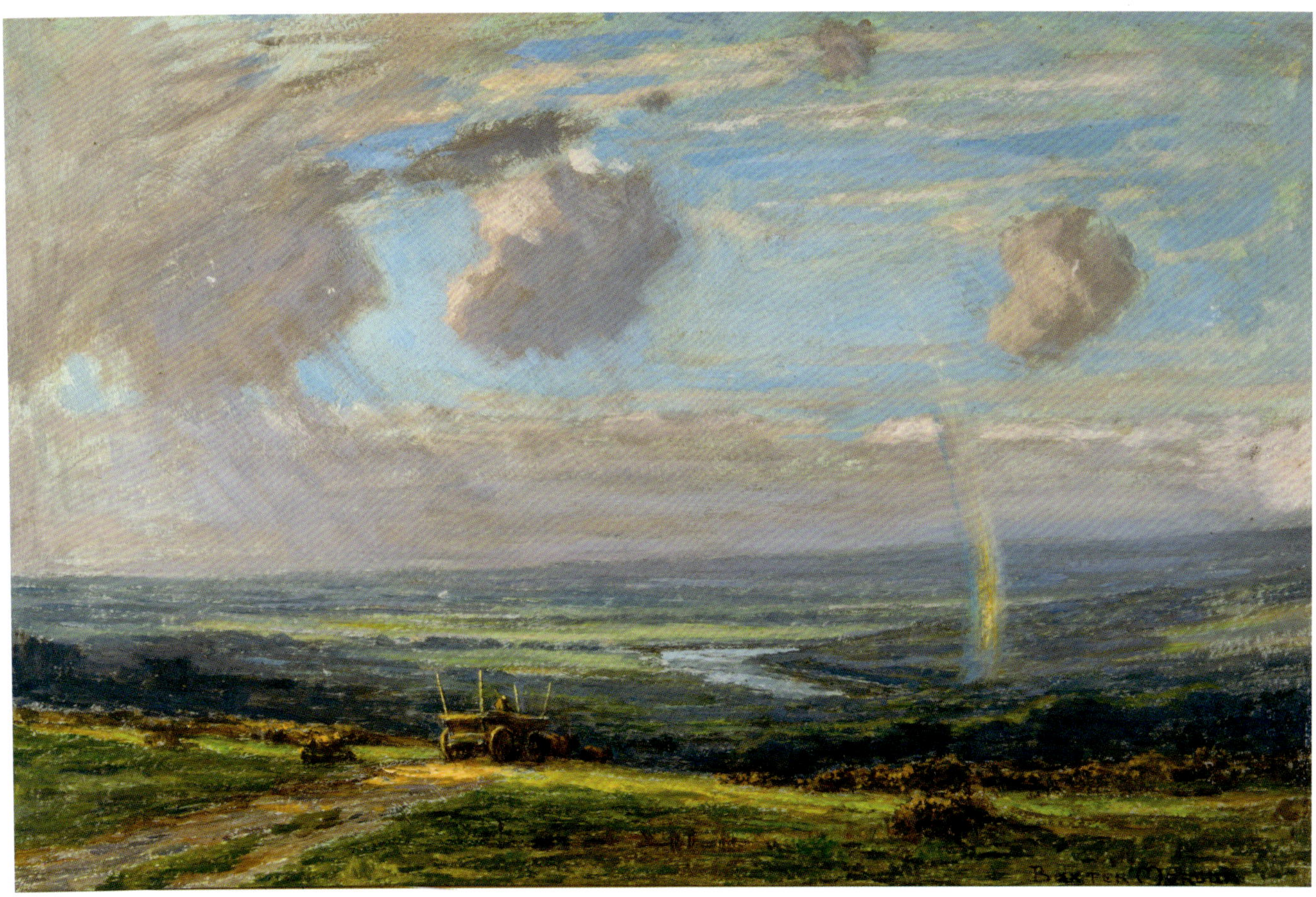

EDWIN ALEXANDER

Edwin John Alexander, RSA RSW RWS SSA (1870-1926)

Edwin Alexander is best remembered for his exquisite, carefully observed watercolours of flora and fauna, and of landscapes of both his native Scotland and North Africa. Often painting on silk, linen or textured paper, he developed a style that reflects the decorative approaches of Joseph Crawhall and other painters of the Glasgow School, and reveals an understanding of their common source, the art of Japan.

For a biography of Edwin Alexander, please refer to page 180.

13 **Dachshund**
Signed with monogram
Watercolour with bodycolour
12 ¾ x 12 inches

14 **Blue Tit on Teasels** (opposite)
Signed with monogram
Watercolour with bodycolour
21 ¾ x 12 ¼ inches

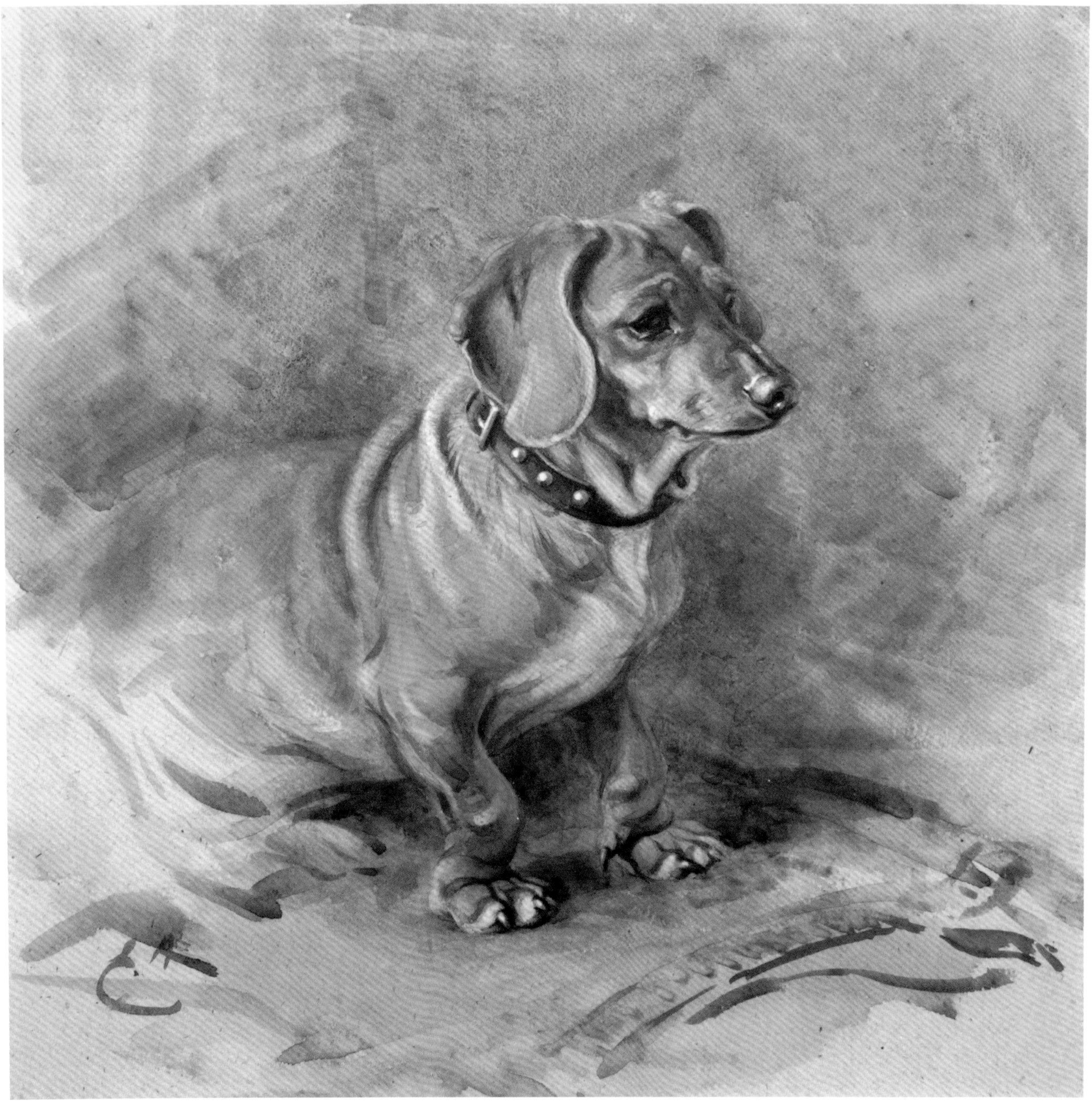

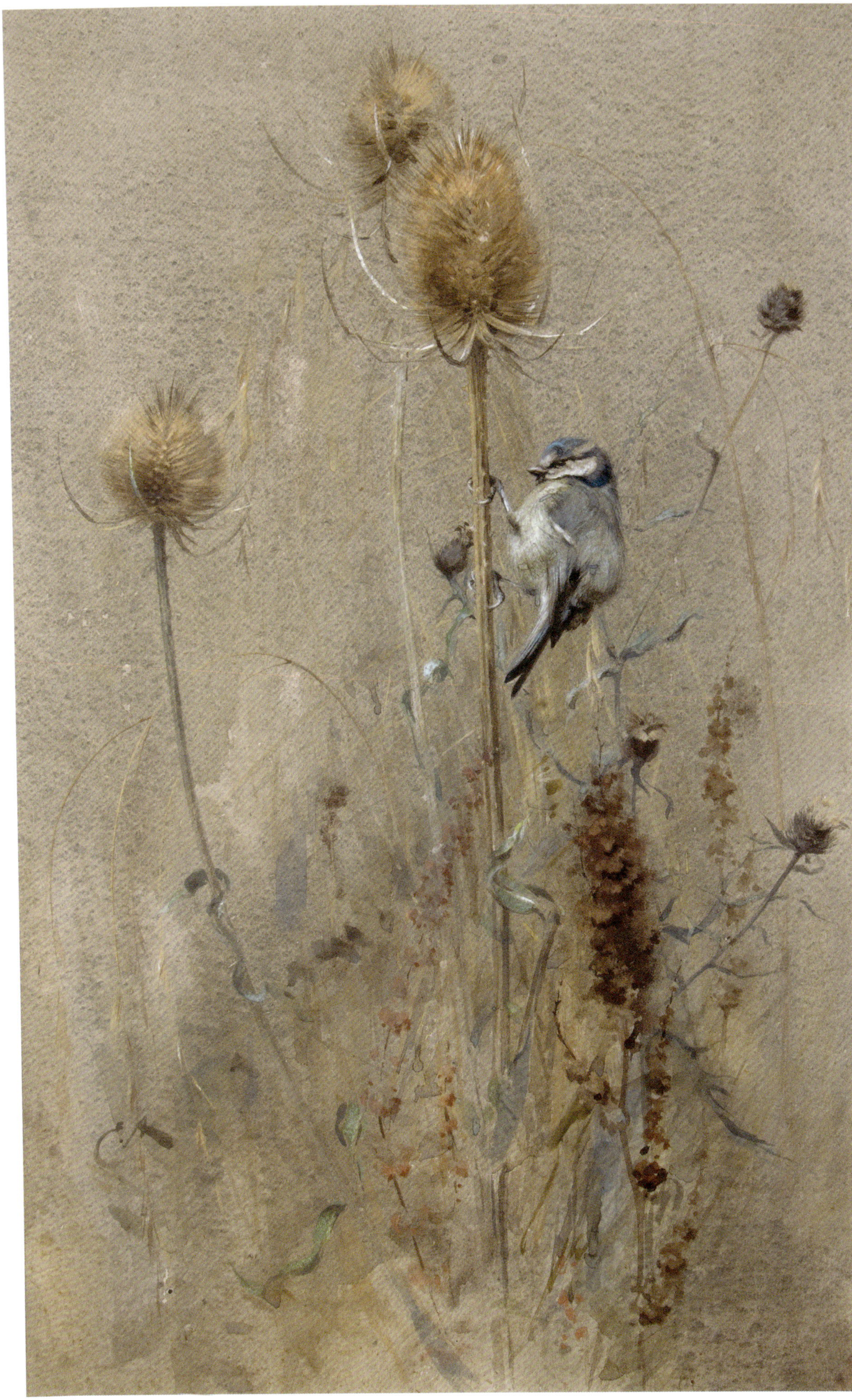

E H SHEPARD

Ernest Howard Shepard, MC OBE (1879-1976)

While E H Shepard is now best remembered for his immortal illustrations to *Winnie-the-Pooh* and *The Wind in the Willows*, he was a wide-ranging artist and illustrator, with an unsurpassed genius for representing children, and an underrated talent for political cartoons.

For a biography of E H Shepard, please refer to page 181.

15 **Florence and Apple Blossom**
Signed with initials
Oil on canvas
24 ¼ x 18 inches
Provenance: Mary Knox, the artist's daughter

Florence Chaplin was the first wife of E H Shepard, and the mother of Mary Knox. They were married from 1904 until her death in 1927.

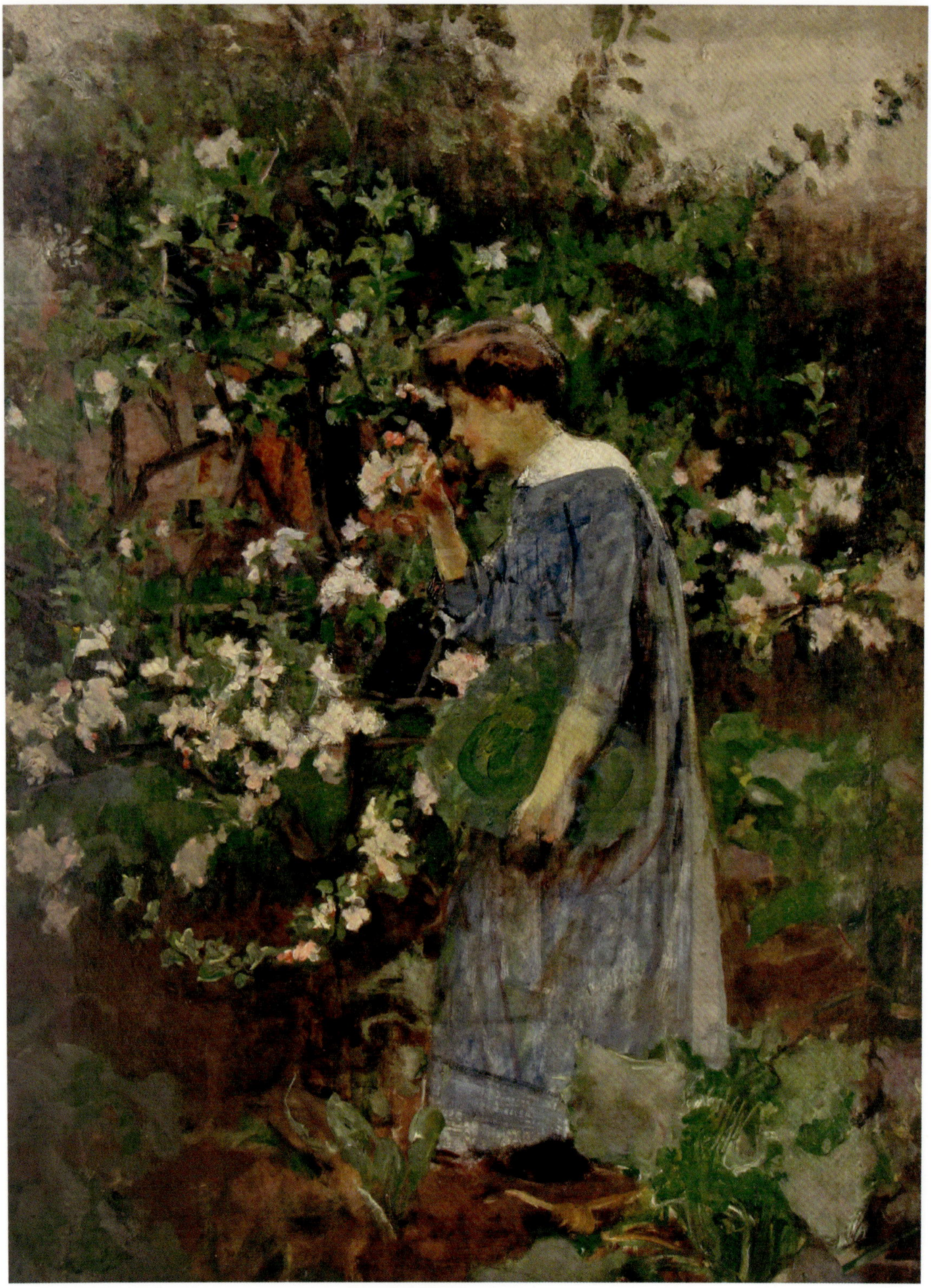

2: DRAWING AND CARICATURE

A PORTRAIT OF THE EARLY TWENTIETH-CENTURY LONDON ART WORLD

As suggested by the contents of the previous section, *Edwardian Impressionism*, the character and status of both the Royal Academy of Arts and the Royal Academy Schools were challenged in the early twentieth century by a new orthodoxy inspired by the French tendencies of Naturalism and Impressionism. This orthodoxy was promoted through the New English Art Club and nurtured at the Slade School of Fine Art by a group of artists that centred on the Slade Professors, Frederick Brown and Henry Tonks. It also included their friends, D S MacColl, William Orpen, Philip Wilson Steer and William Rothenstein (all of whom appear here as artists and/or subjects). This new orthodoxy may in some way even have touched the National Gallery, as its Director from 1916 was the painter and NEAC member, Charles Holmes.

Key to this orthodoxy was an emphasis on strong, accurate, naturalistic draughtsmanship, as a complement – rather than a contrast – to Impressionist painting techniques. It was rooted in the life class of the Parisian atelier, and had a lineage that could be traced back through Edgar Degas to Ingres and beyond. As such, it still involved making copies from prints and antique sculptures, and so refreshed rather than rejected the academic approach. Ultimately, the emphasis on draughtsmanship ensured that the new orthodoxy aligned itself to tradition and emphasised its opposition to Modernist movements, from Post-Impressionism onwards. (However, some of the most talented draughtsmen to train at the Slade, including Percy Wyndham Lewis, would be instrumental in energising the *avant-garde*.)

Draughtsmanship provided a secure foundation rather than a stylistic straitjacket, and a number of artists associated with the Slade stretched their skills by producing caricatures and other forms of cartoon, including comically illustrated letters. Professor Tonks himself was a talented caricaturist, who used satirical sketching as a relief from the responsibilities of his position and an outlet for the sardonic element of his personality. Such students of his as Adrian Allinson and Powys Evans took his lead to parody their contemporaries, both inside and outside the art school, and Evans even turned his talent into a career as the pseudonymous 'Quiz'. Within artistic circles, caricature could act as bond of friendship and, at the New English Art Club, was valued as an artistic genre (as is evidenced by the election of Max Beerbohm to the NEAC in 1909).

Cartooning also played its part in the arsenal of art criticism in both general and specialised print journalism – with comic artists proving a match for those that they lampooned. For instance, E T Reed succinctly summarised the contents of the Royal Academy Summer Exhibition for 1914 in his composite cartoon, *Murdered Masterpieces* [18], which was published in *The Graphic*. In so doing, he provided a more immediate version of many a written review of the show. On the other hand, the young H M Bateman preferred to satirise types that inhabited the contemporary art world rather than particular artists or works. His elegant yet highly dynamic images epitomise the era, from students making copies in the National Gallery to the tortured Bohemian in his Chelsea studio.

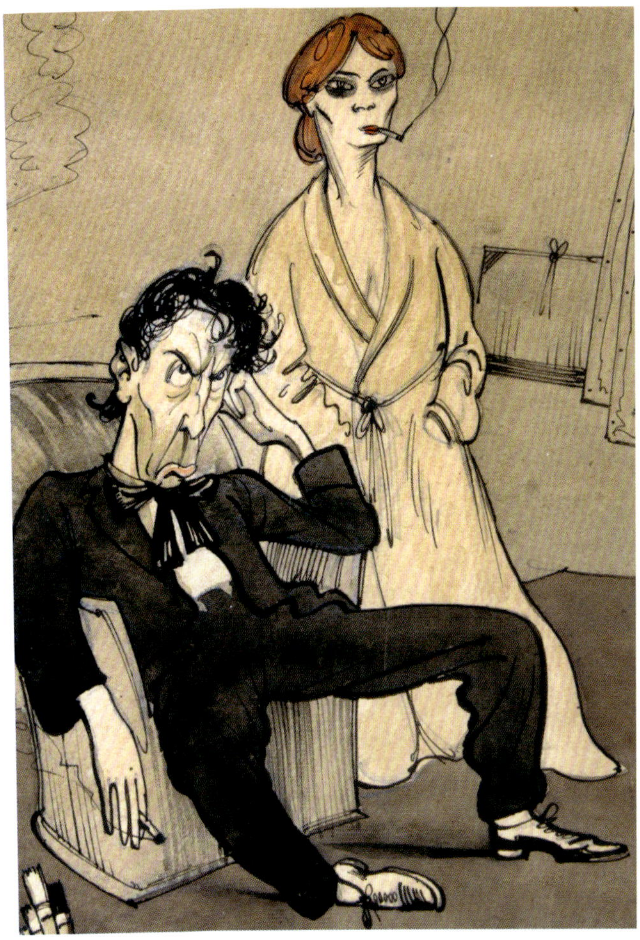

Detail of H M Bateman, *A Bit of Old Chelsea. Is it genius or liver?* [32]

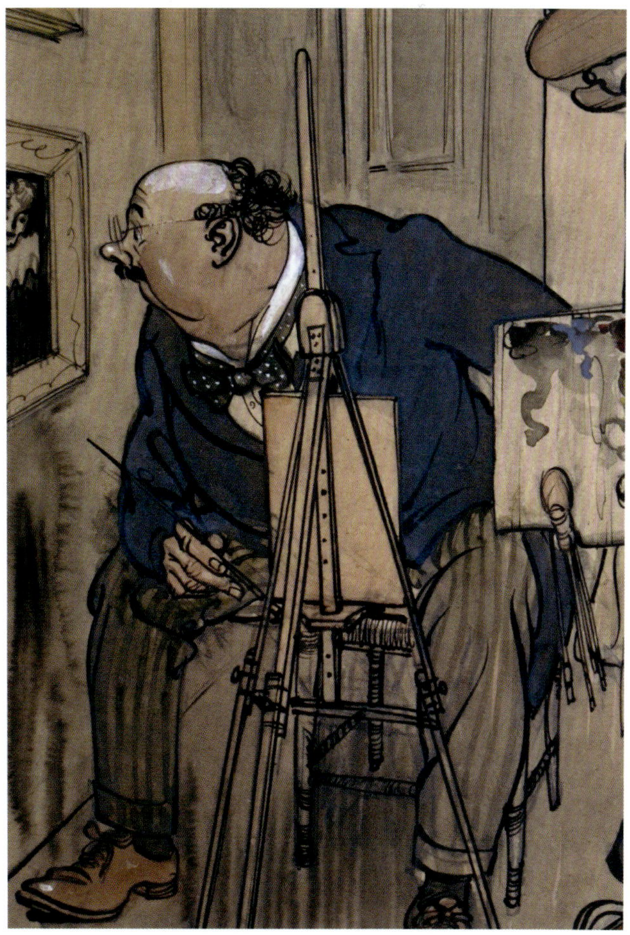

Detail of H M Bateman, *Student Day at the National Gallery* [30]

THE ROYAL ACADEMY OF ARTS

NIBS

Frederick Drummond Niblett, RSA (1861-1928), known as 'Nibs'

Though too little known today, Frederick Drummond Niblett produced some of the most striking caricatures of the Edwardian period in a style reminiscent of the posters and illustrations of William Nicholson and James Pryde, who worked together as the 'Beggarstaff Brothers'.

For a biography of Nibs, please refer to page 182.

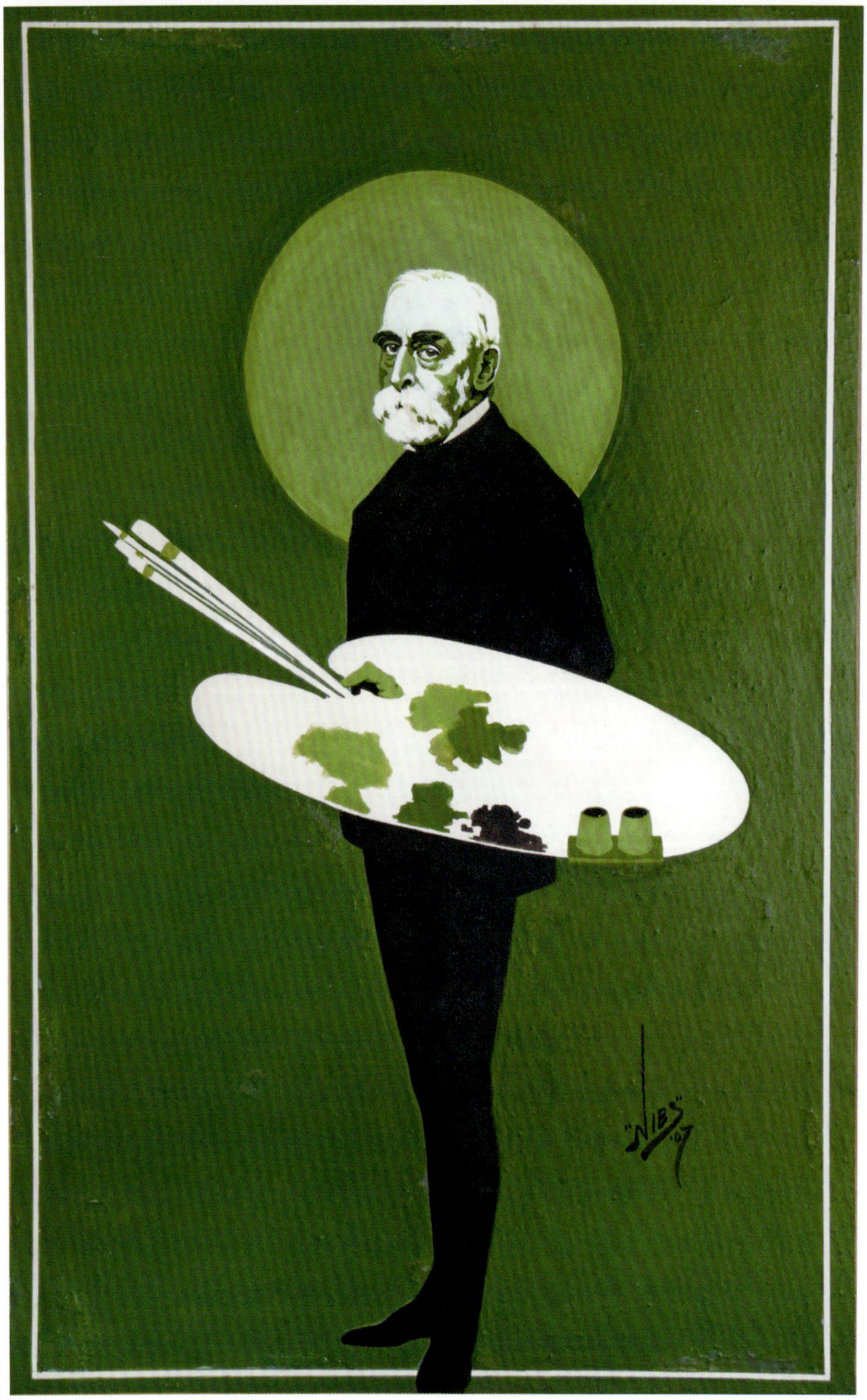

Sir Edward John Poynter, 1st Baronet PRA

One of the leading Classical painters of his generation, Edward John Poynter (1836-1919) was elected President of the Royal Academy of Arts in December 1896, 'in recognition of his experience and talents as an artist, educator and administrator' (Alison Inglis' entry on Poynter in *The Oxford Dictionary of National Biography*). He was knighted in the same year, and raised to the baronetcy in 1902.

Nibs based the head of his caricature on a photographic portrait, which was issued as a card with Ogden's Guinea Gold Cigarettes in about 1902. By the time that the caricature was published in 1907, Poynter represented the old guard, having outlived most of his generation, and becoming the target of artistic progressives. However, his paintings still met with critical approval, and the halo-like sun or moon against which Nibs places Poynter is as likely to be appreciative as satirical.

16 **Sir Edward John Poynter 1st Baronet, PRA**
Signed and dated '07
Watercolour, bodycolour and ink on board
15 ¾ x 10 inches
Illustrated: *The Crown: The Court and County Families Newspaper*

MAX BEERBOHM

Sir Henry Maximilian Beerbohm, IS NEAC PS (1872-1956)

Equally valued as a caricaturist and writer, Max Beerbohm sustained an elegant detachment in art and life. Though the tone of his drawings is often lightly wicked, it is also affectionate, for he hated to wound his subjects, most of whom he knew and liked. As a result, he was on safest ground in satirising artists and writers of the past, and in making many self-caricatures.

For a biography of Max Beerbohm, please refer to page 183.

17 **Cashmere – and again the queue!**

Mr Sargent (to Cook's Interpreter): 'What is it they want? What? ... No! Confound it: really, this is too bad! Don't they know I've made up my mind, absolutely and irrevocably, not to accept any more commissions?'

Signed, inscribed with title and dated 1909
Pen ink, watercolour and pencil
12 ¼ x 16 inches
Provenance: Miss Elizabeth Williamson
Illustrated: Max Beerbohm, *Fifty Caricatures*, New York: E P Dutton & Company, 1913
Literature: Rupert Hart-Davis, *A Catalogue of the Caricatures of Max Beerbohm*, London: Macmillan, 1972, No 1368
Exhibited: New English Art Club, Summer 1909, No 203

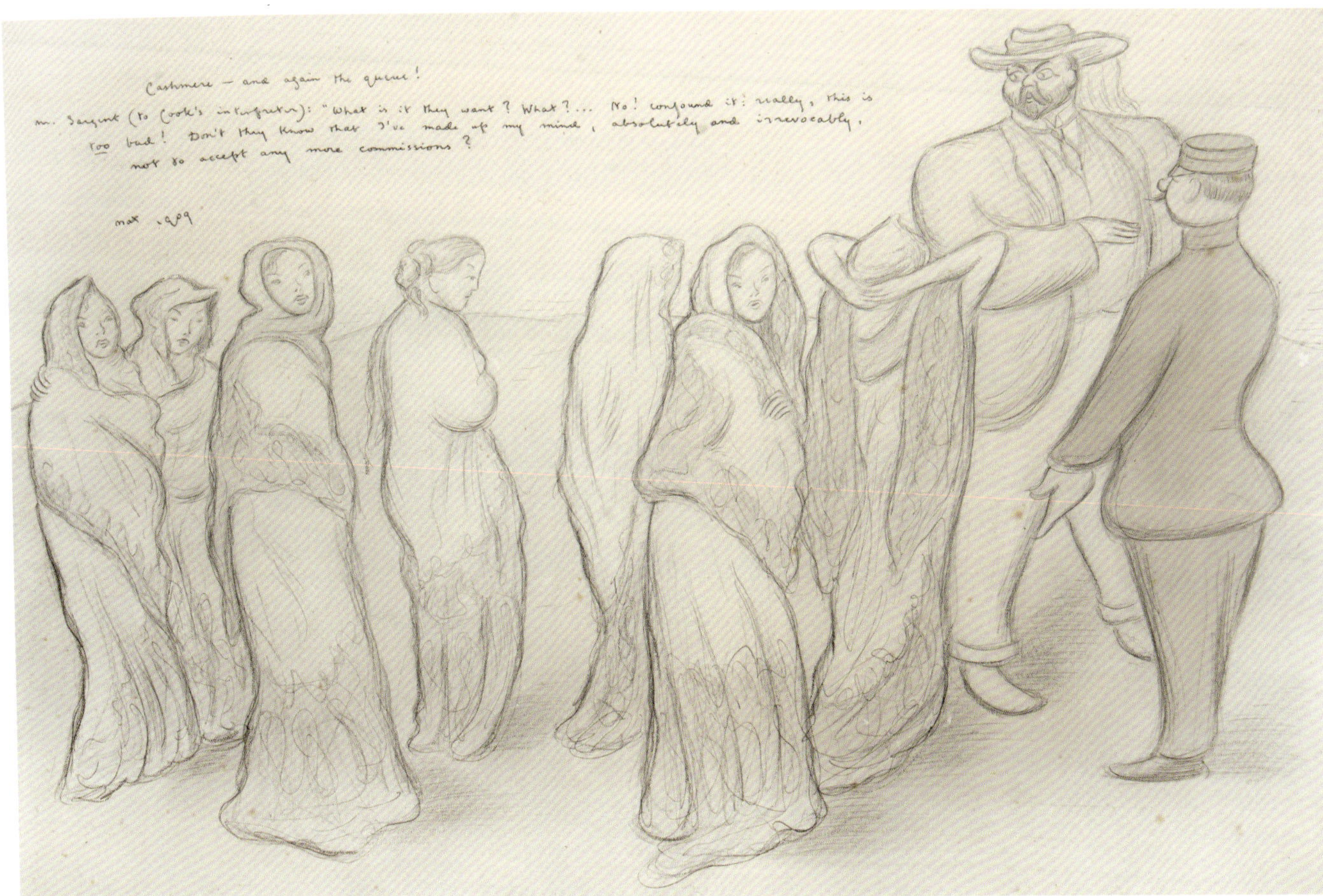

Cashmere – and again the queue!

In the summer of 1908, the American artist, John Singer Sargent (1856-1925), exhibited his oil painting, *Cashmere*, at the Royal Academy (as No 496). It depicted his niece, Reine Ormond, wearing a large exotically-patterned cashmere shawl and standing in seven different positions against a verdant background. The effect is of seven similar women walking together, and is perhaps suggestive of both the Aesthetic paintings of Albert Moore and the Classical friezes that inspired them, though with an Orientalist twist. It also relates to a number of other works that Sargent produced of women in shawls (as Leigh Culver has explored in the fascinating dissertation, 'Performing Identities in the Art of John Singer Sargent', University of Pennsylvania, 1999).

At the time of its exhibition, Sargent's *Cashmere* was the subject of much comment, which attempted both to define and deny a possible meaning. Contributions to this comment were not only written but also drawn, as is epitomised by the present work by Max Beerbohm, who caricatured Sargent some 22 times. Exhibited at the New English Art Club in 1909, a year after *Cashmere* appeared at the RA, it replicates the composition of the painting and adds the figures of Sargent and an interpreter employed by the travel agent, Thomas Cook. In so doing, it locates the setting to the English protectorate of Kashmir, the northernmost region of the Indian subcontinent. Though Sargent never actually visited the place, it was associated with the type of shawl depicted in his painting, which was woven in a distinctive way from the fine wool of particular breeds of goat. The young women comprise a queue of natives keen that Sargent paint their portraits. They may not be aware that Sargent had tired of accepting portrait commissions and, in 1907, had officially closed his studio. From that time, he focussed increasingly on landscapes and architectural subjects, including many in watercolour, and also completed the series of murals for public buildings in Massachusetts, in the United States.

E T REED

Edward Tennyson Reed (1860-1933)

Preferring pencil to pen and ink, E T Reed developed into a superb draughtsman, using his confident line to express a rich imagination. Known equally for his political caricatures and his *Punch* series, 'Prehistoric Peeps', his range of subject and allusion was astonishingly wide.

For a biography of E T Reed, please refer to page 182.

Murdered Masterpieces:
Gems at the Royal Academy Reset

E T Reed epitomises and satirises the state of British art, and specifically the Royal Academy of Arts, on the eve of the First World War. The 146th Summer Exhibition took place at Burlington House between 4 May and 15 August 1914. On 5 May, the suffragette, Mary Wood, attacked John Singer Sargent's portrait of Henry James.

Gallery No II: Oils

99: J J Shannon RA [1862-1923]: *Thomas L Devitt Esq* [Chairman of Lloyd's Register]

109: The Late J H F Bacon, ARA [1868-1914]: *William Nevett, Esq*

South Rooms: Oils

234: David Murray RA [1849-1933]: *The Bora, Venice*

Gallery No III: Oils

350: Edward J Poynter, Bt, PRA [1836-1919]: *The Sea Bath* [also known as *The Champion Swimmer*, this work is now in Wolverhampton Art Gallery]

373: Arthur Hacker RA [1858-1919]: Presentation Portrait: *Rt Hon George Lambert PC MP* [1868-1958; civil lord of the Admirality in the Liberal cabinet of the time, he would be created Viscount Lambert in 1945; private collection]

384: William Orpen ARA [1878-1931]: *Richard B Fudger, Esq of Toronto*

Gallery No IV: Oils

433: Arnesby Brown ARA [1866-1955]: *Dawn*

461: P A de Laszló [1869-1937]: *Lady Richard Wellesley* [1889-1946; the wife of Captain Lord Richard Wellesley (1879-1914), the third child of the 4th Duke of Wellington, who served in the Grenadier Guards and died from wounds received in action during the first battle of Ypres.]

Gallery No V: Oils

539: R Grenville Eves [1876-1941]: *John Gow, Esq*

Gallery No VII: Oils

640: The Late Sir Hubert von Herkomer [1849-1914]: *Arthur Bourchier, Esq* [1863-1927; an actor and theatre manager, he was noted for his roles in Shakespeare's plays, and especially the lead in *Henry VIII*.]

647: F Cadogan Cowper ARA [1877-1958]: *Walter Carlile Esq JP DL* [1862-1950; Conservative MP for Buckingham until 1906, he would be made a baronet in 1928; this work is now in the collection of Buckinghamshire County Council.]

Gallery No VIII

694: Stanhope A Forbes, RA [1857-1947]: *Philip Dawson Esq* [1866-1938; an electrical engineer, he worked for the Ministry of Munitions during the First World War, and was subsequently knighted, while, from 1921, he wold serve as Conservative MP for Lewisham West; in 1977, his family presented this work to the Institute of Fuel, which he had served as President.]

718: John Lavery ARA [1856-1941]: *The Studio of the Painter* [private collection]

Lecture Room: Sculpture

2207: W Reid Dick [1879-1961]: *Femina Victrix* – group, bronze

18 Murdered Masterpieces: Gems at the Royal Academy Reset
Signed with monogram and inscribed with picture captions
Inscribed 'Priceless gems at the Royal Academy' and 'Graphic' and dated 'May 2 1914' on original mount
Pencil
17 x 12 inches

Illustrated: *The Graphic*, 9 May 1914, Page 797
Exhibited: 'The Long Nineteenth Century: Treasures and Pleasures', Chris Beetles Gallery, March-April 2014, No 142

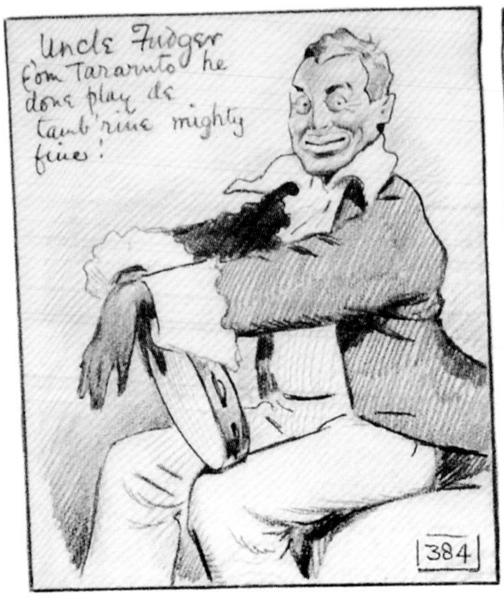
Uncle Fudger fom Tararnto he dons play de tamb'rine mighty fine!
384

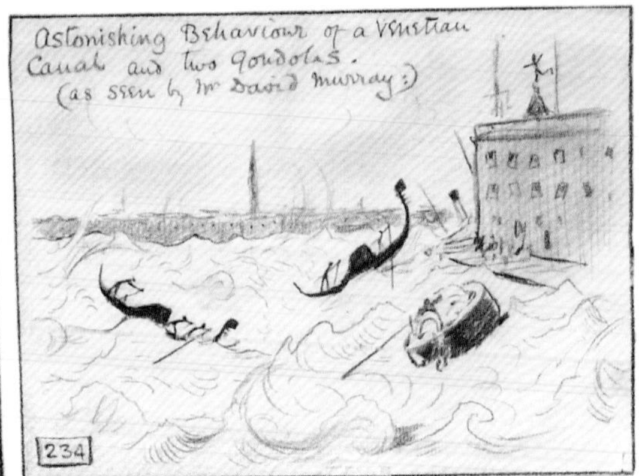
Astonishing Behaviour of a Venetian Canal and two Gondolas.
(as seen by Mr David Murray:)
234

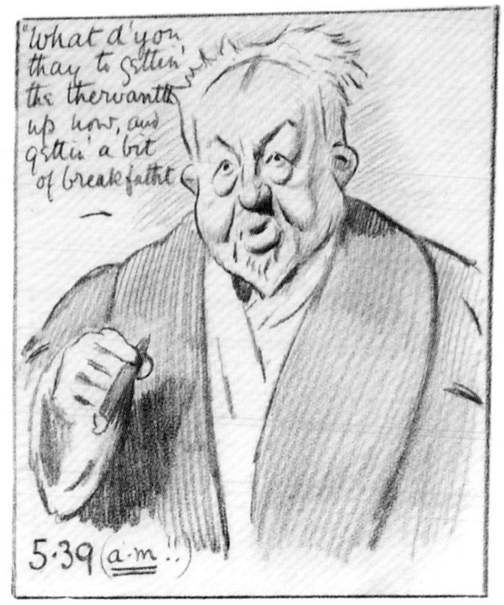
"What d'you thay to gettin' the therwantth up now, and gettin' a bit of breakfatht?
5.39 (a.m.!)

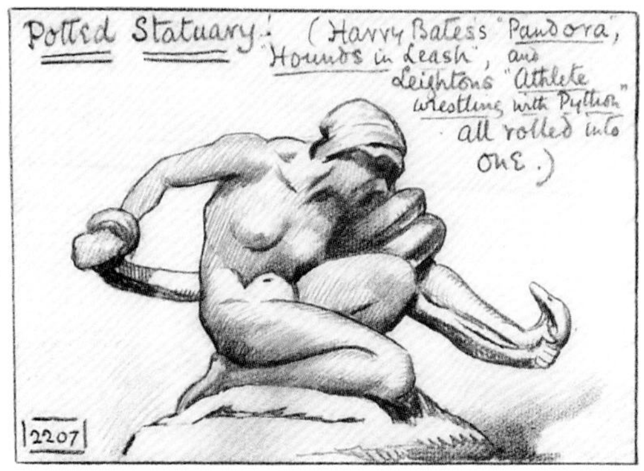
Potted Statuary! (Harry Bates's "Pandora", "Hounds in Leash", and Leighton's "Athlete wrestling with Python" all rolled into one.)
2207

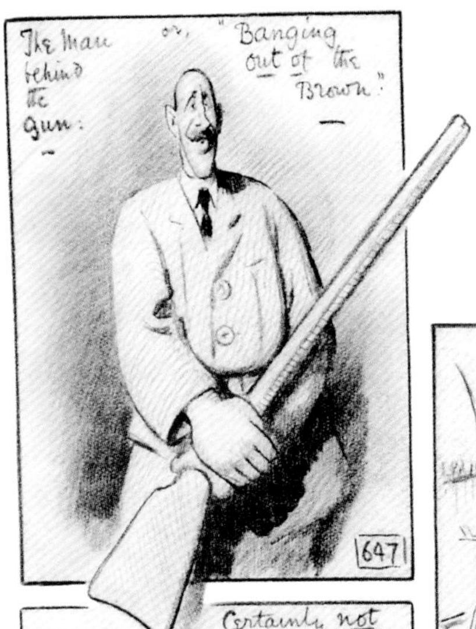
The Man behind the Gun:
or, "Banging out of the Brown."
647

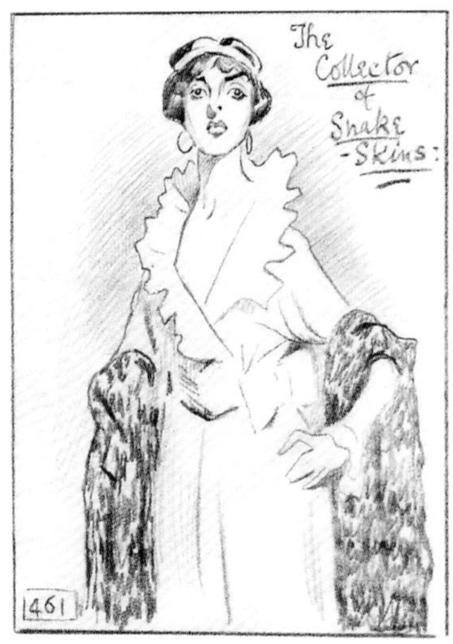
The Collector of Snake-Skins:
461

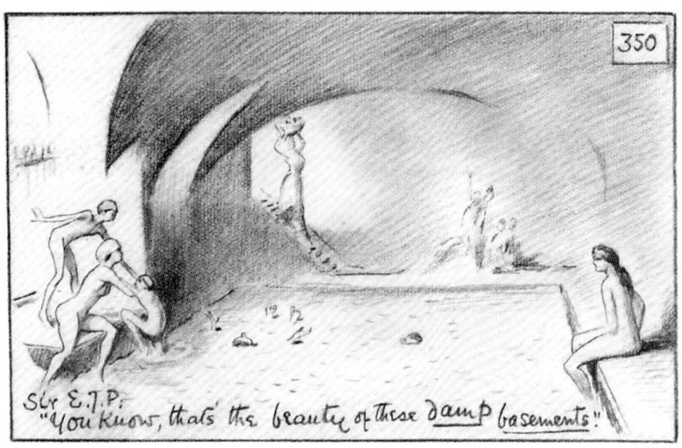
350
Sir E.J.P.
"You know, that's the beauty of these damp basements!"

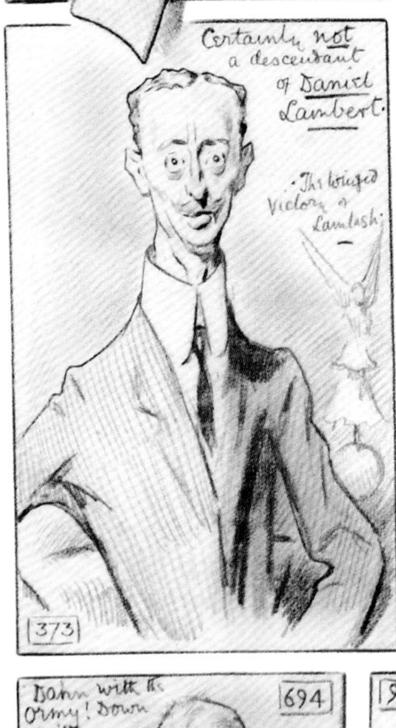
Certainly not a descendant of Daniel Lambert.
373

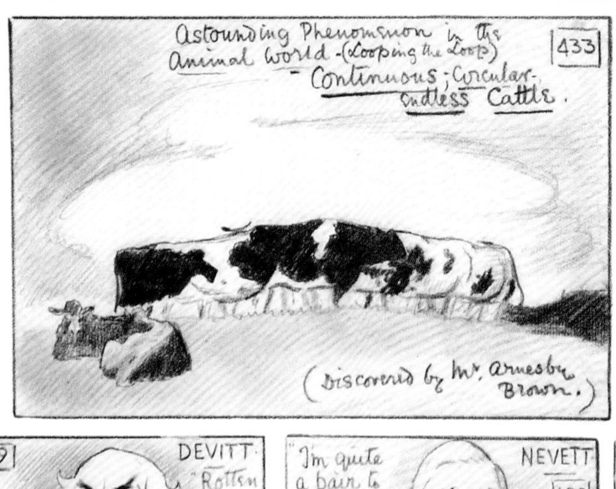
Astounding Phenomenon in the Animal World - (Looping the Loop) - Continuous, Circular-endless Cattle.
433
(Discovered by Mr Arnesby Brown.)

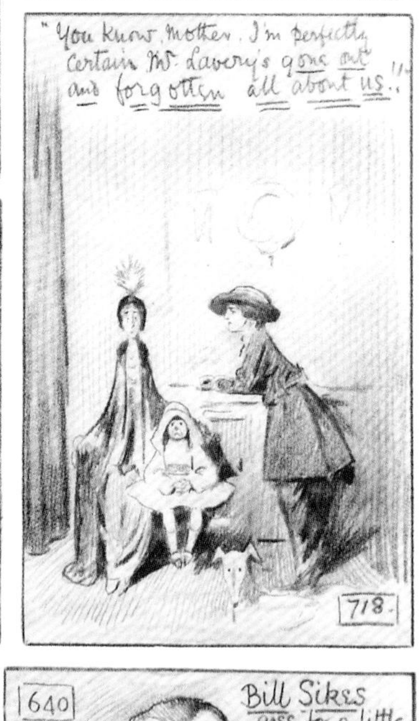
"You know, mother, I'm perfectly certain Mr Lavery's gone out and forgotten all about us!!"
718

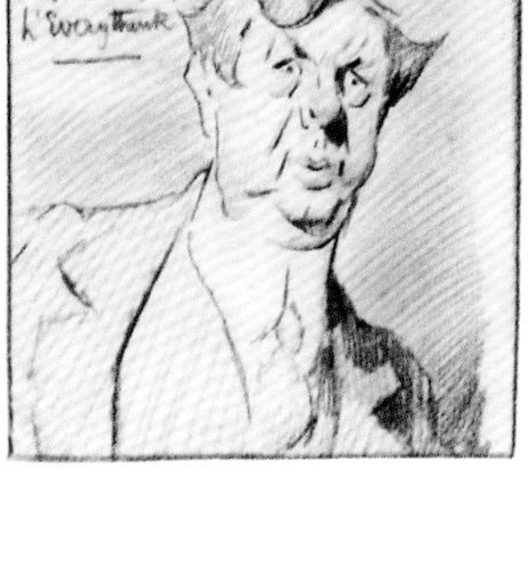
694

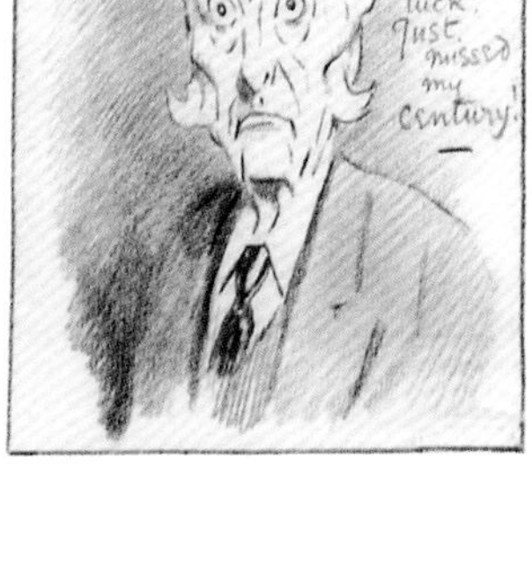
99
DEVITT
"Rotten luck! Just missed my century!"

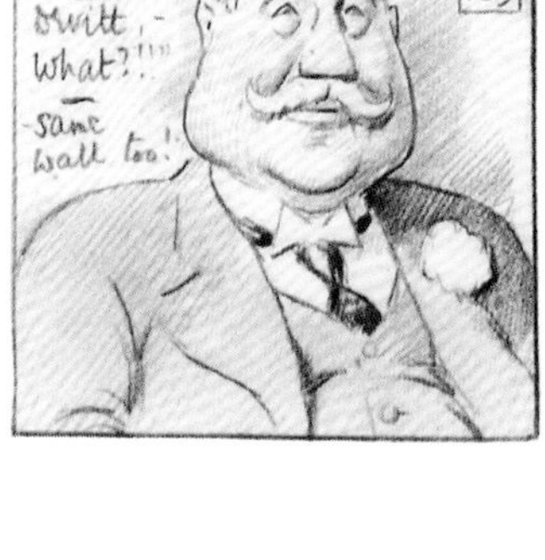
"I'm quite a pair to Devitt,- what?!!"
-same wall too!
NEVETT
109

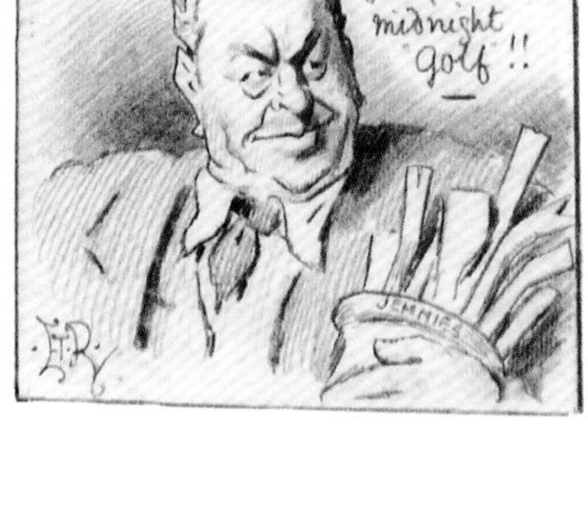
640
Bill Sikes goes for a little midnight "Golf"!!

THE SLADE SCHOOL OF FINE ART AND THE NEW ENGLISH ART CLUB

ADRIAN ALLINSON

Adrian Paul Allinson, RBA ROI LG PS (1890-1959)

One of the hugely talented generation of artists to emerge just before the First World War, Adrian Allinson managed to hold his own through both his personality and his work. He became best known as a painter of strongly modelled, appealingly stylised landscapes, figure compositions and flowers. However, his manifold talents encompassed sculpture, wood carving and pottery; wood engraving, poster design and set design; and, as here, distinctive caricatures.

For a biography of Adrian Allinson, please refer to pages 184-185.

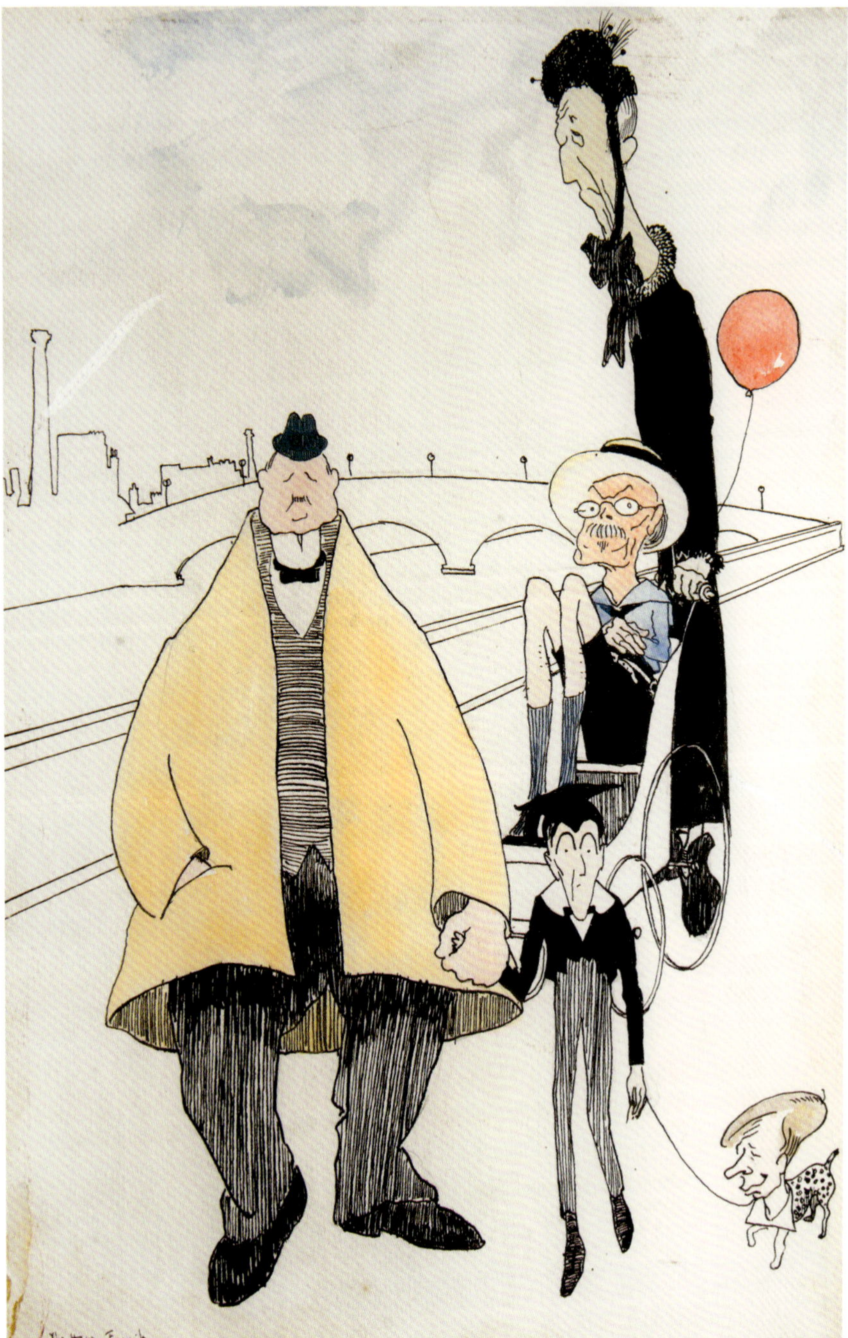

'[Allinson's] "dangerous talent", as Tonks termed it, was turned to good use when he embarked upon caricature especially in those of his fellow artists; one of his earliest submissions to the New English Art Club, entitled The Happy Family, *was in the manner of Max Beerbohm and depicted the teaching staff of the Slade – Steer as the* père de famille *holding Walter Russell by the hand, Tonks pushing a pram containing a sailor-suited Professor Brown with Derwent Lees as a dog completing the group. Not surprisingly with its Slade bias the Jury rejected the caricature but Arthur Clifton sold it at the Carfax Gallery.'*

(Peyton Skipwith, 'Adrian Allinson. A Restless Talent', *The Connoisseur*, August 1978, page 266)

19 The Happy Family
Signed with monogram and inscribed with title
Pen ink and watercolour on board
12 ¾ x 9 inches
Provenance: Carfax Gallery, London

MAX BEERBOHM

Sir Henry Maximilian Beerbohm, IS NEAC PS (1872-1956)

20 Professor Henry Tonks
Signed and inscribed 'Mr Tonks'
Pencil sketch of Winston Churchill on reverse
Pencil and watercolour
12 ½ x 8 ¼ inches
Provenance: Piccadilly Gallery, London;
Thomas Geoffrey Blackwell;
Christie's, London, 6 July 1951, Lot 4, with a Beerbohm of Philip Wilson Steer [see 23]
Literature: Rupert Hart-Davis, *A Catalogue of the Caricatures of Max Beerbohm*, London: Macmillan, 1972, No 1661;
N John Hall, *Max Beerbohm Caricatures*, New Haven & London: Yale University Press, 1997, Plate 115
Exhibited: London Group, 1911;
'The Illustrators: 1800-2008', Portico Library and Gallery, Manchester, November 2008-January 2009

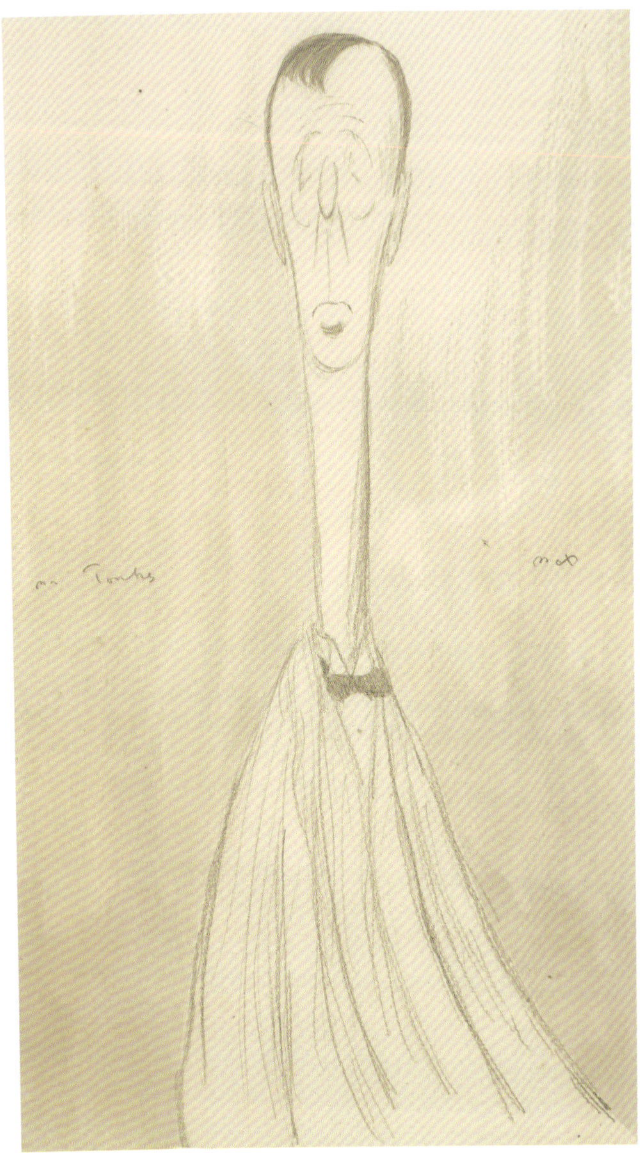

POWYS EVANS

Powys Arthur Lewthall Evans (1899-1982),
also known as 'Quiz'

The artistic talent of Powys Evans was nurtured in the circle of George Sheringham and by a number of teachers that included Henry Tonks at the Slade School of Fine Art. He became best known for his portrait drawings and caricatures, the latter of which he signed with the pseudonym, 'Quiz'. They were sufficiently successful in both exhibition and publication for Max Beerbohm to claim Evans as his heir.

For a biography of Powys Evans, please refer to page 187.

21 Professor Tonks
Signed, inscribed with title and dated 1926
Pen and ink
11 x 9 inches
Probably illustrated in *The London Mercury*

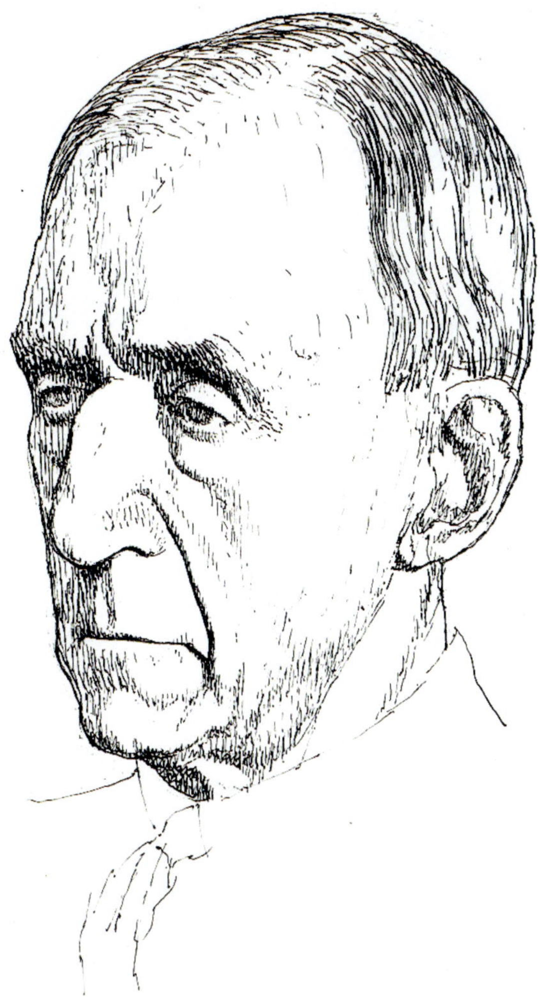

HENRY TONKS

Professor Henry Tonks, NEAC (1862-1937)

Henry Tonks has a special place in the history of twentieth-century British art. Having established himself as a surgeon in the late 1880s, he made great use of his expert knowledge of anatomy in his progression as a draughtsman-painter (and occasional caricaturist). It informed his figure compositions, which synthesised elements of the Rococo, Impressionism and English illustration of the 1860s to distinctively satisfying ends. It also underpinned his almost legendary approach to teaching at the Slade School of Fine Art, when he became assistant to his friend and mentor, Professor Fred Brown, in 1893, and Professor himself, in 1918. He encouraged some of the most talented young artists in the country to use drawing – from the antique, from prints and from life – as the basis for individual development. At the same time, he discouraged them from visiting exhibitions of the avant-garde or engaging with the aesthetic values of its champion, Roger Fry – instead encouraging them to join the Impressionist stronghold that was the New English Art Club. His combination of qualities also made him almost uniquely placed, during the First World War, to record Harold Gillies' pioneering work in reconstructive surgery.

For a biography of Henry Tonks, please refer to pages 186-187.

Eugenics

Among the many gifts of Henry Tonks was one for caricature. He exercised it as a pastime that allowed him to express the satirical, even sarcastic aspect of his character, and experiment with a range of techniques and styles, including the *faux naïf.* He also injected it into some of his painted portraits, particularly those that he made of such close friends as Walter Sickert and Wilson Steer. In turn, his dominating physique and personality made him the object of the skills of other caricaturists, both professional and amateur.

The present drawing may belong to Tonks's earliest datable caricatures, which were produced in about 1905. It is definitely no earlier, for the slogan 'Votes for Women', shouted (as a speech bubble) by a woman standing on the balcony in the image, was adopted in that year. And it may be no later, for it seems to respond to Francis Galton's establishment in 1904 of the Eugenics Record Office at University College London (also home to the Slade School of Fine Art at which Tonks was Assistant Professor). In 1904, the office was reconstituted as the Galton Eugenics Laboratory.

Inspired by Darwinism, Galton developed the theory of improving the human population through selective breeding and, in 1882, named it 'eugenics' from the Greek for 'good growing'. It was popular during the first half of the twentieth century, even among some women, and there was a branch called eugenic feminism. However, it could also prove controversial, and Tonks's former Slade student, the writer, G K Chesterton, would publish *Eugenics and Other Evils* in 1917. The theory has since been discredited and, as recently as January 2021, University College London issued a formal public apology for its own involvement in its history and legacy.

The drawing shows what Tonks has inscribed as the 'Interior of Propagatorium', that is an operating theatre that acts as the embodiment of 'the whole mechanism of reproduction' (the definition of the term Propagatorium given in medical dictionaries of the day). A woman – who says that she is 'happy' – lies on a couch, while a young man is prepared in readiness to join her. One doctor sprays the area of his genitals, while another waits to time him with a stop watch. They are about to engage in an act of medicalised selective reproduction in line with Galton's theory.

While Tonks's exact view of eugenics beyond this caricature is not known, it is likely to have been more informed than that of many, given his medical background. More certainly, he was able to draw on his own experience as both a medical student and surgeon to produce an image of an operating theatre that is at once convincing and amusing. He might possibly also be rehearsing something of his own youthful anxieties about sex through the gangly, somewhat dazed figure of the young man.

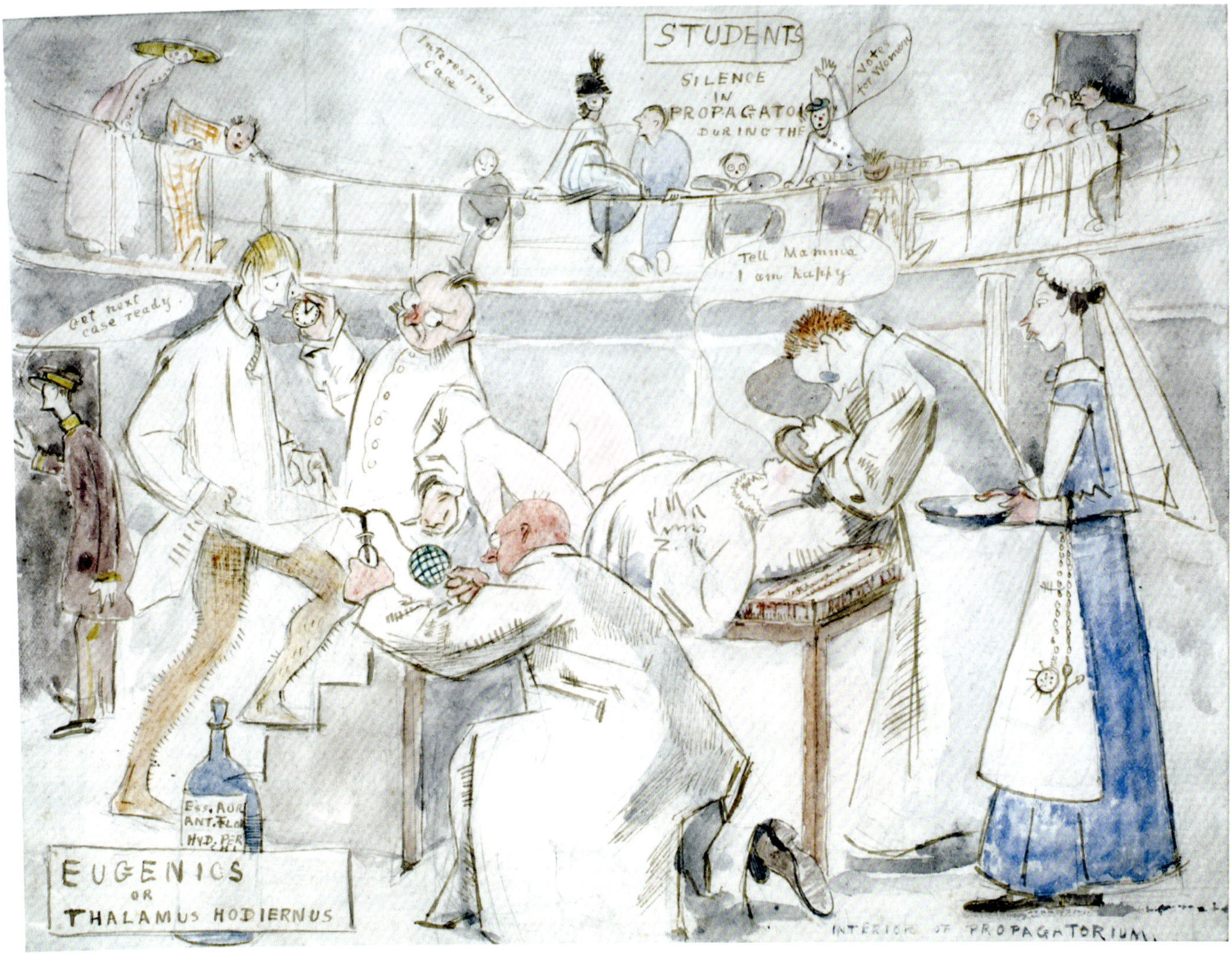

22 Eugenics or Thalamus Hodiernus
Inscribed 'Interior of Propagatorium'
Pen ink and watercolour
7 x 9 inches

MAX BEERBOHM

Sir Henry Maximilian Beerbohm, IS NEAC PS (1872-1956)

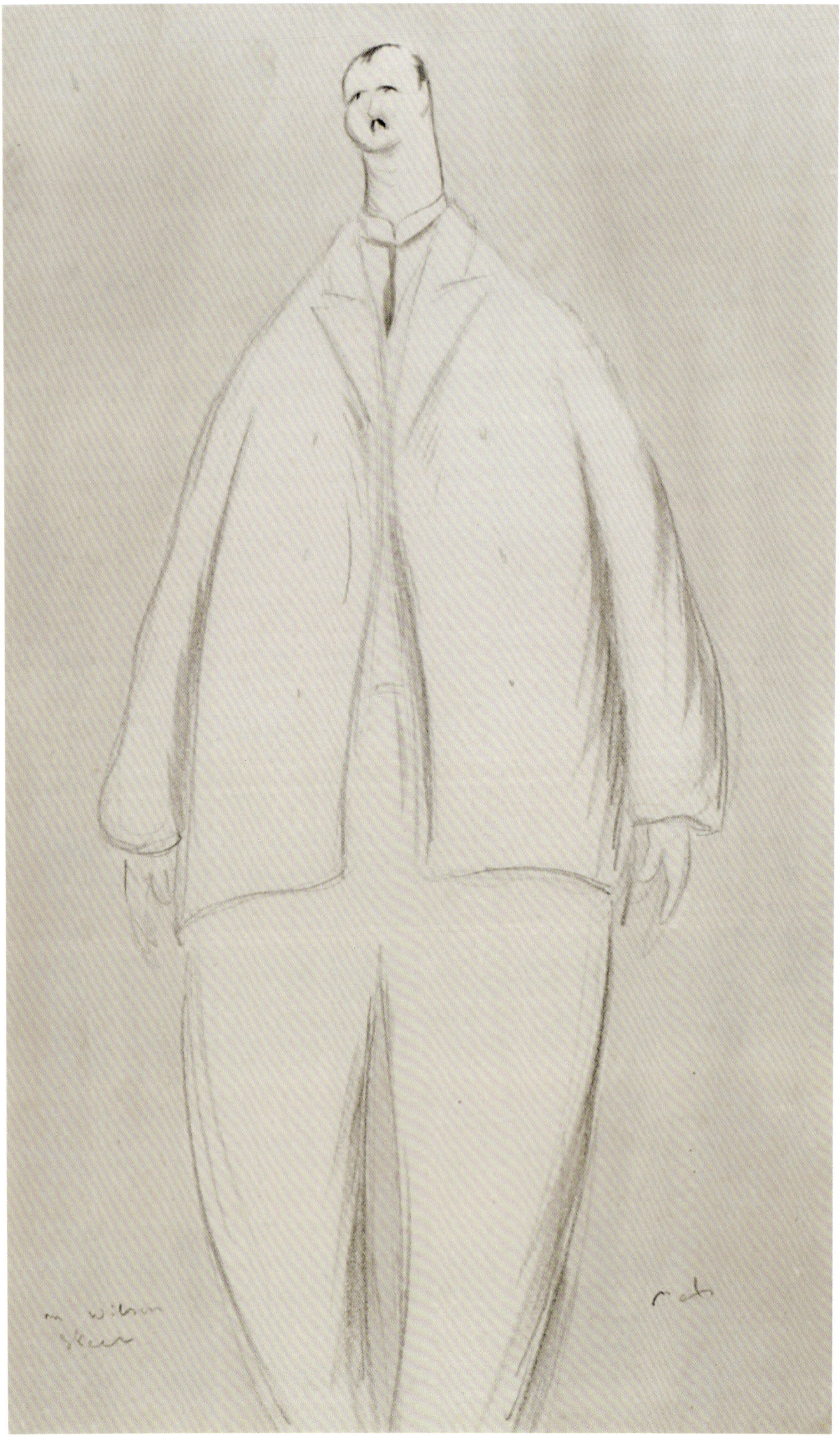

Mr Wilson Steer

Philip Wilson Steer, OM NEAC (1860-1942) was a leading British Impressionist. After studying art in Paris, he returned to England, where he assimilated the influences of James McNeill Whistler and such French painters as Edgar Degas and Jules Bastien-Lepage. In 1886, he helped to establish the New English Art Club as a focus for Impressionist inspired artists. However, by 1894, he had begun to effect a radical change of style by synthesising such French influences with exemplars of the British landscape tradition, notably Constable and Turner. He inculcated the essentials of this singularly British Impressionism, from 1893 to 1910, as a teacher at the Slade School of Fine Art, as an assistant to Professor Fred Brown.

23 Mr Wilson Steer
Signed 'Max' and inscribed with title
Pencil on tinted paper
12 ½ x 7 ¼ inches
Provenance: Piccadilly Gallery, London;
Thomas Geoffrey Blackwell; Christie's, London, 6 July 1951, Lot 4, with a Beerbohm of Henry Tonks [see 20]
Literature: Rupert Hart-Davis, *A Catalogue of the Caricatures of Max Beerbohm*, London: Macmillan, 1972, No 1592

Mr W Rothenstein Doing Nothing

William Rothenstein, RP IS NEAC (1872-1945), studied under Alphonse Legros at the Slade School of Fine Art and then in Paris, where he made the acquaintance of advanced French artists who were promoting Naturalism and Impressionism. He exhibited his own work mainly at the New English Art Club, the home of British Impressionism, and became a member of it in 1894.

Rothenstein met Max Beerbohm in Oxford in 1893; Beerbohm was studying at Merton College and Rothenstein was preparing his book of portraits, *Oxford Characters*, for The Bodley Head. Rothenstein introduced Beerbohm into an artistic circle that included Aubrey Beardsley, and they became close friends corresponding regularly until Rothenstein's death.

Beerbohm also made many caricatures of Rothenstein over the years. The present one shows the inability of Rothenstein to keep still, and so suggests his industriousness. The Italian inscription, 'Dolce far niente', meaning the sweetness of doing nothing, is therefore ironic in this instance. It was popular as a title for paintings during the late nineteenth and early twentieth centuries, especially of languorous women, including one by Rothenstein's friend, Charles Conder.

In the first half of the twentieth century, Rothenstein was a significant force in the British art world, proving influential as an administrator, dealer, teacher and writer. As an artist, he is best remembered for his portraits and for the images that he produced at home and abroad during the First and Second World Wars.

For works by William Rothenstein, please see Nos 37 and 38.

24 Mr W Rothenstein Doing Nothing
Inscribed with title and 'Dolce far niente'
Pencil
7 ¾ x 7 inches
Produced circa 1910-20

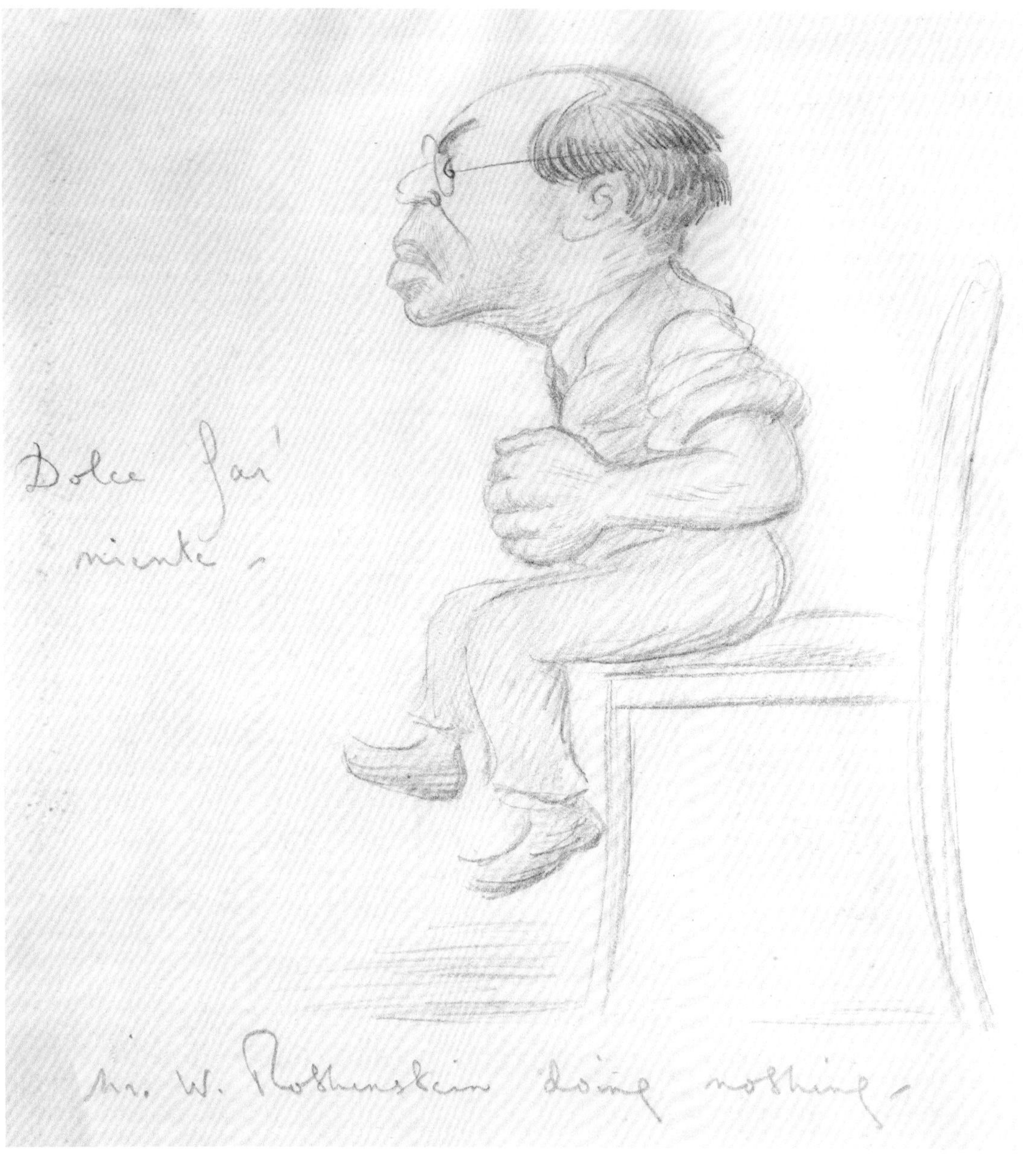

POWYS EVANS

Powys Arthur Lewthall Evans (1899-1982), also known as 'Quiz'

D S MacColl

The Scottish artist, Dugald Sutherland MacColl, NEAC (1859-1948), is best remembered as a critic and curator. He was educated at University College London and then Oxford, and studied painting under Frederick Brown at Westminster School of Art. He was an early enthusiast of both the French and British varieties of Impressionism, and became a member of the New English Art Club in 1896. However, like his friend and fellow member, Henry Tonks, he was critical of Post-Impressionism and its champion, Roger Fry. Both he and Fry lectured in art history at the Slade School of Fine Art while Tonks was Assistant Professor. He also wrote art criticism for *The Spectator* (1890-96) and *The Saturday Review* (1896-1906; 1921-30), and later for *The Week-end Review* (from 1930), and was editor of *The Architectural Review* (1901-5). The driving force behind the foundation of the National Art Collections Fund in 1905, he moved into museum administration, becoming the keeper of the Tate Gallery (1906-11) and then of the Wallace Collection (1911-24). In 1931, he published a collection of criticism, entitled *Confessions of a Keeper*, and, in 1940, his collected poems. The present portrait of him was produced in this later period. His crowning achievement, published in 1945, was the first major monograph on his friend, the British Impressionist, Philip Wilson Steer, which won the James Tait Black Memorial Prize for Biography.

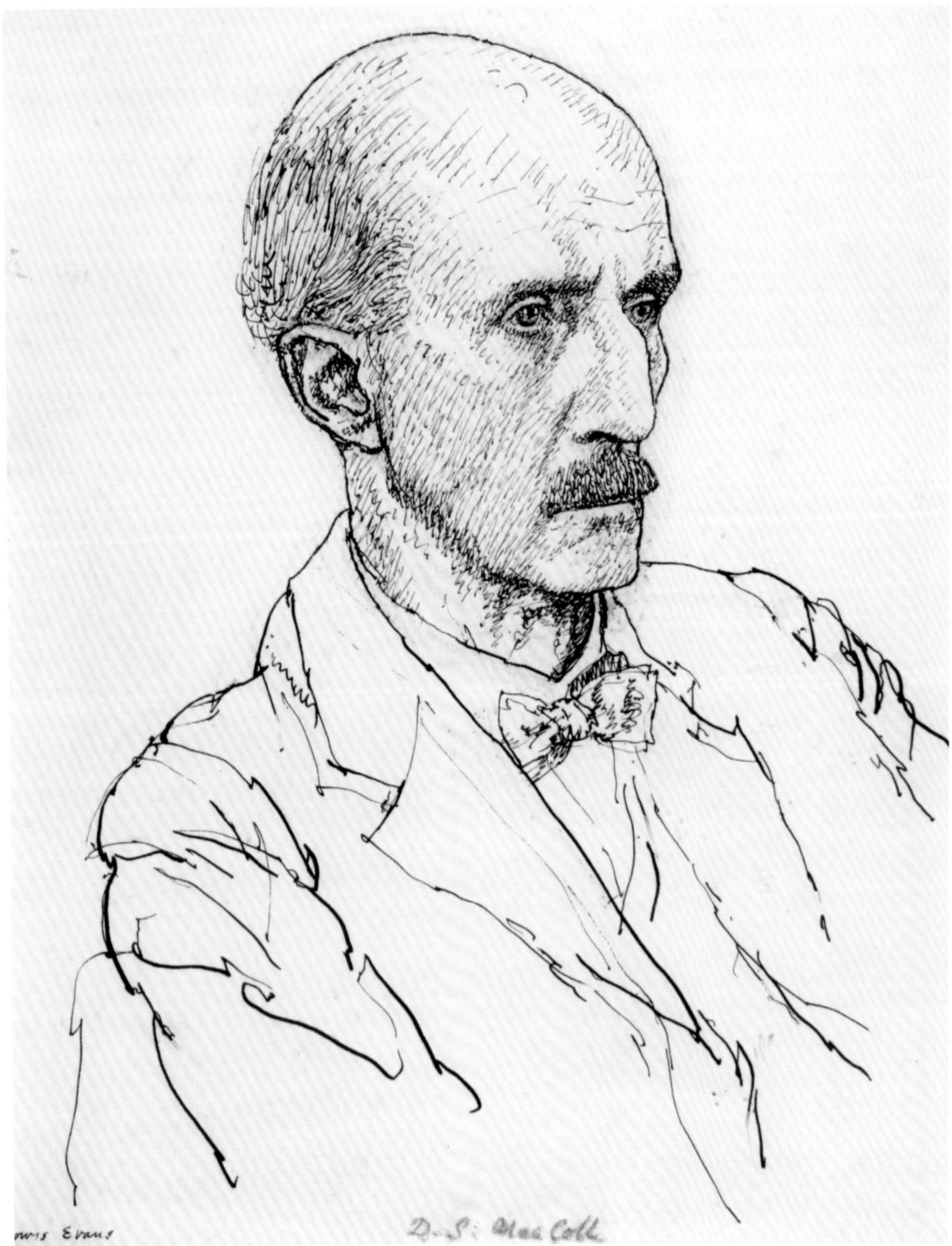

25 D S MacColl
Signed and inscribed with title
Pen and ink
12 x 9 inches
Illustrated: *The London Mercury*, Vol 32, 1935, Page 13

Randolph Schwabe

Randolph Schwabe, RWS LG NEAC (1885-1948), was both a student of the Slade School of Fine Art (1900-5) and its Professor in successor to Henry Tonks (1930-1948). In the years between, he established himself as a painter, printmaker, illustrator, and especially draughtsman, and was elected to the membership of the New English Art Club in 1917, among other societies. As Slade Professor, he followed Tonks' initiative by concentrating on imparting the skill of drawing (while giving responsibility for the teaching of painting to his friend, Allan Gwynne-Jones).

The present caricature by Powys Evans (who studied under Tonks at the Slade) shows that, though Schwabe generally had a reputation for being serious and scholarly, he could also be something of a dandy, almost in the vein of the *Fin de Siècle*. He may have cultivated a particular attention to his appearance during the 1920s, while he was working with Cyril Beaumont and Francis Kelly on such books as Kelly's *Historic Costume*, which was published in 1925, two years after Evans produced this caricature. Schwabe continued to carry a malacca cane throughout his life, and referred to it in his diaries. For instance, on 12 July 1934, he wrote, 'Tate Gallery in the afternoon, after fetching my long malacca from Smiths, with the new top made by Haussen in High Street, St Giles's' (Gill Clarke (ed), *The Diaries of Randolph Schwabe: British Art 1930-48*, Bristol: Sansom & Co, 2016, page 172).

For works by Randolph Schwabe, please see Nos **115-119**, **135**, **137**, **141-142**, **149** and **153**.

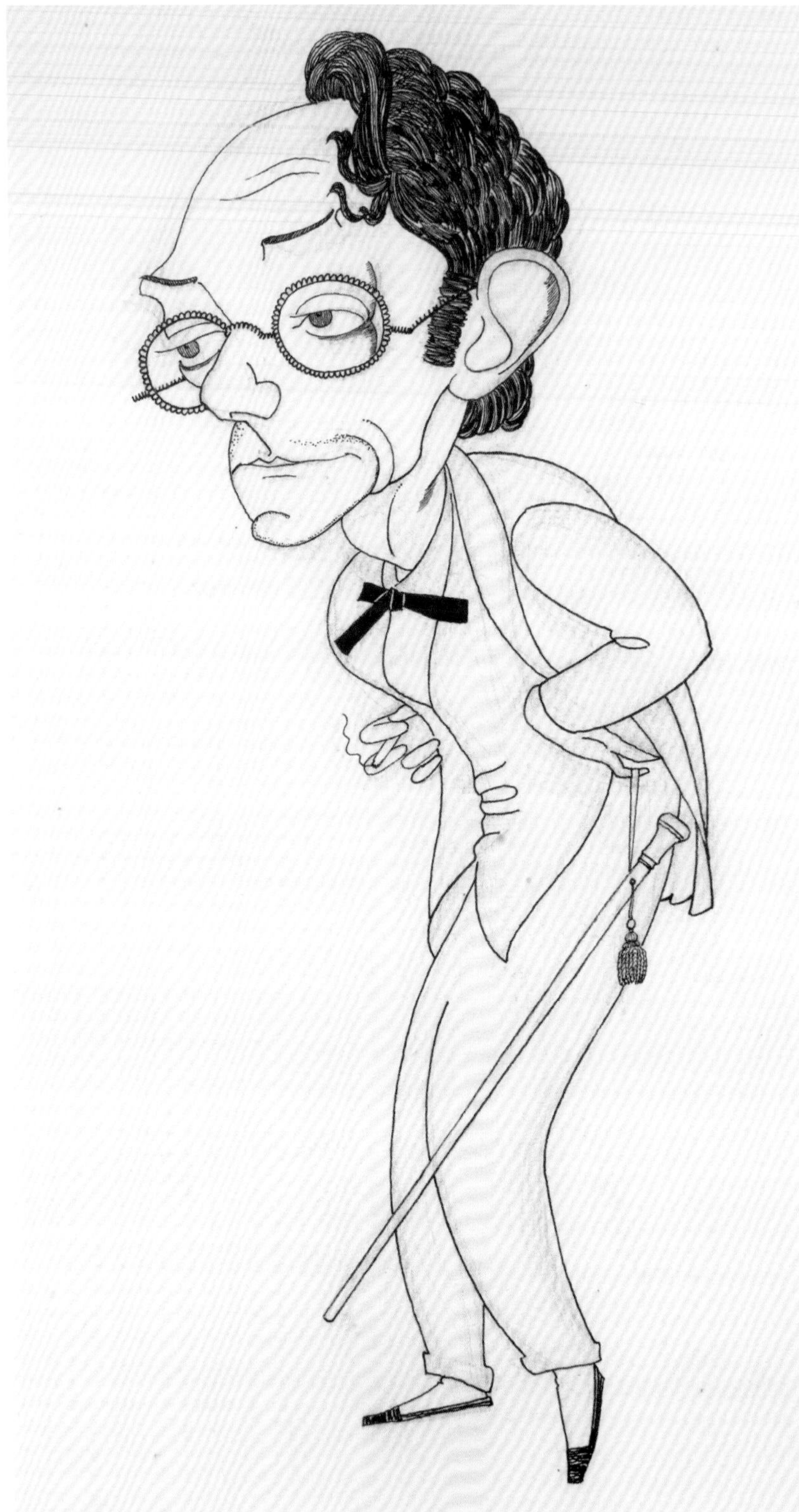

26 Randolph Schwabe
Inscribed with title on reverse
Pen and ink with pencil
15 ½ x 7 inches
Illustrated: *Drawing & Design: The Magazine of Taste*, November 1923, Page 658, 'Quiz' by Kennedy North

WILLIAM ORPEN

Major Sir William Newenham Montague Orpen, RA RWS RHA RI HROI RP PIS NEAC PNPS PS (1878-1931)

Precociously talented and greatly dedicated, the Irish artist, William Orpen, had the potential to succeed in almost any genre or medium of painting and drawing. By 1910, he had established a practice that would make him the most successful and honoured portraitist of his age. Less than a decade later, he was knighted for his significant work as an official war artist.

For a biography of William Orpen please refer to pages 188-189.

The Woman in White

William Orpen's *The Woman in White* was inspired by Wilkie Collins's ground-breaking 'sensation novel' of the same name, which was first published, in serial form in *All the Year Round*, in 1859-60. However, it was more likely intended as an exhibition watercolour than as an illustration for a specific edition of the novel, and was shown at both the New English Art Club, in Winter 1903, as No 9, and the sixth of the Goupil Gallery's 'Salon Series', in November-December 1911 (where it was priced at £31).

The watercolour almost certainly depicts the nocturnal encounter between the upright young drawing-master, Walter Hartright, and the 'woman in white', Anne Catherick (in 'The First Epoch', part one, chapter IV). Anne is the illegitimate half-sister of the novel's heroine, Laura Fairlie, and a victim of Laura's fiancé and later husband, the villainous Sir Percival Glyde. Though the encounter takes place on Hampstead Heath, Orpen's interpretation of the setting is wild and desolate, as if suggesting Anne's vulnerable state and agitated manner, following her escape from the asylum in which Glyde has had her incarcerated.

Collins's novel had an impact on its initial publication in 1859-60 that was immediately reflected in the visual arts. For instance, when James McNeill Whistler's painting, *Symphony in White No 1: The White Girl*, appeared at the Berners Street Gallery in 1862, it was under the title, *The Woman in White*. Perhaps inevitably, F G Stephens, the critic of *The Athenaeum*, took this to indicate that it was illustrative of the novel (28 June 1862). As a result, Whistler was forced to write to the magazine, stating that the title was chosen by the gallery, that he had not read the novel and that the 'painting simply represents a girl dressed in white standing in front of a white curtain' (5 July). However, Frederick Buckstone, the gallery's secretary, subsequently wrote to *The Athenaeum* to say that 'Mr Whistler was aware of … and pleased with the name' (19 July).

A decade later, in 1871, another arresting image returned the novel to the public's conscience, though this time with a more definite intention. Frederick Walker designed what was arguably 'the first high-art poster the world ever knew' (*The Athenaeum*, 27 October 1894) to advertise Wilkie Collins's own dramatisation of his novel, produced at the Olympic Theatre. It shows the back view of Anne Catherick, filling almost all of the picture space, exiting through a doorway and into the night.

When Orpen decided to respond to *The Woman in White*, early in the twentieth century, he may have done so for at least two reasons. Firstly, the trope – of a female figure dressed in white – offered formal and atmospheric possibilities. Secondly, the narrative situation – of an awkward, unequal encounter between a man and a woman – chimed with other literary subjects of interest.

Orpen produced a number of paintings of women dressed in white – sometimes modelled by his wife, Grace – that in all likelihood signalled his approval of the purely painterly qualities of Whistler in particular and of the synthesis of Aestheticism and Impressionism that he had helped to engender. One group of these paintings explores a figure on a beach or cliff, standing in a fresh breeze and sparkling light, and backed by scudding clouds; another, by contrast, has the figure seated at a window, either in reverie or looking out at a deep blue evening sky. To a degree, the present watercolour combines these two modes, the figure standing and on the move but set against the night and illuminated by the unseen moon.

While dedicated to the idea of pure painting, Orpen retained his early interest in literary and theatrical subjects. For instance, in 1901, around the time that *The Woman in White* is likely to have been painted, he produced several works in response to Max Beerhohm's *The Happy Hypocrite*. This 'Fairy Tale for Tired Men', set during the Regency age, was first published as a story in 1897, and then dramatised for a production at the Royalty Theatre in 1900, which Orpen is likely to have seen. The artist chose to focus on the initial encounter between the title character, Lord George Hell, and the dancer, Jenny Mere, when he seems at his most licentious and *she* at her most innocent – rather than on his reform, which proves to be the result of his devoted love for her. This encounter is presented visually as a melodramatic contrast between the erect, dark, brooding presence of Hell and the submissive, even cowering, white-dressed form of Jenny. Though Hell is a more troubling figure than Collins's Hartrick, they share elements of their appearance – including top hats and canes – and comparison with *The Woman in White* is clear.

27 **The Woman in White**
Inscribed with title
Pen ink and watercolour with pencil
18 ½ x 14 inches
Exhibited: New English Art Club, Winter 1903, No 9, and 'Salon Series' No 6, Goupil Gallery, London, November-December 1911 (£31)

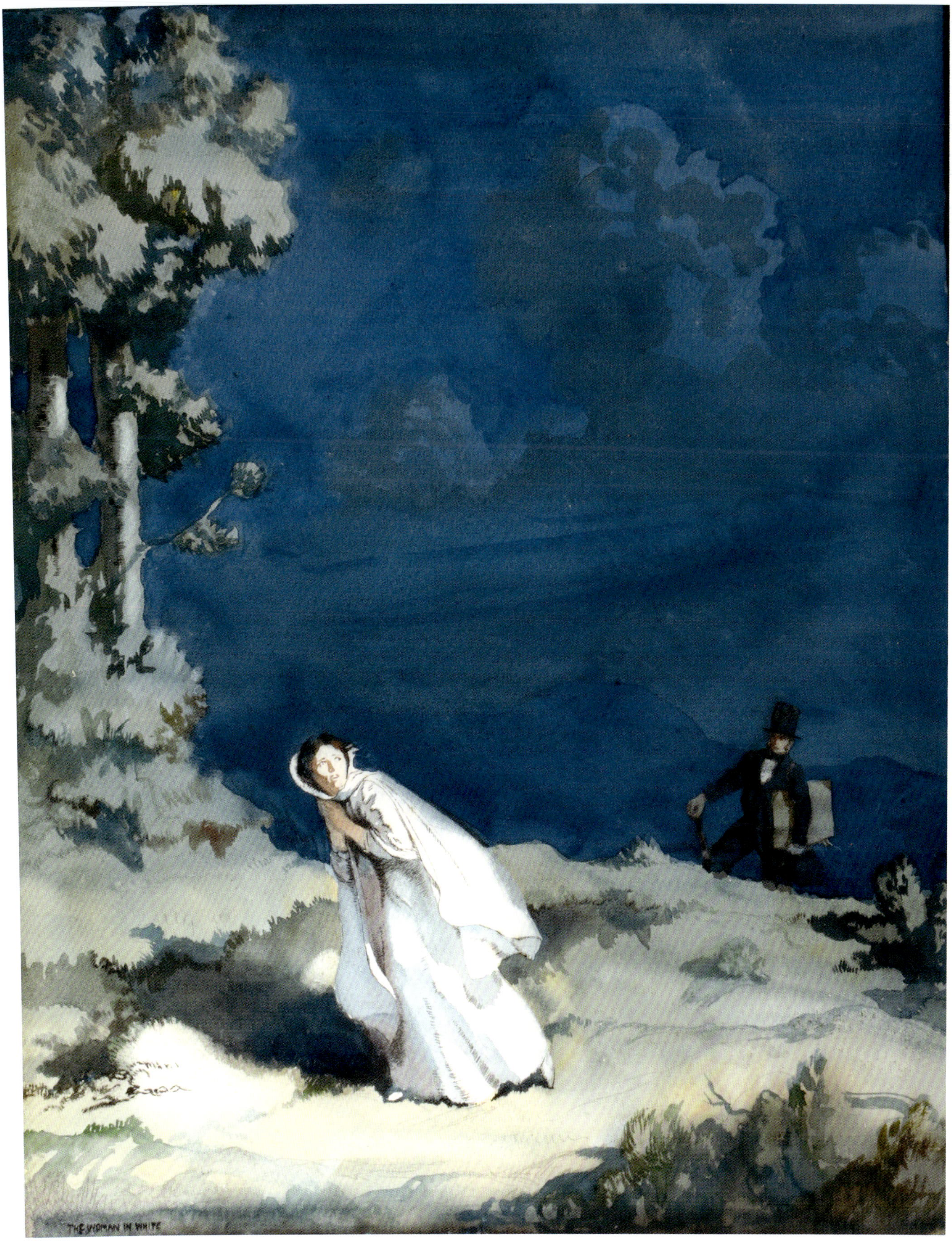
THE WOMAN IN WHITE

WILLIAM ORPEN

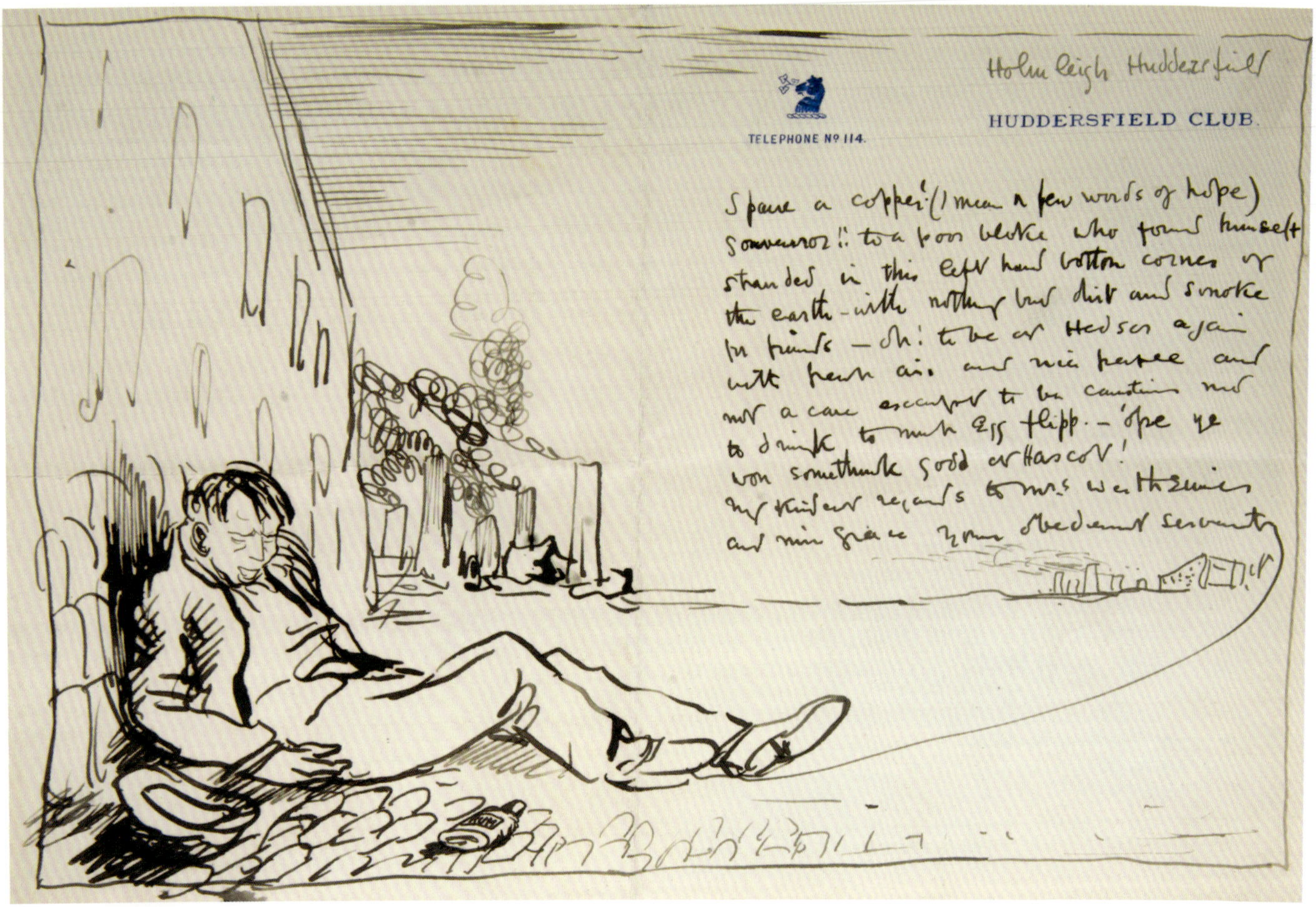

28 Spare a Copper!
Inscribed
Pen and ink on Huddersfield Club writing paper
7 x 9 inches

'Spare a copper! (I mean a few words of hope) governor!! To a poor bloke who found himself stranded in this left hand bottom corner of the earth – with nothing but dirt and smoke for friends – oh! to be a Hedger again with fresh air and nice people and not a care except to be cautious not to drink too much Egg flipp. – 'ope ye won somethink good at Hascot!
My kindest regards to Mrs Wertheimer and Miss Grace
Your obedient servant'

Spare a Copper!

In 1906, William Orpen went to Huddersfield, Yorkshire, to fulfil a commission to paint six-year-old Annie Isobel Lumb, known as 'Lilo'. She was the only child of Joe Lumb, owner of a successful family textile company, and his wife, Ada, who lived at Holmleigh, Park Drive. The completed portrait (now in the collections of Huddersfield Art Gallery) is possibly modelled on James McNeill Whistler's *Harmony in Grey and Green: Miss Cecily Alexander* (1872, Tate).

Orpen seems not to have enjoyed his visit to Huddersfield, as is indicated by letters that he wrote and illustrated at the time, including the present one. In this, he presents himself as a former countryman, who has moved to the industrial city and fallen on hard times. It is written and drawn on the headed paper of the Huddersfield Club, a gentleman's club situated centrally at 22 John William Street. However, he has added the further address of 'Holmleigh', suggesting that he was staying with the Lumbs for at least part of his visit.

While the recipient of this letter is not specified, Orpen does mention both a 'Mrs Wertheimer' and a 'Miss Grace', names that may aid the discovery of Orpen's intended reader. In 1904, the art dealer, Charles Wertheimer, had become Orpen's leading patron, and, in the same year, Orpen showed a portrait of Wertheimer as his first exhibit at the Royal Academy. However, Wertheimer's wife, Frieda, died in that year, so he was a widower when Orpen produced this letter in 1906. Orpen was also in contact with Charles's brother, Asher, another dealer, and, at some point, produced a drawing of the head of his wife, Flora (which he gave to the artist, Alfred Rich). Flora lived until 1922, so it is likely that she is the 'Mrs Wertheimer' mentioned by Orpen, and thus possible that he was writing to Asher. (For more on this branch of the Wertheimer family, and its patronage of John Singer Sargent, see the note on Harold Squire's *Capri* [122].) Less certain is the identification of 'Miss Grace', and her possible connection to the Wertheimers. Orpen's own wife was called Grace, but it seems unlikely that he would have described her as 'Miss' or coupled her with Flora Wertheimer in sending his regards.

THE NATIONAL GALLERY

POWYS EVANS

Powys Arthur Lewthall Evans
(1899-1982),
also known as 'Quiz'

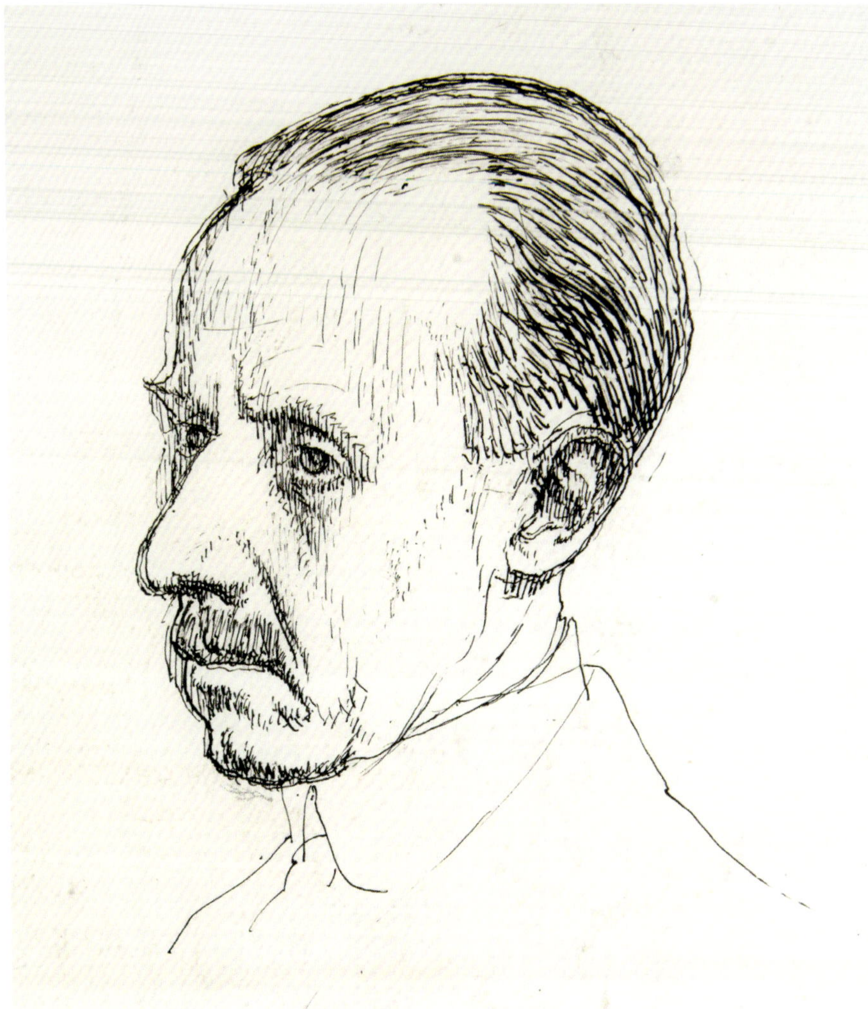

29 Sir Charles Holmes
Inscribed with title below mount
Pen and ink
6 x 6 inches
Illustrated: *The London Mercury*, Vol 29, 1929, Page 295, 'Modern Portraits – LXX: Sir Charles Holmes'

Sir Charles Holmes

Charles John Holmes, RWS NEAC (1868-1936) was both a landscape artist and an art historian. Educated at Eton and Oxford, he initially worked for publishers, including the Vale Press, which was founded by Charles Ricketts. It was Ricketts who encouraged him to develop his self-taught skills of drawing and painting, and, in 1900, he began to exhibit at the New English Art Club, becoming a member four years later (on the same day as John Singer Sargent). By then he had established himself as a significant critic and historian of art, with publications that included *Constable and his Influence on Landscape* (1902). He served as co-editor of the new art periodical, *The Burlington Magazine* (1903-9), and was appointed Slade Professor of Fine Art at Oxford (1904-10). He was Director of the National Portrait Gallery (1909-16) and then the National Gallery (1916-28), and did much to popularise the collection of the latter by establishing departments responsible for photography and publishing. He was knighted in 1921 and appointed KCVO in 1928. In 1929, the year that the present portrait drawing was published, he was elected a full member of the Royal Society of Painters in Water-Colours. As a painter, he is remembered for the landscapes and industrial scenes that he produced in Northern England.

For a work by Charles Holmes, please see No 159.

H M BATEMAN

Henry Mayo Bateman (1887-1970)

H M Bateman established his inimitable style before the First World War when, as he put it, he 'went mad on paper', by drawing people's mood and character. This culminated in 'The Man Who ...', his famous series of cartoons dramatising social gaffes.

For a biography of H M Bateman, please refer to page 190.

Student Day at the National Gallery

In the present cartoon, H M Bateman satirised a long-held practice of the National Gallery. From early in its history, the gallery, opened in 1824, had given special privileges to art students, and allowed them access so that they could copy the works in the collection. By the end of the nineteenth century, that access was allowed on Thursdays and Fridays, which were designated as 'Students' Days', and it was exclusive during the first hour of each of those, so that copyists could set up their easels and start work. Members of the general public could enter on those days, but only from 11 o'clock at the cost of sixpence (while on other days they could enter from 10 o'clock and for free).

If potential copyists had never exhibited at a London gallery, they were required to demonstrate proficiency in oil or watercolour by submitting a specimen of work to the Keeper of the National Gallery, who, throughout the Edwardian period, was Hawes Harison Turner. However, once a card of admission was granted, it remained available for life, so that the numbers of copyists increased each year. These copyists could be divided into three categories: current students, 'artists who come to make copies either on commission or for sale on their own account' and 'dilettante ladies and gentlemen' (a distinction made by Frances A Gerard in *Cassell's Family Magazine* on January 1893, pages 119-20, in one of a number of articles on the subject of the Students' Days published by various authors during the late nineteenth century).

The presence and productivity of these copyists is suggested by the parliamentary report on the National Gallery for 1898, given by Sir Edward Poynter (its Director from 1894 to 1904 as well as President of the Royal Academy until 1918): 'the total number of students' attendances at the Gallery in Trafalgar-square on Thursdays and Fridays was 18,990', and 'independently of partial studies, 841 oil-colour copies of pictures have been made, viz, 357 from the works of 73 old masters, and 484 from the works of 39 modern painters' (*London Evening Standard*, 6 April 1899, page 2).

The institution of Students' Days remained in some form at the National Gallery until the outbreak of the Second World War, after which copyists were allowed to return in 1952.

30 Student Day at the National Gallery
An Impression from Life
Signed and dated 1910
Pen ink and watercolour with bodycolour
14 x 9 ¾ inches
Illustrated: *The Bystander*, 27 April 1910, Page 173

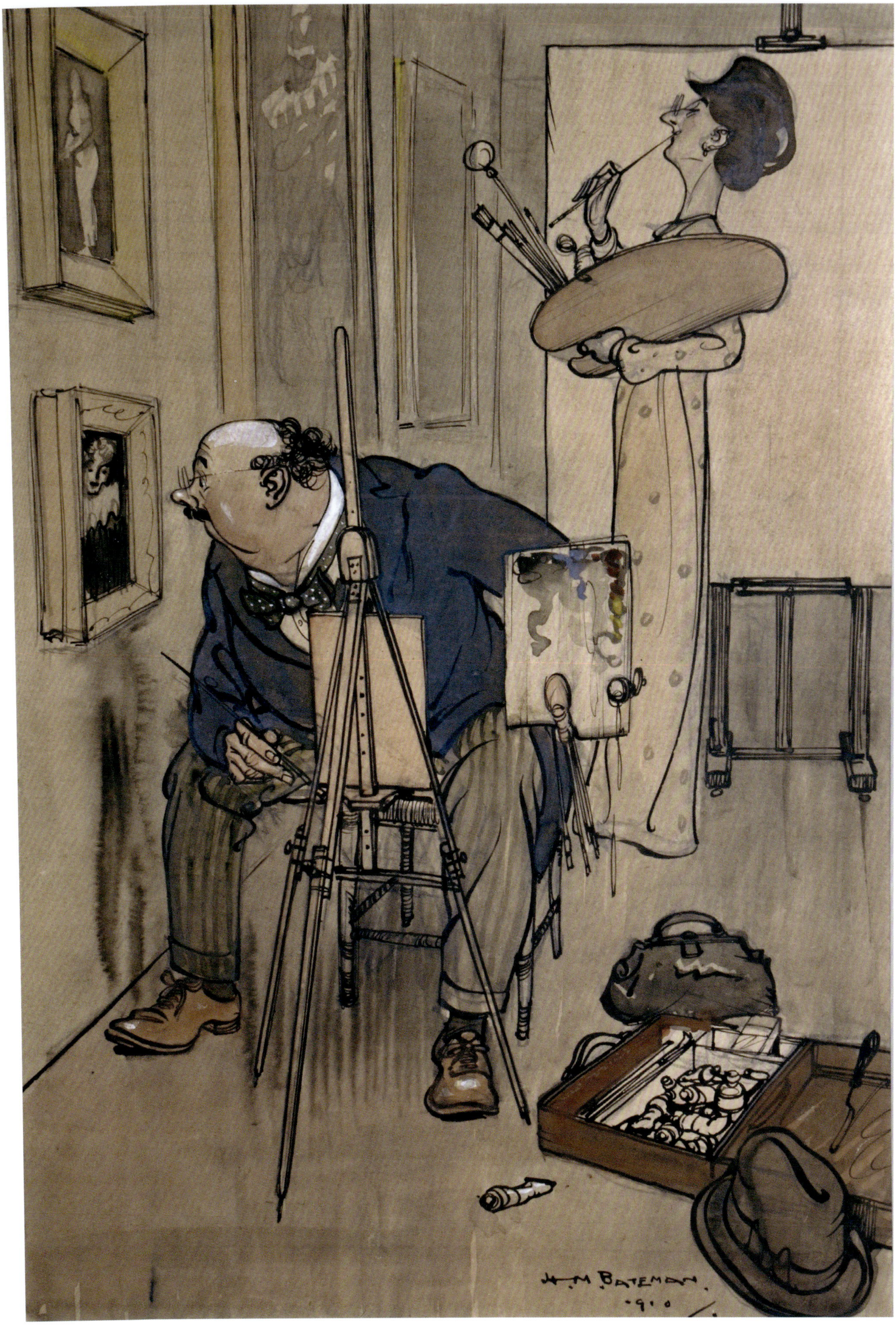
H. M. BATEMAN
·910

BOHEMIANISM IN PARIS AND LONDON

H M BATEMAN

Henry Mayo Bateman (1887-1970)

Nature Lost in Art

By the time that H M Bateman produced the present caricature, the 'Latin Quarter' of Paris had long been frequented by students, and specifically art students, in elements of Bohemian guise: long hair, broad-brimmed hats and loose articles of clothing, including capes and floppy bow ties. These elements had been established by the French Romantics of the 1830s, though they did so more in an attempt to define themselves in opposition to bourgeois conformity than to create a specific look. The British understanding of Parisian Bohemianism and the appeal of it for young would-be British artists was then fostered by a literary tradition that stretched from William Makepeace Thackeray's *The Paris Sketch Book* (1840) to George Du Maurier's *Trilby* (1894) and beyond.

Through the nineteenth century, British art students were increasingly attracted to the more liberal – and more thorough – French system of training. From the mid 1860s, some Paris ateliers even began to cater especially for foreign students, the most popular of which were the Académie Julian and the atelier of Carolus-Duran. Few of these were actually situated in the *Quartier Latin*, the area on the left-bank of the Seine that surrounds the Sorbonne (the historic university of Paris) and includes the Ecole des Beaux-Arts. Nevertheless, it became synonymous with student life, and its bistros and cafes proved a draw for British art students who were working across the city.

31 Nature Lost in Art
Earnest Students of the Famous Quartier Latin
More of the Strange Objects Seen by H M Bateman in Paris
Signed, inscribed with title and dated 1911
Pen ink and watercolour with bodycolour
15 ¼ x 10 inches
Illustrated: *The Bystander*, 28 February 1911, Page 171

Literature: Anthony Anderson, *The Man Who Was H M Bateman*, Exeter: Webb & Bower, 1982, Page 79
Exhibited: 'H M Bateman. The Man Who Went Mad on Paper', Cartoon Museum, London, 2012

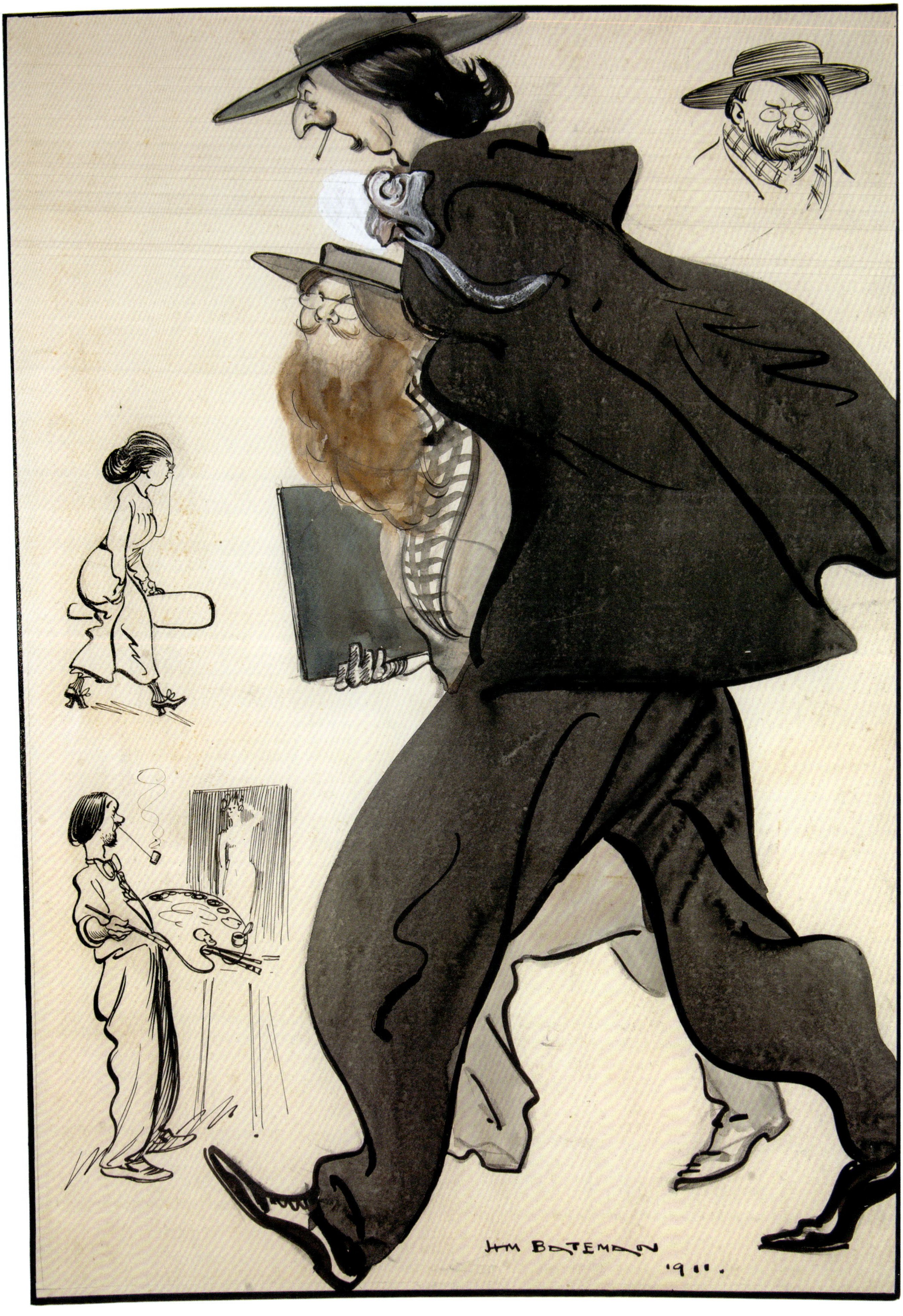
H M BATEMAN
1911.

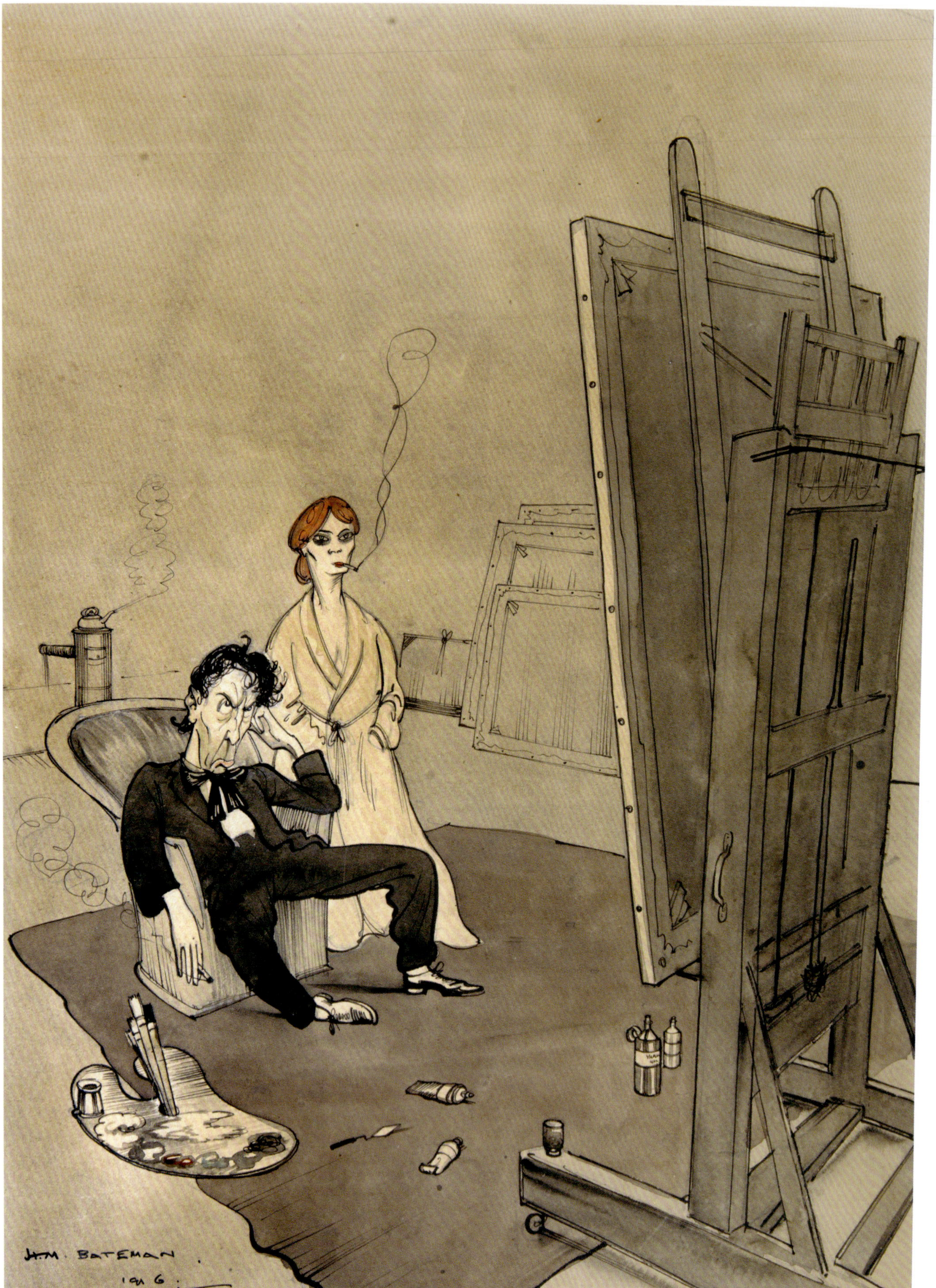
H.M. BATEMAN
1916.

H M BATEMAN

Henry Mayo Bateman (1887-1970)

32 **A Bit of Old Chelsea**
Is it genius or liver?
Signed and dated 1916
Pen ink and watercolour with bodycolour
13 ¾ x 9 ¾ inches
Illustrated: *The Tatler*, 30 August 1916, Page 285

A Bit of Old Chelsea

If British artists were drawn to Paris's *Quartier Latin*, they also created their own equivalent in London's Chelsea. Chelsea was the habitation of a number of artists by the early nineteenth century, and 'From the early 1880s the area where Kings Road met Church Street had become known as The Latin Quarter because of the hundreds of studios in existence and being built' (according to Anne Galbally, *Charles Conder: The Last Bohemian*, Melbourne University Publishing, 2003, page 122). And, while the Bohemian status for Chelsea would be increasingly disputed, with Bloomsbury and later Fitzrovia and Soho being suggested as alternatives or successors, it was sustained in both reality and the popular imagination well into the twentieth century.

By the time that H M Bateman produced *A Bit of Old Chelsea* in 1916 – the title suggesting pottery as well as topography – he himself was an habitué of the area, having become a member of the Chelsea Arts Club in 1910. By 1918, he would also be working there, from 5 Rossetti Studios, Flood Street. A decade earlier, Chelsea Art School had been run from that very studio by Augustus John and William Orpen, two painters who – through their artistic ambitions and flamboyant personalities – may have helped inform Bateman's caricature of the quintessential Chelsea artist. Its questioning subtitle, 'is it genius or liver?, seems to derive ultimately from a humorous verse that was circulating in various American newspapers in the late 1880s:

> Why seems the young poet so weary and sad?
> Existing under constant restraint?
> What is it that shuts out every thought that is glad,
> Is it genius or liver complaint?

POWYS EVANS

Powys Arthur Lewthall Evans (1899-1982), also known as 'Quiz'

33 **Jacob Epstein**
Inscribed with title below mount
Pen and ink
8 x 8 inches

Jacob Epstein

The sculptor and painter, Jacob Epstein (1880-1959), was born in New York to Russian-Polish parents of Orthodox Jewish descent, and initially studied at the Art Students League. On moving to Paris, he attended the Académie Julian, though it was only once he had settled in London in 1905 that he began to define his identity as that of a sculptor. This he achieved from 1907, when he started work on both distinctive modelled portrait busts and carved reliefs for Charles Holden's new headquarters of the new British Medical Association in the Strand. The National Vigilance Society instigated a press campaign to have those reliefs removed on the grounds of obscenity, but the support of key members of the art world ensured their immediate survival and aided the artist's lasting fame. He developed an interest in non-Western sculptural models that aligned him increasingly with Modernists on both sides of the English Channel. And, though he never fully became a member of Percy Wyndham Lewis's Vorticists, he produced, in *Rock Drill* (1913-16, Tate), the movement's most ambitious sculpture. After the First World War, he gradually changed direction, by committing himself more fully to the modelling tradition in Western sculpture, and creating warmly humanist figurative works. Those works eventually received acclaim and led to Epstein being knighted in 1954. Just a year earlier, he had helped found the Society of Portrait Sculptors.

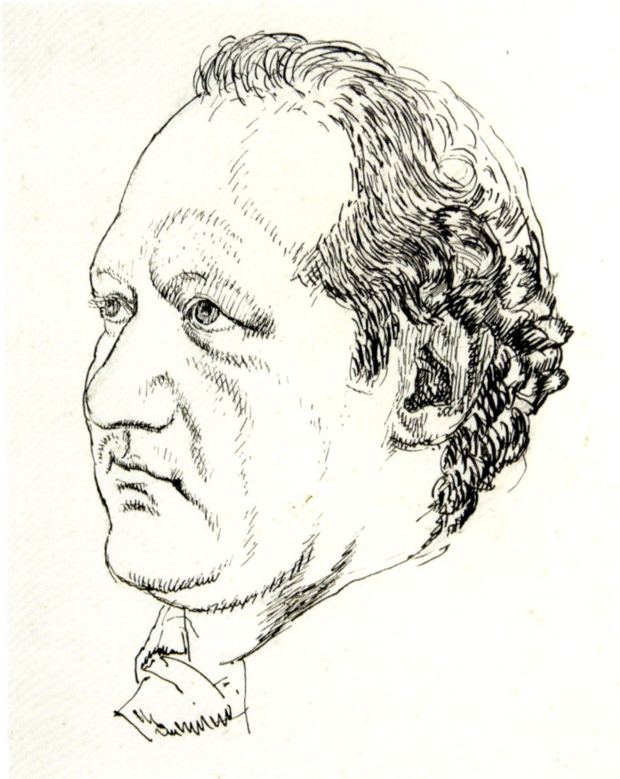

3: EXPERIENCE AND RECOLLECTION OF THE FIRST WORLD WAR

Artists working during the First World War both examined and enriched the long tradition of military imagery. Some of those on active service aided the campaign through such skills as cartography or camouflage, while others recorded their personal experiences in almost the visual equivalent of diaries. As the war persisted, the British government appointed a number of official war artists, in one of several schemes intended to document aspects of the conflict. Those not chosen to serve were often still keen to contribute, and produce images that reflected the martial mood of the age for exhibition and publication. Then, when the war did finally end, artists played a central role in the significant and sensitive task of memorialisation.

Of the artists included here, Joseph Gray, Edward Handley-Read and Gilbert Ledward all saw active service, the first two on the Western Front and the third in Italy. When Gray was invalided out and returned home to Scotland, he became the 'war artist' of *The Graphic*, producing articles and illustrations that were based on his and others' first-hand knowledge of trench warfare. Handley-Read went on to organise a studio that produced diagrams and models for military instruction, before showing his own watercolours in a pioneering series of exhibitions, entitled 'The British Firing-Line'. Ledward was appointed an official war artist, and produced plaster reliefs of men in action that would provide the foundation for his subsequent war memorials. Gray would also continue to rehearse the imagery of war in peacetime, becoming sought after as a military painter.

William Rothenstein and Algernon Talmage were among those who, while not fighting, were able to serve their country, and the wider empire, as official war artists. Rothenstein was of one the artists who had encouraged the War Office to implement the scheme, and he was finally appointed to it late in 1917, spending three months on the Cambrai Front (in the company of Eric Kennington). The British War Memorials committee selected several of the works that he exhibited at the Goupil Gallery in 1918. Like Rothenstein, Talmage went to the Cambrai Front, but for the Canadian Government and attached to the Canadian Army Veterinary Corps. The resulting paintings appeared in a number of international exhibitions of Canadian war art. In 1919, Rothenstein also went to France on behalf of the Canadian War Records.

Samuel Begg and Robert Talbot Kelly had both had very active lives as travelling artists by the time that war broke out in 1914. However, at respectively 60 and 53 years of age, they were too old to be likely to enlist or, from January 1916, liable to be conscripted. Begg had been a staff artist with *The Illustrated London News* since 1895, and a visual reporter of royal and military events in Europe and India. So, he remained well able to work up on-the-spot sketches, whether by professional colleagues or servicemen, of such scenes as the landing of ANZAC troops at Gallipoli. Similarly, Kelly had immersed himself in the life of Egypt – setting up a studio in Cairo, learning Arabic and living with the Bedouin – and had then rehearsed his experience once back in England. So, he was probably able to respond empathetically to the wartime activities of his son, Richard, by producing such watercolours as *War in the Trenches*. Though at one remove from the action, Begg and Kelly used their talents to engage with the reported events and, as with all the artists represented here, communicate them to a wider public through powerful images.

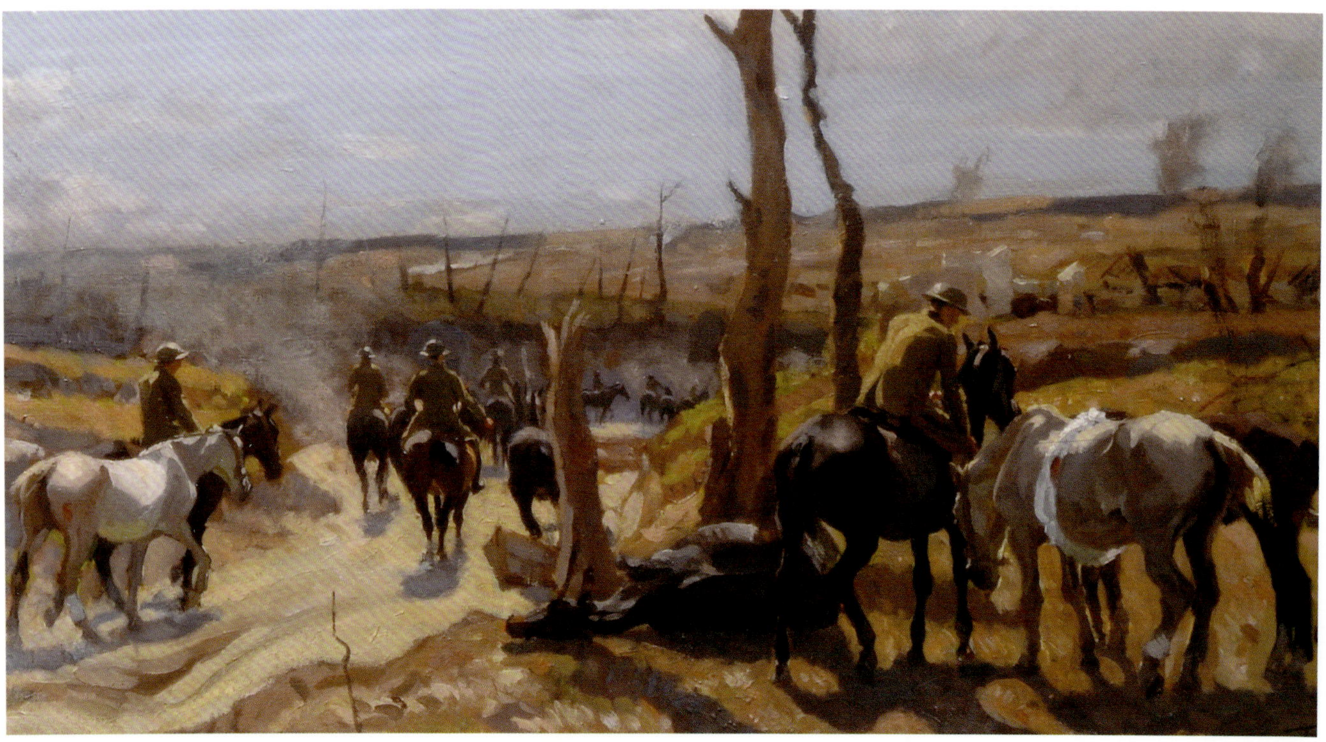

Detail of Algernon Talmage, *Wounded Horses Returning from the Front, France* [41]

GEORGE CLAUSEN

Sir George Clausen, RA RSW RWS HRBA RI ROI NEAC (1852-1944)

George Clausen absorbed a range of Continental influences to become a significant *plein-air* artist of scenes of rural life in oil, watercolour and pastel. The striking, sometime stark naturalism that he learned from Bastien-Lepage and Millet gave way to a light-filled, atmospheric Impressionism. While promoting new developments in painting as a leading member of the New English Art Club, he was eventually accepted by more established societies of artists, including the Royal Academy, becoming a notable Professor of Painting at the Royal Academy Schools. In addition to his distinctive landscapes – both with and without figures – he essayed portraits, nudes, interiors and still life compositions, and produced occasional, but significant murals, one of which was recognised with a knighthood.

For a biography of George Clausen, please refer to pages 176-177

34 **Study for 'Youth Mourning'**
Pencil
13 x 15 inches

Study for 'Youth Mourning'

This pencil drawing of a crouching naked girl was produced as a study for George Clausen's major oil, *Youth Mourning* (1916, Imperial War Museums). The painting provided a sensitive, if stark response to the loss of so many soldiers on the Western Front, by channelling the grief of the artist's daughter, Katharine, at the death of her fiancé, Geraint Payne. A Second Lieutenant in the 1st Highland Light Infantry, Payne had been killed in action at the Battle of Neuve Chapelle, France, on 14 March 1915.

The painting shows a personification of Youth, prostrate before a grave marked by a wooden cross. The distant barren landscape, with its waterlogged craters, suggests a battlefield and evokes a sense of absence. The small plants in the foreground, pushing through the soil, may provide signs of hope.

When *Youth Mourning* was exhibited at the Royal Academy of Arts in 1916, it elicited many positive reviews. It was acquired by C N Luxmoore of Torquay, the owner of at least three other works by Clausen. In 1929, Luxmoore presented it to the Imperial War Museum, and the other works to the Tate Gallery. Since then, it has come to epitomise both grief at those killed in war and a particular phase in Clausen's career. As such, it was included in two major exhibitions: 'Artists & the Great War', held at the Newcastle upon Tyne Polytechnic Art Gallery in 1979 (as No 6), and 'Sir George Clausen RA, 1852-1944', mounted by Bradford Art Galleries and Museums in 1980 (as No 20). As a study for the painting, the present example of Clausen's strength of draughtsmanship holds similar connotations.

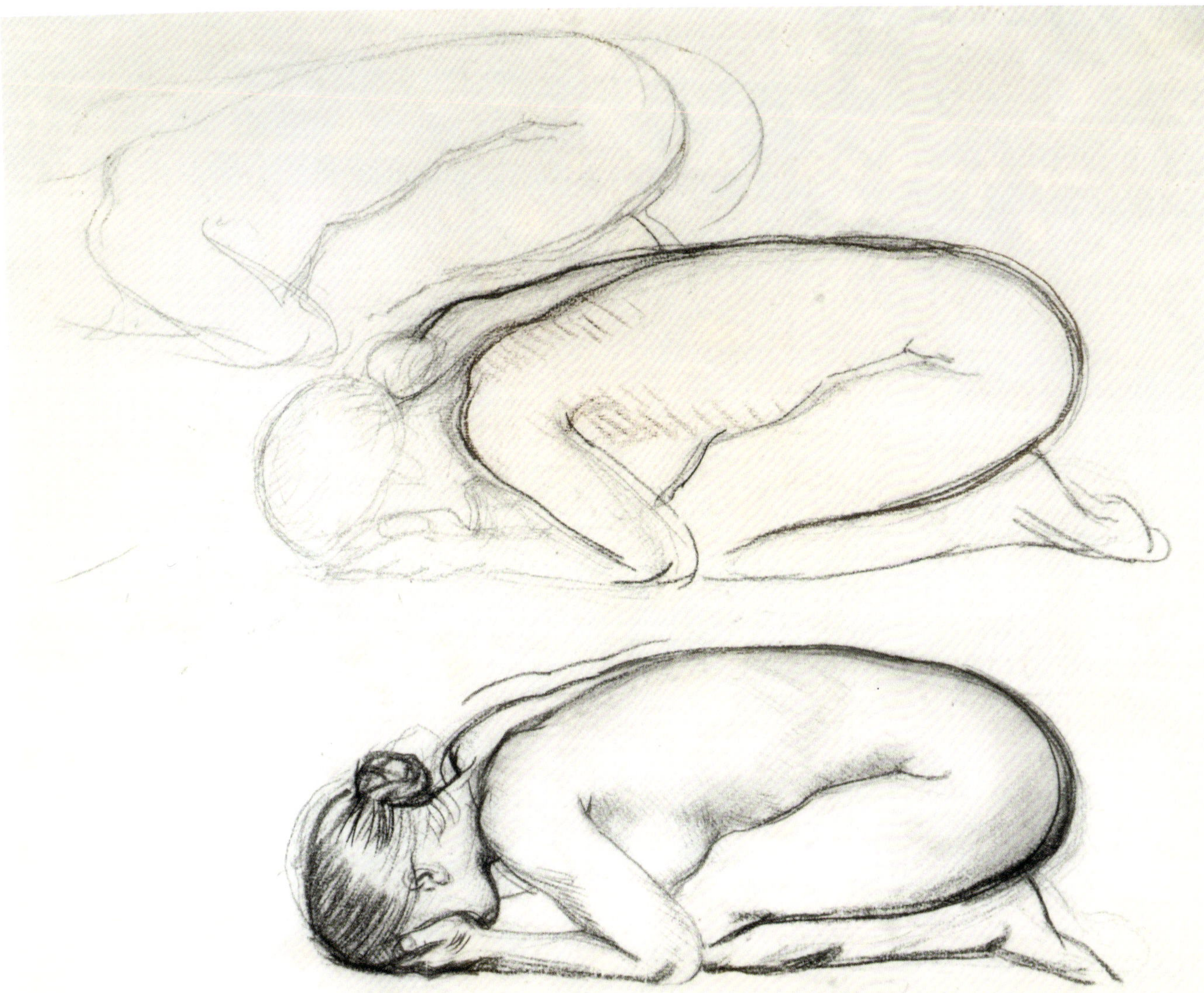

SAMUEL BEGG

Samuel Begg (1854-1936)

Samuel Begg was a significant periodical illustrator, and occasional cartoonist, working initially in his adoptive home of Australasia and then, from 1886, in his native Britain. He became best known as a staff member and special artist for *The Illustrated London News*.

For a biography of Samuel Begg, please refer to page 191.

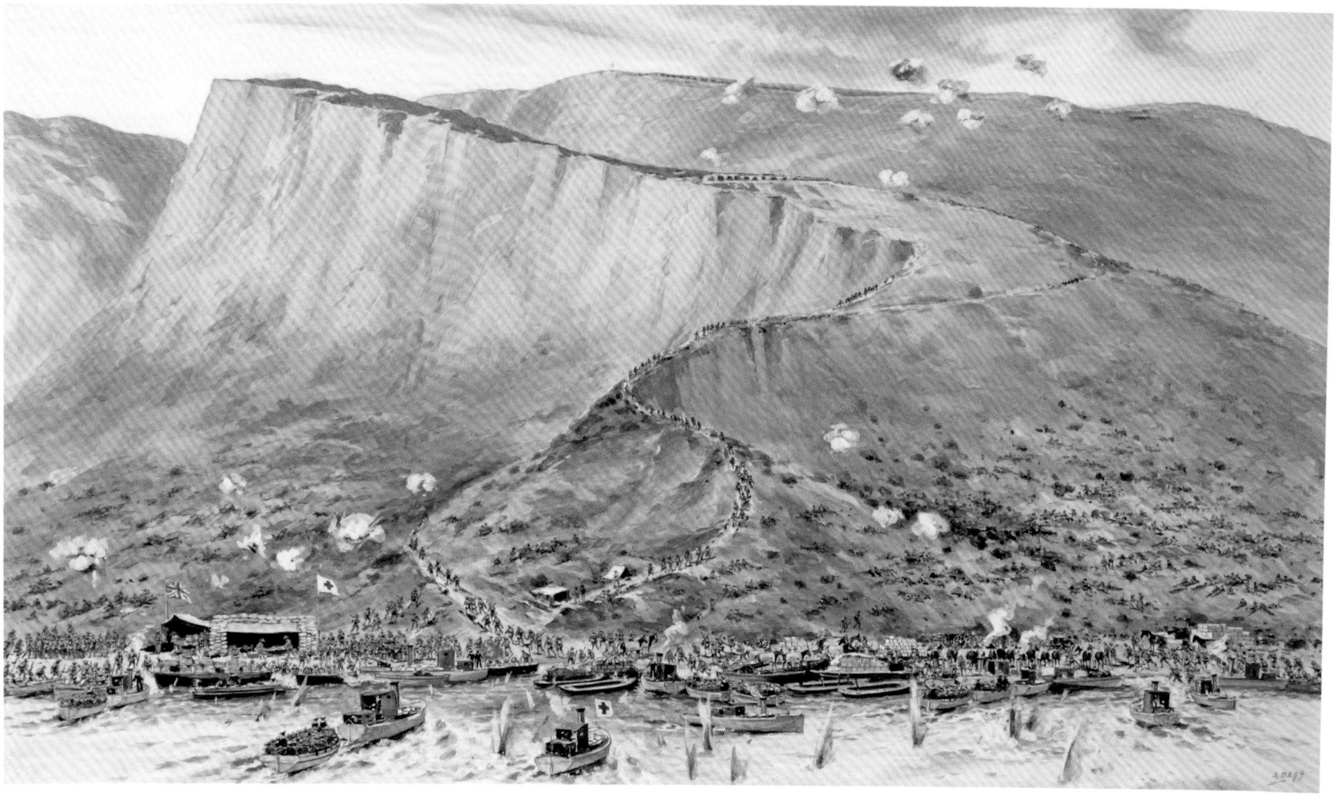

The Great Landing of Troops and Supplies at Gaba Tepe

The Landing at Gaba Tepe, which took place on 25 April 1915, was an amphibious invasion of the Gallipoli Peninsula by Entente forces, mostly composed of the ANZAC (Australian and New Zealand Army Corps). It began the land phase of the Gallipoli Campaign, in which troops planned to overtake the Ottoman forts that controlled the passage of the Dardanelles strait. However, the campaign as a whole proved a failure, with many thousands of casualties and an eventual evacuation in January 1916, which led the Ottomans to consider it a great – if temporary – victory. 25 April is now commemorated in Australia and New Zealand as a national day of remembrance known as Anzac Day.

35 **The Great Landing of Troops and Supplies at Gaba Tepe**
Signed
Inscribed 'Gaba Tepe' and dated '25 April 1915' on reverse
Watercolour and bodycolour
13 x 21 ¾ inches
Illustrated: *The Illustrated London News*, 22 May 1915, Pages 650-651

ROBERT TALBOT KELLY

Robert George Talbot Kelly, RBA RBC RI (1861-1934)

Robert Talbot Kelly was best known as a painter in oil and watercolour of meticulous and atmospheric Egyptian subjects. He settled in Cairo, and absorbed himself in the landscape and culture, learning Arabic and spending time with the Bedouin. As a result, his studio became a destination for foreign visitors and he was eventually awarded an Order by the Kedive of Egypt. However, he was able to broaden his range, and worked with success as far afield as Iceland and Burma.

For a biography of Robert Talbot Kelly, please refer to page 192.

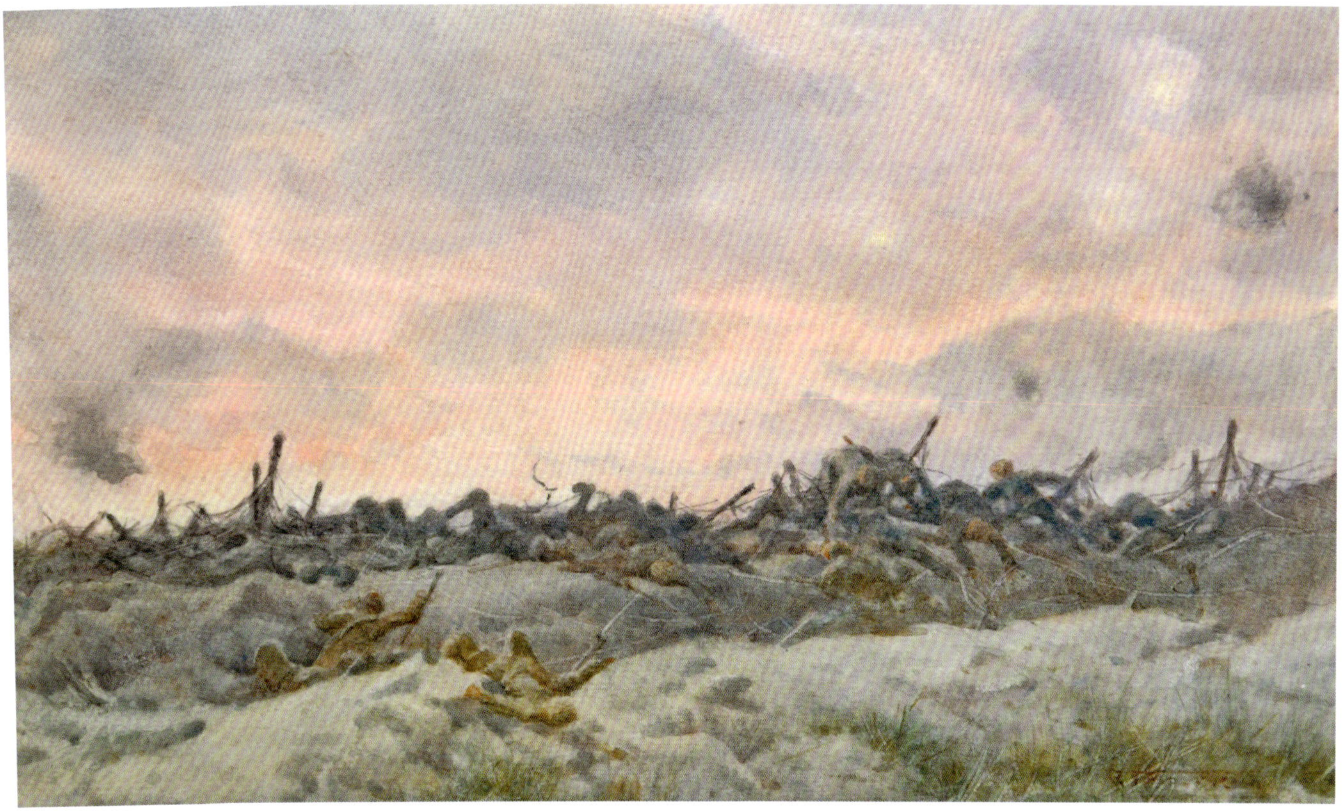

War in the Trenches

Though it is not known whether Robert Talbot Kelly undertook any service during the First World War, his painter son, Richard, served as a Second Lieutenant in the Royal Artillery in France between 1915 and 1918. Richard saw combat in the battles of Loos (1915), the Somme (1916) and Arras (1917), and was awarded a Military Cross in June 1917. Wounded by a shell blast at the Battle of Passchendaele in August 1917, he convalesced at home until April 1918, when he returned to France. Later that year, he taught camouflage at the School of Artillery, Larkhill, Wiltshire. He made a number of watercolours and drawings of his experiences in France (that are now in the National Army Museum), and the present watercolour, by his father, may be based on one of those or on Richard's memories. Richard's memoir, *A Subaltern's Odyssey: Memoirs of the Great War, 1915–1917*, was published posthumously in 1980.

36 **War in the Trenches**
Signed
Watercolour
7 x 10 inches

WILLIAM ROTHENSTEIN

Sir William Rothenstein, RP IS NEAC (1872-1945)

William Rothenstein was a significant force in the British art world of the first half of the twentieth century, proving influential as an administrator, dealer, teacher and writer. As an artist, he is best remembered for his portraits and for the images that he produced at home and abroad during the First and Second World Wars.

For a biography of William Rothenstein, please refer to page 193.

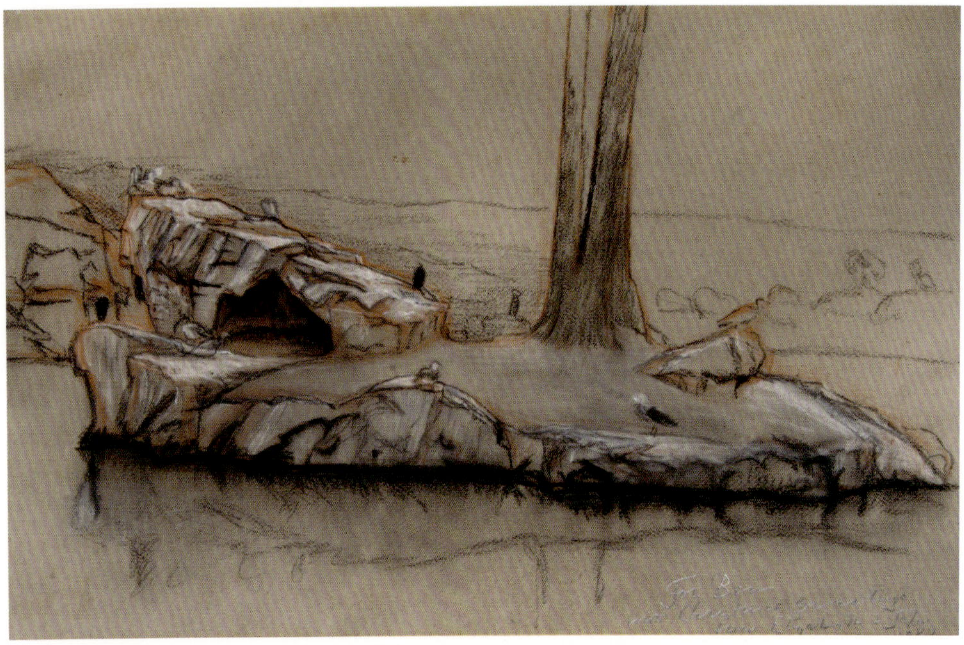

37 **A Battle Field** (left)
Inscribed and dated by the artist's son, John Rothenstein, 'For Ben with Christmas greetings from Elizabeth & John 1982'
Pastel on tinted paper
10 ½ x 15 ½ inches

38 **Montigny Farm** (below)
Signed, inscribed with title and dated 'Dec 1917'
Also signed 'Passed by Censor A N Lee' and dated 29/3/18 by Major Arthur Neale Lee, the Chief Censor for France
Pencil and pastel on tinted paper
14 ¼ x 20 ¾ inches
Exhibited: 'The Long Nineteenth Century: Treasures and Pleasures', Chris Beetles Gallery, March-April 2014, No 179

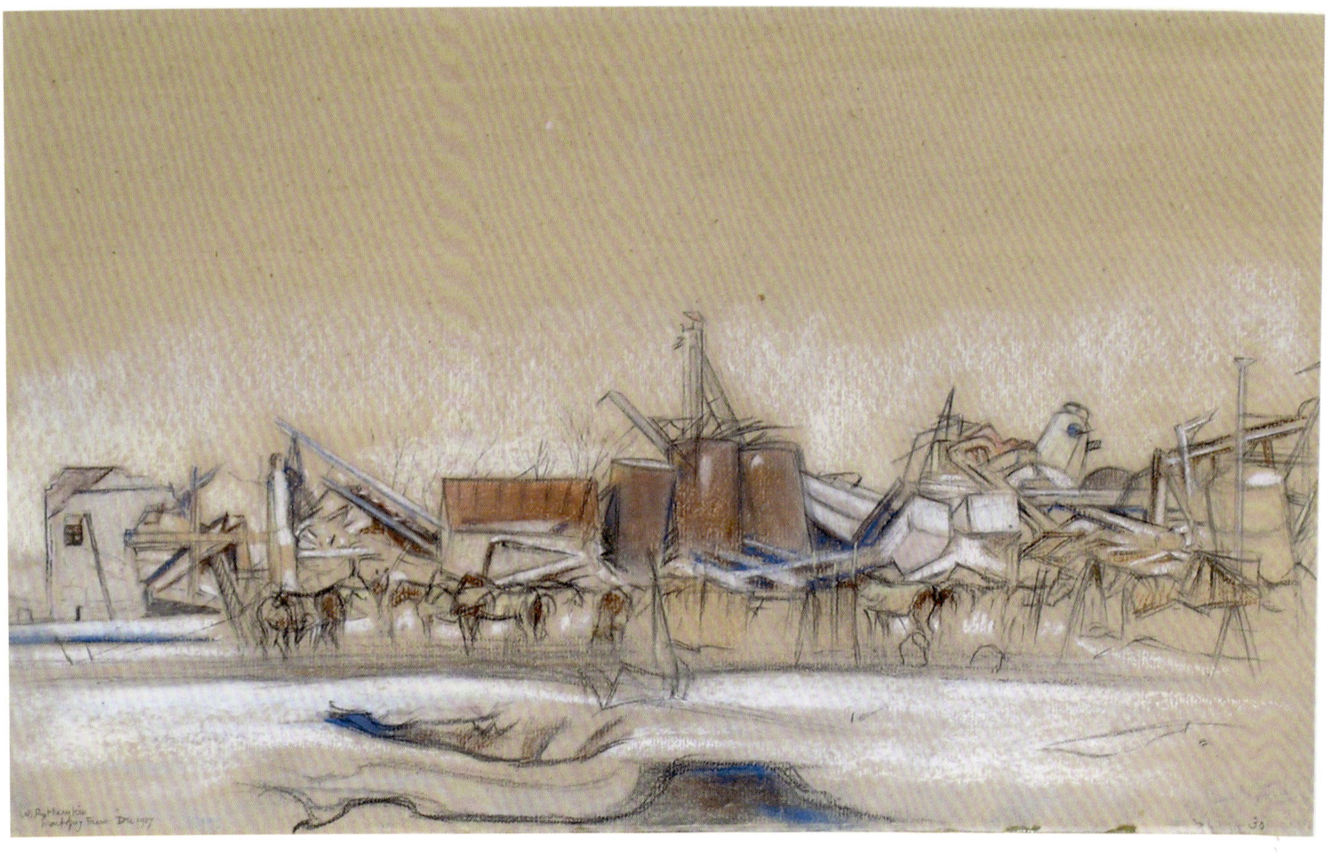

'[Rothenstein] and Kennington were both stationed at Montigny farm, near Roisel, about ten miles from Peronne and twenty from Cambrai, only three to three and a half miles behind the front lines. The troops and their transport were too difficult to draw, so William concentrated on the ruined villages and the landscape under snow. It was often so cold that his brush froze between water-flask and paper, but his energy could still leave a mess-room limp with exhaustion; and Kennington – who was ostensibly in charge of him – found him a law unto himself, refusing the precaution of a gas mask and dealing with superior officers according to his own ideas of their superiority ...
William insisted on sketching under fire, and roamed as widely as he could to discover the ruins that so vividly excited his imagination.'

(Robert Speaight, *William Rothenstein: The Portrait of an Artist in His Time*,
London: Eyre & Spottiswoode, 1962, page 292-293)

EDWARD HANDLEY-READ

Edward Harry Handley-Read, MBE RBA (1870-1935)

Establishing himself as a wide-ranging artist and illustrator during the 1890s, Edward Handley-Read produced pioneering images of the front line during the First World War.

For a biography of Edward Handley-Read, please refer to page 194.

39 A Famous Chateau
Near Ypres – Boesinghe – 1916
Quite Demolished Later
Signed and inscribed with title
Watercolour and charcoal on laid paper watermarked 'vidalon ingres'
19 x 24 ½ inches
Exhibited: 'The Long Nineteenth Century: Treasures and Pleasures', Chris Beetles Gallery, March-April 2014, No 176

A Famous Château

Home to the Flemish noble family, De Thibault de Boesinghe, the eighteenth-century château of Boesinghe stood close to the village of the same name, north of the city of Ypres, in Belgium. A shelter to refugees from early in the First World War, Boesinghe was attacked during the First Battle of Ypres, in October-November 1914, and almost destroyed in the Second Battle in April 1915. Close to the Allies' Front line, the area remained central to further action, and the damaged château became symbolic of the devastation of war through dissemination of its photographed and painted image. It was rebuilt after the war and still remains in the De Thibault family.

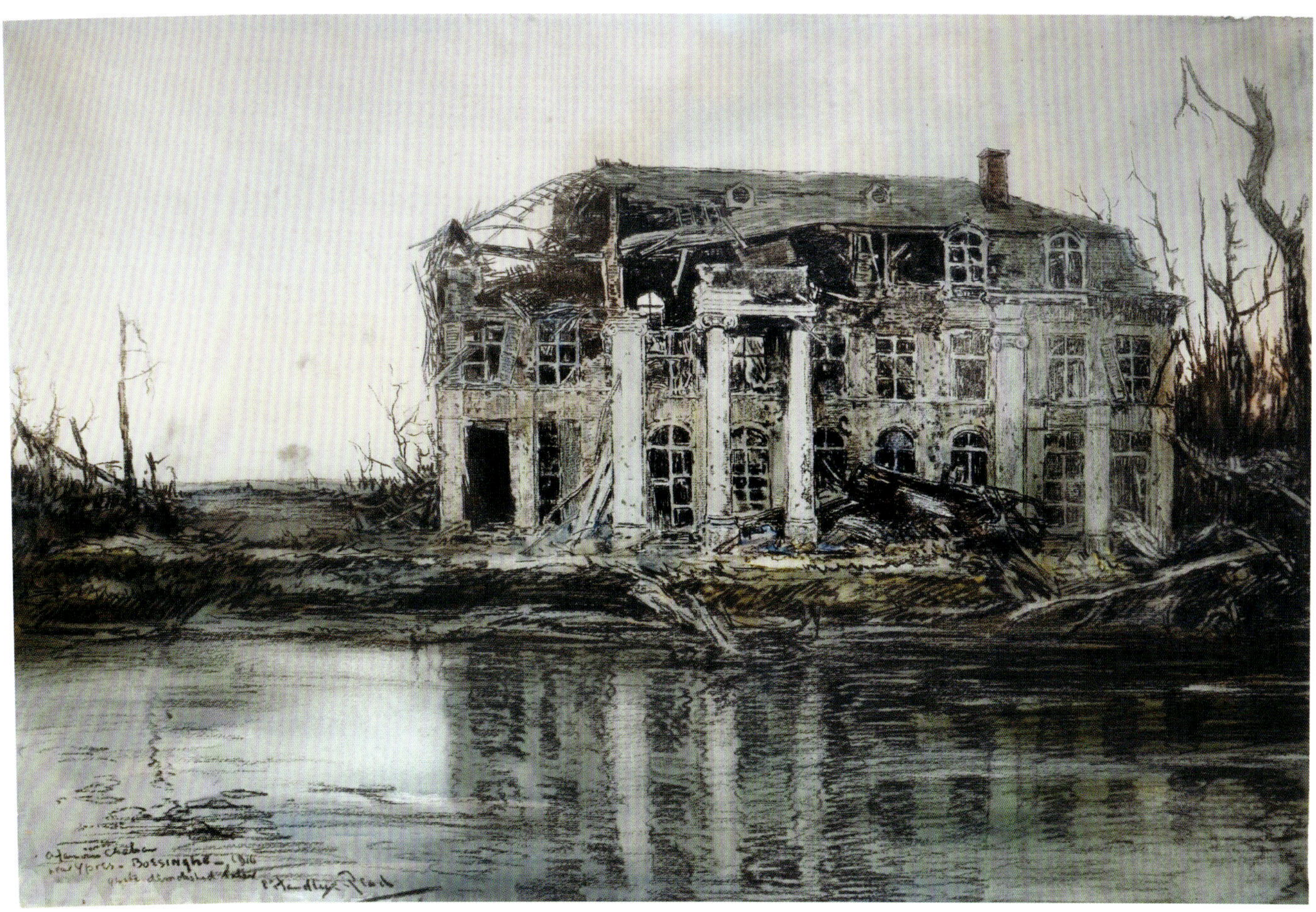

JOSEPH GRAY

Joseph Gray (1890-1963)

Joseph Gray, is now best remembered as an evocative war artist. During the First World War, he produced detailed drawings based on direct experiences in the Black Watch on the Western Front, and was subsequently sought after – by regiments and museums – as a painter of military subjects. Then, in the Second World War, he employed his expertise to develop large-scale forms of camouflage, while also creating drypoints of blitz-torn London, an indication of his broader interest in, and talent for, landscape and architectural subjects.

For a biography of Joseph Gray, please refer to pages 194-195.

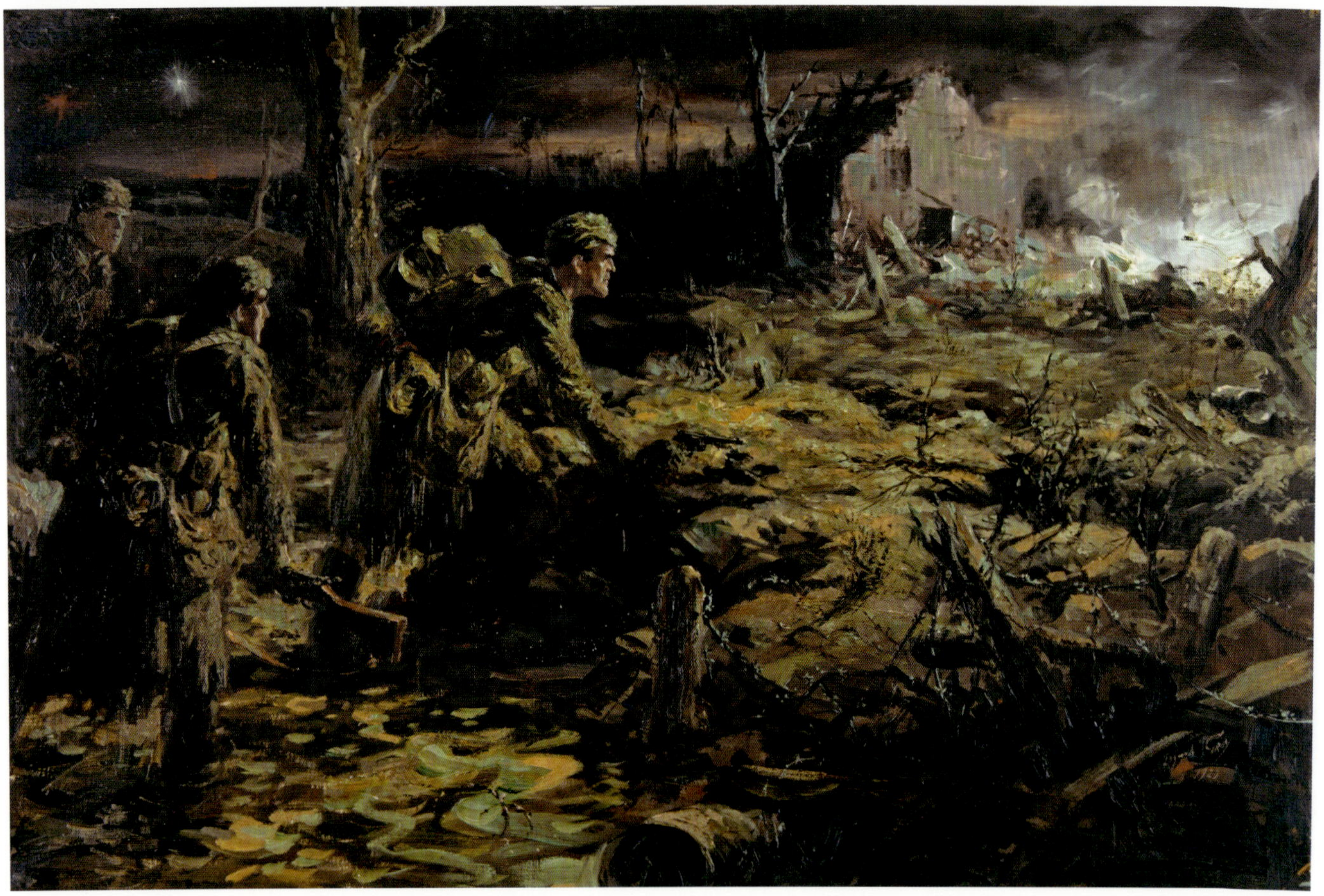

40 **Night Manoeuvres**
Signed and dated 1920
Oil on canvas
20 x 30 inches

ALGERNON TALMAGE

Algernon Mayow Talmage, RA RBA HRE ROI RWA (1871-1939)

Talmage is principally known as a painter of plein-air pastorals and equestrian subjects in a restrained yet sparkling Impressionist manner. During the First World War, he applied his passion for painting animals in landscape settings to his work as an official war artist for the Canadian Government.

For a biography of Algernon Talmage, please refer to page 196.

Wounded Horses Returning from t

In 1918, Algernon Talmage was commissi
War Memorials Fund to go to France to
though he produced 25 in all. Between tl
he spent nearly three months in Le Havre at the No 1 Canadian Veterinary Hospital. He then travelled to the Cambrai front, remaining there until mid October.

This painting depicts a scene on the road to Héninel, near the Cambrai front. A Canadian Mobile Veterinary Unit is taking wounded horses to an evacuating station, so that they may be returned by train to a base hospital. The smoke from German shelling can be seen on the horizon.

A larger version of this composition, entitled *A Mobile Veterinary Unit in France*, and produced in 1919, is held in the collections of the Canadian War Museum, Ottawa, and has hung in the Senate Chamber of the Canadian Houses of Parliament. It was exhibited as No 53, 'The Road to Henin', in four exhibitions of Canadian war art held in London, New York, Montreal and Toronto in 1919, and in later, similar exhibitions.

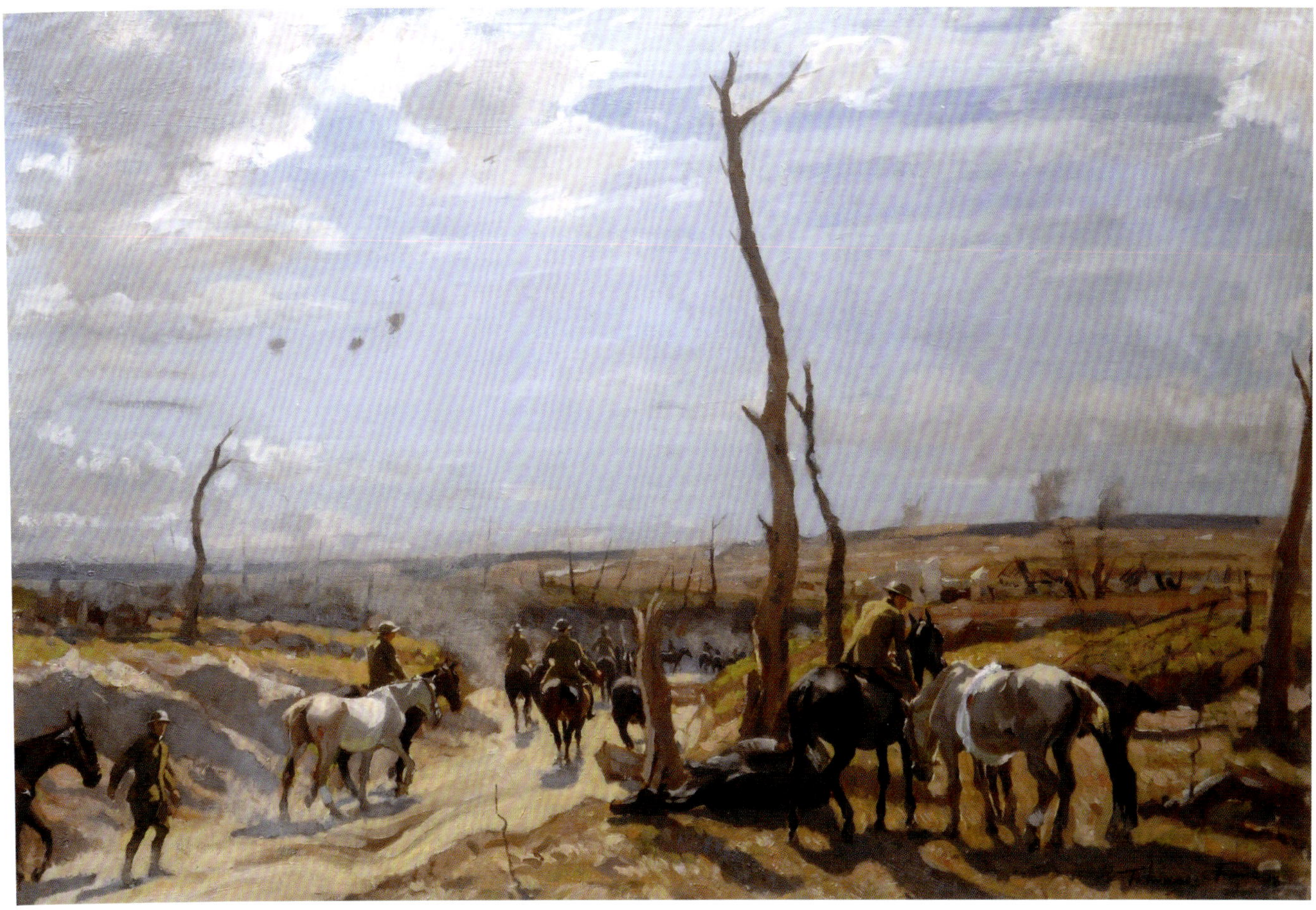

41 **Wounded Horses Returning from the Front, France**
Signed and dated 18
Oil on canvas
30 x 42 ½ inches
Exhibited: 'Home Lad, Home. The War Horse Story',
St Barbe Museum & Art Gallery, Lymington, Hampshire, 1 March-25 April 2014

…ILBERT LEDWARD

Gilbert Ledward, OBE RA PRBS (1888-1960)

Gilbert Ledward was a highly skilled sculptor in stone and metal of portraits, figure subjects and, most notably, majestic war memorials. Trained in the conventions of the late nineteenth century, he remained loyal to academic traditions and to the representational values that were suited to public projects of commemoration. As a Royal Academician and eventually a President of the Royal British Society of Sculptors, he became involved in discussions on the roles of both sculpture and the sculptor in society.

For a biography of Gilbert Ledward, please refer to pages 198-199.

Remembering the War: Gilbert Ledward and the Guards Memorial

The traumatic impact of the First World War prompted a strong and widespread desire to commemorate its events and casualties. The resulting memorials embraced cemeteries, large national monuments and smaller memorials, both civic and private, and they took a variety of forms, including buildings, cenotaphs, works of art and parks. Most of the constructed and sculpted memorials were traditional in design, though they included such novel features as lists of the names of those who had died. The presence of these memorials provided a focus for mourning, reflection, ceremony and pilgrimage.

Some memorials were created while the war persisted, including works by artists commissioned during 1918 by the British War Memorials Committee. However, a more thorough and widespread process of commemoration developed once the conflict had ceased. This was marked, in part, by the Imperial War Graves Commission establishing large-scale cemeteries close to the fields of battle. In Britain itself, the Cenotaph was constructed in 1919 in London's Whitehall, to a design by Sir Edwin Lutyens, as a focus for national remembrance. Thousands of other memorials were established across the kingdom, often as the result of focussed fundraising.

The Guards Division Memorial here represents those many memorials. It commemorates the 14,000 Guardsmen who died in France and Belgium between 1915 – when the division was formed from battalions of the Guards regiments of the regular army – and the end of the war in 1918. It also commemorates the soldiers of the Household Cavalry, Royal Regiment of Artillery, Corps of Royal Engineers, Royal Army Service Corps, Royal Army Medical Corps and other units that served with the Guards.

A committee of high-ranking Guards officers began to raise funds for the memorial in 1920, and mounted a competition in order to select the designers. The submissions were assessed by two prominent artists, the sculptor, Sir Thomas Brock, and the architect, Sir Reginald Blomfield. In December 1921, the committee selected the design of the sculptor, Gilbert Ledward, and the architect, H Chalton Bradshaw, both of whom had served in the war (Bradshaw having been gassed and wounded). Their design underwent many modifications, as the result of the involvement of the committee in general, and Blomfield in particular.

The committee vetoed stone figure groups, intended to go at either side of the monument, as being too costly, and images of corpses on the relief of artillery in action as being inappropriate. Blomfield not only defended what he liked in the original design but – in the opinion of Lord Crawford, First Commissioner of Works – took it over, and influenced, and even limited, Ledward's sculptural contribution. However, Blomfield and Ledward had already collaborated successfully in 1920 on a memorial – admittedly smaller – to Dean H D M Spence-Jones for Gloucester Cathedral. Also Crawford's view is belied by the prominence of Ledward's resonant sculptures on the resulting memorial, which was unveiled on the eastern edge of St James's Park, London, on 16 October 1926 by the Duke of Connaught, Senior Colonel of the Guards.

The memorial comprises a Portland stone truncated obelisk surmounting a base. Five bronze sculptures of foot soldiers, each slightly larger than life size, stand easy in a row on a platform on the east side, facing Horse Guards Parade. Each of the other three sides supports a bronze relief depicting military equipment, that to the west showing artillery in action. Above the statues and reliefs, the obelisk bears a number of inscriptions, including, most prominently, one written by Rudyard Kipling, whose only son, John, was killed in action in 1915, while serving in the Irish Guards at the Battle of Loos. The monument was built by the Birmingham Guild, the lettering cut by Ernest Gillick and the sculptures and reliefs cast by the William Morris Art Bronze Foundry using bronze taken from German guns.

Ledward took to heart the brief to provide realistic imagery, and modelled his statues on serving Guardsmen. These were Sergeant R Bradshaw MM of the Grenadier Guards, Lance Corporal J S Richardson of the Coldstream Guards, Guardsman J McDonald of the Scots Guards, Guardsman Simon McCarthy of the Irish Guards and Guardsman A Comley of the Welsh Guards. However, it is said that McCarthy became frustrated with having to pose, and that the legs of the Irish Guardsman were modelled on those of Lance Sergeant W J Kidd.

If Ledward created these indomitable yet individualised figures as a focus for mourning, the relief on the west side of the monument provided him with the opportunity to introduce a dynamic, even narrative element into its imagery. Centring on the wheel of an 18-pounder gun, it depicts, on the left, gunners loading and firing, and, in the foreground right, a signaller communicating via a field telephone. The present detailed drawing is a study for that signaller, and clearly shows that, as with the statues, he was modelled on a serving Guardsman (though one as yet unidentified).

Ledward produced work of a consistently high quality, and was consequently much valued as a sculptor of war memorials. His particular contribution to the Guards Division Memorial – the most prominent example of his art in London – was recognised in July 1927, when he was awarded a silver medal by the Royal Society of British Sculptors for the best work of sculpture publicly exhibited in the capital in the previous 12 months.

42 **Study for the Guards Division Memorial**
Signed and inscribed 'Study for the signaller represented on the bronze panel on the west face of the Guards Division Memorial – Horse Guards Parade. London SW' and dated 1925
Pencil and chalk
11 ½ x 15 ¾ inches

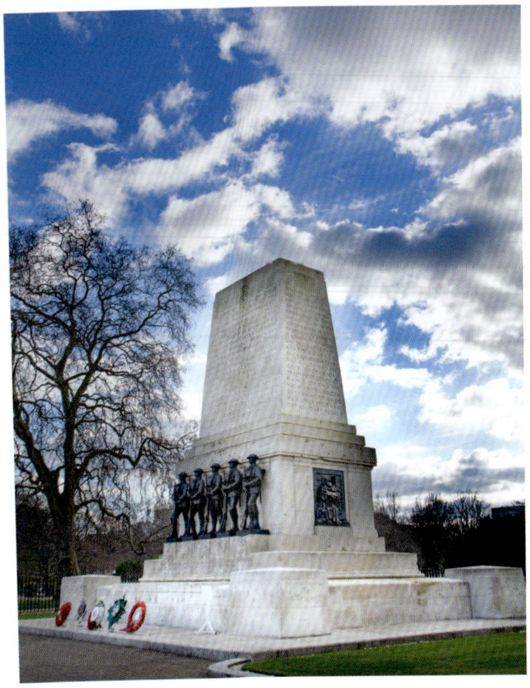

The Guards Division Memorial, Horse Guards Parade, London, by H Chalton Bradshaw and Gilbert Ledward, 1921-26: General View (left); West Facing Relief (below)

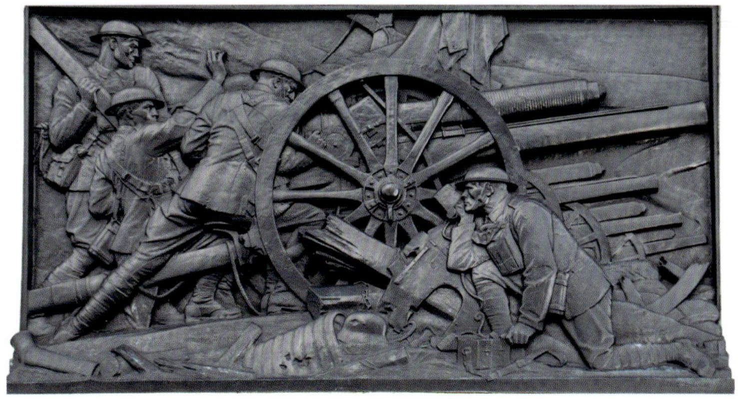

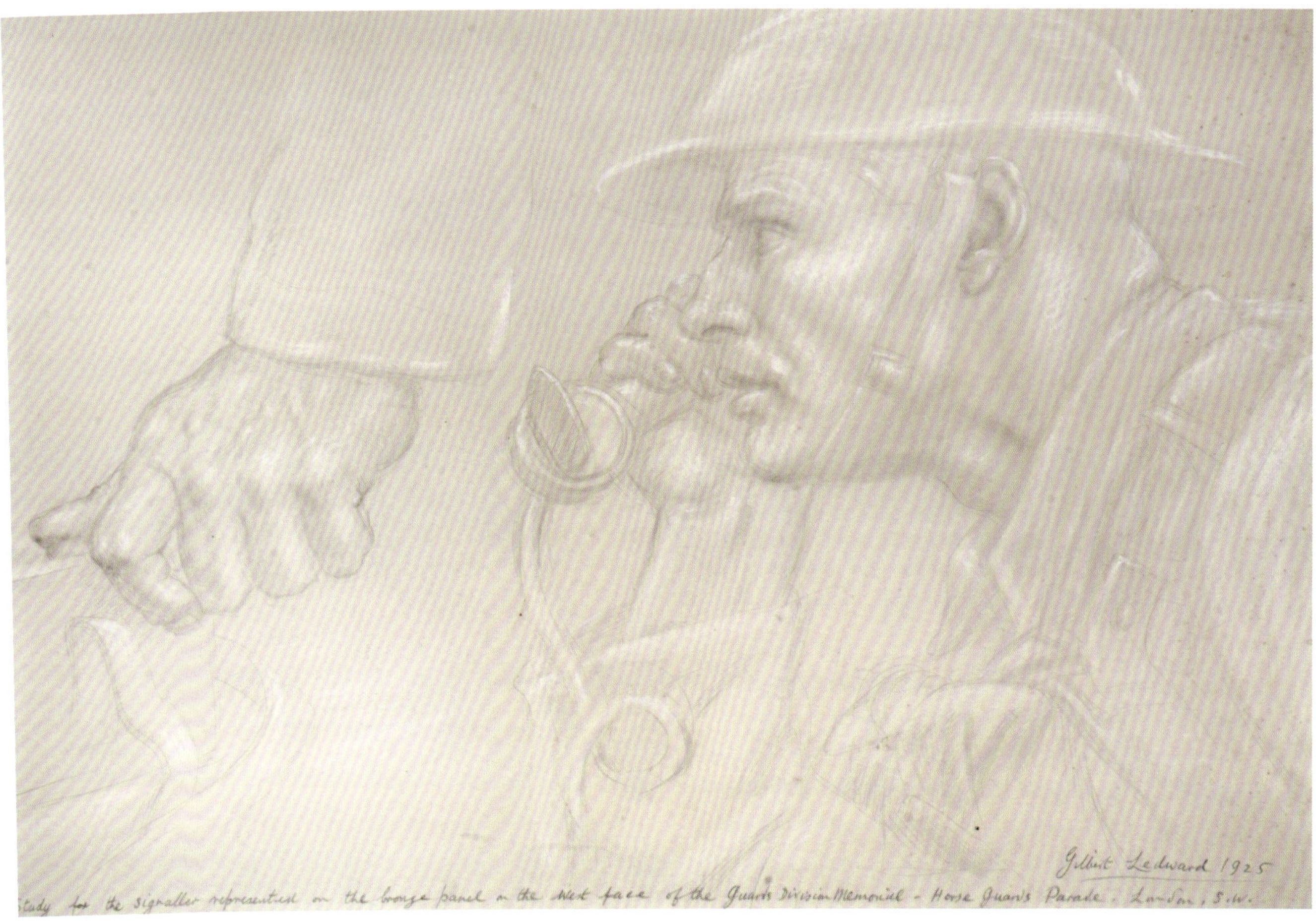

4: THE ETCHING REVIVAL AND THE ETCHING BOOM

A revival of interest in etching as an original form of printmaking took place in Britain between the 1860s and the 1920s. It acted as an artistic reaction against the highly-worked reproductive engravings that replicated paintings. Perhaps the greatest catalyst to change was the arrival from Paris, in 1859, of the American artist, James McNeill Whistler. He and his English brother-in-law, Francis Seymour Haden, initially worked closely together to produce and promote etchings. However, they soon took opposing stances, Whistler emphasising qualities of tone and Haden the expression of line. In 1880, Haden became founder and first President of the Society of Painter-Etchers and Engravers, but Whistler was not invited to join. As President, Haden carefully controlled the creativity and originality of its members for 30 years, until his death in 1910. (The society received its Royal Charter in 1888, from which date fellows placed the initials RE after their names.)

Haden's successor as President of the Painter-Etchers was Frank Short. He was also influential as a teacher of etching at the Royal College of Art, so strengthening the revival of the medium by nurturing a new generation of talent (including George Soper and Stanley Anderson). As such, he may be considered the father of the 'Modern Etching Boom', in which contemporary printmakers gained increasing commercial success. During the 1920s, opportunities for collectors to invest inexpensively in etchings soon developed into a phenomenal bubble of speculation, with some prints selling in auction for the price of a house. This was encouraged and guided by such institutions as the Print Collectors' Club (established by the Painter-Etchers in 1921) and such publications as Malcolm Salaman's annual *Fine Prints of the Year* (1923-38).

Masterly etchers employed every technique at their disposal to represent the world memorably in black and white. In their different ways, George Soper (RE 1920), Edmund Blampied (RE 1921) and S R Badmin (RE 1935) revealed aspects of the rural life and landscape that had survived the First World War. Badmin also shared with Henry Rushbury (RE 1922) and William Walcot (RE 1920) in surveying the contemporary urban scene. As a practising architect, Walcot produced decorative, often large-scale etchings that could equally capture the spirit of the modern city [50] and conjure up an ancient civilisation [47-49]. By contrast, Rushbury's close friend, Gerald Brockhurst (RE 1921), focussed compellingly on the human form, and most notably the female face and figure. George Soper's daughter, Eileen, had similar success in conveying the life of the child, gaining an international reputation at the age of only 16.

The boom was essentially brought to an end by the Wall Street Crash in October 1929 and the consequent economic depression. Printmakers could no longer lightly undertake the creation and printing of editions of etchings, and publishers could no longer incur financial risks. However, artists continued to make etchings of quality, and also explored other forms of printmaking.

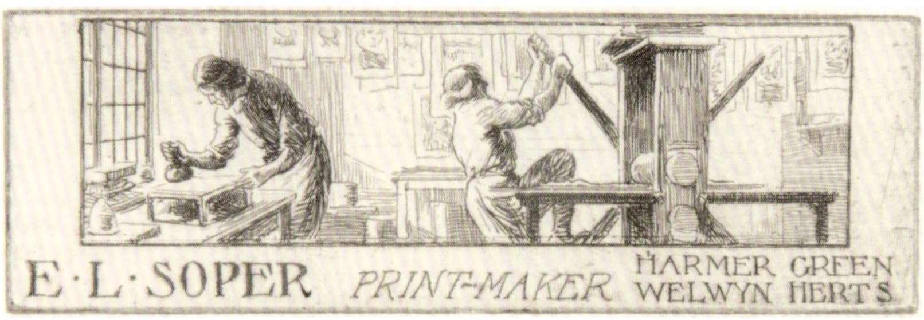

43 E L Soper Print-Maker
Etching (laid-wove)
1 ¾ x 5 ¼ inches
Provenance: The Estate of George and Eileen Soper
Literature: *The Catalogue Raisonné of the Etchings of George and Eileen Soper*, London: Chris Beetles Ltd, 1995, No 219

George Soper executed this in about 1921 for his daughter, Eva Soper. The image is derived from Abraham Bosse's 1642 etching entitled 'Intaglio Etching'.

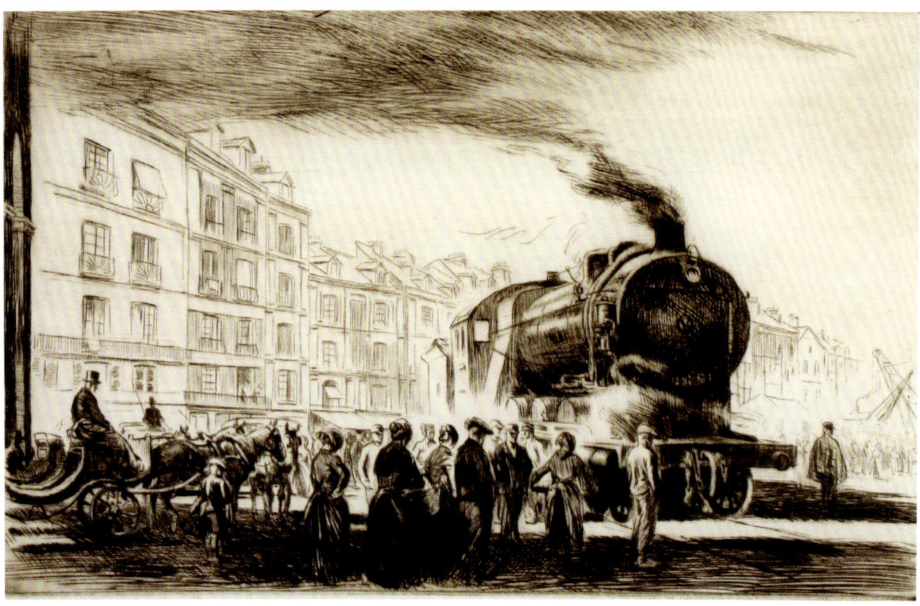

44 Waiting For the Boat, Dieppe Harbour
Signed
Drypoint on laid paper
7 x 11 ¼ inches
Executed in about 1927
Provenance: The Estate of George and Eileen Soper
Literature: *The Catalogue Raisonné of the Etchings of George and Eileen Soper*, London: Chris Beetles Ltd, 1995, No 403

GEORGE SOPER

George Soper, RE (1870-1942)

While beginning his career as an illustrator at the turn of the twentieth century, George Soper established a reputation as a painter and, especially, a printmaker of a wide range of rural subjects. In turn, his daughter, Eileen, was influenced by his skills and sympathies from an early age.

For a biography of George Soper, please refer to page 197.

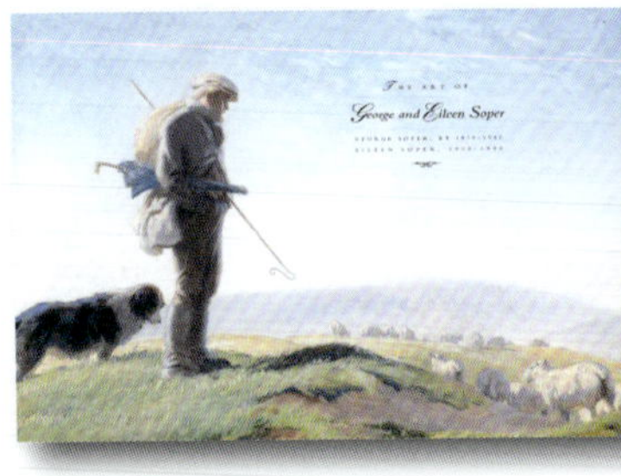

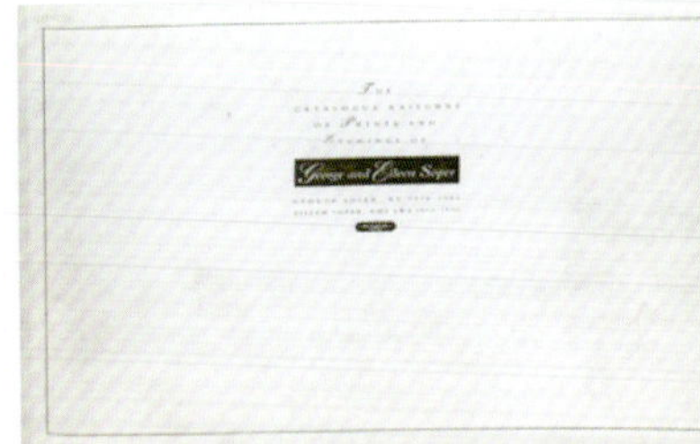

In 1995, Chris Beetles Gallery mounted a highly successful major retrospective of the work of George Soper and his daughter, Eileen. It was accompanied by these two substantial, fully-illustrated volumes: a 128-page catalogue, including extensive biographical information, and a 160-page catalogue raisonné of prints and etchings.

For works by Eileen Soper, please see Nos **103-106**.

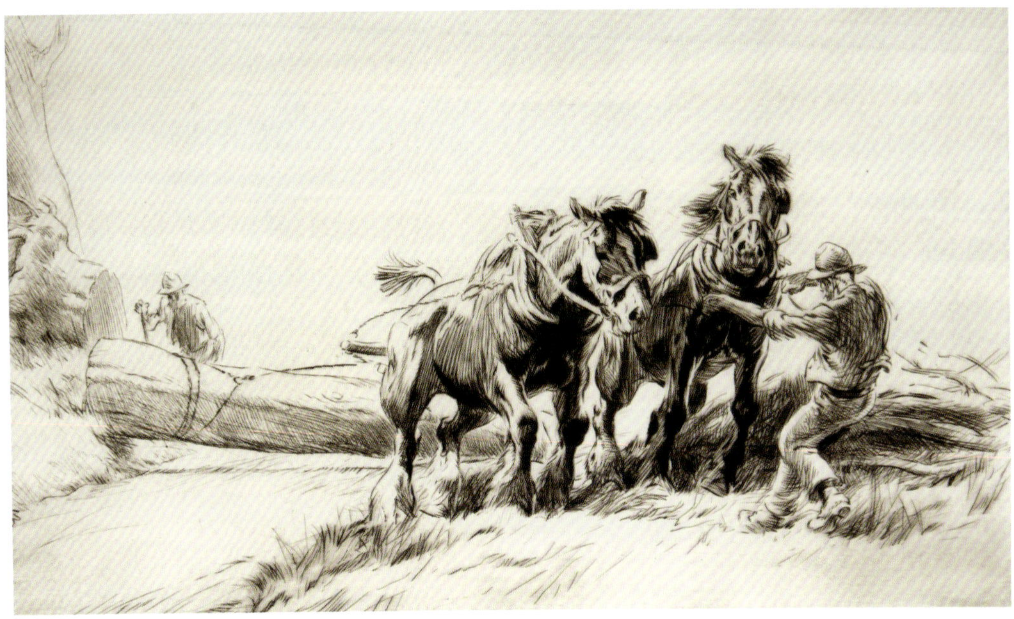

45 **After the Storm**
Signed and inscribed with title
Drypoint on laid paper
7 ¾ x 13 ¼ inches
Executed in 1929
Provenance: The Estate of George and Eileen Soper
Literature: *The Catalogue Raisonné of the Etchings of George and Eileen Soper*, London: Chris Beetles Ltd, 1995, No 434

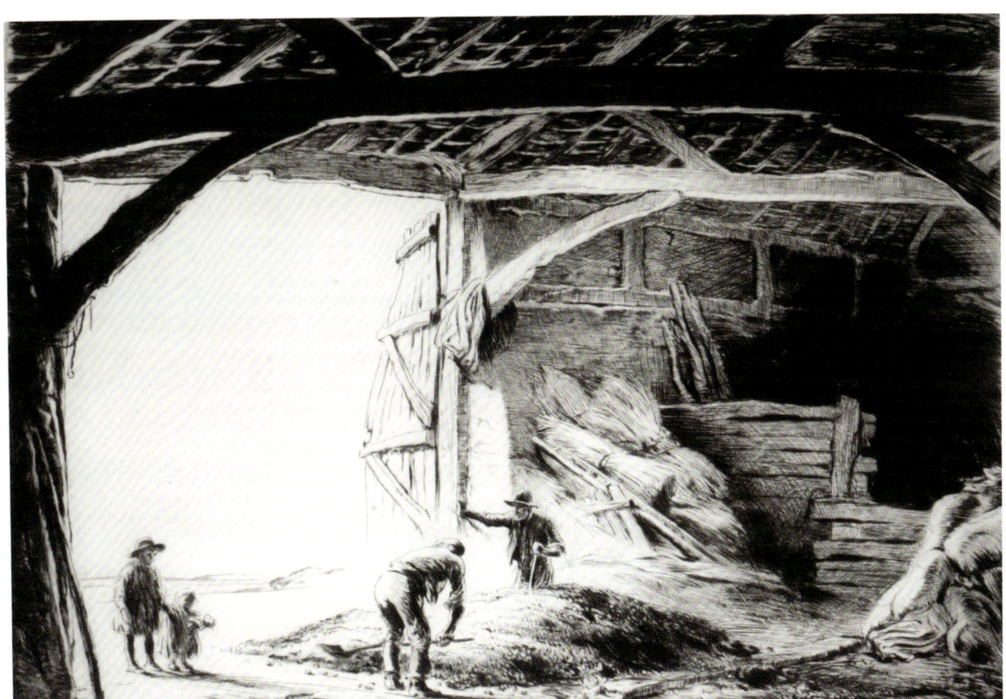

46 **The Cider Harvest**
Signed
Drypoint on laid paper
8 ¼ x 10 ½ inches
Executed in 1924
Provenance: The Estate of George and Eileen Soper
Literature: *The Catalogue Raisonné of the Etchings of George and Eileen Soper*, London: Chris Beetles Ltd, 1995, No 314

WILLIAM WALCOT

William F Walcot, RBA RE (1874-1943)

Working as a painter and printmaker, William Walcot became the most celebrated architectural artist in England during the 1920s and 30s.

For a biography of William Walcot, please refer to page 200.

48 **Babylon** (opposite above)
Signed
Inscribed with title
Etching with drypoint
13 ½ x 21 ¾ inches
Published by H C Dickins in 1918 in an edition of 50, originally priced at 12 guineas
Literature: Sir Reginald Blomfield (intro), *Architectural Water-Colours and Etchings of W Walcot*, London: H C Dickins & Technical Journals, 1919, Page 79;
H C Dickins, 'Chronological List of Etchings', as it appears in Blomfield, 1919, No 49;
Elizabeth Harvey-Lee, William Walcot Catalogue Raisonné, online, No 70
Exhibited: 'Paintings, Watercolours and Etchings by William Walcot', James Connell & Sons, London, April 1918, No 24;
Royal Academy, Summer Exhibition, 1919, No 1208, as 'Babylone';
'Original Engravings, Etchings and Drypoints by Younger Contemporary Gravers', Beaux Arts Gallery, London, April-May 1929;
'William Walcot: Artist & Architect', Chris Beetles Gallery, October 2018, No 23

47 **At the House of a Patrician**
Signed
Etching
16 ¼ x 17 ¾ inches
Published by H C Dickins in 1913 in an edition of 65, originally priced at 6 guineas
Literature: Sir Reginald Blomfield (intro), *Architectural Water-Colours and Etchings of W Walcot*, London: H C Dickins & Technical Journals, 1919, Page 59;
H C Dickins, 'Chronological List of Etchings', as it appears in Blomfield, 1919, No 2;
Elizabeth Harvey-Lee, William Walcot Catalogue Raisonné, online, No 15
Exhibited: Royal Academy, Summer Exhibition, 1913, No 1548;
'Etchings by William Walcot', Fine Art Society, London, May 1914;
'Paintings, Water-Colours and Etchings by William Walcot', James Connell & Sons, London, April 1918, unnumbered, in the Folio (watercolours entitled *The House of a Patrician* were exhibited as Nos 8 & 10);
'William Walcot: Artist & Architect', Chris Beetles Gallery, October 2018, No 18

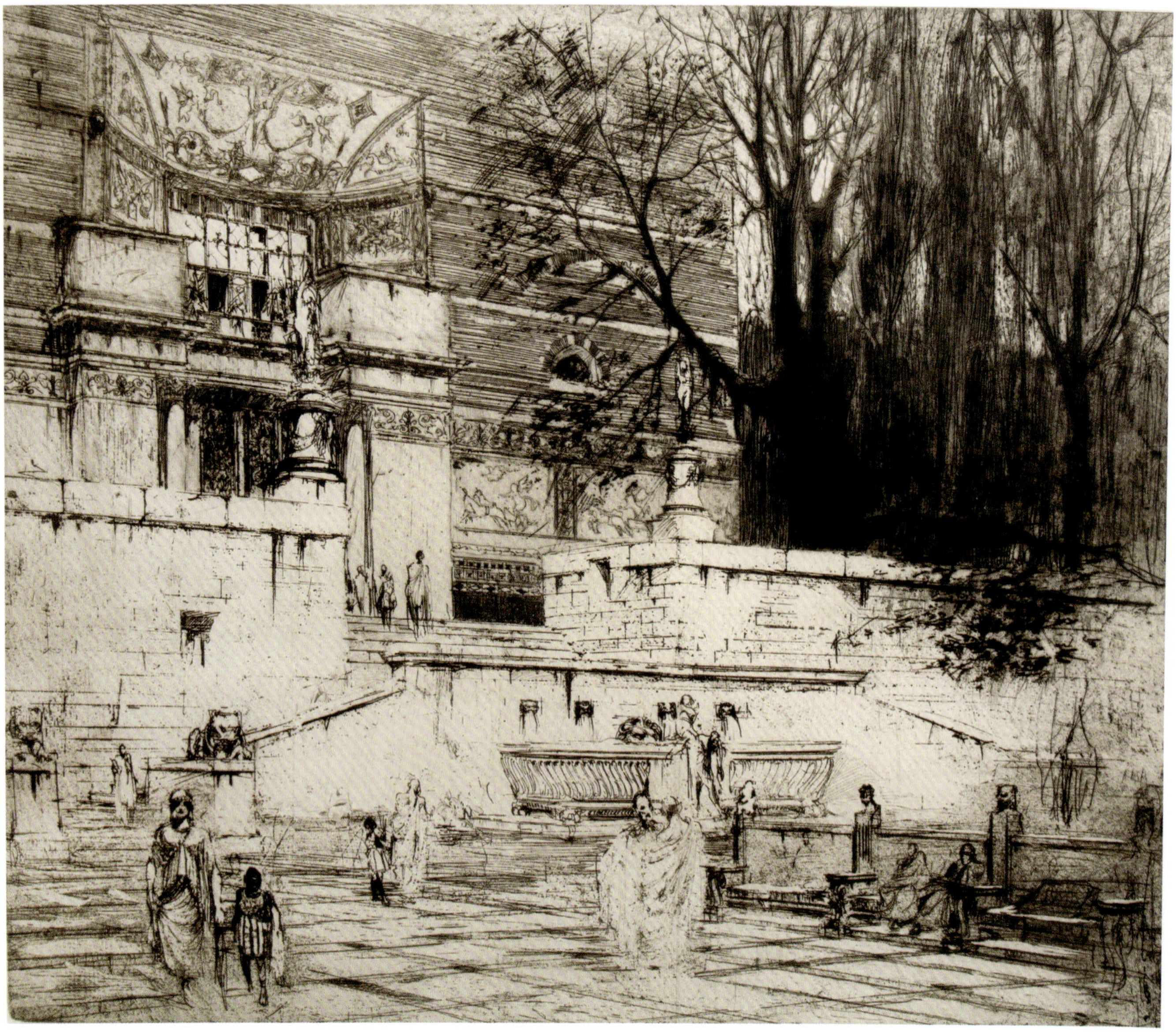

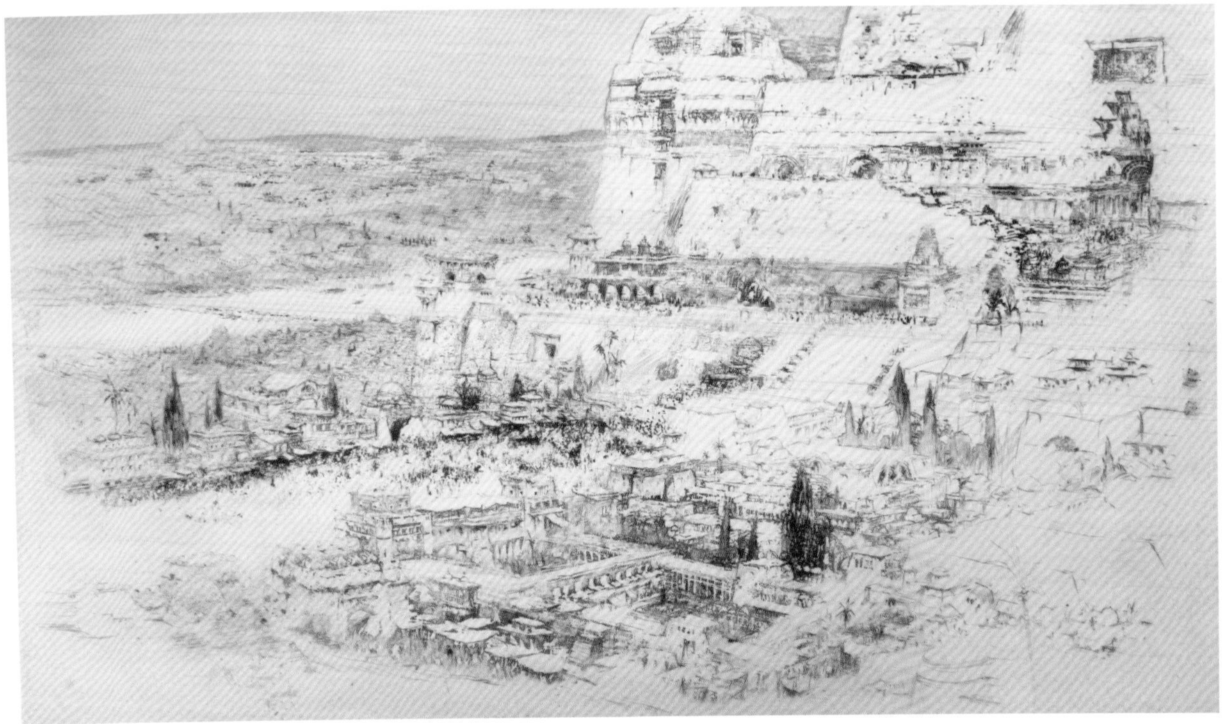

49 **Villa Quintilii** (below)
Signed
Drypoint with etching and aquatint
7 x 10 inches
Published by H C Dickins in 1921 in an edition of 300 (UK) and 100 (USA), originally priced at 8 guineas
Literature: Malcolm C Salaman (intro), *William Walcot RE (Modern Masters of Etching No 16)*, London: The Studio, 1927, Plate II;
H C Dickins, manuscript, 'Chronological List of Etchings', 1920-1924, No 71;
Elizabeth Harvey-Lee, William Walcot Catalogue Raisonné, online, No 98

Exhibited: 'Summer Exhibition of Original Etchings (A Selection From the Gallery's Portfolios)', Fine Art Society, London, July-September 1922;
'Original Etchings by Leading Artists', Fine Art Society, London, November 1923;
'Paintings, Water-Colours and Etchings by William Walcot', Fine Art Society, London, June 1924;
'Modern Etchings', Beaux Arts Gallery, London, October 1926;
'Etchings by Leading Artists', Fine Art Society, London, December 1927;
'William Walcot: Artist & Architect', Chris Beetles Gallery, October 2018, No 24

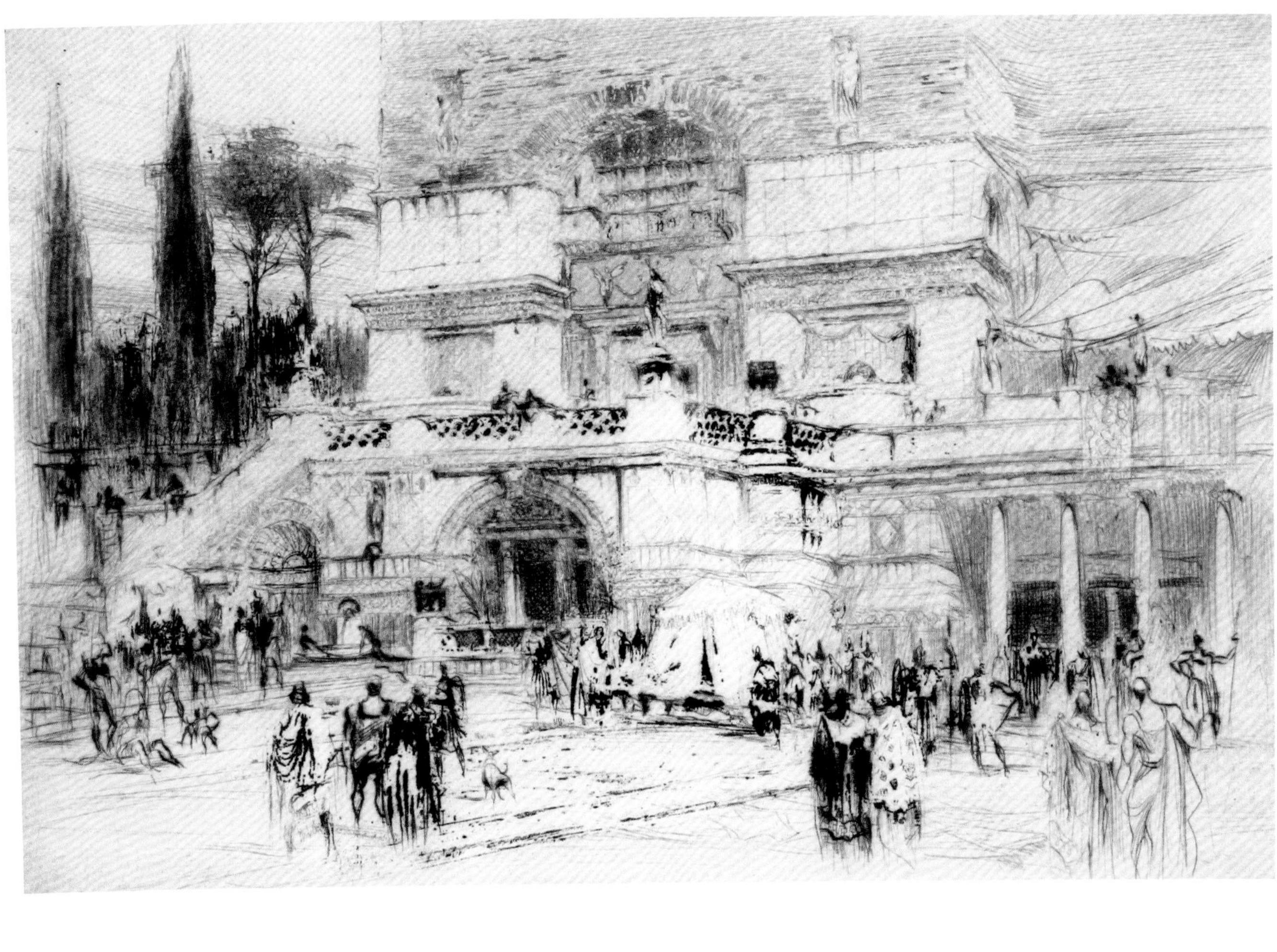

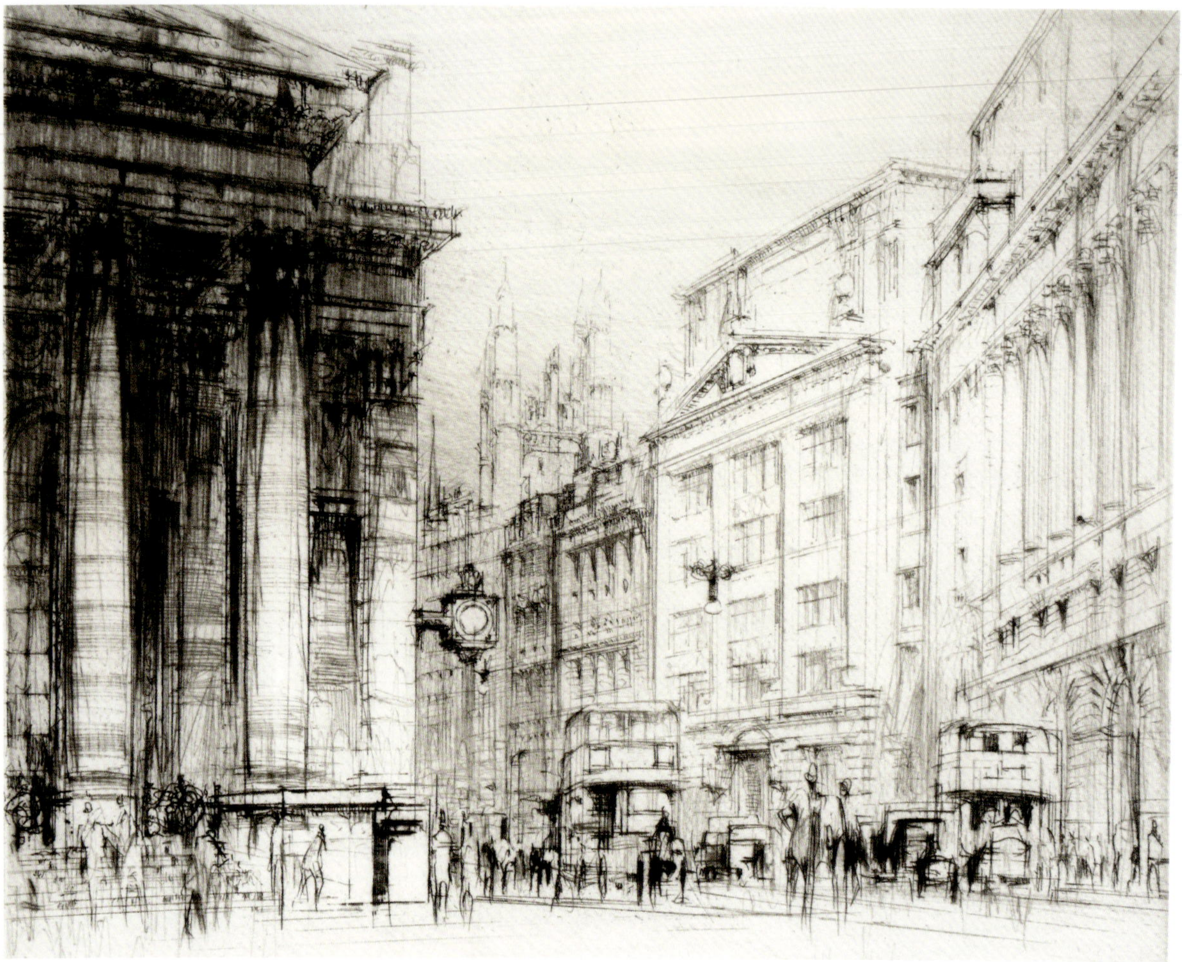

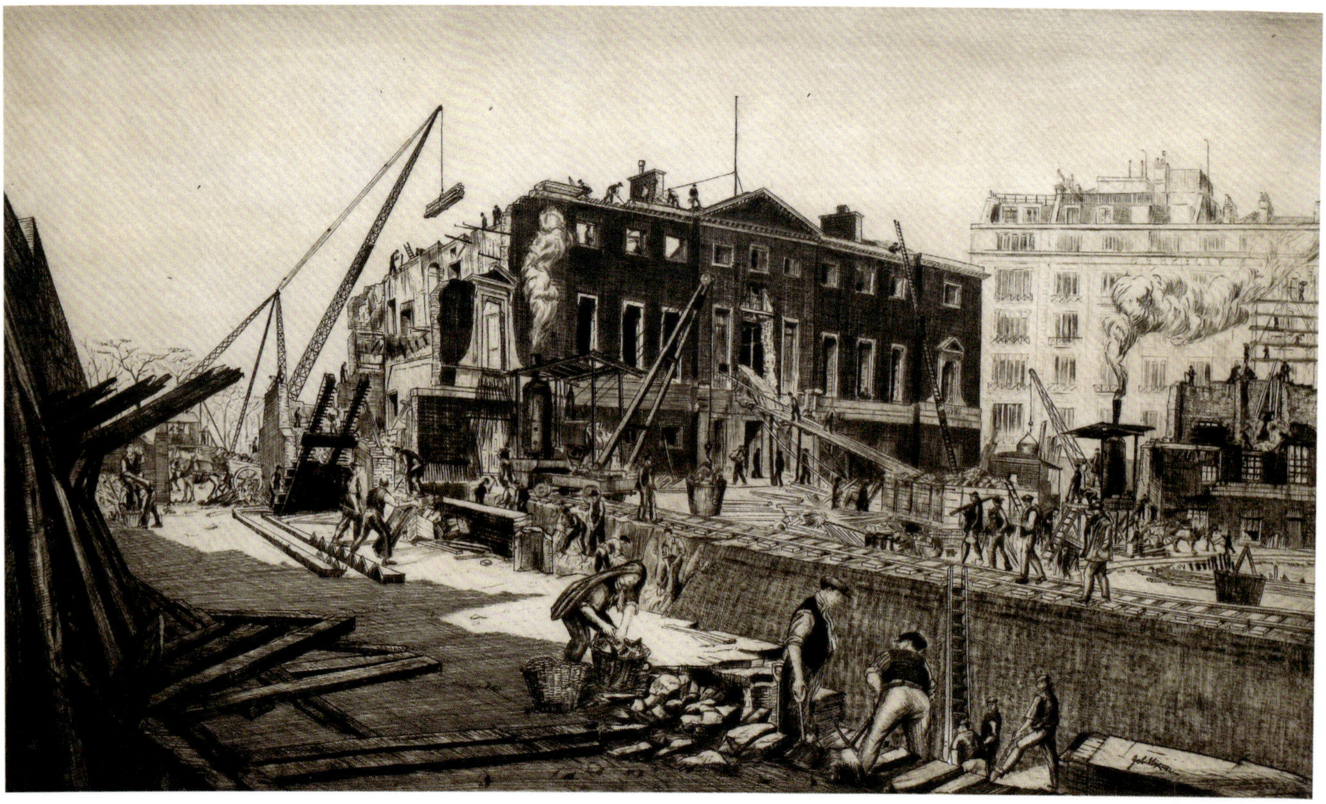

WILLIAM WALCOT

50 Cornhill and the Royal Exchange (opposite above)
Signed
Etching and drypoint
7 x 7 ¾ inches
Executed in 1933
Literature: Elizabeth Harvey-Lee, William Walcot Catalogue Raisonné, online, No 170
Exhibited: 'William Walcot: Artist & Architect', Chris Beetles Gallery, October 2018, No 72

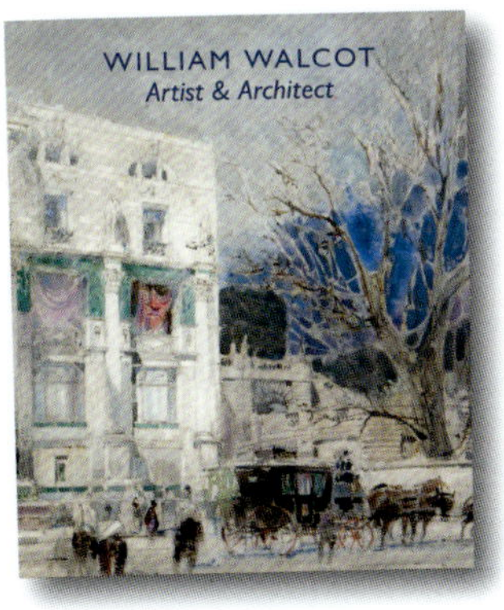

In 2018, Chris Beetles Gallery mounted a major retrospective of the work of William Walcot. It was accompanied by this beautifully designed, fully-illustrated, 50-page catalogue, which includes biographical information and a topographical index.

JOB NIXON

Job Nixon, RWS RE NEAC (1891-1938)

Though a painter as well as a printmaker, Job Nixon was best known as an etcher of landscapes and figure subjects. He was the first to win the scholarship for engraving at the British School at Rome, and during his time in Italy he produced *An Italian Festa*, the large and complex plate that made his name. On his return to London, he soon became assistant to Malcolm Osborne in the engraving school of the Royal College of Art. During the later years of his short career, he worked in Cornwall and taught at the Slade School of Fine Art.

For a biography of Job Nixon, please refer to page 201.

51 The Demolition of Devonshire House (opposite below)
Signed
Inscribed with title below mount
Signed in plate
Etching with drypoint
9 ¼ x 14 ¾ inches
Literature: Harold Wright, 'A Chronological List of the Etchings, Drypoints and Engravings of Job Nixon ARE', *The Print Collector's Quarterly*, 1927, Vol XIV
Devonshire House was demolished in 1924.

MALCOLM OSBORNE

Malcolm Osborne, CBE RA RBC PRE (1880-1963)

Malcolm Osborne is best known as an etcher and engraver of portraits, figure subjects and townscapes. An influential teacher, he was head of the Engraving School at the Royal College of Art for many years.

For a biography of Malcolm Osborne, please refer to page 200.

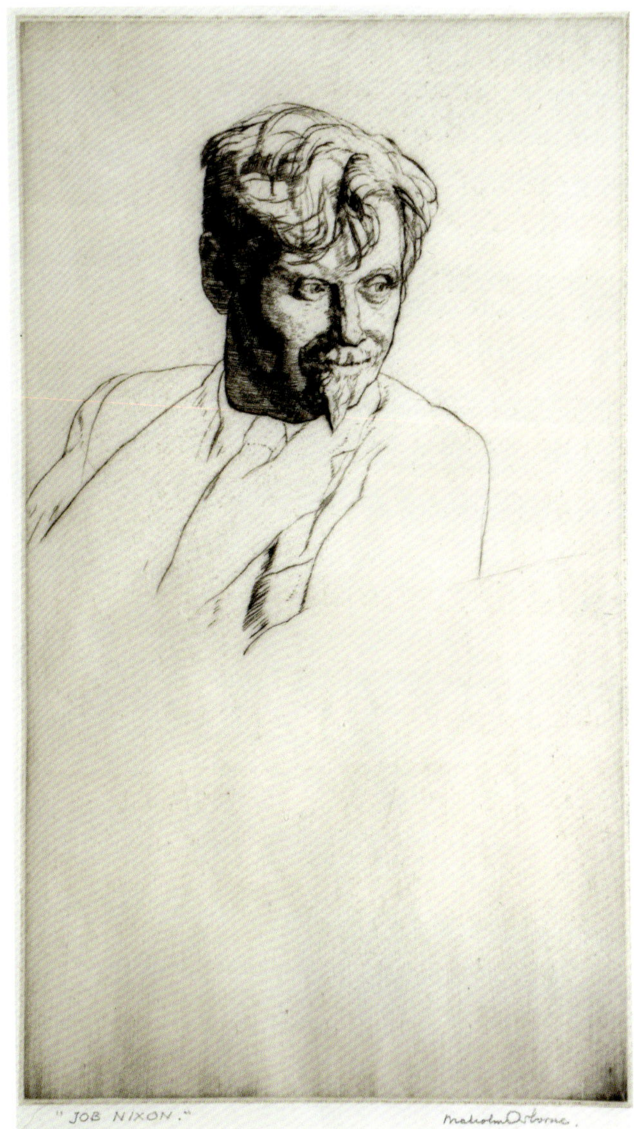

52 Job Nixon
Signed and inscribed with title in pencil
Drypoint
13 x 8 inches
Probably excecuted in about 1926

STANLEY ANDERSON

Alfred Charles Stanley Anderson, RA RE (1884-1966)

The printmaker and painter, Stanley Anderson, was a major figure in the revival of line engraving between the wars. Though a long career allowed for a diverse range of subjects, his skill was displayed particularly well in a series of prints of farm workers and rural craftsmen.

For a biography of Stanley Anderson, please refer to page 202.

Nos 53-55 Literature: Martin Hardie, 'The Etchings and Engravings of Stanley Anderson', *The Print Collector's Quarterly*, July 1933

Nos 55-62 Literature: Robert Meyrick and Harry Heuser, *Stanley Anderson. Prints: A Catalogue Raisonné*, London: Royal Academy of Arts, 2015, Page 197

Nos 55-61 Exhibited: 'An Exhibition of Etchings and Engravings by Stanley Anderson RA RE', Cheltenham Art Gallery and Museum, 1949

53 The Fallen Star
Signed
Inscribed with title and 'Edition 85 proofs' below mount
Signed in plate
Engraving
7 ¼ x 8 ½ inches
From an edition of 85
Executed in 1929 and published by P & D Colnaghi (4gns)
Literature: Martin Hardie, July 1933, No 129;
Robert Meyrick and Harry Heuser, 2015, Page 190, Catalogue Raisonné No 187

Exhibited: Royal Academy, Summer Exhibition, 1929, No 1096;
Royal West of England Academy, Bristol, 1929, No 769 (5gns);
'Twelve Recent Prints by Stanley Anderson', P & D Colnaghi, London, 1930, No 14 (4gns);
'An Exhibition of Paintings, Drawings and Prints and Stanley Anderson RE', P & D Colnaghi, London, October 1932, No 1 (4gns);
Royal Society of Painter-Etchers and Engravers, 1930, No 110 (4gns);
Cheltenham, 1949, No 79

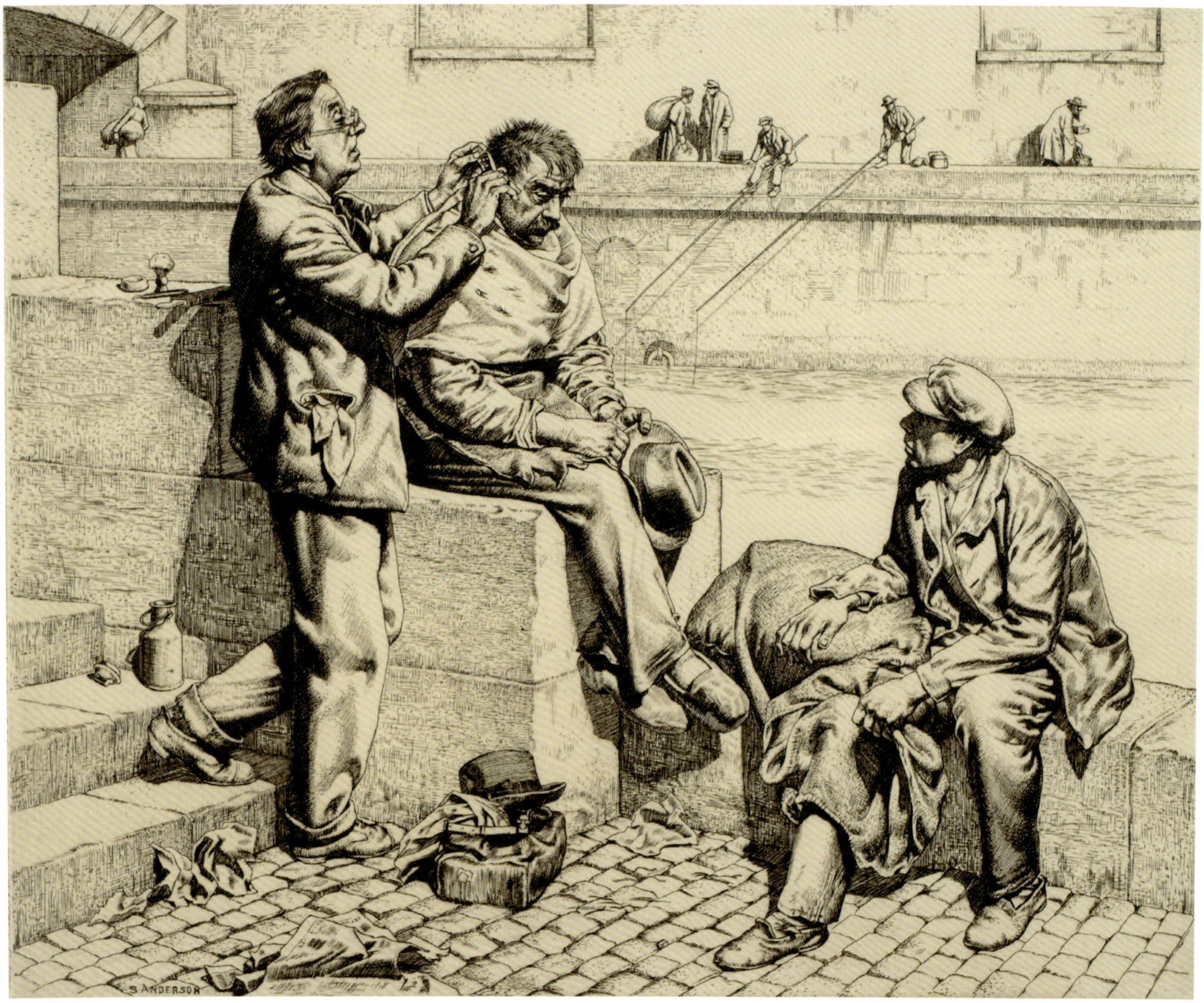

54 **Within the Ramparts, St Malo**
Signed in pencil
Signed in plate
Drypoint; 11 ¼ x 9 inches
Literature: Martin Hardie, July 1933, No 128;
Robert Meyrick and Harry Heuser, 2015, Page 188, No 185
Exhibited: Royal Society of Painter-Etchers and Engravers, 1929, No 40;
Royal West of England Academy, Bristol, 1929, No 737;
Colnaghi, London, 1930, No 6, 1932, No 26;
Cheltenham, 1949, No 54

55 **The Reading Room** (below)
Signed
Inscribed with title, 'Line Engraving' and 'Edition 85 proofs' below mount
Signed and inscribed with title, artist's address and 'No 2 line engraving' on reverse
Signed in plate
Engraving
6 ½ x 8 ½ inches
From an edition of 85
Executed in 1930 and published by P & D Colnaghi (4gns)
Literature: Malcolm C Salaman (ed), *Fine Prints of the Year*, London: Halton & Company, 1931, Plate 4;
Martin Hardie, July 1933, No 134;
Robert Meyrick and Harry Heuser, 2015, Page 197, Catalogue Raisonné No 192
Exhibited: Royal Society of Painter-Etchers and Engravers, 1931, No 14 (4gns);
Royal Academy, Summer Exhibition, 1931, No 1278;
Royal West of England Academy, Bristol, 1931, No 738 (£4. 17s. 6d);
'An Exhibition of Paintings, Drawings and Prints and Stanley Anderson RE', P & D Colnaghi, London, October 1932, No 6 (4gns);
Cheltenham, 1949, No 40

The setting is Hammersmith Library.

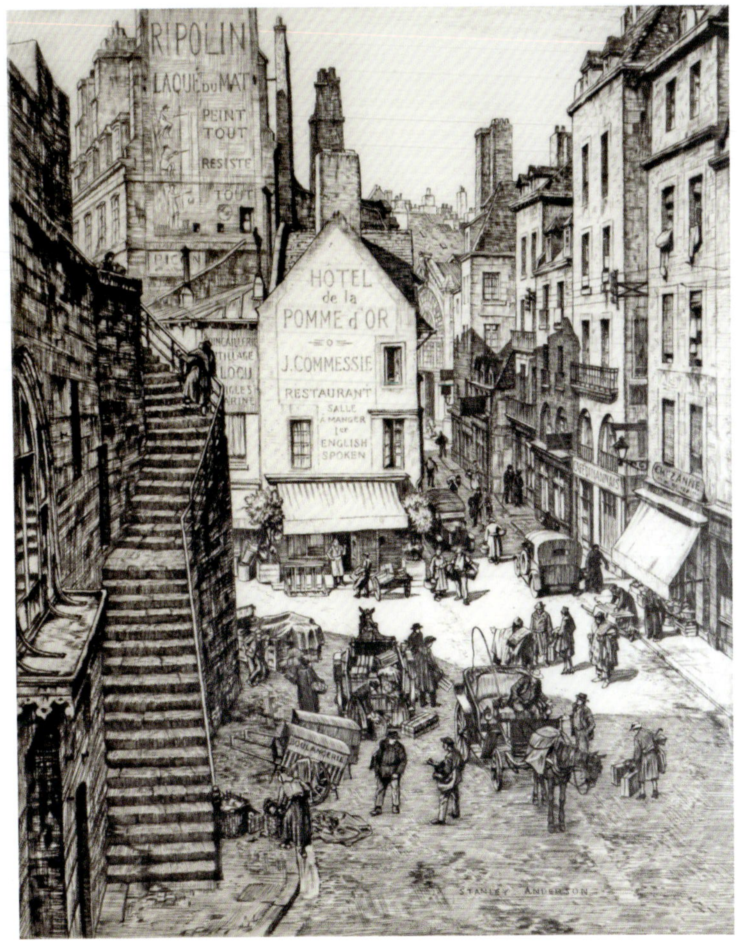

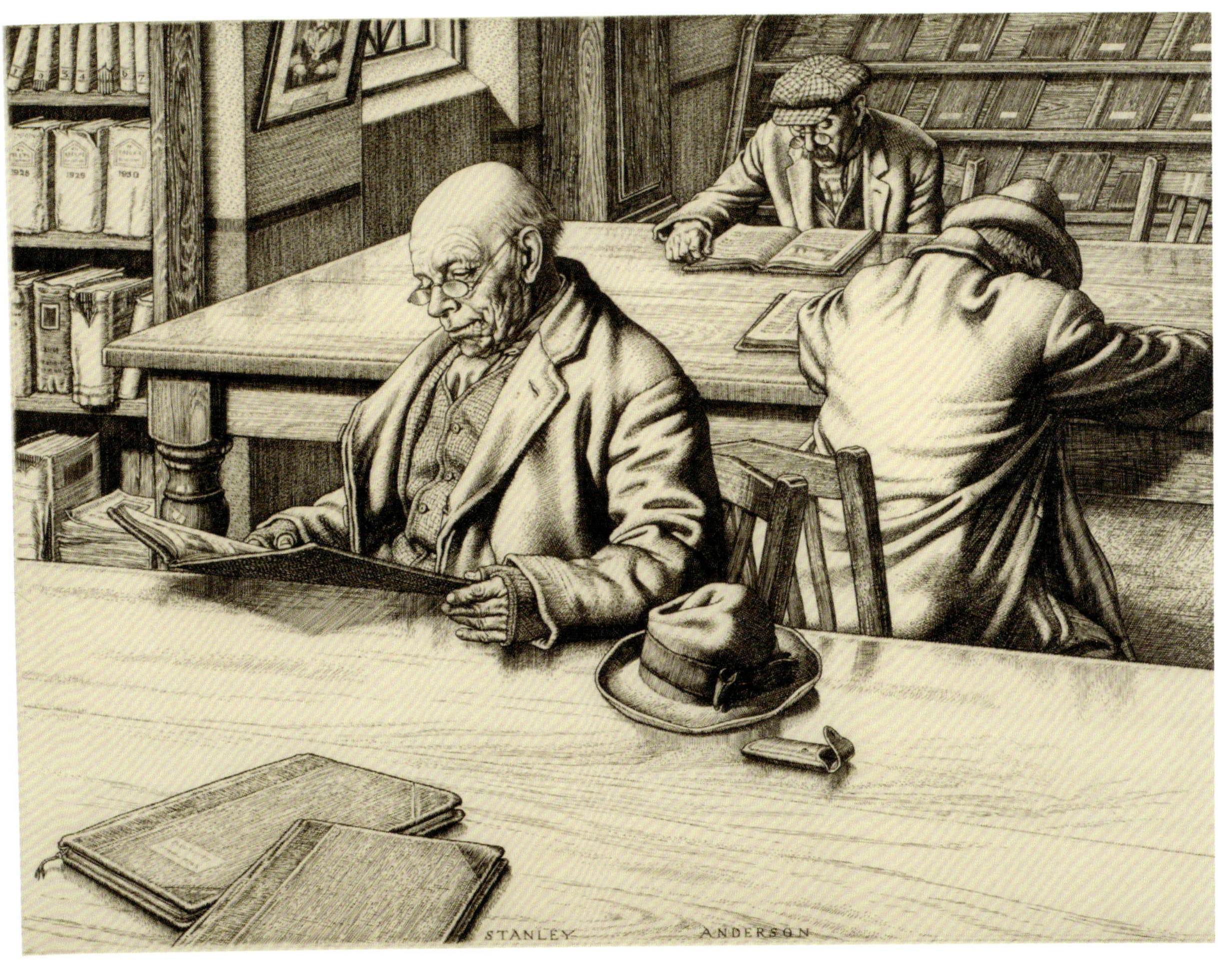

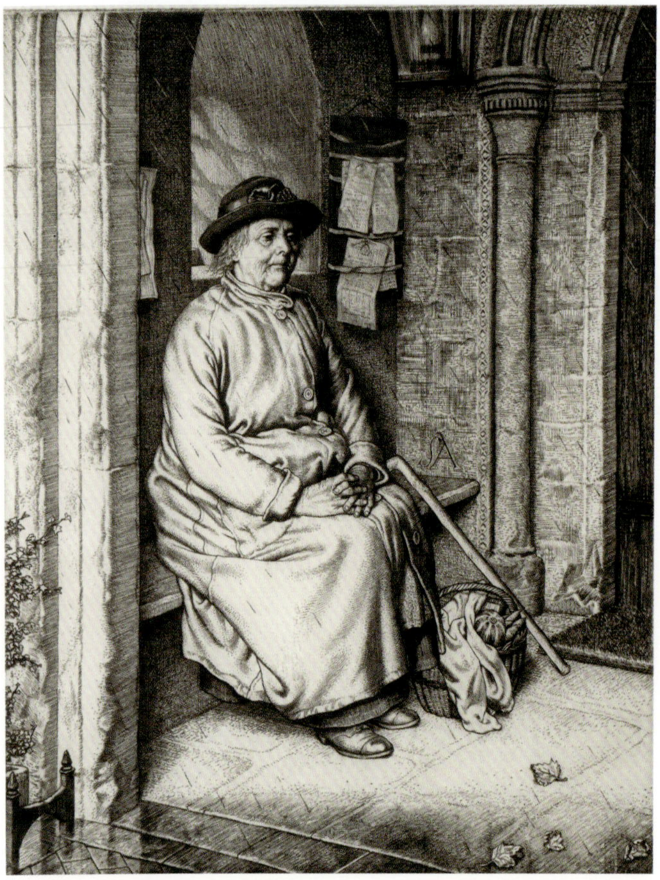

56 Shelter
Signed
Engraving
8 x 6 ½ inches
Executed in 1935 and published by P & D Colnaghi
Literature: Robert Meyrick and Harry Heuser, 2015, Page 218, Catalogue Raisonné No 214
Exhibited: Royal Academy, Summer Exhibition, 1925 No 1302; Royal West of England Academy, Bristol, 1935, No 703; Royal Society of Painter-Etchers and Engravers, 1936, No 64; Royal Society of Painter-Etchers and Engravers, 1946, No 165; Cheltenham, 1949, No 90

57 The Basket Maker (below)
Signed and inscribed 'ed:50'
Inscribed 'The basket maker', '(line-engraving)' and 'edition 50 prints' below mount
Engraving, from an edition of 50
6 ¾ x 6 ½ inches
Executed in 1942 and published by P & D Colnaghi
Literature: Robert Meyrick and Harry Heuser, 2015, Page 237, Catalogue Raisonné No 234
Exhibited: Royal Academy, Summer Exhibition, 1942, No 518; Cheltenham, 1949, No 10

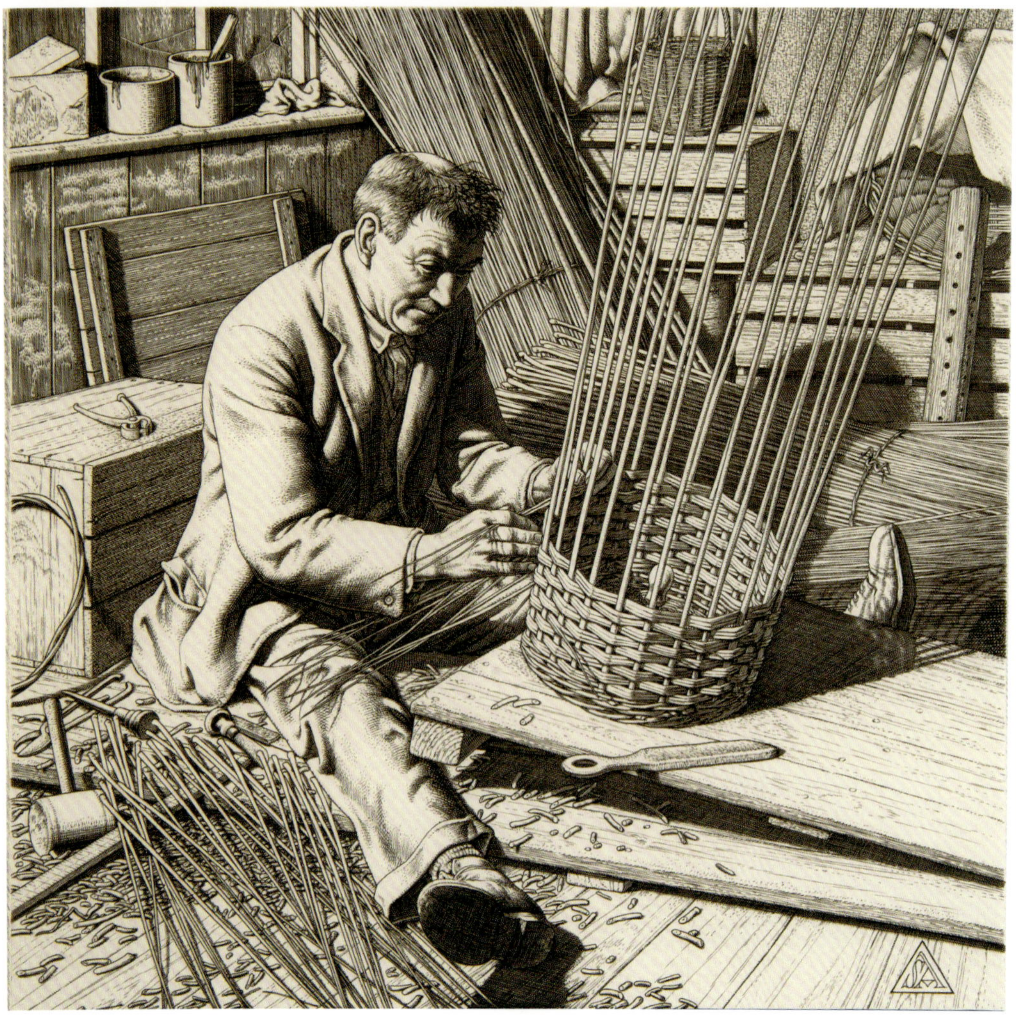

58 The Saddler
Engraving
7 ½ x 6 ¼ inches
Executed in 1946 and published by
P & D Colnaghi
Literature: Robert Meyrick and Harry
Heuser, 2015, Page 250,
Catalogue Raisonné No 248
Exhibited: Royal Academy,
Summer Exhibition, 1946, No 1030;
The Royal Society of Painter-Etchers and
Engravers, 1947, No 46;
Royal West of England Academy, Bristol,
1947, No 5;
Cheltenham, 1949, No 59

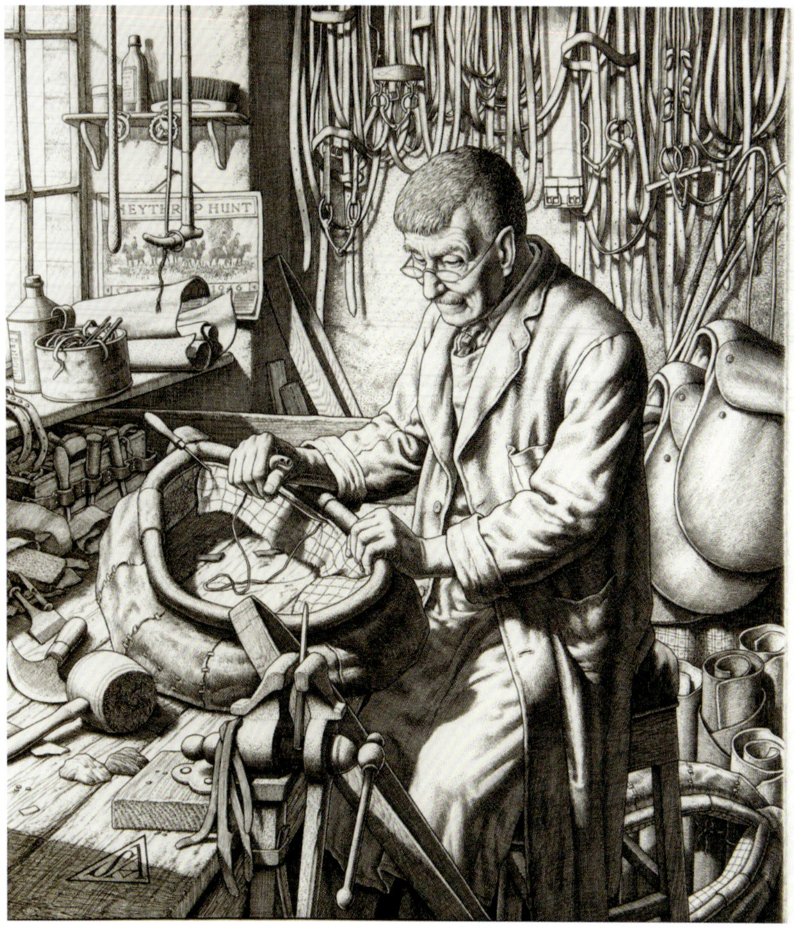

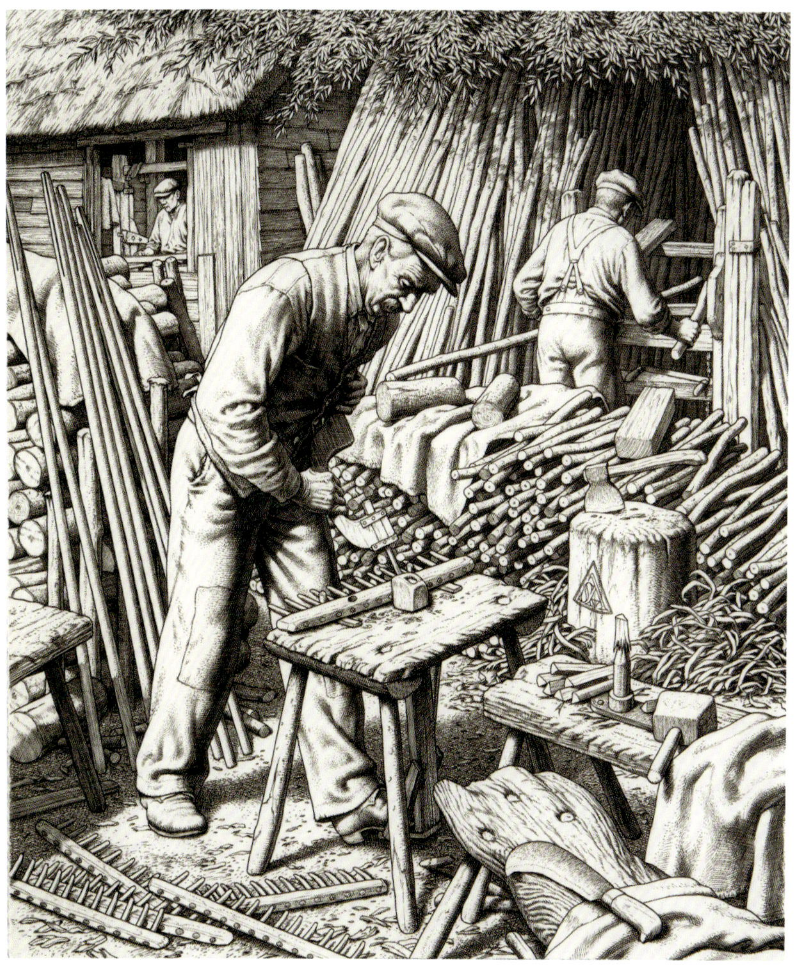

59 The Rake Makers
Signed and inscribed 'ed:65'
Inscribed with title below mount
Engraving
7 ½ x 6 inches
Executed in 1948 and published
by P & D Colnaghi
Literature: Robert Meyrick and Harry
Heuser, 2015, Page 254,
Catalogue Raisonné No 253
Exhibited: Royal Academy,
Summer Exhibition, 1948, No 1065;
The Royal Society of Painter-Etchers and
Engravers, 1949, No 193;
Cheltenham, 1949, No 100

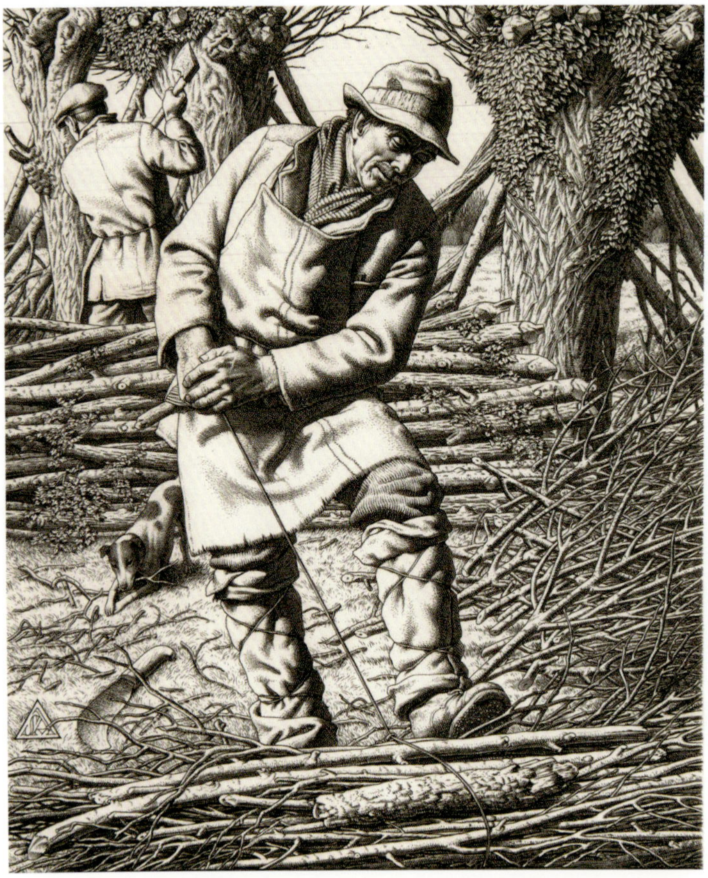

60 Trimming and Faggoting
Signed and inscribed 'ed:50'
Inscribed with title below mount
Engraving
8 x 6 inches
Executed in 1943 and published by P & D Colnaghi
Literature: Robert Meyrick and Harry Heuser, 2015, Page 240, Catalogue Raisonné No 238
Exhibited: Royal Academy, Summer Exhibition, 1943, No 805; The Royal Society of Painter-Etchers and Engravers, 1944, No 15;
Cheltenham, 1949, No 65

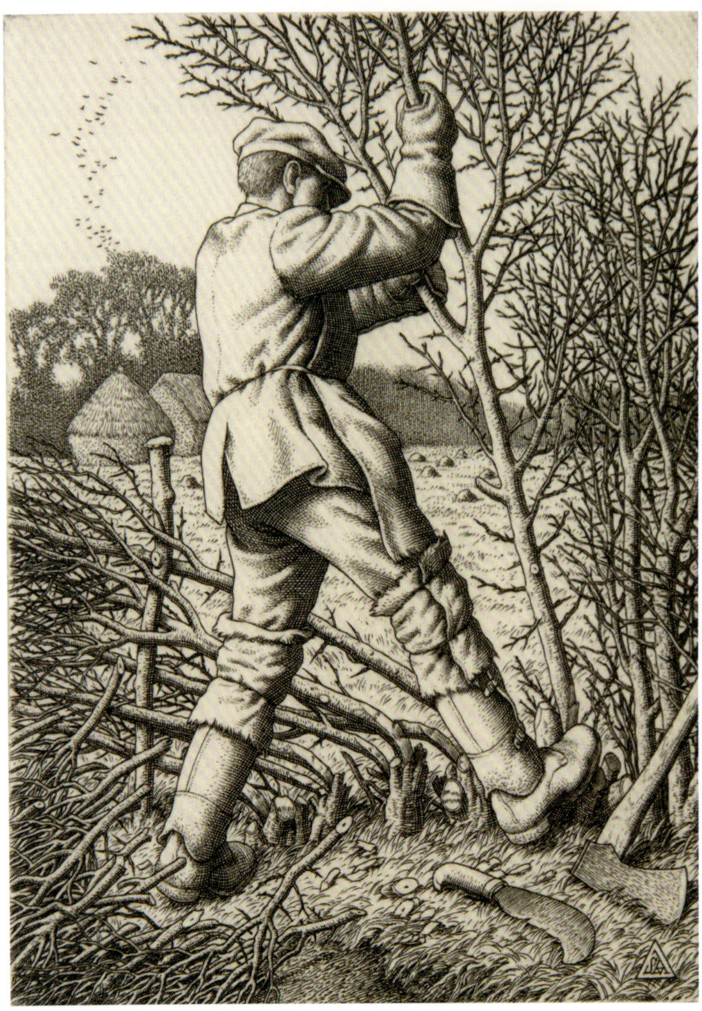

61 Hedge Laying
Signed
Signed with monogram in plate
Engraving
4 x 3 inches
From an edition of 260 (with an additional 12 on old paper)
Published by The Miniature Print Society, Alexandria, Virginia (December 1945)
Literature: Robert Meyrick and Harry Heuser, 2015, Page 249, Catalogue Raisonné No 246
Exhibited: Royal Society of Painter-Etchers and Engravers, 1946, No 35 (2gns);
Cheltenham, 1949, No 41

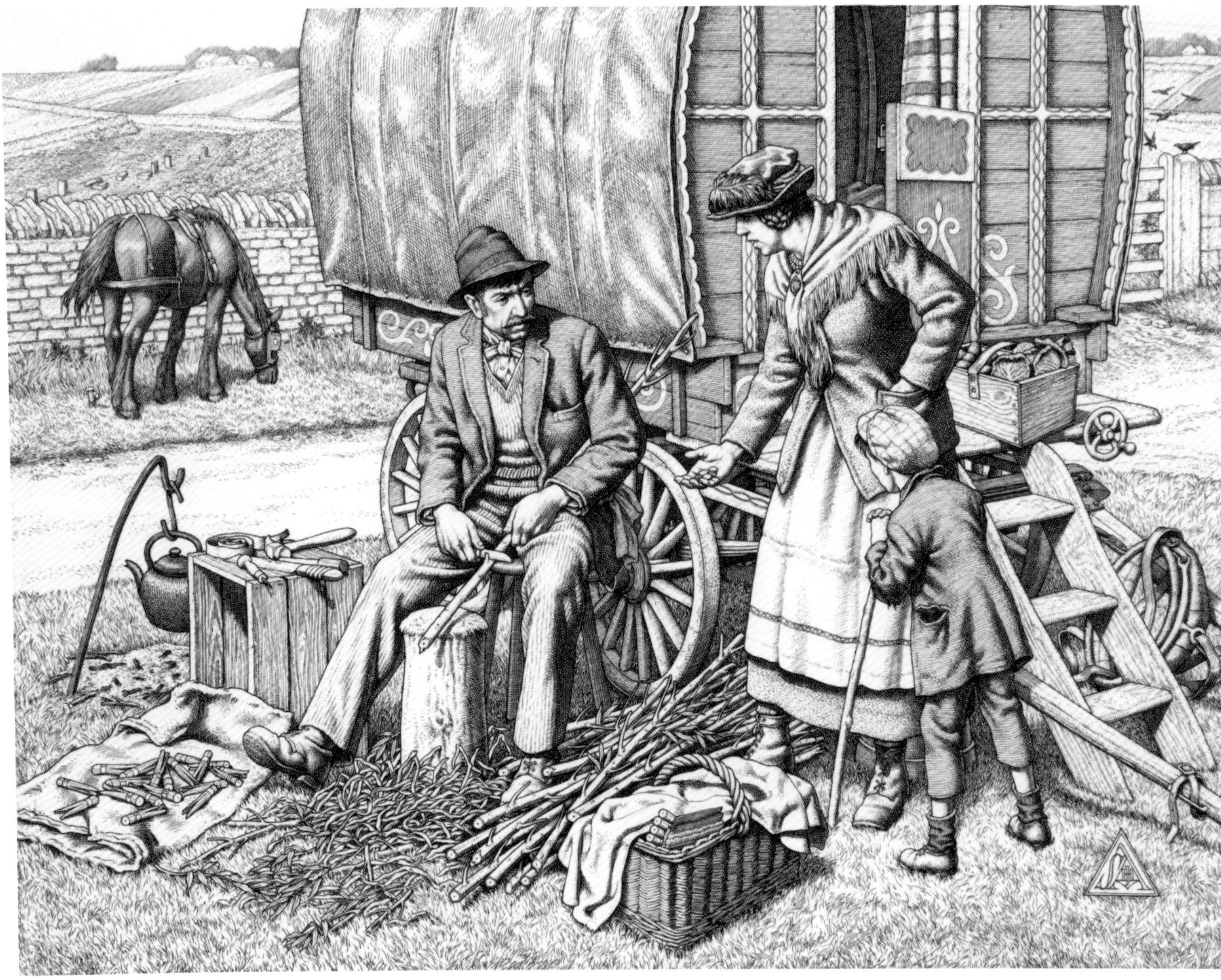

62 **The Clothes Peg Maker**
Signed with monogram, incorporating the collector John Hart's initials, in plate
Engraving
7 x 9 inches
Literature: Robert Meyrick and Harry Heuser, 2015, Page 263, Catalogue Raisonné No 260
Exhibited: Royal Academy, Summer Exhibition, 1953, No 1027

The Clothes Peg Maker

This is Stanley Anderson's final print. He dedicated it to the print collector, John Hart. Hart's initials are incorporated into the artist's monogram.

EDMUND BLAMPIED

Edmund Blampied, RBA RE (1886-1966)

Edmund Blampied is one of the most significant artists to have hailed from the Channel Islands. Greatly versatile, he worked as a painter, illustrator, and occasional sculptor, though is best remembered as a printmaker and, especially, an etcher. Having been born on a farm, he produced some particularly evocative etchings of agricultural and peasant subjects. Their fluidity of line, strong sense of humanity and Gallic humour suggest a kinship with Daumier and Gavarni.

For a biography of Edmund Blampied, please refer to page 203.

63 **En Pension** (below)
Signed and numbered 24/100
Signed and dated 'Oct 30. 1929' in plate
Drypoint
8 ½ x 12 inches
From an edition of 100
Executed 1929-30
Literature: Malcolm C Salaman (ed), *Fine Prints of the Year*, London: Halton & Truscott Smith, 1930;
Kenneth M Guichard, *British Etchers 1850-1940*, London: Robin Garton, 1981, Page 26;
Jean Arnold & John Appleby, *A Catalogue Raisonné of Etchings, Drypoints & Lithographs of Edmund Blampied*, St Ouen: John Appleby Publishing, 1996, No 142

64 **Joy Ride** (opposite above)
Signed
Signed in plate
Drypoint
8 ½ x 10 ½ inches
From an edition of 100
Literature: Malcolm C Salaman (ed), *Fine Prints of the Year*, London: Halton & Truscott Smith, 1925, Plate IV;
E L Allhusen, 'The Etchings of Edmund Blampied', *The Print Collectors' Quarterly*, 1926, Vol 13, No 56;
Campbell Dodgson, *A Complete Catalogue of The Etchings and Drypoints of Edmund Blampied*, London: Halton & Trustcott Smith, 1926, No 81;
Malcolm C Salaman, *Modern Masters of Etching, Vol 10, Edmund Blampied*, London: The Studio, 1926, Plate VI;
Jean Arnold & John Appleby, *A Catalogue Raisonné of Etchings, Drypoints & Lithographs of Edmund Blampied*, St Ouen: John Appleby Publishing, 1996, No 89

65 **Purring and Snoring** (opposite below)
Signed
Signed and dated 1921 in plate
Drypoint
7 ½ x 9 ½ inches
Literature: E L Allhusen, 'The Etchings of Edmund Blampied', *The Print Collectors' Quarterly*, 1926, Vol 13, No 39;
Campbell Dodgson, *A Complete Catalogue of The Etchings and Drypoints of Edmund Blampied*, London: Halton & Trustcott Smith, 1926, No 62;
Malcolm Salaman, *Modern Masters of Etching, Vol 10, Edmund Blampied*, London: The Studio, 1926, Plate III;
Harold J Baily, 'Blampied, Artist & Philosopher', *The Print Collectors' Quarterly*, Vol 24, No 5, 1937, Page 386;
Jean Arnold & John Appleby, *A Catalogue Raisonné of Etchings, Drypoints & Lithographs of Edmund Blampied*, St Ouen: John Appleby Publishing, 1996, No 87

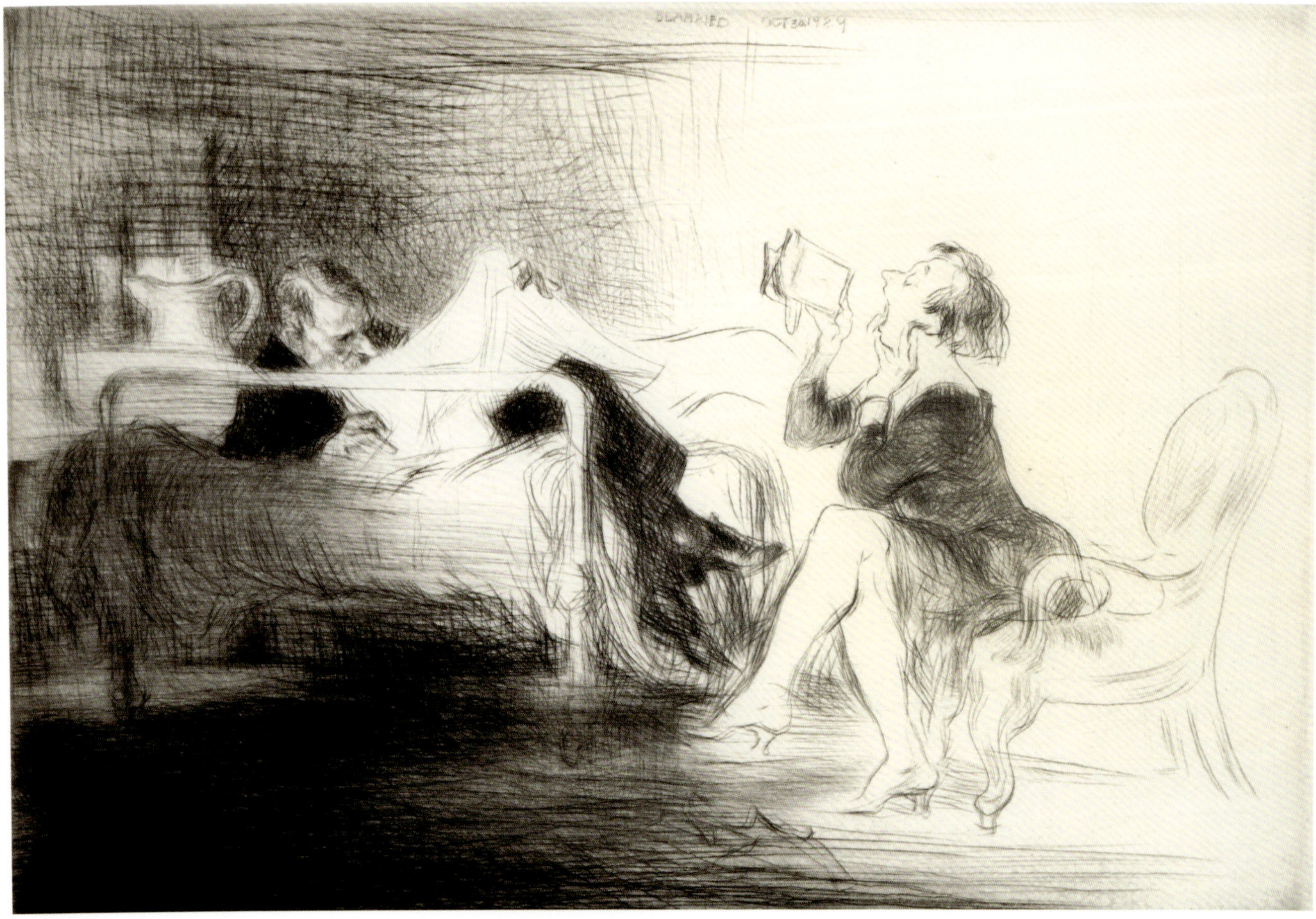

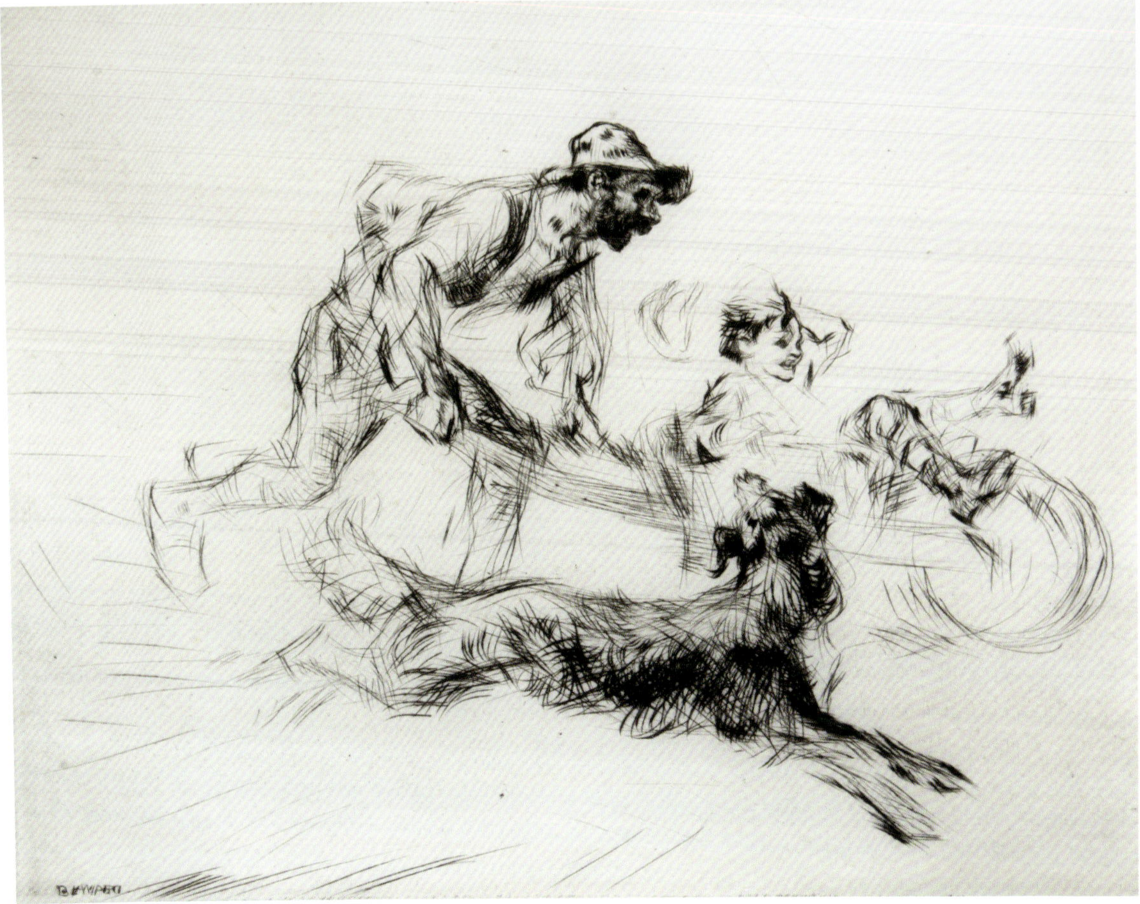

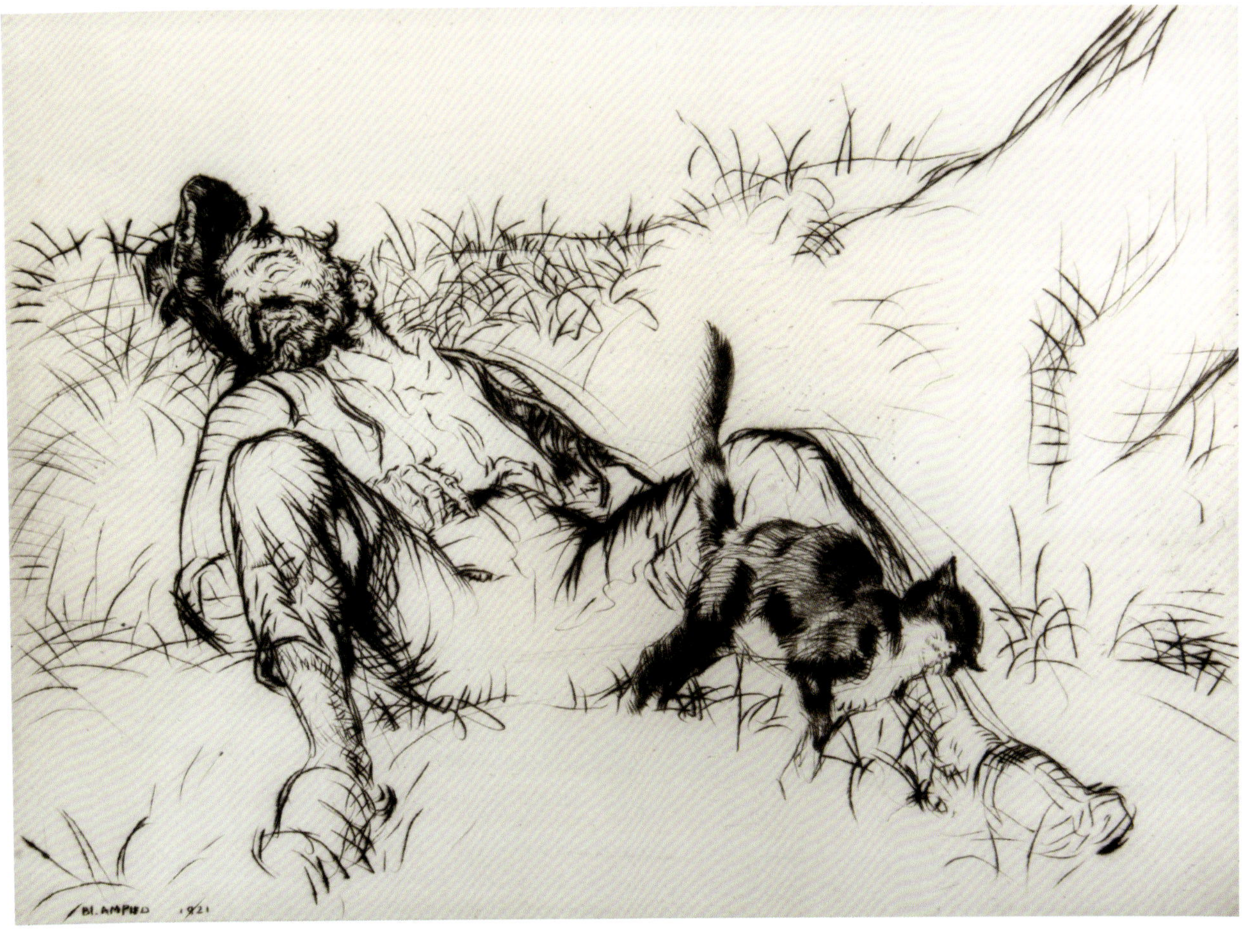
BLAMPIED 1921

HENRY RUSHBURY

Sir Henry George Rushbury, RA VPRWS RE HonRIBA NEAC (1889-1968)

A painter, draughtsman and printmaker, Henry Rushbury was one of the finest artists of the twentieth century to specialise in architectural and other topographical subjects. He had a great ability to capture the spirit as well as the appearance of a place through the use of light and shade and the introduction of elements of everyday life.

For a biography of Henry Rushbury, please refer to page 204.

Nos **66-69**
Literature: Julia Rushbury, *Henry Rushbury, Prints: A Catalogue Raisonné*, London: Royal Academy of Arts, 2010

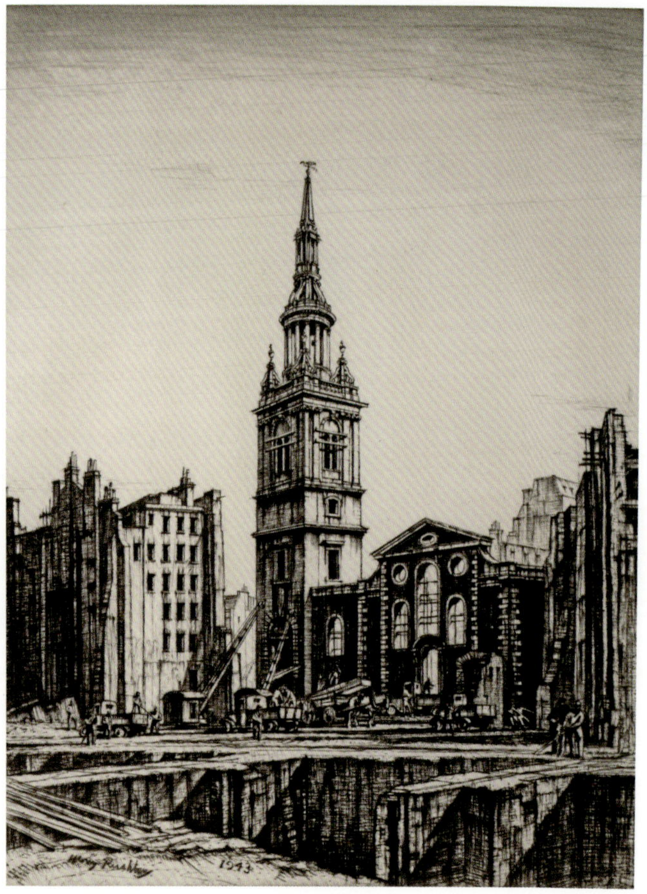

66 St Mary-Le-Bow
Signed
Signed and dated 1943 in plate
Drypoint
11 x 8 ¼ inches
Literature: Julia Rushbury, 2010, No 81
Exhibited: Royal Academy, Summer Exhibition, 1944, No 1067, as 'Bow Church from Bread Street';
Royal Society of Painter-Etchers and Engravers, 1944

67 St Victor, Marseilles
Signed; Drypoint
7 ¾ x 9 inches
Literature: Julia Rushbury, 2010, No 38

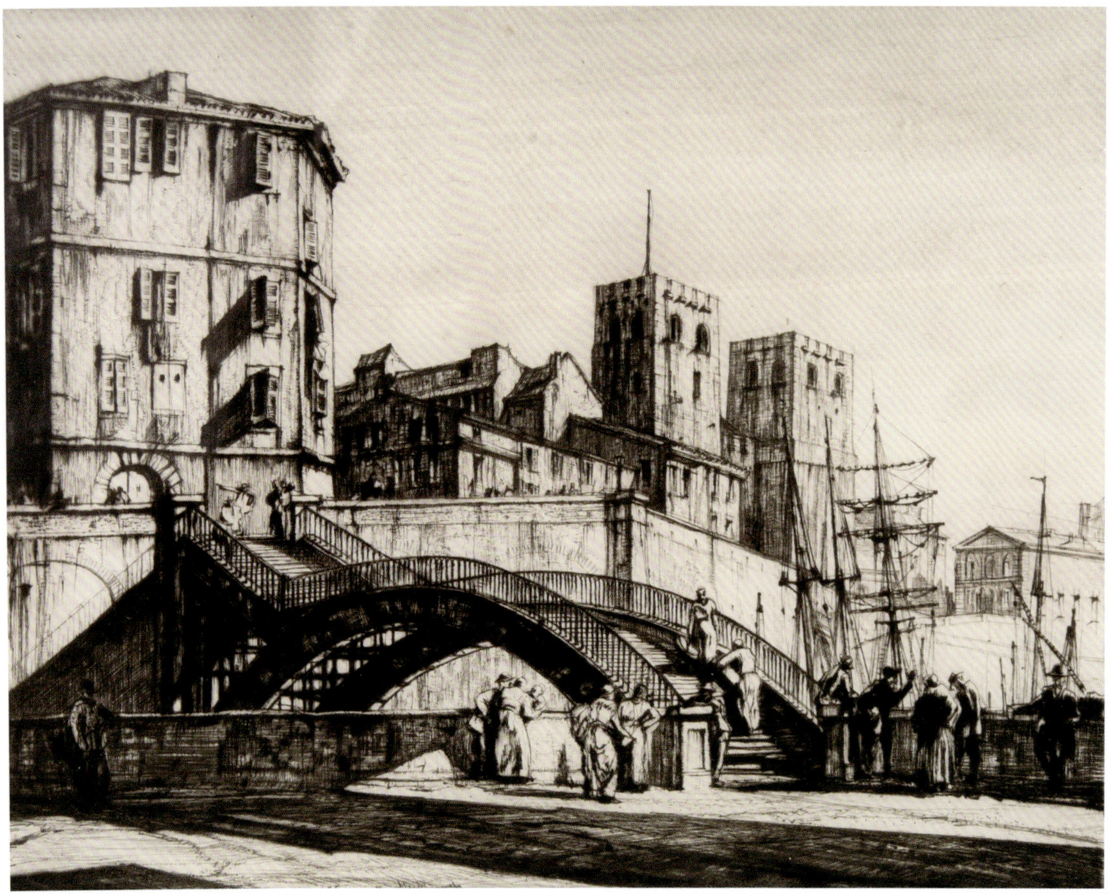

68 Viterbo
Signed
Inscribed with title below mount
Signed in reverse in plate
Drypoint
7 ¾ x 11 ¾ inches
Literature: Malcolm C Salaman (ed), *Fine Prints of the Year*, London: Halton & Truscott Smith, Vol 7, 1929, Pages 9 & xii;
Julia Rushbury, 2010, No 63

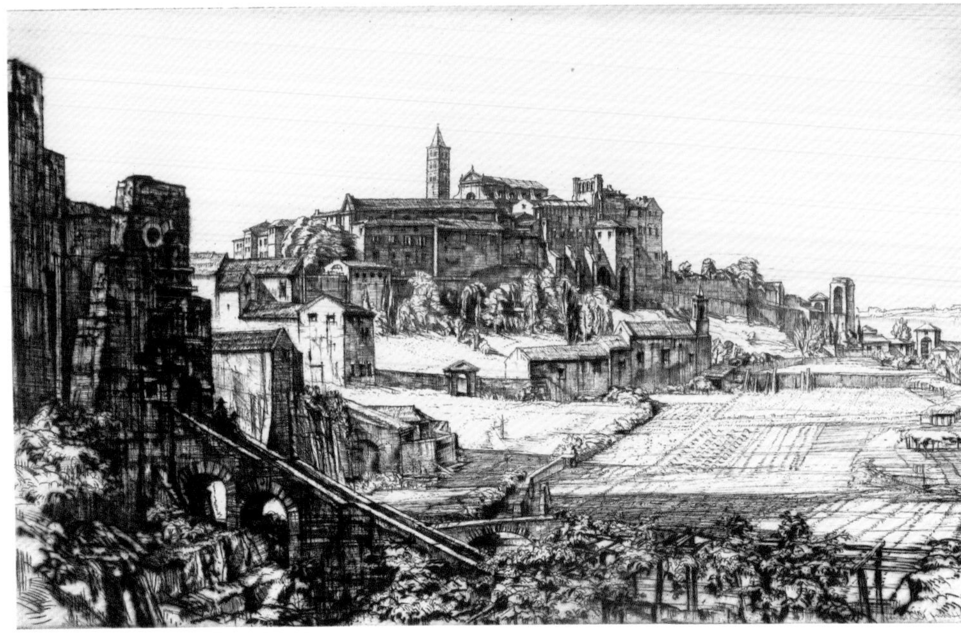

69 Lothbury Court, Bank of England, 1929
Signed
Drypoint
14 ½ x 14 ½ inches
Illustrated: *The Sphere*, 17 November 1949, Christmas Number
Literature: Julia Rushbury, 2010, No 65

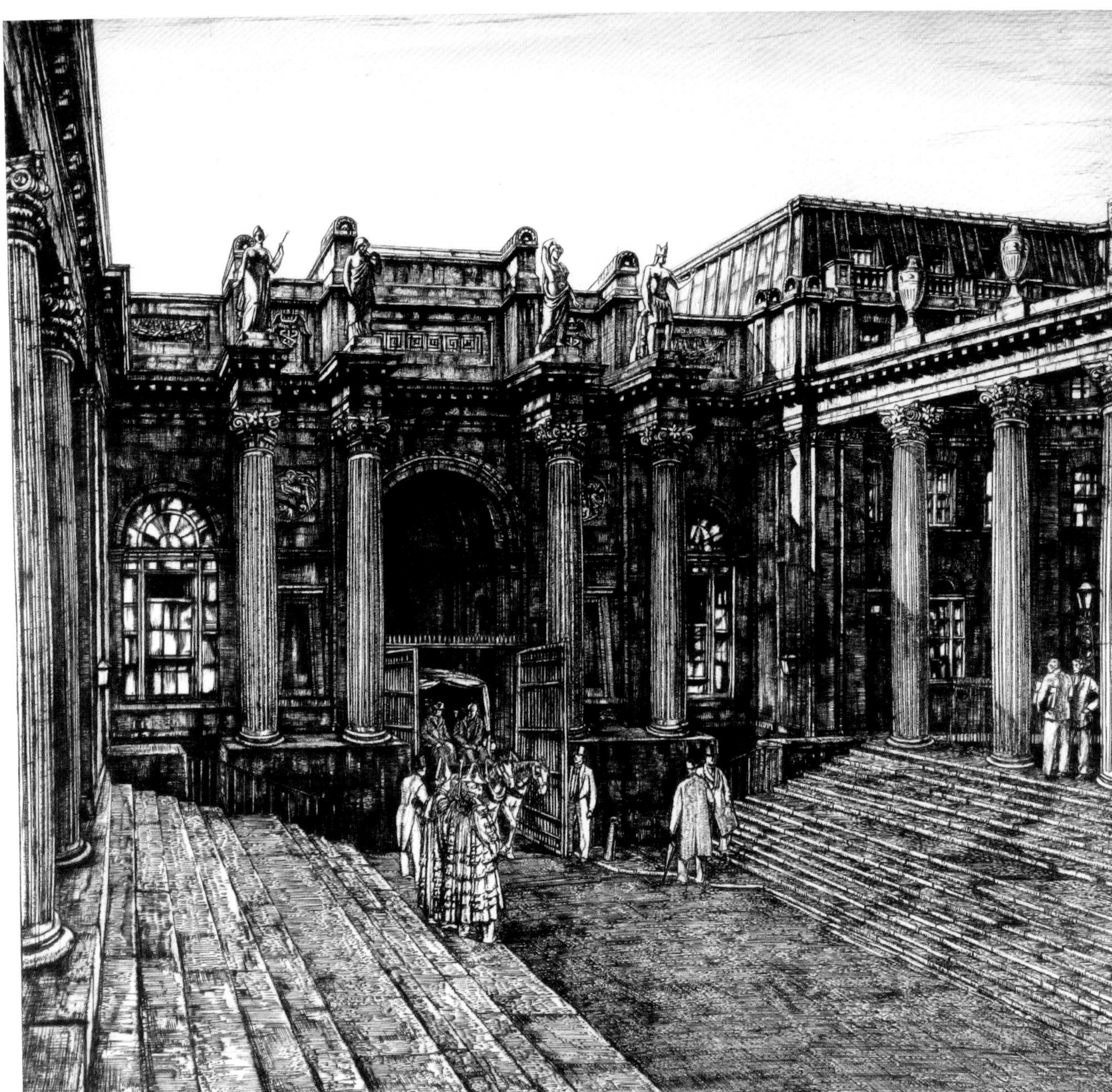

JOHN AUSTEN

John Archibald Austen, RBA (1886-1948)

Early influenced by the work of Aubrey Beardsley, John Austen developed into an illustrator of wit and elegance by the mid 1920s, producing unusually decorative images that are associated with Art Deco. Both craftsman and auto-didact, he mastered a range of media, including etching and wood-engraving, and absorbed a variety of styles and motifs.

For a biography of John Austen, please refer to page 207.

70 **Black Venus**
Signed and inscribed with title and edition number
Woodcut
8 x 5 inches
Number 7 from an edition of 25
Executed in 1932

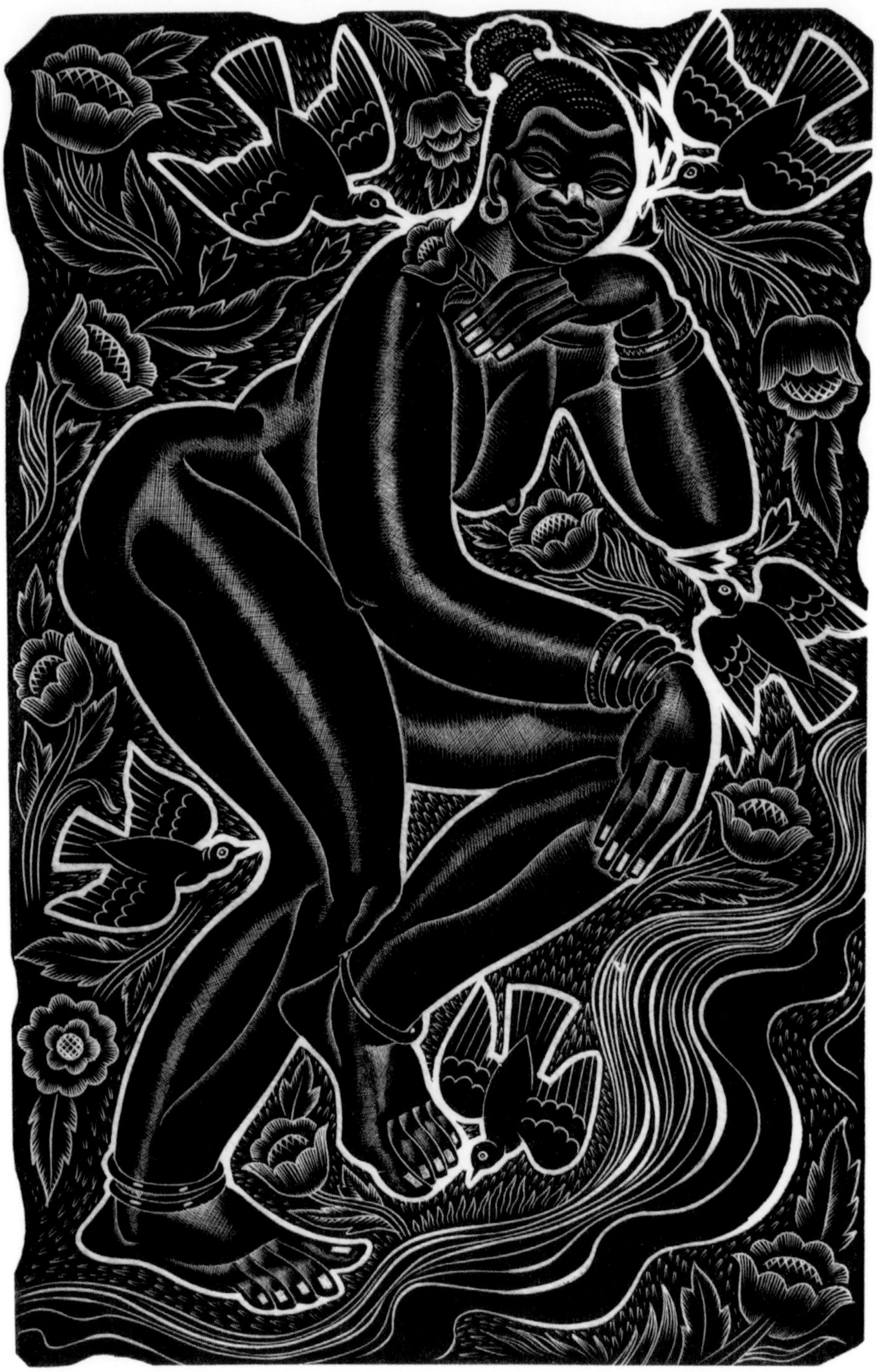

GERALD BROCKHURST

Gerald Leslie Brockhurst, RA RE RP SGA (1890-1978)

Gerald Brockhurst was a precociously gifted painter, draughtsman and printmaker, who is best known for his portraits of women, including his two wives and a number of celebrities. The work of Italian Renaissance artists informed his developing style, which at its most mature was intensely, even unnervingly, realistic.

For a biography of Gerald Brockhurst, please refer to page 205.

71 L'Eventail (Anaïs), also called The Fan
Signed
Signed in reverse in plate
Etching
6 ½ x 4 ½ inches
From an edition of 76
Literature: Hugh Stokes, 1924, Page 418;
Harold Wright, 1935, Page 64, Catalogue Raisonné No 22;
William Dolan Fletcher, 1984, Page 34, Catalogue Raisonné No 22
Exhibited: Royal Society of Painter-Etchers and Engravers, 1921, No 189;
Fine Art Society, 1986, No 75

Executed in 1921, this etching shows the artist's first wife, Anaïs.

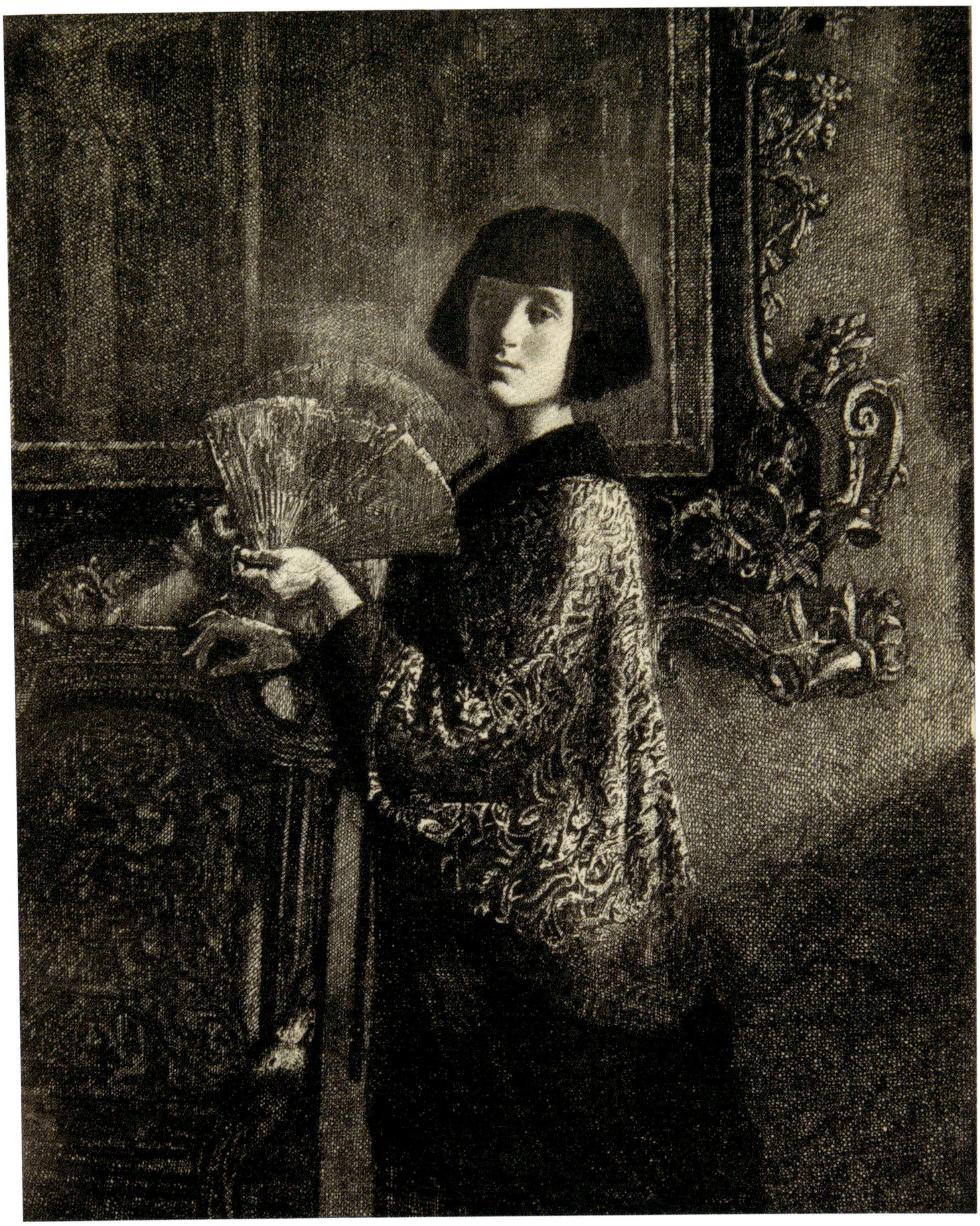

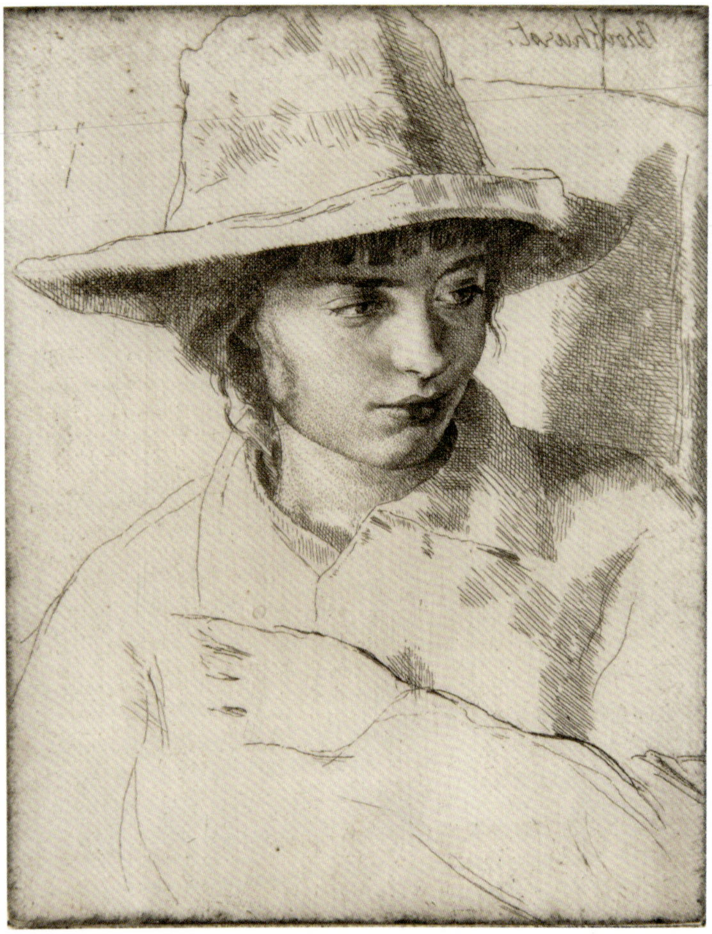

72 Yolande
Signed
Signed in reverse in plate
Etching
4 ½ x 3 ½ inches
From an edition of 55
Literature: Hugh Stokes, 1924, Page 427;
Harold Wright, 1934, Page 317;
Harold Wright, 1935, Page 64, Catalogue Raisonné No 12;
William Dolan Fletcher, 1984, Page 27, Catalogue Raisonné No 12
Exhibited: Royal Society of Painter-Etchers and Engravers, 1922;
Fine Art Society, 1986, No 68;
Fine Art Society, 2018, No 2

Executed in 1920, this etching is a study of Florence Rushbury (née Layzell), whom the artist, Henry Rushbury, married in 1914.

Nos **71-72** Literature: Hugh Stokes, 'The Etchings of G L Brockhurst', *The Print Collector's Quarterly*, December 1924, Vol XI, No 4

Nos **72, 80, 82-93** Literature: Harold Wright, 'The Later Etchings by G L Brockhurst', *Print Collector's Quarterly*, 1934, Vol XXI, No 4

Nos **71-93** Literature: Harold Wright, 'Catalogue of the Etchings of G L Brockhurst', *The Print Collector's Quarterly*, 1935, Vol XXII, No 1, Page 64, Catalogue Raisonné No 12

Nos **71-93** Literature: William Dolan Fletcher, *Complex Simplicity, Gerald Leslie Brockhurst and his Graphic Work*, Connecticut: Eastern Press 1984

Nos **71-72, 74, 76, 78, 80, 82-84, 86, 88-90, 93** Exhibited: 'Gerald Brockhurst: A Dream of Fair Women', Fine Art Society, London, 1986

Nos **72, 90** Exhibited: 'Gerald Brockhurst, A Private Collection', Fine Art Society, London, February 2018

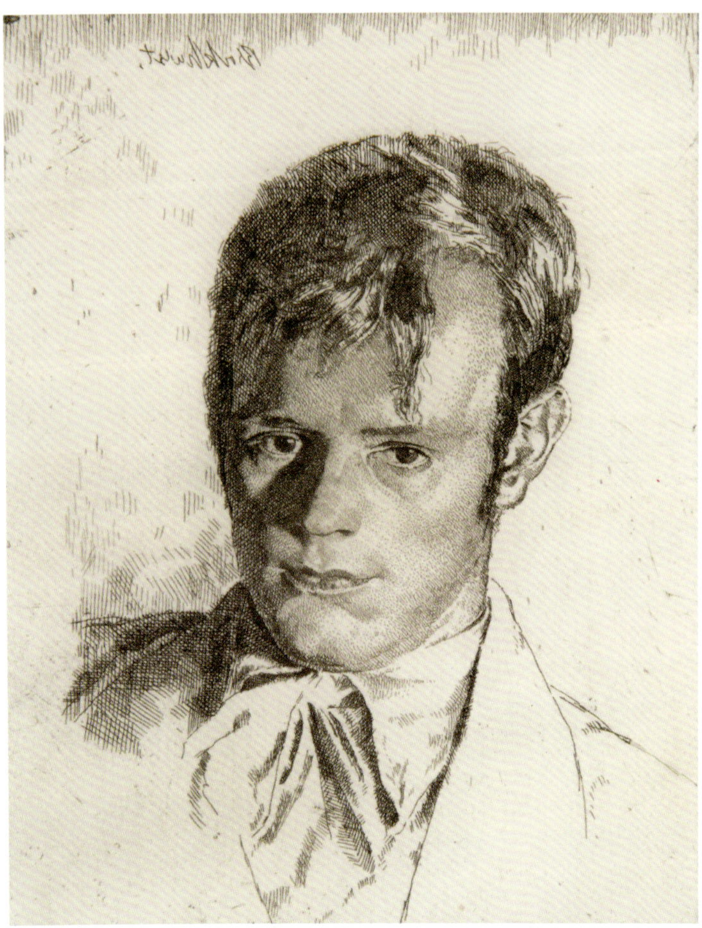

73 Henry Rushbury, No 1
Signed
Signed in reverse in plate
Etching
4 ¾ x 3 ½ inches
From an edition of 55
Literature: Harold Wright, 1935, Page 64,
Catalogue Raisonné No 17;
William Dolan Fletcher, 1984, Page 30,
Catalogue Raisonné No 17

Executed in 1920, this etching was based on two paintings by Gerald Brockhurst of Henry Rushbury

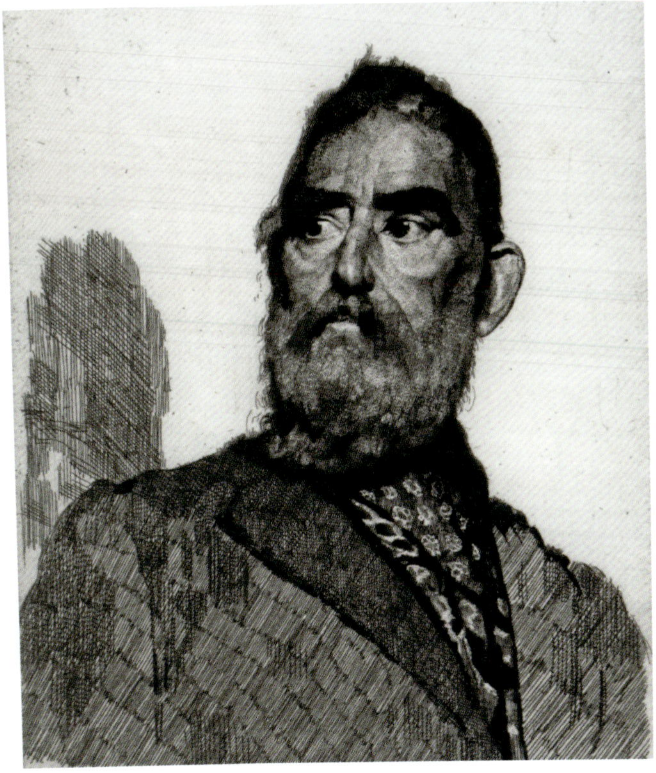

74 An Old Corsican
Signed
Signed and dated 1921 in reverse in plate
Etching
6 ½ x 4 ½ inches
From an edition of 76
Literature: Harold Wright, 1935, Page 64, Catalogue Raisonné No 27;
William Dolan Fletcher, 1984, Page 36, Catalogue Raisonné No 27
Exhibited: Fine Art Society, 1986, No 77

'The model is Mr Marquett, a well-known figure in Chelsea art circles and one of the last of the Dalziel school of wood-engravers.'
(Harold Wright, *The Print Collector's Quarterly*, 1924)

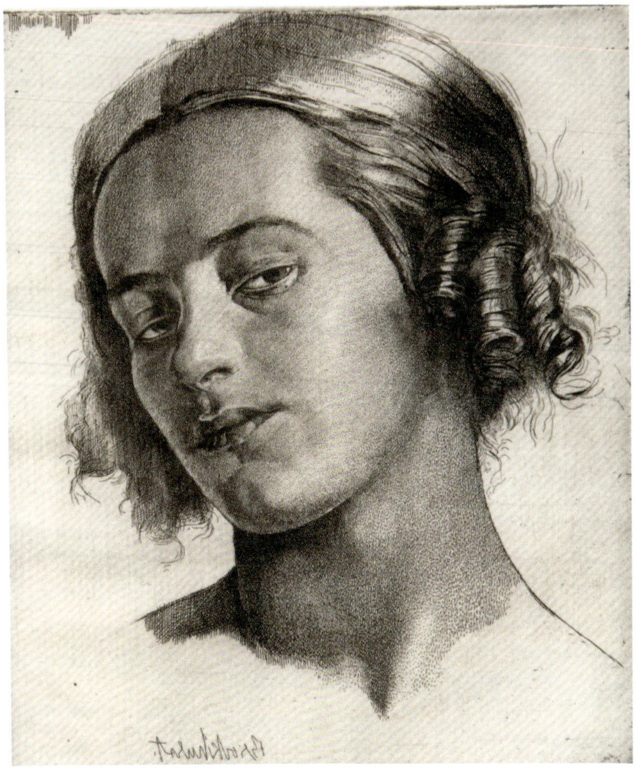

75 Nadia
Signed
Signed in reverse in plate
Etching
5 ½ x 4 ½ inches
From an edition of 55
Executed in September 1921
Literature: Harold Wright, 1935, Page 64, Catalogue Raisonné No 26;
William Dolan Fletcher, 1984, Page 37, Catalogue Raisonné No 26

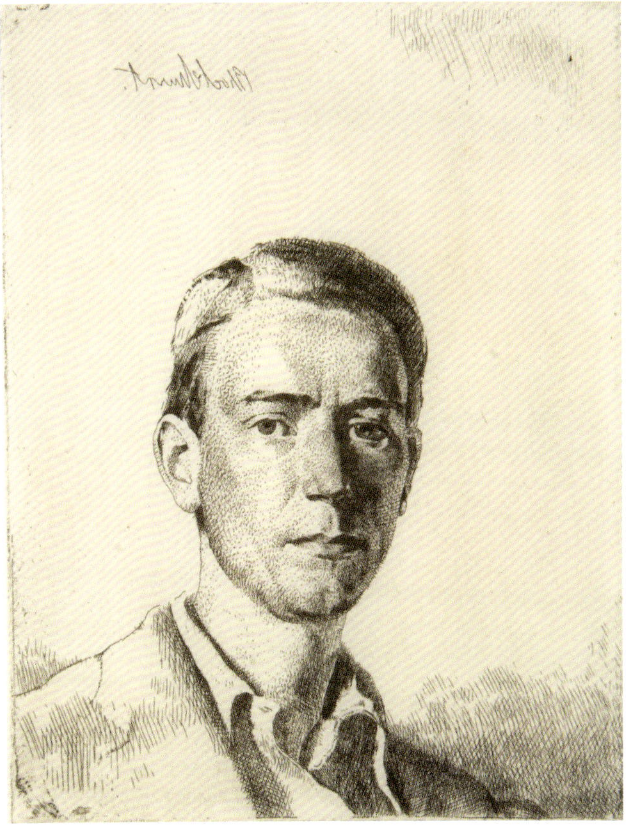

76 Francis MacNamara
Signed
Signed in reverse in plate
Etching
5 x 4 inches
From an edition of 55
Literature: Harold Wright, 1935, Page 63, Catalogue Raisonné No 3;
William Dolan Fletcher, 1984, Page 21, Catalogue Raisonné No 3
Exhibited: Fine Art Society, 1986, No 64

Executed in 1920, this etching was based upon a painting by Gerald Brockhurst of the Irish poet, Francis MacNamara, in the National Gallery of Ireland, Dublin.

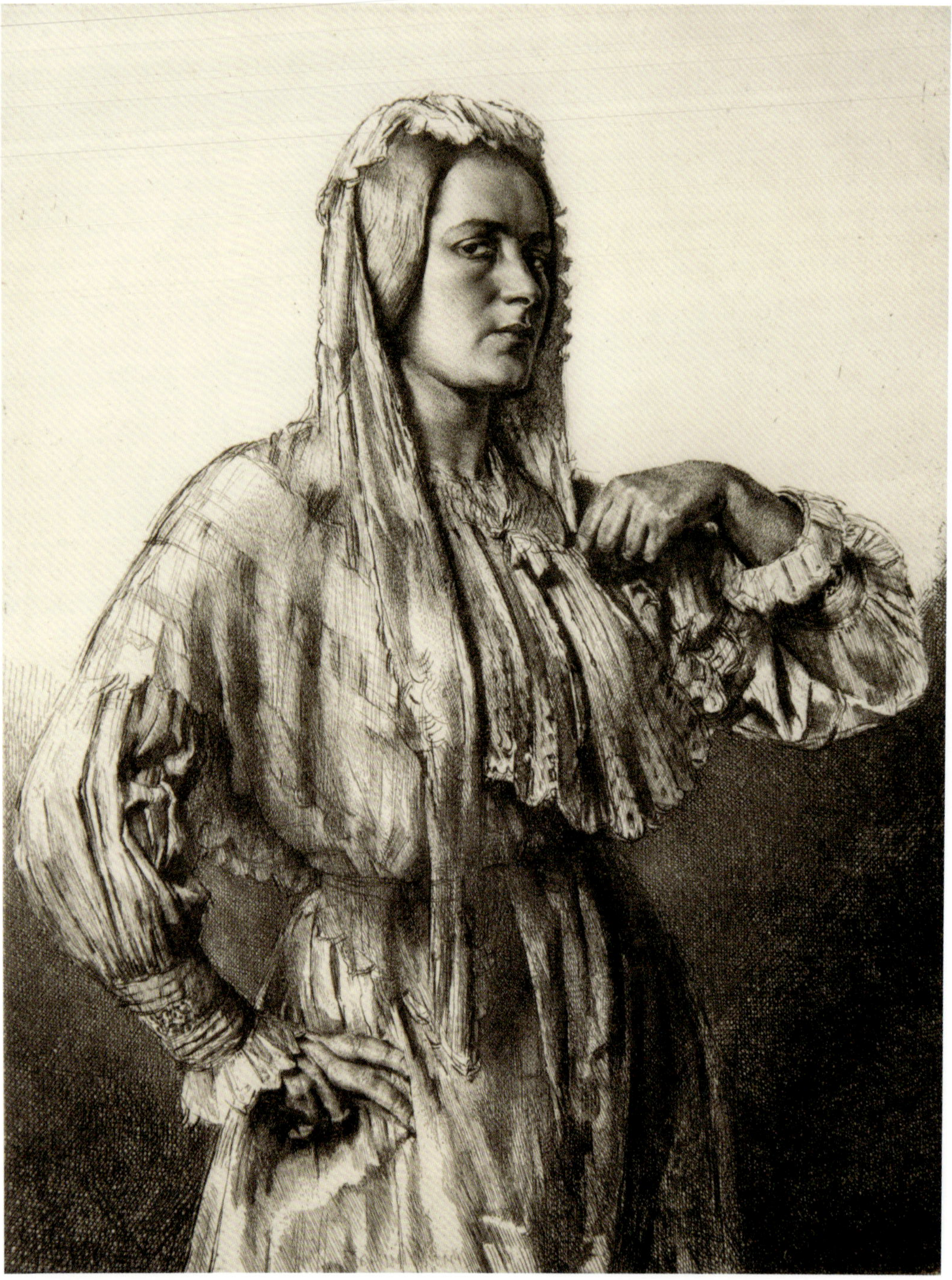

77 Almina
Signed
Signed in reverse in plate
Etching
7 x 5 ¼ inches
Executed in 1924
Literature: Harold Wright, 1935, Page 67, Catalogue Raisonné No 48;
William Dolan Fletcher, 1984, Page 50, Catalogue Raisonné No 48

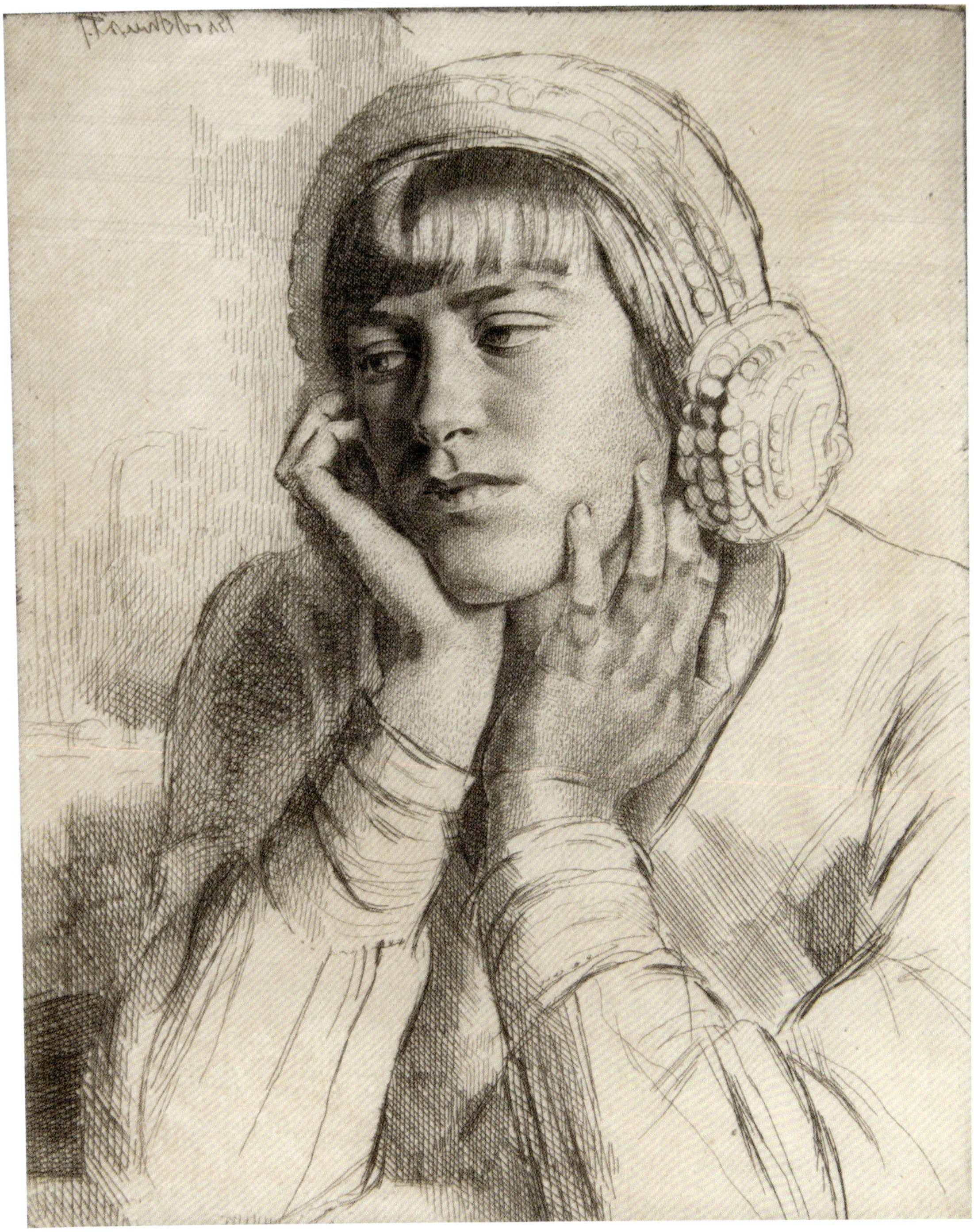

78 **Le Beguin (Anaïs)**
Signed
Signed in reverse in plate
Etching
5 ½ x 4 ½ inches
From an edition of 76
Literature: Harold Wright, 1935, Page 65, Catalogue Raisonné No 33; William Dolan Fletcher, 1984, Page 41, Catalogue Raisonné No 33
Exhibited: Fine Art Society, 1986, No 79

Le Beguin (Anaïs)
Produced in 1922, this etching shows the artist's first wife Anaïs. The title of the plate is taken from the French-Moorish cap or head band worn by women from Anaïs's home town of Dax, in southwest France. Beguin means bonnet and also, colloquially, an infatuation.

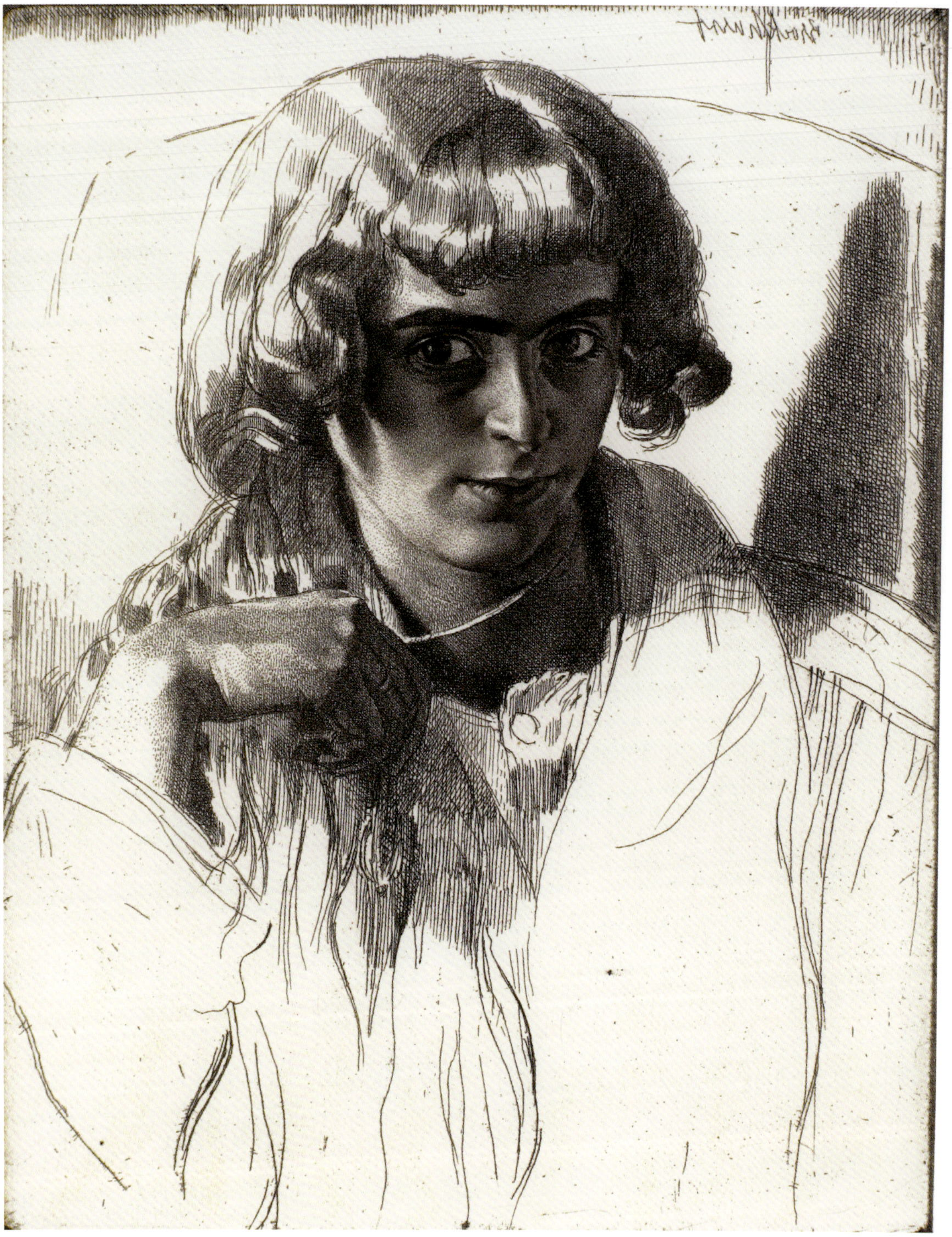

79 Xenia (Marguérite)
Signed
Signed in reverse in plate
Etching
8 x 6 inches
Executed in 1923
Literature: Harold Wright, 1935, Page 65, Catalogue Raisonné No 39;
William Dolan Fletcher, 1984, Page 44, Catalogue Raisonné No 39

80 Marquett
Signed
Signed in reverse in plate
Etching
8 ½ x 7 inches
From an edition of 106
Executed in December 1925
Literature: Harold Wright, 1934, Page 321;
Harold Wright, 1935, Page 68, Catalogue Raisonné No 51;
William Dolan Fletcher, 1984, Page 51, Catalogue Raisonné No 51
Exhibited: Fine Art Society, 1986, No 86

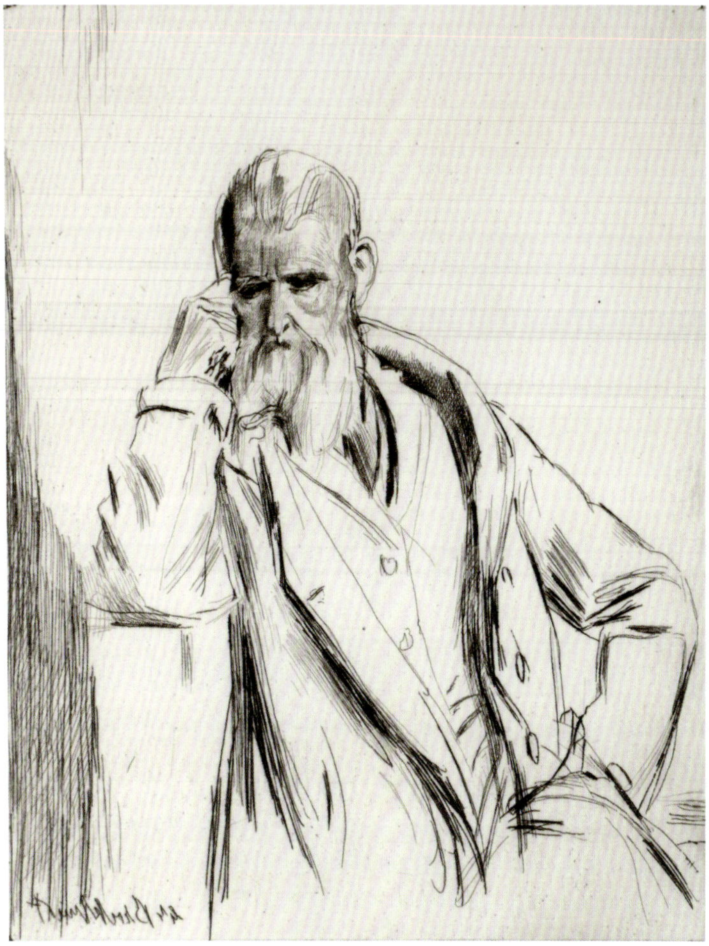

81 Lassitude
Signed
Signed in reverse in plate
Etching
5 ½ x 7 ¼ inches
Literature: Harold Wright, 1935, Page 67,
Catalogue Raisonné No 43;
William Dolan Fletcher, 1984, Page 46, Catalogue Raisonné No 43

Executed in 1923-24, this etching is a portrait of Brockhurst's first wife, Anaïs.

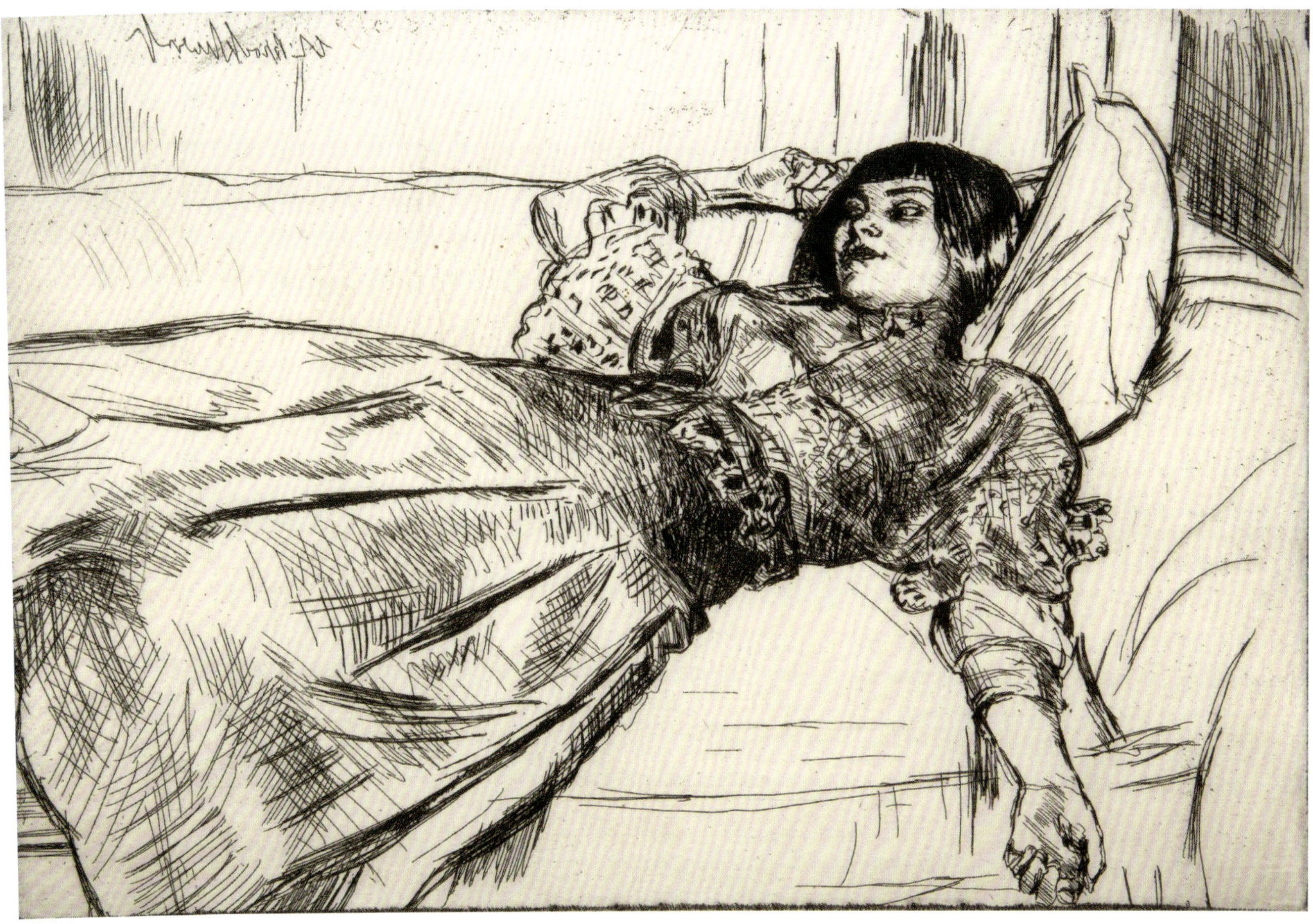

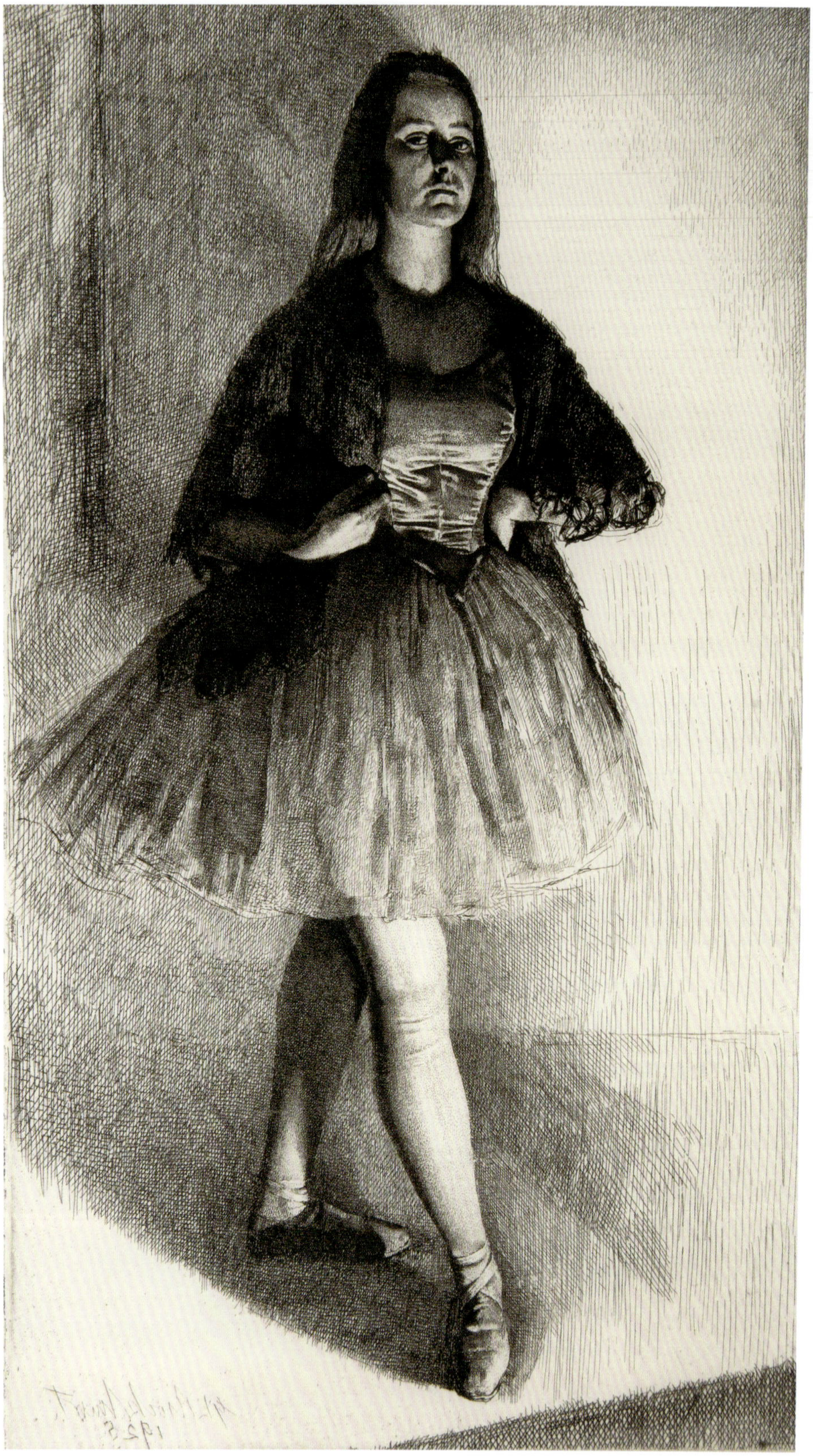

82 **The Dancer (Anaïs)**
Signed and dated 1925 in reverse in plate
Etching
9 ½ x 5 ½ inches
Literature: Malcolm C Salaman (ed), *Fine Prints of the Year*, London: Halton & Truscott Smith, Vol 4, 1926;
Harold Wright, 1934, Page 319, Plate 52;
Harold Wright, 1935, Page 68, Catalogue Raisonné No 52;
William Dolan Fletcher, 1984, Page 52, Catalogue Raisonné No 52
Exhibited: Fine Art Society, 1986, No 87

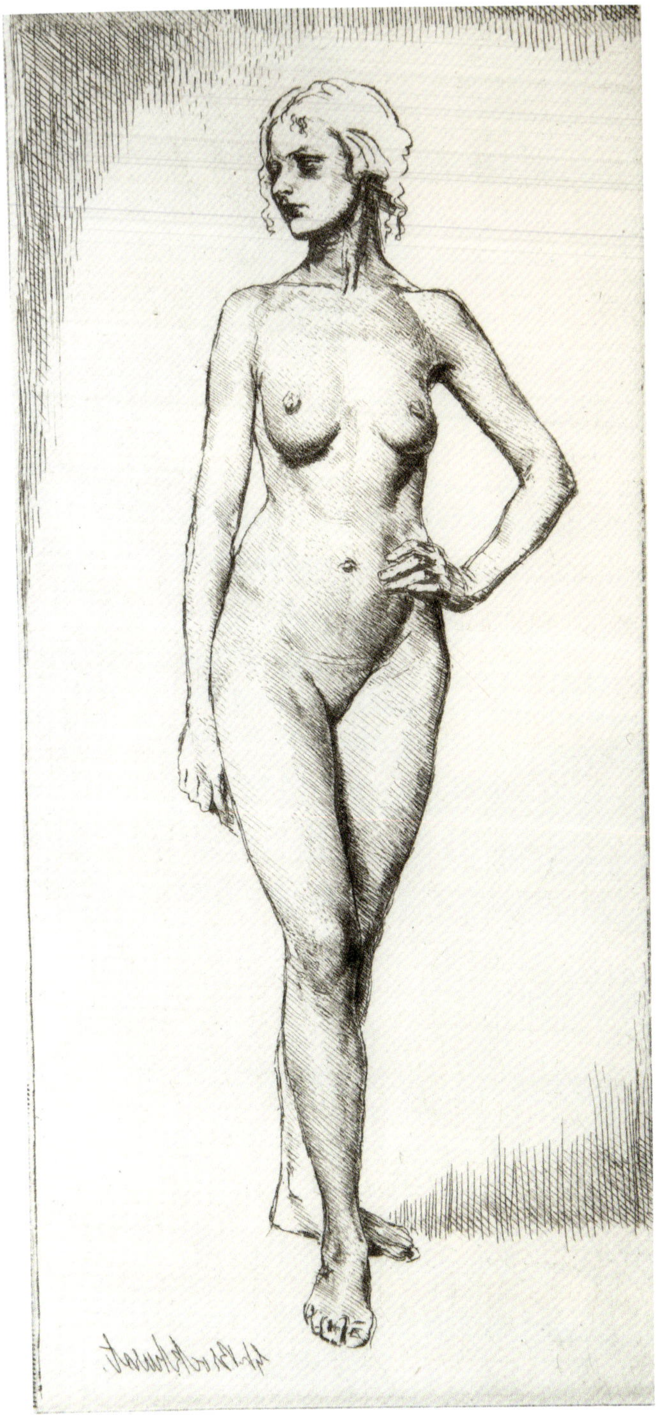

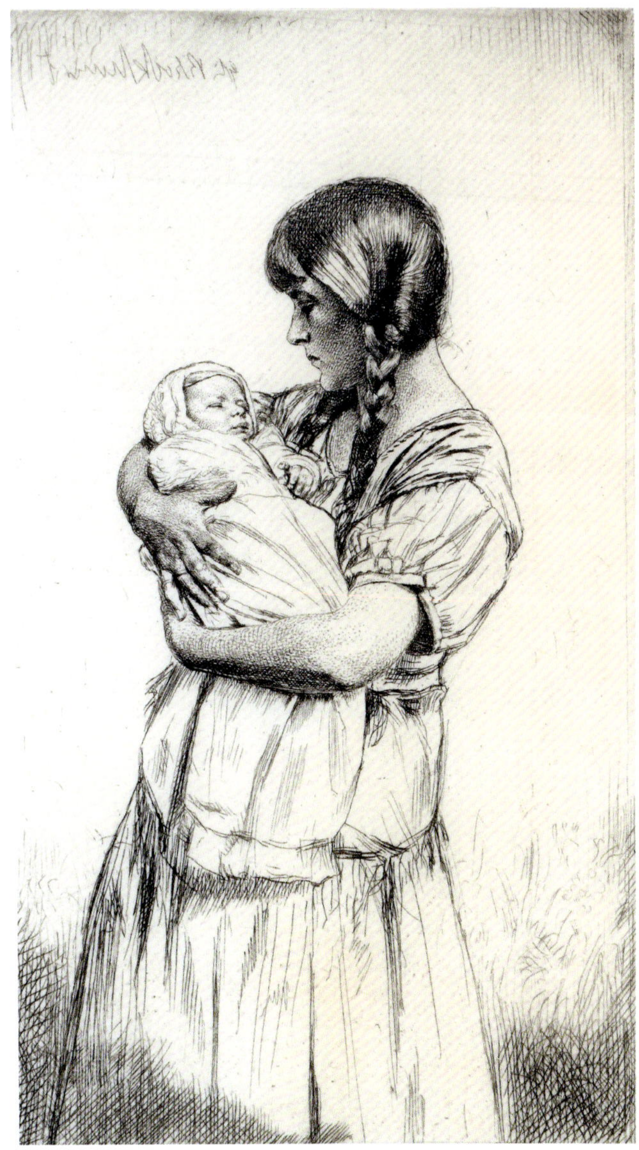

83 **Ursula**
Signed
Signed in reverse in plate
Etching
6 x 3 inches
From an edition of 111
Executed in October 1926
Literature: Harold Wright, 1934, Page 324;
Harold Wright, 1935, Page 69, Catalogue Raisonné No 55;
William Dolan Fletcher, 1984, Page 54, Catalogue Raisonné No 55
Exhibited: Royal Society of Painter-Etchers and Engravers, 1927, No 3;
Fine Art Society, 1986, No 90

84 **The Two Mélisandes**
Signed
Signed in reverse in plate
Etching
6 x 3 ½ inches
Literature: Harold Wright, 1934, Page 327, Plate 60;
Harold Wright, 1935, Page 71, Catalogue Raisonné No 60;
William Dolan Fletcher, 1984, Page 58, Catalogue Raisonné No 60
Exhibited: Royal Society of Painter-Etchers and Engravers 1929, No 145;
Fine Art Society, 1986, No 93

This portrait of the artist's first wife, Anaïs, and their daughter, Melisande, was executed in February 1928.

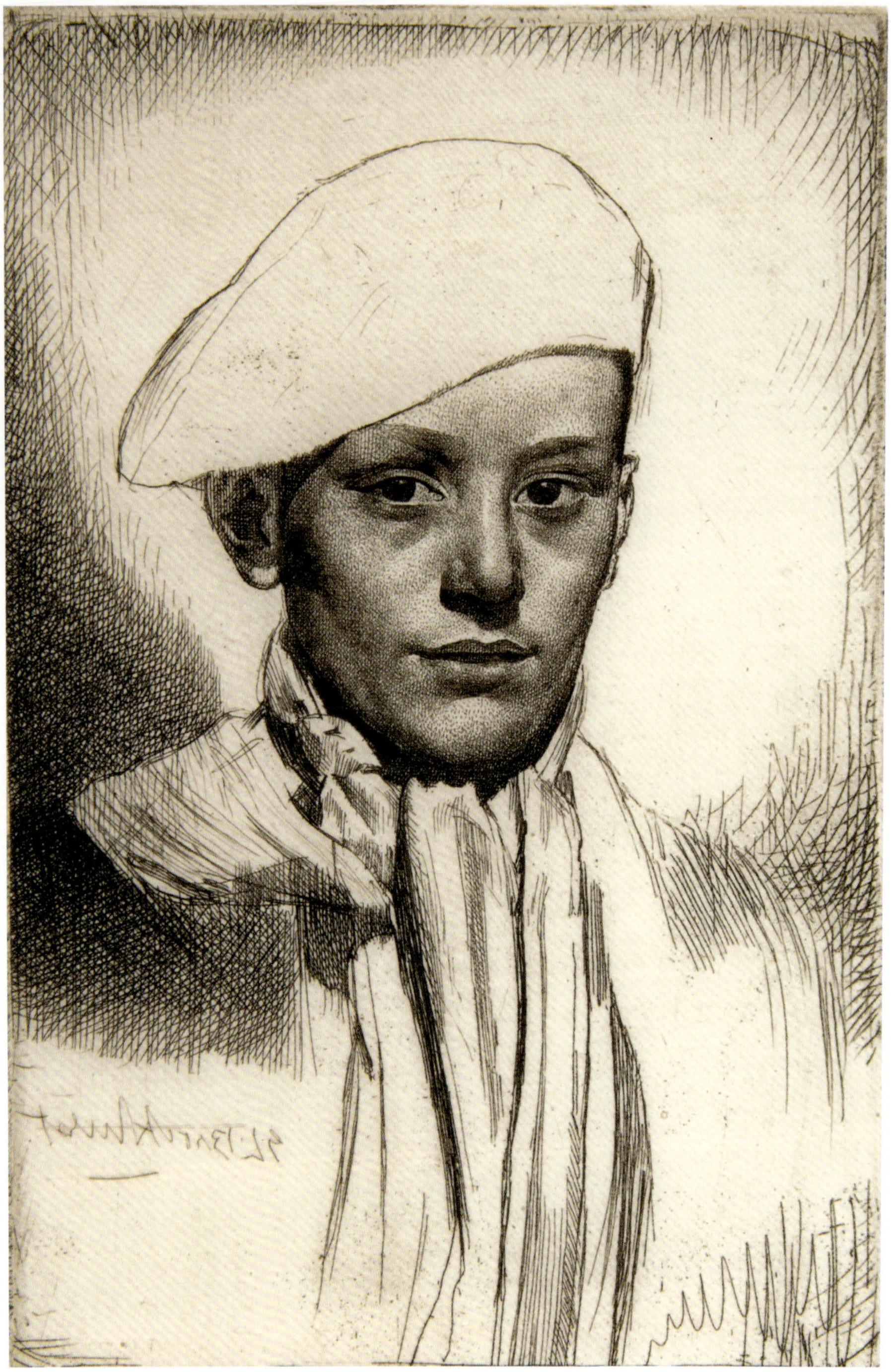

85 **Cypriano**
Signed
Signed and signed with initials, and inscribed '9th state' below mount
Signed in reverse in plate
Etching
6 ½ x 3 ¾ inches
Ninth state of 10, one of only five impressions of this state, produced in 1927. The final edition was printed in February 1928.
Literature: Malcolm C Salaman, *Modern Masters of Etching, Vol 19, G L Brockhurst*, London: The Studio, 1928;
Harold Wright, 1934, Page 326;
Harold Wright, 1935, Page 71, Catalogue Raisonné No 59;
William Dolan Fletcher, 1984, Page 56, Catalogue Raisonné No 59

This etching is a study of a Basque boy who lived near Bayonne.

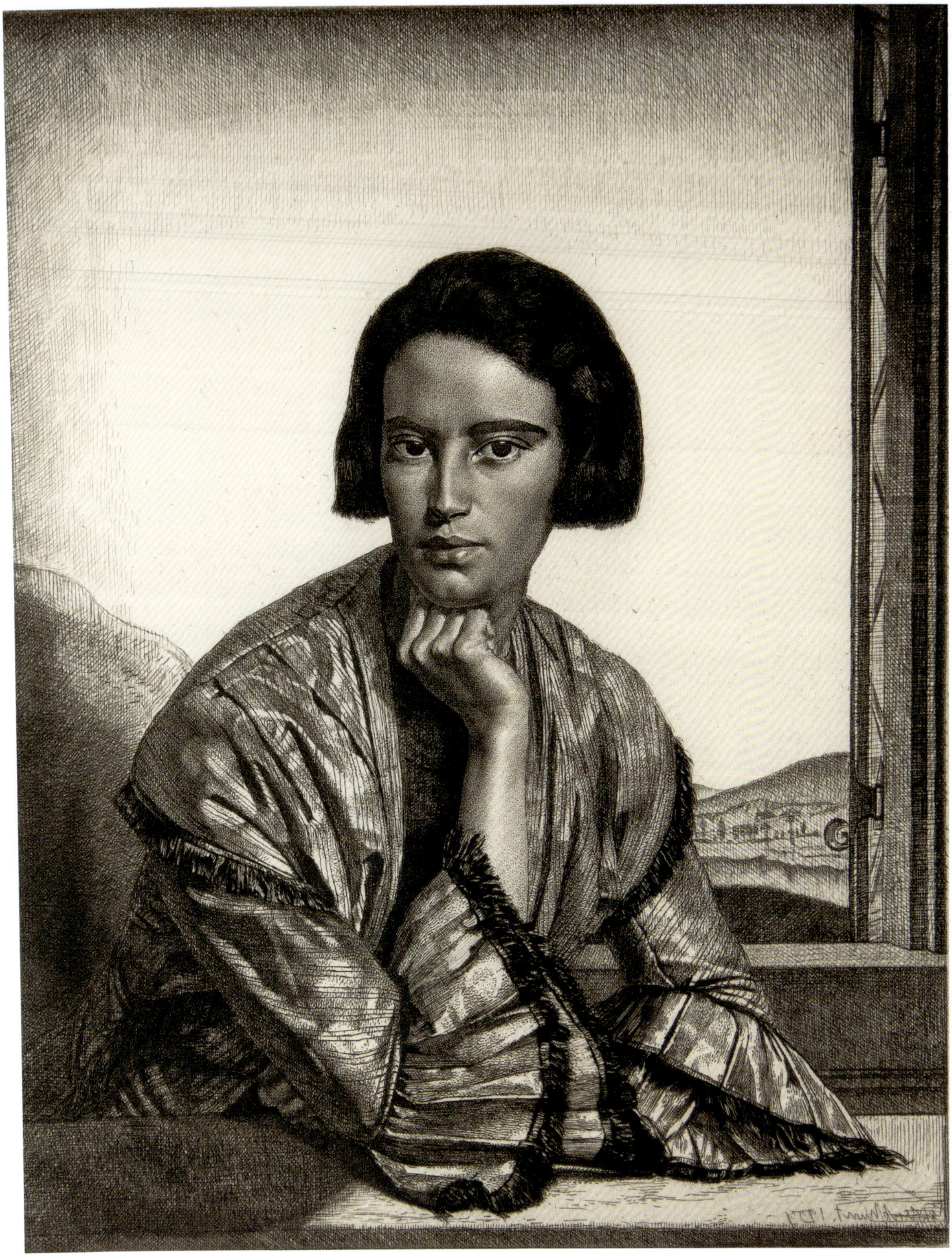

86 **Viba**
Signed
Signed and dated 1929 in reverse in plate
Etching
8 ½ x 6 ¾ inches
Final state of 8 from an edition of 111
Literature: Malcolm C Salaman (ed), *Fine Prints of the Year*, London: Halton & Truscott Smith, Vol 7, 1929, Pages 2 & iii, Plate 8;
Harold Wright, 1934, Page 328;
Harold Wright, 1935, Page 72, Catalogue Raisonné No 63;
William Dolan Fletcher, 1984, Page 59, Catalogue Raisonné No 63

Exhibited: Royal Academy, Summer Exhibition, 1929, No 991;
Royal Society of Painter-Etchers and Engravers, 1929, No 30;
Fine Art Society, London, 1986, No 95

Executed in March 1929, this etching shows Mrs Bobby Hazleton Ross.

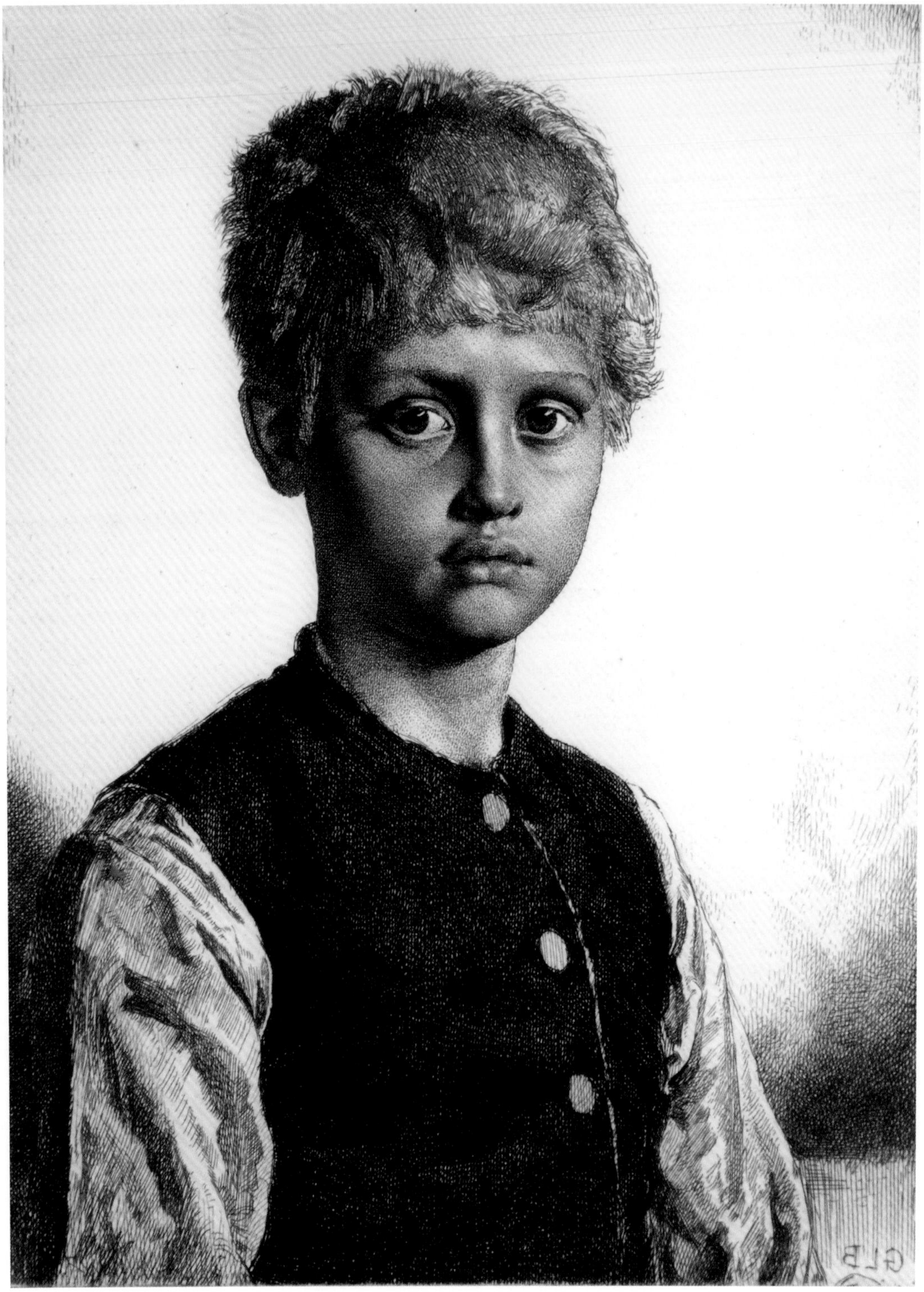

87 Casper, also called Casper, Son of 'Chenil'
Signed
Signed with initials in reverse in plate
Etching
7 ¾ x 5 ¾ inches
From an edition of 91
Literature: Harold Wright, 1934, Page 336;
Harold Wright, 1935, Page 77,
Catalogue Raisonné No 76;
William Dolan Fletcher, 1984, Page 66,
Catalogue Raisonné No 76

Executed in 1933, this etching was based on a 1920 painting used as a cover for *Colour*, July 1920.

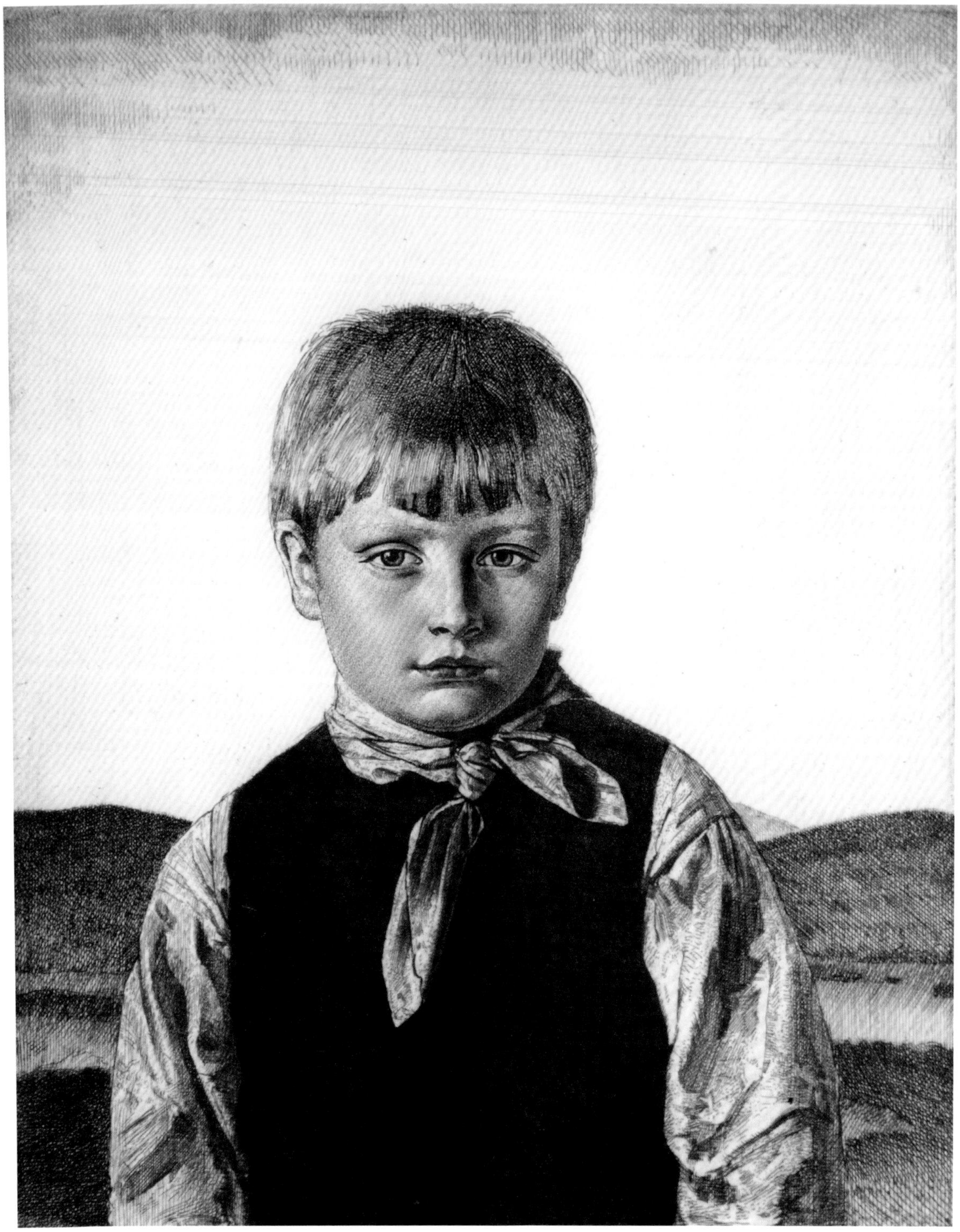

88 **The Amberley Boy, No 2**
Signed
Signed in reverse in plate
Etching
7 ¾ x 5 ¾ inches
Executed in 1928
Literature: Harold Wright, 1934, Page 328;
Harold Wright, 1935, Page 72, Catalogue Raisonné No 62;
Kenneth M Guichard, *British Etchers 1850-1940*, London: Robin Garton, 1981, Plate 11;
William Dolan Fletcher, 1984, Page 58, Catalogue Raisonné No 62
Exhibited: Fine Art Society, 1986, No 74

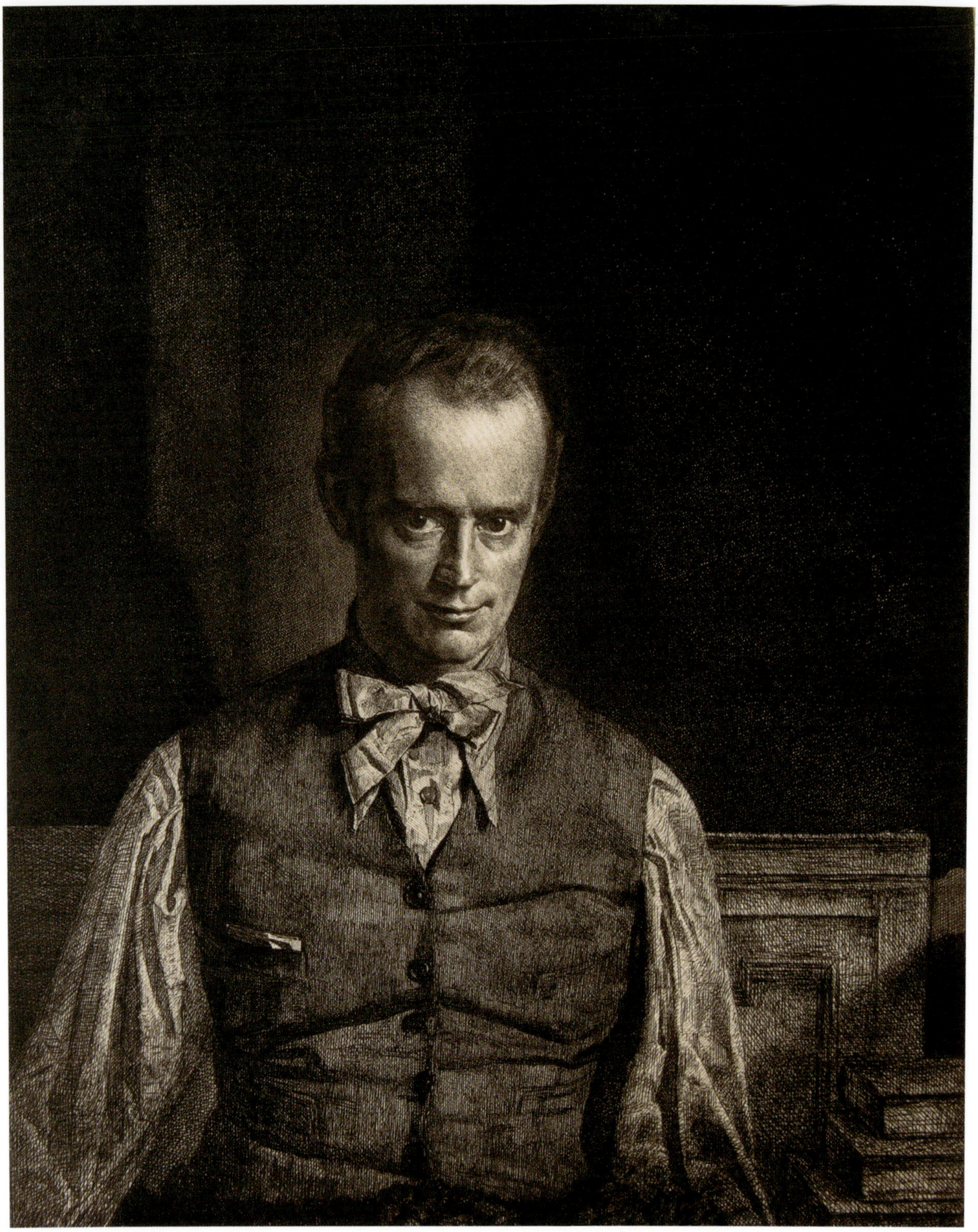

89 **Henry Rushbury No 2**
Signed
Inscribed 'Henry Rushbury Esq ARA', and signed and dated 1930 in reverse in plate
Etching
10 x 7 ¼ inches
Executed in March 1930
Literature: Malcolm C Salaman (ed), *Fine Prints of the Year*, London: Halcott & Truscott Smith, Vol 8, 1930;
The Royal Academy Illustrated, London: Walter Judd, 1930, No 1059;
Harold Wright, 1934, Page 331, Plate 66;
Harold Wright, 1935, Page 73, Catalogue Raisonné No 66;
William Dolan Fletcher, 1984, Page 63, Catalogue Raisonné No 66
Exhibited: Royal Academy, Summer Exhibition, 1930, No 1059;
Royal Society of Painter-Etchers and Engravers, 1931, No 86;
Fine Art Society, 1986, No 97

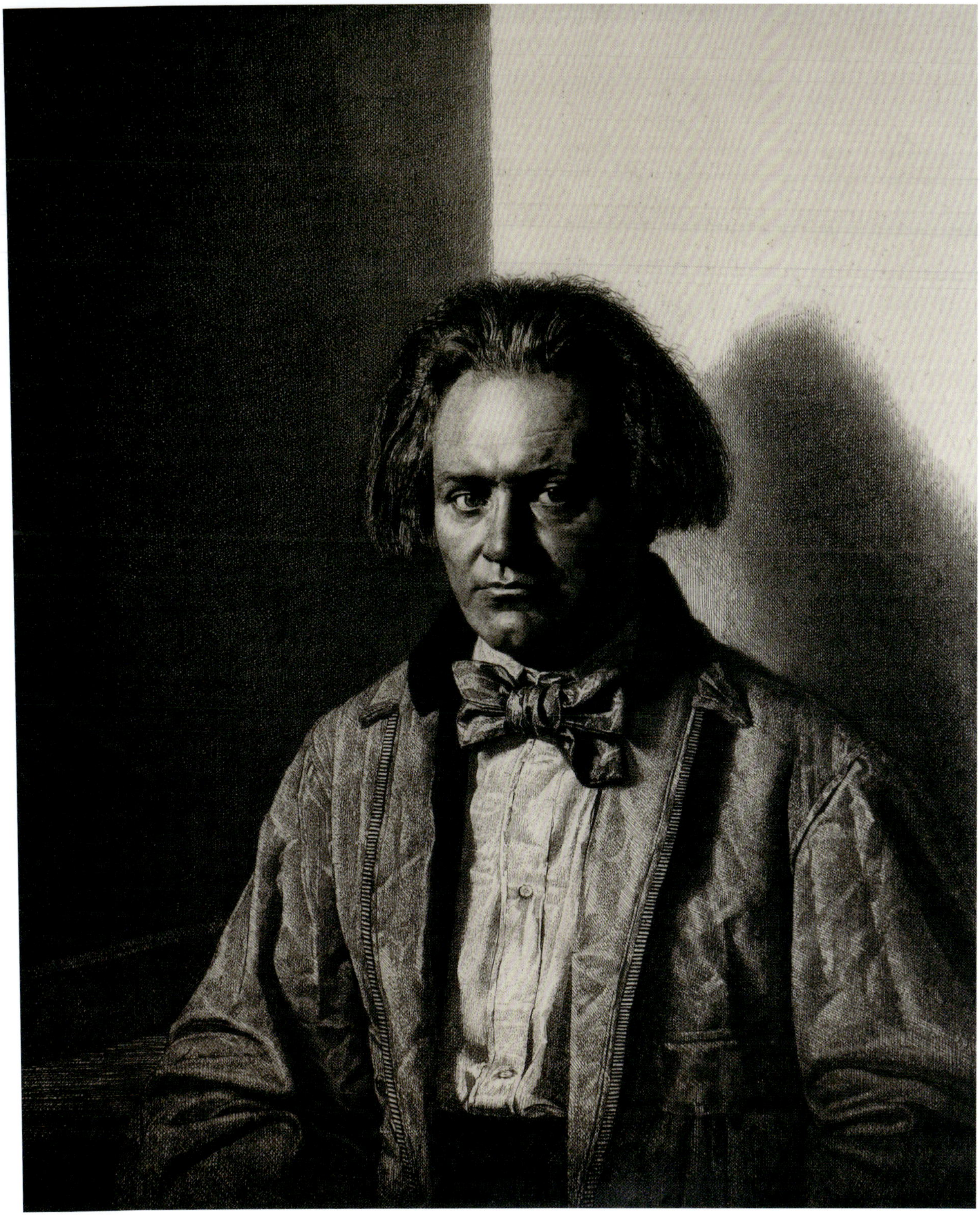

90 James McBey
Signed
Signed with initials and inscribed '6th state' below mount
Etching
10 ½ x 7 ½ inches
Sixth state of 9
Executed in 1931
Literature: Malcolm C Salaman (ed), *Fine Prints of the Year*, London: Halcott & Truscott Smith, Vol 9, 1931;
Harold Wright, 1934, No 4, Page 330;
Harold Wright, 1935, Page 75, Catalogue Raisonné No 31;
William Dolan Fletcher, 1984, Page 63, Catalogue Raisonné No 69
Exhibited: Fine Art Society, 1986, No 98;
Fine Art Society, London, February 2018, No 40

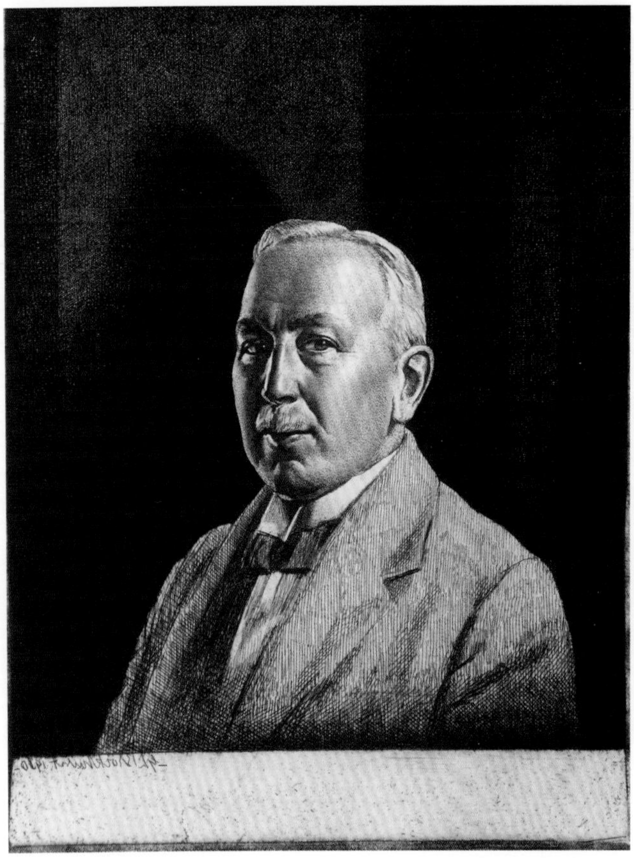

91 Henry Bell
Signed
Signed and dated 1930 in reverse in plate
Etching
8 ½ x 6 ¼ inches
From an edition of 68
Literature: Harold Wright, 1934, Page 330;
Harold Wright, 1935, Page 75, Catalogue Raisonné No 68;
William Dolan Fletcher, 1984, Page 62, Catalogue Raisonné No 68

'This was a private commission and the Bells offered hospitality to Brockhurst when he came to the United States in 1939.'

(W D Fletcher, *Complex Simplicity, Gerald Leslie Brockhurst and his Graphic Work*, Connecticut: Eastern Press 1984)

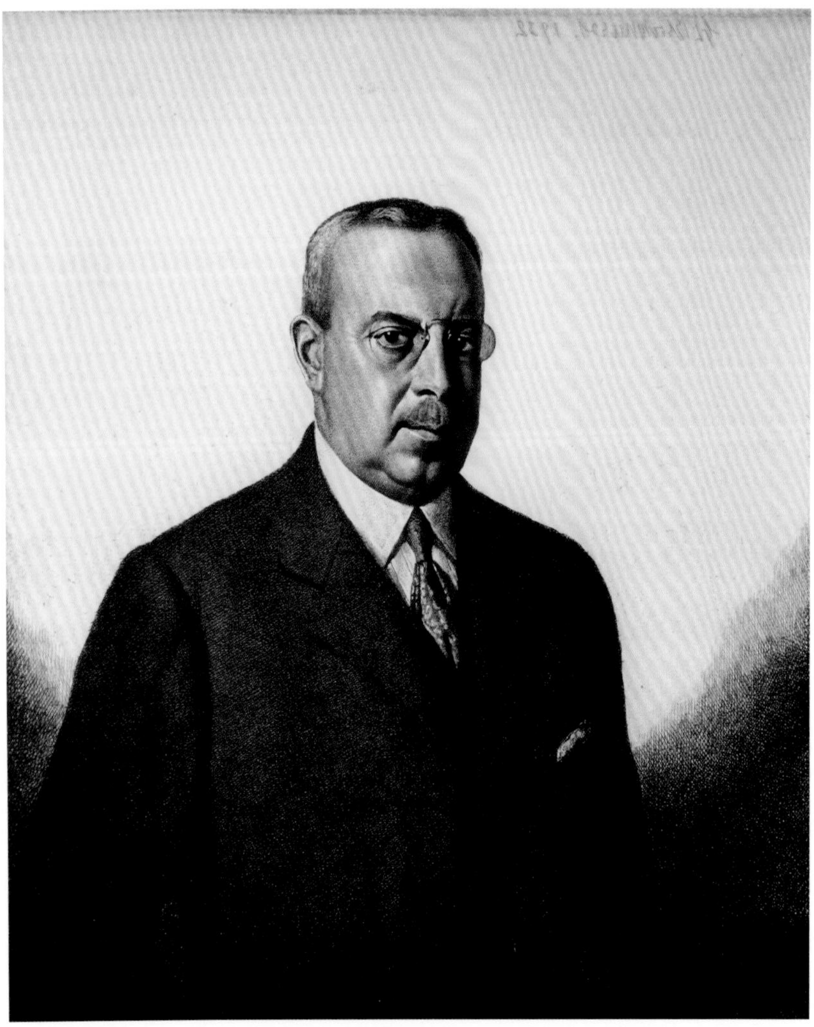

Albert H Wiggin Esq (of New York)
Albert Henry Wiggin (1868-1951) was President of the Chase National Bank, retiring in 1932. He began collecting prints, drawings and books in 1911, and donated his collection of several thousand pieces to Boston Public Library. He also endowed a number of other important American museums and institutions.

92 Albert H Wiggin Esq (of New York)
Signed
Signed and dated 1932 in reverse in plate
Etching
9 ¾ x 7 ½ inches
From an edition of 58
Literature: Harold Wright, 1934, Page 334;
Harold Wright, 1935, Page 76,
Catalogue Raisonné No 73;
William Dolan Fletcher, 1984, Page 65,
Catalogue Raisonné No 73

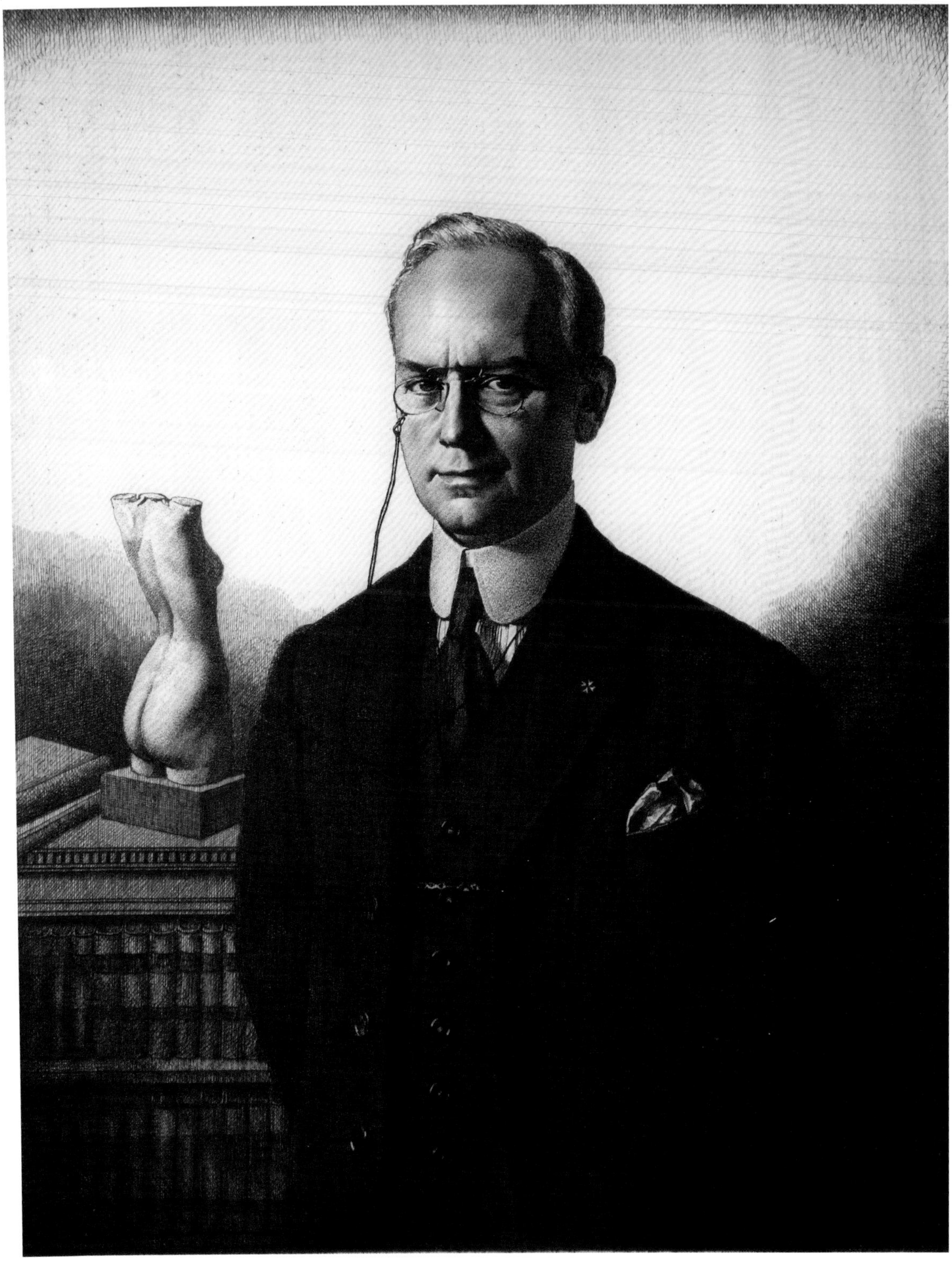

93 Charles Claude Carpenter
Signed
Signed and dated 1931 in reverse in plate
Etching
11 ¾ x 8 ¾ inches
From an edition of 80
Literature: Harold Wright, 1934, Page 332;
Harold Wright, 1935, Page 76, Catalogue Raisonné No 71;
William Dolan Fletcher, 1984, Page 64,
Catalogue Raisonné No 71
Exhibited: Fine Art Society, 1986, No 101

Charles Claude Carpenter

Charles Claude Carpenter (1858-1938) was a collector of sculpture, books and prints, and privately commissioned this etching. Allegedly, he had commissioned a nude sculpture of Dorette, the young model who was to become Brockhurst's second wife. Although the sculpture remained unfinished, Brockhurst included it on the bookcase in the background in this portrait. Carpenter was some time President of the South Metropolitan Gas Company. Although there were 80 impressions of this plate in all (including proofs) only 20 were ever offered for sale, Carpenter retaining the balance with their fate unknown.

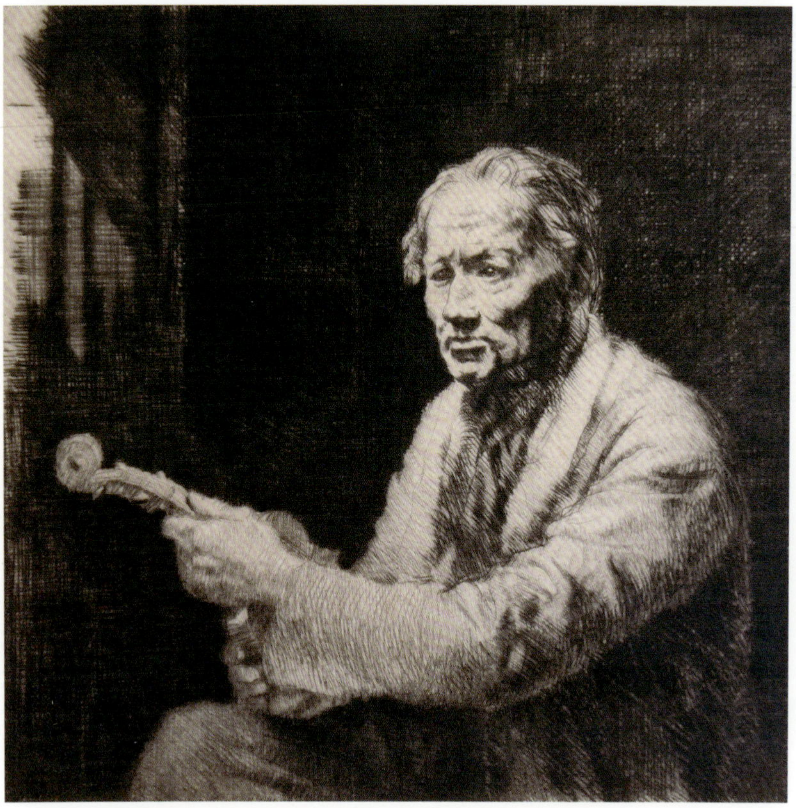

94 **The Forgotten Melody**
Signed
Drypoint
4 ¾ x 5 inches

A R MIDDLETON TODD

Arthur Ralph Middleton Todd,
RA RWS RE RP NEAC (1891-1966)

Middleton Todd has been described, by fellow artist, Robert Buhler, as 'by far the most sensitive and accomplished painter of his generation' (Foreword to *Works from the Studio of A R Middleton Todd*, Stow on the Wold: Fosse Gallery, 1985). His mature achievement as a portraitist was founded on a versatile *oeuvre*, in which he produced paintings, drawings and etchings of a wide range of subjects that included figures, landscapes and still life compositions. He particularly enjoyed drawing nudes in pastel, in emulation of his hero, Degas. Though modest and self-critical, he passed on many artistic insights as a successful teacher.

For a biography of Middleton Todd, please refer to page 206.

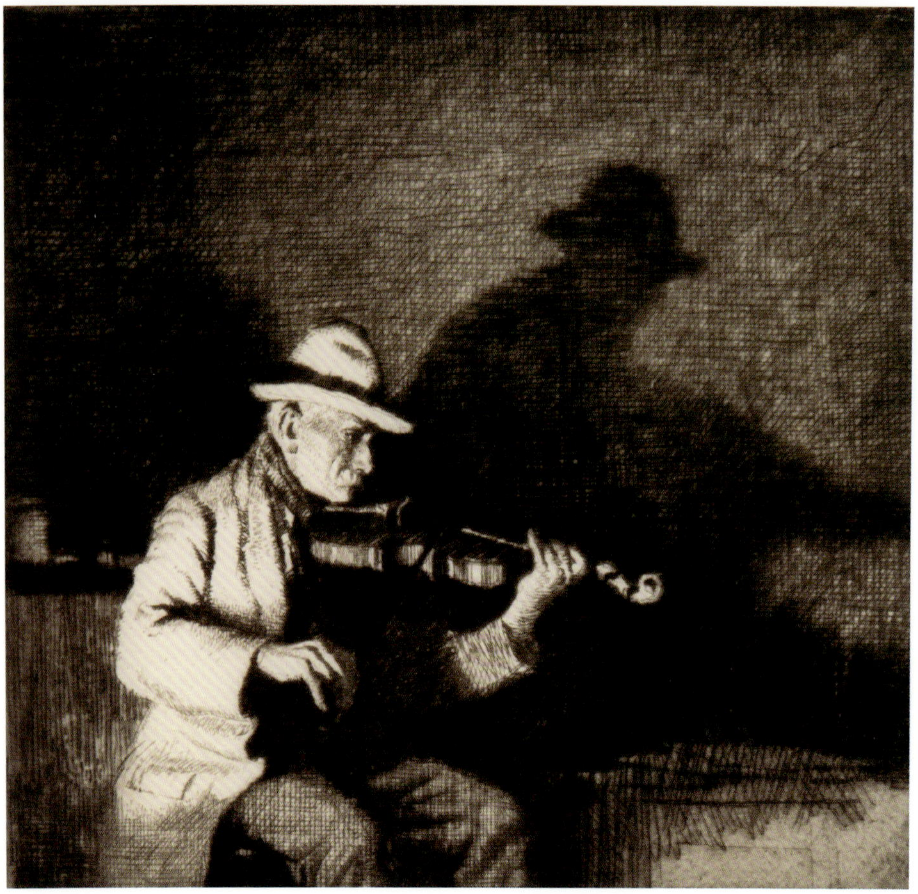

95 **The Fiddler** (left)
Signed
Drypoint
4 ¼ x 4 ½ inches

98 **The Listener** (opposite left)
Signed
Drypoint
6 ¾ x 5 inches
From the special edition as issued to the members of the Print Collectors' Club and with their stamp in the plate

99 **Interior of a Barn** (opposite right)
Signed
Etching and drypoint
10 x 7 inches

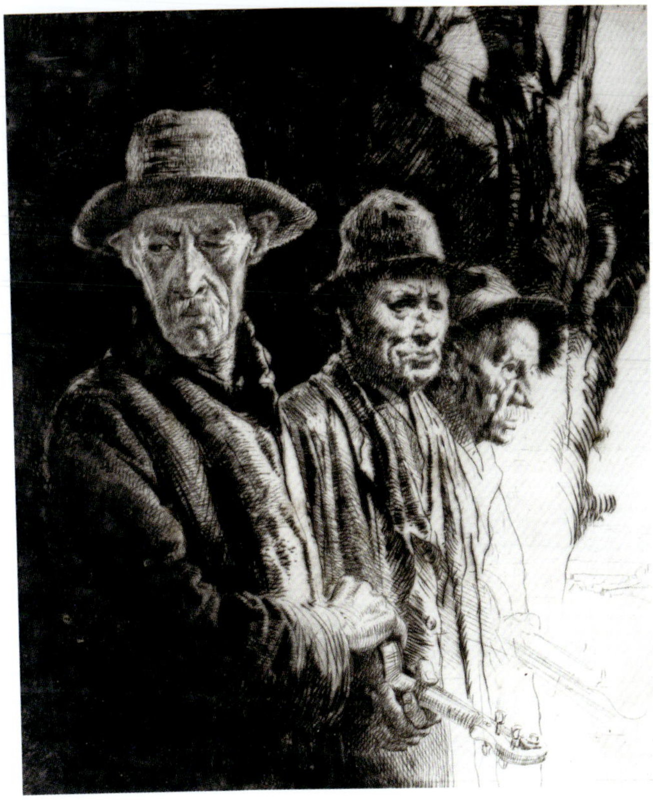

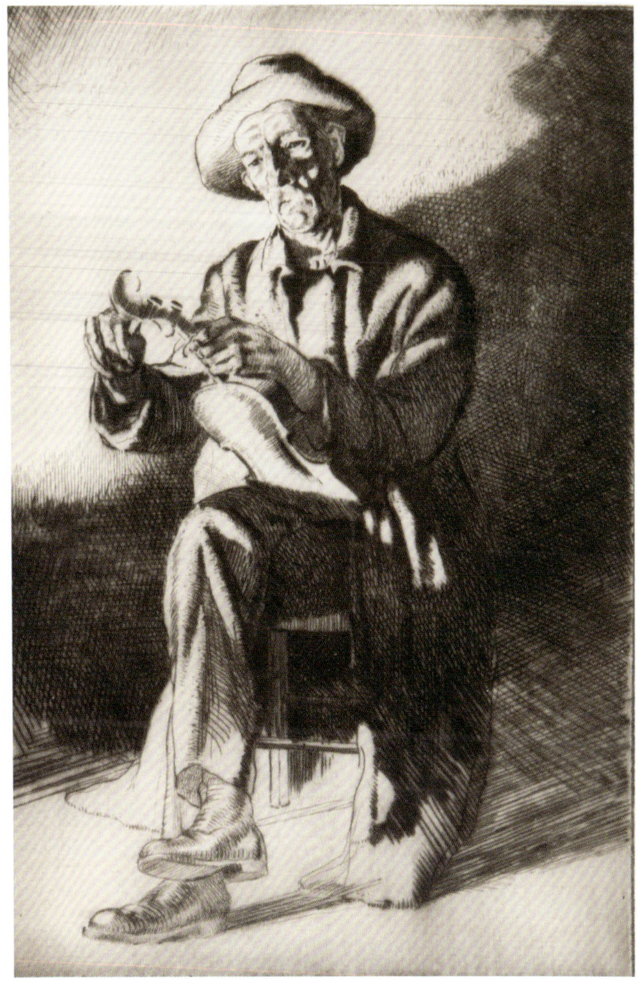

96 Strolling Players (above)
Signed
Signed in plate
Drypoint
6 ¾ x 5 ¾ inches

97 A New String for an Old Tune (above right)
Signed
Drypoint
6 ¾ x 4 ½ inches
This is a study for a larger print of the same title, which includes an interior and window.

99

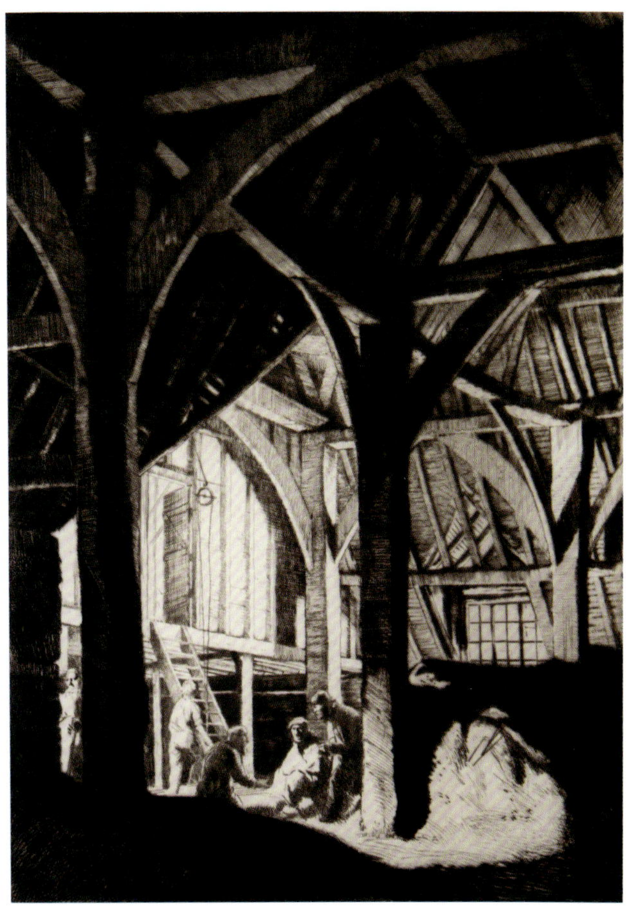

98

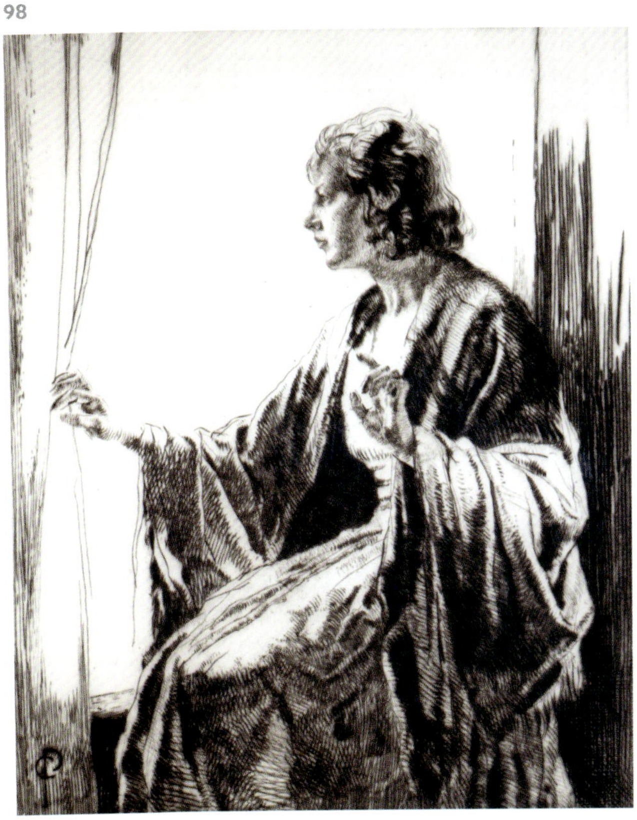

A R MIDDLETON TODD

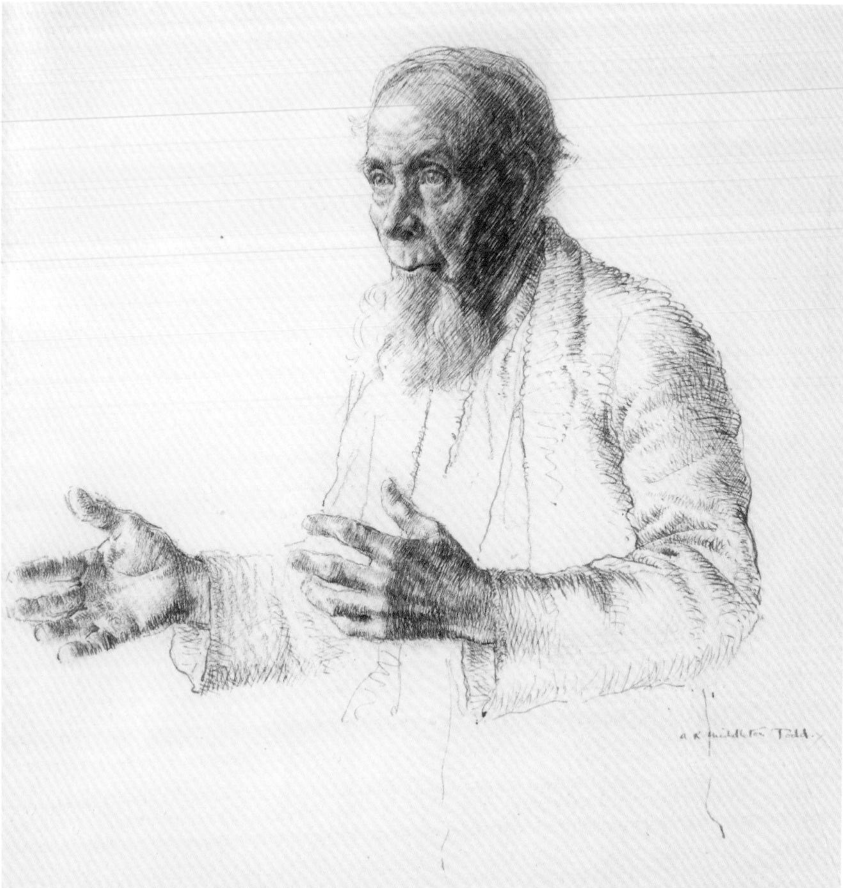

100 Old Man
Signed
Ink and pencil
10 ¼ x 8 ¾ inches

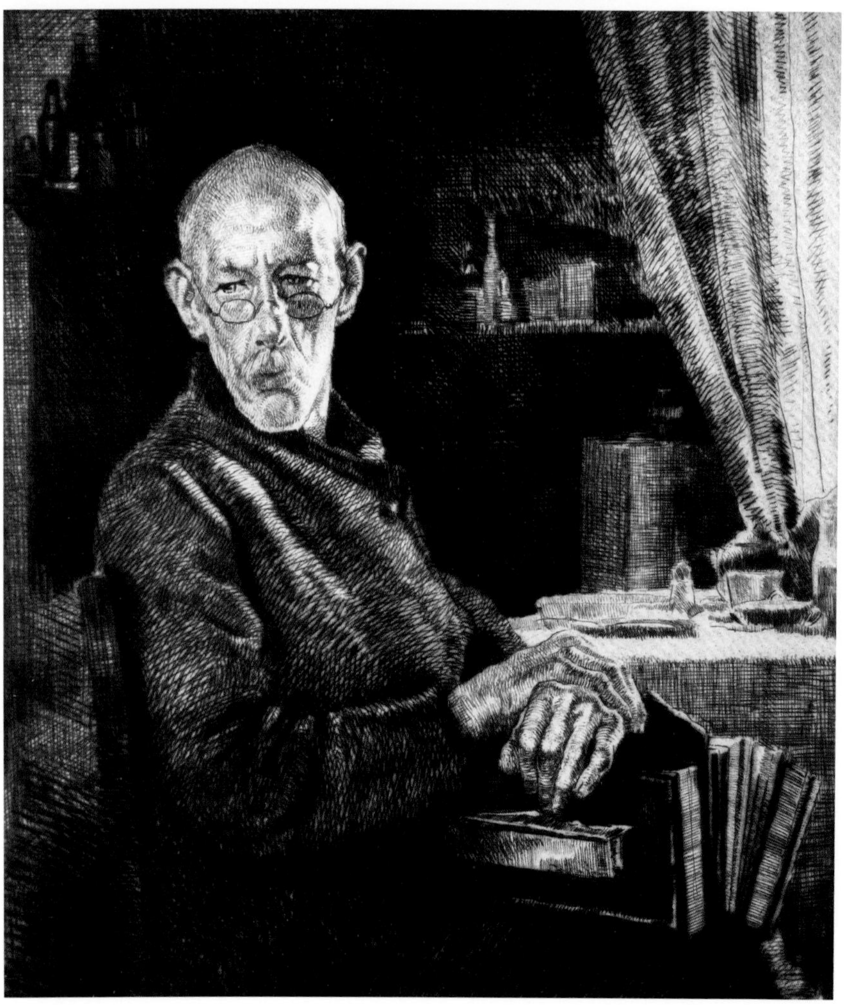

101 The Accordion Player
Signed
Drypoint
6 x 5 inches
From an edition of 25
Executed in 1924

MARJORIE SHERLOCK

Alice Marjorie Sherlock, SGA WIAC (1891-1973)

A pupil of Walter Sickert, Marjorie Sherlock established herself with paintings and etchings of urban scenes, including a striking series of images of railway stations. Later, she was much inspired by trips abroad – including those to Egypt and India – which were often made in the company of, and financed by, her close friend and fellow artist, Orovida Pissarro.

For a biography of Marjorie Sherlock, please refer to page 207.

102 **Liverpool Street Station**
Signed, inscribed 'To JE' and dated 1917
Etching and drypoint
10 ¾ x 8 inches

This work is a study for Liverpool Street Station of which Marjorie Sherlock painted at least two versions. The one that most closely resembles the present etching is in the collections of the National Railway Museum, York, while another is in the Government Art Collection.

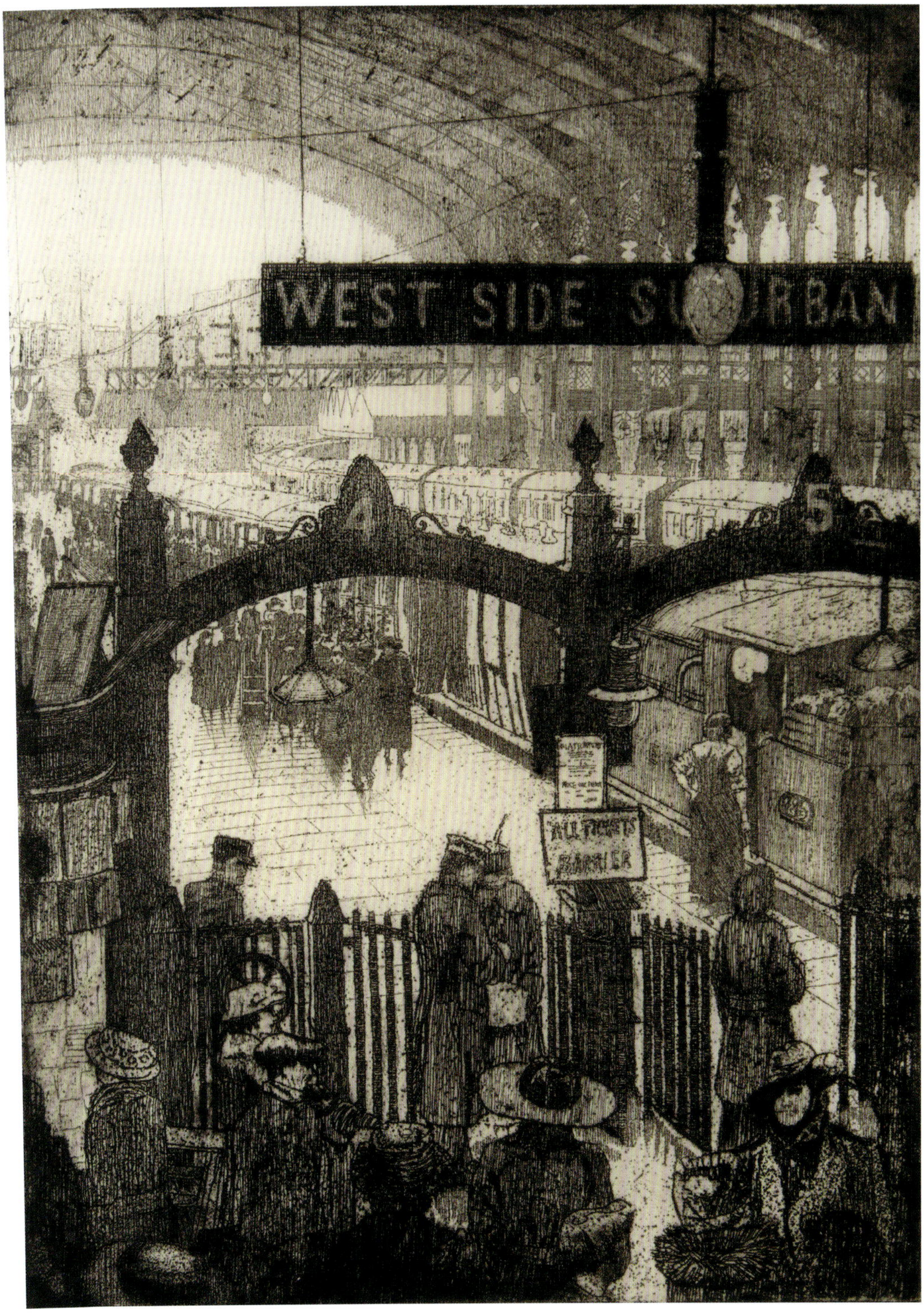

EILEEN SOPER

Eileen Alice Soper, RMS SWLA (1905-1990)

The work of Eileen Soper – like that of her father, George – comprises some of the most popular strands of British art in the twentieth century. She placed emphasis on subjects that have diverted and delighted a large percentage of the population, and presented them directly and precisely. In working extensively as a printmaker and illustrator, she ensured wide dissemination of her images through exhibition and publication.

For a biography of Eileen Soper, please refer to page 208.

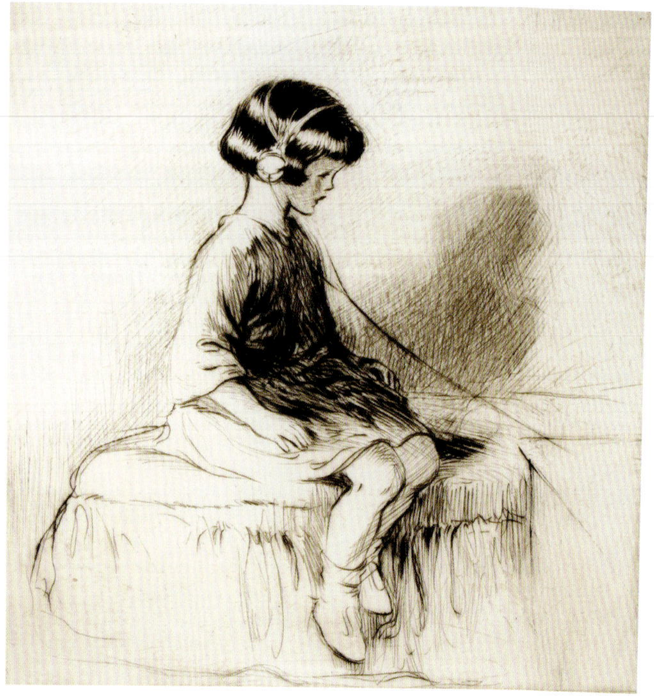

103 The Fair (below)
Signed
Etching with drypoint on laid paper, with a 'J Whatman' watermark
8 ¼ x 10 ¾ inches
Provenance: The Estate of George and Eileen Soper
Literature: *The Catalogue Raisonné of the Etchings of George and Eileen Soper*, London: Chris Beetles Ltd, 1995, No 85

104 Children's Hour (above)
Signed
Drypoint on laid paper
7 ½ x 6 ½ inches
Provenance: The Estate of George and Eileen Soper
Literature: *The Catalogue Raisonné of the Etchings of George and Eileen Soper*, London: Chris Beetles Ltd, 1995, No 80

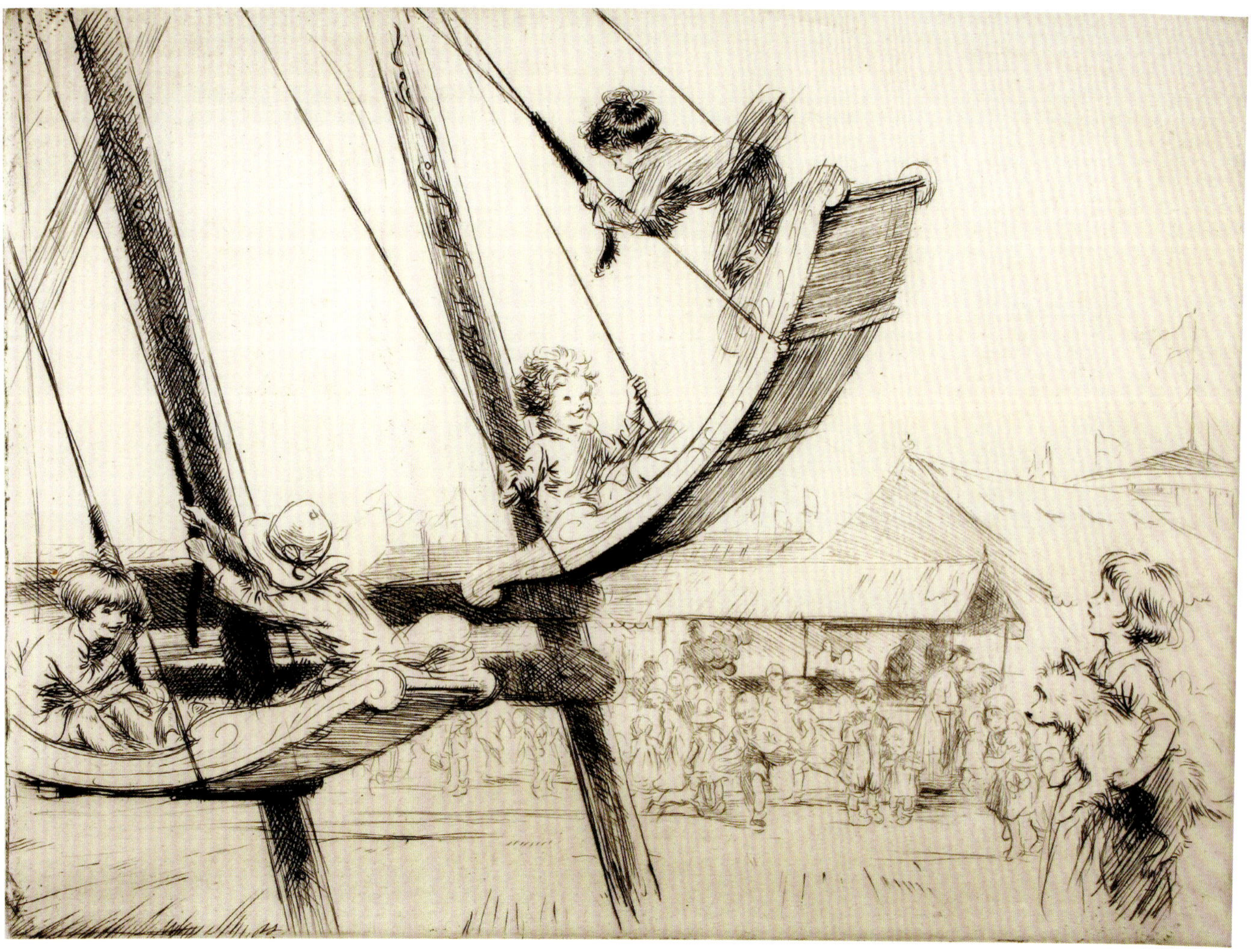

105 Peg-Tops
Signed
Etching on laid paper
6 x 7 ¾ inches
Provenance: The Estate of George and Eileen Soper
Literature: *The Catalogue Raisonné of the Etchings of George and Eileen Soper*, London: Chris Beetles Ltd, 1995, No 119

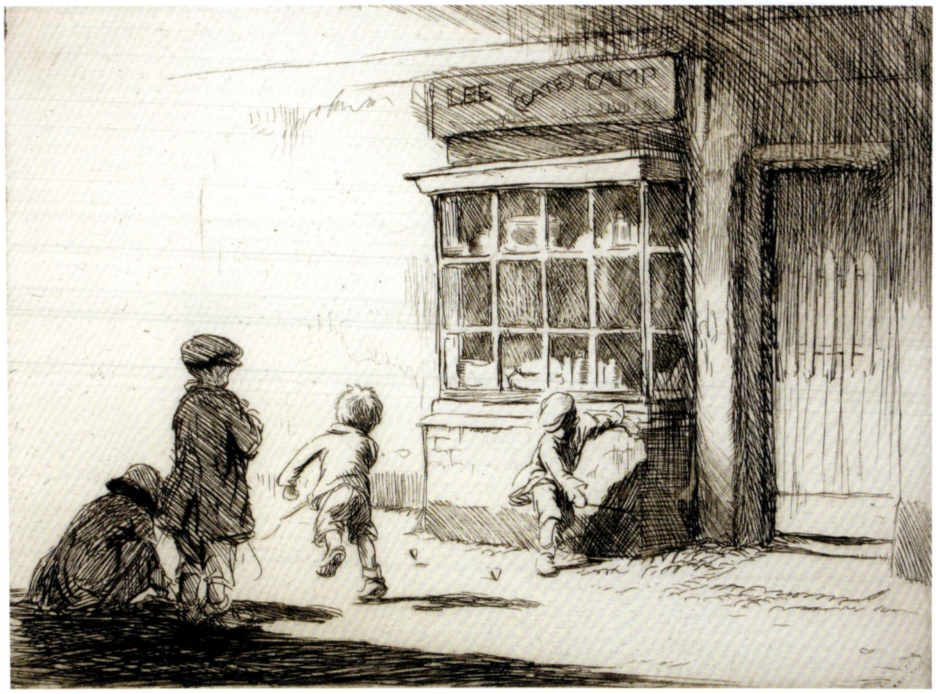

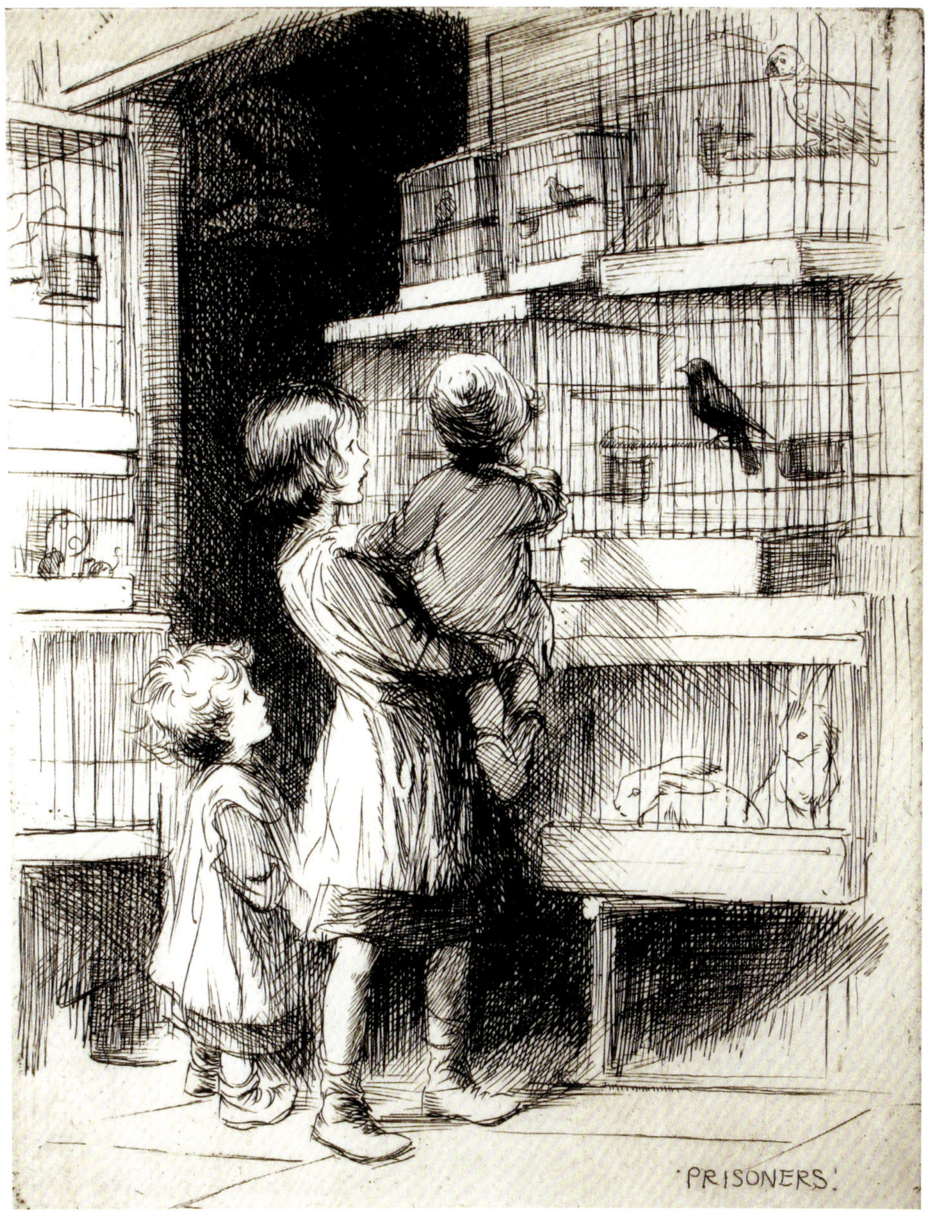

106 Prisoners
Signed and inscribed with title in plate
Etching on laid paper watermarked 'F J Head'
7 ½ x 5 ½ inches
Second state
Provenance: The Estate of George and Eileen Soper
Literature: Duff Hart-Davis, *Wildings*, London: Witherby, 1991; *The Catalogue Raisonné of the Etchings of George and Eileen Soper*, London: Chris Beetles Ltd, 1995, No 124

S R BADMIN

Stanley Roy Badmin, RWS RE AIA FSIA (1906-1989)

Throughout his career, S R Badmin used his great talents – as etcher, illustrator and watercolourist – to promote a vision of the English countryside and thus of England itself. By underpinning his idealism with almost documentary precision and detail, he was able to produce images that appealed to all, and could be used for a great variety of purposes, from education through to advertising. The wellbeing suggested by each rural panorama is all the more potent, and pleasing, for the accuracy of each tree and leaf, and the plausibility of the slightest anecdotal episode.

For a biography of S R Badmin, please refer to pages 208-209.

Nos **107-109**
Literature: Chris Beetles,
S R Badmin and the English Landscape,
London: Collins, 1985

108 Evening Light, near Sevenoaks, Kent (opposite above)
Signed and inscribed with title and numbered 29/40
Etching on laid paper
5 x 6 ½ inches
This artist's proof was done on fine Dutch laid paper in December 1929.
Published by the Twenty One Gallery in 1930.
Literature: Chris Beetles, 1985, Page 53, Catalogue Raisonné No 16
Exhibited: Fine Art Society, London, February 1933, No 13;
McDonald's Gallery, New York, March 1936;
Royal Society of Painter-Etchers and Engravers, 1956;
Worthing Art Gallery, 1967, No 2

109 Swinbrook Bridge (opposite below)
Signed and inscribed with title and '7th St'
Signed with initials in plate
Etching
3 ¾ x 5 ½ inches
Executed in 1931 and published by the Twenty-One Gallery.
Swinbrook Bridge is near Burford, Oxfordshire; it was replaced during the Second World War. An edition of 45 was taken from the 8th state.
Literature: Chris Beetles, 1985, Pages 54 and 63,
Catalogue Raisonné No 22
Exhibited: Royal Society of Painter-Etchers and Engravers, 1931, No 72;
Royal Academy, Summer Exhibition, 1932, No 1109;
Fine Art Society, London, February 1933, No 40;
McDonald's Gallery, New York, 1936;
Fine Art Society, London, July 1937, No 49;
Leicester Galleries, London, 1955, No 2, as 'Old Swinbrook';
Worthing Art Gallery, 1967, No 9

107 Wareham, Dorset
Signed, inscribed with title and numbered A/P
Inscribed 'Ed of 50 for Print Collectors Club. Artist Proof final state' below mount
Signed with initials, inscribed 'PC' and dated 1934 on shop sign in plate
Etching
5 ¼ x 6 ¼ inches
Published by the Print Collectors' Club in 1934. 'PC' had been inserted with slight addition of sepia in the final state. Six Artist's Proofs.
Literature: Chris Beetles, 1985, page 60, Catalogue Raisonné No 36
Exhibited: Fine Art Society, London, February 1933, No 20;
Royal Academy, Summer Exhibition, 1934, No 1322;
Royal Society of Painter-Etchers and Engravers, 1934;
McDonald's Gallery, New York,1936; Worthing Art Gallery, 1967, No 4;
Royal Society of Painter-Etchers and Engravers, 1979, No 71;
'S R Badmin RWS, Paintings, Drawings & Prints', Chris Beetles Gallery, 2015, No 203

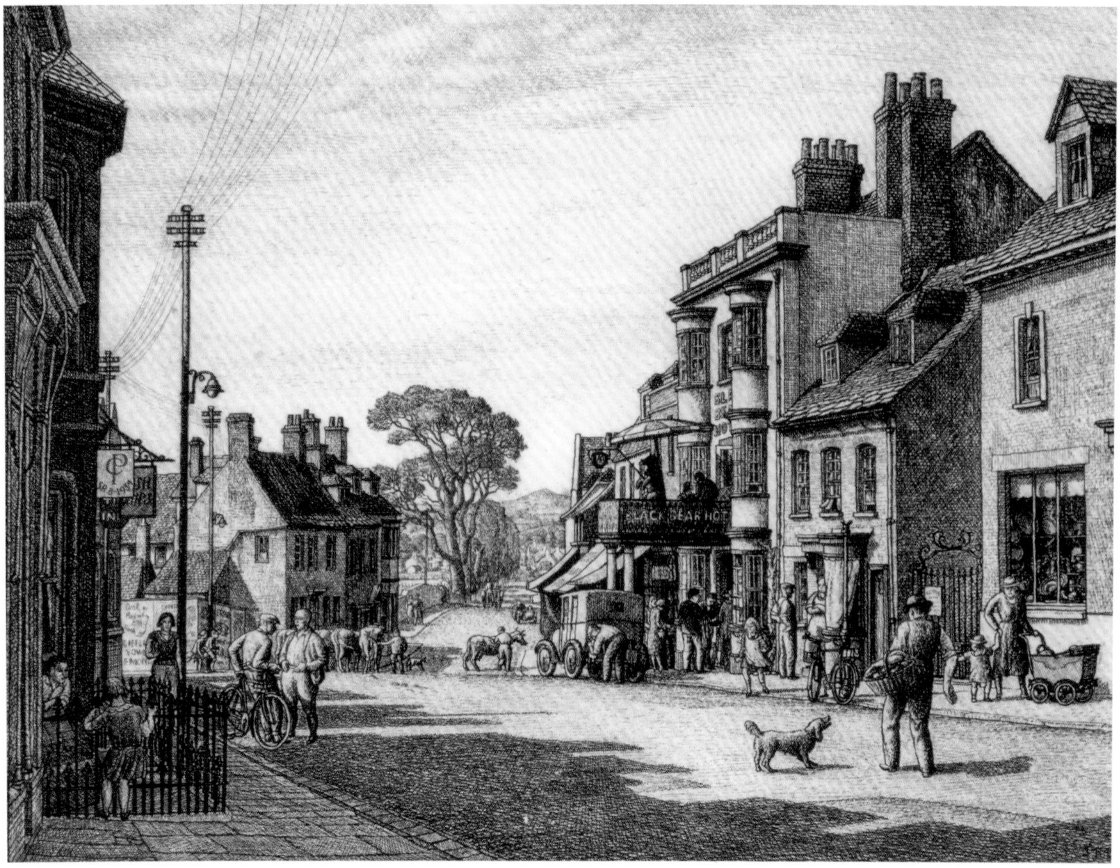

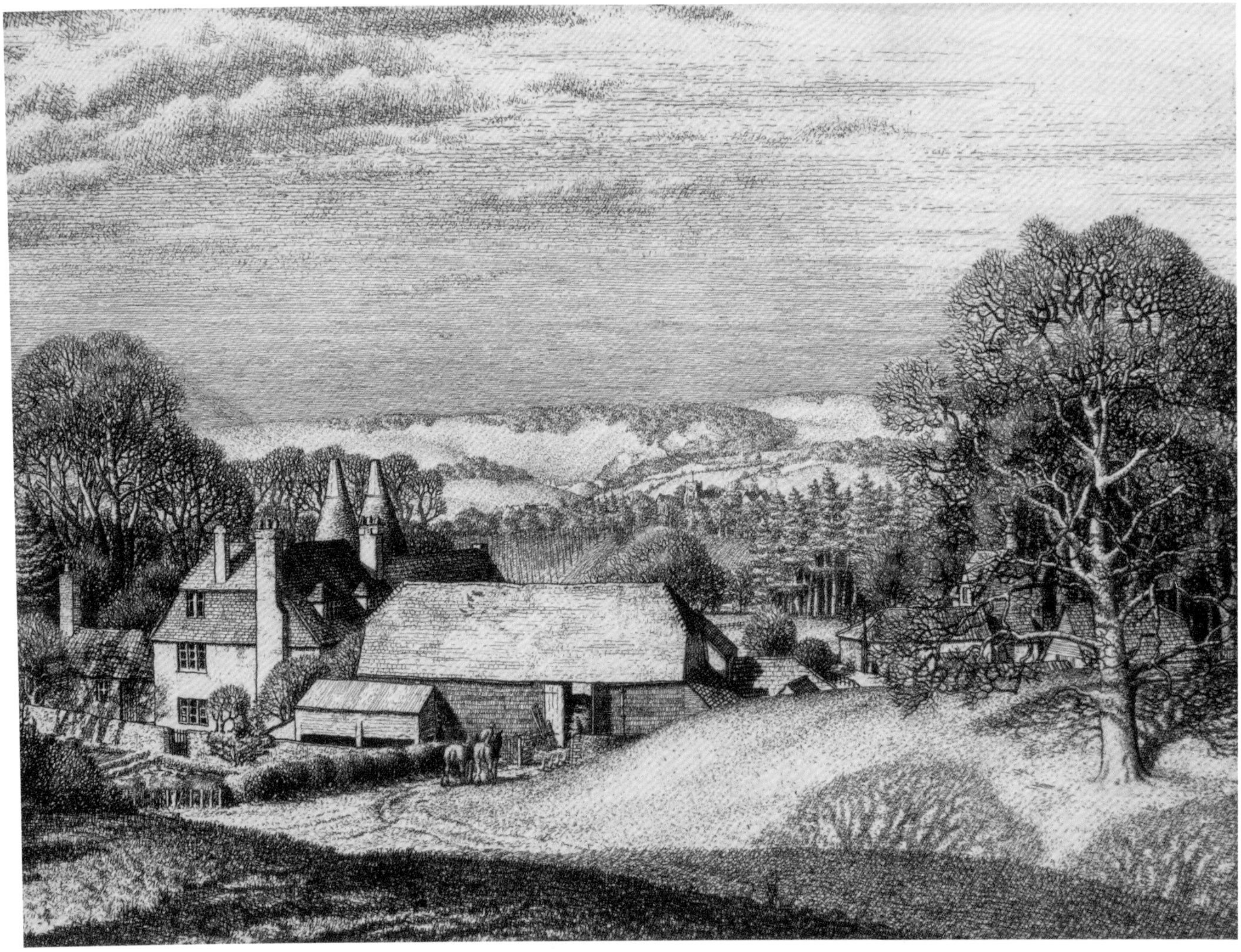

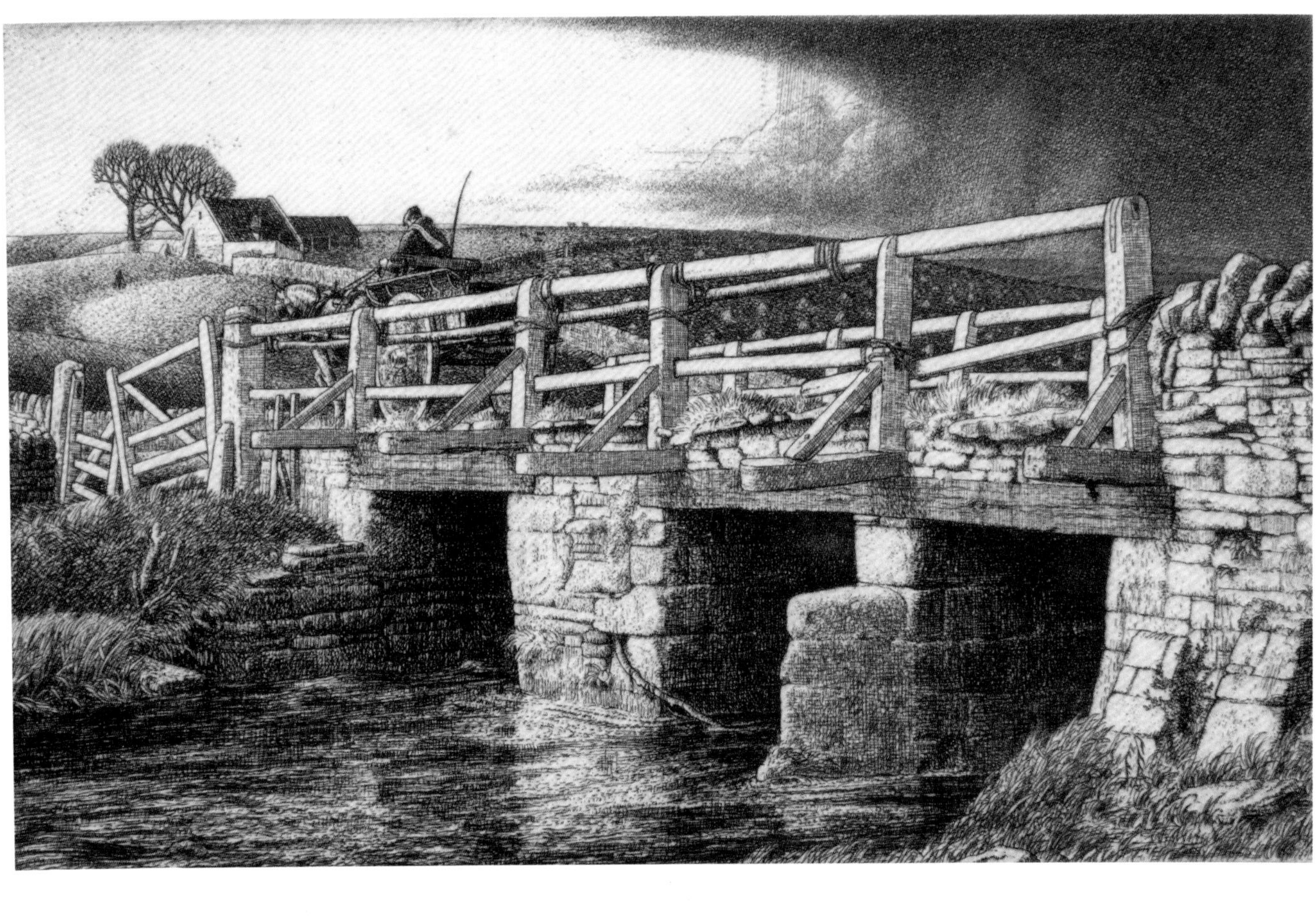

5: THE CONTINENTAL SCENE

Artists had been among the most enterprising of British travellers before the First World War; and so they were among the first to take advantage of the renewed freedom to travel in Europe, and elsewhere, once the war had ended, and once the 'Spanish Flu' epidemic was in decline. However, they were now joined by a greater percentage of the wider population encouraged by new opportunities, and especially by improved communications. Rail travel reached its peak of popularity during the 1930s, gradually to be replaced by motor transport and, from the end of that decade, by the first commercial air flights. Following a dip during the Great Depression, travel generally increased again through the late 1930s, before it was halted by the outbreak of the Second World War.

Many artists had gained their taste for European travel by choosing to study in key cultural centres, and especially Paris, in the late nineteenth and early twentieth centuries. So, for example, Randolph Schwabe had studied at the Académie Julian, in Paris, from 1906 to 1908, and from there had travelled to Italy, to absorb its art, architecture and landscape. Between the wars, he returned frequently to France, to holiday with his family and draw alongside artist friends, and was particularly fond of such picturesque Provençal communities as Moustiers-Sainte-Marie [**115-116**] and Sisteron [**117-119**].

Others had made their first sketching tours before war broke out in 1914, including Cecil Arthur Hunt, who had taken one major trip to Italy in 1910-11. This prepared him for extensive travel across the continent from 1920, which took in France [**114**] and Greece [**124**], as well many further stays in Italy [**123**].

Talmage had frequented France from as early as 1894, and knew it well by 1918, the last year of the war, when he worked in the country as an official war artist for the Canadian Government. That wartime experience was seminal for him and other artists, including some who were encountering foreign soil for the first time. Nevertheless, when he was able to return to France in peacetime, he recaptured much of the earlier carefree spirit of the pre-war period [**110-111**].

There was a younger generation that had not known Europe before the war and had been too young to fight. Charles Knight, for instance, was first introduced to Northern France in 1918, when he was only 17, on the first of four trips made in the company of his mentor, Canon Elliott. This gave him access to a landscape replete with associations, including the Abbey of Jumièges and Rouen Cathedral, which had both been painted by Knight's artistic hero, John Sell Cotman.

Those who were students after the First World War were aided in their desire to explore Europe by an increasing number of travel scholarships. Important among these were those awarded by the British School at Rome. Winners of the various Prix de Rome – including Job Nixon [**51**], Thomas Monnington [**192**] and Frank Archer [**179-181**] – were given the opportunity to study in Italy for three years (though Archer's stay was cut short by another impending war).

As a cradle of civilisation, it was perhaps inevitable that Italy in general, and Rome in particular, should continue to provide a base for outstanding students of art, and especially those with a Classical turn of mind. When the Scottish artist, William Wilson, went travelling in 1932, as the result of winning a Carnegie Travelling Scholarship, he certainly included Italy on his itinerary. However, he also visited Spain, which was still known to too few British artists, and made much of its astonishing architecture heritage [**121**]. This was only four years before the outbreak of the Spanish Civil War, which led to the rise of General Franco and was, retrospectively, a signpost on the road to the Second World War. Karl Hagedorn also worked in Spain on the eve of the Spanish Civil War, and then, once it had begun, transferred his attention, while he could, to the relatively peaceful, neutral Portugal [**120**].

110 A French Harvest [I]
Watercolour
8 x 10 ½ inches

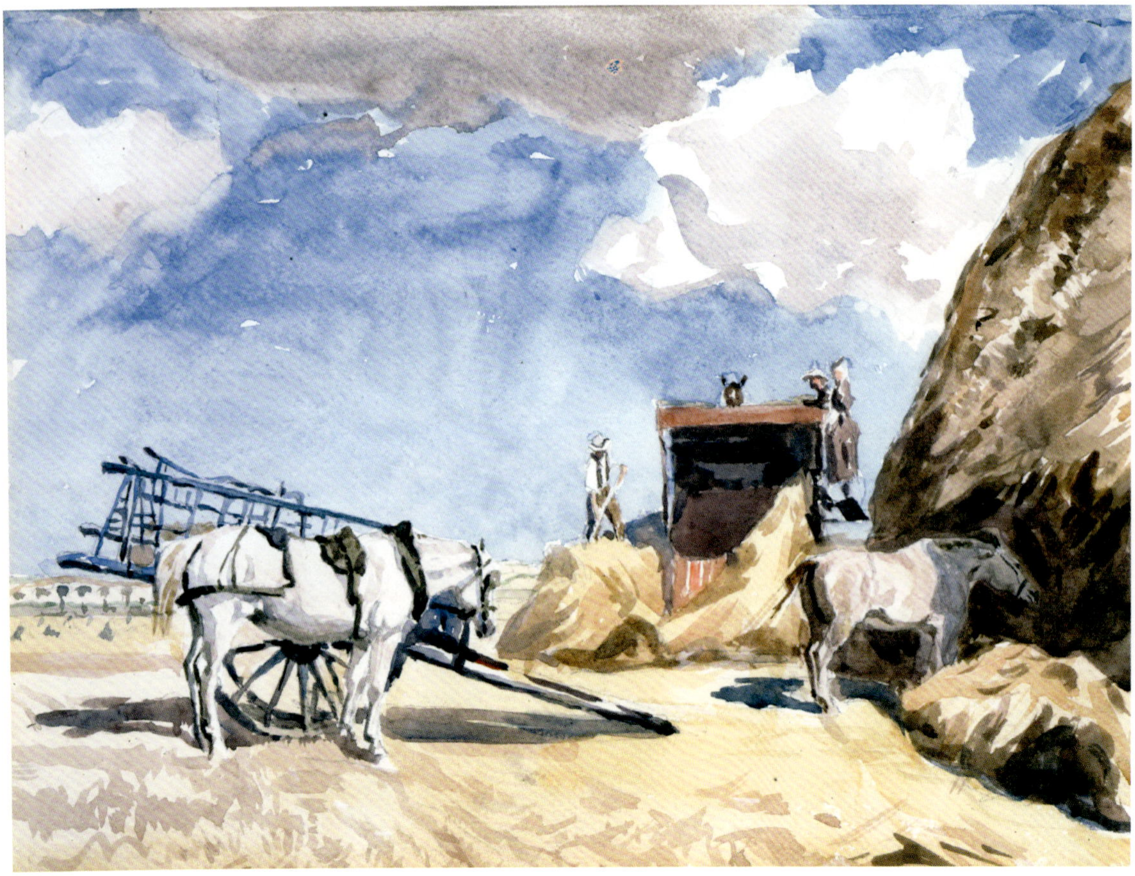

ALGERNON TALMAGE

Algernon Mayow Talmage, RA RBA HRE ROI RWA
(1871-1939)

Talmage is principally known as a painter of plein-air pastorals and equestrian subjects in a restrained yet sparkling Impressionist manner. During the First World War, he applied his passion for painting animals in landscape settings to his work as an official war artist for the Canadian Government.

For a biography of Algernon Talmage, please refer to page 196.

FRANCE

111 A French Harvest [II]
Signed and dated 26
Oil on canvas
25 ¾ x 32 inches
Exhibited: Royal Academy, Summer Exhibition, 1927, No 329

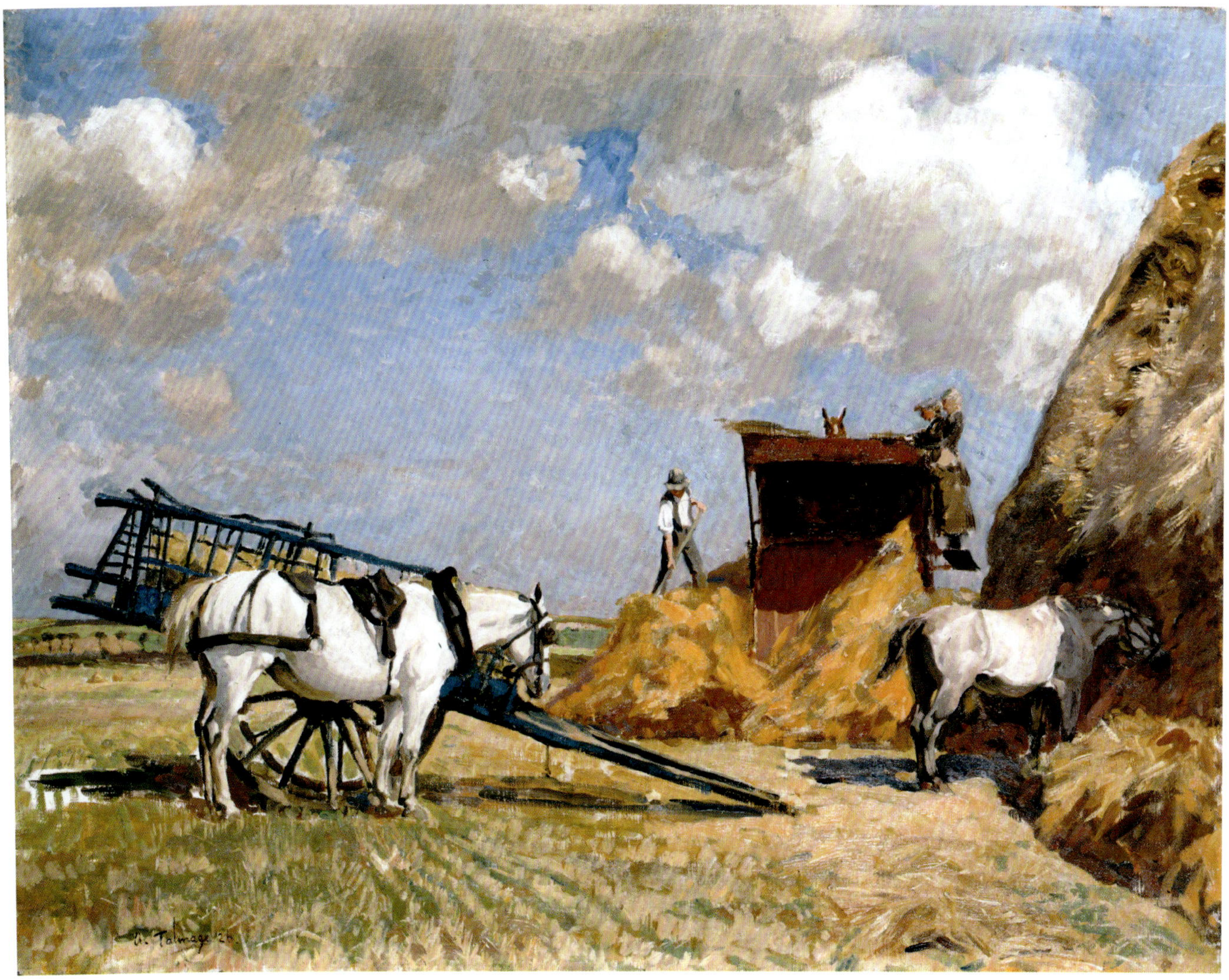

CHARLES KNIGHT

Charles Knight, VPRWS ROI (1901-1990)

The Sussex landscape painter, Charles Knight, channelled the tradition of English watercolour painting in order to produce his own original contribution. As a result, he became a pillar of the Royal Society of Painters in Water-Colours and received acclaim, from William Russell Flint, as the 'star turn' of the Recording Britain scheme.

For a biography of Charles Knight, please refer to page 210.

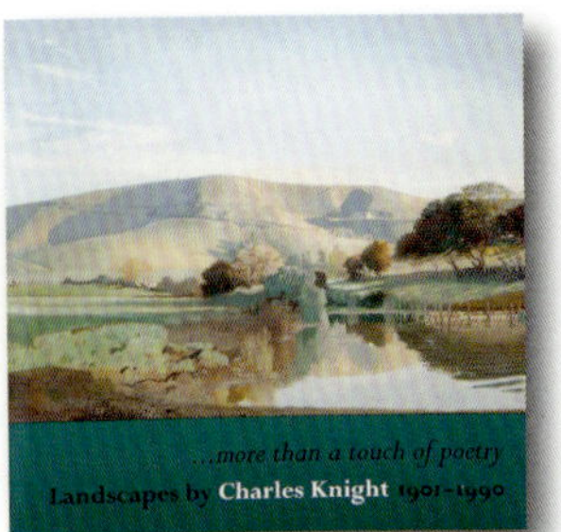

In 1997, the Chris Beetles Gallery hosted '... More Than a Touch of Poetry', an important retrospective exhibition of the work of Charles Knight, organised in conjunction with the Towner Gallery, Eastbourne, and Hove Museum and Art Gallery. It was accompanied by this 96-page fully-illustrated catalogue, which included a biographical essay and lists of works shown at leading exhibiting societies.

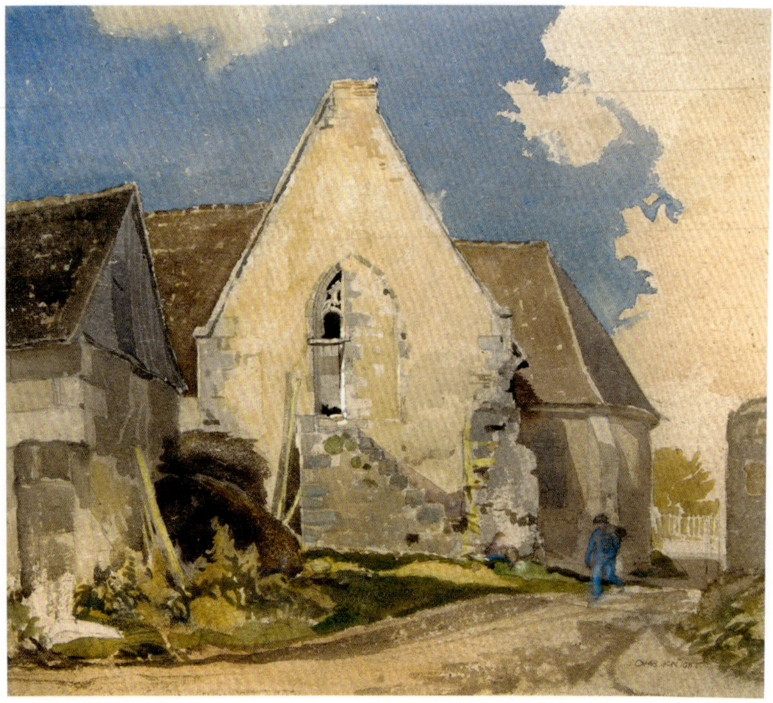

112 **Farm Buildings at Montoire** (above)
Signed
Watercolour
13 x 13 inches
Produced in 1930
Literature: Michael Brockway, *Charles Knight RWS ROI*, Leigh-on-Sea: F Lewis, 1952, Catalogue No 48
Exhibited: Royal Society of Painters in Water-colours, Winter 1934, No 56

113 **At Chartres** (below)
Signed
Watercolour with pencil
11 ½ x 17 ½ inches
Produced in 1934
Similar to the watercolour, *At Chartres*, illustrated in Michael Brockway, *Charles Knight RWS ROI*, Leigh-on-Sea: F Lewis, 1952, Catalogue No 100 (Plate 12), and listed as in the Collection of Henry Barran

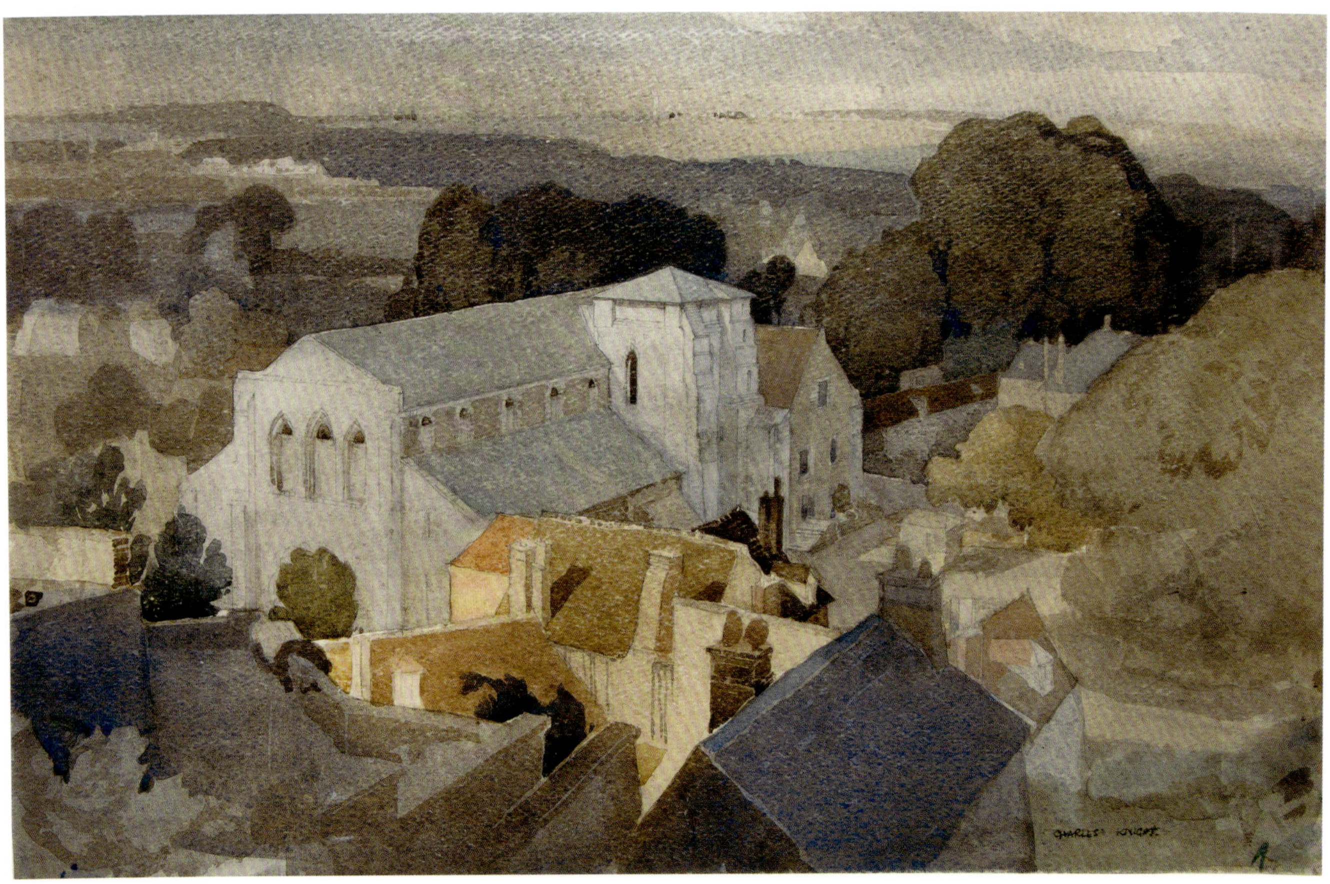

CECIL ARTHUR HUNT

Cecil Arthur Hunt, VPRWS RBA (1873-1965)

Once elected a full member of the Royal Society of Painters in Water-Colours in 1925, Cecil Arthur Hunt retired from his career as a barrister and turned his serious pastime of painting into a profession. While he had first established himself as a painter of mountains, especially the Alps and the Dolomites, he soon proved himself a master of a great variety of topographies. The impressive, often stark, effects that he achieved rival those associated with his friend and mentor, Frank Brangwyn.

For a biography of Cecil Arthur Hunt, please refer to page 210.

In 1996, the Chris Beetles Gallery mounted a large-scale retrospective exhibition of the work of Cecil Arthur Hunt (on the exact site of the artist's first substantial show in 1901). The retrospective was accompanied by this definitive 112-page fully-illustrated catalogue, which included a biographical essay and a detailed list of exhibitions.

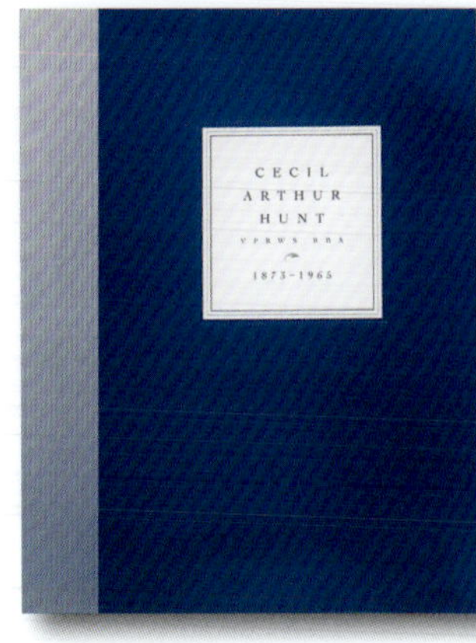

Dawn
Le Puy-en-Velay

Hunt travelled to Le Puy-en-Velay in the Haute-Loire region of France in 1926. It is the start of one of the pilgrimage routes to Santiago de Compostela, and the majesty and theatricality of its surroundings, and the spirituality of its setting, inspired him to dedicate this watercolour to the memory of his son, Esmond Moore Hunt, who died in 1927 at the age of 19. The pinnacle in the foreground is surmounted by the Chapel of Saint Michel d'Aiguilhe, while the Rocher Corneille in the distance is topped by the Notre-Dame de France, an imposing statue of the Madonna and Child. Hunt made a visual record of his visit to Le Puy-en-Velay in his sketchbooks of 1926 (sb18 and sb19).

114 **Dawn**
Le Puy-en-Velay
Signed
Watercolour with pencil
15 ½ x 22 inches

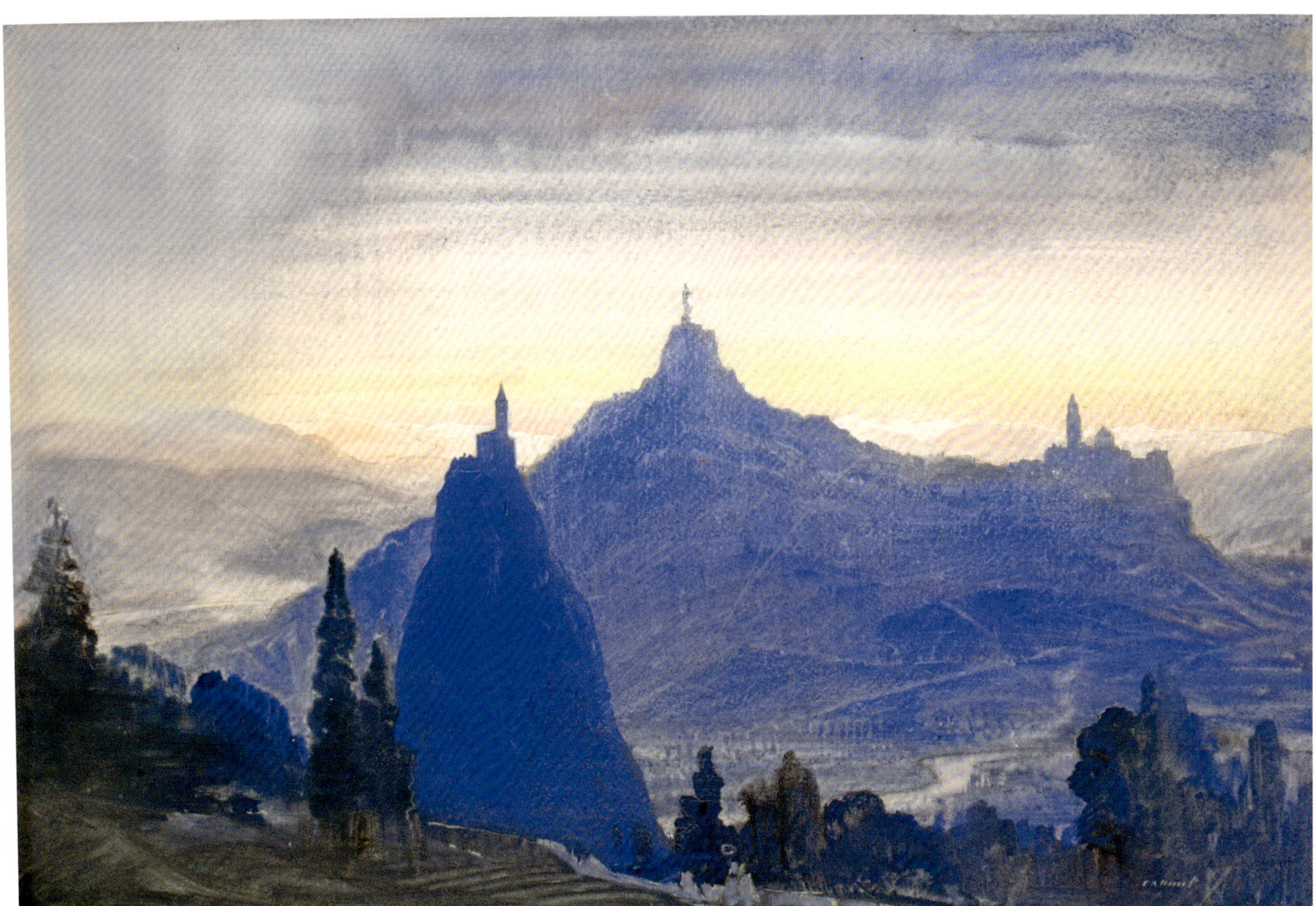

RANDOLPH SCHWABE

Randolph Schwabe, RWS LG NEAC (1885-1948)

A clear eye and sure hand enabled Randolph Schwabe to produce drawings, etchings and lithographs of consistent clarity and strength. Trained at the Slade School of Fine Art, he would return there to become an influential Principal and Professor. He also held a significant position as an official war artist in both world wars. Though he is best remembered for his attentive, absorbing images of buildings and landscapes, his subjects included figures and still life compositions, and he also produced illustrations and designs for the theatre.

For a biography of Randolph Schwabe, please refer to pages 212-213.

115 Ancien Château de Sabran, Moustiers-Ste Marie
Signed and inscribed 'Sabran'
Signed and inscribed with title and artist's address on original backboard
Pen ink and watercolour
14 x 15 inches
Exhibited: Imperial Gallery of Art, Imperial Institute, South Kensington, London (which was founded in connection with the British School at Rome)

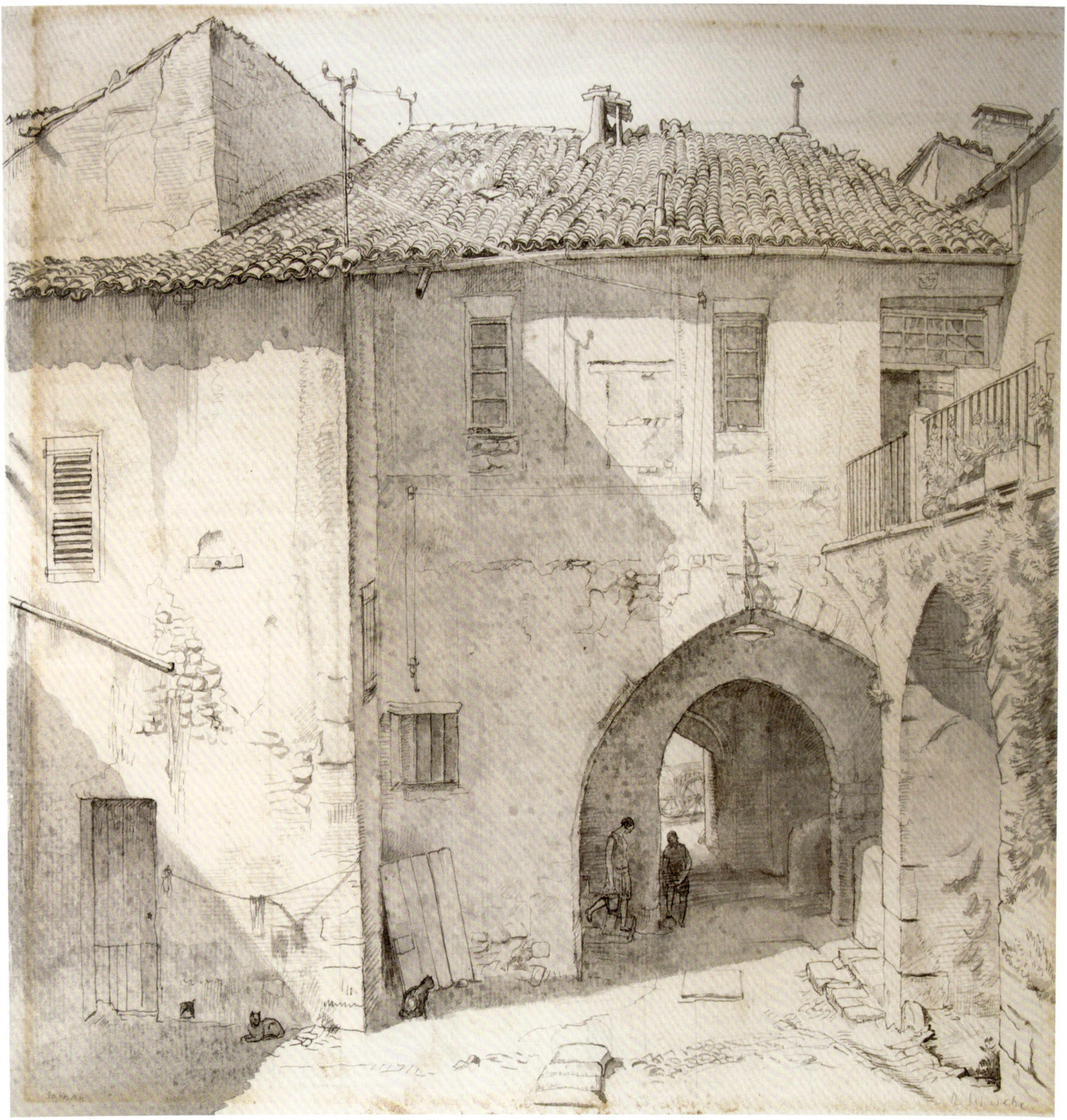

Moustiers-Sainte-Marie

Randolph Schwabe holidayed with his family in the village of Moustiers-Sainte-Marie, Provence, on a number of occasions. He made several drawings of the place, being attracted by 'such a combination of mountain scenery and architectural features' (as he was quoted as saying in C Geoffrey Holme and G S Sandilands, *Artists' Country*, London: The Studio, 1932, page 98).

A friend of the Schwabes, Laura Millicent Russell, always known as 'Russell', lived mainly in Moustiers for many years, until 1941. The Schwabes not only saw her while they were there, but also combined their stays with visits to other friends living in France. These included Charles Rennie Mackintosh and Margaret Macdonald Mackintosh, who, between 1923 and 1927, were based in and around Port-Vendres, on the Mediterranean coast, close to the border with Spain.

Schwabe exhibited his drawings of Moustiers in London and internationally. The international exhibitions included the solo show, 'Exposicion de Obras de Randolph Schwabe en el Museo Nacional de arte Moderno', which was held in Madrid in 1935, and featured three views of Moustiers. Their inclusion suggests that Schwabe considered his drawings of Moustiers to comprise an important and characteristic element of his output.

With thanks to Gill Clarke for her help in the compilation of this note.

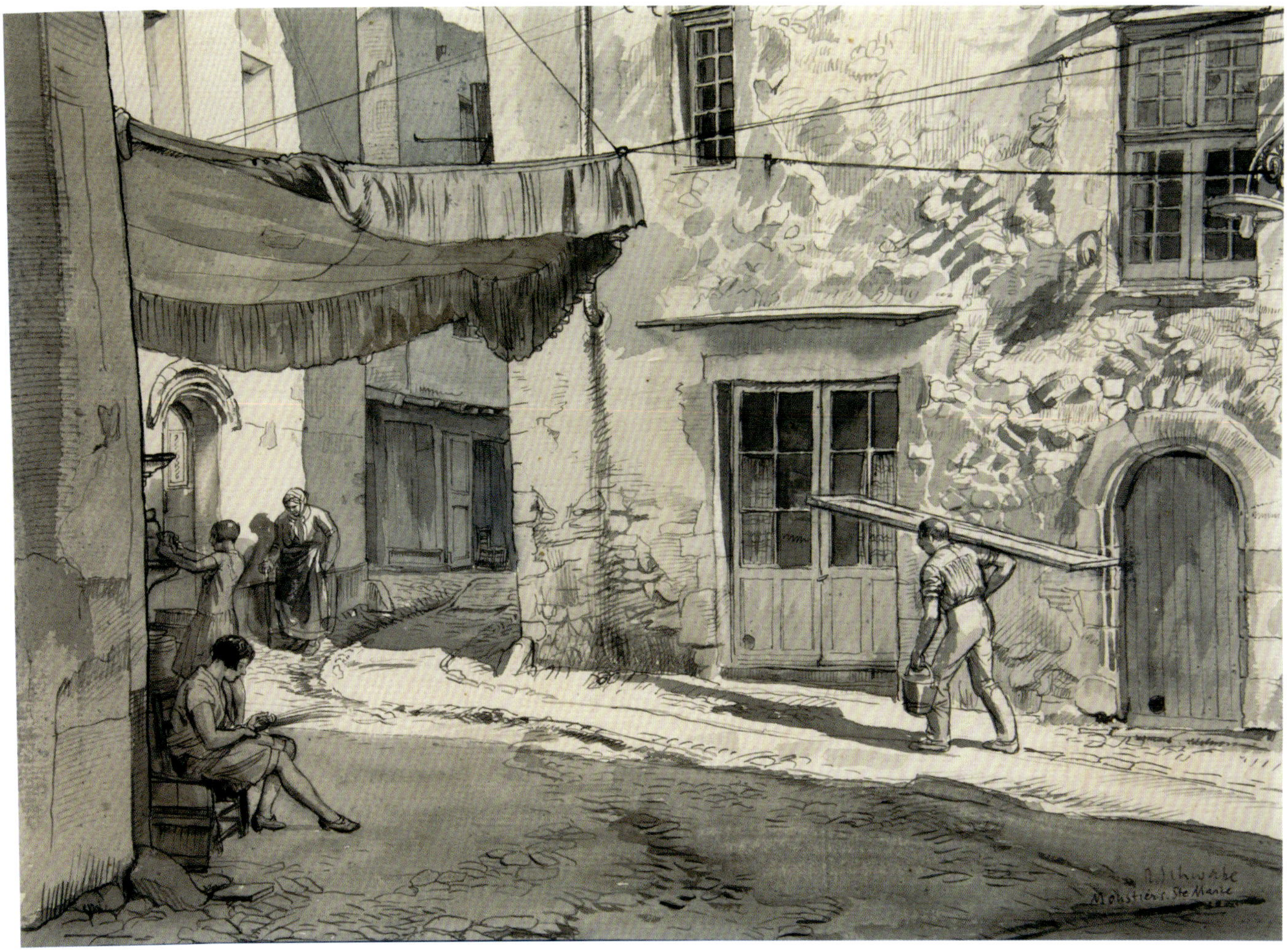

116 Figures on a Street in Moustiers-Sainte-Marie, France
Signed and inscribed 'Moustiers Ste Marie'
Pen ink and watercolour
10 ¼ x 13 ½ inches
Provenance: The Estate of Randolph Schwabe

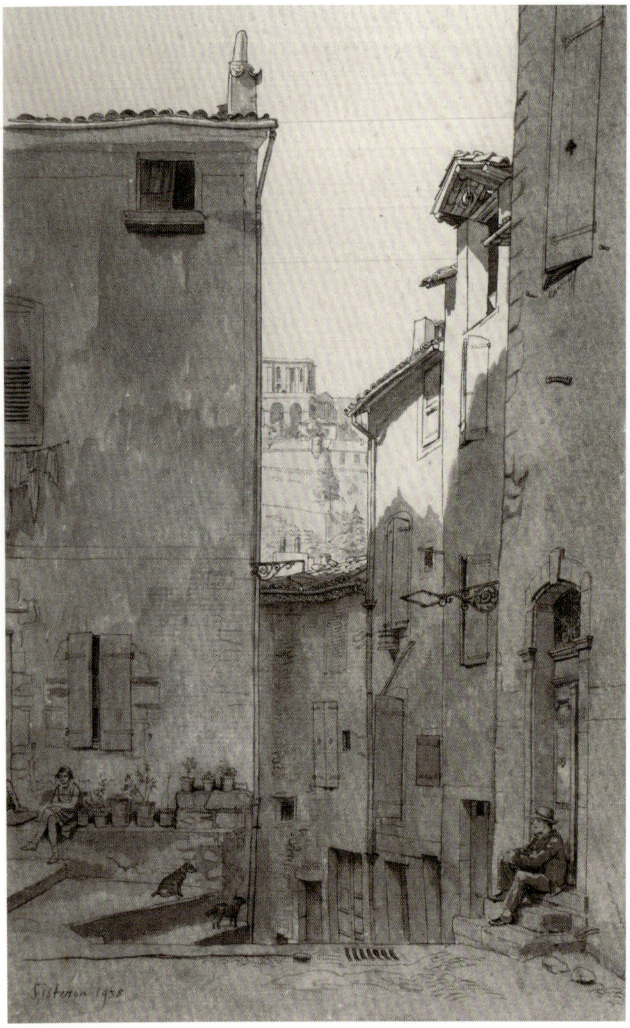

Sisteron

In September 1938, Randolph Schwabe went on a sketching tour of France with his friends, the architect, Maxwell Ayrton, and Ayrton's artist son, Tony. They based themselves in the austerely picturesque Provençal town of Sisteron, which is situated on the River Durance, in a gap between two mountain ridges. Schwabe enjoyed drawing both its dark, narrow streets and wider views of the surrounding light-filled countryside.

117 Sisteron (left)
Inscribed with title and dated 1938
Pen ink and watercolour
14 ¼ x 9 inches
Provenance: The Estate of Randolph Schwabe

118 Sisteron above the Durance (below)
Signed, inscribed 'Sisteron' and dated 1938
Pen ink and watercolour
9 ¼ x 9 inches
Provenance: The Estate of Randolph Schwabe

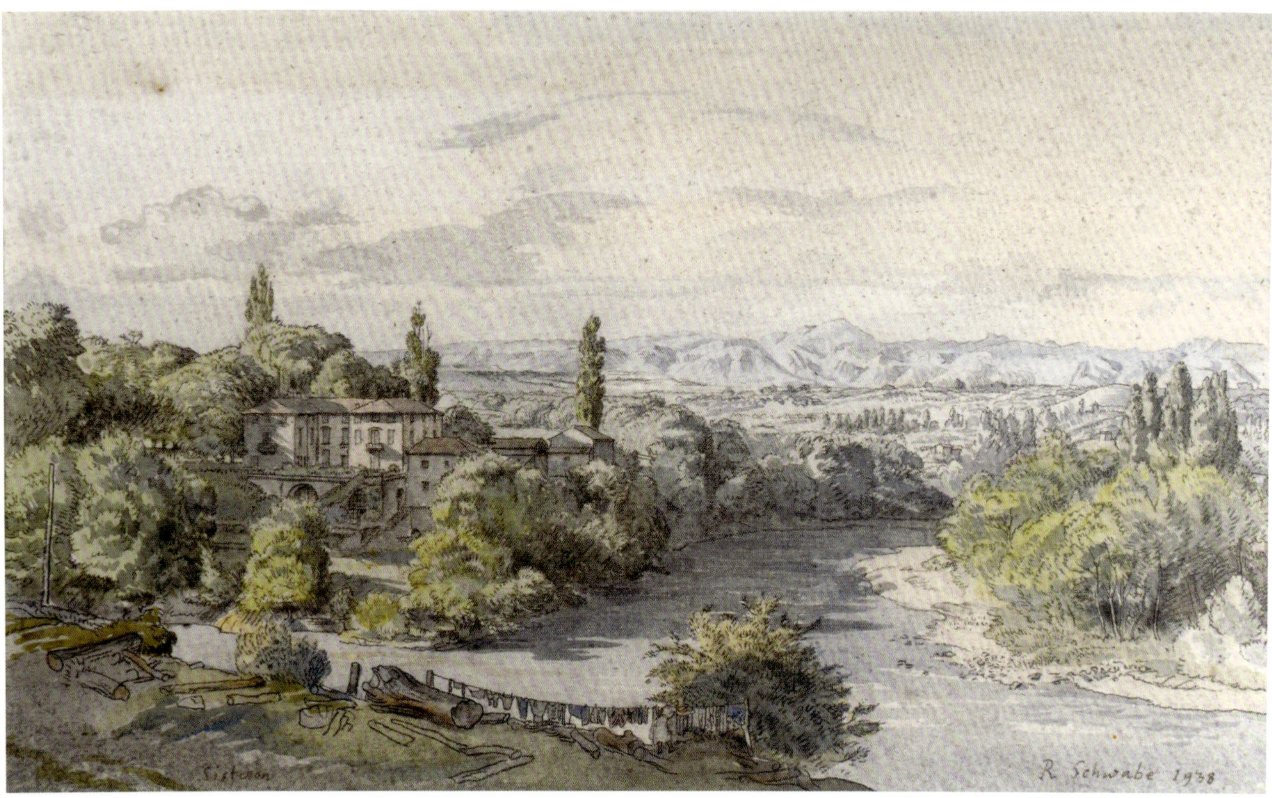

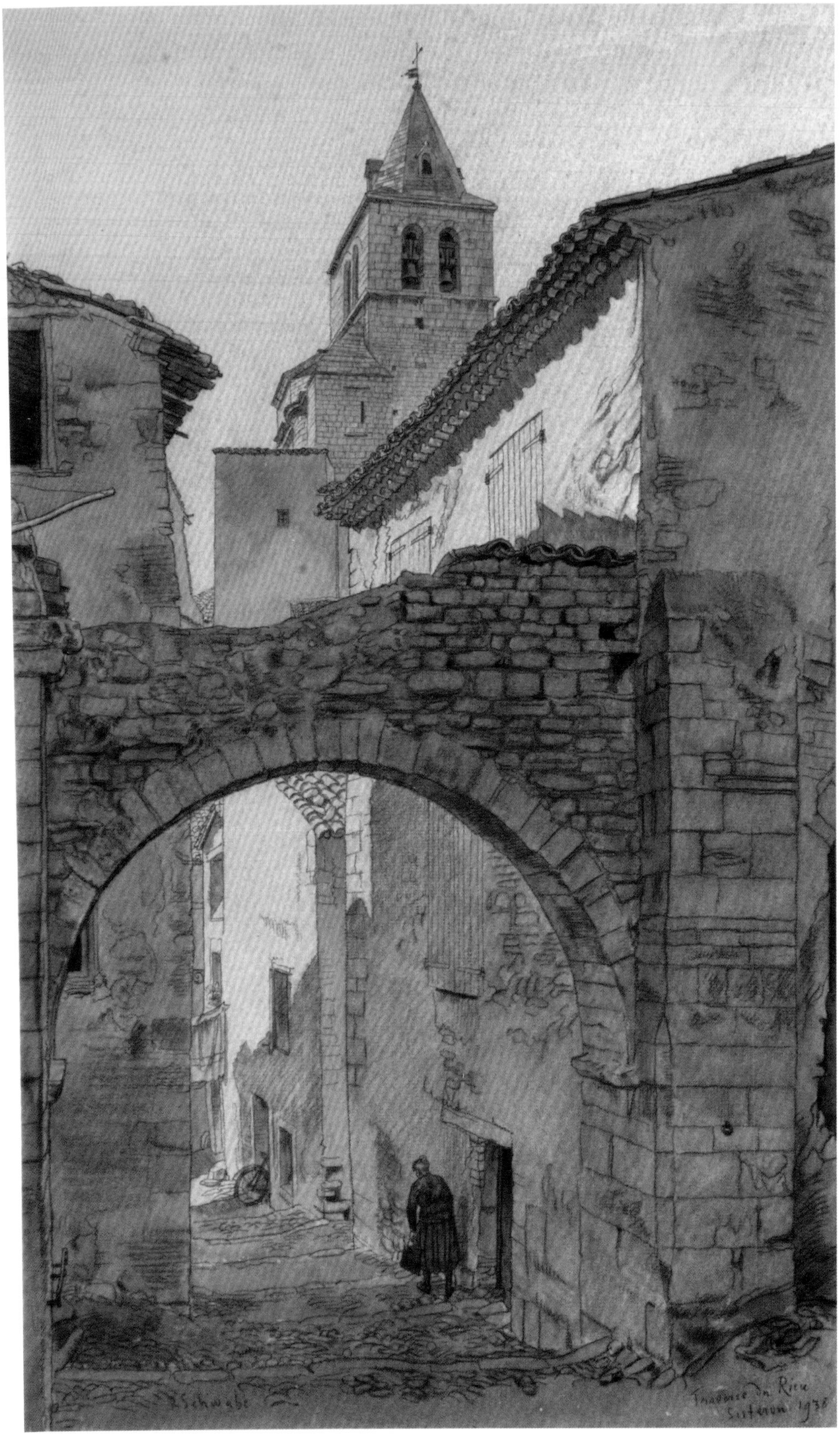

119 **Traverse du Rieu, Sisteron**
Signed, inscribed with title and dated 1938
Pencil and watercolour
21 x 12 ¼ inches
Provenance: The Estate of Randolph Schwabe

PORTUGAL AND SPAIN

KARL HAGEDORN

Karl Adolph Hagedorn,
RBA RI RSMA NEAC NS (1889-1969)

German-born Karl Hagedorn made a consciously pioneering attempt to introduce Modernism to Manchester in the early decades of the twentieth century, through his work as a painter and designer. Later, he tempered his style so that it fitted more easily into England's naturalistic watercolour tradition.

For a biography of Karl Hagedorn, please refer to page 211.

In 1995, the Chris Beetles Gallery hosted 'Manchester's first Modernist', an important retrospective exhibition of the work of Karl Hagedorn, organised in conjunction with the Whitworth Art Gallery of the University of Manchester. It was accompanied by this 72-page fully-illustrated catalogue, which included a number of biographical and evaluative essays.

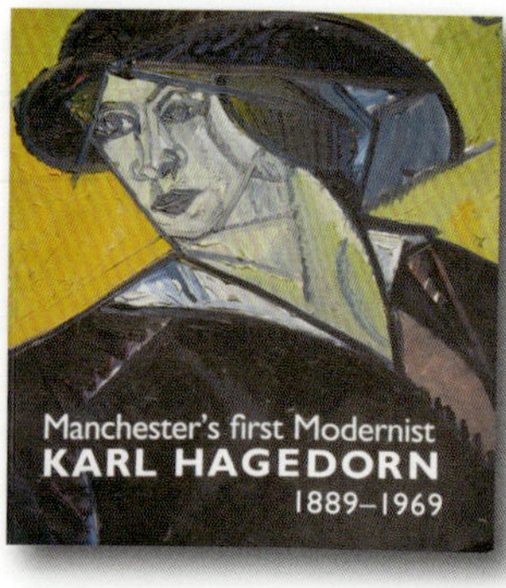

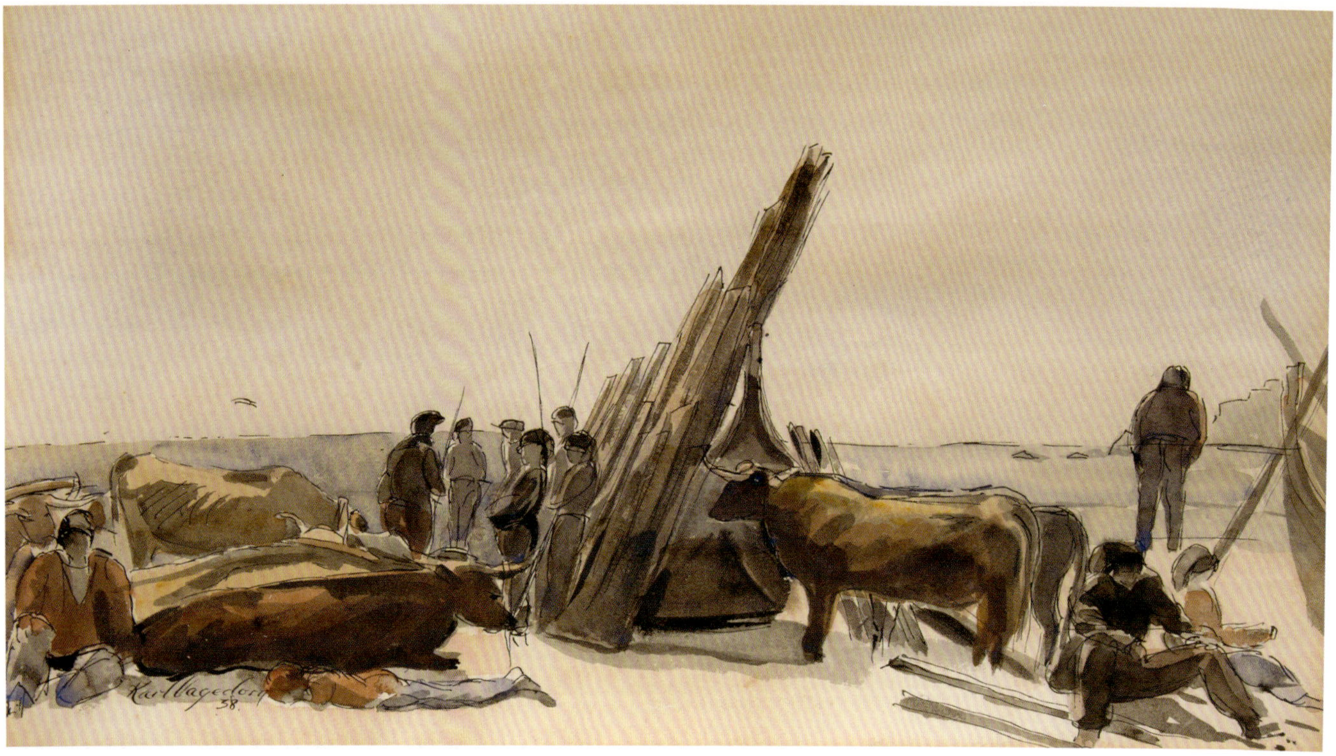

120 Bulls, Algarve, Portugal
Signed and dated 38
Inscribed with title on reverse
Pen ink and watercolour
10 x 17 inches

Bulls, Algarve, Portugal
From the mid 1920s, Karl Hagedorn made sketching trips to the Mediterranean coasts of France and Spain, including one to Tossa de Mar, on the Costa Brava, in 1935. The outbreak of the Spanish Civil War in 1936, led him – along with several other artists – to turn his attention from Spain to Portugal. He is known to have spent time drawing in Nazaré, on the Atlantic coast, north of Lisbon, and on the southern coast of the Algarve. As at his favourite sketching ground of Hastings, in Kent, he was attracted to the activities of the fishermen. An article in *The Studio Annual of Fine Art in Colour*, of 1937, noted that 'Recently in Portugal he found a beach similar to that at Hastings where boats were pulled ashore by a team of bullocks' (page 36), and it is that beach, on the Algarve, that is shown in the present watercolour. A contributor to the magazine, *The Artist*, considered him 'outstanding among the male contributors' (page 140) to an exhibition of Portuguese subjects that was held in London in 1937, and opened by the Portuguese ambassador.

WILLIAM WILSON

William Wilson, OBE RSA RSW SAP SSA (1905-1972)

William Wilson has a reputation as the outstanding Scottish printmaker and stained glass artist of the twentieth century. Underpinning these achievements are his substantial skills as a draughtsman and painter.

For a biography of William Wilson, please refer to page 214.

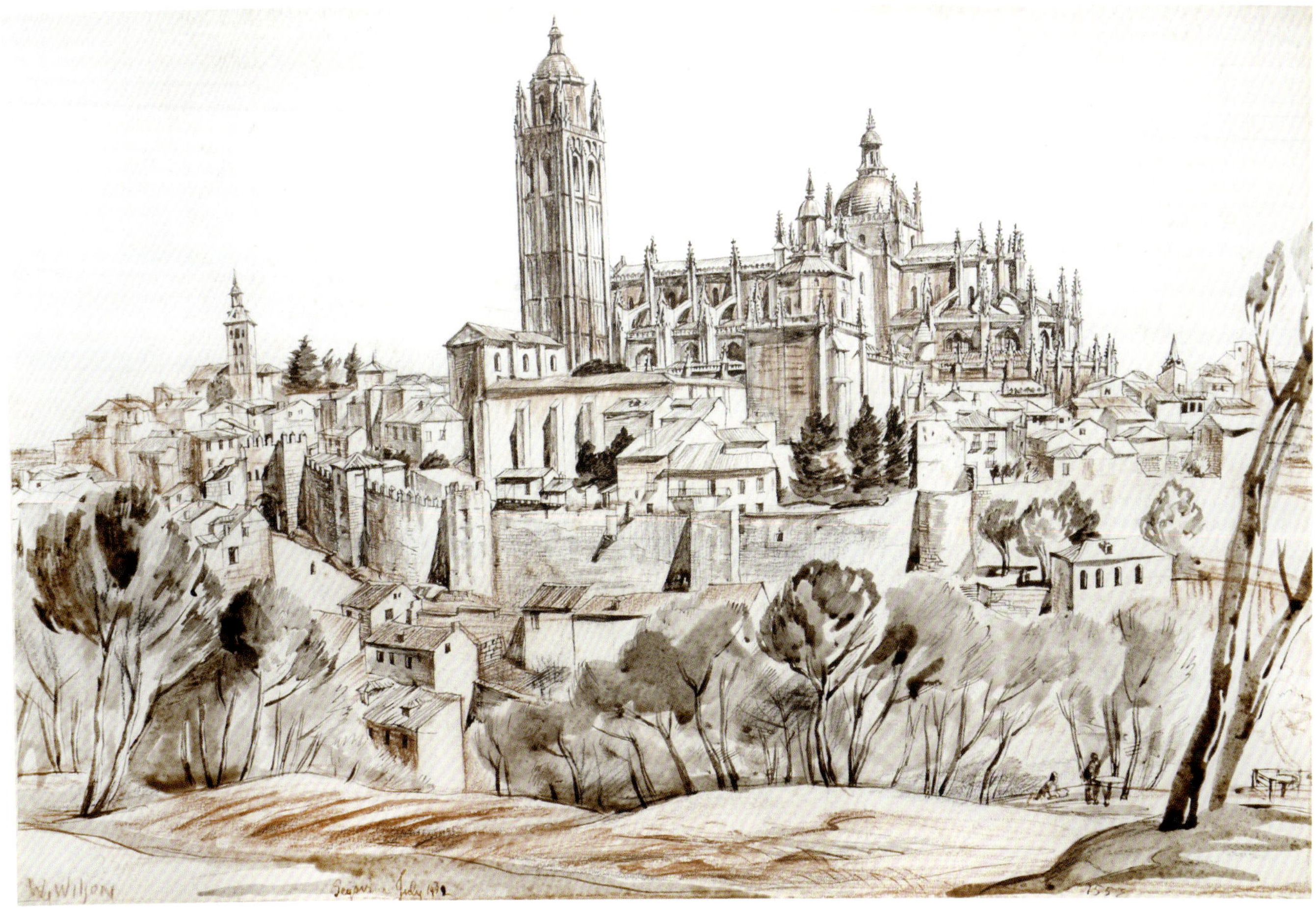

121 Segovia
Signed, inscribed with title and dated 'July 1932'
Pen and ink
13 x 18 inches

Segovia

In 1932, William Wilson won the Royal Scottish Academy Carnegie Travelling Scholarship. As a result, he took leave from his employer – the stained glass manufacturer, James Ballantine – to study full-time at Edinburgh College of Art and travel to Spain and Italy. In Spain, he produced views of Madrid, Toledo and Segovia (in Castille), and Granada and Ronda (in Andalucia).

The present drawing of Segovia was made from a hill – then outside the city – that provides a magnificent panoramic view that centres on the late Gothic cathedral dedicated to the Virgin Mary. To the left is the tower of the earlier, Romanesque church of San Andrés, while beyond that, and excluded from this drawing, is the royal palace known as the Alcázar. Wilson produced a separate drawing of the Alcázar, which, in 1935, won the Guthrie Award, presented by the Royal Scottish Academy.

In 1937, during the Spanish Civil War, the Republicans were thwarted by the air power of the Nationalists in their attempt to occupy Segovia. The attempt, known as the 'Segovia Offensive', was described by Ernest Hemingway in his novel, *For Whom the Bell Tolls* (1940).

ITALY

HAROLD SQUIRE

Harold Squire, LG NEAC (1881-1959)

Harold Squire was a painter of landscapes, flowers and occasional figure subjects in a refined Post-Impressionist style. Having taken lessons from Augustus John, he often employed spare landscape motifs similar to those of John Dickson Innes and Derwent Lees, artists in John's circle. However, his handling is more comparable to that of Lucien Pissarro, who exhibited with him in 1913 in a show of independence from the London Group. In addition to easel painting, he displayed an interest in interior design, and associated with a number of key artist-designers of the age, including the architect, Charles Rennie Mackintosh (who designed a studio-house for him), and members of the Bloomsbury Group.

For a biography of Harold Squire, please refer to page 215.

122 **Capri**
Signed and inscribed with title on reverse
Oil on board
13 x 16 inches
Provenance: Mrs Robert Mathias, 15 Montagu Square, Marylebone, London

Capri

Harold Squire is likely to have made his first visit to the isle of Capri, in the Bay of Naples, not long before the First World War. He showed two views of Monte Solaro, the island's highest point, at the New English Art Club in the winter of 1913, and a painting of the mainland from the island at 'Twentieth Century Art: A Review of Modern Movements', held at Whitechapel Art Gallery in the spring of 1914. However, his largest group of paintings of Capri was possibly that shown at the Goupil Gallery in 1919, some of which were purchased for Johannesburg Art Gallery. Either the visit before the war had proved so inspiring to Squire that he continued to generate compositions of the island, or he returned there soon after the war had ended.

The present example of Squire's paintings of Capri shows a spot high above Matermania with a view across to Punta Campanella on the mainland. Its great appeal as an image is almost matched in this instance by the interest of its provenance.

The work was once owned by Mrs Robert Mathias (1874-1935) of 15 Montagu Square, Marylebone, who was born Helena Wertheimer, and known as Ena. She was the third child of the antiques dealer, Asher Wertheimer, who had a gallery at 158 Bond Street. He commissioned a series of 12 portraits of members of his family from John Singer Sargent, which comprised the largest private commission that the artist ever received. Ten of these are now in the collection of the Tate, including the two of Ena. The first, from 1901, shows her with her younger sister, Betty, while the second, from 1905, shows her alone. Entitled *A Vele Gonfie*, which is Italian for 'in full sail', this second painting was a wedding gift from her father. ☞

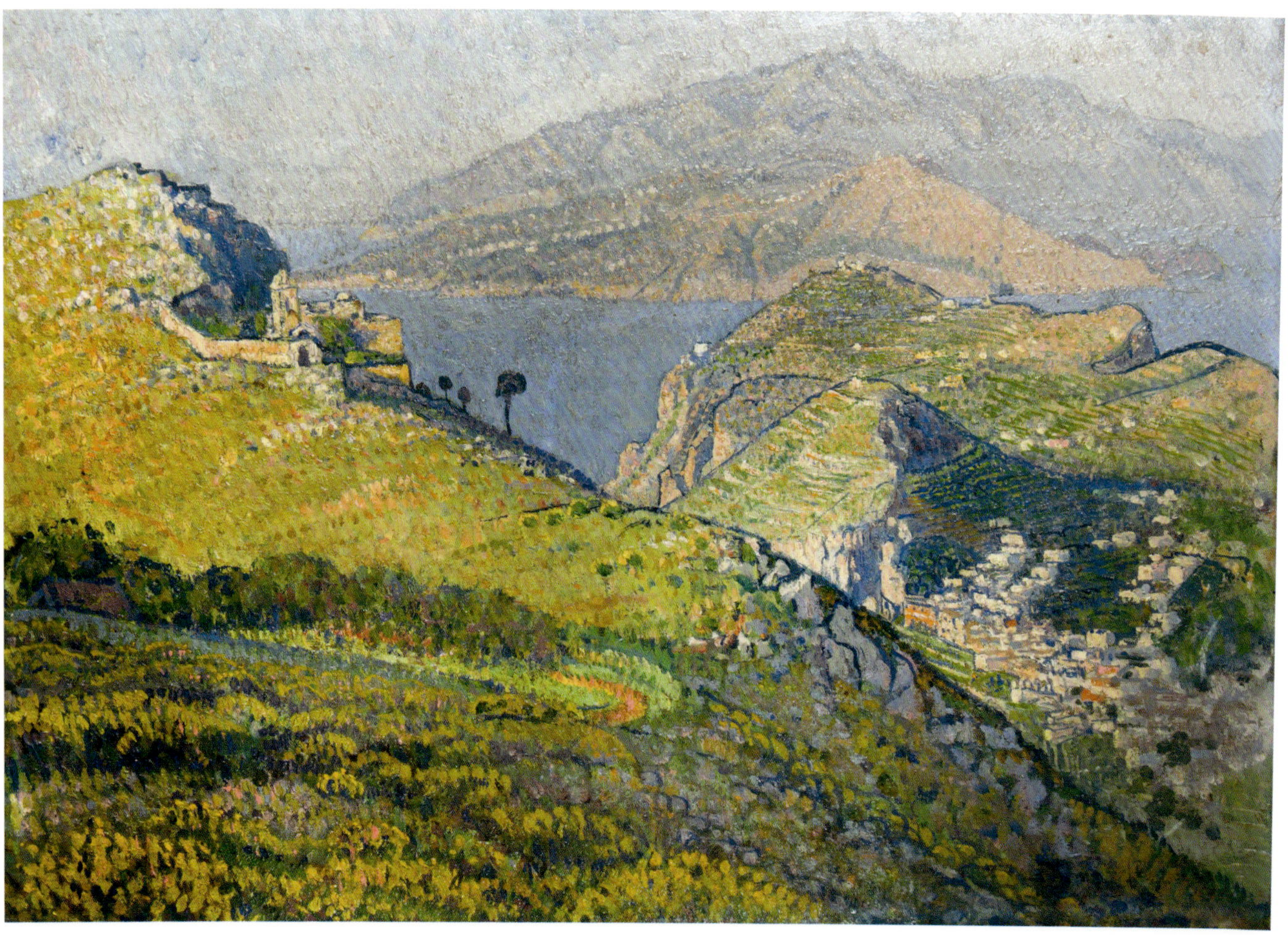

Capri note continued

Ena Wertheimer married Robert Moritz Mathias in 1905 at the West London Synagogue, Upper Berkeley Street. Mathias worked for his uncle, the distinguished industrial chemist, Ludwig Mond (who is also remembered for the collection of old masters that he bequeathed to the National Gallery). They would have five children.

Like her sister Betty, Ena studied at the Slade School of Art, and developed a great passion for the arts, becoming a collector, hostess and patron (known for her support of the Ballets Russes). Among her various roles, she was the owner of the Claridge Gallery, Brook Street, which, during the late 1920s and early 30s, mounted a wide range of exhibitions of contemporary artists. These included one in 1926 of flower paintings, which featured works by Harold Squire.

CECIL ARTHUR HUNT

Cecil Arthur Hunt, VPRWS RBA (1873-1965)

Arco Near Lake Garda

In 1923 Hunt travelled to northern Italy and sketched many of the villages encircling Lake Garda, including the magnificent mountain town of Arco on its northern shore. The town is faced on one side by sheer limestone cliffs and is crowned by the high tower of the medieval Castello di Arco, clearly visible on this work. (sb9 and sb10). It is likely that this work is one that Hunt exhibited at the Royal Society of Painters in Water-Colours, either 'Arco in the Valley of the Sarca', Winter 1923, No 101 (bought by Wrenacre for £31) or 'Arco', Summer 1926, No 40 (bought by the Rt Hon C Allen for £52.10.0).

123 **Arco Near Lake Garda** (below)
Signed
Signed and inscribed with title on reverse
Oil on canvas
20 x 26 inches

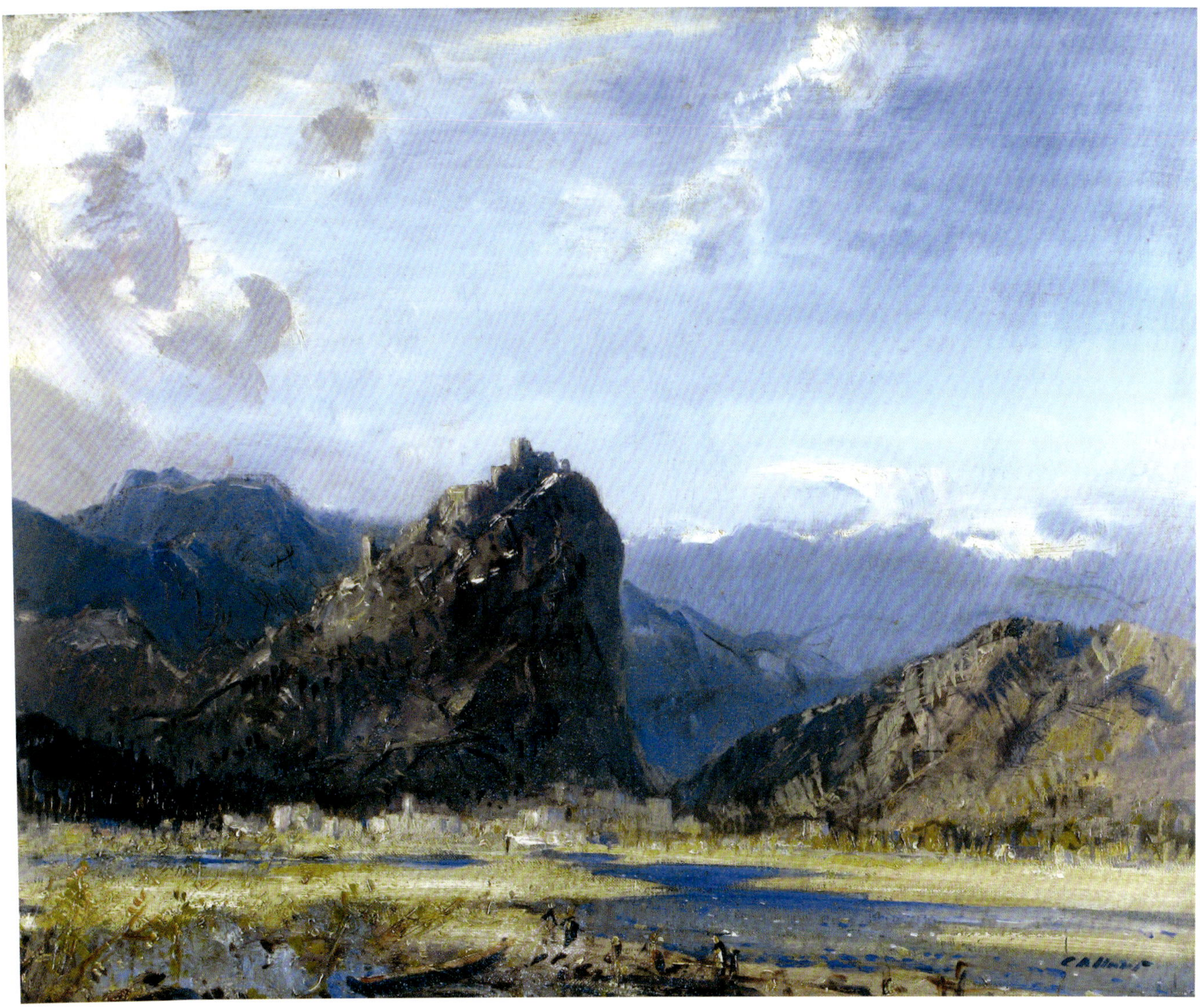

GREECE

CECIL ARTHUR HUNT

Cecil Arthur Hunt, VPRWS RBA (1873-1965)

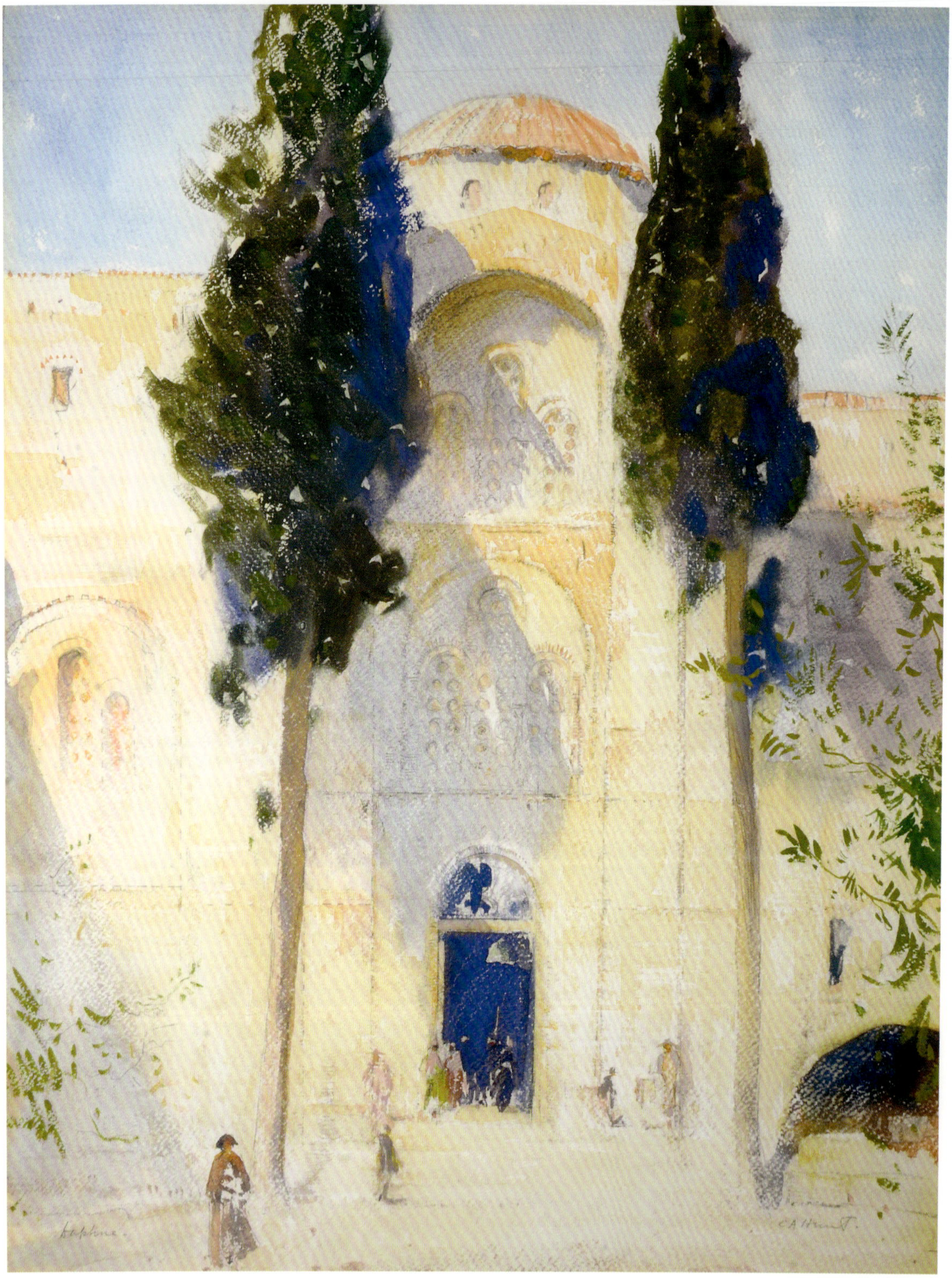

124 **Byzantine Church, Daphni**
Signed and inscribed 'Daphne'
Signed, inscribed with title and exhibition number, and dated 1930 on Fine Art Society label on original backboard
Watercolour, bodycolour and pencil
19 x 14 ¼ inches
Exhibited: 'The Isles of the Aegean and Beyond, Recent Watercolours', Fine Art Society, London, 1930, No 7

Byzantine Church, Daphni

Hunt travelled to Greece and Italy in May 1931, his sketchbook (sb30) of that tour contains a sketch of 'Daphne' [sic] and is inscribed 'with Curtis Green RA & Mrs G. Venice in a few days then steamer to Athens via Corinth canal. voyage in Greece & car to hanging monasteries of Meteora etc etc back from Brindisi up east coast of Italy to Stresa on L Maggiore'.

6: S R BADMIN IN LONDON

S R Badmin is best known for his highly-distinctive, meticulous drawings, watercolours and etchings of the British countryside, which were the result of both a penetrating eye and a deep knowledge of natural history, vernacular architecture and traditional customs. However, he was a Londoner by birth, and he lived in the capital for the first two-thirds of his life, a period that encompassed his artistic training, his first marriage, the establishment of his career as a painter and illustrator, and his entire practice as a printmaker. At various points in his life, he applied his skills to recording his own local environment, and this was especially true of the late 1920s and early 30s. During those years, he produced a number of fine images that bring London vividly to life, and make a case for him being as significant an artist of the urban scene as he was of the rural one.

Badmin was born in Sydenham, in Southeast London, in 1906, and during the next 50 years he lived at seven different addresses in the area, ranging geographically from 162 Croydon Road, Anerley (in the south) to 45 Thorpewood Avenue, Sydenham (in the north, and bordering Forest Hill). It was at the latter that his father had the house, 'Aleroy', built for him, following his marriage to Peggy Colbourn in 1925 [131]. His first serious study of art also took place in Southeast London, at Camberwell School of Arts and Crafts, in the years from 1919. Then, in 1924, a studentship enabled him to graduate to the Royal College of Art, which, at the time, was adjacent to the Victoria and Albert Museum. This brought him to South Kensington and other more central areas of the city. He would hold his first solo show at the Twenty-One Gallery, at 15 Mill Street, just off Regent Street, in 1930, and later solo shows at the Fine Art Society, in Bond Street. By 1932, he had a studio near Clapham Common (on which he liked to watch and draw the model yacht racing [125]). Part-time teaching at art schools took him further afield, both westwards to Richmond (1934) and northwards to St John's Wood (1936).

Badmin's abilities allowed him to capture almost any London location or event, and populate it with a convincing variety of people and activity. His attention to detail has him delineate not only each building, but also each shop sign along the Strand, and his love of contrast has him distinguish between the stylish flapper and the old-fashioned flower seller, and the horse-drawn cart and the latest motor car [127]. He can instil a crowd with the appropriate degree of interest or excitement, whether it is welcoming a pilot at the end of a record flight [126], or enjoying works of art at a prestigious exhibition [133]. And he is particularly good at documenting workers at their tasks, be they pruning trees in Exhibition Road [129] or sprucing up boats in Richmond [132]. He understands that these jobs are as much a sign of seasonal change as the trees themselves bursting into leaf.

In retrospect, Badmin's images also evidence more permanent changes to London's infrastructure and affairs. The hall that used to house the London County Council may survive on the South Bank, but the buildings that frame it in Badmin's view from Victoria Tower Gardens [126] have long gone; the northernmost block of old St Thomas's Hospital was destroyed by wartime bombing, while the Shot Tower of Lambeth Lead Works was demolished to make way for the Queen Elizabeth Hall. Badmin's Strand [127] may have a passing resemblance to that which exists today, but entire blocks were removed in order to widen it, while the French School in South Kensington [128] has been replaced by the Ismaili Centre. It is all credit to Badmin that, while chronicling the losses, he manages to convince the viewer that life goes on as he observed it.

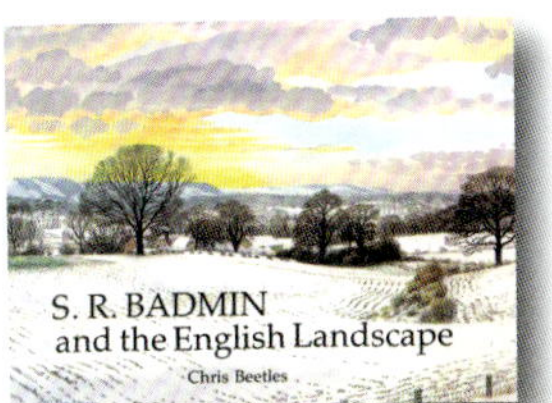

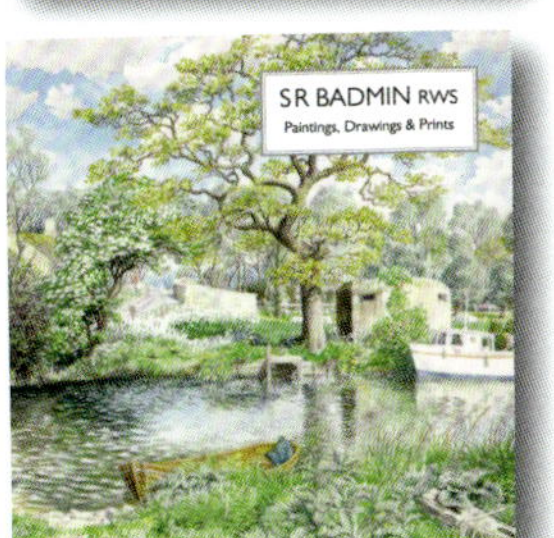

Chris Beetles has done much to promote the work of S R Badmin, notably through the monograph, *S R Badmin and the English Landscape* (Collins, 1985), which includes a catalogue raisonné of etchings, and a series of exhibitions. The most recent of those exhibitions, held in 2015, was accompanied by a 48-page fully-illustrated catalogue.

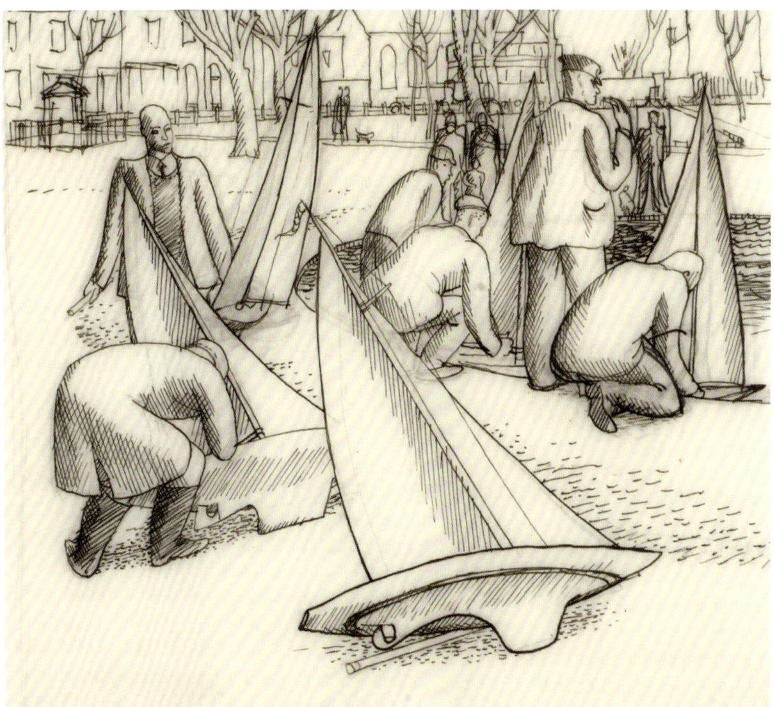

125 **Model Yacht Racing, Clapham Common**
Inscribed with title
Pen and ink on tracing paper; 6 ¼ x 6 ¼ inches
Exhibited: 'S R Badmin RWS', Chris Beetles Gallery, June 1985, No 205;
'S R Badmin RWS, Paintings, Drawings & Prints', Chris Beetles Gallery, March-April 2015, No 3

S R BADMIN

Stanley Roy Badmin, RWS RE AIA FSIA (1906-1989)

Throughout his career, S R Badmin used his great talents – as etcher, illustrator and watercolourist – to promote a vision of the English countryside and thus of England itself. By underpinning his idealism with almost documentary precision and detail, he was able to produce images that appealed to all, and could be used for a great variety of purposes, from education through to advertising. The wellbeing suggested by each rural panorama is all the more potent, and pleasing, for the accuracy of each tree and leaf, and the plausibility of the slightest anecdotal episode.

For a biography of S R Badmin, please refer to page 208-209.

1926

126 Sir Alan Cobham Returning to London from His Record Breaking Flight to Australia
Signed and dated 'Oct 1926'
Inscribed 'from Australia. Cobham turning preparatory to landing. LCC County Hall' and dated 'Oct 1926' below mount
Pen ink and watercolour
12 ¼ x 9 ½ inches
Exhibited: 'S R Badmin RWS, Paintings, Drawings & Prints', Chris Beetles Gallery, March-April 2015, No 1

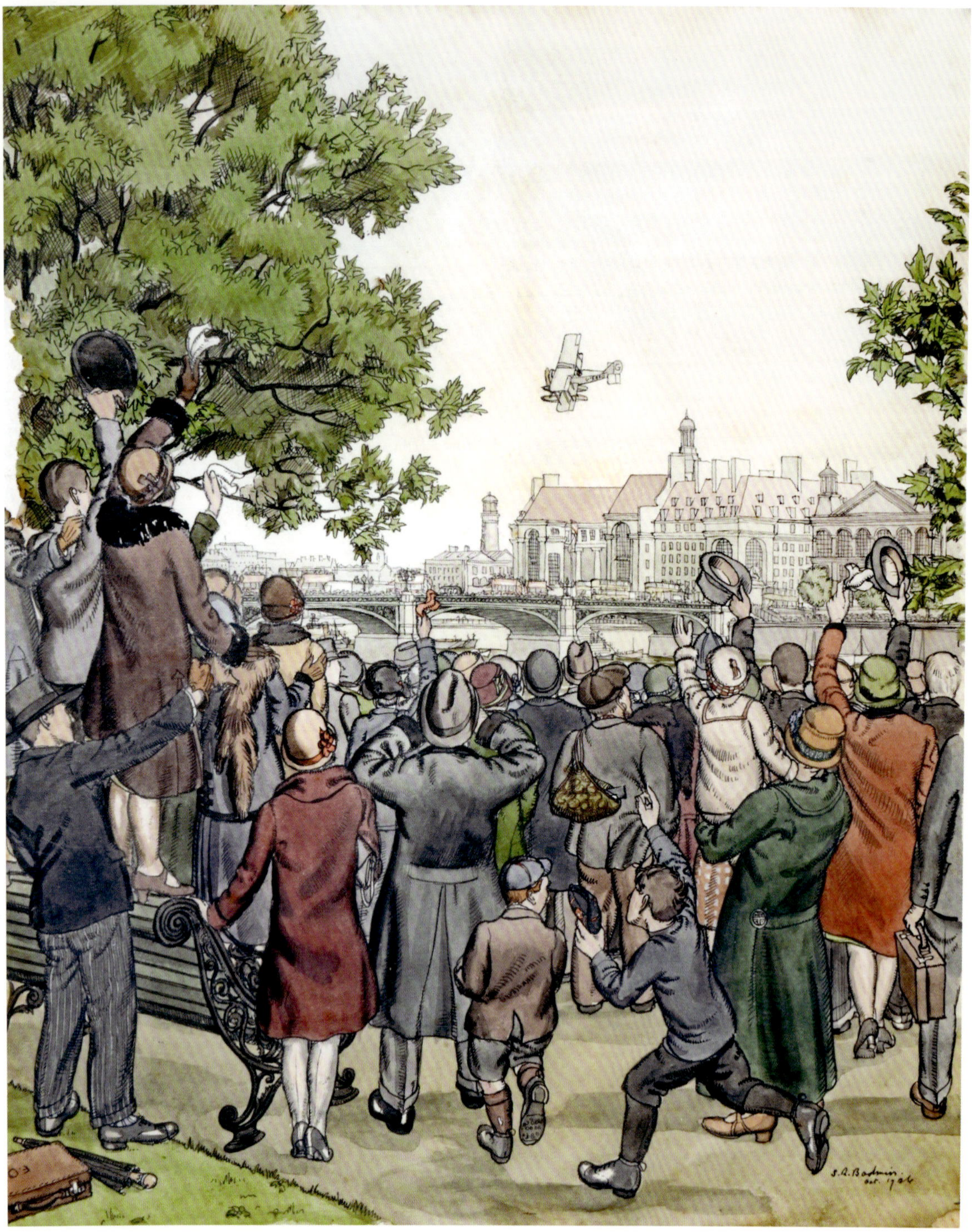

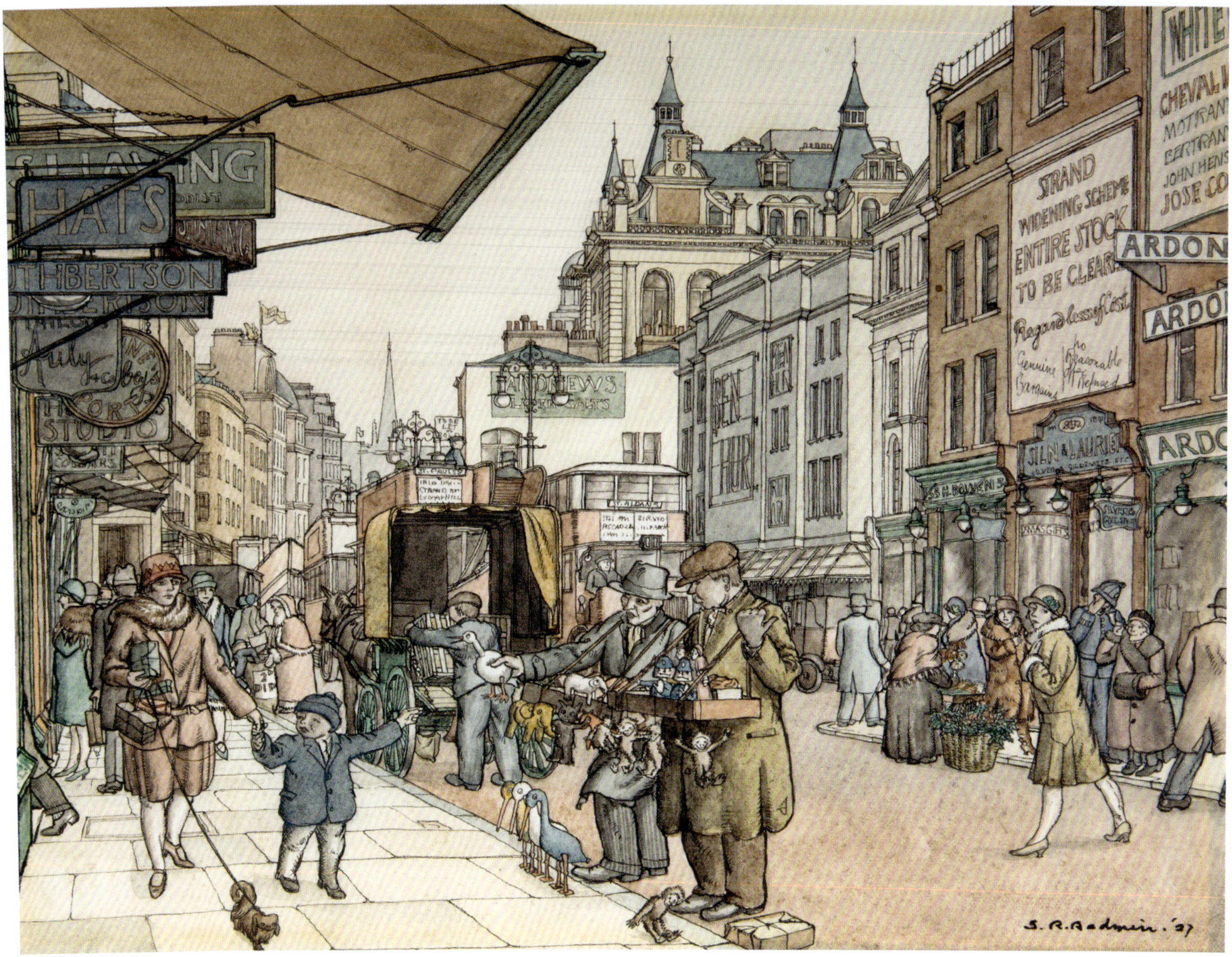

1927

Sir Alan Cobham Returning to London from His Record Breaking Flight to Australia (opposite)
Alan Cobham won the prestigious Britannia Trophy in 1923 for his 12,000 mile flight around Europe, the Middle East and North Africa. He won the trophy again in 1925 when he became the first person to fly to India and back in 1924-25. This painting depicts the third and final time he won the trophy, in 1926, when he became the first person to fly to Australia and back in his De Havilland DH 50 biplane.

Alan Cobham began his Australia flight on 30 June 1926, which was marred when his faithful mechanic, Arthur Elliott, was shot and killed whilst flying over Basra, Iraq. Cobham continued his flight with a replacement mechanic reaching Melbourne, Australia on 15 August 1926 where a record breaking crowd of 150,000 people gathered to meet him. He left Australia for England on 29 August 1926 and landed on the river Thames by the Houses of Parliament 34 days later on 1 October 1926. This painting commemorates his triumphant return to crowds of around a million who clustered on the bridges and embankments to watch him land. He received a knighthood within days of returning. The view is from the Victoria Tower Gardens south of the Houses of Parliament looking towards the old London County Council County Hall.

Fiona Nickerson

127 **Street Hawkers, Strand, Xmas**
Signed and dated '27
Signed, inscribed with title and 'Strand now altered 1931', and dated 'June 1927' below mount
Pen ink and watercolour
7 ¾ x 9 inches

Street Hawkers, Strand, Xmas
The present watercolour shows the central section of the Strand, in London's West End, as it looked in 1927, while the road was subject to a widening scheme. The project had begun in 1899 with the rebuilding of the Strand frontage of the Hotel Cecil, which can be seen looming over the other buildings. Following the hiatus of the First World War and its aftermath, work continued in 1923 with the rebuilding of the Tivoli Theatre of Varieties as a 'Picture Theatre'. The Tivoli sits at the centre of the image, and is identified by the words 'Ben Hur', advertising the British premiere of the American silent epic, which ran there from November 1926 to October 1927. The buildings between the Cecil and the Tivoli, and those at the far right of the image, were demolished soon after S R Badmin completed his visual document.

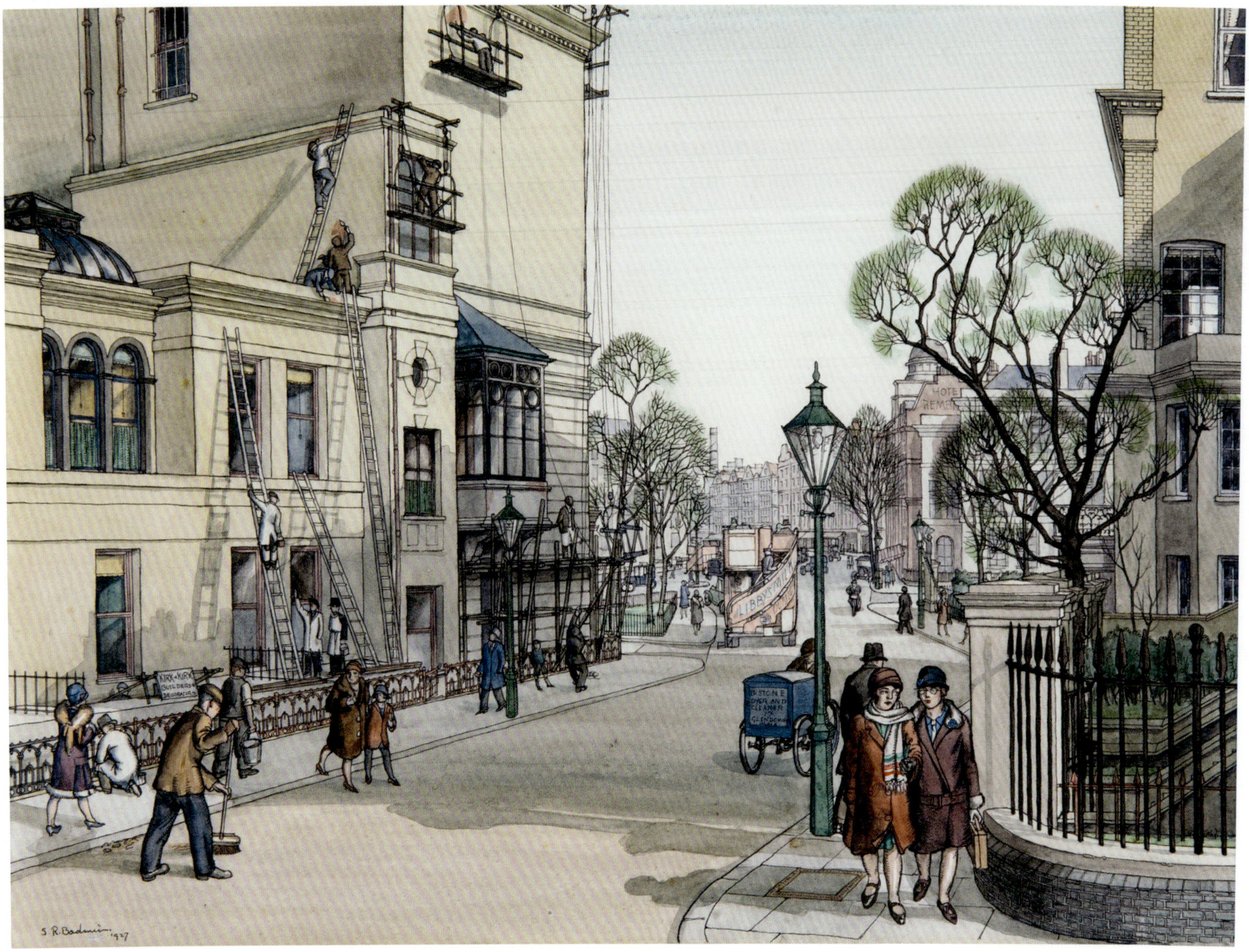

128 The Back of the French School, Cromwell Gardens, South Kensington
Signed and dated 1927
Inscribed with title and 'grey wash on trees altered for Graphic to green. published in May 1927', and dated 'Jan 197' [1927] below mount
Inscribed 'reproduced in colour 'May 21st 1927' and 'original to be returned to R P Gossop after reproduction' on reverse
Pen ink and watercolour
9 ¼ x 11 ¾ inches
Illustrated: *The Graphic*, 21 May 1927

The Back of the French School, Cromwell Gardens, South Kensington

The seven large houses that originally comprised Cromwell Gardens were designed by Alfred Williams and built by John Spicer in the 1860s. Though impressive, the heavy traffic that developed around them made them far less attractive by 1912. At that date, they were purchased by the Office of Works, so that they could make way for a new Royal College of Art. That plan never materialised and, in 1920, the houses were leased to the Institut Français and its attached Lycée (the French School of Badmin's title). Over the following decade, these institutions outgrew the site and, in 1936, they moved into purpose built premises further west along the Cromwell Road. The plot was then purchased as the location for a National Theatre to be designed by Sir Edwin Lutyens and Cecil Masey, architect of the Phoenix Theatre. However, the Second World War delayed construction and, in 1942, an agreement was drawn up in which the Kensington site was exchanged for a newer, less restrictive site on the South Bank of the Thames. Cromwell Gardens was then used to house advertising hoardings, and later a car-hire depot and a pre-fabricated office. Then, in the 1970s, the land was secured by Mawlana Hazar Imam for the establishment of the first Ismaili Centre in the Western world, as a religious, social and cultural meeting place for British members of Ismailism, one of three branches of Shia Islam. It was designed by the Casson Conder Partnership, which included Sir Hugh Casson, nephew of the actor and director, Sir Lewis Casson, who had been a member of the committee for the National Theatre that was to have been built on the same site. It opened in 1985.

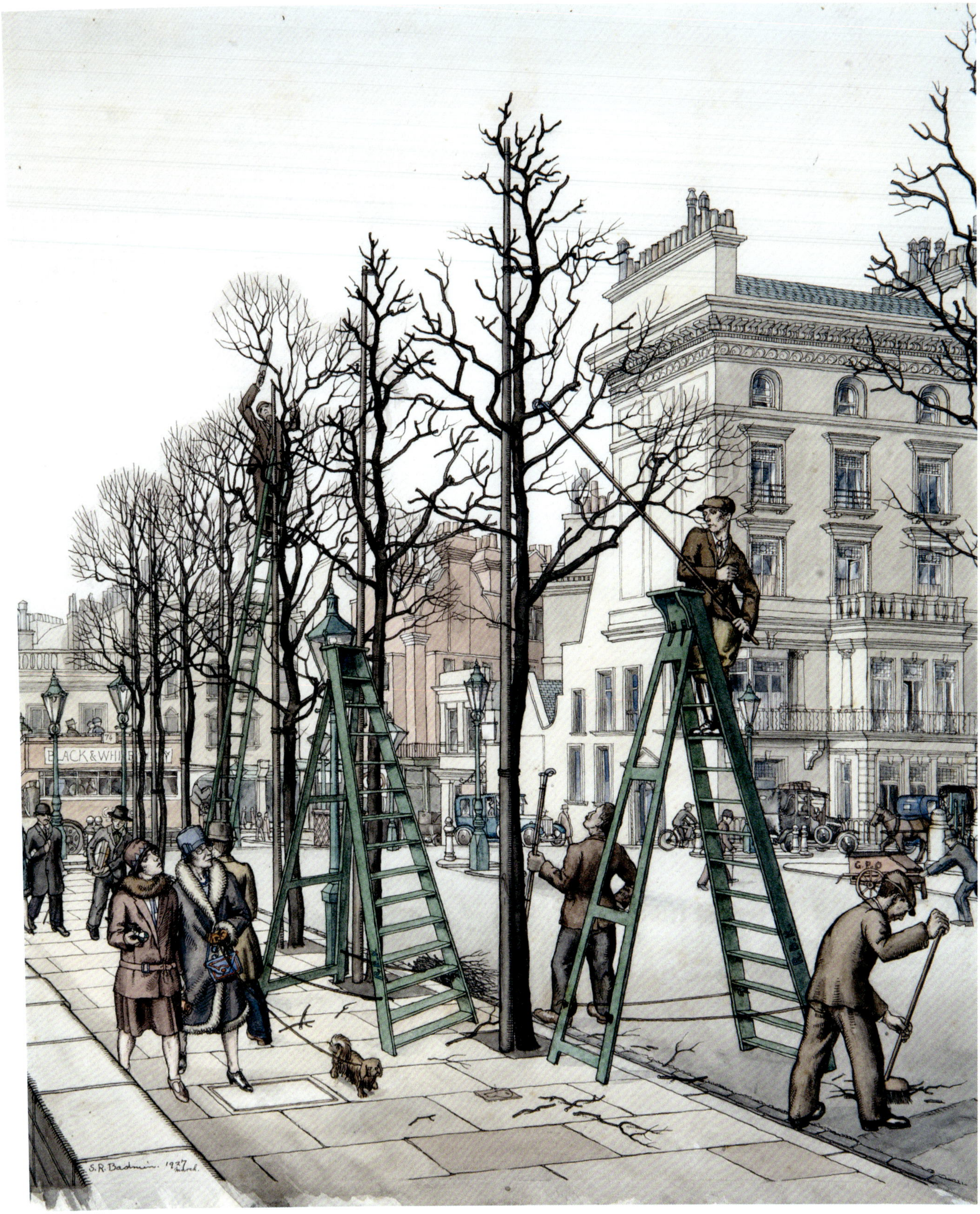

129 Preparing London for the Summer:
Exhibition Road, South Kensington
Signed and dated 'March 1927'
Signed with initials, inscribed 'from a sketch made in Exhibition Rd S Kensington'
and 'published in Graphic 1927', and dated 'March 1927' below mount
Pen ink and watercolour
11 ¼ x 9 inches
Illustrated: *The Graphic*, 23 April 1927, Front Cover, 'Preparing London for the Summer'

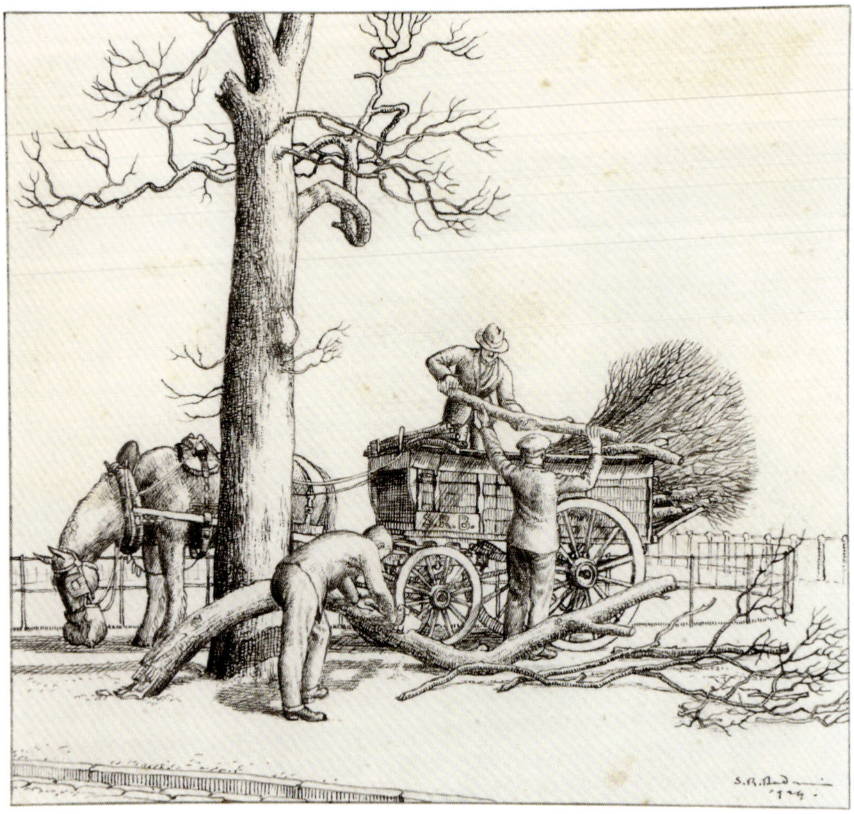

130 The Fallen Bough in Hyde Park, London
Signed, inscribed 'The Fallen Bough' and dated 1929
Inscribed with title and 'Drawing for engraving from a sketch in Hyde Park', and dated 'Dec 1928' below mount
Pen and ink
4 x 4 ¼ inches
Exhibited: 'S R Badmin RWS, Paintings, Drawings & Prints', Chris Beetles Gallery, March-April 2015, No 2

131 Thorpewood Avenue, Sydenham (below)
Signed and dated 1927
Watercolour
7 x 10 ¼ inches

Thorpewood Avenue, Sydenham

In 1925-26, S R Badmin's father, Charles James Badman, built 'Aleroy', 45 Thorpewood Avenue, Sydenham, London, SE26, for Badmin and his first wife, Peggy.

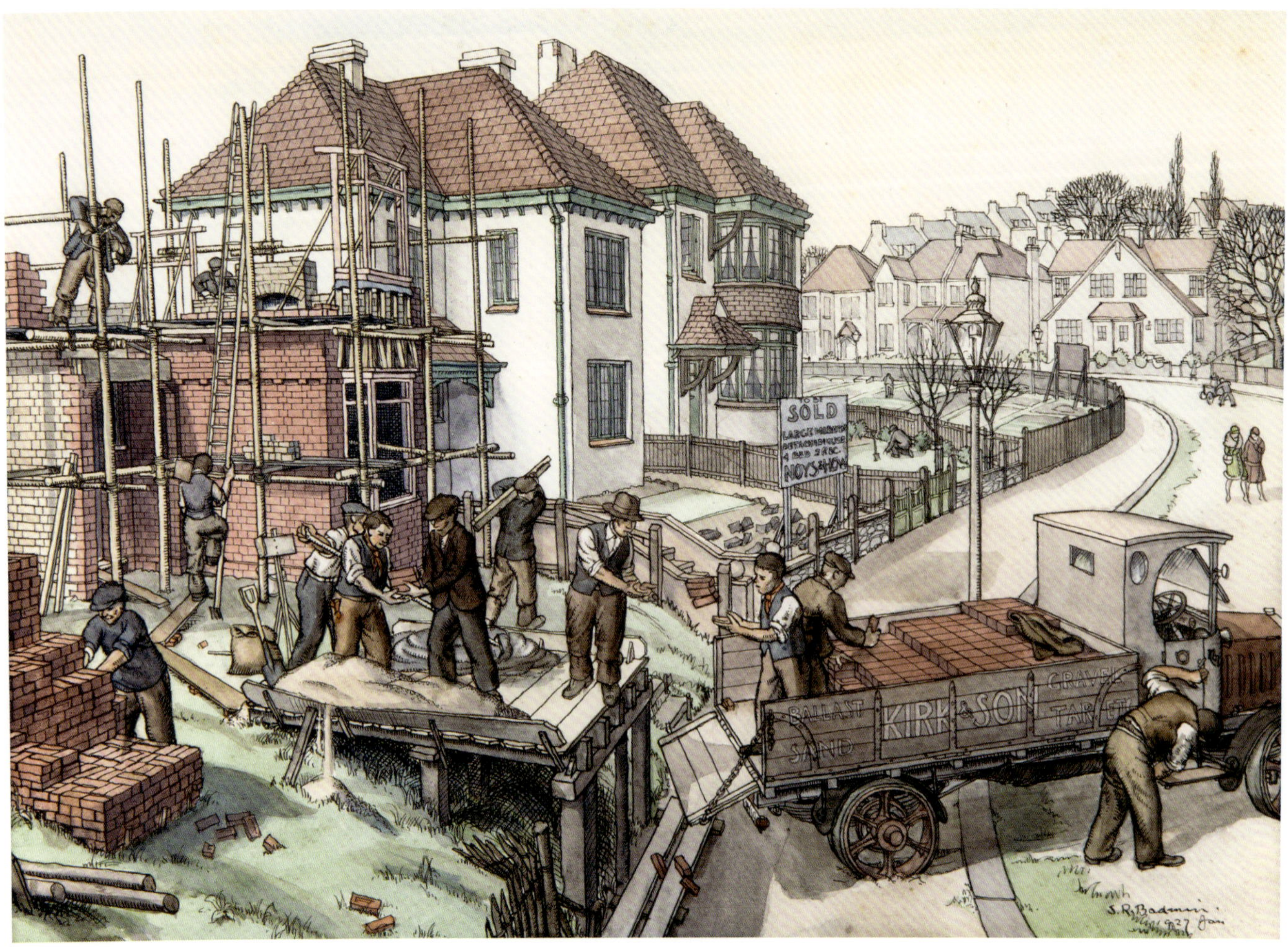

1931

'If Mr Badmin is put first it is because he accepts more completely than the others the convention of line and wash ... Mr Badmin makes no bones about his tone and the result is that drawings like "Mill Street W" and "The Season Commences – Richmond" give complete satisfaction.'

(*The Times*, review of The Royal Society of Painters in Water-Colours, Summer 1932)

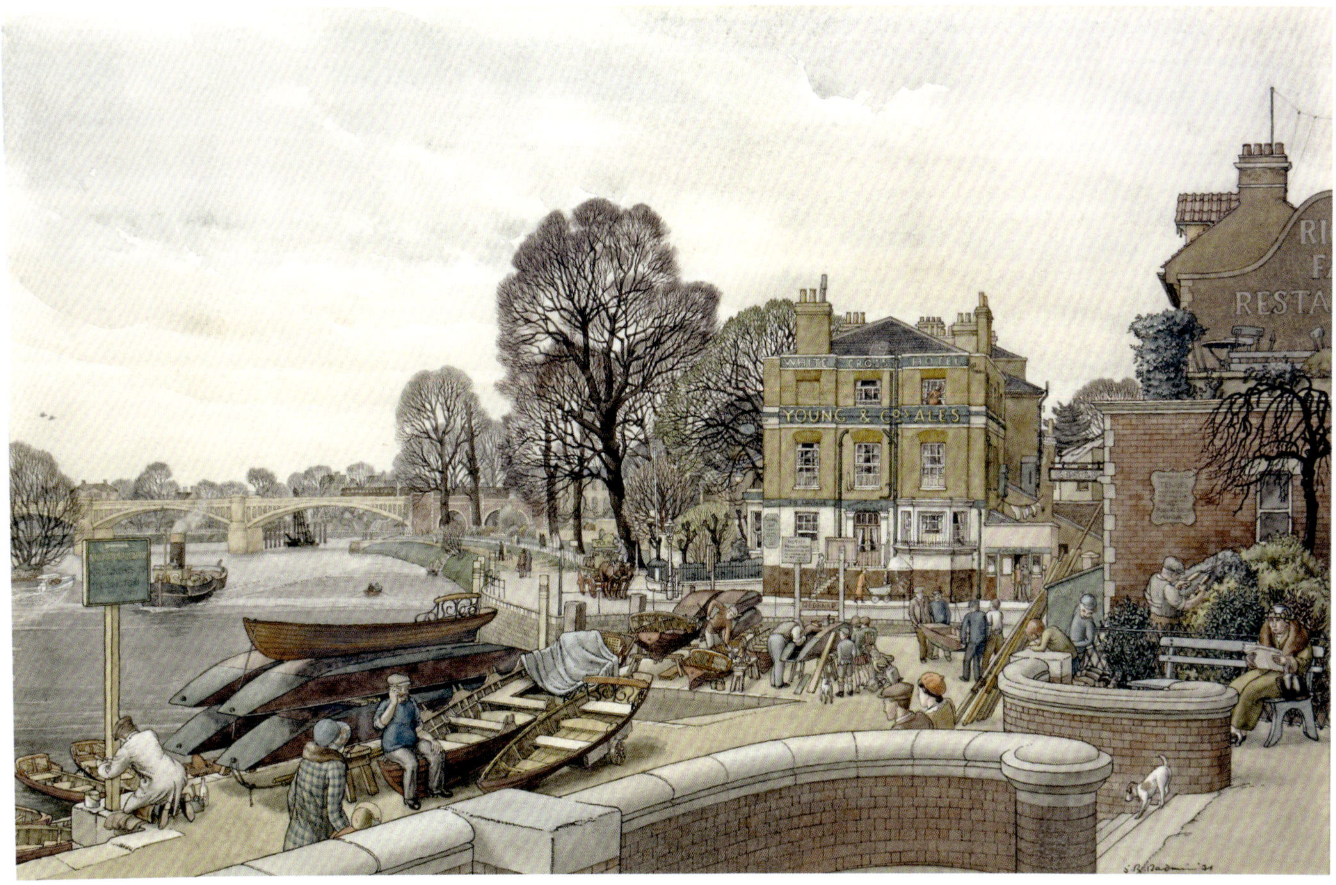

132 The Season Commences – Richmond
Signed and dated '31
Signed and inscribed with title and medium on original back label
Pen ink and watercolour
7 ½ x 11 ¾ inches
Provenance: Inns & Blake, London EC4
Exhibited: The Royal Society of Painters in Water-Colours, Summer 1932, No 48

1932

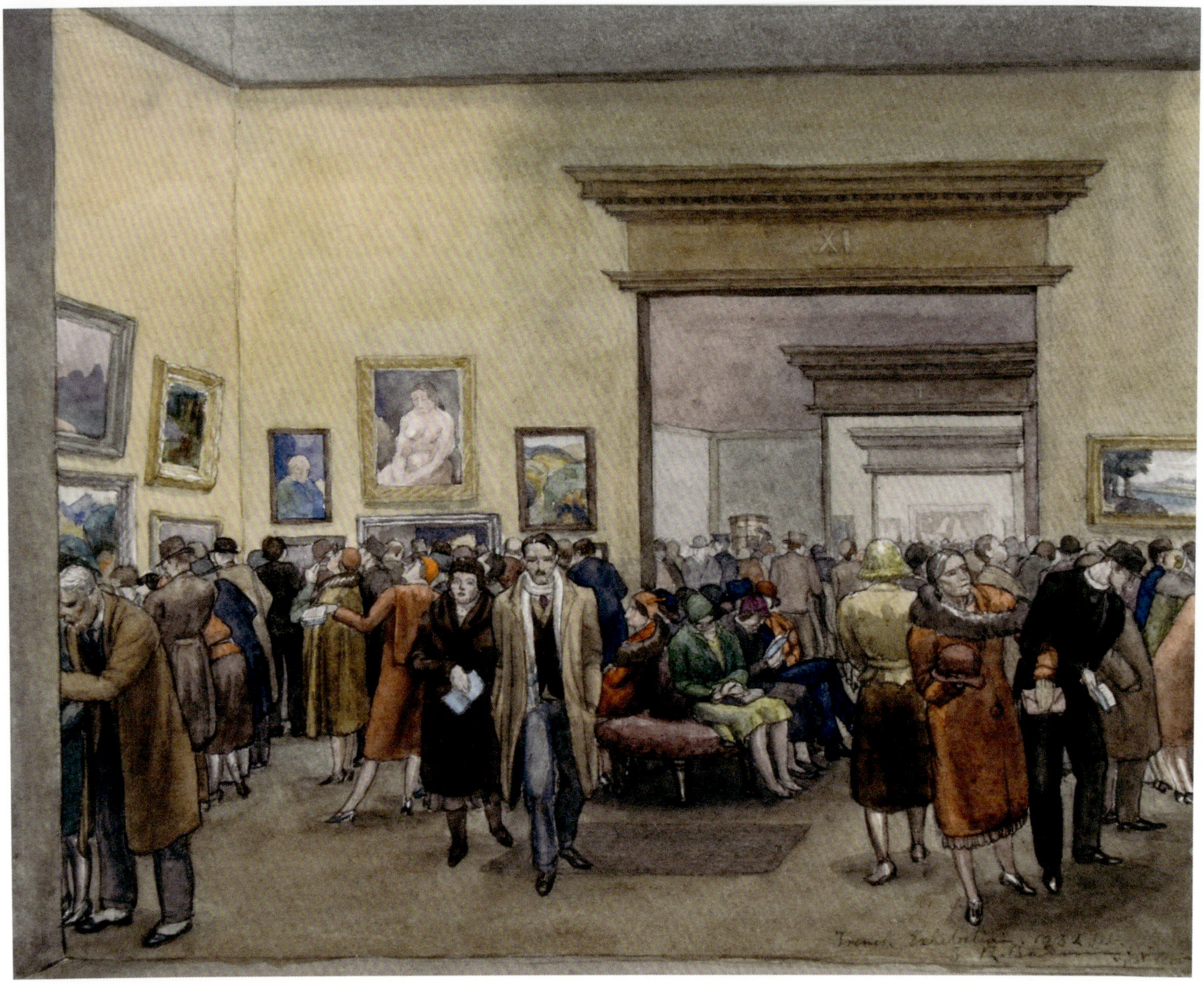

133 French Exhibition, 'First' Room
Signed, inscribed with title and dated '1932 Feb'
Watercolour with pen and ink
6 x 6 ¾ inches
Exhibited: 'S R Badmin RWS, Paintings, Drawings & Prints', Chris Beetles Gallery, March-April 2015, No 4

French Exhibition, 'First' Room

The exhibition of French Art 1200-1900 was held at the Royal Academy of Arts between January and March 1932. Though S R Badmin describes this as the 'first' room, it is actually gallery XI, containing nineteenth century paintings and especially those by Impressionists and Post-Impressionists. It is seen from the doorway to Gallery X, with the Vestibule and Galleries I and II beyond. In the same year, S R Badmin showed several of his own etchings in the Royal Academy Summer Exhibition.

7: LANDSCAPES IN BRITAIN

Following the end of the First World War, there was a revival of interest in the British countryside – its landscapes, its history and myths, and its customary ways of life – both generally and among artists. In reconsidering the countryside as a subject, many of those artists chose to return to the values of naturalistic painting and explore its native traditions. The reputations of such figures as Francis Towne and John Sell Cotman were revaluated, and they were placed alongside Thomas Gainsborough, J M W Turner and John Constable to create an enhanced canon of landscape art.

The use that Towne and Cotman had made of strong outlines and flat washes helped to inspire the absorption of a greater element of refined design into the naturalistic approaches of many artists. While Charles Knight has been described as the 'twentieth-century Cotman', this element of design can be seen equally well in such works as Averil Burleigh's *The Spring (Oxford)* [152] and S R Badmin's *Cliff Path, Richmond, Yorks* [158].

However, other, more contemporary factors may also have influenced the element of design in many of the landscapes produced between the wars. There was the residual survival of Modernist formalism (as exemplified by the work of Karl Hagedorn [134]). There was the strong interplay between the fine and decorative arts, as the Arts and Crafts morphed into Art Deco. And, not unrelated to this, there was the fact that many of the landscape painters also worked as graphic artists, and produced prints and illustrations.

S R Badmin is a supreme example of such a multi-disciplinary artist. This section alone includes examples of his work as a designer of posters (from a series published by the Eastern National Omnibus Company, 1932 [155]) and as an illustrator of guide books (*Highways and Byways in Essex*, 1939 [144-147]). These indicate his involvement in the spate of publication projects developed at this time to examine and promote rural England. Others included the Shell Guides and the particular Puffin Picture Books on which he worked (*Village and Town*, 1939; *Trees in Britain*, 1942; *Farm Crops in Britain*, 1955).

Within the emotional range of landscapes produced in Britain between the wars, those by Badmin tend to the intimate rather than the sublime, though he could certainly vary the mood when he felt the need. His preference for the inhabited landscape was shared by Randolph Schwabe, whose tinted drawings in the eighteenth-century mode are given scale and life by the inclusion of people going about their business; so a cleaner sweeps a church path in Cerne Abbas [135], and a groom leads a horse along the road in South Hinksey [153]. By contrast, William Thomas Wood [138] and Charles Knight [139] painted highly atmospheric, isolated woods, and Cecil Arthur Hunt scaled the heights with his depiction of the cliffs and mountains of Scotland [160-161].

The constant, lively reassessment of British topography that took place during the 1920s and 30s was given something of a summation at the start of the Second World War in the outline and contents of 'Recording Britain'. This scheme, funded by the Pilgrim Trust, commissioned artists to record the face of Britain at a time of rapid change as the result of urbanisation and developments in agriculture, and also the threat of bombing and other war damage. Many of the artists who took part are also represented here, including Charles Knight, whom William Russell Flint considered the scheme's 'star turn'.

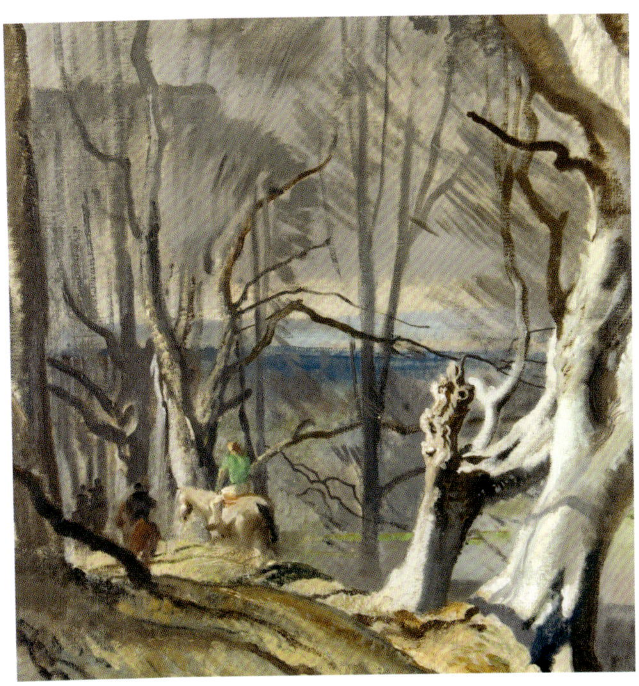

Detail of Charles Knight, *Winter Beeches Near Poynings* [139]

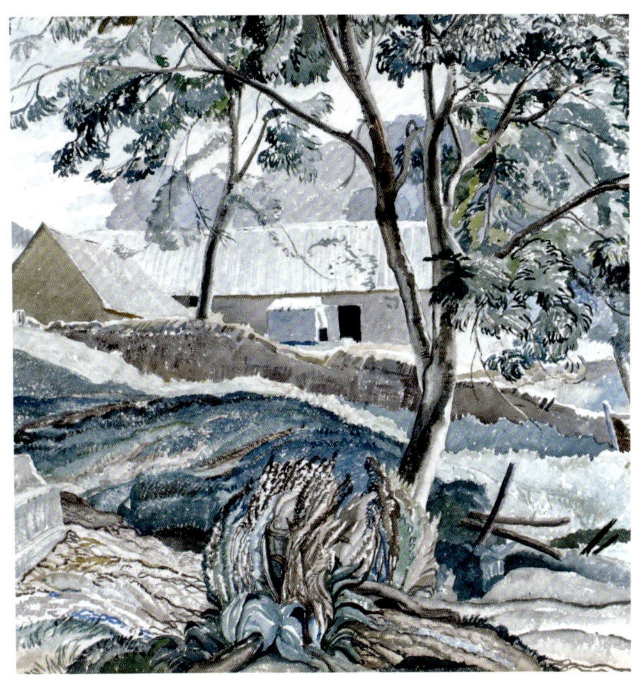

Detail of Averil Burleigh, *The Spring (Oxford)* [152]

KARL HAGEDORN

Karl Adolph Hagedorn,
RBA RI RSMA NEAC NS (1889-1969)

German-born Karl Hagedorn made a consciously pioneering attempt to introduce Modernism to Manchester in the early decades of the twentieth century, through his work as a painter and designer. Later, he tempered his style so that it fitted more easily into England's naturalistic watercolour tradition.

Hagedorn contributed watercolours of Middlesex and Derbyshire to Recording Britain.

For a biography of Karl Hagedorn, please refer to page 211.

CORNWALL

Polruan

In the summer of 1932, Karl Hagedorn, Randolph Schwabe and their wives holidayed on the south coast of Cornwall. The drawings that they made – including Hagedorn's *Polruan, Cornwall* and Schwabe's *Hall Farm and Hall Chapel, Bodinnick, Cornwall* – suggest that they stayed on or near the River Fowey, and probably on a farm at Pont. They may have been drawn to the area by the enthusiasm of fellow artist, Frances Hodgkins, who had stayed at The Rook, Bodinnick, for two periods of the winter and spring of 1931-32, and had written to Hagedorn of the 'sheer enjoyment' that she had experienced when spending days painting in the woods (Linda Gill (ed), *Letters of Frances Hodgkins*, Auckland University Press, 1993, page 464: 6 March 1932). Schwabe exhibited his drawings at a solo show at Barbizon House, London, in November 1932.

134 **Polruan, Cornwall**
Inscribed 'Polruan' and dated 1932 below mount
Inscribed with title and dated 1932 on reverse
Watercolour and pencil
12 ¾ x 19 ½ inches

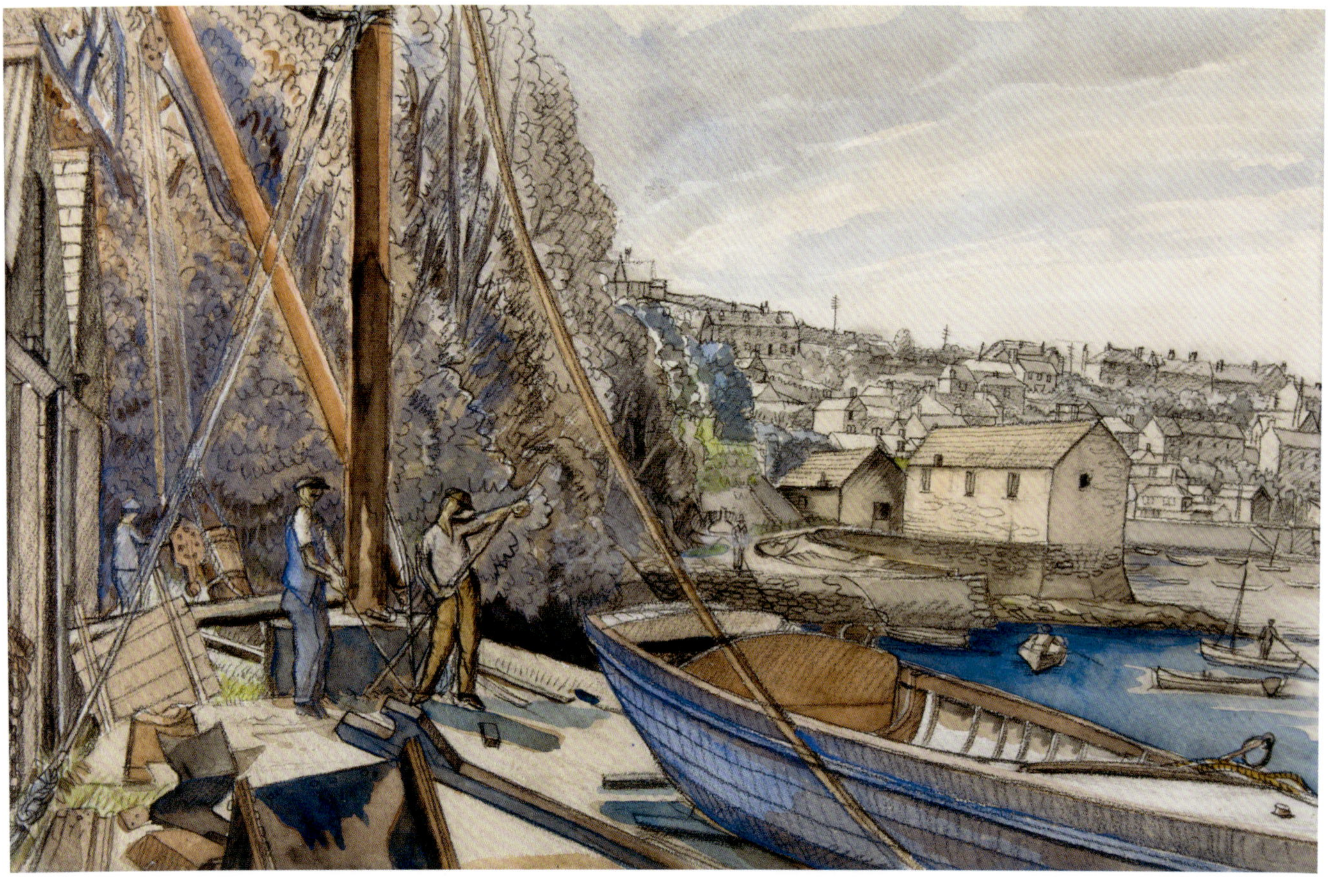

RANDOLPH SCHWABE

Randolph Schwabe, RWS LG NEAC (1885-1948)

A clear eye and sure hand enabled Randolph Schwabe to produce drawings, etchings and lithographs of consistent clarity and strength. Trained at the Slade School of Fine Art, he would return there to become an influential Principal and Professor. He also held a significant position as an official war artist in both world wars. Though he is best remembered for his attentive, absorbing images of buildings and landscapes, his subjects included figures and still life compositions, and he also produced illustrations and designs for the theatre.

For a biography of Randolph Schwabe, please refer to pages 212-213.

DORSET

Cerne Abbas

Randolph Schwabe spent a considerable part of the summer of 1937 drawing in Cerne Abbas, Dorset, which was one of his favourite places. He noted in his diary for Saturday 31 July:

> Left for Cerne Abbas …We stay at the Pitch Market, facing the Church door in Abbey Street. It is a half-timbered house, with a little 15th century carving left on it, and two 15th-century fireplaces. Mrs Jarrett runs it as a 'guest-house'.

The present drawing was made from the first floor of the Pitch Market, and shows the south side of the former abbey church of St Mary and the roofs of houses in Long Street.

135 Cerne Abbas
Signed, inscribed with title and dated 1937
Pencil and watercolour
11 x 15 ½ inches

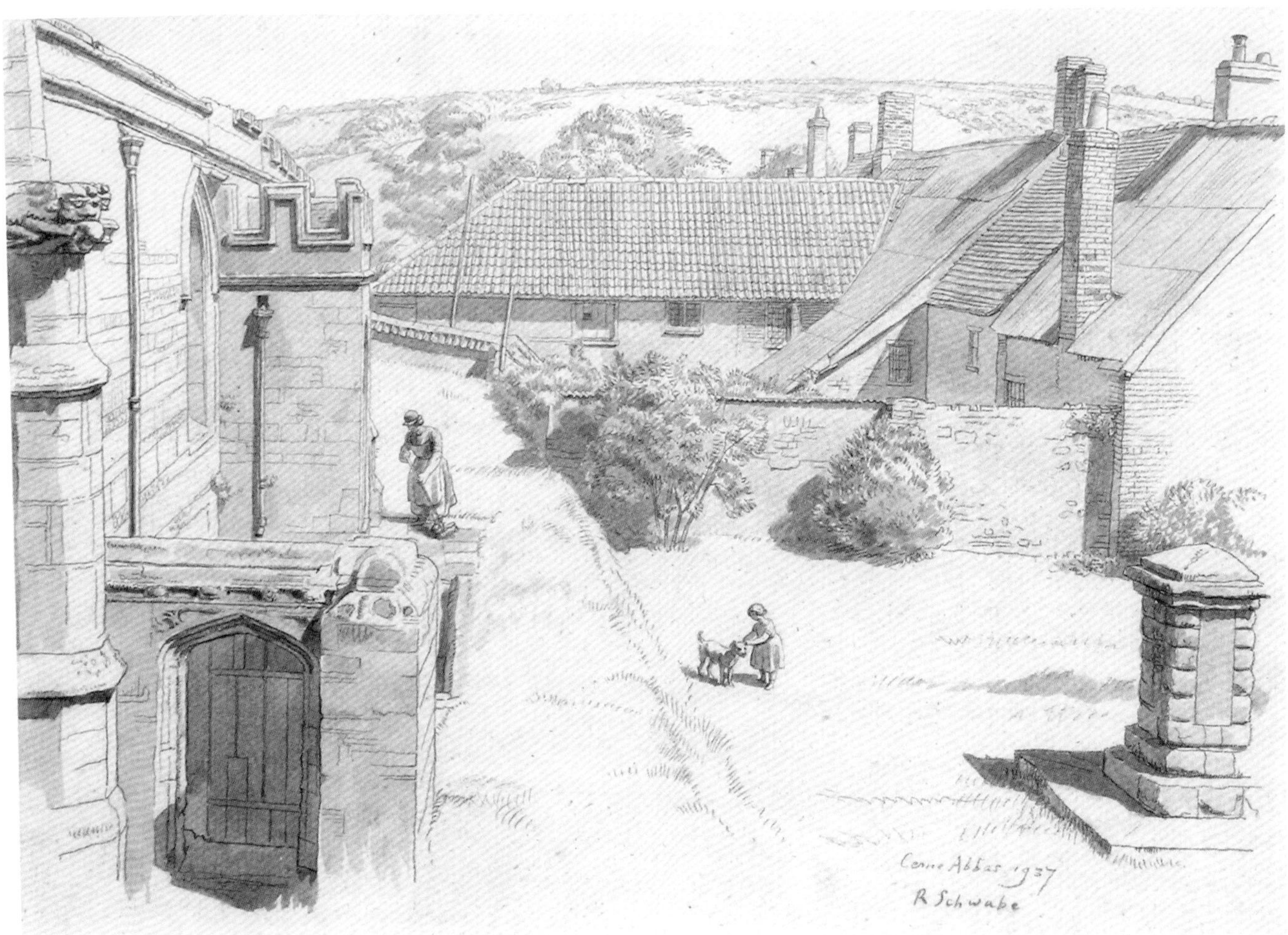

SAM HARTLEY BRAITHWAITE

Samuel Hartley Braithwaite (1883-1947)

The artist and musician, Sam Hartley Braithwaite, first established himself in London as a performer and teacher, and then gradually as a composer, mainly of short, evocative works for piano or orchestra. Following his move to Bournemouth at the end of the First World War, he developed a parallel career as a painter and printmaker, in which he produced landscape watercolours and etchings of clarity, economy and brilliance.

For a biography of Sam Hartley Braithwaite, please refer to page 216.

HAMPSHIRE

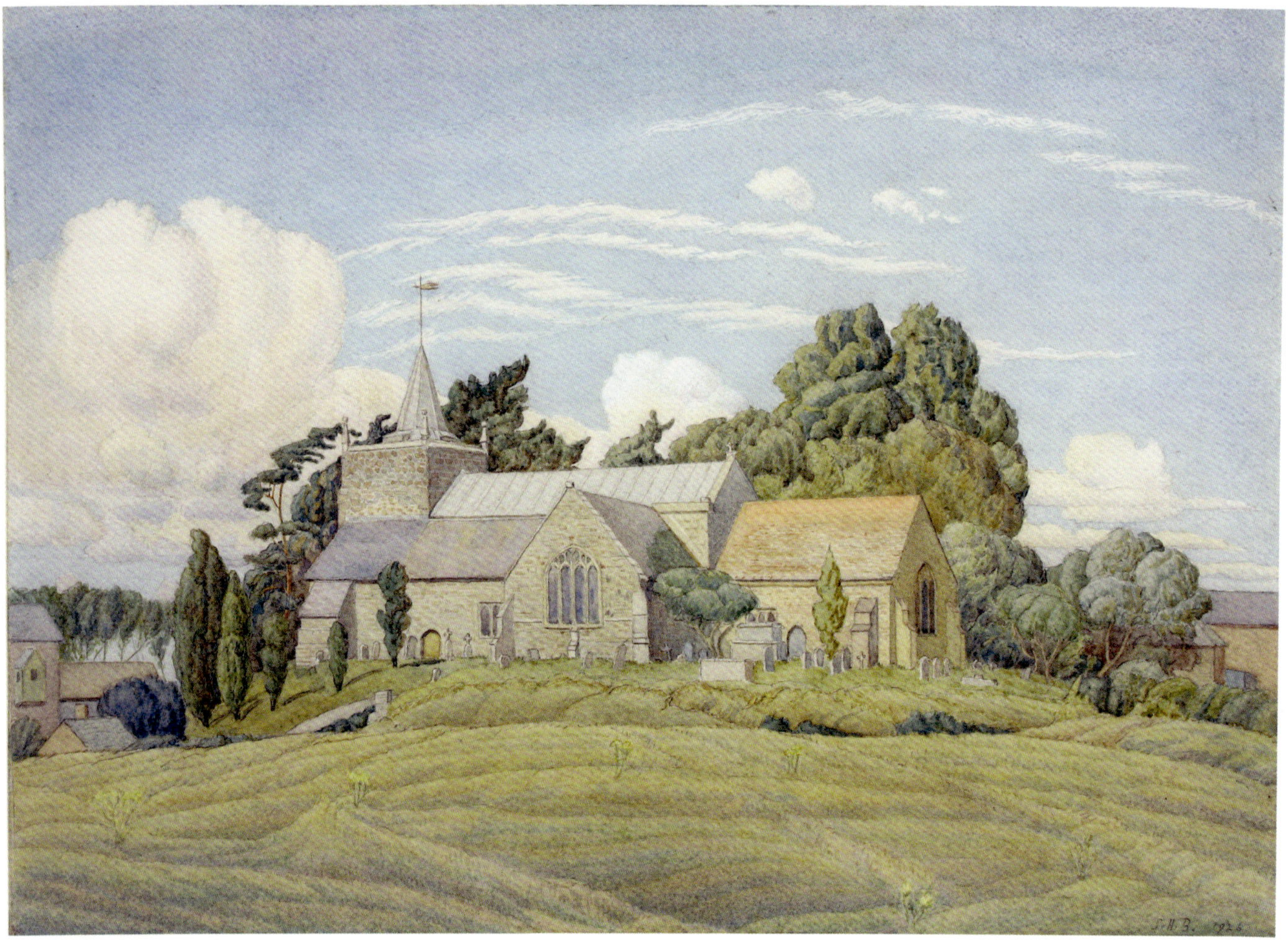

136 Sopley Church, Hampshire
Signed with initials and dated 1926
Watercolour with pencil
7 ¾ x 10 ½ inches
Exhibited: 'A Mirror of the Times'; 100 years of British Art. Bournemouth Arts Club 1920-2020', 8 May-21 October 2020

Sopley Church, Hampshire

The Mediaeval church of St Michael and All Angels, in the Hampshire village of Sopley, overlooks the River Avon (which is indicated by the mill on the far left of the present watercolour). The mound on which it stands may have been either the site of an earlier, pagan temple or the camp of Jute invaders.

RANDOLPH SCHWABE

Randolph Schwabe, RWS LG NEAC (1885-1948)

THE ISLE OF WIGHT

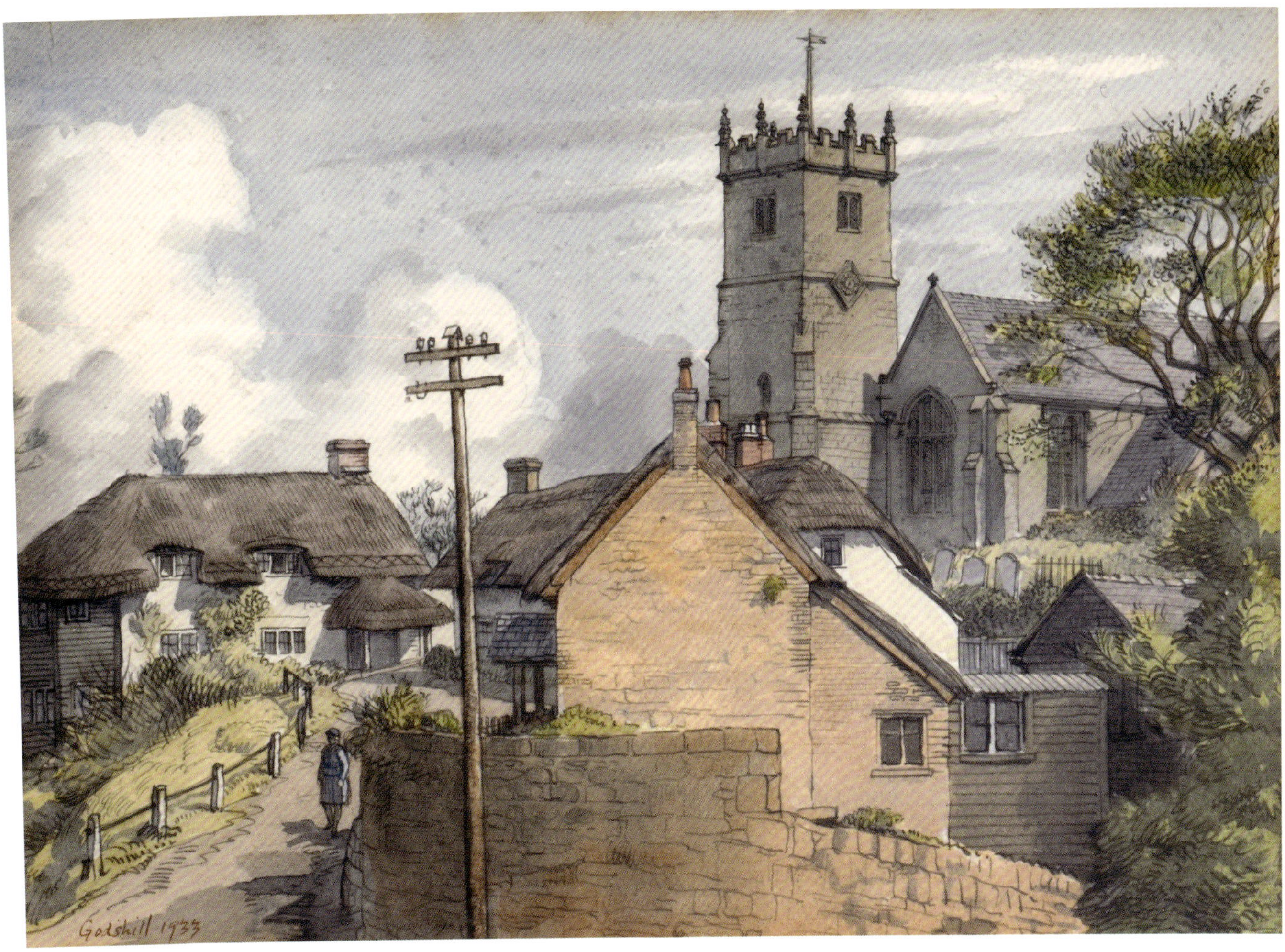

137 Godshill
Inscribed with title and dated 1933
Pen ink and watercolour
8 ¾ x 11 inches
Provenance: The Estate of Randolph Schwabe

Godshill

In April 1933, Randolph Schwabe spent a fortnight at the Royal Marine Hotel, Ventnor, on the Isle of Wight, in the company of Karl Hagedorn and his wife. During their stay, Schwabe made a number of watercolours, including the present one of the pretty inland village of Godshill, with the tower of the Mediaeval church of All Saints dominating a cluster of thatched cottages.

WILLIAM THOMAS WOOD

William Thomas Wood, VPRWS ROI NS (1877-1958)

A painter in both oil and watercolour, William Thomas Wood became particularly well known for atmospheric landscapes of Sussex, as well as flower still lifes. During the First World War, he served on the Balkan Front, both in the Royal Flying Corps and as an official war artist. He returned to images of aerial warfare in the Second World War, during which he served in the Home Guard.

For a biography of William Thomas Wood, please refer to page 214.

SUSSEX

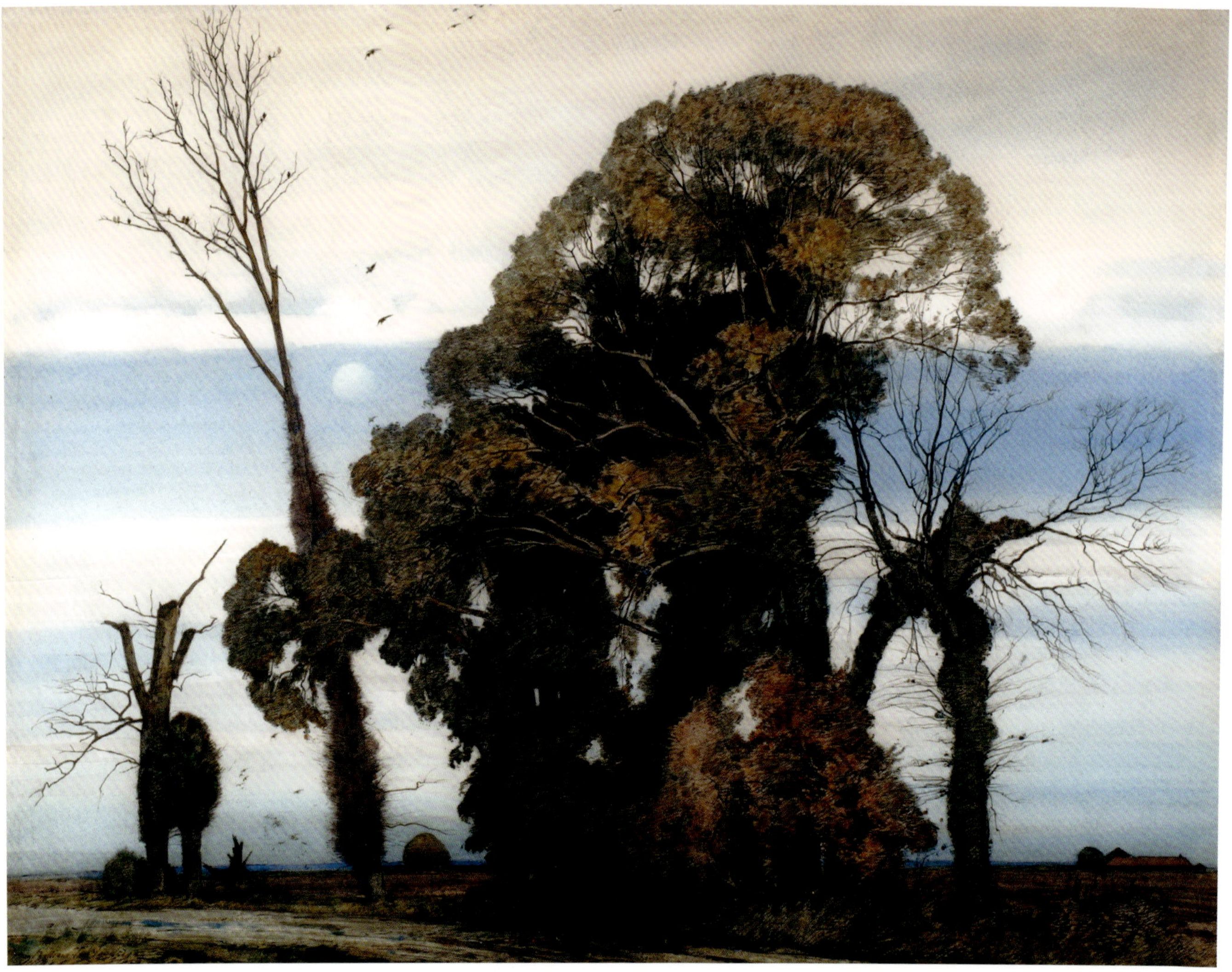

138 **Autumn Trees, Sussex**
Signed
Signed and inscribed with title on label on backboard
Pen ink and watercolour
21 ¼ x 27 inches
Literature: *The Old Water-Colour Society's Club*, Vol IV, 1926-27, Plate xxxiii;
Adrian Bury, *Water-Colour Painting of To-Day*, London: The Studio, 1937, No 118
Exhibited: Royal Society of Painters in Water-Colours, Summer 1926, No 76

CHARLES KNIGHT

Charles Knight, VPRWS ROI (1901-1990)

The Sussex landscape painter, Charles Knight, channelled the tradition of English watercolour painting in order to produce his own original contribution. As a result, he became a pillar of the Royal Society of Painters in Water-Colours and received acclaim, from William Russell Flint, as the 'star turn' of Recording Britain. He contributed 40 watercolours of Sussex to the scheme.

For a biography of Charles Knight, please refer to page 210.

SUSSEX

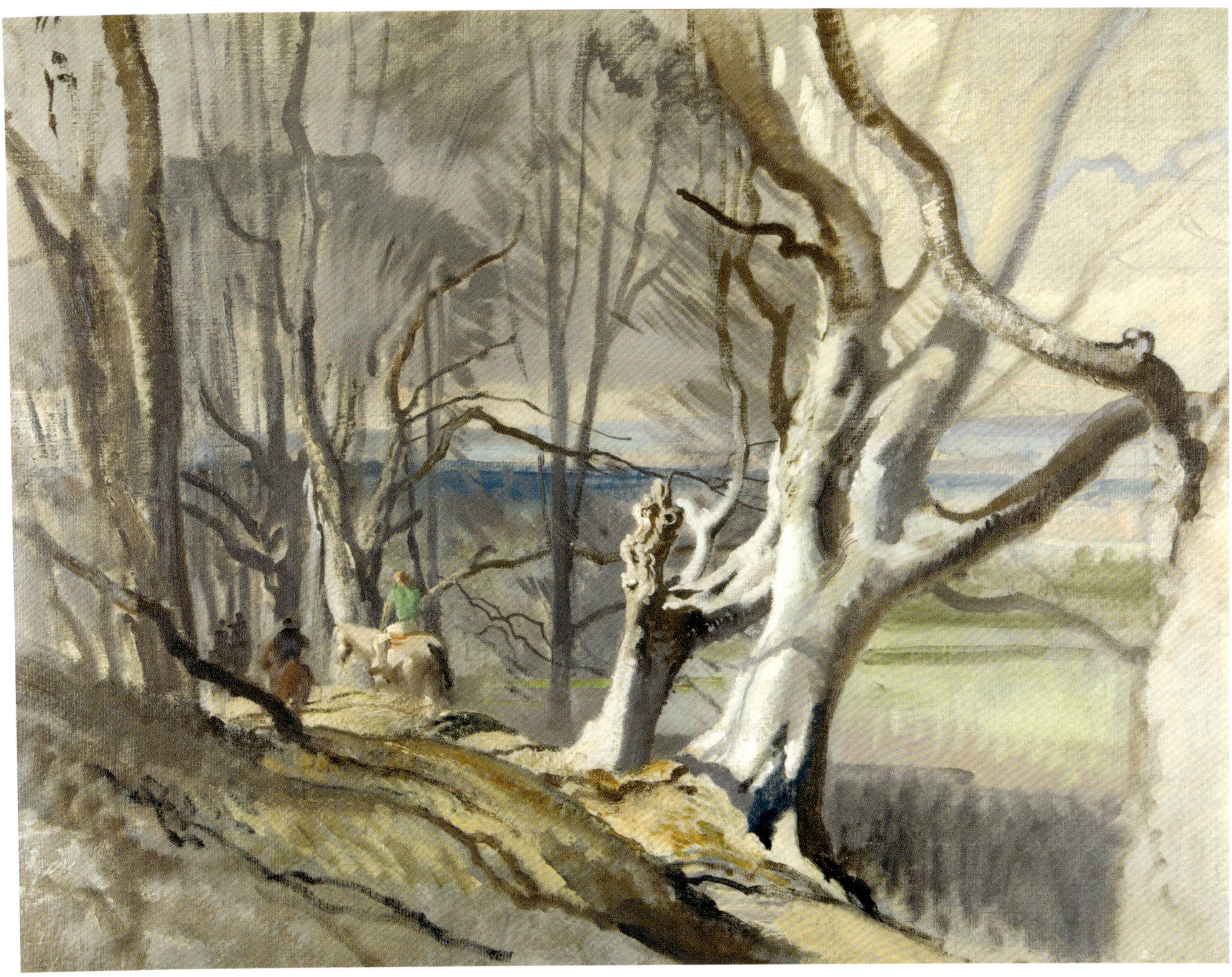

139 **Winter Beeches Near Poynings**
Oil on canvas
23 x 29 ½ inches
Provenance: The Artist's Studio
Literature: Michael Brockway, *Charles Knight RWS ROI*, Leigh-on-Sea: F Lewis, 1952, Plate 26
Exhibited: '... More Than a Touch of Poetry. Landscapes by Charles Knight RWS ROI 1901-1990', No 83: Towner Art Gallery, Eastbourne, March-May 1997, Chris Beetles Ltd, June 1997, Hove Museum and Art Gallery, July-August 1997

ROWLAND HILDER

Rowland Frederick Hilder, OBE PRI RSMA (1905-1993)

A highly fluent watercolourist, Rowland Hilder became synonymous with the Kent countryside that he painted for much of his life. However, he was a wide-ranging painter and illustrator, who tackled cityscapes, marines and figure subjects with equal confidence and success.

Hilder contributed watercolours and drawings of Sussex to Recording Britain.

For a biography of Rowland Hilder, please refer to page 217.

KENT

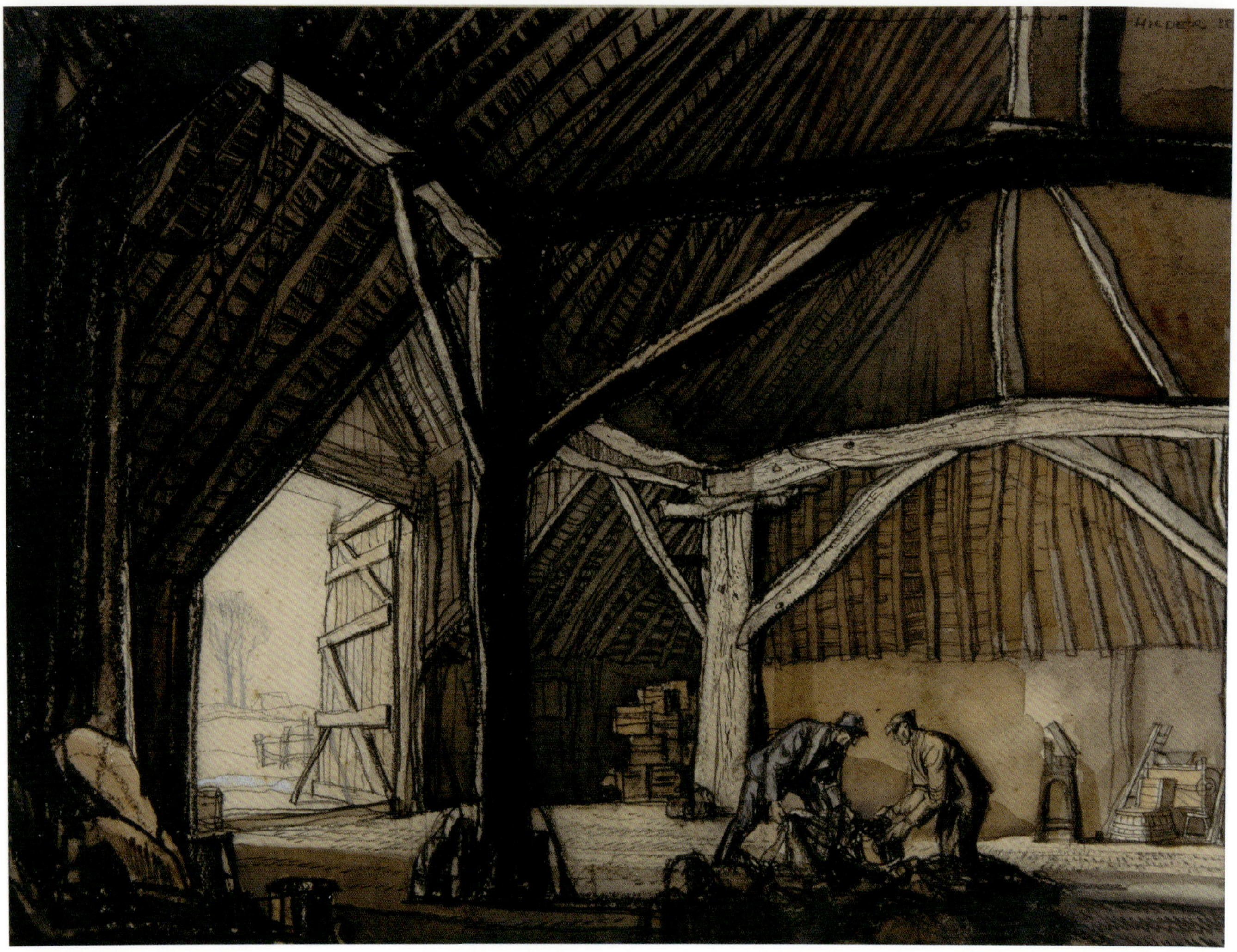

140 The Barn in Winter
Signed and dated 38
Chalk, ink and watercolour with bodycolour
12 x 15 ¾ inches
Exhibited: Fine Art Society, London, March 1945

RANDOLPH SCHWABE

Randolph Schwabe, RWS LG NEAC (1885-1948)

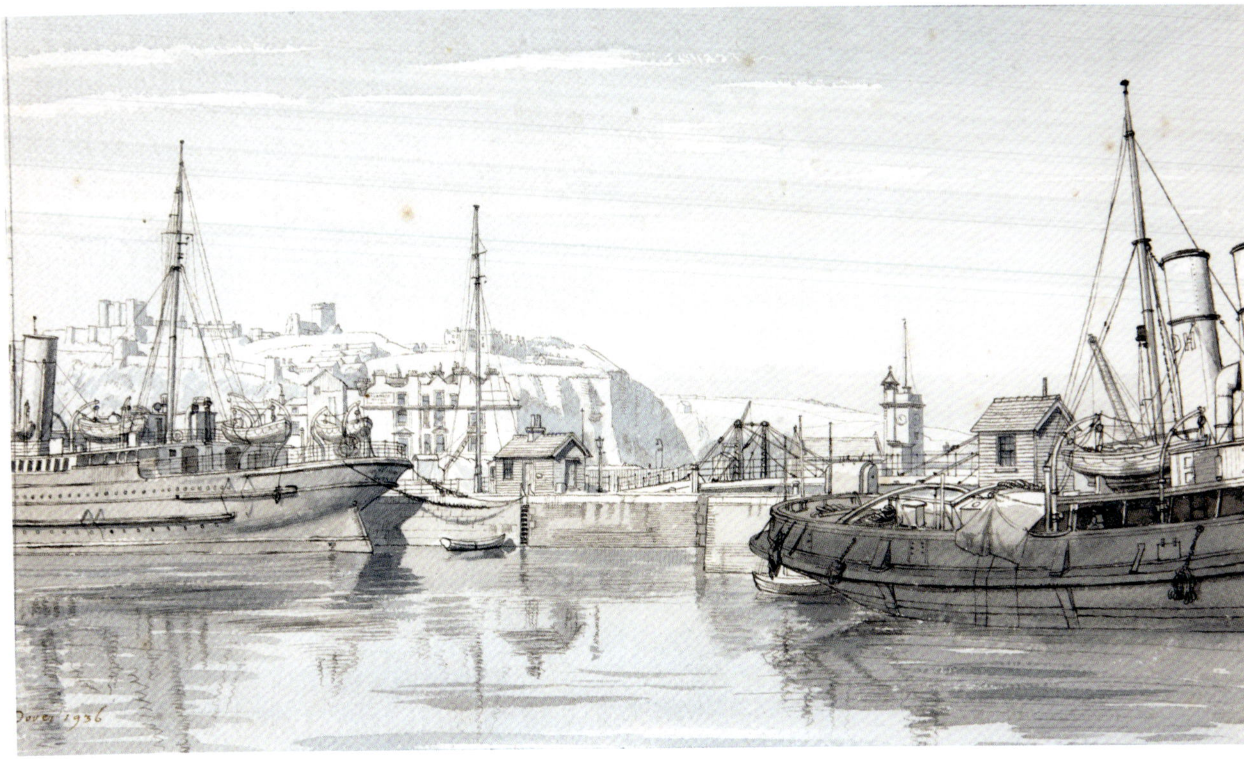

141 **Dover Harbour, with the Castle Beyond** (above)
Inscribed 'Dover' and dated 1936
Pen ink and watercolour; 8 ½ x 13 ¼ inches
Provenance: The Estate of Randolph Schwabe

142 **Wellington Basin, Dover** (below)
Signed and dated 1928
Pen ink, watercolour and pencil; 14 x 18 ½ inches
Provenance: The Estate of Randolph Schwabe

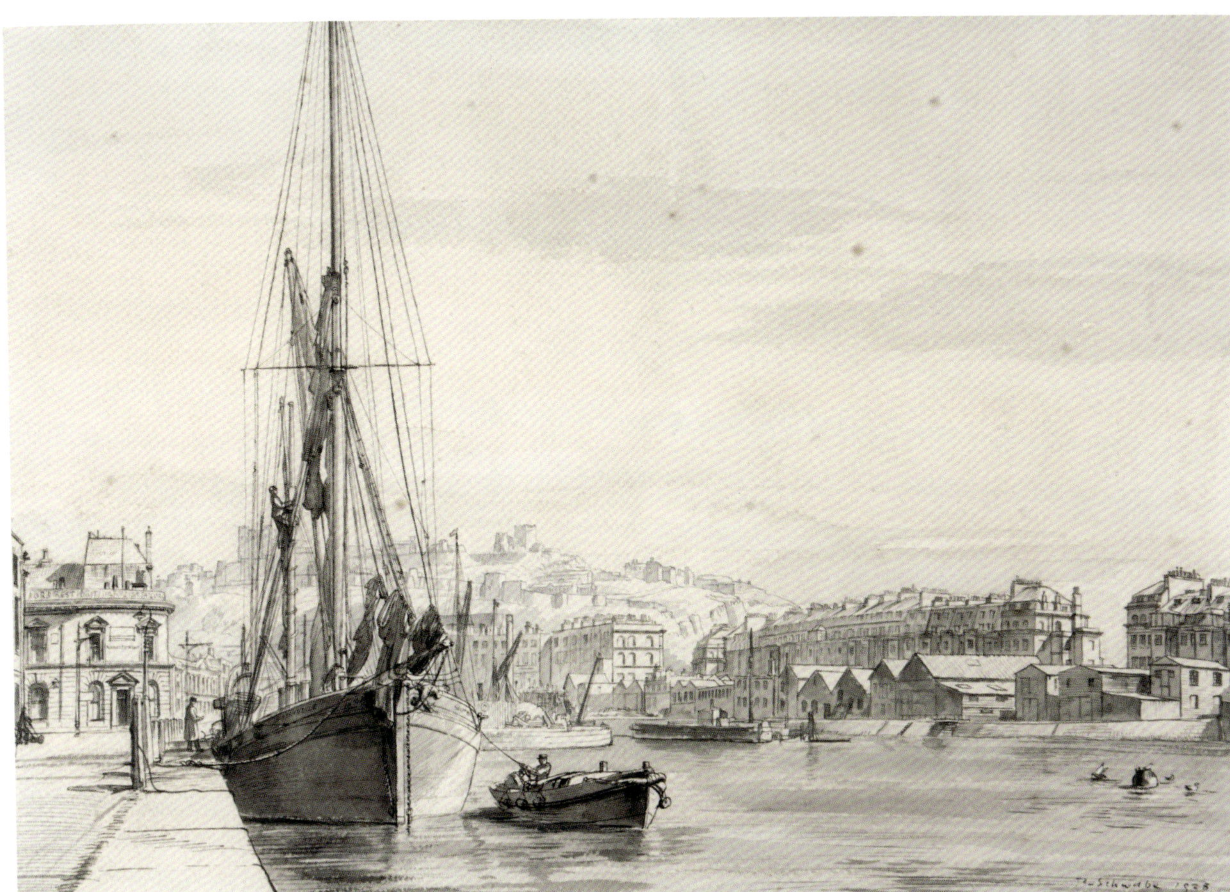

S R BADMIN

Stanley Roy Badmin, RWS RE AIA FSIA (1906-1989)

Throughout his career, S R Badmin used his great talents – as etcher, illustrator and watercolourist – to promote a vision of the English countryside and thus of England itself. By underpinning his idealism with almost documentary precision and detail, he was able to produce images that appealed to all, and could be used for a great variety of purposes, from education through to advertising. The wellbeing suggested by each rural panorama is all the more potent, and pleasing, for the accuracy of each tree and leaf, and the plausibility of the slightest anecdotal episode.

Badmin contributed watercolours and drawings of Buckinghamshire, Hertfordshire, Kent, London, Northamptonshire and Suffolk to Recording Britain.

For a biography of S R Badmin, please refer to pages 208-209.

ESSEX

'In 1927 Badmin received his fee from Macmillan for his illustrations for Highways and Byways in Essex … Started by F L Griggs, this was the last of a prestigious series of nineteen Highways and Byways *begun by Griggs for Macmillan in 1900. Due to his illness and death, the Essex volume was finished by Badmin.*

The commission was a welcome one and the task enjoyable: Badmin had just paid £9 to buy his father's car … and in this he travelled about Essex doing his sketching.

He already knew some parts of Essex from the previous year when he had occasionally gone to stay in the Assington area, north-west of Colchester, with fellow-artist Percy Horton at his country cottage …

Badmin's peopled drawings give life to village green and country seats alike … This early example of purely illustrative work establishes that unaffected and inviting quality that marked Badmin's later topographical and travel books.'

(Chris Beetles, *S R Badmin and the English Landscape*, 1985, pages 21 & 48)

143 Epping Forest
Signed, inscribed with title and dated 1940
Pen and ink
5 ½ x 9 ½ inches
Exhibited: 'S R Badmin RWS, Paintings, Drawings & Prints', Chris Beetles Gallery, March-April 2015, No 17

'And so we come to Epping Forest, where there is record of romance and peril. Even now it is easy enough to lose your way among those old, mute trees; and if a fog is rising, you will be lucky if you can find a main road. The great forest was, for centuries, royal property, and that, they say, is why for so long a time the road to London from Newmarket was so indirect.'

(Clifford Bax, *Highways and Byways in Essex*, London: Macmillan and Co, 1939, Page 146)

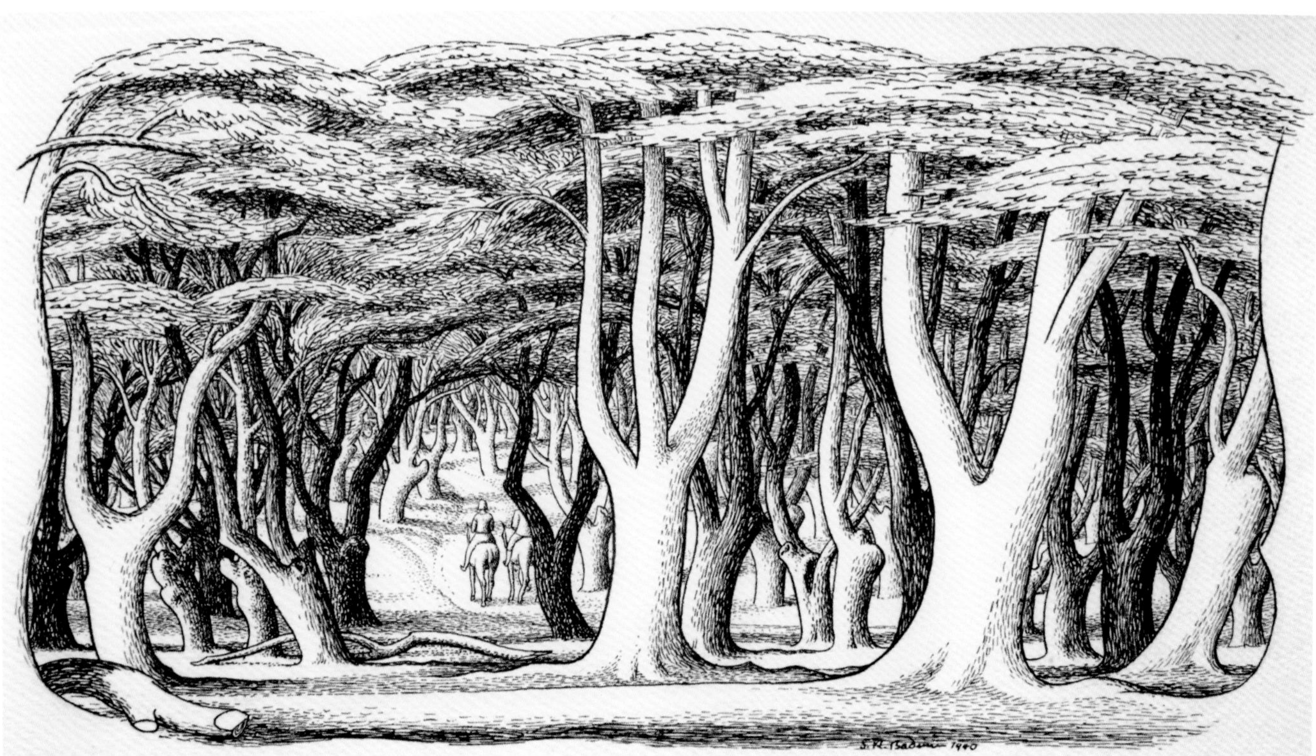

144 Steeple Bumpstead (right)
Signed and inscribed with title and 'Near Chelmsford'
Pen and ink
6 x 4 ¾ inches
Illustrated: Clifford Bax, *Highways and Byways in Essex*, London: Macmillan and Co, 1939, Page 117
Exhibited: 'S R Badmin RWS, Paintings, Drawings & Prints', Chris Beetles Gallery, March-April 2015, No 99

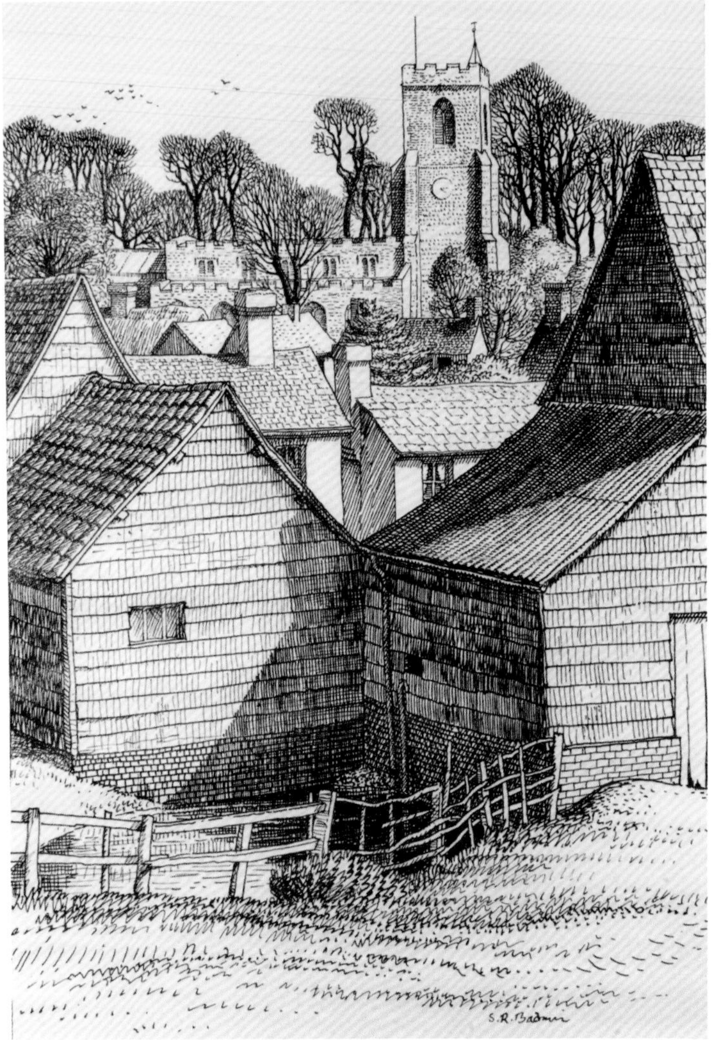

145 Audley End (below)
Signed and inscribed with title and 'Saffron Walden'
Pen and ink with coloured crayon
5 ¼ x 8 ¼ inches
Illustrated: Clifford Bax, *Highways and Byways in Essex*, London: Macmillan and Co, 1939, Page 120
Exhibited: 'S R Badmin RWS, Paintings, Drawings & Prints', Chris Beetles Gallery, March-April 2015, No 100

'At one point of the road from Newport to Cambridge there is a gap in the high hedges, and many a passenger in a motor-car must have exclaimed "Oh, look, look!" and many a walker must really have looked: for through this gap, across two broad meadows which are divided by a stretch of the River Cam, we may gaze upon the proud Italianate splendour of Audley End.'

(Clifford Bax, *Highways and Byways in Essex*, London: Macmillan and Co, 1939, Page 119)

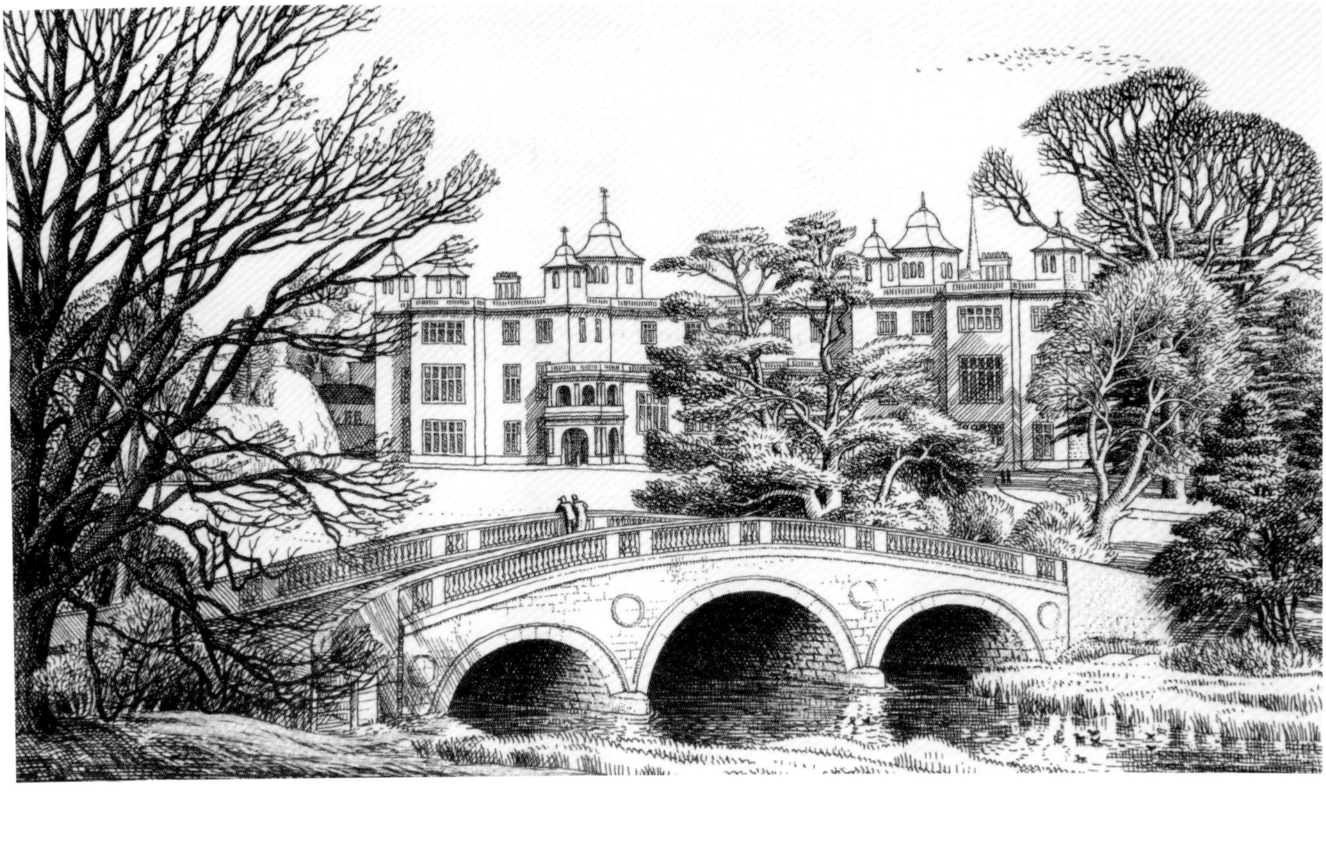

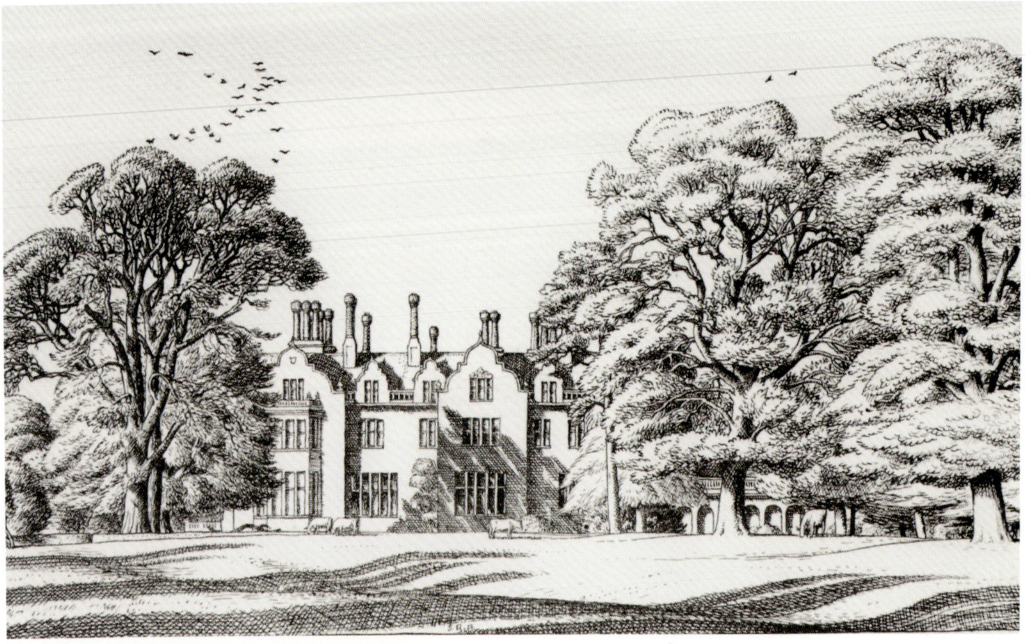

ESSEX

146 Stansted Hall
Signed with initials and inscribed 'Stansted Hall, Essex'
Pen and ink
4 ½ x 7 inches
Illustrated: Clifford Bax, *Highways and Byways in Essex*, London: Macmillan and Co, 1939, Page 72
Exhibited: 'S R Badmin RWS, Paintings, Drawings & Prints', Chris Beetles Gallery, March-April 2015, No 94

'Stansted is now a place of little honour to English builders ; nor does it seem likely that many travellers will want to examine the earthworks which are all that remains of the castle built by the Norman family of Montfitchet: but so late as 1870 Stansted possessed a remarkable monument of the past. This was a pre-Reformation "wayside chapel", probably built by John de Vere, twelfth Earl of Oxford, in the middle of the fifteenth century. A photograph, taken when the chapel was being demolished shows that it must have been a beautiful building, richly beamed … Stansted Hall, a noble pile, does what it can to rebuke the vandals of sixty years ago.'

(Clifford Bax, *Highways and Byways in Essex*, London: Macmillan and Co, 1939, Page 71)

147 Henham, Essex
Inscribed with title and 'copyright with Macmillans' on reverse of original backboard
Pen and ink
5 x 8 inches
Illustrated: Clifford Bax, *Highways and Byways in Essex*, London: Macmillan and Co, 1939, Page 75
Exhibited: The Fine Art Society, London, January 1940, No 1

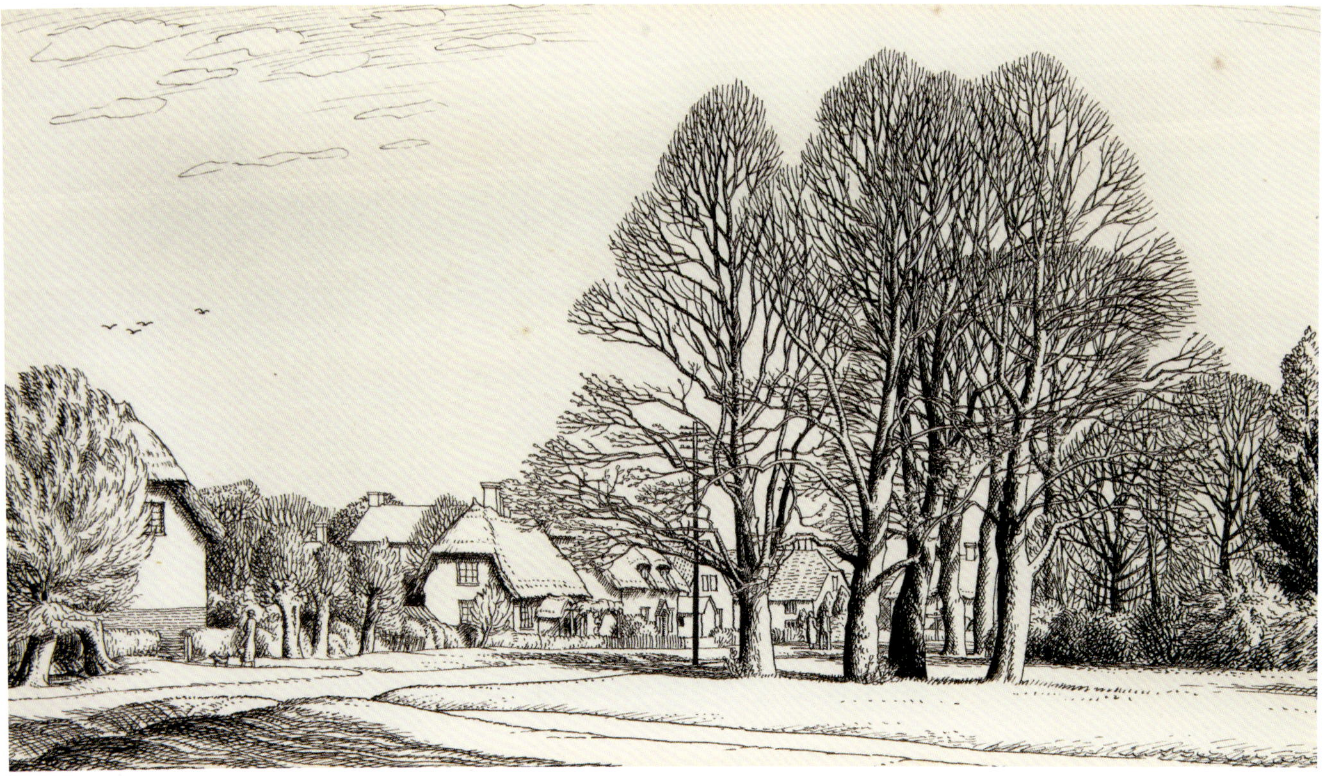

ALFRED HAYWARD

Alfred Robert Hayward, ARWS RP IS NEAC (1875-1971)

Alfred Hayward was a painter of landscapes, portraits and figure subjects in oil and watercolour, and also a mural decorator. His landscapes, in particular, show a strong influence of Impressionism, and his loose application of watercolour was especially suited to his studies of such aquatic subjects as the River Thames and the city of Venice, which he worked in on several occasions. Indeed, he had a great love of Italy and of travel in general and, in the years before the First World War, went as far afield as the West Indies and Central America.

Hayward contributed watercolours and drawings of Sussex to Recording Britain.

For a biography of Alfred Hayward, please refer to page 218.

LONDON AND THE THAMES VALLEY

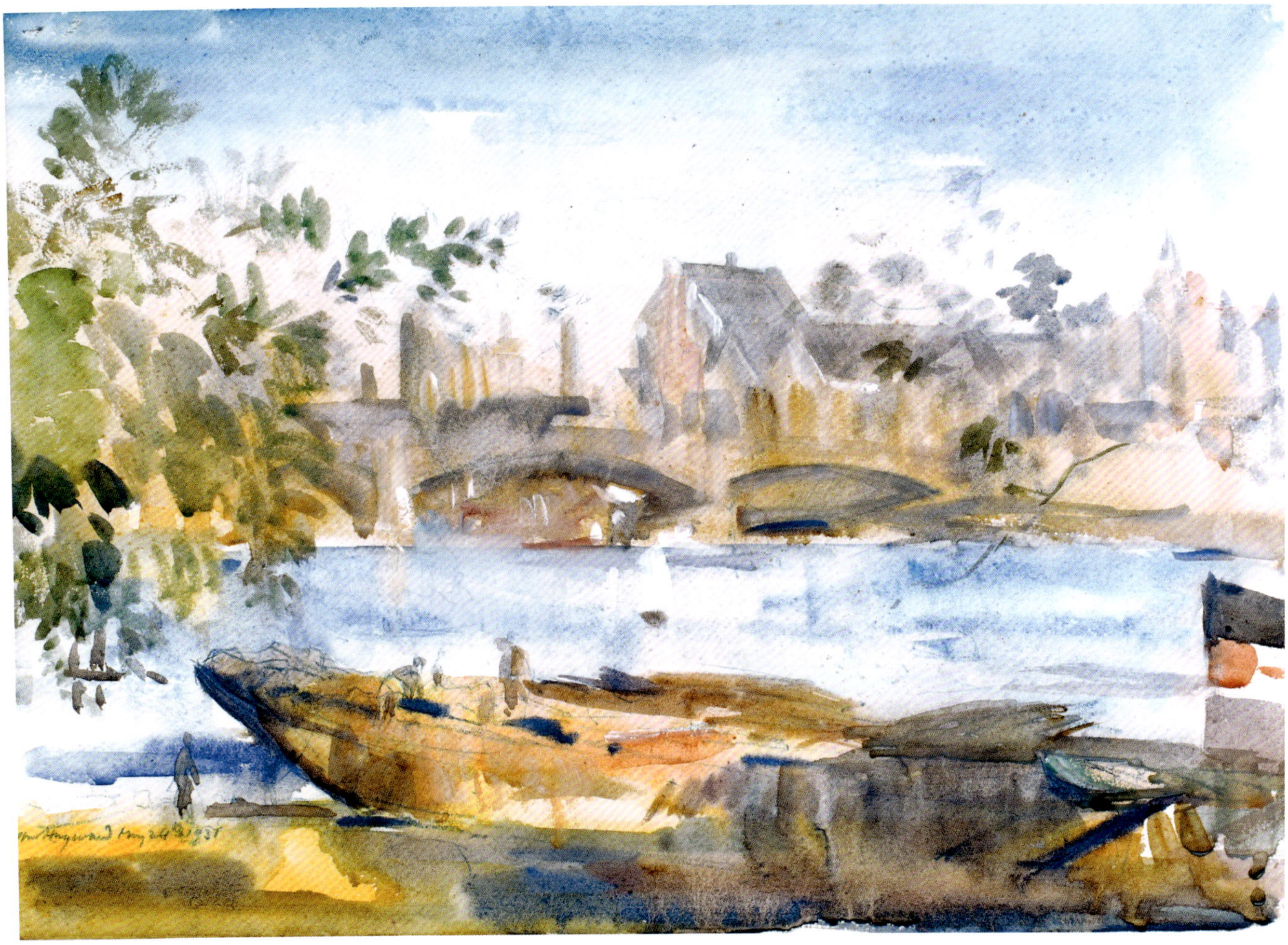

148 Battersea Reach from Cheyne Walk
Signed and dated 'May 24th 1931'
Inscribed with title below mount
Watercolour with bodycolour
10 x 13 ¾ inches

RANDOLPH SCHWABE

Randolph Schwabe, RWS LG NEAC (1885-1948)

LONDON AND THE THAMES VALLEY

'Went to Sunbury with H [Hagedorn] and drew there with him, on the eyot, looking towards the church, which has been so barbarously added to in Victorian days ...'

(Randolph Schwabe's Diary, Monday 8 April 1946)

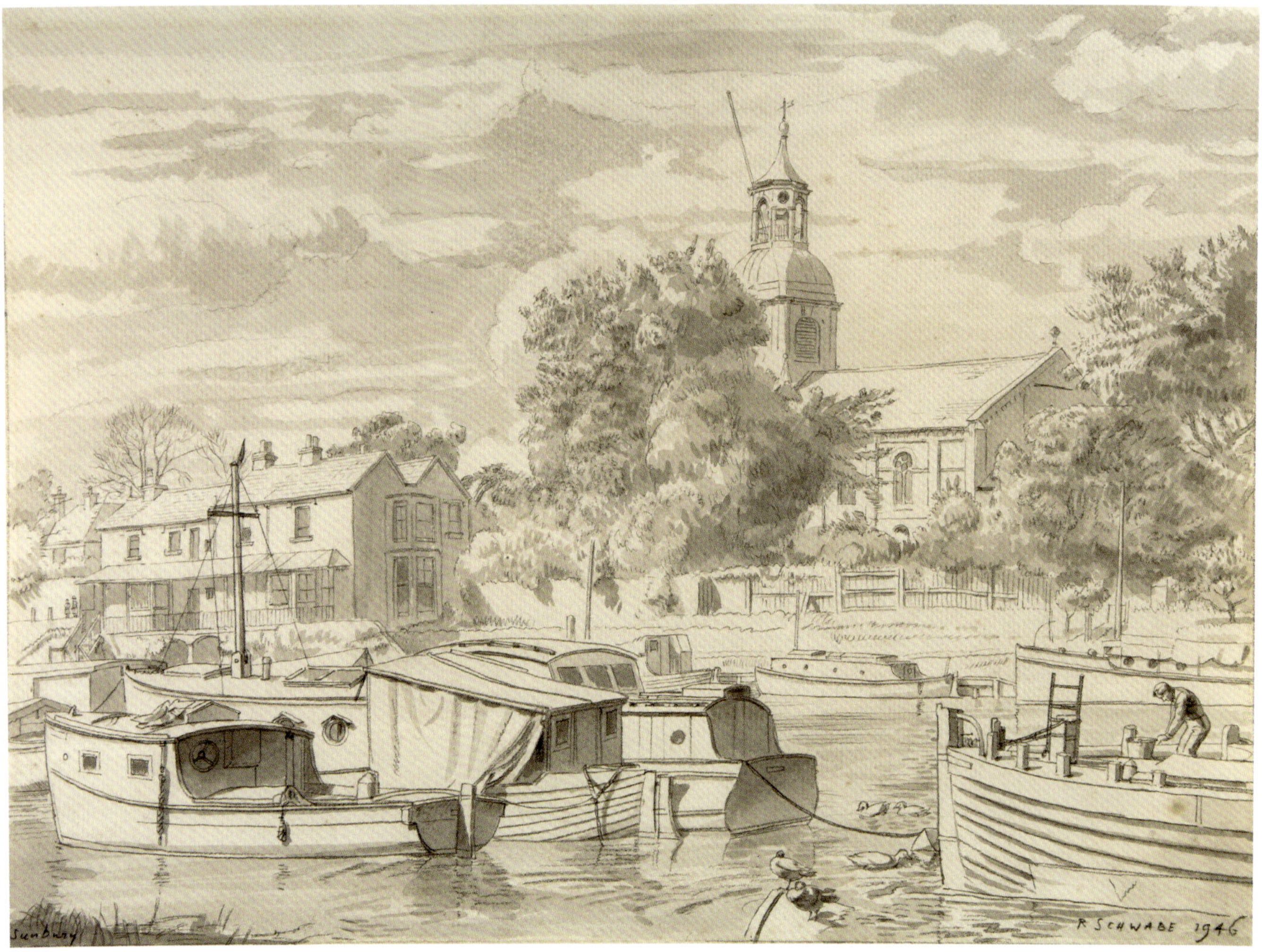

149 St Mary's Church, Sunbury-on-Thames
Signed, inscribed 'Sunbury' and dated 1946
Watercolour, pencil and chalk
9 ¾ x 13 inches
Provenance: The Estate of Randolph Schwabe

NORMAN JANES

Norman Thomas Janes, RWS RE RSMA (1892-1980)

Norman Janes was a wide-ranging painter and printmaker, who had a particular affinity with the London scene, from the busyness of railway stations and Thames embankments to the tranquil spots around his Hampstead home.

Janes contributed watercolours and drawings of London to Recording Britain.

For a biography of Norman Janes, please refer to page 219.

'Mr Janes has not far to go for subjects for he lives near Hampstead Heath, one of the last remaining woodlands in Greater London. The Vale of Health, which he has painted, has memories of Leigh Hunt, Keats, Coleridge and Shelley, who sometimes congregated there.'

(Adrian Bury, *Oil Painting To-Day*, London: The Studio, 1938, page 32)

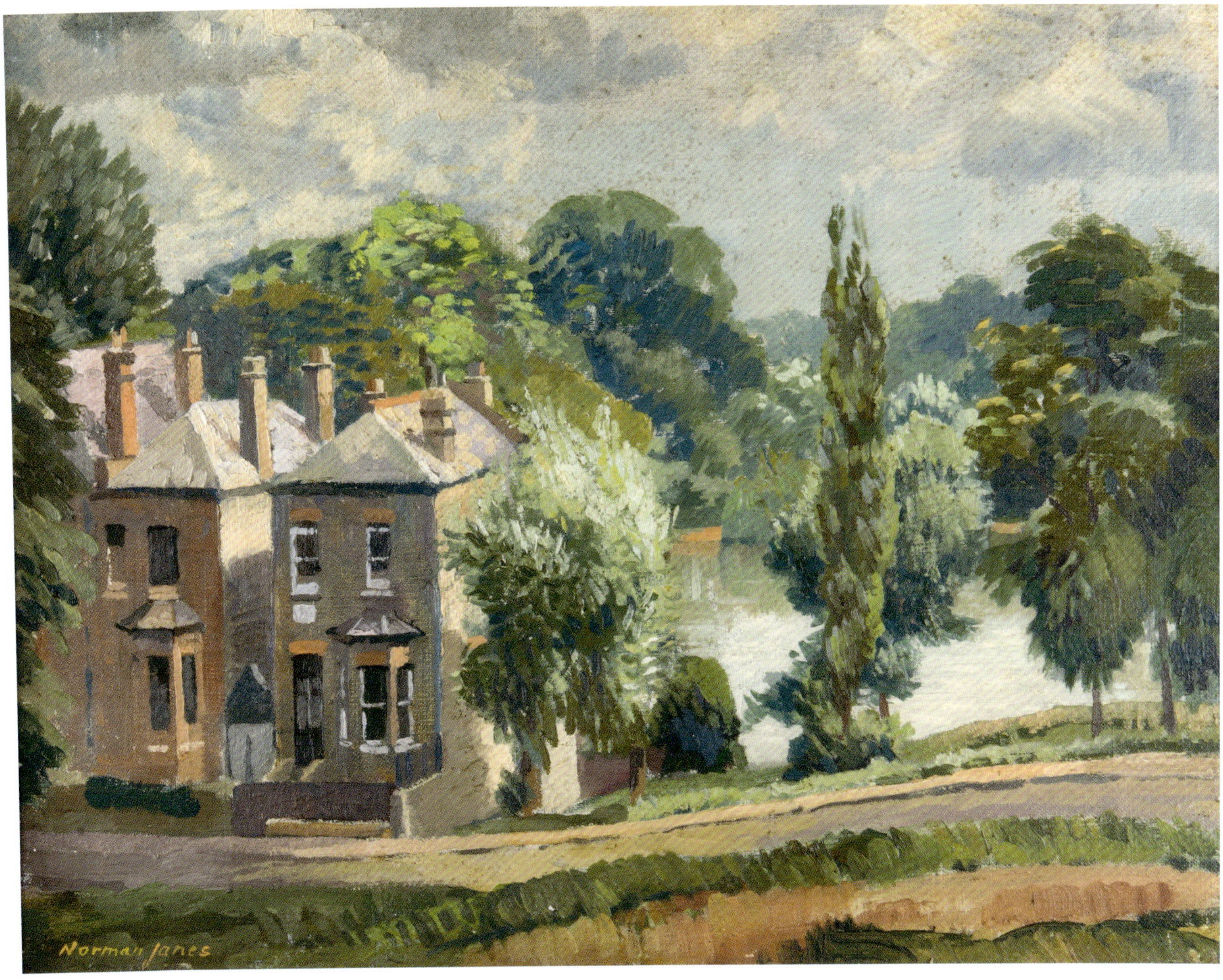

150 **The Vale Pond, Hampstead**
Signed
Oil on canvas
15 ½ x 19 ½ inches

STANLEY ANDERSON

Alfred Charles Stanley Anderson, RA RE (1884-1966)

The printmaker and painter, Stanley Anderson, was a major figure in the revival of line engraving between the wars. Though a long career allowed for a diverse range of subjects, his skill was displayed particularly well in a series of prints of farm workers and rural craftsmen.

Anderson contributed watercolours of market towns in Buckinghamshire and Oxfordshire to Recording Britain.

For a biography of Stanley Anderson, please refer to page 202.

OXFORDSHIRE

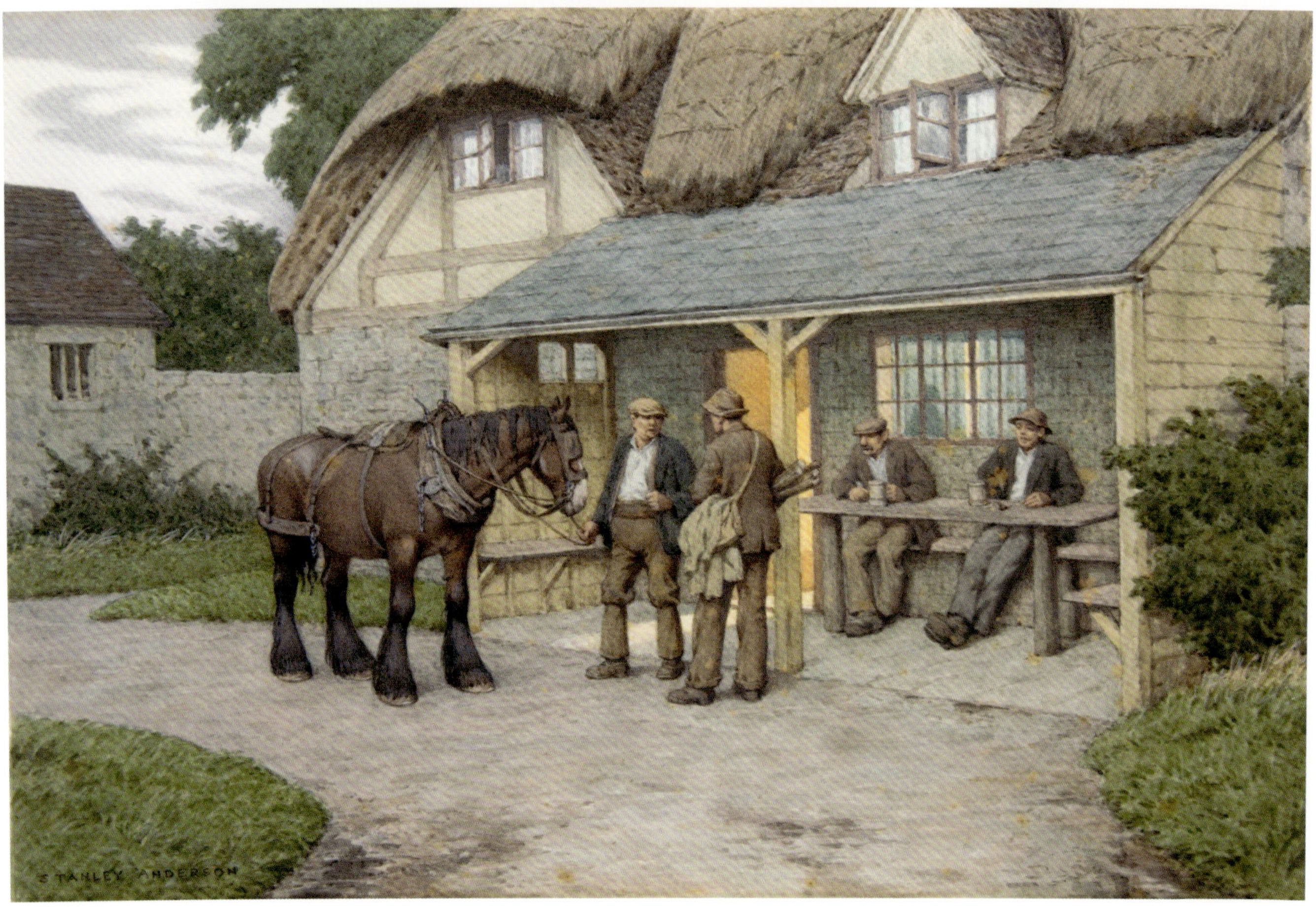

151 Homeward Bound
Signed
Inscribed with title below mount
Watercolour
8 x 11 ½ inches

AVERIL BURLEIGH

Averil Mary Burleigh (née Dell),
ARWS RI SWA (1882-1949)

The versatile art of the painter and illustrator, Averil Burleigh, is distinguished by its strong sense of design. Initially influenced by the Pre-Raphaelites and drawn to Mediaeval subject matter, she became increasingly known for her luminous temperas and watercolours.

For a biography of Averil Burleigh, please refer to page 217.

OXFORDSHIRE

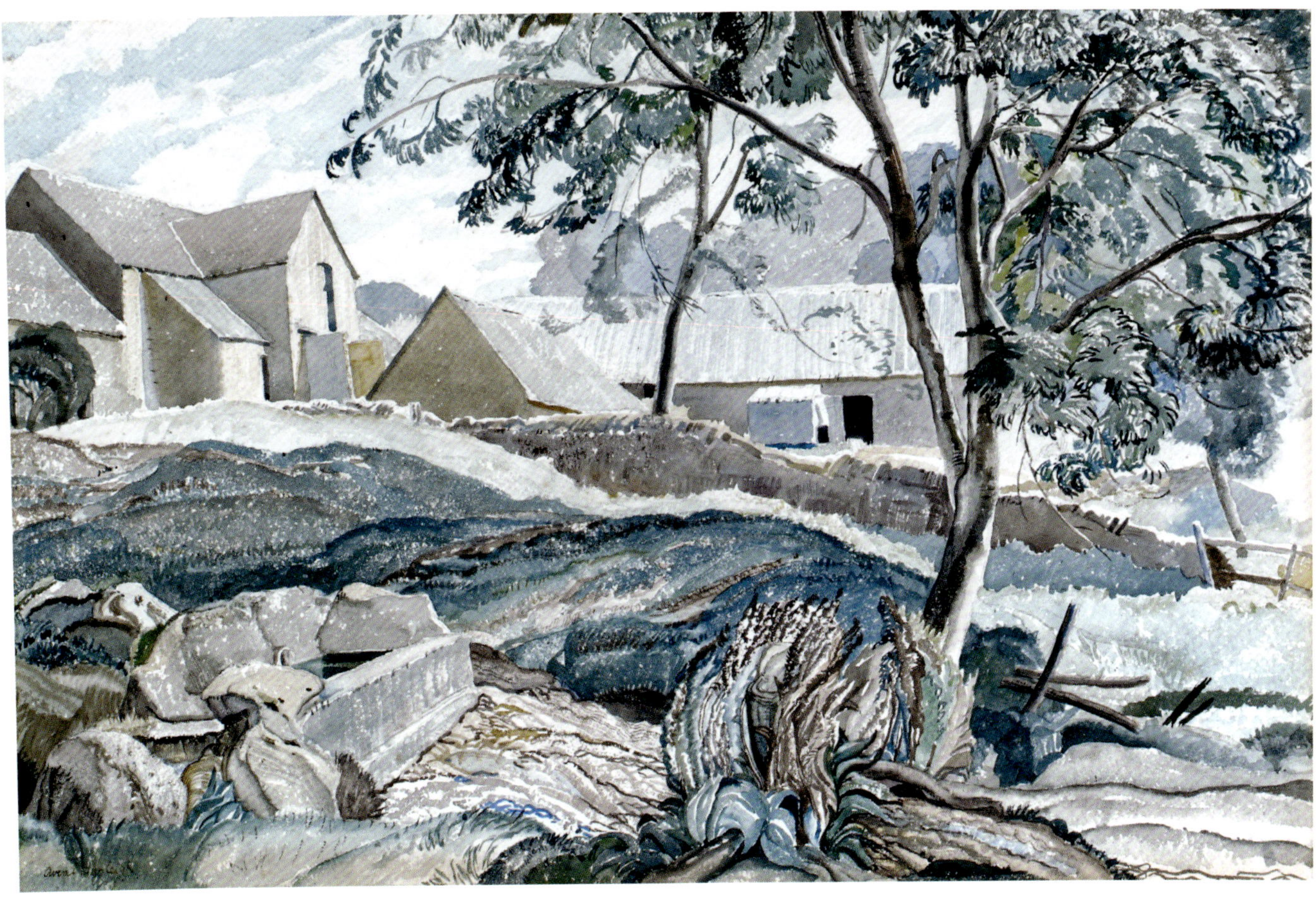

152 The Spring (Oxford)
Signed
Watercolour with pencil
14 x 21 inches

The Spring (Oxford)
The Oxfordshire farm buildings in the present watercolour also appear in oils painted by Averil Burleigh's husband, Charles Burleigh, and their daughter, Veronica Burleigh. Notable among these is Veronica's *Self Portrait with the Artist's Parents* (circa 1937, Brighton and Hove Museums and Art Galleries).

RANDOLPH SCHWABE

Randolph Schwabe, RWS LG NEAC (1885-1948)

OXFORDSHIRE

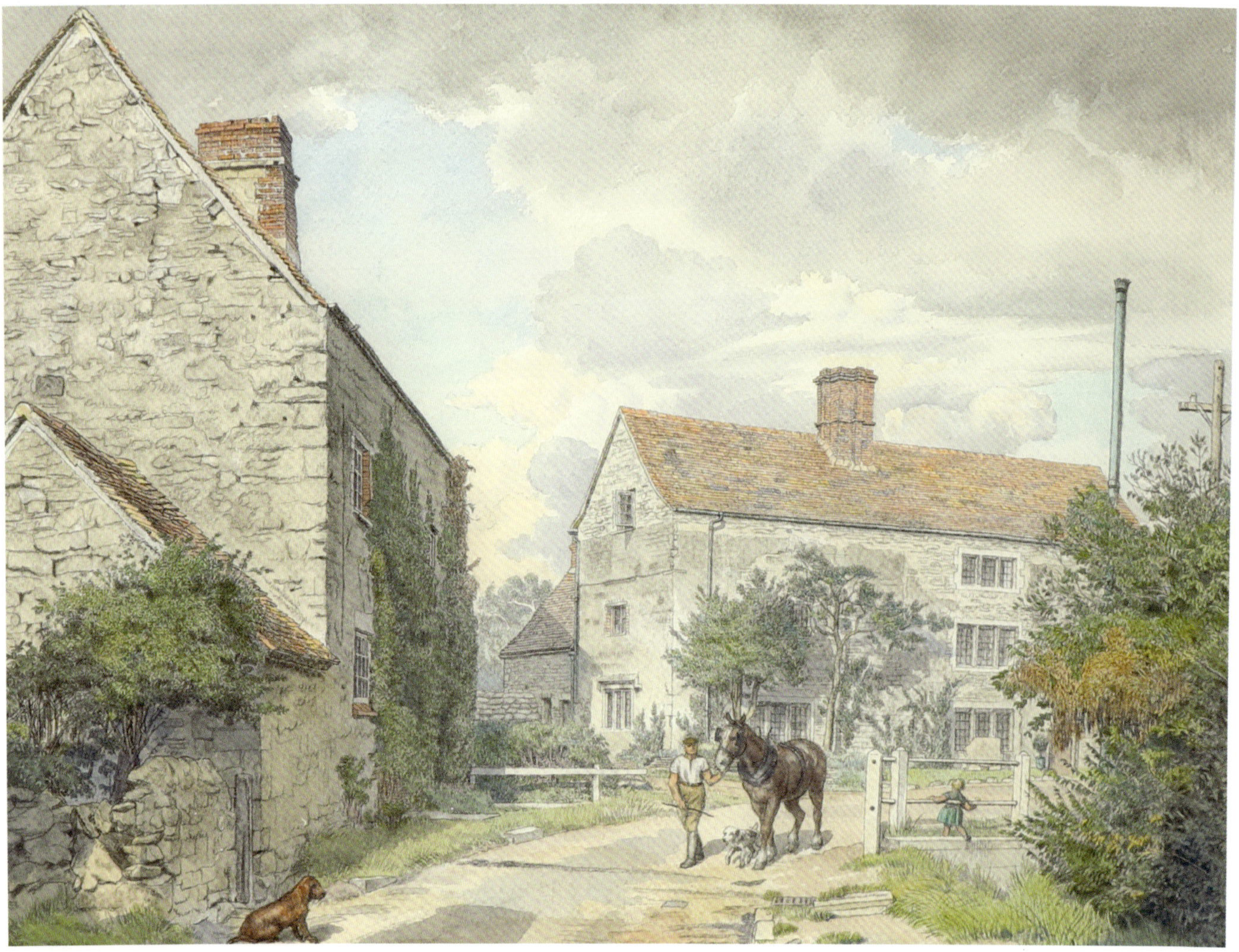

153 South Hinksey
Signed, inscribed with title and dated 1942 below mount
Watercolour and pencil
13 ½ x 16 inches

South Hinksey

Following the outbreak of the Second World War, the Slade School of Fine Art, under the Professorship of Randolph Schwabe, shifted its operations from London to Oxford. There it shared premises with the Ruskin School of Art, and Schwabe ran the amalgamated school with Albert Rutherston, the Ruskin Master of Drawing.

During his sojourn in Oxford, Schwabe made watercolours of the surrounding countryside , including the present one of the village of South Hinksey, which is immediately to the west of the city. It shows three houses in Manor Road, South Hinksey: Nos 1 & 3 (to the left) and No 7 (known as Stonecroft). Schwabe has taken a little artistic licence with Stonecroft, in terms of the dimensions of its windows and other features, and has somehow made it look even more impressive than it does in reality. At the time, it was the home of Clement Cyril Carter (1875-1949), a geography lecturer at Oxford and the author of several books.

CHARLES KNIGHT

Charles Knight, ROI VPRWS (1901-1990)

THE COTSWOLDS

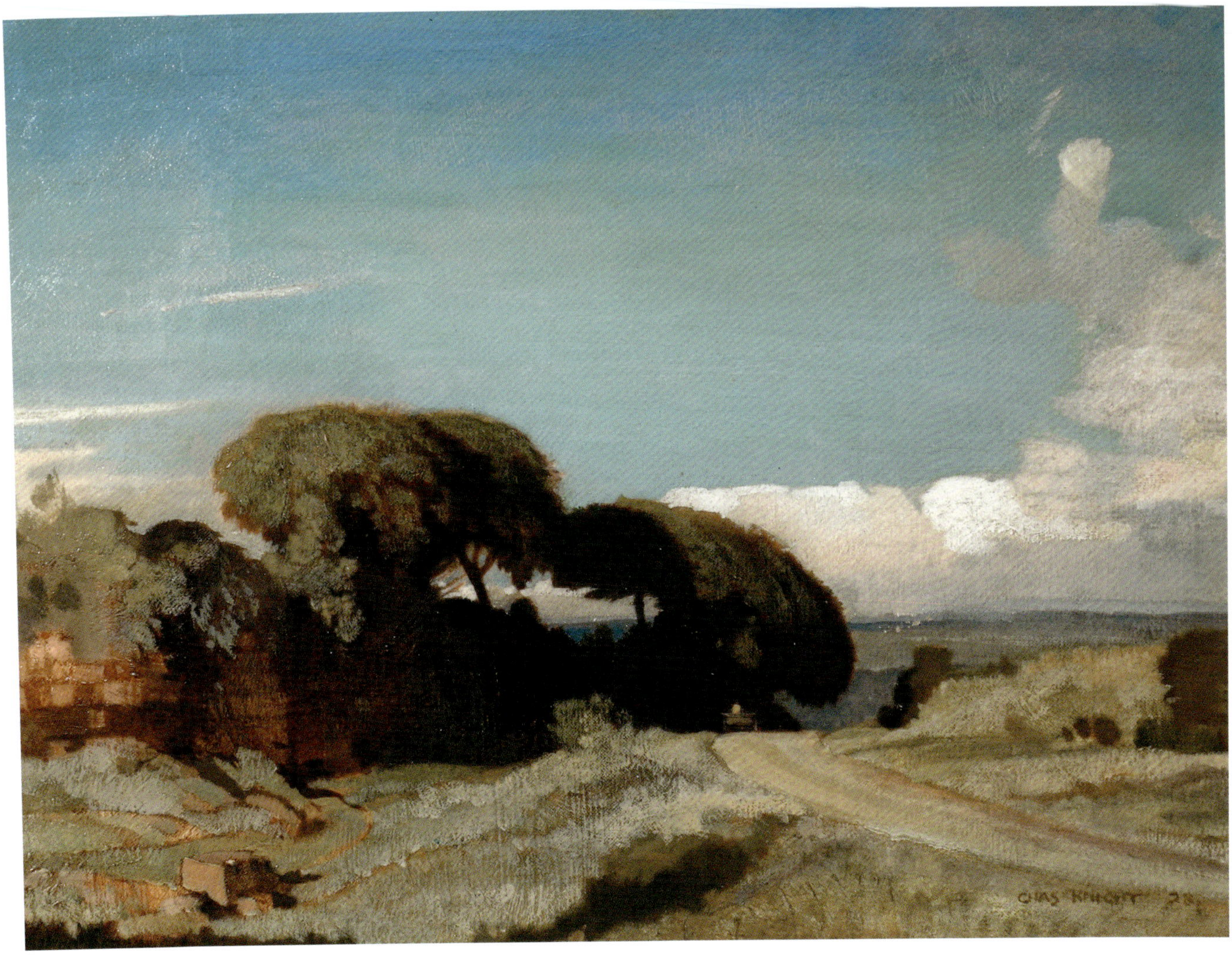

154 The Edge of the Cotswolds
Signed and dated '28
Inscribed on remnants of label on reverse
Oil on canvas
14 x 17 ½ inches

S R BADMIN

Stanley Roy Badmin, RWS RE AIA FSIA (1906-1989)

SHROPSHIRE

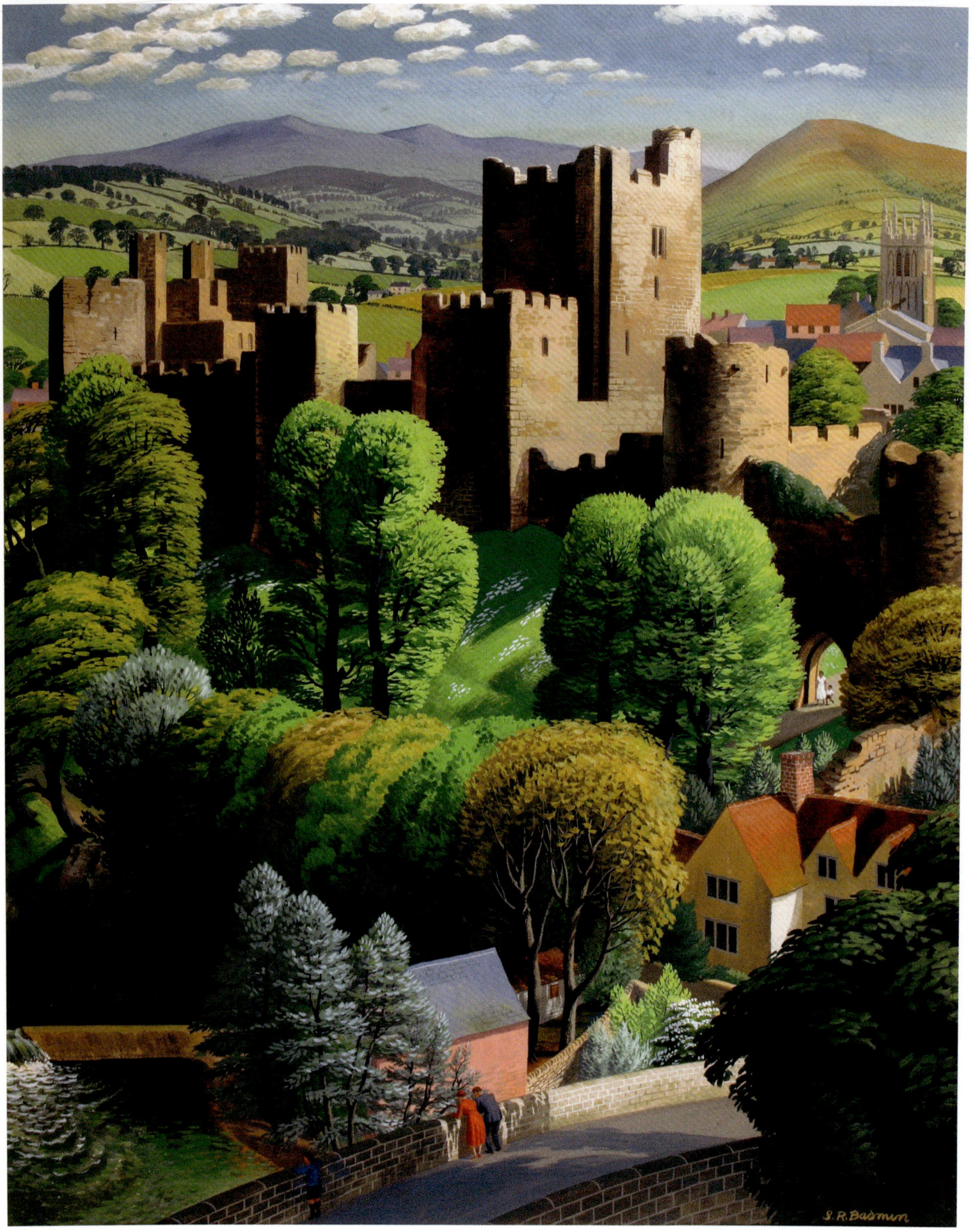

155 Ludlow, Shropshire
Signed
Signed, signed with initials and inscribed 'British Castles. I suggest 1 inch (minimum width) white border and dark blue lettering underneath' below mount
Bodycolour
25 x 19 ½ inches

Illustrated: This is the design for one of the series of posters, 'Enjoy the Riches of Britain', published by the Eastern National Omnibus Company and various others in 1932
Exhibited: 'S R Badmin RWS. Paintings, Drawings & Prints', Chris Beetles Gallery, March-April 2015, No 5

EDWARD STEEL HARPER

Edward Steel Harper, RBSA (1878-1951)

The work of the Birmingham artist, Edward Steel Harper, possesses a distinctive quality that combines late Pre-Raphaelitism with something more modern.

For a biography of Edward Steel Harper, please refer to page 220.

WALES

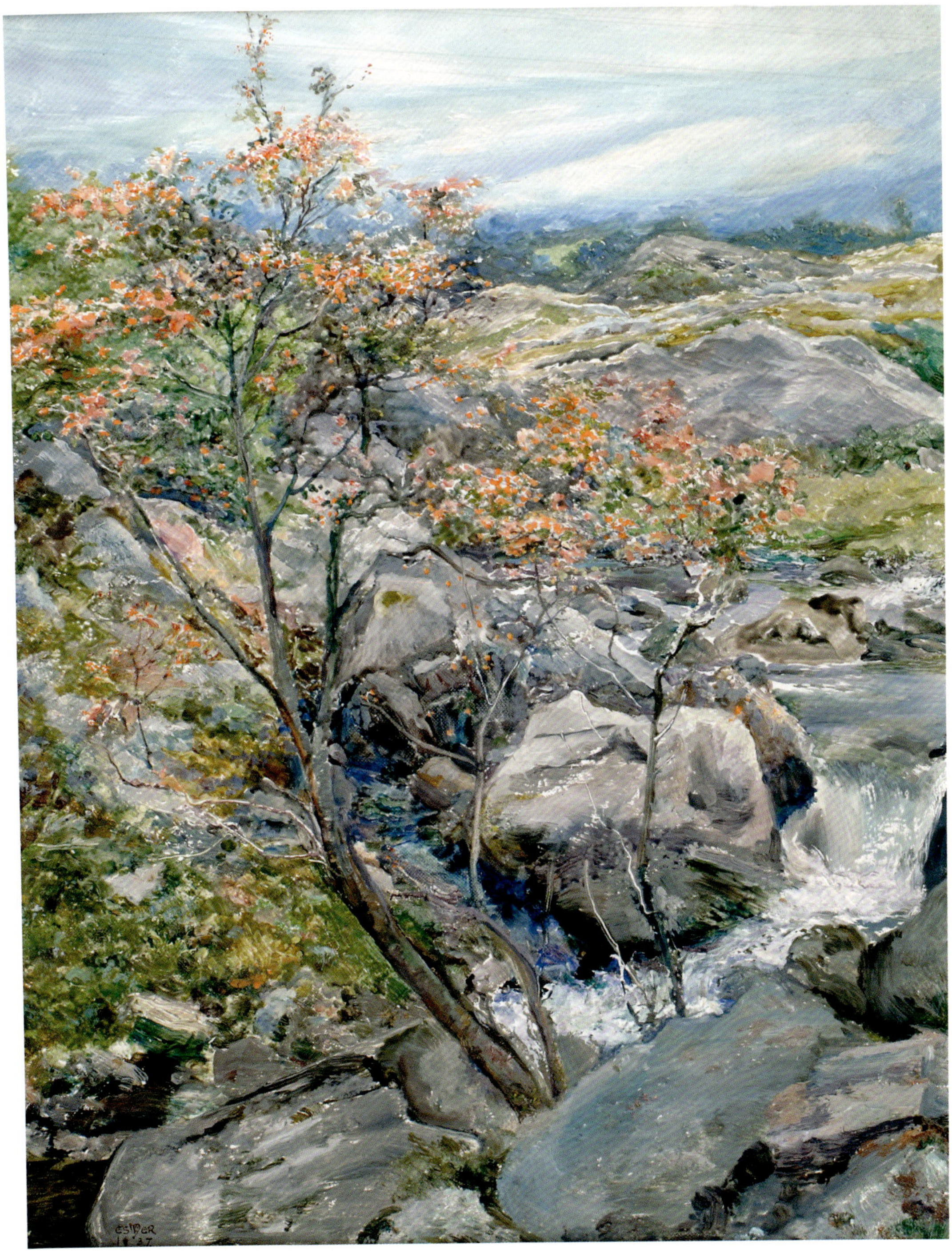

A Rowan; Nant Col, Llanbedr

The countryside around Llanbedr, in the historic Welsh county of Merionethshire, was a favourite painting ground of Edward Steel Harper. In the present work, he focussed upon a hardy little rowan tree growing to the east of Llanbedr, close to the River Nant Col (or, to give it its current Welsh name, Cwmnantcol).

156 **A Rowan; Nant Col, Llanbedr**
Signed with monogram and dated 1937
Signed, inscribed with title and artist's address, and dated '4 Dec 1938' on label on backboard
Oil on board
15 ¼ x 11 ½ inches

HARRY TITTENSOR

Harry Tittensor, RI (1887-1942)

Beginning his career as a ceramic painter and designer, Harry Tittensor concentrated on oils and watercolours from 1925. He then specialised in atmospheric topographical subjects, with and without figures, seeing himself as 'a translator of objects into light and shade, tone and colour' (Cole, Heap and Lynn, *York through the Eyes of the Railways*, York: National Railway Museum, 1994, page 41).

For a biography of Harry Tittensor, please refer to page 220.

STAFFORDSHIRE

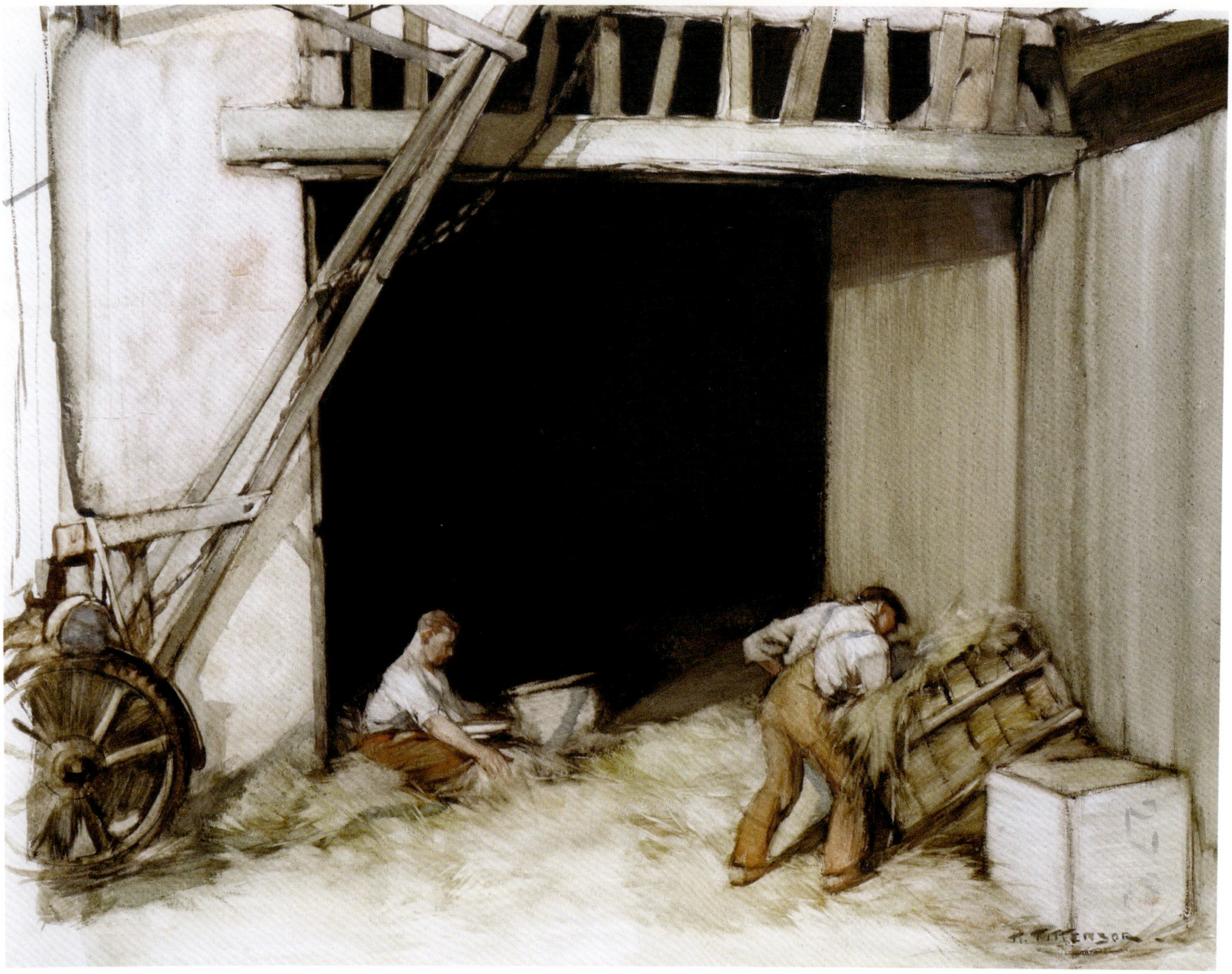

157 Farm Workers in a Barn
Signed
Watercolour
13 x 16 inches

S R BADMIN

Stanley Roy Badmin, RWS RE AIA FSIA (1906-1989)

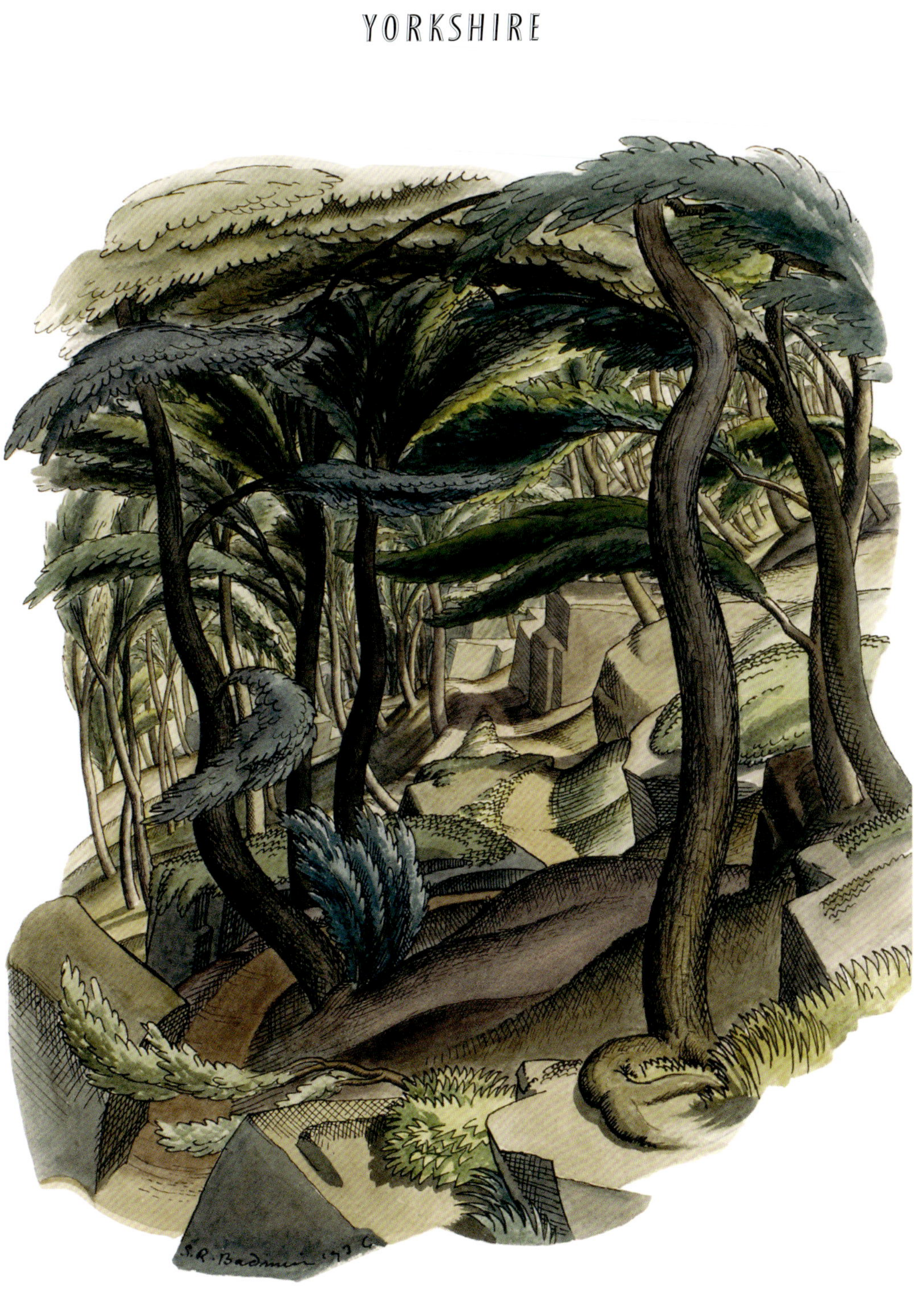

158 **Cliff Path, Richmond, Yorks**
Signed, signed with initials, inscribed with title
and dated 1936 twice
Pen and ink and watercolour
12 x 9 inches
Literature: Chris Beetles, *S R Badmin and the English Landscape*,
London: Collins, 1985, Page 40, as 'Yorkshire Wood'

CHARLES HOLMES

Sir Charles John Holmes, VPRWS NEAC (1868-1936)

As a painter and printmaker, Charles Holmes is best remembered for the strong forms and clear light of his landscapes and industrial scenes of the North of England. He was also central to the artistic life of Britain in the early twentieth century, as a publisher, editor, critic, historian, professor and museum director.

For a biography of Charles Holmes, please refer to page 221.

LANCASHIRE

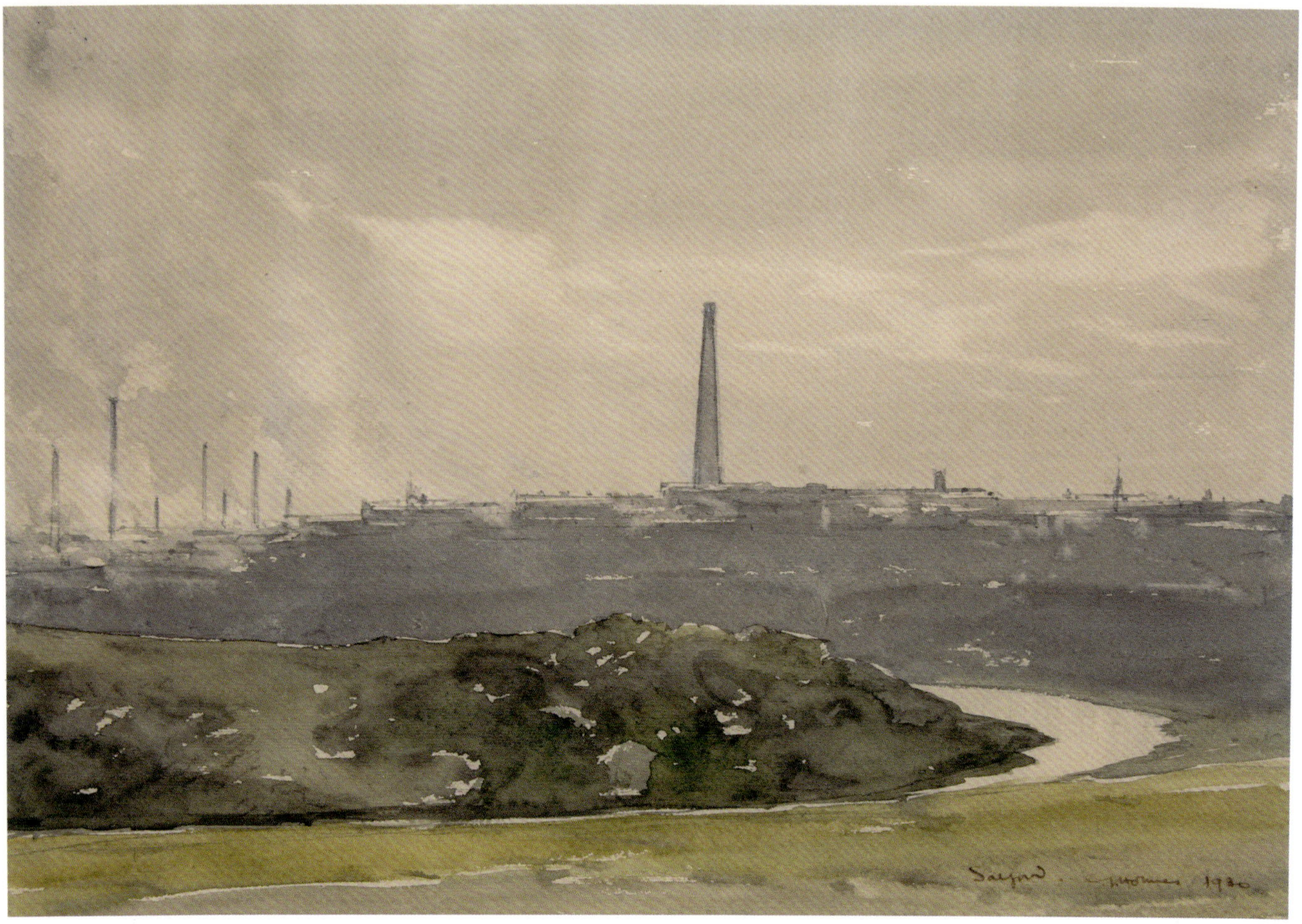

159 Salford
Signed, inscribed with title and dated 1930
Watercolour
9 ¾ x 14 ¼ inches

Salford
Though Sir Charles Holmes rose to become Slade Professor of Fine Art at Oxford and Director of both the National Portrait Gallery and the National Gallery, he remained close to his Lancashire roots by frequently choosing the industrial north as the subject matter of his own distinctive art. The present late watercolour shows mill and other factory chimneys on the Salford skyline as a dynamic and atmospheric background to a – seemingly more rural – bend in the River Irwell.

CECIL ARTHUR HUNT

Cecil Arthur Hunt, VPRWS RBA (1873-1965)

Once elected a full member of the Royal Society of Painters in Water-Colours in 1925, Cecil Arthur Hunt retired from his career as a barrister and turned his serious pastime of painting into a profession. While he had first established himself as a painter of mountains, especially the Alps and the Dolomites, he soon proved himself a master of a great variety of topographies. The impressive, often stark, effects that he achieved rival those associated with his friend and mentor, Frank Brangwyn.

For a biography of Cecil Arthur Hunt, please refer to page 210.

SCOTLAND

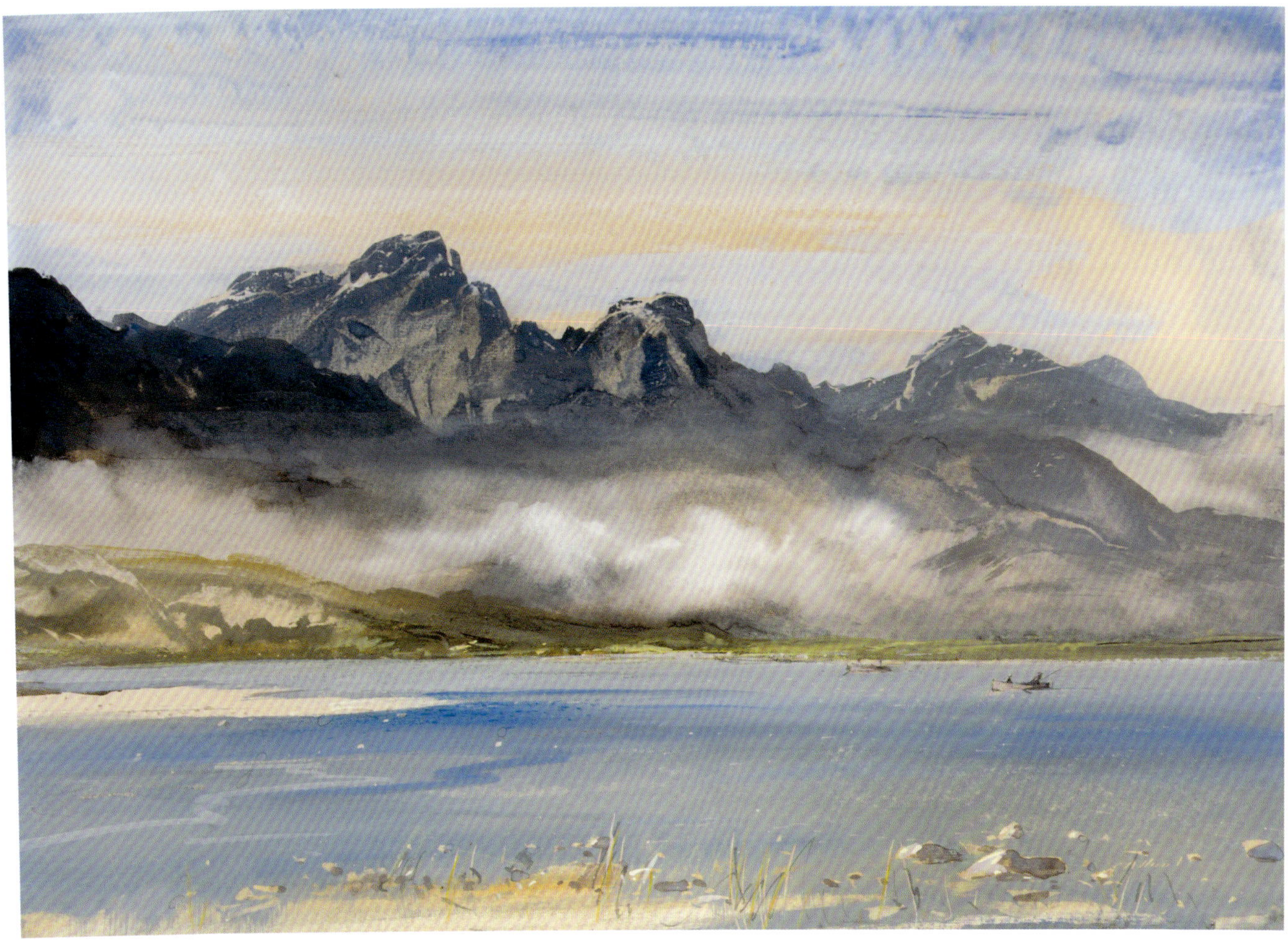

160 **Blaven from Loch Slapin, Skye**
Signed
Inscribed with title on reverse
Signed, inscribed with title, 'No1 Blaven from Skye' and the artist's address on labels on the original backboard
Watercolour and bodycolour
15 ½ x 20 inches
Provenance: J T Drew
Exhibited: Royal Society of Painters in Water-Colours, Spring 1946, No 46

Blavin from Loch Slapin, Skye

Hunt made many trips to Scotland and Skye, but in 1932 and again in 1933 he visited Skye and made sketches of Blaven and Loch Slapin. (Sketchbooks 34 & 42). Blaven, or Bla Bheinn (thought to mean 'Blue mountain') is a Monro on the edge of the Cuilins, and rises to 3,048 feet. This work was painted from the shores of Loch Slapin by the village of Torrin, looking West.

CECIL ARTHUR HUNT

SCOTLAND

'Dear Mr Macdonald,
What a truly delightful letter I received from you this morning. Thank you so much. Such appreciation from a Scot of course thrills me, as I always have loved your western highlands, & particularly the fairy land of Skye, & further north the bleak precipices of Suilven. How lovely they are! I used to motor and walk these a lot.
Well now I should like to help you if I can about methods and colours. What I have been using in some years is Winsor and Newton's designers superfine Gouache in tubes. They just have the strength & body I like, but which are anathema to the purely transparent watercolourist!
I enclose a scribble [not the work below] painted with ultramarine, red ochre, raw sienna & spectrum yellow. & you can see how brilliant the effect is. The lighter parts are taken out with a palette knife when the colour is still damp, & you can see what fascinating accidents appear! I find from one of my sketch books that I was at Dunthulm [sic] in 1932, but I have been there since.
Yours sincerely, Cecil A Hunt'

(Letter of Provenance from Cecil Hunt to William Macdonald, dated '1 July 1954')

161 **Duntulm Castle, Skye**
Signed
Watercolour, bodycolour and chalk
15 ½ x 22 inches
Provenance: William Macdonald
Exhibited: Royal Glasgow Institute of Fine Arts, 1935, No 706
as 'Ruins at Duntholm [sic], Skye' (£12)

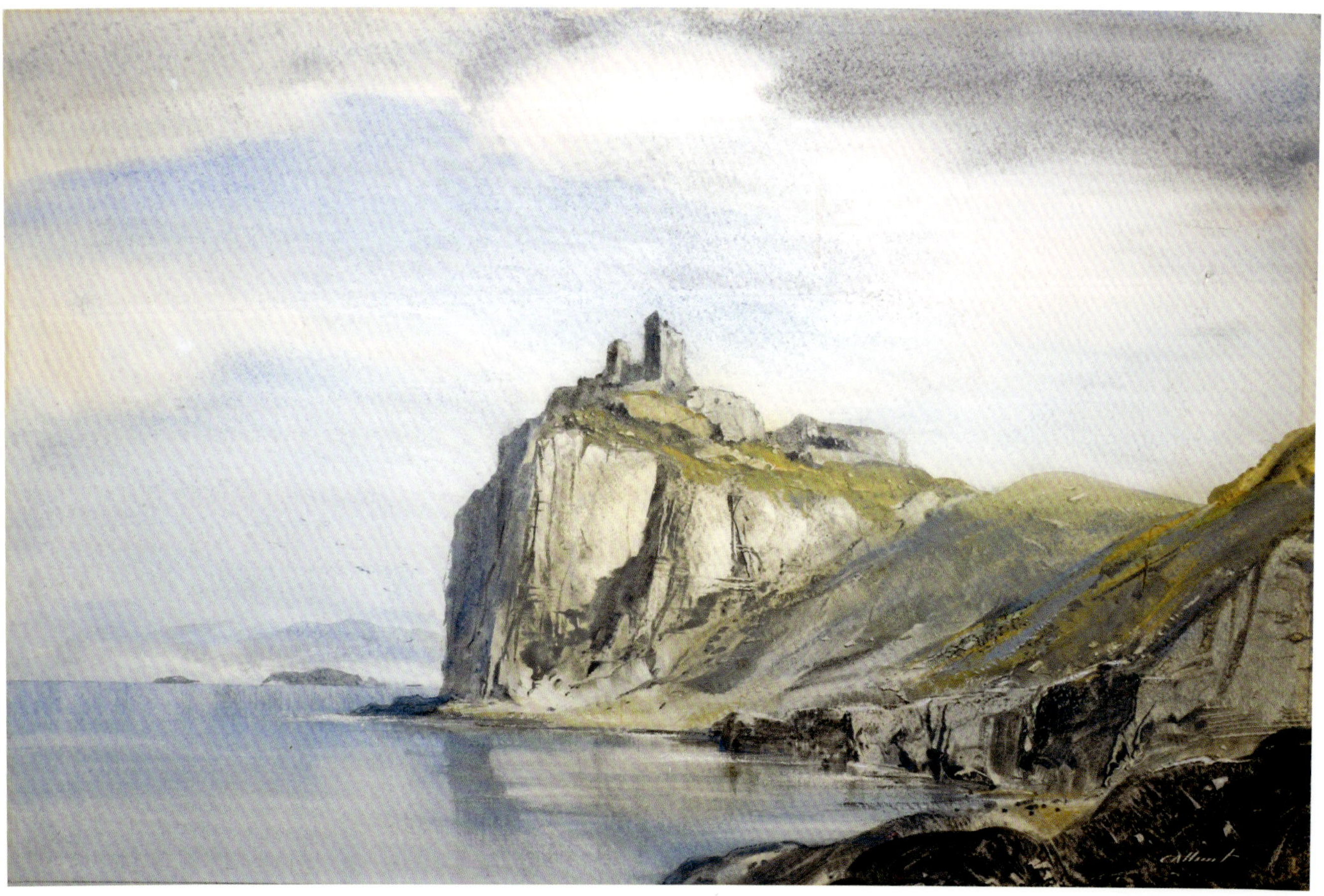

8: THOMAS HENNELL IN PEACE AND WAR

The artist and writer, Thomas Hennell, lived through periods of national peace and world war, and died in 1945 while working as an official war artist. He also experienced periods of war and peace within himself, in suffering and recovering from a nervous breakdown. He responded creatively to all that happened around and within by harnessing an intense, individual vision, comparable to those of the poet, John Clare, and the painter, Vincent Van Gogh, both of whom he admired.

Hennell was born in a very distinctive place, the tiny neighbouring parishes of Ridley and Ash, set in the chalk hills of northwest Kent. The son of the local vicar, he was brought up in a loving family and developed a strong Christian faith. He learned from an early age to value his particular surroundings and its inhabitants, and, by extension, the natural world and country life. So he understood the spirit of a place, and its ability to nurture and heal, and he gained the skills to communicate that spirit in memorable word and image.

Hennell drew and painted in a variety of rural areas of England, including Essex, Herefordshire [171] and Somerset [164]. However, he tended to gravitate back towards Kent, and considered it a refuge. So, while studying art in London in 1921, he recorded his home county in a series of early watercolours, including Saltwood Castle [162], close to the coast at Hythe. In the following decade, in 1935, on his release from a stay at Claybury Mental Hospital, in Essex, he settled at Orchard Cottage, Ridley, across the fields from his first home, and took to working in its garden. The images that he produced of it, through the changing seasons, suggest that it melded harmoniously into the countryside beyond, and echoed his own oneness with nature [167-168].

Hennell's landscapes are not necessarily empty ones. They often provide the context for authentic and vigorous depictions of labour, which capture the closing days of a long tradition of agriculture, being brought to an end by economic depression. Hennell was fascinated by the tasks of rural workers, both in themselves and as subjects for his art. His dynamic brushstrokes replicate the rhythmic movements of men taking down a hay rick at West York Farm, Ash [165], and emphasise the closeness to the earth of women weeding onions, in the same locale [174].

Both Hennell's subject matter and his approach to it prepared him well for his work as an official war artist in the period between 1942 and 1945. He was used to documenting large groups of people, working with machinery out on the land. His clear eye and steady hand ensured his accurate delineation of the damaged vehicles at a tank graveyard in Normandy [177]. However, there is something almost pastoral about the way that the soldiers walk among them or rest by the side of the road [176]. Even in the midst of war, Hennell never forgot that the land on which it was being fought had once been farmed and would be so again. While he was acutely aware of change and loss, he also took the long view, and achieved an art that now seems almost timeless.

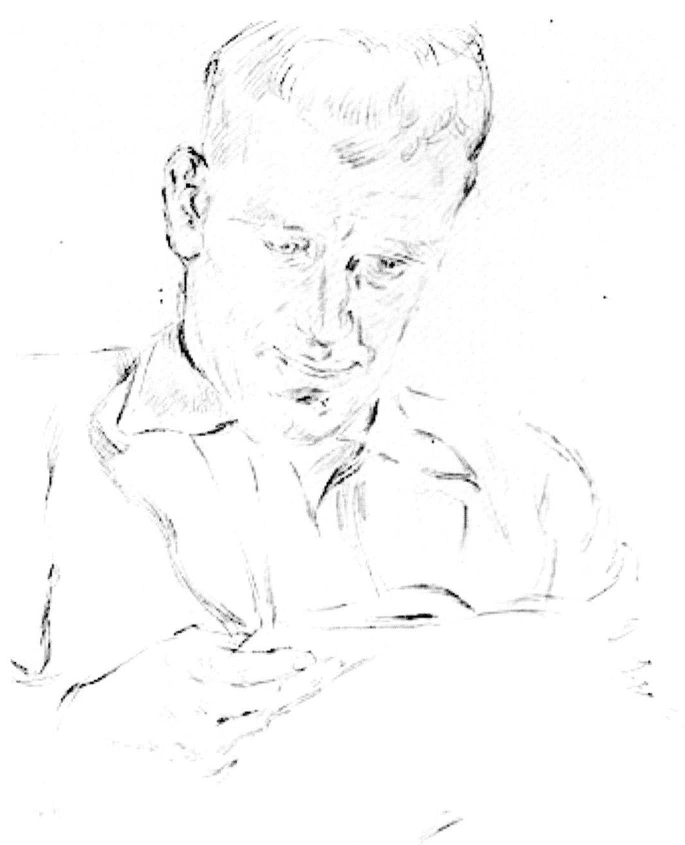

Self-Portrait
Pencil
(Private Collection)

Thomas Hennell drew this self-portrait on 18 July 1936, almost nine months after his release from Claybury Mental Hospital, Essex. By then, he was living at Orchard Cottage, near his childhood home in Ridley, Kent, and had embarked on a period of five stable years, in which he made his name as an artist and poet.

THOMAS HENNELL

Thomas Barclay Hennell, RWS NEAC (1903-1945)

Thomas Hennell expressed his love of landscape and rural life in words and images that were at once accurate and intense. Late in his short career, he became an official war artist, and presented aspects of the international conflict through his unique vision, from Iceland to Java, where he is presumed to have been killed.

For a biography of Thomas Hennell, please refer to page 222.

1922

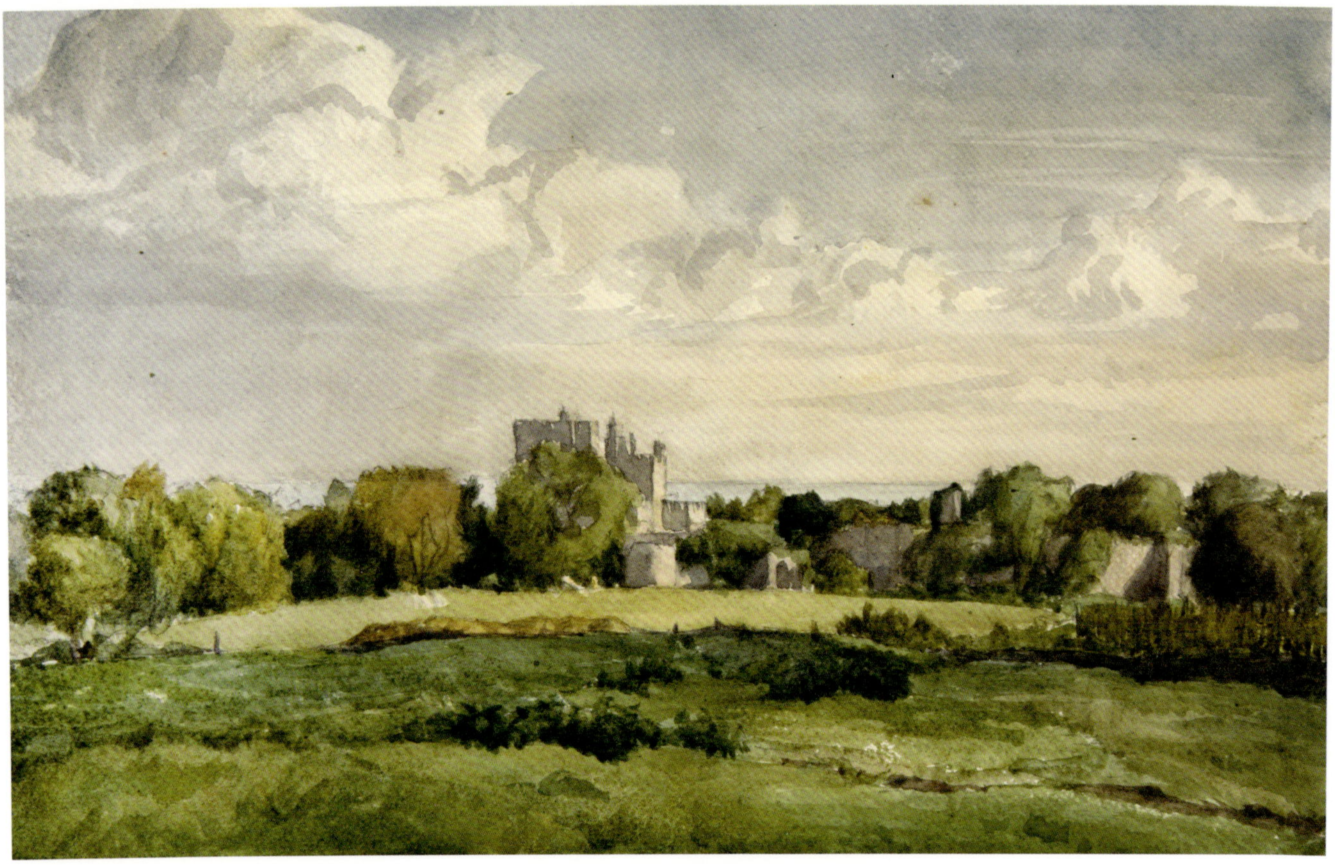

162 Saltwood Castle, Nr Hythe
Inscribed with title and dated 1922 below mount
Watercolour and pencil
7 ½ x 11 inches

Saltwood Castle, Nr Hythe, and The Fallen Tree

Thomas Hennell produced these two watercolours soon after he began to study at Regent Street Polytechnic, London, in 1921, at the age of eighteen.

Situated in Hennell's home county of Kent, Saltwood Castle was built near Hythe in the eleventh century, and expanded in the thirteenth and fourteenth centuries. In 1953, it became the home of the art historian, Sir Kenneth Clark (1903-1983), who had long recognised Hennell's talents. While Clark was Director of the National Gallery, he had both chosen Hennell to contribute to the scheme, 'Recording Britain', in 1940, and helped appoint him an official war artist in 1943.

163 The Fallen Tree
Watercolour
7 ¾ x 10 ¾ inches

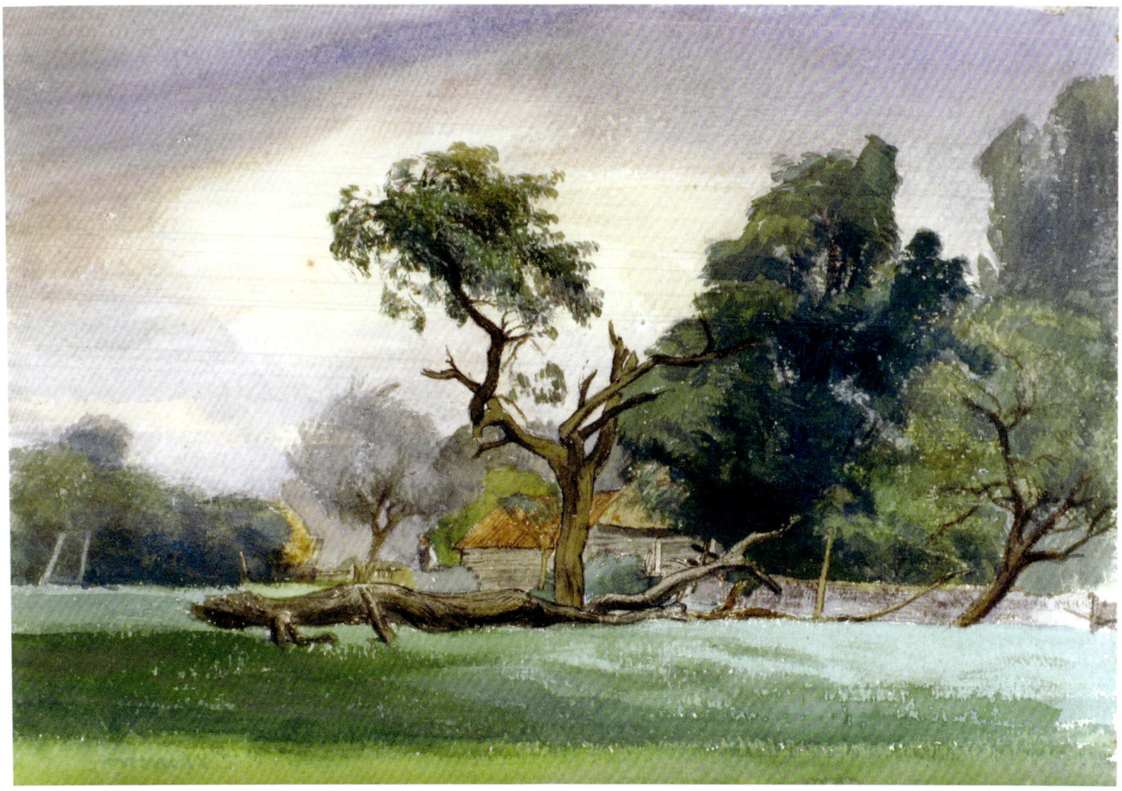

1929

164 Corston
Signed, inscribed with title and dated 'March 9th 1929'
Pen ink and monochrome watercolour
11 ¼ x 15 ½ inches

Corston

Between 1928 and 1930, Thomas Hennell lived in Bath, and taught art at Kingswood School. While there, he made many drawings in and around the city, including the present one, of men at work in the village of Corston.

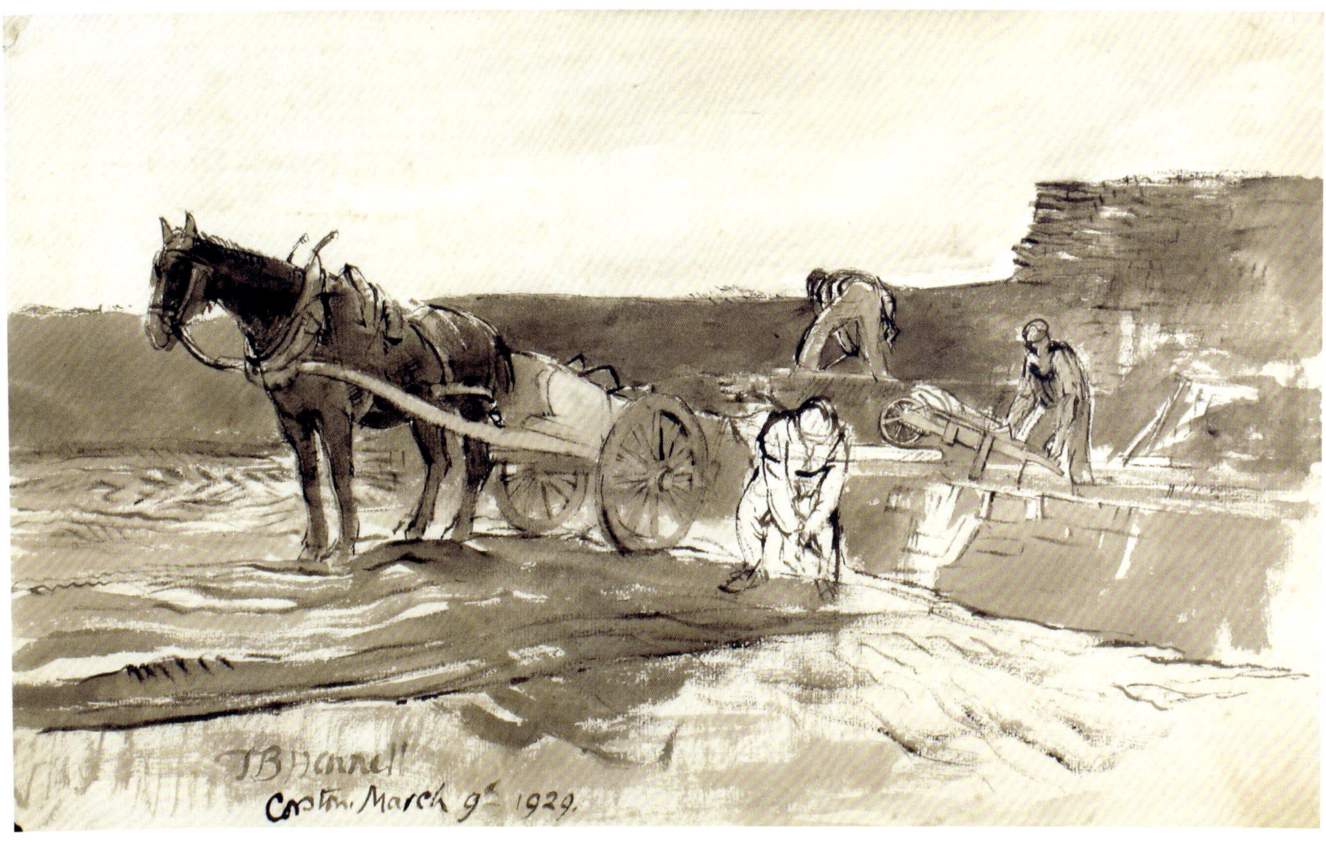

1935

Taking Down a Hay Rick

Thomas Hennell produced this work at West Yoke Farm in Ash-next-Ridley, close to his family home. It is a very similar composition to the watercolour, *Taking Down a Rick and Threshing* (private collection), which he made there on Sunday 25 August 1935, while on a 'probationary weekend' away from Claybury Mental Hospital, Essex. Jessica Kilburn's comments on that watercolour, in her study of Hennell, may equally apply to the present one:

> Hennell ... confidently painted a scene which is a celebration of work, each figure portrayed busily going about his job. The painting conveys the joy Hennell took in their activity. At West Yoke Farm in August 1935, many men may have been involved in 'taking down a rick and threshing', but during the interwar years hundreds of thousands of farmworkers 'were forced off the land by farmers attempting to reduce costs by cutting back on labour'. Scenes like the one Hennell painted were becoming less prevalent.

(*Thomas Hennell: The Land and the Mind*, London: Pimpernel Press, 2021, page 122, quoting Jeremy Burchardt, *Paradise Lost: Rural Idyll and Social Change since 1800*, London: I B Tauris & Co, 2002, page 107)

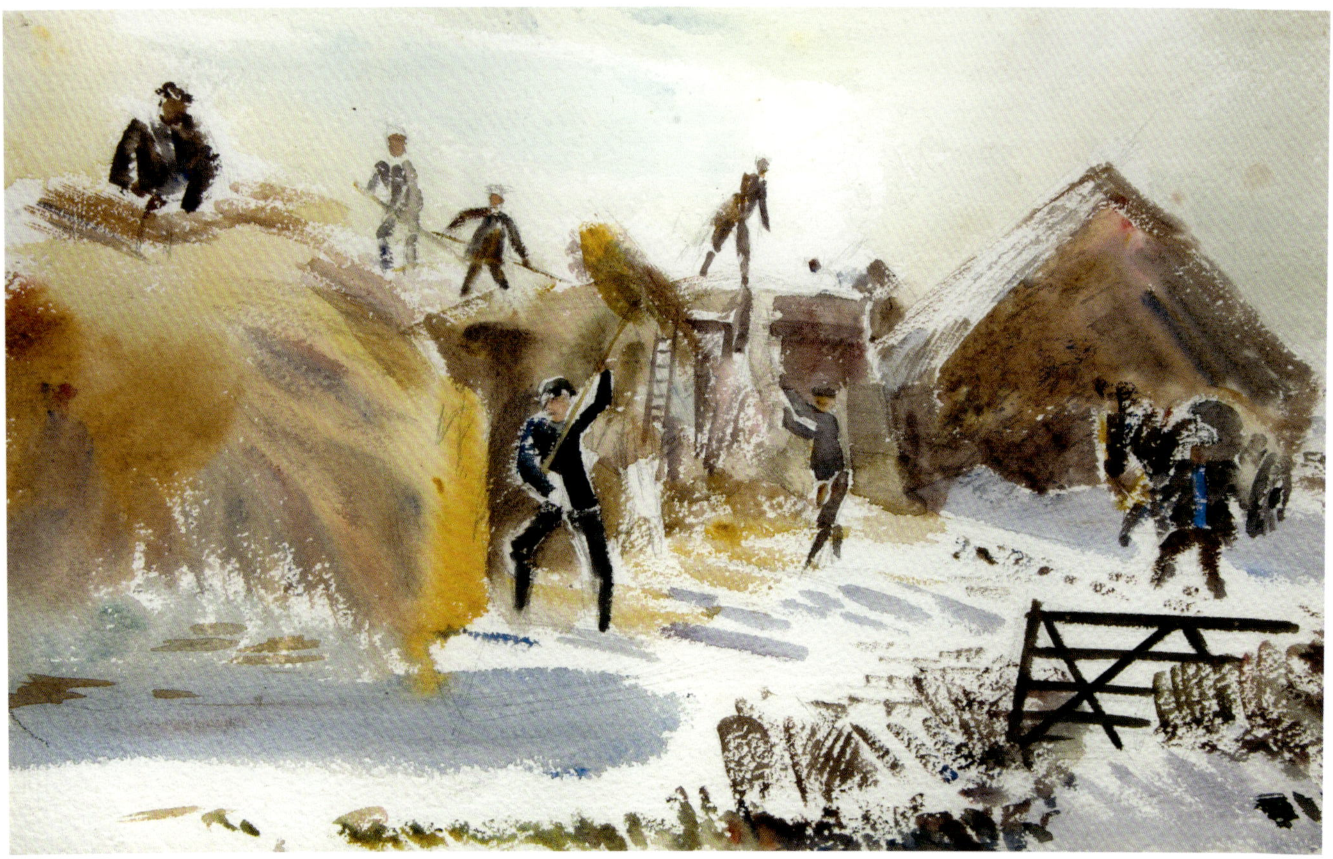

165 Taking Down a Hayrick
Watercolour on reverse of 'Loading the Farm Cart'
Watercolour and pencil
11 ¼ x 19 ¾ inches

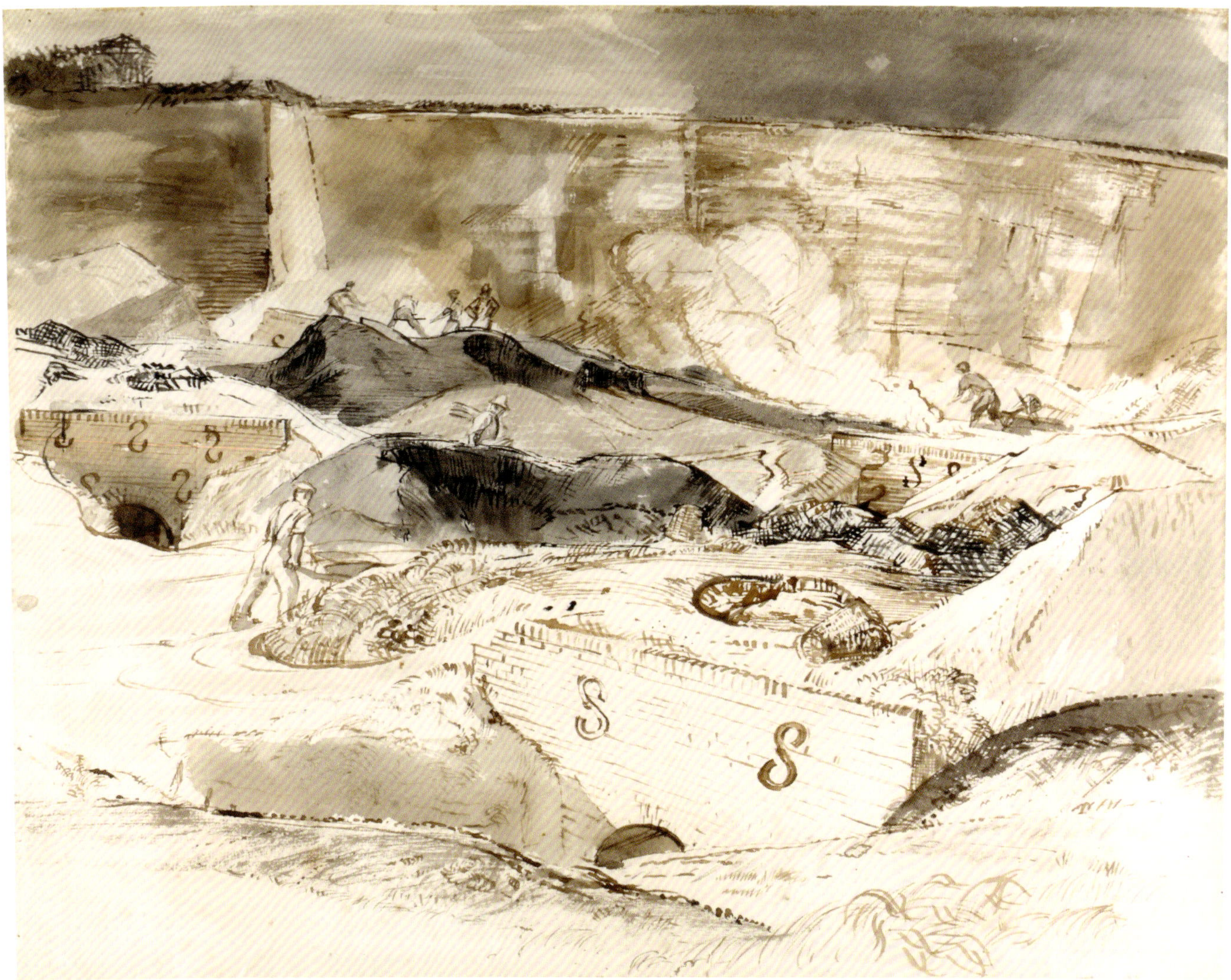

166 Marl Pit
Inscribed with title on reverse
Pen and ink
15 ½ x 17 ¾ inches

1937

Two Views from Orchard Cottage

These two watercolours by Thomas Hennell show views from Orchard Cottage, Ridley, Kent, which became the artist's home following his release from Claybury Mental Hospital, Essex, in 1935. As described by Jessica Kilburn, the cottage was

> a Victorian property which stood across the fields from Ridley Rectory, Hennell's beloved childhood home … [It] had been left to the Revd Hennell by one of his parishioners … who had known the children since their infancy, and expressed 'the hope that one of them should live there'
> (*Thomas Hennell: The Land and the Mind*, London: Pimpernel Press, 2021, page 112, quoting an unpublished reminiscence of Hennell's sister, Betty)

Hennell gained particular pleasure from the cottage's garden, which can be seen here, both from a first floor window, covered in March snow, and from ground level, in spring or summer.

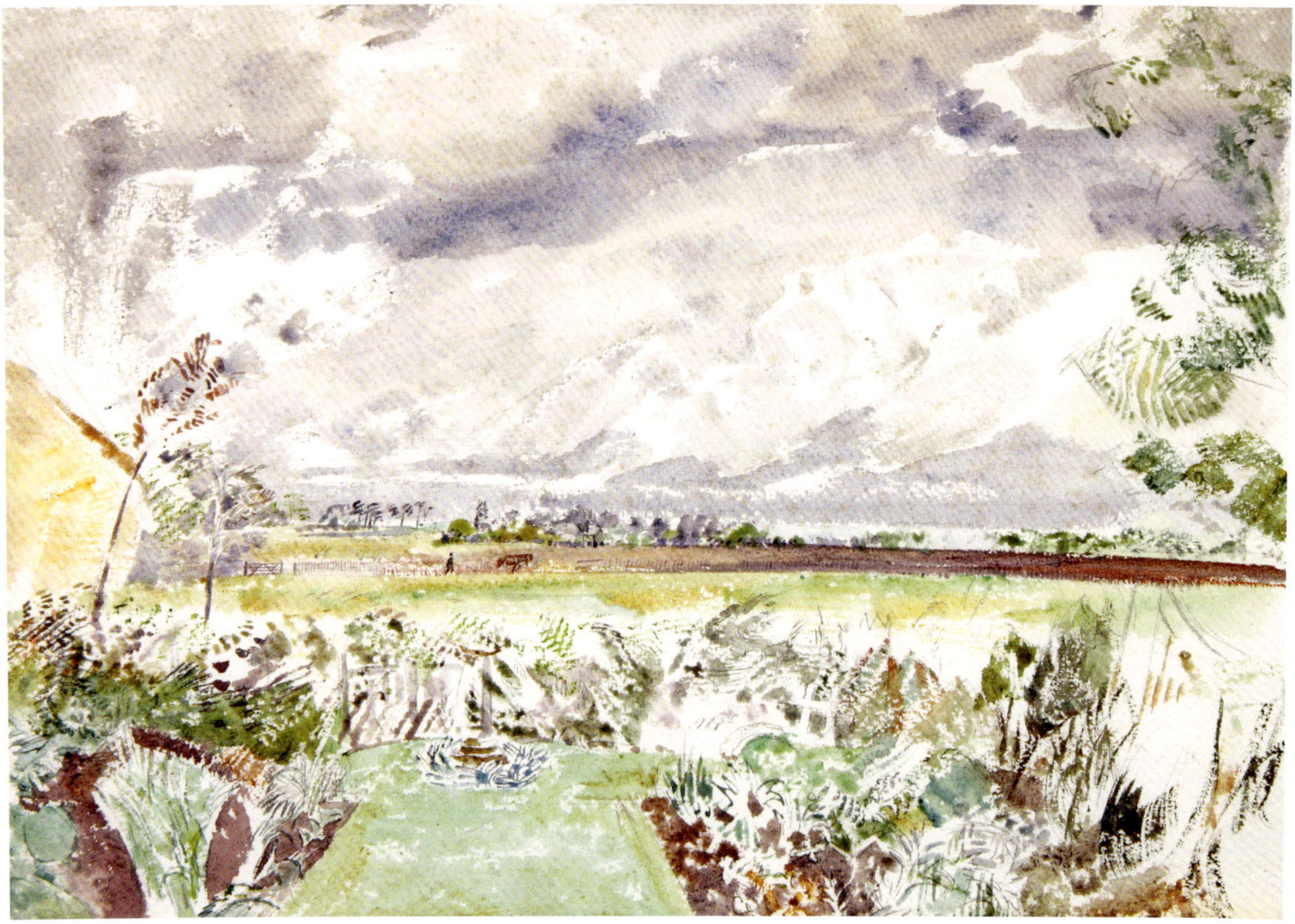

167 View from Orchard Cottage
Faint pencil drawing of village on reverse
Watercolour
11 ¼ x 15 ½ inches
Produced circa 1936-37
Illustrated: Jessica Kilburne, *Thomas Hennell: The Land and the Mind*, London: Pimpernel Press, 2021, Page 117
Exhibited: 'The Watercolour Tradition in Landscape', Nunnington Hall, Yorkshire, April-June 2013

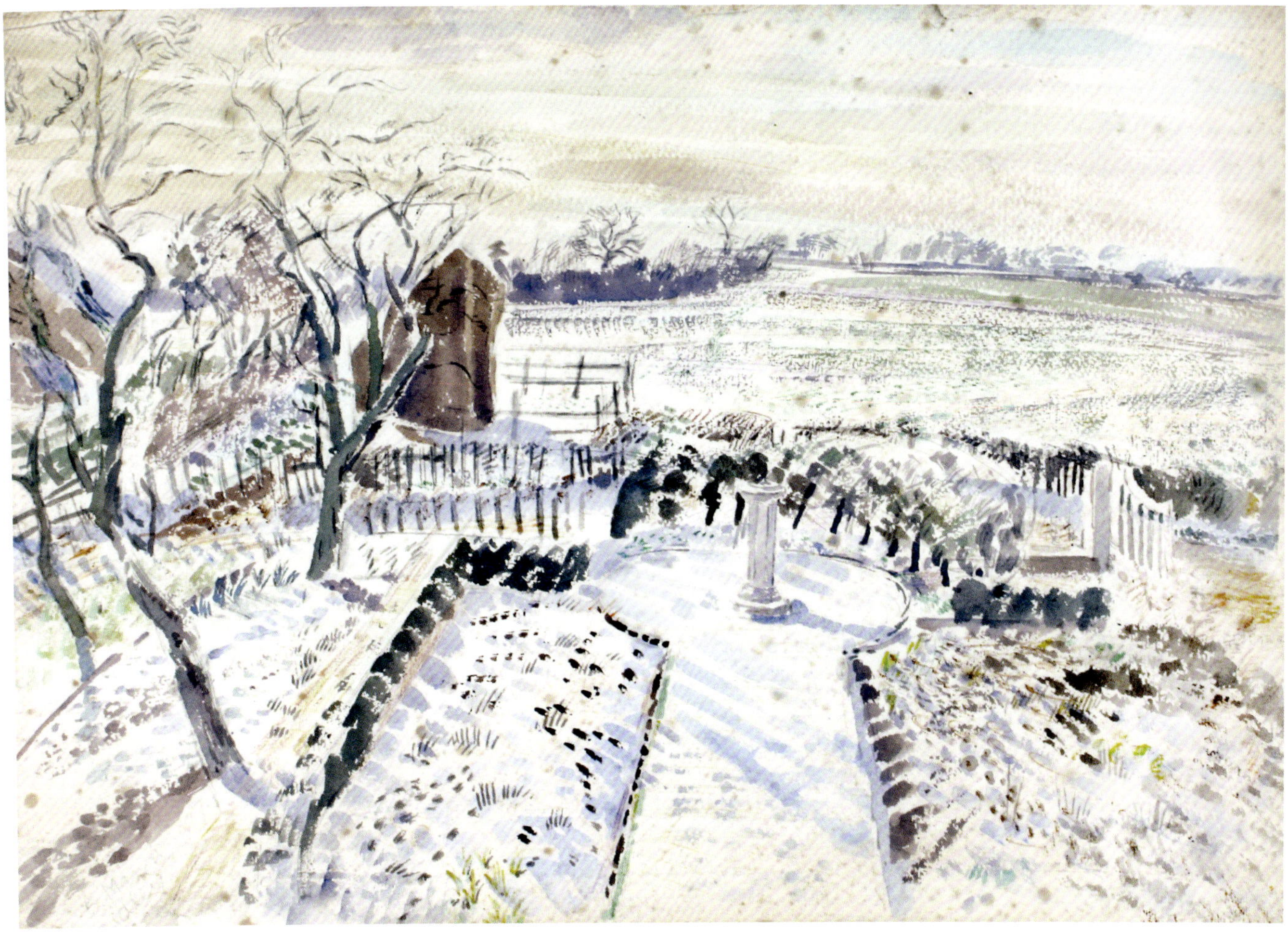

168 View from Orchard Cottage, Ridley
Inscribed 'Ridley' and dated '5 March 1937'
Watercolour with pencil
14 x 19 ¼ inches

1939

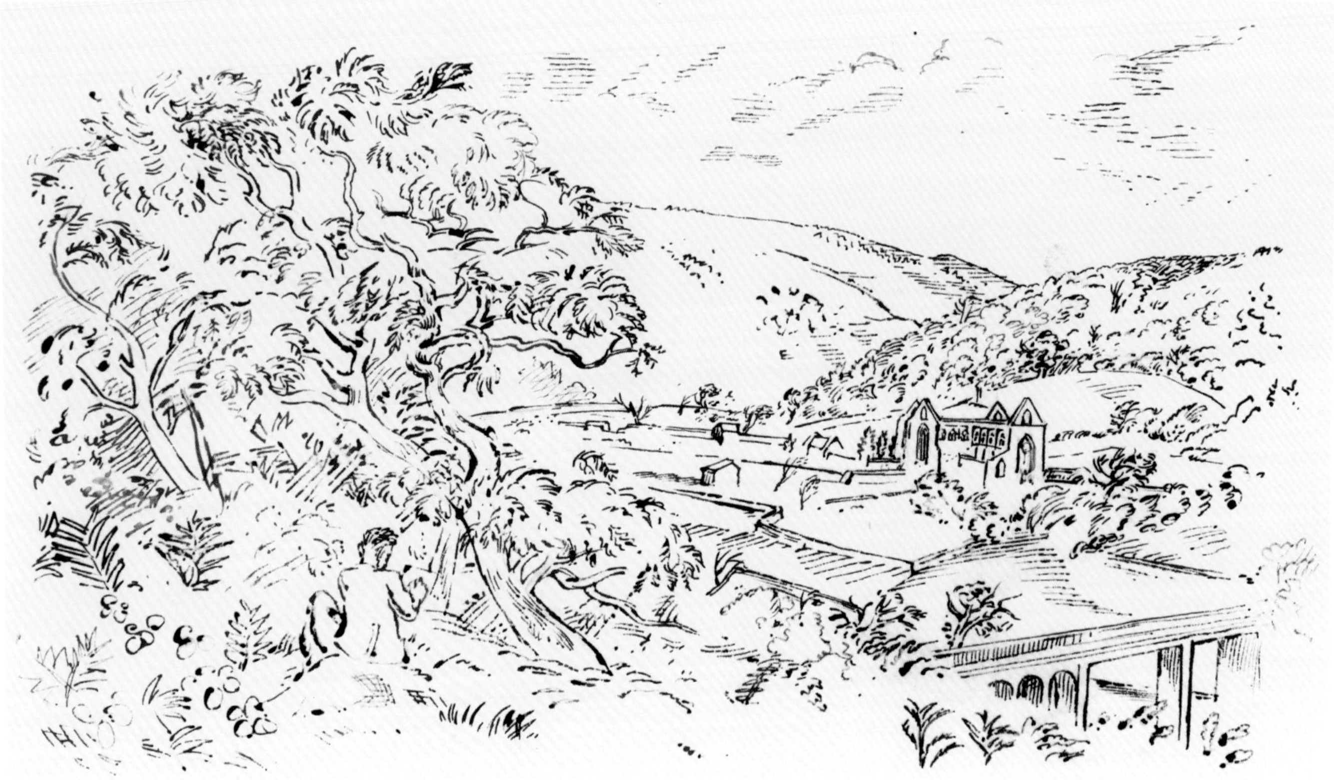

169 Tintern with Vincent Lines Painting
Inscribed with title below mount
Pen and ink
9 x 13 ½ inches
Illustrated: H J Massingham, *A Countryman's Journal*, London: Chapman & Hall, 1939, Page 15;
Jessica Kilburne, *Thomas Hennell, The Land and the Mind*, London: Pimpernel Press, 2021, Page 15
Exhibited: 'Thomas Hennell, 1903-1945. Kent Artist, Painter of Rural Life; Circle of Ravilious and Bawden', Folkestone Art Trust, University Centre Folkestone, April 2012, No 27

Tintern with Vincent Lines Painting

Thomas Hennell first met Vincent Lines (1909-1968) in the late 1920s in the London studio of the artist and teacher, Archibald Standish Hartrick (1864-1950), who had once been the friend of both Vincent Van Gogh and Paul Gauguin. Hennell and Lines would themselves become close friends and frequently accompany each other on sketching expeditions. One of these took in Tintern, on the River Wye, which had been made famous by Romantic painters and poets, but also had a personal association for Hennell, his father having been rector there before his move to Ridley, Kent. In the present work, Hennell has given as much emphasis to a portrait of Lines, himself engaged in drawing or painting, as to a view of Tintern Abbey. It would be published in *A Countryman's Journal*, the second of four books by the ruralist writer, Harold John Massingham (1888-1952), that Hennell illustrated. The book collected articles by Massingham that had first appeared in *The Field* magazine, including one on Tintern Abbey.

For information on another of the sketching tours that Thomas Hennell undertook with Vincent Lines, please see *Hop Picking* [171].

1940

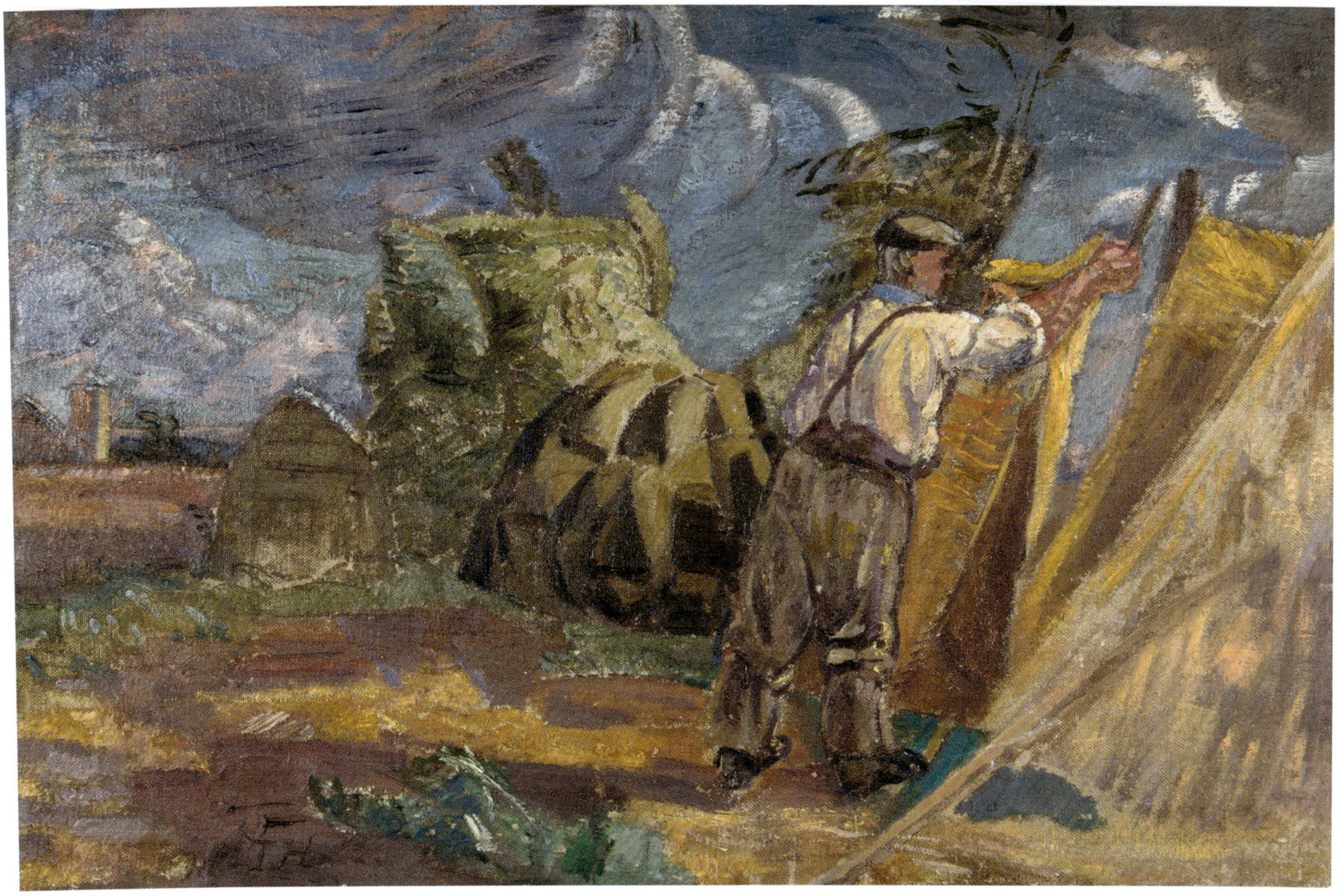

170 The Charcoal Burner
Signed with initials
Signed and inscribed 'Ridley, Wrotham, Kent' and '£21' on label on stretcher
Oil on canvas
20 x 30 inches
Produced circa 1940
Exhibited: Probably exhibited at the National Gallery, London, during the Second World War;
'Thomas Hennell, 1903-1945. Kent Artist, Painter of Rural Life; Circle of Ravilious and Bawden', Folkestone Art Trust, University Centre, Folkestone, April 2012, No 39

The Charcoal Burner

Thomas Hennell probably painted this oil of a charcoal burner near his home in Ridley, Kent, in about 1940. Its frame bears labels that indicate that it was produced as the result of support from an 'RAF Scheme' and the 'Central Institute of Art and Design/National Gallery London', for which Sir Kenneth Clark was responsible.

1941

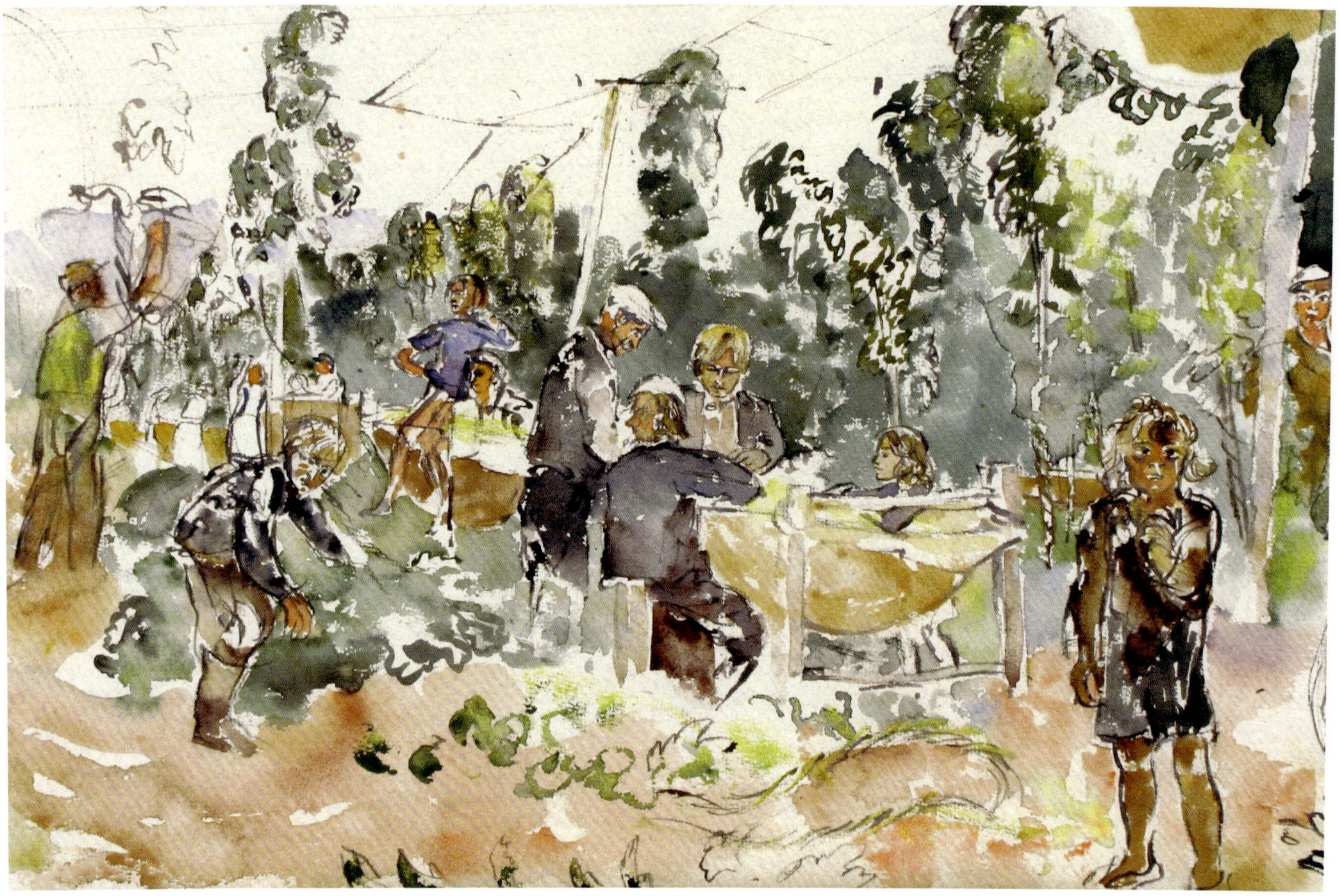

171 Hop Picking
Inscribed with title and '(Mr Davis's Brierley Farm Nr Leominster)' and dated 'Sept 15th, 1941' on reverse
Watercolour and pencil on tinted paper
11 ¾ x 17 inches

Hop Picking

In September 1941, Thomas Hennell spent ten days with Vincent Lines at the home of Lines's mother, at Whitney-on-Wye, Herefordshire, close to the Welsh border. This gave him the opportunity to fulfil a commission from the War Artists' Advisory Committee to produce some drawings of the harvest, which was the key component of wartime domestic food production. As Jessica Kilburn explains in her study of Hennell,

> the harvest in Herefordshire occurred 'somewhat later' than in other areas and brought him 'no lack of fine possibilities' … Painting alongside Lines enabled him 'to tackle more harvest subjects than I would otherwise have attempted'.
>
> (*Thomas Hennell: The Land and the Mind*, London: Pimpernel Press, 2021, page 238, quoting letters from Hennell to Gwyneth Lloyd Thomas and H J Massingham)

Near the end of their stay, they visited Brierley Court, a hop farm owned by William Davies, that was situated just south of Leominster, and about 15 miles from Whitney-on-Wye. The Kent-born Hennell would have been familiar with such scenes of hop picking as the one that he captured in the present watercolour. The WAAC purchased seven of the watercolours that he produced of the harvest, plus another of Scythe Smithy, Belbroughton, Worcestershire (and most of these are now in the Government Art Collection).

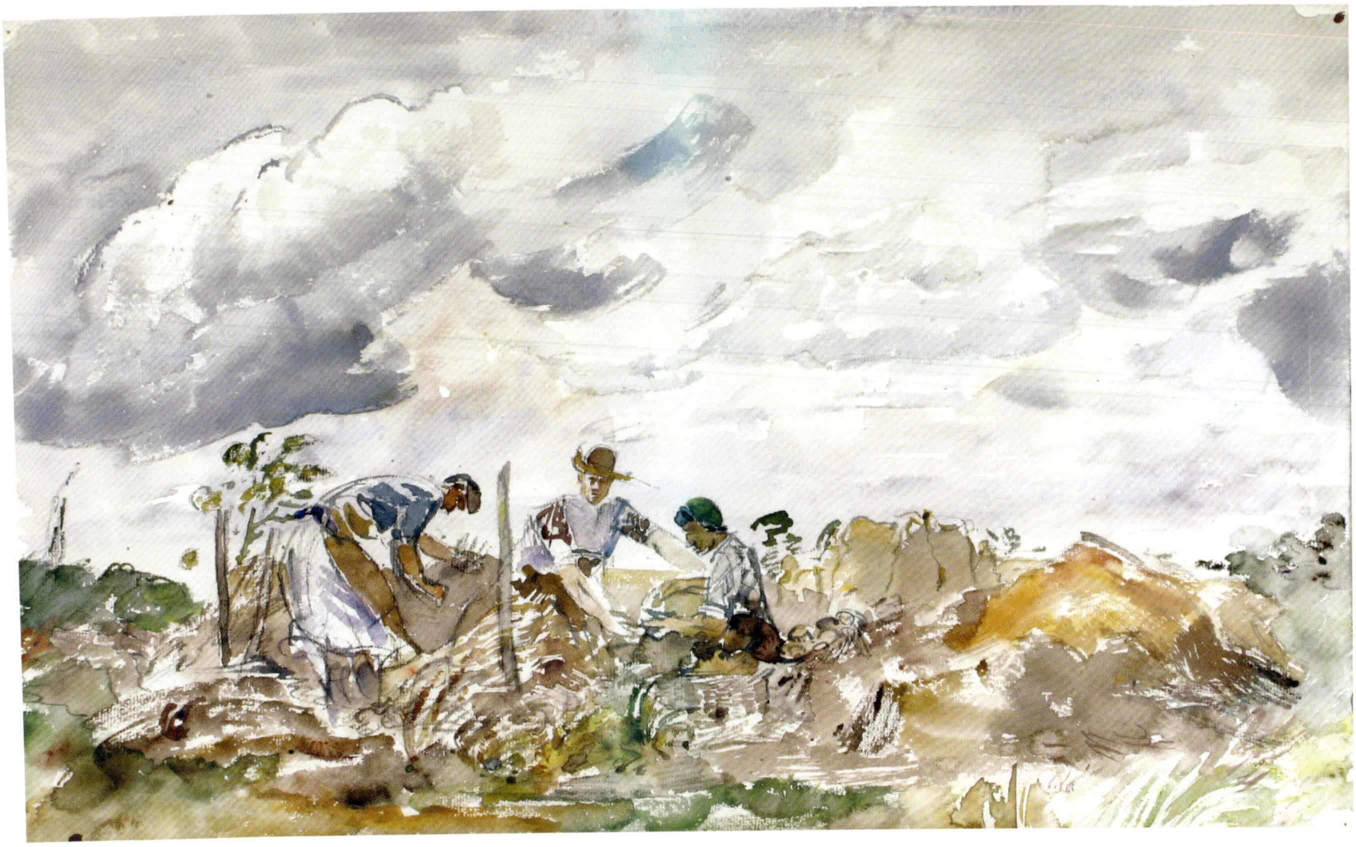

172 Women Working the Land (above)
Watercolour and pencil
12 ¼ x 19 ¼ inches

173 Gipsies at the Roadside (below)
Pen ink and watercolour with pencil
12 ½ x 17 ½ inches

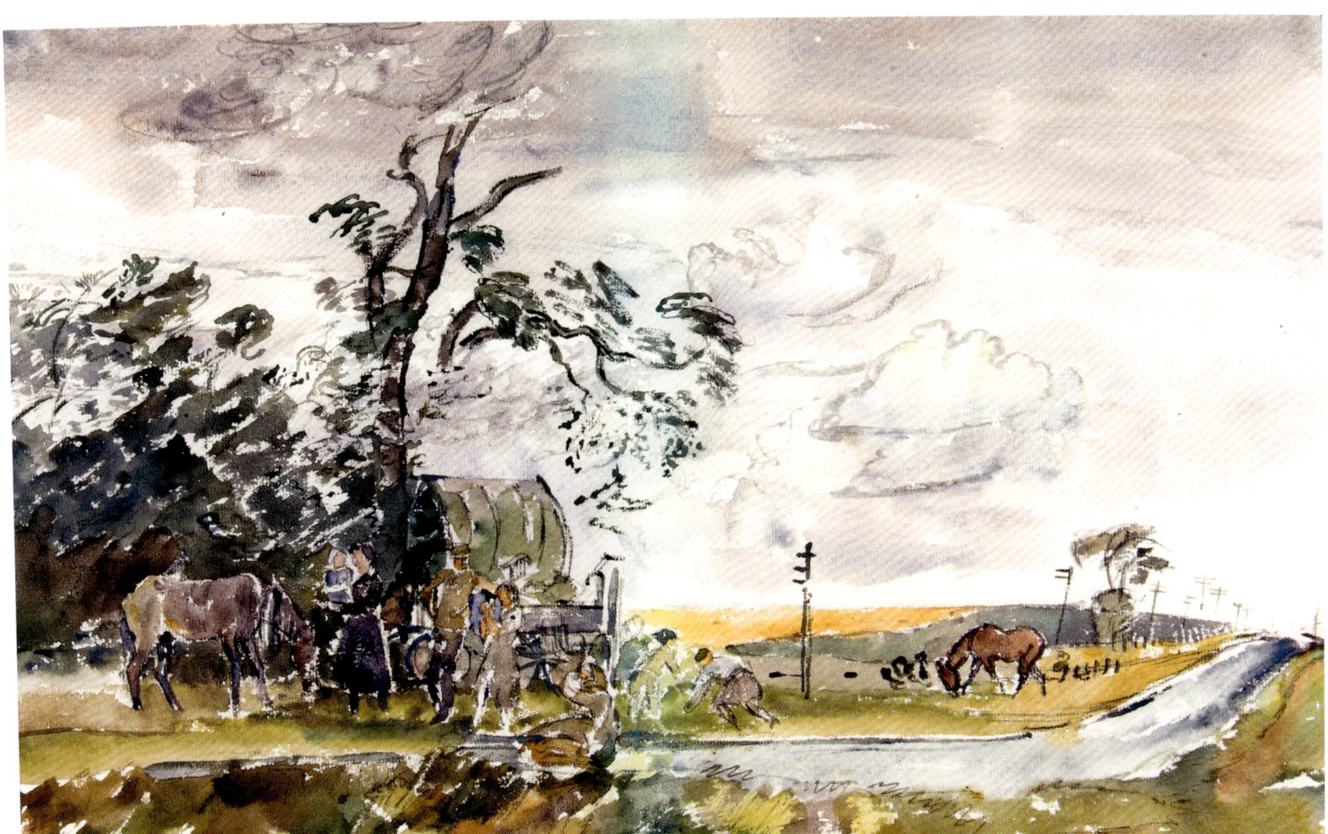

1943

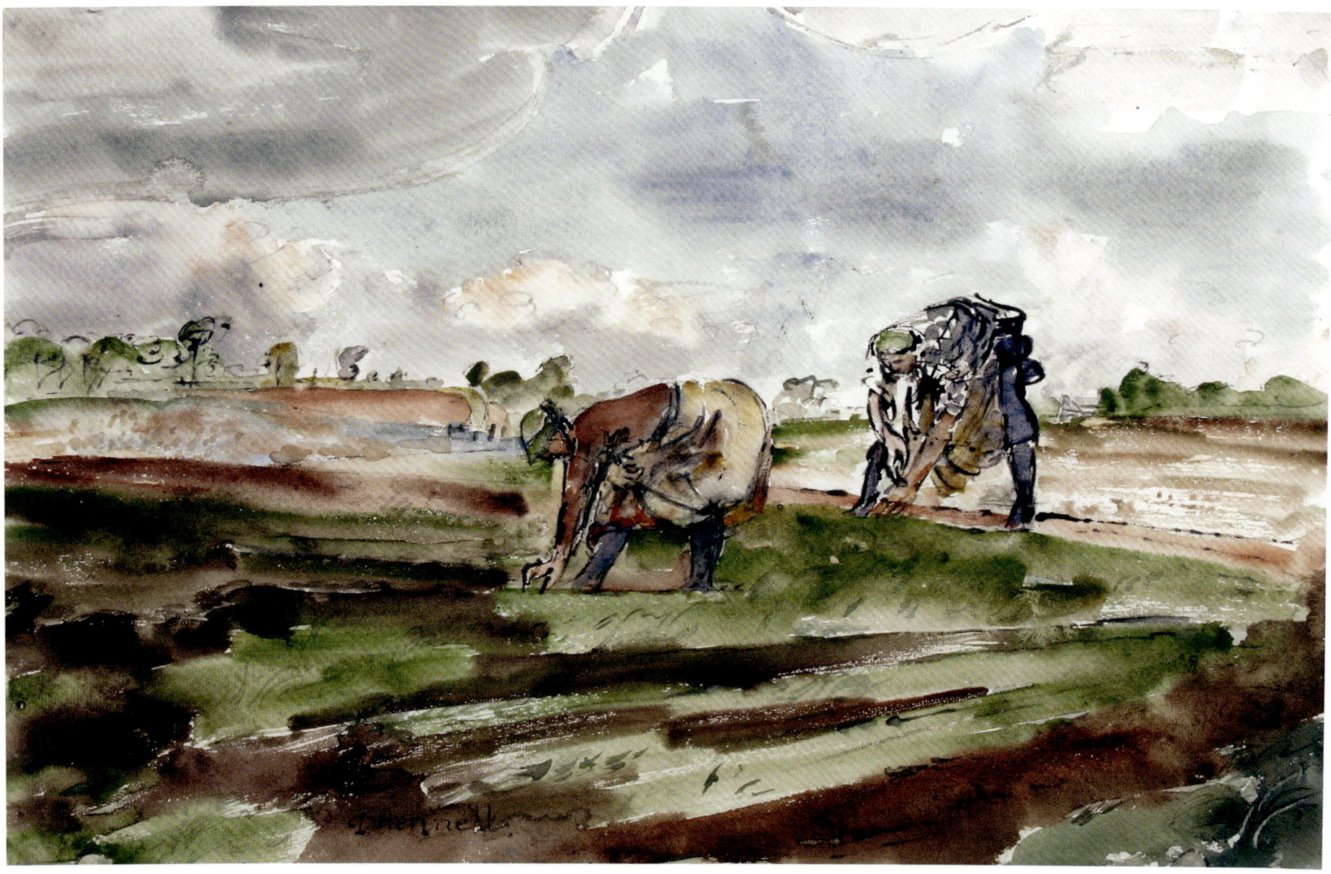

174 Weeding Onions
Signed
Inscribed with title and dated '25 May 1943' on reverse
Watercolour with pencil
12 ½ x 18 ¾ inches
Exhibited: 'The Seasons: Art of the Unfolding Year', St Barbe Museum and Art Gallery, Lymington, 11 September 2020-9 January 2021

Weeding Onions

Early in 1943, Thomas Hennell was busy working on the illustrations to *The Land is Yours*, the first of two collaborations with the ruralist writer, Clarence Henry Warren (1895-1966), the focus of which was corn growing in Essex. He completed these in April, and by late May – when he painted *Weeding Onions* – he is likely to have been back in Kent, at Orchard Cottage, Ridley. He would certainly have wanted to be close to home at that time, as his beloved brother, David, was then seriously ill and sadly died, aged only 32, in hospital in Tunbridge Wells at the beginning of June.

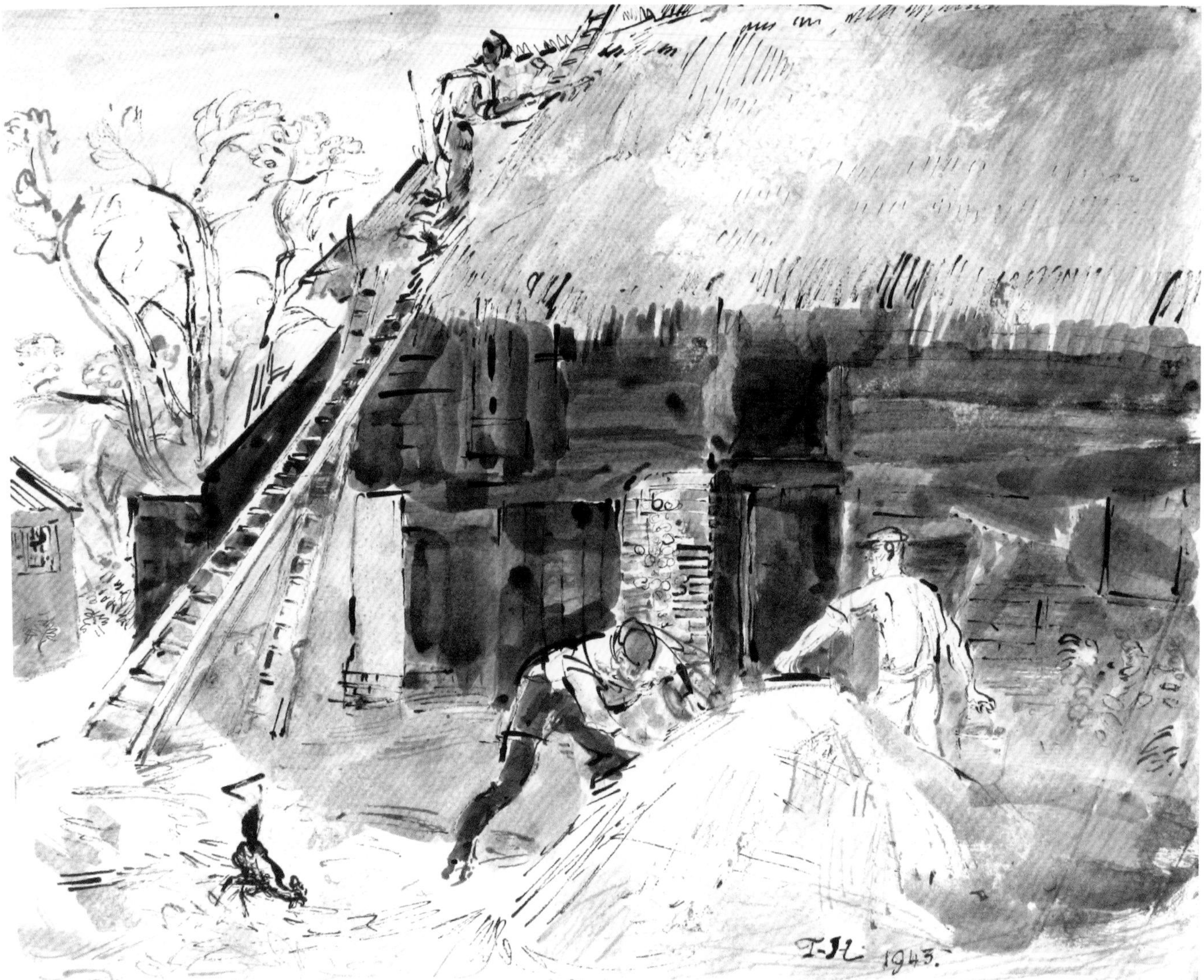

175 Thatching
Signed with initials and dated 1943
Pen ink, watercolour and pencil
11 ¼ x 13 ¼ inches

1944

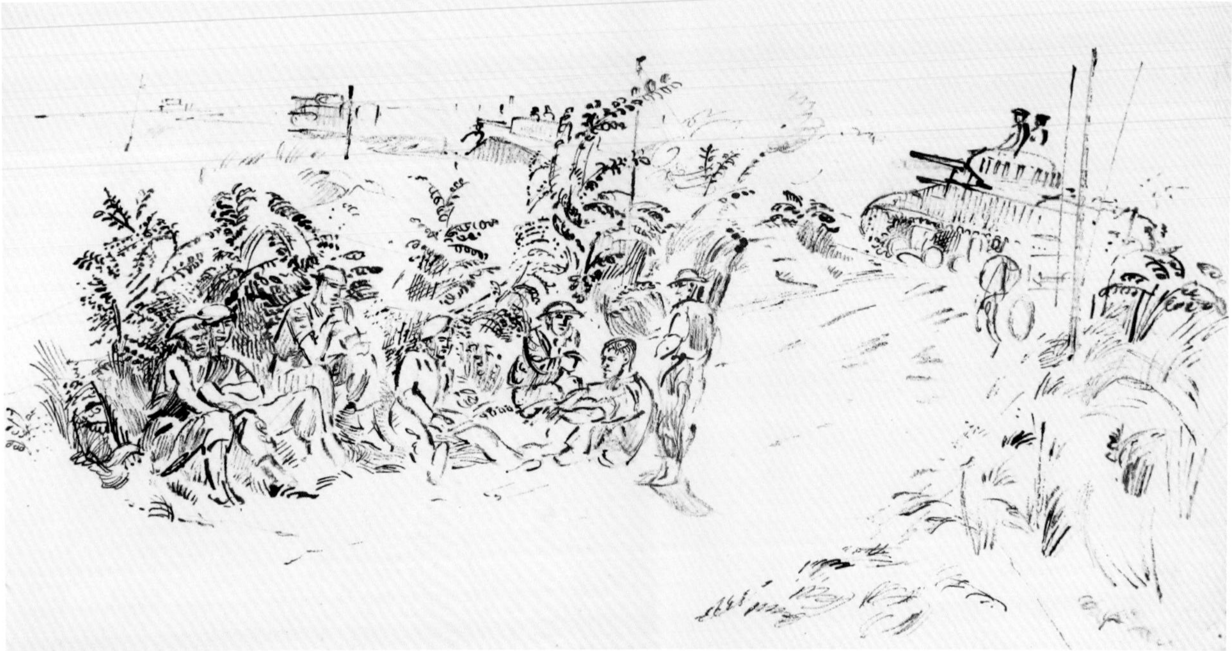

176 Dusty Road, Tanks Passing to Bénouville
Inscribed with title on reverse
Admiralty and Supreme Headquarters Allied Expeditionary Force stamps, the latter dated '1 Aug 1944' on reverse
Pen and ink; 4 ½ x 9 ¾ inches

177 Tank Graveyard Near La Délivrande
Inscribed with title on reverse
Admiralty stamp on reverse
Pen and ink; 11 ¼ x 19 ½ inches
Exhibited: 'Thomas Hennell, 1903-1945. Kent Artist, Painter of Rural Life; Circle of Ravilious and Bawden', Folkestone Art Trust, University Centre, Folkestone, April 2012, No 49;
Royal Watercolour Society, Spring 2014

'Inevitably, broken down vehicles and useless armaments had to be cleared out of the way of the advancing army. Hennell would recognise the aesthetic potential of such rubbish heaps.'

('Thomas Hennell, 1903-1945. Kent Artist, Painter of Rural Life; Circle of Ravilious and Bawden', Folkestone Art Trust, April 2012)

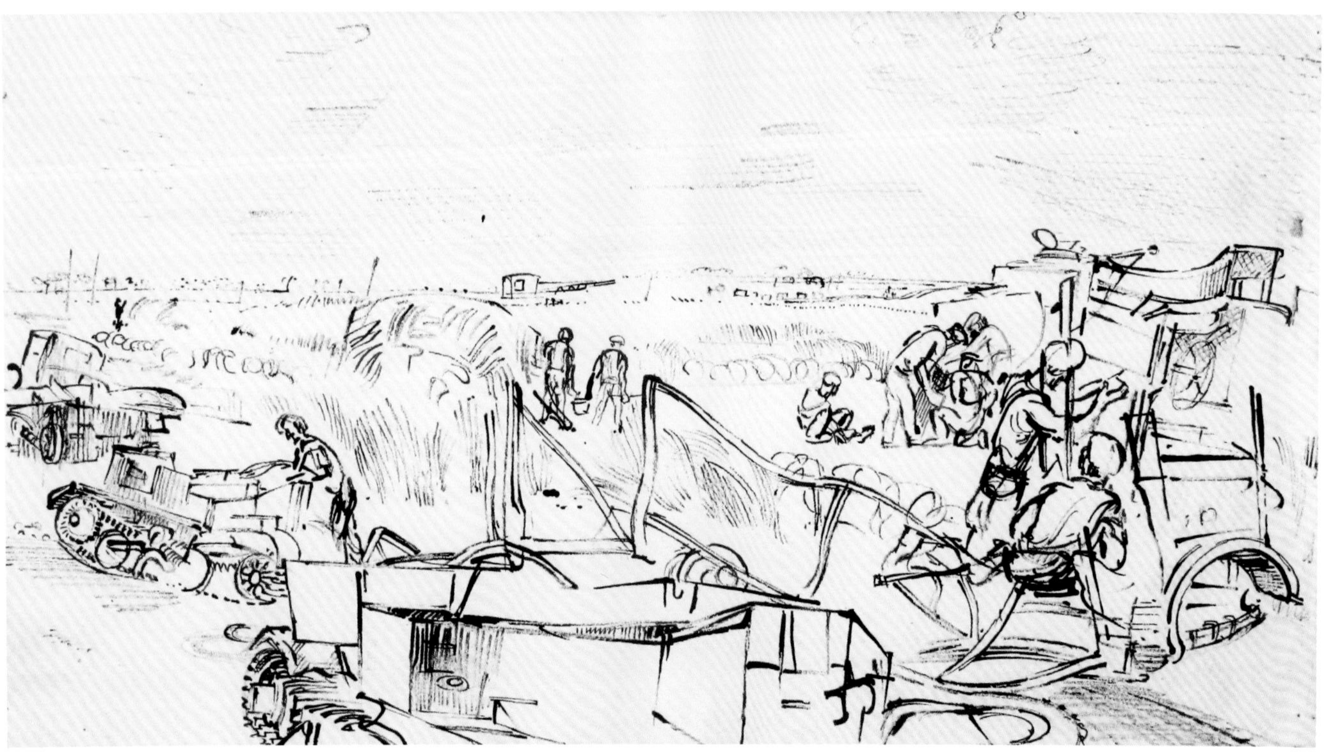

Dusty Road. Tanks Passing to Bénouville (opposite)
Following the death of Eric Ravilious in 1942, Thomas Hennell replaced him as an official war artist, and spent several months, from August to November 1943, in Iceland. In the following year, he was made a temporary lieutenant in the Royal Naval Volunteer Reserve, and on 12 June 1944 sent to Normandy on a three-month commission to record the military action, which would include the Battle of Normandy. He lodged at a small house near Caen, with Captain Derrick Knight of the Army Film Unit, and was allowed a good deal of freedom to draw what he wanted. The two drawings here give an indication of the kinds of subject that appealed to him.

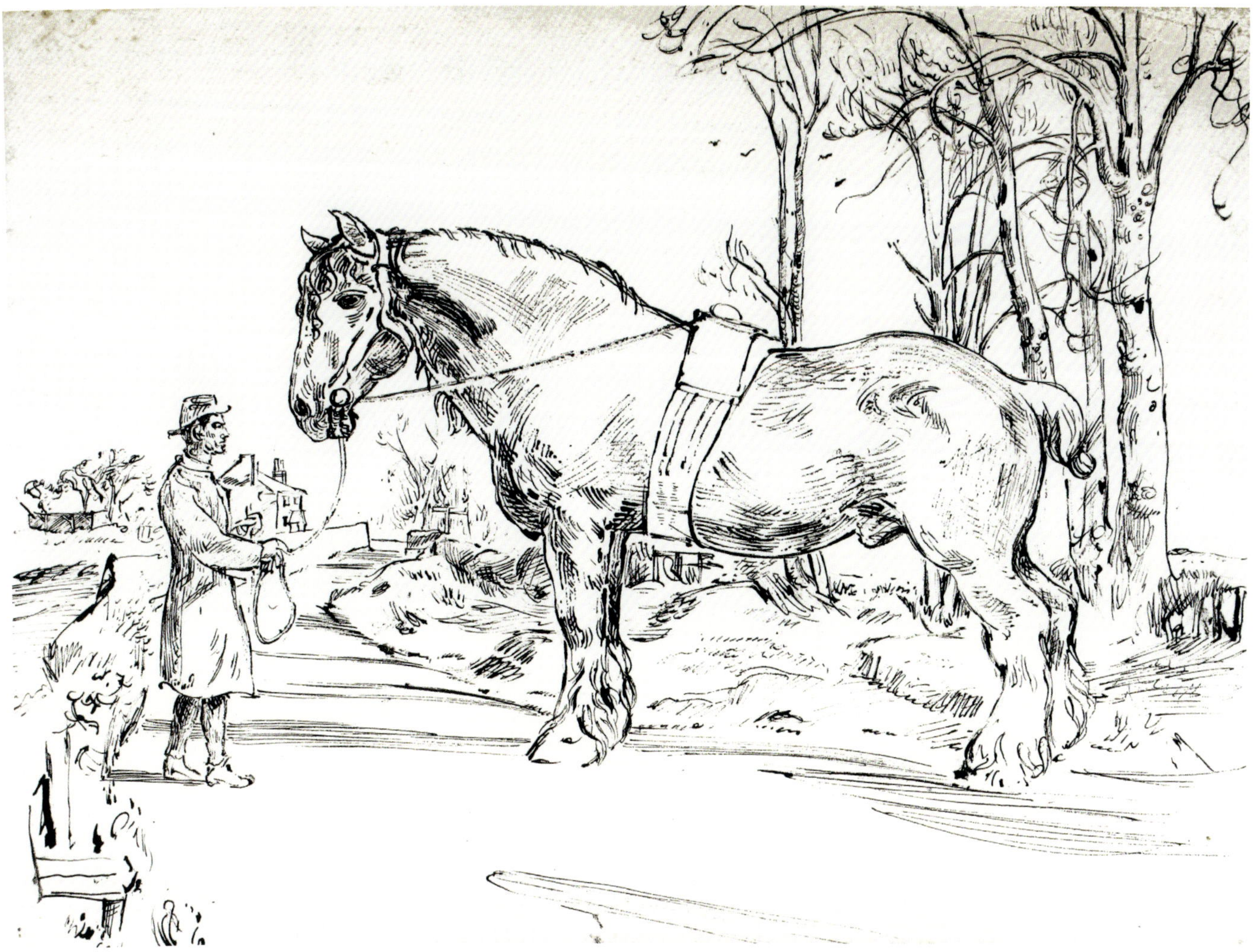

178 The Travelling Stallion
Inscribed 'Stallion Travelling the Road' on backboard
Pen and ink
15 ½ x 20 ¼ inches
Illustrated: C Henry Warren, *Miles From Anywhere*, London: Eyre and Spottiswoode, 1944, Page 50

The Travelling Stallion
Thomas Hennell produced the present work for *Miles from Anywhere* (1944), his second collaboration with C Henry Warren. The book concerns the area around Warren's home in Finchingfield, Essex, though Hennell made some of the drawings for it near his own home in Ridley, Kent.

9: THE SECOND WORLD WAR

The opportunities that British artists had to employ their talents during the second of the two World Wars developed out of those that had been afforded to them in the first. The role of the 'official war artist' was revived at the outset of the conflict, in 1939, and its responsibilities were widened and made more flexible. Artists were appointed by the War Artists' Advisory Committee, a government agency within the Ministry of Information that was headed by Sir Kenneth Clark, who was also Director of the National Gallery. They received either full-time or temporary contracts, and their achievements were supplemented by the acquisition of individual works from other artists, in order to create a comprehensive record of Britain at war. While the majority were employed to respond to aspects of life on the home front, more than 30 artists – such as Thomas Hennell [176-177] and Thomas Monnington [192] – were commissioned to work overseas.

However, the drawings and watercolours gathered here show that there were many ways for artists to engage with the war. William Thomas Wood may have failed in his application to the WAAC, but he was not deterred from demonstrating how military motifs could be incorporated effectively into traditional forms of landscape and seascape, and so provide a distinctive sense of uplift [185-186]. Cecil Arthur Hunt stayed close to his home, in Chelsea, and, guided by his own curiosity, charted the effects of enemy bombing on the surrounding architecture [182].

Other artists communicated with as wide as possible an audience by disseminating their images through a variety of printed means. For instance, S R Badmin detailed the necessary change that war was bringing to Clapham Common as a contribution to a series of affordable prints that were issued by the Artists International Association [183]. Feliks Topolski and Mervyn Peake provided their services to periodicals, and so followed in the footsteps of the Victorian 'special artists' by reporting visually on international events that ranged from an exhibition of Soviet war trophies in Moscow in 1941 [190] to the imprisonment of a German war criminal in the Rhineland in 1945 [191]. Cartoonists could also play their part, by establishing and articulating archetypal caricatures of the leaders involved in the conflict, by raising morale through humour and by helping to underpin a humane national consciousness [184,187-188].

FRANK ARCHER

Frank Joseph Archer, RWS RE (1912-1995)

As both a painter and printmaker, Frank Archer combined his talent as a draughtsman with a sensitive understanding of light. His early work was highly structured, being rooted in his experience of the British School at Rome. Later, his handling became looser and his approach more personal, as he absorbed the inspiration of historic stained glass and mosaics in order to produce vividly-coloured visual parallels to music.

For a biography of Frank Archer, please refer to page 223.

179 Composition for 'We have piped unto you and you have not danced' (opposite above)
Signed and dated 38
Pen ink, watercolour and bodycolour on tinted paper
8 ½ x 14 ½ inches

180 The Town Square (opposite below)
Signed and dated 38
Pen ink and watercolour with bodycolour
17 ½ x 22 inches

Frank Archer in Italy

In 1938, Frank Archer won the coveted Prix de Rome in Engraving, which allowed him to study for three years at the British School at Rome. His stay in Italy was unfortunately cut short by the outbreak of the Second World War in 1939. Nevertheless, the months that he spent in the country initiated 'a life-long association with [it] and a deep love for its landscape and architecture' (as he explained in 'a brief autobiography' in the catalogue to his retrospective at London's Bankside Gallery in 1990).

Two of the works included here were produced by Archer soon after his arrival in Italy in 1938. Their strong sense of design, in which solid figures are well integrated into architectural settings, show how he adjusted his abilities as a draughtsman to fit the traditions and aspirations of students of the British School at Rome. They also reveal his love for his new, if temporary home, while suggesting the potential vulnerability of its way of life and a tension presaging conflict.

The works are possibly studies for murals, and the quotation from the Gospel According to St Matthew – 'We have piped unto you and you have not danced' – is typical of the subjects set for mural projects at art schools at the time. However, it is one that would have particularly appealed to Archer, who said that the Bible was, from an early age, 'by far the most potent influence in my life'.

The third work, *Refugees* [181], was produced two years later, in 1940, by which time Archer had joined the Royal Pioneer Corps. If its location is inexplicit, it clearly draws on the settings of his Italian images, while intensifying their mood, through the use of a stronger palette and a thrusting, dynamic vertical composition. In each of its elements, down to the fragility of the fence, it epitomises the disruption of war.

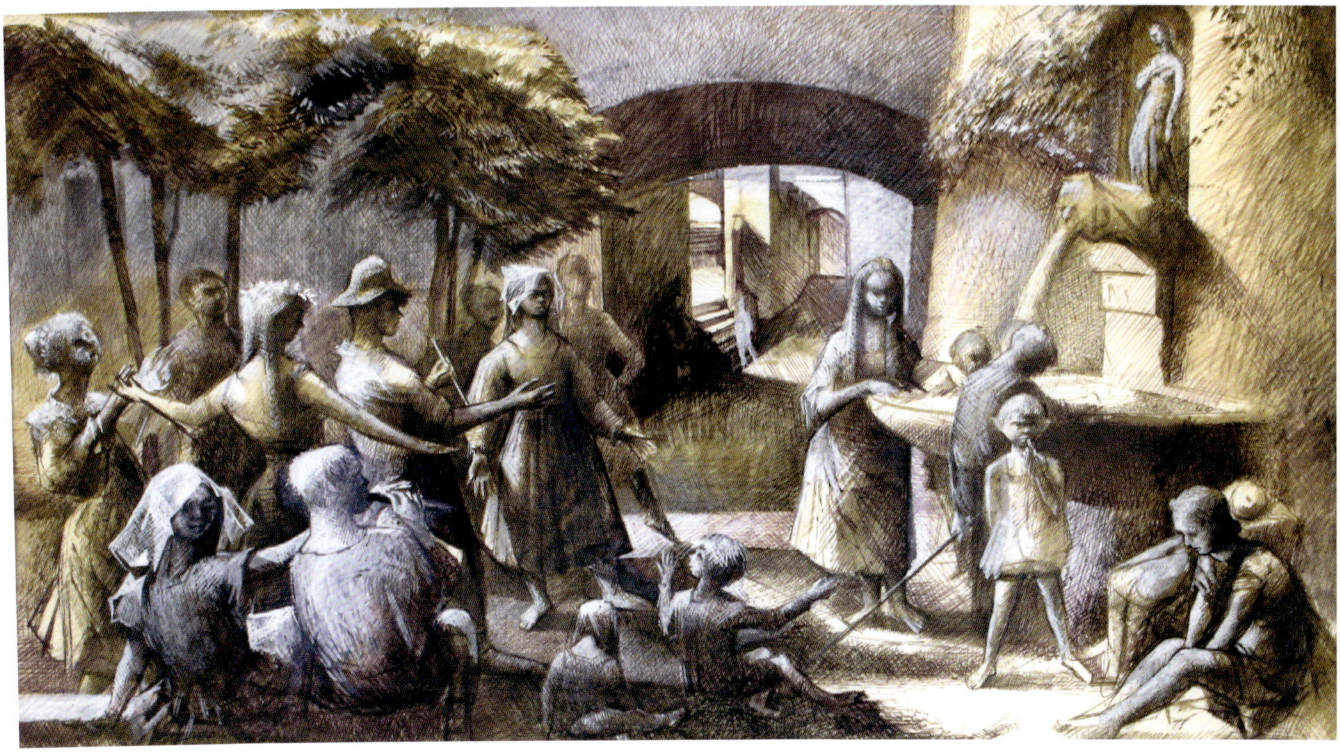

179

180

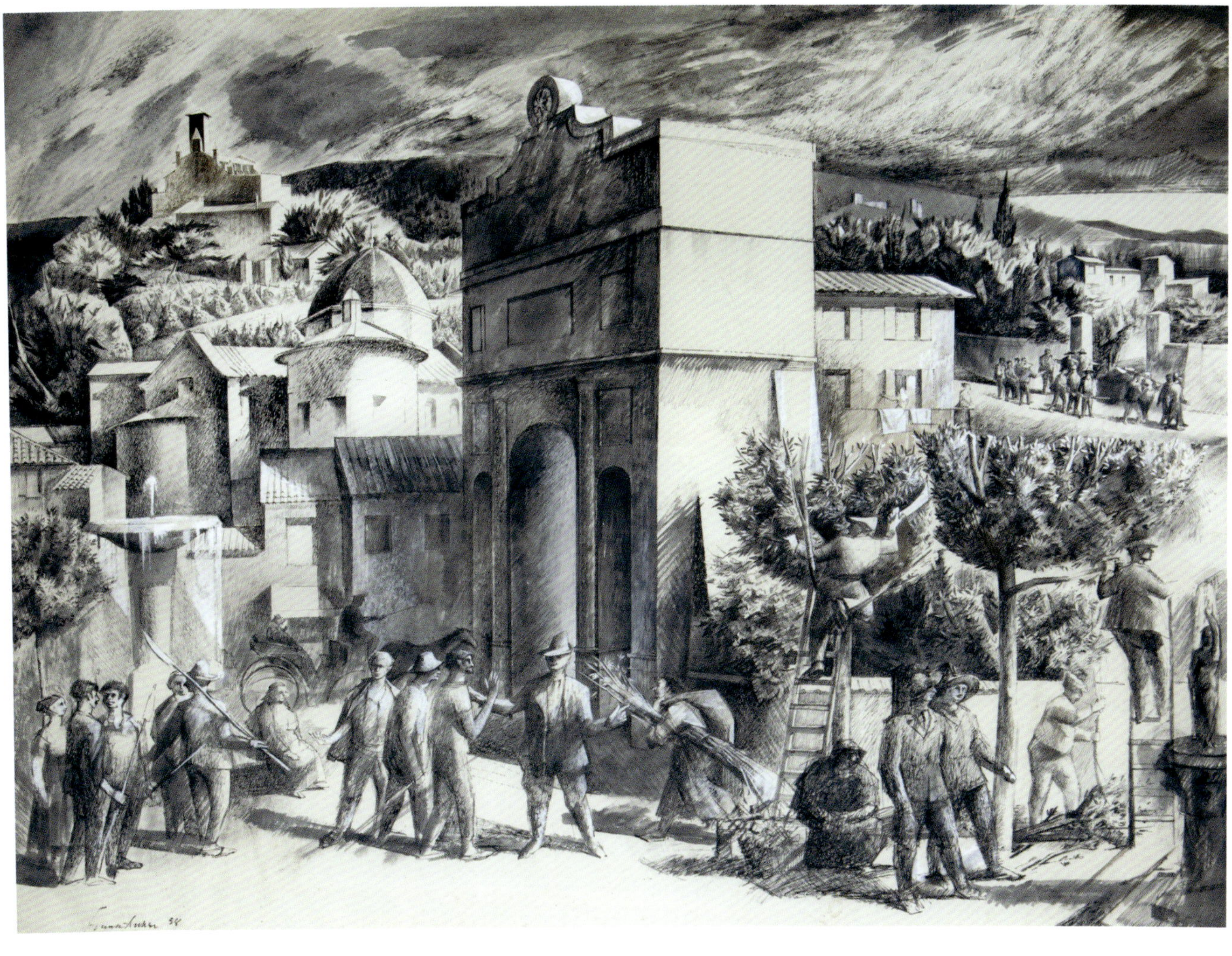

FRANK ARCHER

181 Refugees
Signed and dated 1940
Watercolour and bodycolour
15 ½ x 12 ½ inches

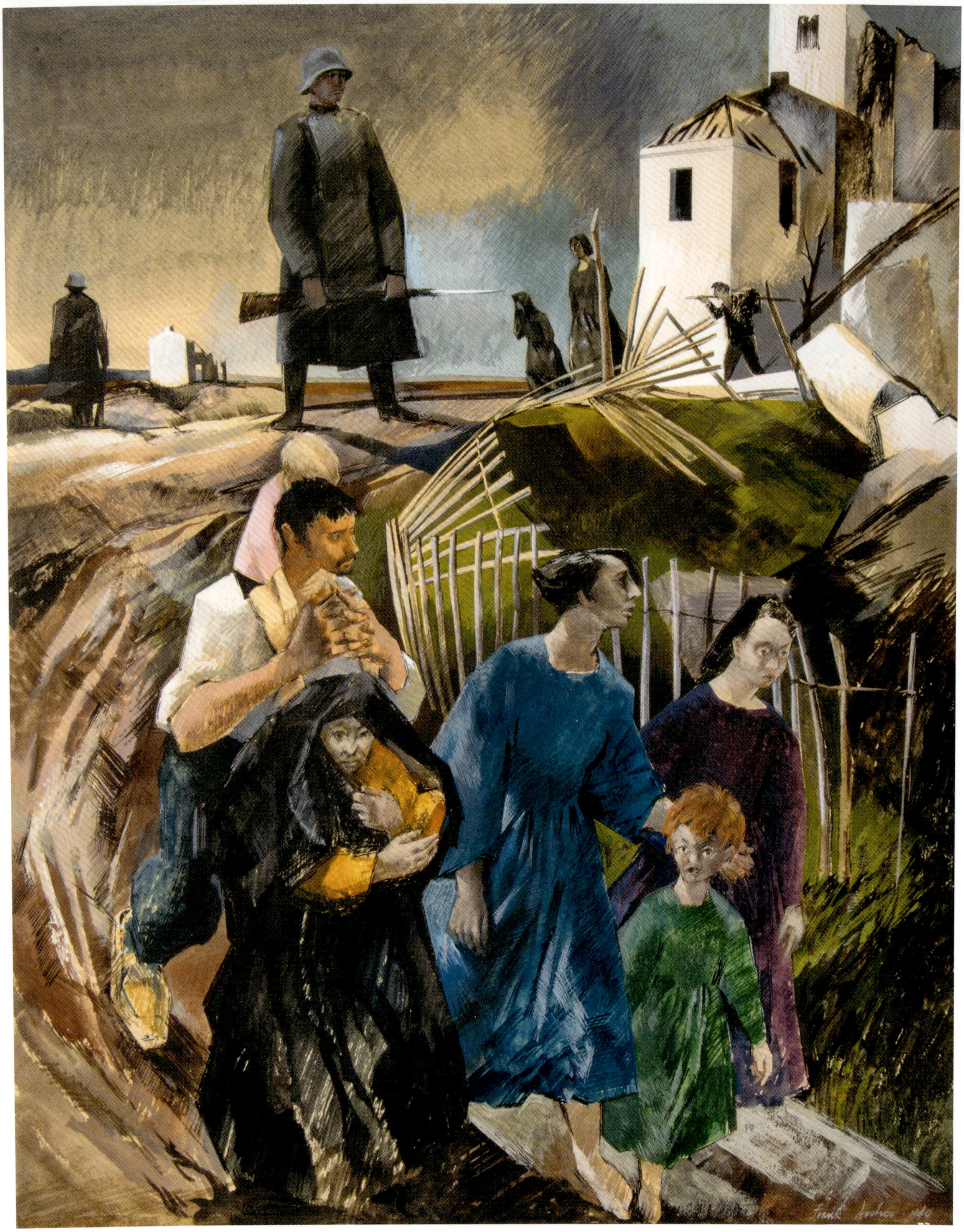

CECIL ARTHUR HUNT

Cecil Arthur Hunt, VPRWS RBA (1873-1965)

Once elected a full member of the Royal Society of Painters in Water-Colours in 1925, Cecil Arthur Hunt retired from his career as a barrister and turned his serious pastime of painting into a profession. While he had first established himself as a painter of mountains, especially the Alps and the Dolomites, he soon proved himself a master of a great variety of topographies. The impressive, often stark, effects that he achieved rival those associated with his friend and mentor, Frank Brangwyn.

For a biography of Cecil Arthur Hunt, please refer to page 210.

Enemy Action in Chelsea

From 1911 until his death in 1965, Cecil Arthur Hunt lived at Mallord House, on the corner of Mallord Street and Old Church Street, Chelsea, London. It was designed for him by the architect, Ralph Knott, who was later responsible for County Hall. Remaining there throughout the war, he drew bomb damaged buildings in his neighbourhood. Always attracted to the drama and pathos of a subject, he added bomb ruins to the list of distinctive manmade structures that he recorded – including slag heaps and quarries, bridges and castles – which paralleled his beloved mountains.

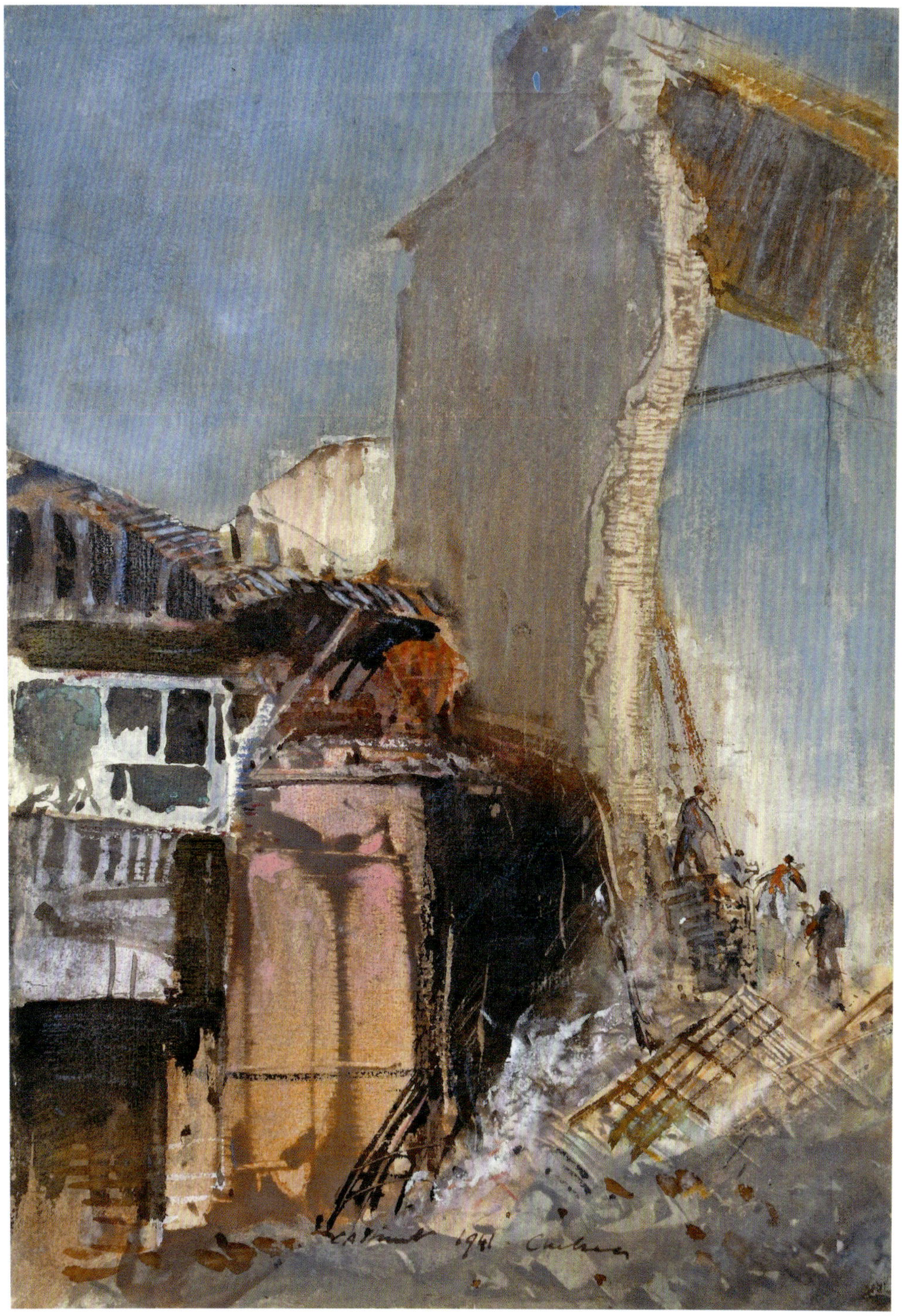

182 **Enemy Action in Chelsea**
Signed, inscribed 'Chelsea' and dated 1941
Inscribed with title and 'On the Embankment', and dated 1941 on original backboard
Watercolour with bodycolour
15 x 10 ¾ inches
Exhibited: Royal Society of Painters In Water-Colours, Spring 1943, No 20;
'Cecil Arthur Hunt VPRWS RBA', Chris Beetles Gallery, October 1996, No 15

S R BADMIN

Stanley Roy Badmin, RWS RE AIA FSIA (1906-1989)

Throughout his career, S R Badmin used his great talents – as etcher, illustrator and watercolourist – to promote a vision of the English countryside and thus of England itself. By underpinning his idealism with almost documentary precision and detail, he was able to produce images that appealed to all, and could be used for a great variety of purposes, from education through to advertising. The wellbeing suggested by each rural panorama is all the more potent, and pleasing, for the accuracy of each tree and leaf, and the plausibility of the slightest anecdotal episode.

For a biography of S R Badmin, please refer to pages 208-209.

183 **A British Common [Clapham Common]**
Signed with initials, inscribed 'London Common' and dated 1939
Pen ink and watercolour
6 x 9 ¼ inches
Exhibited: 'S R Badmin RWS, Paintings, Drawings & Prints', Chris Beetles Gallery, March-April 2015, No 105
Preliminary drawing for the Artists International Association Everyman print produced as a zinc lithoplate in 1939.

A British Common

From the early 1930s, S R Badmin had rented a studio at Clapham Common, in South London, and so had become familiar with the area. It is therefore only natural that, in designing a print for the Artists International Association in 1939, he should have chosen to depict the changes to the appearance of the common that had been wrought by wartime conditions.

Badmin was a member of the Artists International Association, which had been founded in 1933 with the aims of fighting for peace against Fascism, establishing a social role for artists, and broadening the audience for the contemporary visual arts. In 1939, the AIA devised a series of artists prints that could be reproduced by offset lithography and so mass produced and sold cheaply. Badmin contributed three designs, the others being *Down for a Refill* (showing a barrage balloon on Clapham Common) and *Dulwich Park* (showing skaters on the pond). In all, there would be 52 'Everyman Prints' by more than 40 artists.

A British Common shows the digging of a gunsite on what had been the children's playground on Clapham Common. (Included, as an ironic commentary, is the playground's former sign, announcing that 'the use of this ground is restricted to children under the age of 14'.) This was to be anti-aircraft command ZS16, with 4.5-inch guns manned by members of the Royal Artillery's Heavy Anti-Aircraft Regiment. The guns have arrived and are to the right, behind a fence and beside the bandstand. The construction of the site was the responsibility of Air Raid Precaution wardens, and the initials 'ARP' are painted on the sides of the diggers and lorries. Another part of Clapham Common, close to Holy Trinity Church, was used as an allotment during the war, and Badmin recorded it in a watercolour as one of his contributions to the scheme, 'Recording Britain' (1940, V&A).

In 1942, Badmin would be called up to active service with the Royal Air Force, and work on operational model-making at RAF Medmenham, near Henley-on-Thames.

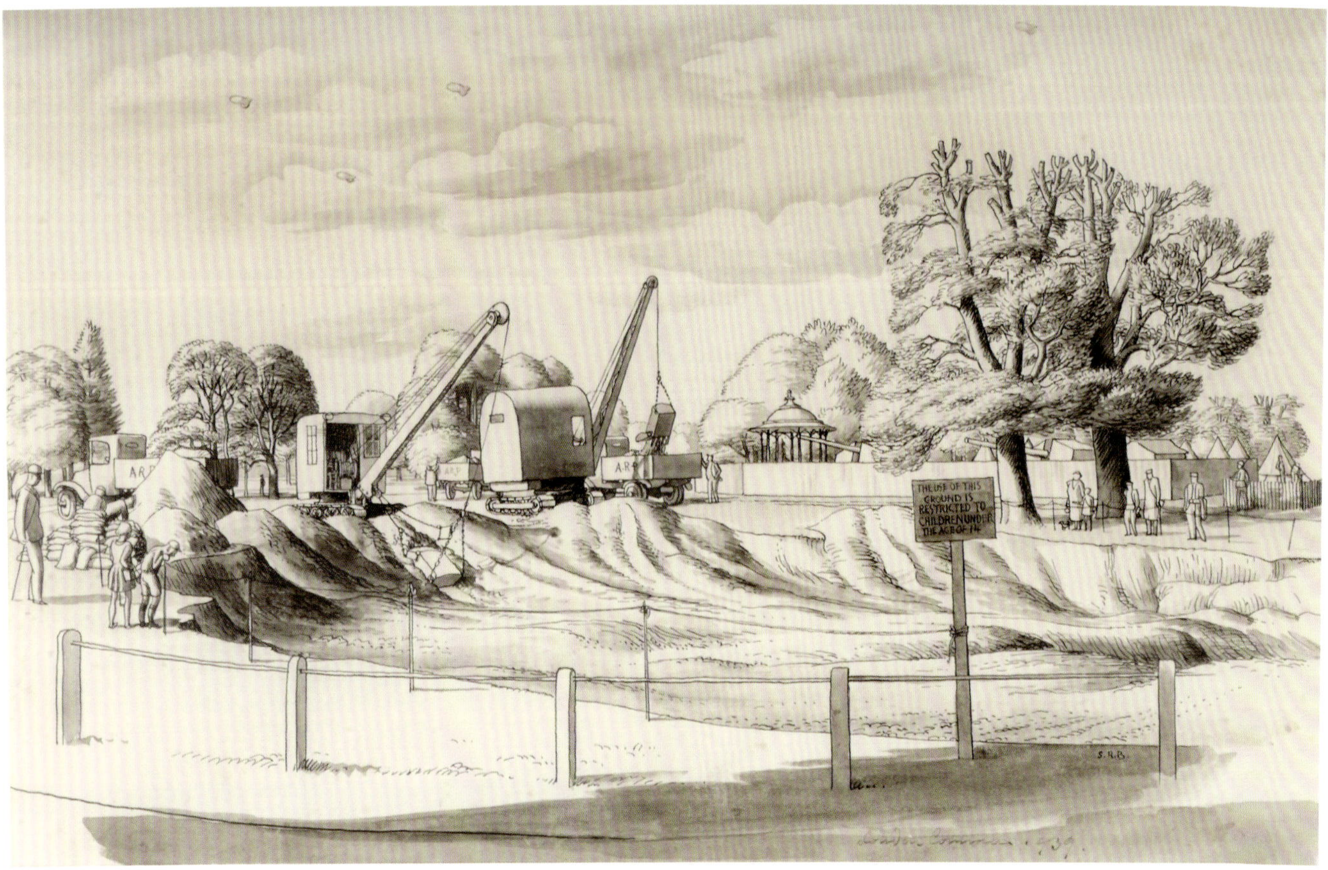

WILLIAM HEATH ROBINSON

William Heath Robinson (1872-1944)

Heath Robinson is a household name, and a byword for a design or construction that is 'ingeniously or ridiculously over-complicated' (as defined by *The New Oxford Dictionary of English*, 1998, page 848). Yet, he was also a highly distinctive and versatile illustrator, whose work could touch at one extreme the romantic watercolours of a Dulac or Rackham, at another the sinister grotesqueries of a Peake, and at yet another the eccentricities of an Emett.

For a biography of William Heath Robinson, please refer to page 224.

The Ubiquitous Winston: a cowardly attempt to kidnap Lord Haw-Haw

In 1940, William Heath Robinson contributed a series of cartoons to *The Sketch*, with the overarching title of 'The Ubiquitous Winston'. As always with Heath Robinson, the humour resides in part in the detailed, and delicate, delineation of complicated, even impossible, manoeuvres. However, this series adds a degree of gentle irony, both verbal and visual, by presenting events from the enemy's point of view, and casting Britain's wartime Prime Minister, Winston Churchill, as the villain of the piece – so here calling him 'cowardly'. The underlying purpose of the series was to bolster morale among the British people by suggesting that Churchill was in complete control of all events, even at the micro-level. In this example, he is seen kidnapping William Joyce (1906-1946), the American-born fascist, who, during the war, broadcast Nazi propaganda to Britain from Germany. Joyce was the best known of the broadcasters to be identified as 'Lord Haw-Haw', a nickname coined by Jonah Barrington, the radio critic of the *Daily Express*.

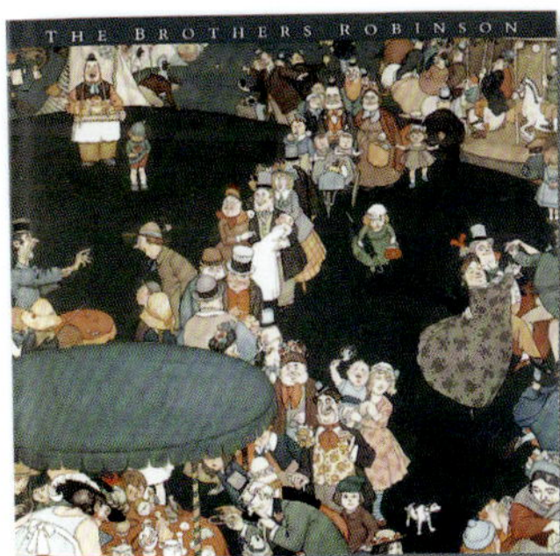

The Chris Beetles Gallery has mounted a number of significant exhibitions of the work of William Heath Robinson. These include 'The Brothers Robinson', which was shown at the Chris Beetles Gallery and the Royal Festival Hall in February 1992. It was accompanied by this 240-page, fully-illustrated, limited-edition catalogue, written by the Heath Robinson expert, Geoffrey Beare.

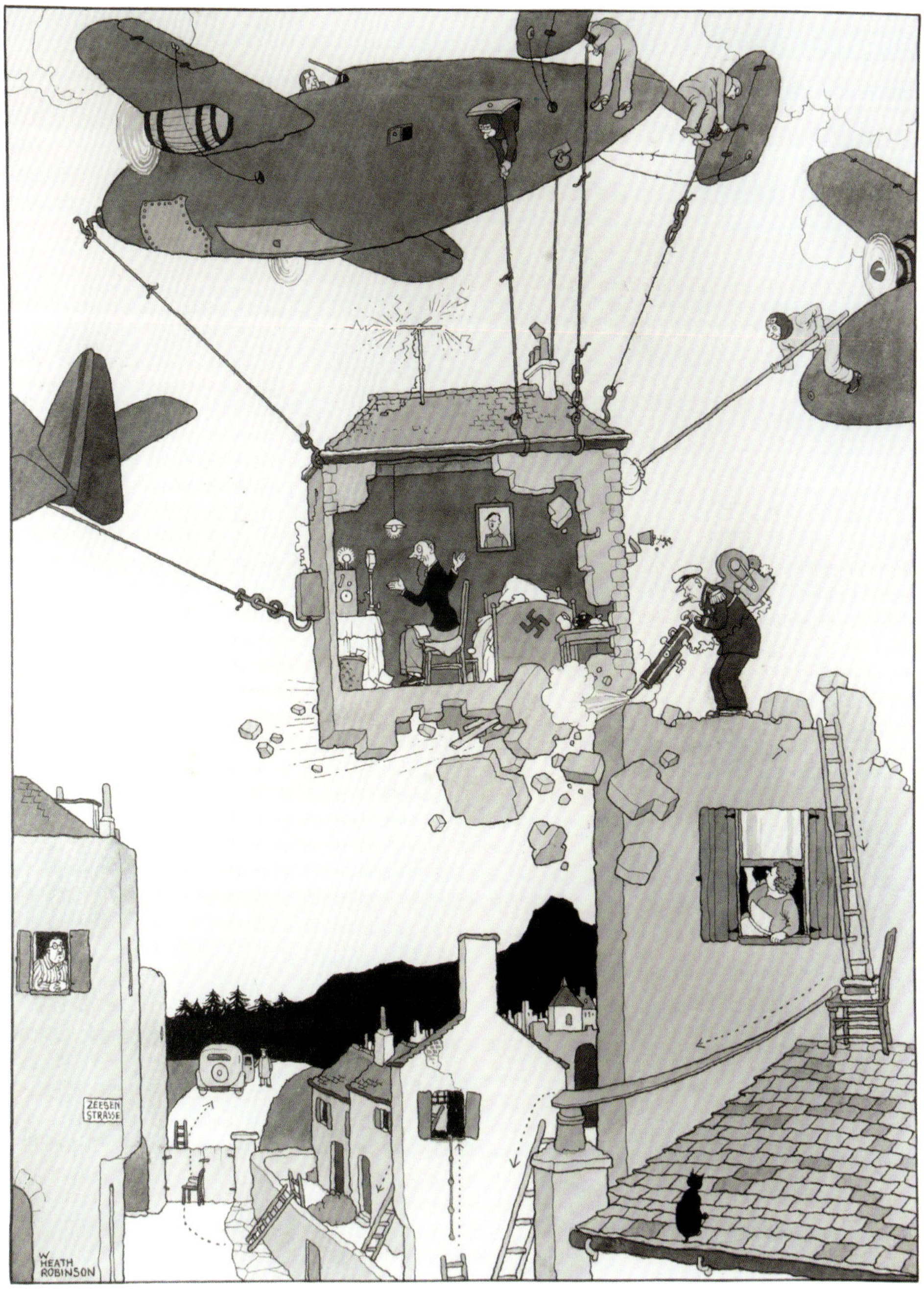

184 **The Ubiquitous Winston: a cowardly attempt to kidnap Lord Haw-Haw**
Signed and inscribed 'Cowardly Manoeuvre by the First Lord to Kidnap Lord Haw Haw'
Inscribed 'To Oliver and Evelyn with love from Mother' (Josephine Heath Robinson [William's wife]) [/] 'To Donald and Lucy: We are delighted for you to have this original – Oliver and Evelyn'
on reverse
Pen and ink on board
16 ¼ x 12 ½ inches
Illustrated: *The Sketch*, 24 January 1940, Page 99

WILLIAM THOMAS WOOD

William Thomas Wood, VPRWS ROI NS (1877-1958)

A painter in both oil and watercolour, William Thomas Wood became particularly well known for atmospheric landscapes of Sussex, as well as flower still lifes. During the First World War, he served on the Balkan Front, both in the Royal Flying Corps and as an official war artist. He returned to images of aerial warfare in the Second World War, during which he served in the Home Guard.

For a biography of William Thomas Wood, please refer to page 214.

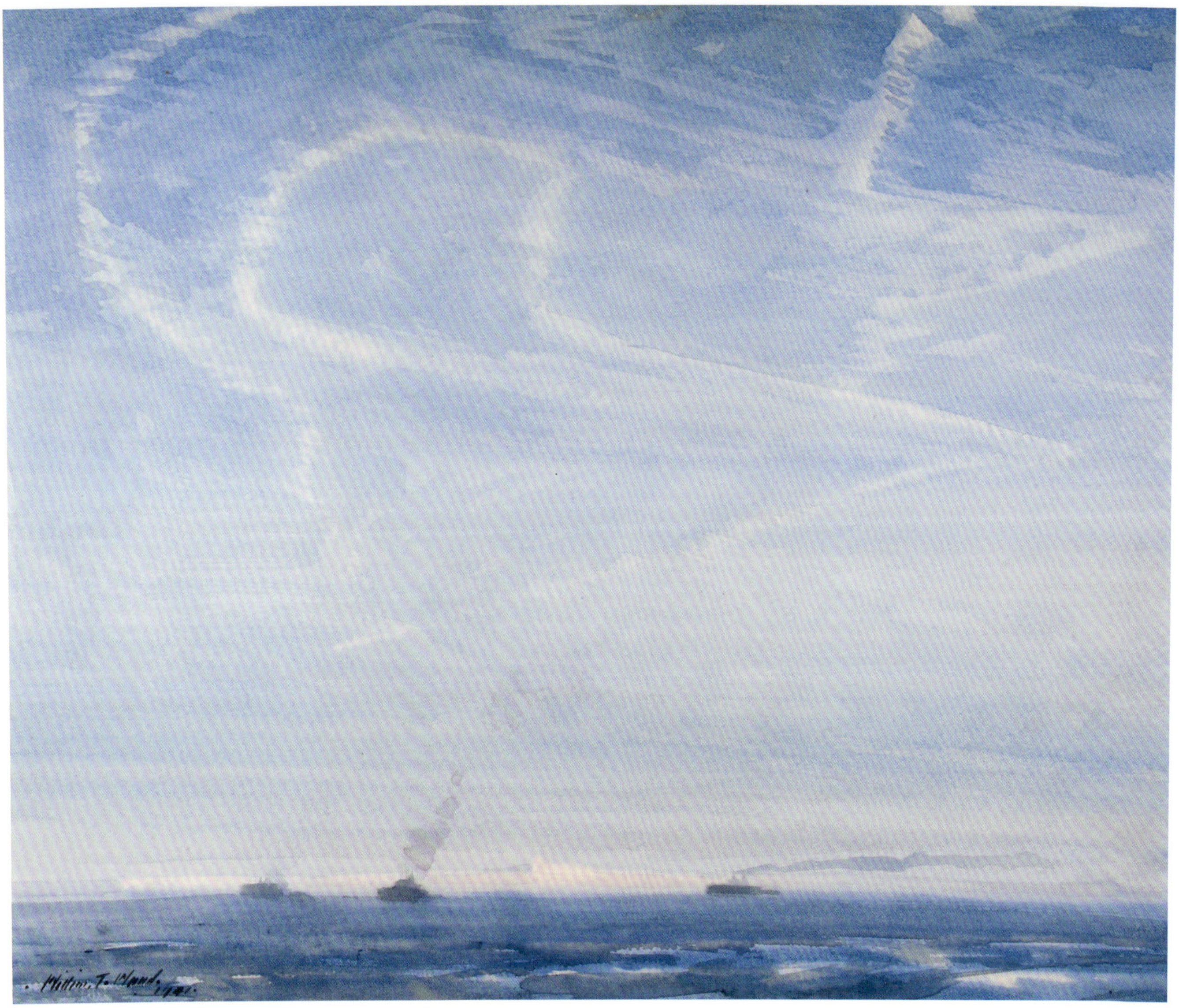

185 **Aeroplane Trails**
Signed and dated 1941
Inscribed with title on reverse
Watercolour
12 x 14 inches

William Thomas Wood in Dover

Given that he had been an official war artist during the First World War, William Thomas Wood must surely have been disappointed when, on 30 May 1940, he failed in his application to provide work to the War Artists Advisory Committee. Nevertheless, he pursued his distinctive vision of war. Having recorded aerial dogfights over Salonika in 1918, he now captured aeroplanes and their trails over Dover, using a square format and a light touch to create a great sense of height and space. Having worked in Dover before the Second World War, and painted Shakespeare's Cliff in 1937, among other subjects, he was drawn back there as a result of its symbolic quality and strategic position. The other paintings that he produced during the war range from his impressions of London as a member of the Home Guard to pastoral landscapes that suggest what it was that people were fighting for.

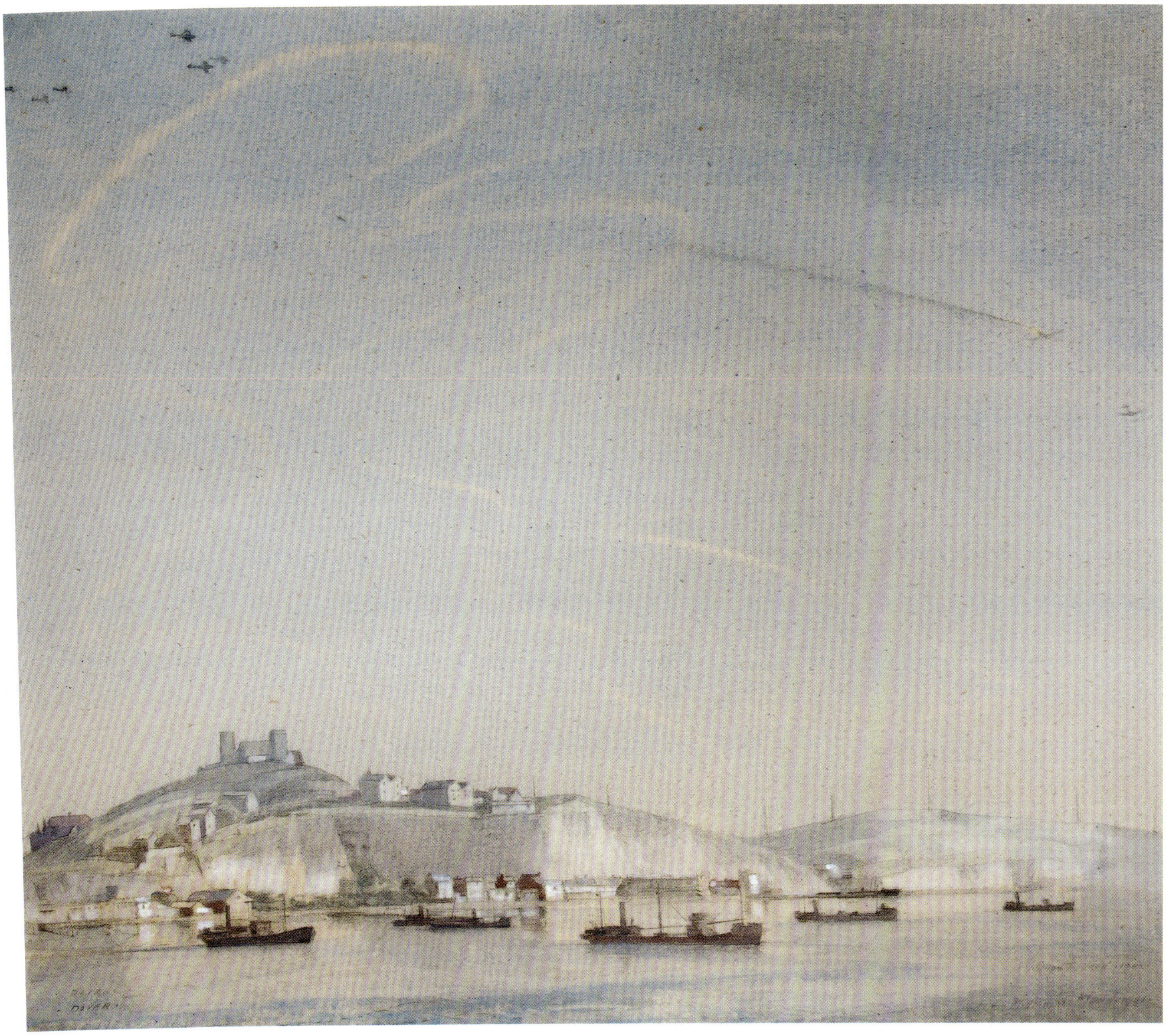

186 Dover
Signed twice, inscribed with title twice and dated 1940 and 1941
Watercolour with bodycolour
18 ¾ x 20 inches
Exhibited: A work entitled 'Dover' was exhibited at the Royal Academy Summer Exhibition in 1942, No 125

E H SHEPARD

Ernest Howard Shepard, MC OBE (1879-1976)

While E H Shepard is now best remembered for his immortal illustrations to *Winnie-the-Pooh* and *The Wind in the Willows*, he was a wide-ranging artist and illustrator, with an unsurpassed genius for representing children, and an underrated talent for political cartoons.

For a biography of E H Shepard, please refer to page 181.

Accident to the Axis
'United we stood'

The fall of Beda Fomm, Libya, on 7 February 1941 marked the end of Operation Compass, the first major Allied offensive of the North African campaign. In the ten weeks of the campaign, Allied forces had decisively defeated the Italian 10th Army, advancing 800 kilometres, destroying or capturing some 400 tanks and 1290 artillery pieces and capturing approximately 130,000 Italian and Libyan POWs.

This was a crippling blow to Italian control in North Africa, at a time when the combined Axis powers of Nazi Germany, Italy and Japan were attempting to consolidate their position in Europe, Africa and the Far East. In Europe, the Nazis were massing troops on the Soviet border in preparation for an invasion of the Soviet Union, which occurred in June 1941 under the name Operation Barbarossa. In the Far East, Japan had successfully invaded French Indochina, and was planning to take advantage of the war in Europe by seizing resource-rich European possessions in Southeast Asia.

Shepard depicts Adolf Hitler and a Japanese soldier, representing Nazi Germany and Japan respectively, standing tall in their respective theatres of war, while Benito Mussolini, representing Italy, is shown sinking into the mud.

(It is possible that the muddiness of the ground that Hitler and Mussolini are standing on/sinking into represent the ground of the 'Near East' muddied by war, whilst the Japanese soldier stands on solid, unmuddied ground, perhaps representing the fact that the Far East had not yet become a major theatre of war. If this is the case, Shepard seems to be ignoring the Second Sino-Japanese War from 1937, in which thousands had already died. The sinking of Mussolini, despite clinging desperately onto Hitler, seems to indicate a belief that this defeat signaled the end of Italy as a significant member of the Axis. This was a little premature, as the reinforcement of North African Italian troops by the German Afrika Korps allowed a continuation of hostilities in North Africa, until the Axis finally were defeated in May 1943.)

Alexander Beetles

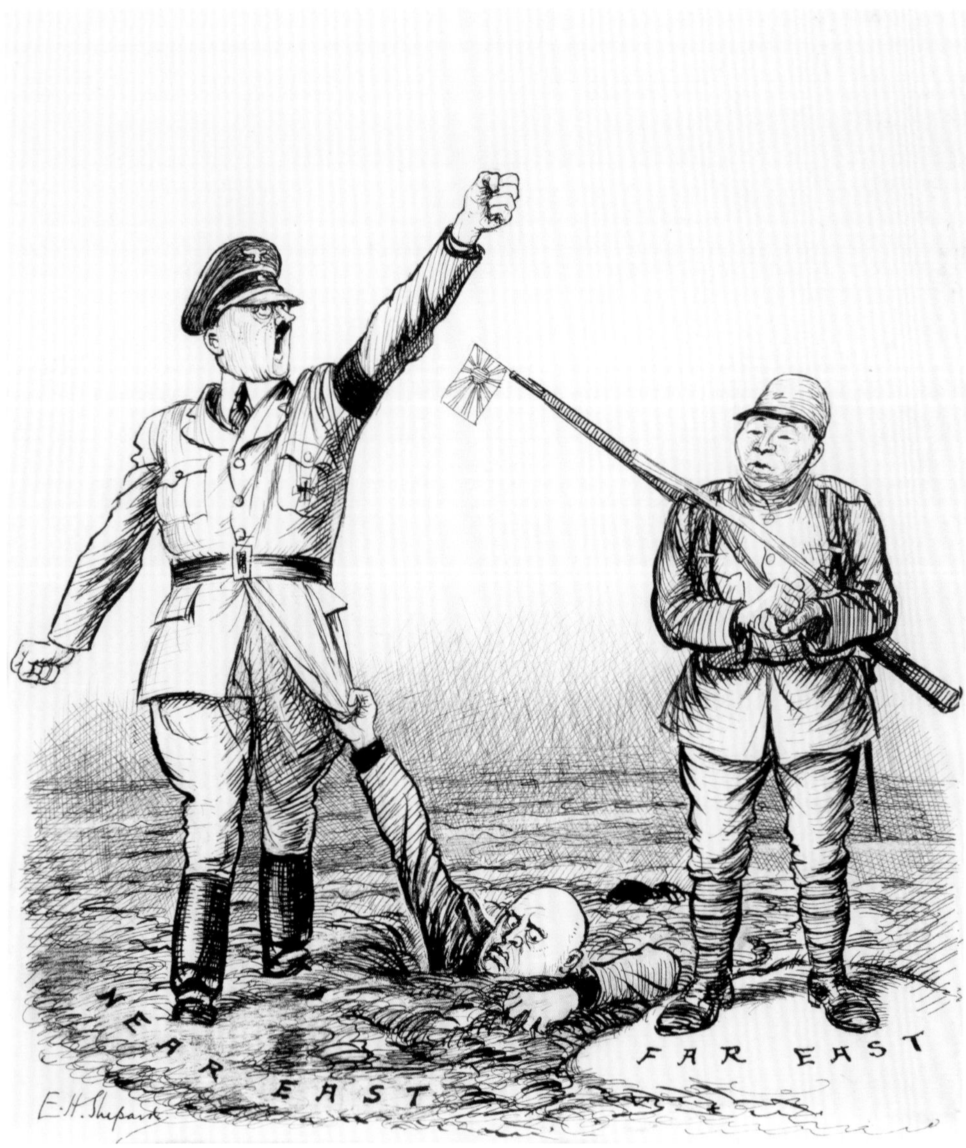

187 **Accident to the Axis**
'United we stood'
Signed and inscribed with title
Pen and ink with bodycolour
12 x 9 ½ inches
Provenance: 'The Political Cartoon Collection of Jeffrey Archer', Sotheby's, London, 14 March 2018, Lot 89
Illustrated: *Punch*, 5 March 1941, Page 231
Exhibited: 'Images of Power: From the Jeffrey Archer Cartoon Collection', Monnow Valley Arts, 3 September-30 October 2011; 'Comedy and Commentary', Mottisfont, Hampshire, January-April 2020

DAVID LOW

Sir David Alexander Cecil Low (1891-1963)

David Low was considered the most outstanding British political cartoonist of his generation. Able to capture recognisable likenesses with great economy, he produced the definitive image of a number of leading figures of the day. And he did so with a subtle combination of ridicule and insight, rather than exaggeration and condemnation. A key feature of his approach was the use of such symbols as the strong but stubborn TUC carthorse and the reactionary Englishman, Colonel Blimp.

For a biography of David Low, please refer to page 225.

188 **Reconnaissance Flight**
Signed
Pen and ink with watercolour and crayon
14 ½ x 17 ¼ inches
Illustrated: *Evening Standard*, 2 December 1943
Exhibited: 'Comedy and Commentary', Mottisfont, Hampshire, January-April 2020

Reconnaissance Flight

By December 1943, it was clear that the war had turned decisively against Nazi Germany. The liberation of Stalingrad in February 1943 had been followed by a Soviet counter-offensive and, following Italy's armistice with the Allies, British and US forces invaded the Italian mainland in September. Franz von Papen had served as Vice-Chancellor of the German Reich from 1933 to 1934, but had been quickly marginalised by Hitler. Though he survived the purge of the Night of the Long Knives in the summer of 1934, he was forced to resign as Vice-Chancellor. Hitler was keen to remove von Papen and his influence from Berlin, so he was named first Ambassador to Austria and then, from 1939, Ambassador to Turkey.

In November 1943, von Papen visited Berlin and met with Hitler. David Low's cartoon suggests there was a belief in the British press that von Papen had met with Hitler to discuss the possibility of negotiating peace. Low indicates the types of peace Hitler may consider, while von Papen appears to stealthily attempt to fix the accoutrements of peace to Hitler and a Nazi General. It would later emerge that von Papen had flown to Berlin to reveal to Hitler that he had a spy working in the British embassy in Ankara.

Alexander Beetles

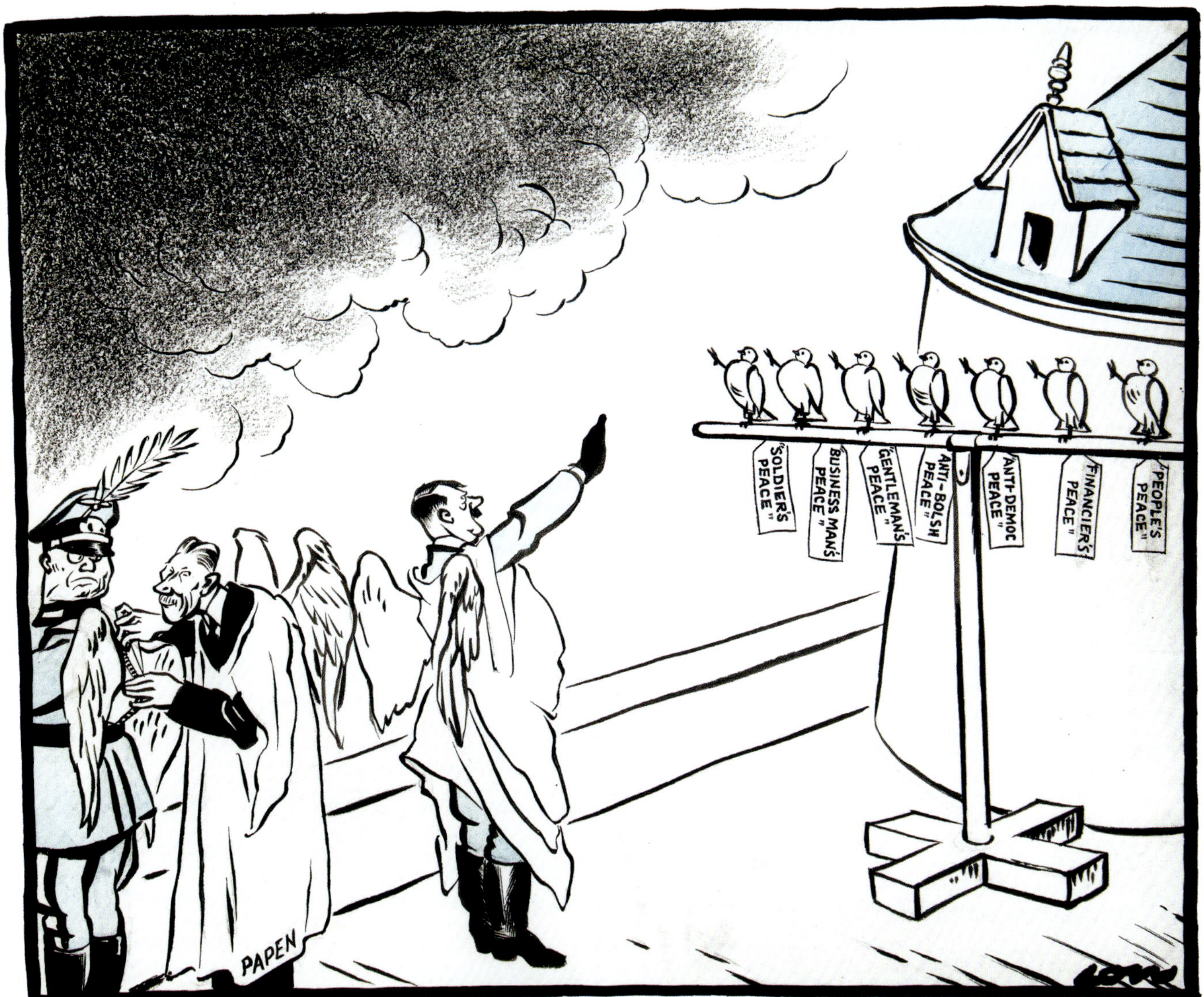

RECONNAISSANCE FLIGHT

FELIKS TOPOLSKI

Feliks Topolski (1907-1989)

The significance of Feliks Topolski is suggested by those projects that were closest to his heart: the regular broadsheet, *Topolski's Chronicle* (1953-82), and the sequence of murals, *Memoir of the Century* (1975-89); for his drawings and paintings comprise a uniquely comprehensive yet impartial record of the age in which he lived. He employed a swift, expressionist style for all of his projects, from illustrations to stage designs. This gave an emotional unity to his oeuvre, and even the smallest of his figures – such as a vignette for his edition of Bernard Shaw's *Pygmalion* (1941) – seems to speak volumes.

For a biography of Feliks Topolski, please refer to pages 228-229.

189 Passport Control (opposite above)
Pen ink and crayon with pencil
12 x 15 inches
Illustrated: Drawn for the title sequence of Sidney Gilliat and Frank Launder's film, *The Rake's Progress,* 1945

The Rakes' Progress

The Rakes' Progress is a 1945 British film written and produced by Frank Launder and Sidney Gilliat, and directed by Sidney Gilliat. It has been described as 'part satiric critique, part ironic elegy' and 'one of the most fascinating films of the classical British cinema's richest period'. Feliks Topolski's 'atmospheric and somewhat lonely' drawings for the title sequence suggest that satire will not wholly dominate (Bruce Babington, *Launder and Gilliat: British Film Makers*, Manchester University Press, 2002, pages 94 & 98).

Based on a story by Val Valentine, who contributed to the screenplay, *The Rake's Progress* traces the decline of a modern upper-class playboy, Vivian Kenway, through a life of womanising, heavy drinking and running into debt, from being sent down from Oxford to causing the death of his father. Inspired in part by William Hogarth's series of paintings and engravings of the same name, the film departs from its source by allowing Kenway to redeem himself by dying in combat during the Second World War (as shown in the opening moments). Rex Harrison's sympathetic portrayal of Kenway is considered one of the best performances of his career.

170 **The War Trophies**

When war broke out in 1939, Polish-born Feliks Topolski remained in London. While nominally serving as an officer in the Polish army, he became an official war artist to both the Polish government in exile and the British. For the British, he recorded bombed London streets during the Battle of Britain and the Blitz, in May 1941, and, while doing so, received serious wounds that led him to spend six weeks in hospital. As some compensation, his efforts resulted in the book, *Britain in Peace and War* (1941).

In August 1941, Topolski received a commission from *Picture Post* to travel as a member of the first allied Arctic convoy to Russia. He arrived in Moscow as the German army moved towards the city, in an advance that led to the gruelling struggle of the Battle of Moscow, and eventual Russian victory. Many of the drawings that he made there were published in 1942, in *Russia in War*, including the present one, which shows one of the highlights of the tour. This was an exhibition of captured German war trophies held at Moscow's Gorky Central Park of Culture and Leisure, along the banks of the River Moskva. One American, who visited the exhibition in the following year, described it thus:

> Here, spreading over many acres is a vast but systematically organized collection of armament and equipment captured from the Germans. There are special sections for each classification – tanks, planes, trucks, artillery, uniforms, mines, bombs etc … The Russian Major General who personally conducted me had special technicians elaborating details in each section … [They] explained the differences in German and Soviet equipment and indicated how much more mobile a great deal of the Russian equipment is.
> (Edward C Carter, Chair of the American Committee for Russian War Relief, in a letter written to his son, John, on 15 November 1943)

By contrast, the present image focusses on the visitors to the exhibition rather than the exhibits themselves, and creates a sense of occasion by including a number of large and impressive flags – both German and Soviet – in motion above the crowd.

Following his return from Moscow, Topolski made further travels, which took in Egypt and the Levant, and India, Burma and China. In the final year of the war, he accompanied the Polish 2nd Corps in the advance up the Adriatic coast, and other Polish forces in the Low Countries. He was in Bergen-Belsen concentration camp two weeks after its liberation in April 1945, and later worked as an official war artist at the Nuremberg Trials. The record of these years appeared as *Three Continents 1944-45* (1946).

190 The War Trophies (opposite below)
Signed, inscribed 'Park of Culture – War Trophies' and dated 'September 1941'
Pen ink and watercolour
12 ¾ x 15 ¾ inches
Illustrated: Sir Stafford Cripps (intro), *Feliks Topolski, Russia in War*, London, Methuen, 1942, Page 55

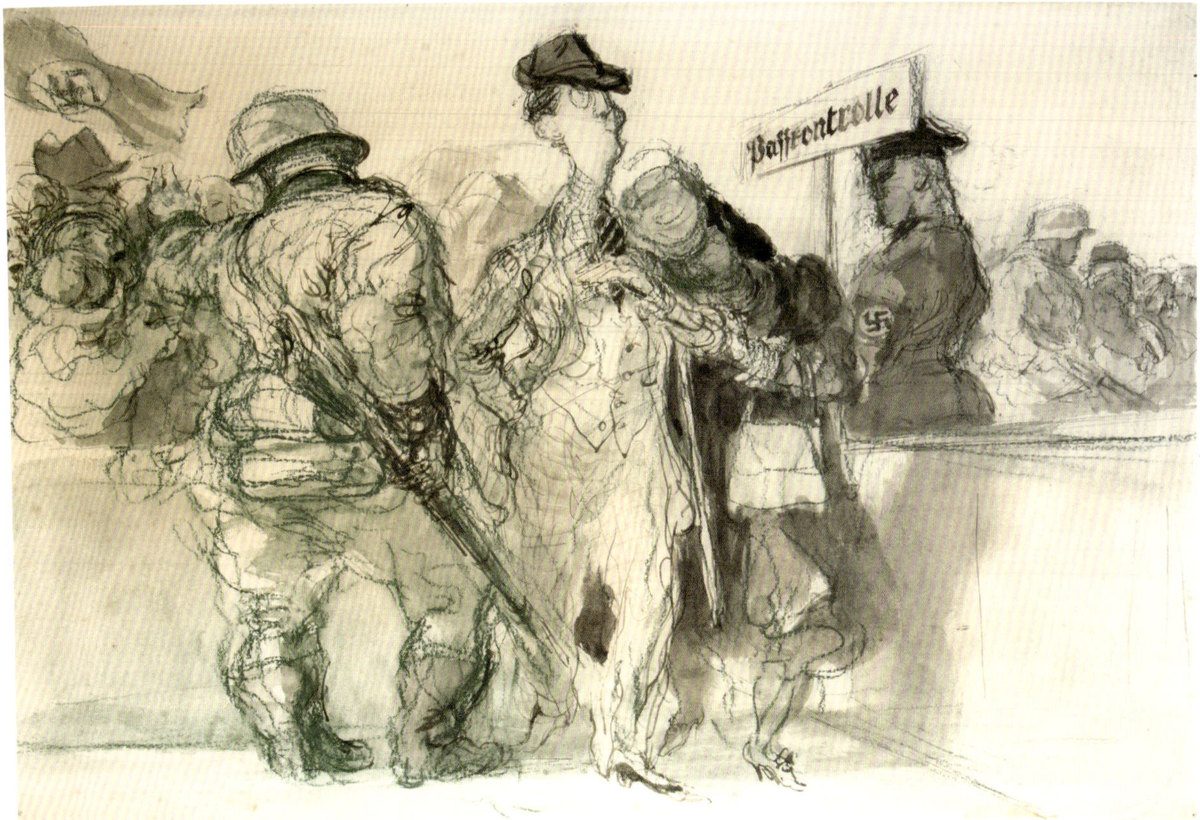
Paßkontrolle

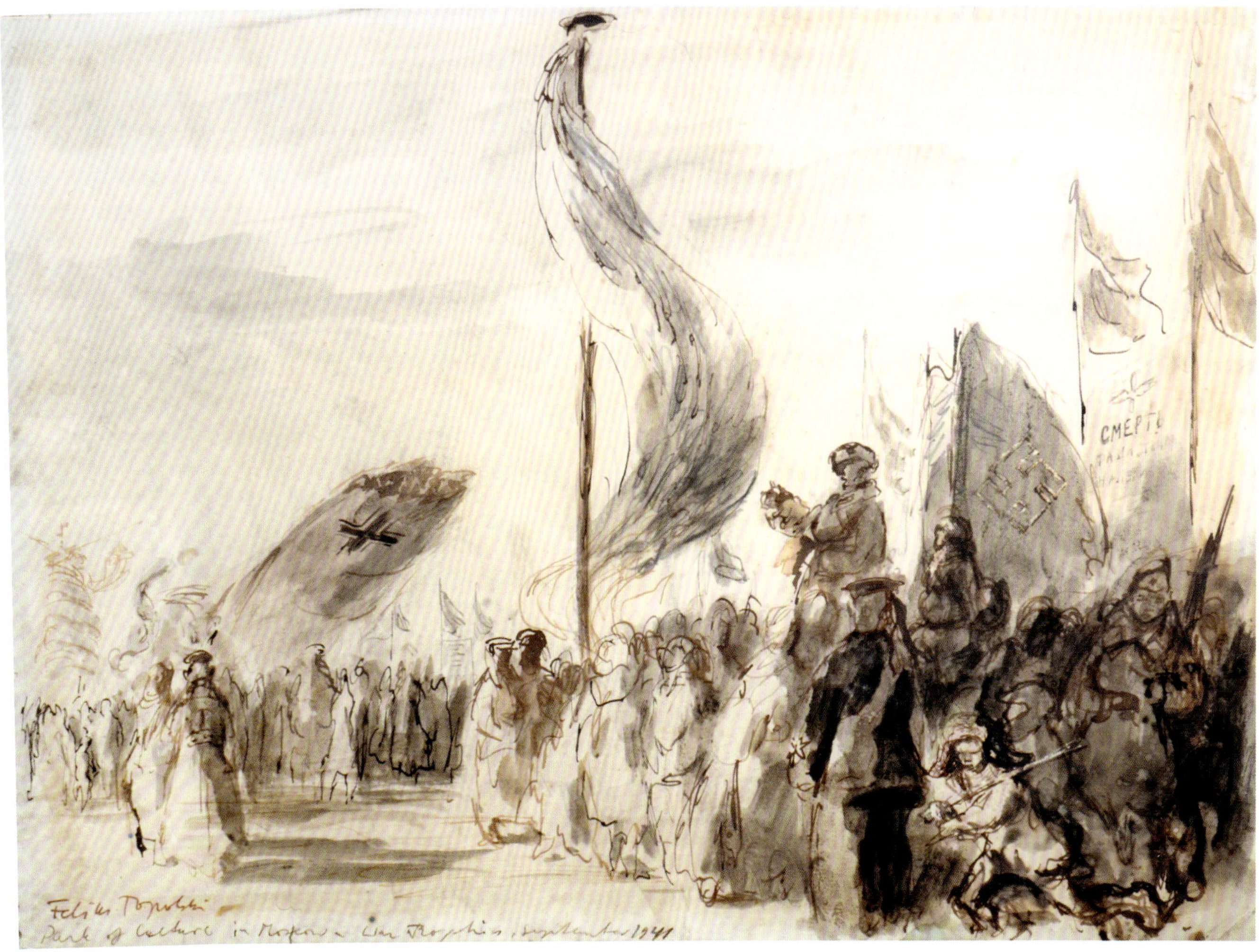
Feliks Topolski
Park of Culture in Moscow – War Trophies, September 1941

MERVYN PEAKE

Mervyn Peake (1911-1968)

Though already developing as a painter, Mervyn Peake established himself as a writer and illustrator in 1939, with *Captain Slaughterboard Drops Anchor*, a comic fantasy intended for children. This revealed that he had an outstanding talent for the grotesque, and was ready to align himself to Romantic tendencies in British art. He applied that talent to a broad range of visual and verbal forms, central to which was his 'Gormenghast' trilogy, an extraordinary imaginative achievement detailing a parallel world.

For a biography of Mervyn Peake, please refer to page 227.

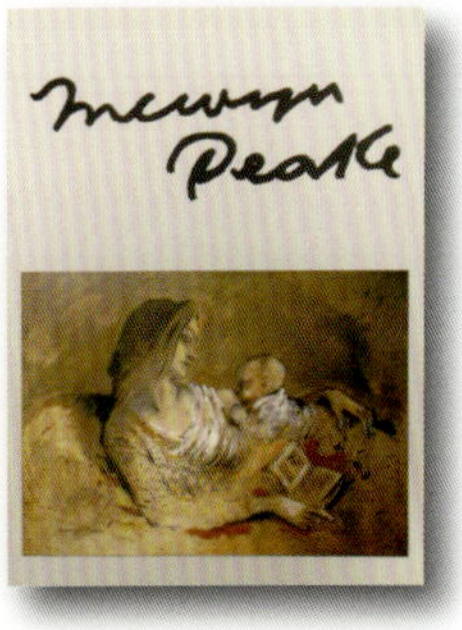

The Chris Beetles Gallery's championship of Mervyn Peake has included a number of exhibitions, including a major show in 1994, which was accompanied by this 24-page fully-illustrated catalogue.

Peter Back, a Condemned War Criminal at Rheinbeck Prison, 1945

In 1945, Mervyn Peake offered his services as a war artist to Charles Fenby, the editor of *Leader*, a weekly current affairs magazine. Fenby agreed that he could go to Germany to make drawings. However, as Peake was not recognised in Fleet Street as a writer but only as an artist, Fenby asked the journalist, Tom Pocock, to accompany him. Pocock would later recall their tour in *1945: The Dawn Came Up Like Thunder* (London: Collins, 1983), including their attendance of the first war crimes trial in Germany, at Ahrweiler, and their visit to Peter Back, one of the accused, in a prison at Rheinbeck in the Rhineland. As Peake wrote in a letter to his wife, Maeve, his intention was 'to make records of what humanity suffered through war' (quoted in Pocock 1983, page 128). He was therefore reluctant to draw Peter Back in his cell, and did so only at the urging of public relations officers. Pocock remembers that, 'Mervyn suggested to the interpreter that Back should sit ... and he did so, while the sketching was done as quickly as the pencil could move. We left in a few minutes, the doomed man thanking us' (op cit, page 134). The story of Back's crime was reported in *Life* magazine, as can be read here:

'[On 15 August 1944], an American Liberator began to smoke ... over the Rhineland village of Preist. Three Americans bailed out. One American landed in a tree in a wheat field. Two German soldiers started to help him out of his parachute when a crowd, headed by a paralytic much resembling Goebbels himself, tore into the wheat field. The paralytic was the Nazi leader of Preist, and he had clearly in mind Goebbels' pronouncement, "It is far too much for us to ask that we call on German police to protect these murderers from the fate they deserve." Goebbels was referring to US airmen, described in the Nazi press as "Air Huns" and "pleasure murderers." The little man, one Peter Back, shot the American twice. Twice the American stood up again and came on. Another German, [Peter] Kohn, clubbed the wounded man and he fell on his face. A third, [Matthias] Gierens, swung a stone hammer into his head. A fourth, [Matthias] Krein, whose home-guard responsibility was to guard prisoners, stood by. The airman did not rise again. His body has been found but not identified. One old German, a veteran of World War I, had protested, "This man is a prisoner: this is no way to treat him." Peter Back sneered, "You can bury him and put forget-me-nots on his grave."

The trial of three men, not including Peter Back, was held in Ahrweiler [on 1 June] by a military commission named by Lieut General Gerow of the Fifteenth Army. The prosecution cited the Ten Commandments, the laws of decency, the Laws and Customs of War and Nazi German regulations for the treatment of prisoners. All three were sentenced to death by hanging, but General Gerow commuted Krein's sentence to life imprisonment. Back was caught [on 6 June] and sentenced [16 June]. [He was hanged on 29 June.]'

(*Life*, 16 July 1945, Page 17, 'US Army Justice Falls on Germans')

191 **Peter Back, a Condemned War Criminal at Rheinbeck Prison, 1945**
Signed
Watercolour, ink, pencil and chalk on tinted paper
13 ½ x 10 inches
Literature: Gordon Smith, *Mervyn Peake, A Personal Memoir*, London: Gollancz 1984, Page 122, where it is incorrectly described as 'Condemned Cell at Belsen with Nazi War Criminal'

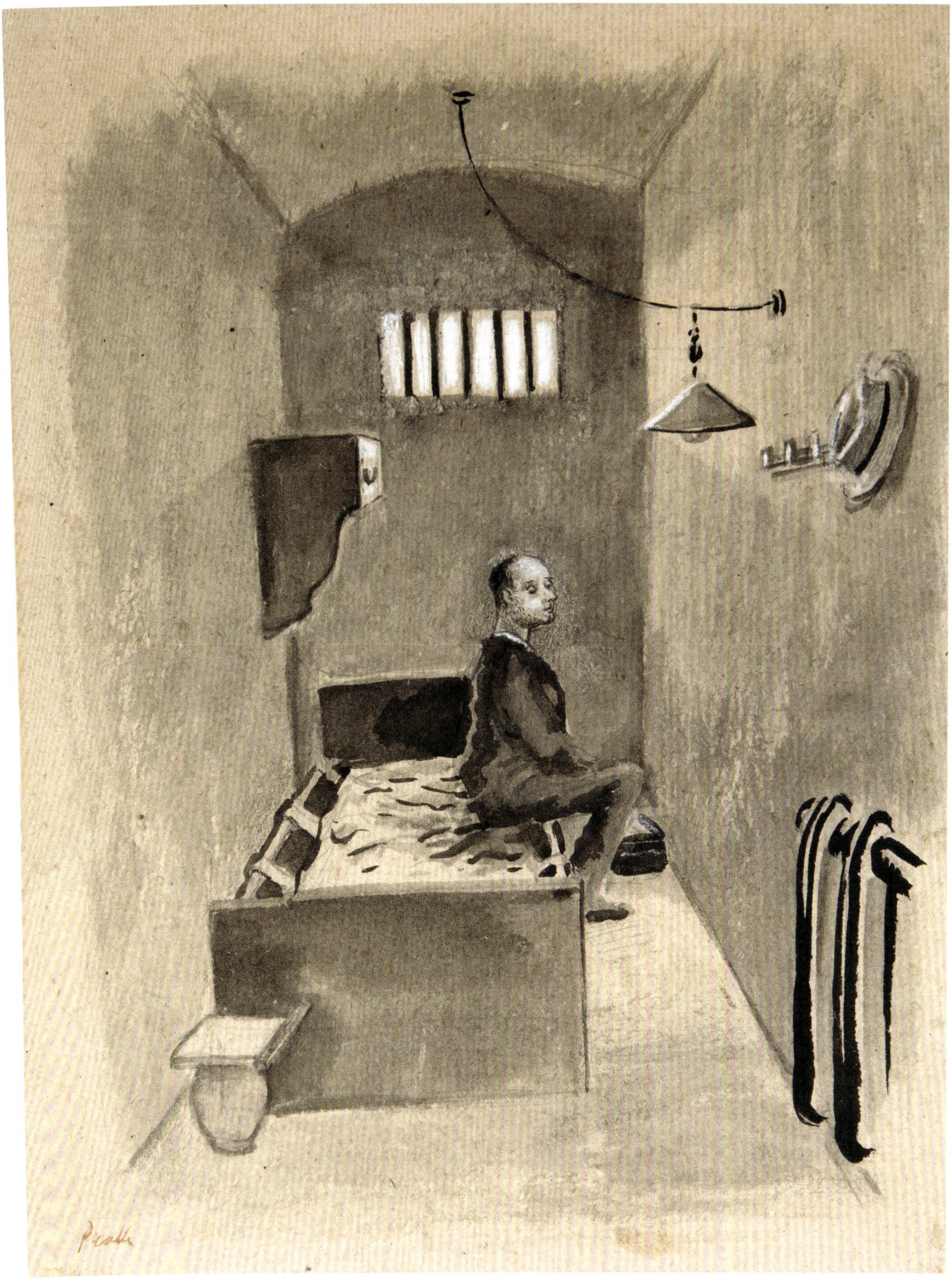

THOMAS MONNINGTON

Sir Walter Thomas Monnington, PRA NEAC (1902-1976)

One of the outstanding draughtsmen of his generation, Thomas Monnington gained a particular reputation for his figure compositions, both easel paintings and large-scale decorations. His cool, analytical approach was honed at the Slade School – where he would return to teach – and was influenced by his encounter with artists of the Italian Quattrocento, while at the British School at Rome. That approach would later affect both his decision to turn to abstraction, and the appearance of the works that resulted. Able as an administrator as well as an artist and teacher, he became one of the most effective Presidents of the Royal Academy.

For a biography of Thomas Monnington, please refer to page 226.

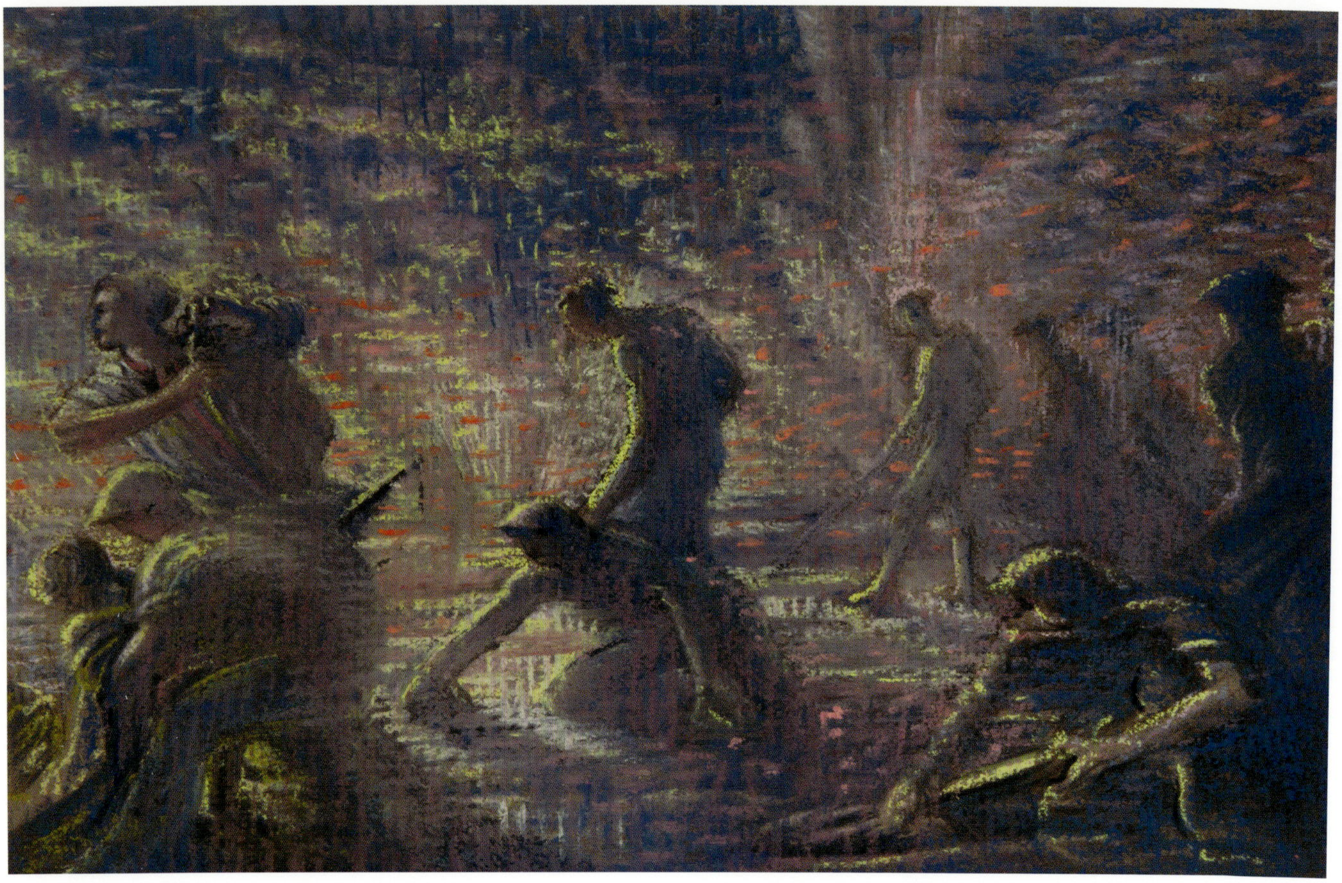

192 Clearing the Minefields at El Alamein
Pastel and chalk
7 x 10 inches

Clearing the Minefields at El Alamein

The present work is one of at least two similar compositions that Thomas Monnington produced in pastel and chalk during the Second World War. The other version (in a private collection) has been given the completely different, if less convincing, title of *ARP Wardens Rescuing Casualties of Bomb Blast*. This discrepancy suggests that there is some uncertainty as to the subject. However, close scrutiny of the image reveals that the majority of the figures are engaging with the ground in a delicate operation, and some appear to be holding mine detectors.

The earliest portable mine detector, invented by the Polish signals officer, Jósef Kosacki, was used for the first time in action by the allied Eighth Army during the Second Battle of El Alamein, in Egypt, in October 1942. Handled by mine sweepers, which included Reconnaissance Corps troops and sappers, these detectors helped double the speed of detection and removal of the many mines that had been laid by the Axis troops led by Generalfeldmarschall Erwin Rommel. As a result, they played a key role in a decisive victory of the war.

Thomas Monnington is not known to have been present at the Second Battle of El Alamein, or to have visited North Africa at all during the war. Therefore, it seems more likely that he based this drawing (and its pair) on reports, and possibly sketches by others, of the demining operation.

Monnington spent the early years of the war, including 1942, as a member of the design team of the Civil Defence Camouflage Operation Establishment, based at Leamington Spa, in Warwickshire. During this time, he was chiefly responsible for the design of camouflage for aircraft production airfields. In 1943, he was appointed an official war artist with Royal Air Force, and documented war from the air. Latterly, in 1944-45, he was in Holland, with the 2nd Tactical Air Force, drawing pioneer mobile radar equipment.

BIOGRAPHIES

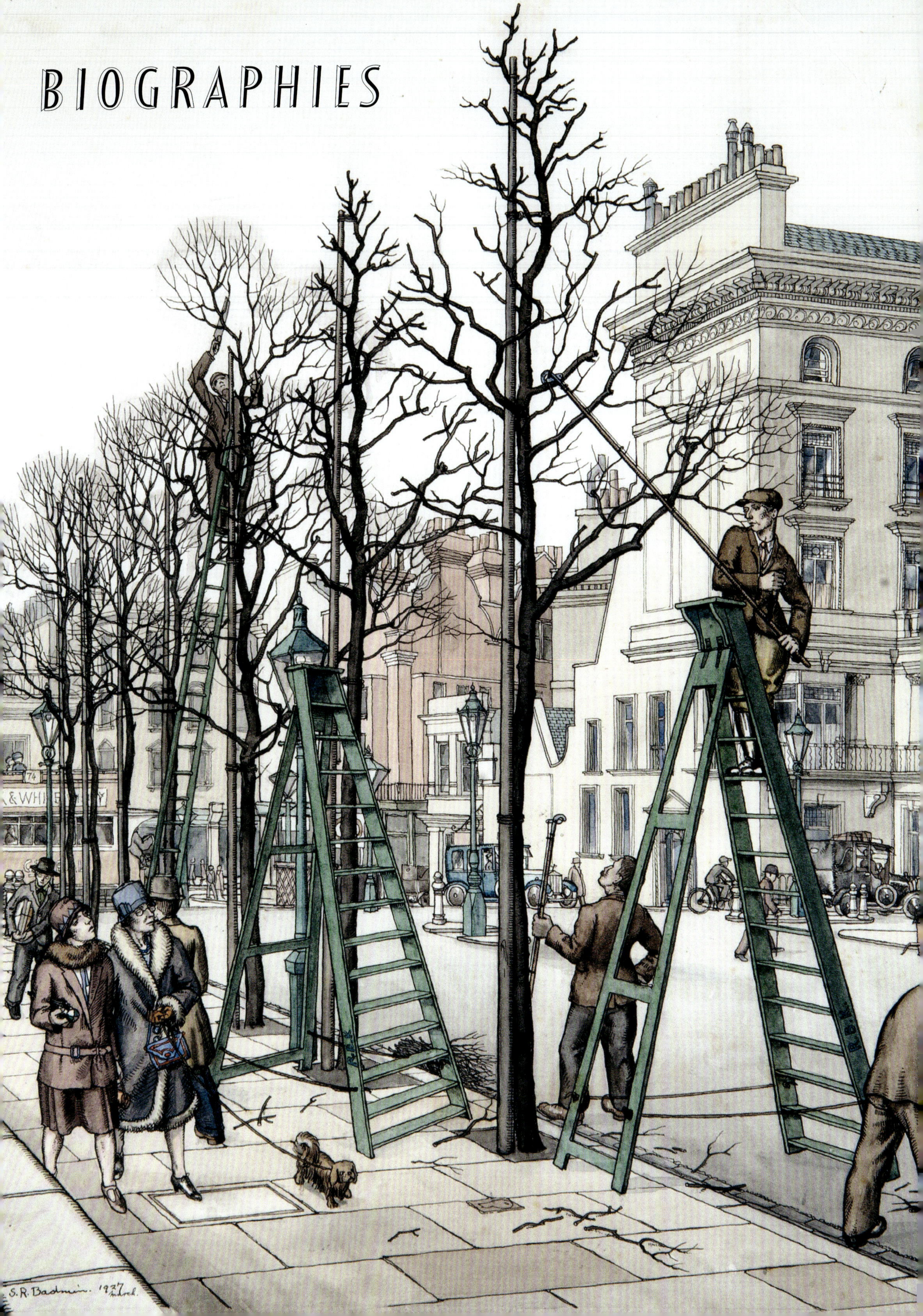

GEORGE CLAUSEN

Sir George Clausen, RA RSW RWS HRBA RI ROI NEAC (1852-1944)

George Clausen absorbed a range of Continental influences to become a significant *plein-air* artist of scenes of rural life in oil, watercolour and pastel. The striking, sometime stark naturalism that he learned from Bastien-Lepage and Millet gave way to a light-filled, atmospheric Impressionism. While promoting new developments in painting as a leading member of the New English Art Club, he was eventually accepted by more established societies of artists, including the Royal Academy, becoming a notable Professor of Painting at the Royal Academy Schools. In addition to his distinctive landscapes – both with and without figures – he essayed portraits, nudes, interiors and still life compositions, and produced occasional, but significant murals, one of which was recognised with a knighthood.

George Clausen was born at 8 William Street, Regent's Park, London, on 18 April 1852, the second of five children of the Danish decorative painter, Jurgen (George) Johnson Clausen, and his wife, Elizabeth (née Fillan).

On leaving St Mark's School, King's Road, Chelsea, in 1867, Clausen became an apprentice in the drawing office of Messrs Trollope & Sons, a leading firm of decorators. While there, he also took drawing lessons with John Leghorn, which prepared him for a course of evening classes, on a two-year scholarship, at the National Art Training School, South Kensington. During his time there, he won two of its gold medals for design (in 1868 and 1870). By 1871, he had moved with his family to 9 Stafford Terrace, Fulham Road.

As the result of a commission to decorate the house of the history painter, Edwin Long, Clausen became the artist's researcher, and received assistance from him in his development as an artist. Taking Long's advice, Clausen visited Belgium and Holland during the years 1875-76. He studied briefly at the Royal Academy of Fine Arts in Antwerp under Joseph Van Lerius and, absorbing the influence of painters of the Hague School, began to take an interest in working *en plein air*. The results included *High Mass at a Fishing Village on the Zuider Zee* (Nottingham Castle Museum), which he showed successfully as his first exhibit at the Royal Academy of Arts in 1876. In the same year, he was elected an associate of the Royal Institute of Painters in Water Colours (becoming a full member in 1879).

Believing that he could learn more from a formal art education, Clausen went to Paris in 1876, in the hope of entering the atelier of Jean-Léon Gérôme, but found it closed. He then considered working under Carolus-Duran, only to be shocked by 'sloppy paint and bitumen all over the place', and so returned to London. There he learned not only from the successful genre works of William Quiller Orchardson, Marcus Stone and James Tissot, but also from the experiments of James McNeill Whistler. By the end of the 1870s, he and his family were living at 4 The Mall, Park Road, Haverstock Hill, and he was establishing himself in his own studio.

In 1881, Clausen married fellow artist, Agnes Webster, in Kings Lynn, and they settled first in the village of Childwick Green, near St Albans, Hertfordshire, moving to Grove House, Fag End Road, Cookham Dean, Berkshire, in 1885. They would have three sons and two daughters; Margaret would marry the artist, Thomas Derrick, while Katharine would herself become an artist.

Clausen's move to the country marked his increasing focus on rural themes, interpreted through a broad technique that involved the use of square-headed brushes. He was influenced in this approach by developments in France, which he visited on painting trips, including that to Brittany in 1882, and for further study, spending a term at the Académie Julian under Bouguereau and Robert-Fleury in 1883 (the year that he was elected to the new Institute of Painters in Oil Colours). He was especially inspired by the example of Jules Bastien-Lepage, whose work he had first seen at the Grosvenor Gallery, and would do much to promote him in England, as exemplified by the article, 'Bastien-Lepage and Modern Realism', published in *The Scottish Art Review* in 1888. He also had his own French success, when he was awarded a silver medal at the Exposition Universelle, in Paris, in 1889.

In 1884, critics had attacked the harsh realism of Clausen's painting, *Labourers after Dinner* (private collection), when it was shown at the Royal Academy. This encouraged him to help found the New English Art Club in 1886, and he – like his friend and fellow member, Henry La Thangue – would remain a keen advocate of the reform of the Royal Academy after he returned to exhibiting there regularly in 1891. In that year, he and his family moved to Bishops Farm House, Widdington, near Newport, Essex, and many of the local farmyards, barns and fields would feature his work.

Attracted to a range of modern painting, Clausen tempered his monumental depictions of the agricultural labourer, influenced by Jean-François Millet, with an increasingly bright palette, derived from the Impressionists, and an atmospheric use of pastel, inspired by Edgar Degas. However, he strengthened his association with more established institutions, and was elected to the Royal Society of Painters in Water-Colours (ARWS 1889; RWS 1898) and the Royal Academy (ARA 1895; RA 1908). His standing at home was confirmed by a series of solo shows – the first of which was held at the Goupil Gallery, London, in 1902 – while his wider reputation was consolidated through the award of medals at a number of international exhibitions, notably those in Chicago (1893), Brussels (1897) and Paris (1900). He also visited Hungary in 1894 and Italy in both 1898 and 1903.

Having taught at the Royal Academy Schools since the mid 1890s, Clausen became its Professor of Painting during the years 1903-6 (and would become temporary Director and Master of the Painting School in 1926-27). This academic position gave him the opportunity to urge the traditional study of the Old Masters in lectures that were published as *Six Lectures on Painting* (1904) and *Aims and Ideals in Art* (1906). From 1905, he maintained a London home and studio at 61 Carlton Hill, St John's Wood. In 1909, he was master of the Art Workers' Guild.

Clausen's own work, exhibited in solo shows at the Leicester Galleries (1909 and 1912), demonstrated how tradition and innovation could complement each other, and it seemed no contradiction for an exponent of Impressionism to undertake public commissions. He was an original member of the Faculty of Painting for the British School at Rome (1912), an official war artist during the First World War (assigned to Woolwich Arsenal) and later a mural decorator of, especially, St Stephen's Hall, Westminster (1927). The last of those projects led to his being knighted (1927) in a period in which he continued to be elected to exhibiting societies. He became an honorary member of the Royal Society of British Artists (1923) and a member of the Royal Scottish Society of Painters in Water-Colours (1926). Retrospectives of his work were held at Barbizon House in 1928 and 1933. In these later years, he painted numerous landscapes around the Essex village of Duton Hill, where, from 1917, he maintained 'Hillside' cottage. Following the outbreak of the Second World War, he and Lady Clausen left their London home to live with their daughter, Margaret, and her husband, Thomas Derrick, at St Finians Farm, Cold Ash, Thatcham near Newbury, Berkshire. He died there on 22 November 1944, eight months after his wife.

His work is represented in the collections of the Royal Academy of Arts and numerous public collections, including the British Museum, Tate and the V&A; Birmingham Museums Trust, Bristol Museum & Art Gallery, Holburne Museum (Bath), Laing Art Gallery (Newcastle upon Tyne), Leeds Museums and Galleries (including both Leeds Art Gallery and Lotherton Hall), Manchester Art Gallery, the Usher Gallery (Lincoln) and the Walker Art Gallery (Liverpool); and National Museum Wales (Cardiff).

Further reading:

Kenneth McConkey, 'Clausen, Sir George (1852-1944)', H C G Matthew and Brian Harrison (eds), *Oxford Dictionary of National Biography*, Oxford University Press, 2007, https://doi.org/10.1093/ref:odnb/32435;
Kenneth McConkey, 'Clausen, Sir George (*b* London, April 18, 1852; *d* Newbury, Berks, Nov 22, 1944)', *Grove Art Online*, 2003, https://doi.org/10.1093/gao/9781884446054.article.T018054;
Kenneth McConkey, *George Clausen and the picture of English rural life*, Edinburgh: Atelier Books, 2012;
Kenneth McConkey (intro), *Sir George Clausen, RA, 1852-1944*, Bradford: City of Bradford Metropolitan District Council and Tyne and Wear County Council, 1980

OWEN BAXTER MORGAN

Owen Baxter Morgan (1873-1920)

Owen Baxter Morgan was a painter, in oil and watercolour, of gently impressionistic poetic pastoral landscapes, including sunsets and nocturnes. Sometimes they incorporated figures of farmworkers, involved in such activities as guiding animals and making hay.

Owen Baxter Morgan was born at Grove Lodge, Gloucester Grove (now Clareville Grove), Kensington, London, on 9 April 1873. He was the fifth of the six children of the artist, Alfred Morgan, and his wife, Jessey (née Roe), who was sister-in-law of the painter, Henry B Hagreen. His elder brother, Alfred Kedington (1868-1928), and younger sister, Ethel Mahala (1875-1926), also became artists. Their father is best remembered for the painting, *An Omnibus to Piccadilly Circus: Mr Gladstone Travelling with Ordinary Passengers* (1885). This includes portraits of young Owen, his parents and his elder sister, Jessie.

By 1891, the Morgan family had moved to 12 Albert Road (now Albert Bridge Road), Battersea. Two years later, in January 1893, Owen began to study at the Royal Academy Schools, and during his time there twice won a silver medal for his painting of a head from life (1895 & 1897). However, following completion of his studies in January 1898, he soon began to specialise in landscapes, as exemplified by the two works that he exhibited at the Royal Academy in 1898 and 1901, and others shown at the Royal Society of British Artists. By 1901, he had moved to 30 Palewell Park, East Sheen, with his parents and two of his siblings. It would be his home for the remainder of his life. He died on 29 August 1920.

JAMES HAMILTON HAY

James Hamiton Hay, LG (1874-1916)

The painter and printmaker, James Hamilton Hay, applied his sophisticated tonal approach to a range of subjects that included landscapes, seascapes, townscapes and portraits. While absorbing the influences of James McNeill Whistler, Japanese printmakers and various teachers and friends, he made an original contribution to art – and cultural life – at the turn of the century, in the Liverpool area and more widely.

James Hamilton Hay was born at 98 Bridge Street, Birkenhead, on 6 December 1874, the second of four children of Scots-born James Murdoch Hay, and his wife, Annie Wilhelmina Hamilton Lothian Hogg. James Murdoch Hay was an architect, working in partnership with his elder brother, William, as W & J Hay, and specialising in churches. Early in their marriage, James and Annie lived with William and his wife, Mary Ann, at Bridge Street, moving to 8 Carlton Terrace, Great Meolse, Wirral, Cheshire, as their family grew.

For a short time, James Hamilton Hay worked in the family firm, with his father and uncle, but soon enrolled at Birkenhead School of Art. In the late 1890s, he travelled to St Ives, in Cornwall, to take lessons from Algernon Talmage and Julius Olsson, and would consider the latter the best of his teachers. On returning to Liverpool, he continued his studies at Liverpool School of Art under John Finnie, David Muirhead and Augustus John, the last of whom became a friend.

In 1895, Hay had work included for the first time in the prestigious Liverpool Autumn Exhibition, and would continue to contribute annually to these exhibitions until 1915. The other leading venues at which he exhibited included the Royal Academy of Arts, the Royal Scottish Academy, the Liverpool Royal Institution and the Liverpool Academy, of which he became a member in 1904. In that year, he also curated 'The Independent Exhibition' at The Studio, which included work by E A Hornel, Augustus John and James McNeill Whistler (who was an influence upon him).

By the early 1900s, Hay's work had started to sell, the poet, Gordon Bottomley, becoming the first major collector of his paintings. Then, in 1909, he made a public breakthrough when the Walker Art Gallery, Liverpool, bought his painting, *The Lovers*, from the Liverpool Autumn Exhibition, and another in the following year.

In 1907, Hay collaborated with the writer, Walter Dixon Scott, on Liverpool for A & C Black's series of colour plate books. In the same year, he married the artist, Enid Rutherford, daughter of William Rutherford who, at the time, was the Conservative Member of Parliament for Liverpool West Derby. They soon settled at Taintree House, Heathfield Road, Audlem, near Nantwich. Like James, Enid was a member of both the Liverpool Academy and the Sandon Studio Society. James was also a member of the committee that selected the works for the Sandon's ground-breaking exhibition, which, in 1911, introduced the Post-Impressionists and other Modernist artists to the Liverpool public. Sadly, Enid died in the same year.

In 1912, Hay moved to London and took lodgings at 18 Trafalgar Square, Chelsea (now Chelsea Square). Having already held a solo show at the Baillie Gallery in 1910, he showed work with various dealers and societies, including the Camden Town Group, where he appeared as a guest, and the London Group, of which he became a member in 1915. His later work shows the influence of the Camden Town members, Spencer Gore and Robert Bevan.

In 1914, Hay was one of the 90 artists selected to represent Britain at the Venice Biennale. The other artists included his friend, Francis Dodd, who produced a drypoint portrait of Hay.

Alongside the Japanese printmaking tradition, it was the example of Dodd that influenced the decision of Hay to turn his own hand to drypoint, and make it the main focus of his work during his last few years. Following diagnosis with lung cancer, his health began to deteriorate and, in 1915, he returned to Cheshire, where he settled at his family home at Foenum Lodge, Oldfield Road, Heswall, Wirrall. His father died there in October 1915, and he followed him to the grave a year later on 7 October 1916, aged 42. The Goupil Gallery held a 'Memorial Exhibition of Paintings and Drawings by J Hamilton Hay' in March 1917.

His work is represented in numerous public collections, including the Walker Art Gallery (Liverpool) and the Williamson Art Gallery and Museum (Birkenhead).

With acknowledgements to the researches of David Brown, Secretary, past-President and committee member of the Liver Sketching Club.

FRANCIS E JAMES

Francis Edward James, RWS RBA NEAC (1849-1920)

'Perhaps the revelation of the season to the public ... are the watercolours of Mr Francis E James. I am deliberately convinced that watercolour has never been used more brilliantly and to more purely artistic effect by any master, living or dead.' (Walter Sickert, 'The New English Art Club', *New York Herald*, 14 June 1889)

Francis James was a watercolourist of exceptional delicacy and freedom, and contemporaries likened his landscapes and flower subjects to the work of the Japanese. He developed his art in the orbit of both James McNeill Whistler and Hercules Brabazon Brabazon, and joined the New English Art Club as an associate of the Impressionist nucleus, becoming one of the club's most regular exhibitors.

Francis James was born in Willingdon, Sussex, on 16 February 1849, the youngest of five children of the Reverend Henry James, Rector of St Mary Willingdon, and his wife, Eliza Mary Mann (née Eliot), the daughter of Lieutenant Colonel William Granville Eliot. His father died in 1850, following a fall while climbing Beachy Head, and by 1851 the family had moved to 7 Richmond Terrace, Brighton. By 1861, it had settled at Valebrook, a large eighteenth-century house situated just outside Hastings. This remained in the family at least until the artist's death.

Though Francis James was educated privately, little more is known of his development before 1871, when he turned 22. According to the Census for that year, he was a student lodging at 7 Hogarth Terrace, Chiswick, though, again, nothing is known of the subject of his studies. During the decade, he served for some time as a Midshipman in the Royal Navy, but had resigned his position by 1881, when he was living with his mother and an aunt at Valebrook. He is said to suffered from illness for most of his life, and it may have been his health that led him to give up an active life and focus on watercolour painting.

James taught himself to paint by studying works in major galleries in Britain and abroad (and he often wintered on the Continent for the sake of his health). He was influenced at first by Peter de Wint, and then by the Impressionists. By the late 1870s, he had entered the circle of James McNeill Whistler, and became a frequent visitor to the artist's studios in Cheyne Walk and, later, Tite Street, both in Chelsea. With Theodore Roussel, he became one of Whistler's closest friends, and was one of the few men never to quarrel with him. As the result of his association with Whistler, he was elected to the Royal Society of British Artists in 1884, and became a member of the New English Art Club in 1888. He was one of the artists represented in the key exhibition of London Impressionists mounted at the Goupil Gallery in December 1889, and held his first solo show at the Dudley Gallery in 1890 (Walter Sickert, a fellow protégé of Whistler, writing the preface to its catalogue). By this time, he may have taken a studio at 39a Queen Square, Bloomsbury.

During the 1890s, James became a friend of his Sussex neighbour, Hercules Brabazon Brabazon, who lived at Oaklands, Sedlescombe, and he developed his characteristic style under Brabazon's influence. When Philip Wilson Steer proposed Brabazon as a member of the New English Art Club in 1891, it was James who seconded. James's development was showcased in solo shows at E J van Wisselingh's Dutch Gallery, Brook Street, in 1893, 1896 and 1901, and also in Frederick Wedmore's article, 'Mr Francis E James's Watercolours', published in *The Studio* in 1898. Illustrations and references in Wedmore's article indicate the range of James's sketching tours by this time, from the shopfronts of Bewdley, Worcestershire, to the churches of Germany and Italy. Wedmore noted that he had also spent 'several months' sojourn' at the nursery of the 'orchid king', H F C Sander, in St Albans, Hertfordshire (page 266). Certainly, he became as well known as a flower painter as a landscapist – favourite blooms including roses, wallflowers and geraniums – and there is evidence that he was also a serious gardener.

From about 1900, James was increasingly attracted by the coastline of Devon. Early in 1901, he painted at Kingswear, on the estuary of the Dart, in the south of the county. Then, later the same year, he settled at Windycroft, a house on the outskirts of Instow, on the north coast, on the estuary of the Torridge. In 1903, in Chelsea, he married Annie Georgiana, widow of the late Philip Scholfield of Maltby Hall, and daughter of T S Gooch, who had been a Captain in the Royal Navy. In 1905, he began a correspondence with the Irish dealer, collector and gallery director, Sir Hugh Lane (which is held in the collections of the National Library of Ireland).

Continuing to exhibit in London, James was lodging at 14/16 Milner Street, Chelsea, in April 1911. His later solo shows include those at the Dutch Gallery (1905), the Leicester Galleries (1909), E J van Wisselingh's Gallery, Grafton Street (1913), and the Fine Art Society (1919). From 1906, he also contributed to the annual exhibitions of flower paintings organised by the Baillie Gallery. He was elected an associate of the Royal Society of Painters in Water-Colours in 1908, and a full member in 1916. In 1911, Frederick Charles Mulock, who lived in Instow, exhibited a portrait of James at the New English Art Club. It showed him in his studio, seated in a wheelchair and holding a crutch.

In 1913, Francis James and his wife moved up the River Torridge to settle in an eighteenth-century house at 42 South Street, Great Torrington. He lived his last years in this small market town, dying there on 25 August 1920. A memorial exhibition was held at the Leicester Galleries in May 1921.

His work is represented in numerous public collections, including the British Museum and the V&A; and Manchester Art Gallery.

EDWIN ALEXANDER

Edwin John Alexander, RSA RSW RWS SSA (1870-1926)

Edwin Alexander is best remembered for his exquisite, carefully observed watercolours of flora and fauna, and of landscapes of both his native Scotland and North Africa. Often painting on silk, linen or textured paper, he developed a style that reflects the decorative approaches of Joseph Crawhall and other painters of the Glasgow School, and reveals an understanding of their common source, the art of Japan.

Edwin Alexander was born in Edinburgh, Scotland, on 1 February 1870, the only son, and second of five children, of the animal painter, Robert Lowe Alexander RSA, and his English wife, Anne Sarah (née Jennings). During his early childhood, they lived at 13 Bell Place, and at other addresses in Edinburgh and its environs. By 1879, his father had taken Jemima Jane (née Martin) as his second wife, and together they would have four children. In that year, the family settled at 'Plewlands', a large detached house to the south of Edinburgh. It would subsequently live at other properties in the area, including 'Greenbank', Lothian Burn (1882-84), 'Canaan Grove', 82 Newbattle Terrace, Morningside (1885-87), and addresses in Craiglockhart (1887-93).

From an early age, Edwin Alexander was encouraged by his father in both his talent for art and his love of plants and animals. In 1886, he began to study at the schools of the Royal Scottish Academy, though would never take a formal qualification in art. In the following year, he participated in a sketching trip to Tangier with his father and two other artists, Joseph Crawhall and Pollock Nisbet. Crawhall would have a particularly strong influence on the development of his art, in both the subject matter and handling of his refined watercolour studies of animals and birds. He also learned from other painters of the Glasgow School, with whom he mixed at the Society of Scottish Artists, of which he became a member soon after its foundation in 1891.

It was in 1891 that Alexander went to Paris to study for a few months under the eminent animal sculptor, Emmanuel Frémiet, who was professor of animal drawing at the Muséum national d'histoire naturelle. Then, between 1892 and 1896, he made two extended trips to Egypt with fellow artist, Erskine E Nicol. They lived and worked on a houseboat on the Nile, near Cairo, and also with the Bedouin in the desert, learning Arabic in the process. Some years later, Alexander would return to the Mediterranean to visit Granada and the Balearic Islands.

Once back in Edinburgh in 1896, Edwin Alexander continued to live with his father and his family, who had settled at Hailes Cottage, on the Union Canal, beyond the southwest edge of the city. While there, he began to exhibit his work regularly, in both Scotland and England and, from 1897, was promoted by The Scottish Gallery, the Edinburgh dealership run by Aitken Dott and his son, Peter McOmish Dott. He was elected an associate of the Royal Society of Painters in Water-Colours in 1899, an associate of the Royal Scottish Academy in 1902, and an associate of the Royal Scottish Society of Painters in Water Colour by 1904. In 1902, he contributed to the album of work by members of the RWS given to King Edward VII and Queen Alexandra in order to mark their coronation.

In 1904, Edwin Alexander married Dorothea Maclellan (known as Dora), and they settled at Shepherd House, Inveresk, just outside Musselburgh, the coastal town to the east of Edinburgh. They would have a son, Harry, born in 1906, and a daughter, Sarah (known as Sally), born in 1909. In the 'tumble-down outhouses and stables' of Shepherd House, Alexander created a menagerie of animal models that 'contained not merely ordinary fowls and farmyard animals, goats, kids and turkey-cocks, but peacocks, twenty varieties of sea-gulls and at one time a nine-foot python' (Martin Hardie, *Water-Colour Painting in Britain*, London: Batsford, vol 3, 1968, page 207). However, plants remained as important as animals as a subject of his painting and, in 1909, he illustrated J H Crawford's *The Wild Flowers*. In 1910, he and his family moved into Musselburgh, and settled at Links Lodge, 10 Links Place (now Balcarres Road), between the golf course and the River Esk. It would remain his home for the rest of his life.

Following the move, Alexander initially worked hard and continued to exhibit widely, and was elected a full member of the RWS in 1910 and of the RSW in 1911, and a Royal Scottish Academician in 1913. In that latter year, he visited Amsterdam to carry out some drawings at the Royal Zoo. However, by 1914, he had 'virtually ceased painting', becoming involved 'in voluntary work and in teaching at Edinburgh College of Art in place of David Alison' (Julian Halsby, *Scottish Watercolours 1740-1940*, 1986, page 148). In 1915, he donated a group of his watercolours of birds to the British Museum, a suggestion that he was putting his affairs in order. In February 1918, he was healthy enough to be 'an officer in the 1/1st MVR, E Company, Musselburgh' (according to the *Musselburgh News*). However, he soon suffered a stroke, which left him paralysed on his left side and subject to persistent ill health.

Edwin Alexander died in Musselburgh on 23 April 1926. In the following year, The Scottish Gallery mounted a memorial exhibition of Alexander's work, while Gurney & Jackson published an edition of Charles St John's *Wild Sports and Natural History of the Highlands*, which included illustrations by both Edwin Alexander and his father's friend, George Denholm Armour.

Edwin Alexander's daughter, Sarah Dorothea (known as Sally), became a painter and sculptor. In 1940, she married the paediatrician, Dr Eric Dott, a son of Peter McOmish Dott, and grandson of Aitken Dott.

His work is represented in numerous public collections, including the British Museum; and Glasgow Museums.

E H SHEPARD

Ernest Howard Shepard, MC OBE (1879-1976)

While E H Shepard is now best remembered for his immortal illustrations to *Winnie-the-Pooh* and *The Wind in the Willows*, he was a wide-ranging artist and illustrator, with an unsurpassed genius for representing children, and an underrated talent for political cartoons.

Ernest Howard Shepard was born at 55 Springfield Road, St John's Wood, London, on 10 December 1879, the youngest of the three children of the architect and amateur watercolourist, Henry Dunkin Shepard, and his wife, Jessie, the daughter of the watercolourist, William Lee. He was initially educated at St John's Wood Preparatory School. Then, following his mother's death in 1890, and the family's move to Hammersmith, he attended Colet Court School and St Paul's School. He was encouraged in his early talent for drawing at St Paul's, and took extra classes at Heatherley's School of Art. In 1897, he was awarded a scholarship to the Royal Academy Schools, and studied there until 1902, winning the Landseer Scholarship, the British Institution Prize and other awards.

Receiving much pleasure from his work as an oil painter, Shepard exhibited at the Royal Academy of Arts for the first time in 1901, while he was living at 52 Glebe Place, Chelsea. In 1904, his painting, *Followers*, was bought from the RA by Durban Art Gallery. In the same year, he married fellow artist, Florence Chaplin, the granddaughter of the engraver, Ebenezer Landells, one of the founders of *Punch*. They settled at Arden Cottage, Shamley Green, near Guildford, Surrey, and had two children, Graham and Mary, both of whom would become illustrators. (Mary famously illustrated P L Travers' series of books featuring the character, Mary Poppins.)

Shepard developed a great interest in the illustrators of the 1860s and, while still a student, began to contribute cartoons and illustrations to various publications. He illustrated books from the turn of the century and, fulfilling a particular hope, had his first cartoon accepted by *Punch* in 1906.

Shepherd served as an officer in the Royal Artillery during the First World War, and saw action in France, Belgium and Italy, being awarded the Military Cross in 1917. During this time, he kept several sketchbooks and worked up some of these drawings for memorable inclusion in *Punch*.

Shepard was elected to the *Punch* table in 1921 and made good friends with both Frank Reynolds, the magazine's new art editor, and the writer E V Lucas. It was Lucas who introduced Shepard to A A Milne, thus initiating several immortal projects, most obviously *When We Were Very Young* (1924) and *Winnie-the-Pooh* (1926). Shepard also illustrated Lucas's writing in *Playtime and Company* (1925) and *As the Bee Sucks* (1937), his own selection of Lucas's essays. His range as an illustrator could encompass such historical works as *Everybody's Pepys* (1926) and such children's classics as Kenneth Grahame's *The Wind in the Willows* (1931). By 1926, he was holding solo shows of his illustrations at the Sporting Gallery, Covent Garden.

Shepard succeeded Leonard Raven-Hill as second political cartoonist on *Punch* in 1935, and produced some of his most impressive cartoons during the Second World War. He succeeded Bernard Partridge as principal cartoonist in 1945, but handed over the position to Leslie Illingworth four years later. However, he remained with *Punch* until 1953. Continually sketching and reworking, he still managed to retain the appearance of spontaneity in his finished work, and excelled at the depiction of both movement and character.

Shepherd's first wife, Florence, had died suddenly in 1927. In 1944, he married Norah Carroll, a nurse at St Mary's Hospital, Paddington. In 1955, they moved to 'Woodmancote', Lodsworth, Sussex.

Late in life, Shepard turned to himself as a subject and illustrated his autobiographical reminiscences, *Drawn from Memory* (1957) and *Drawn from Life* (1961). An exhibition devoted to his illustrations to *Winnie-the-Pooh* was held at the Victoria and Albert Museum in 1969. Having received various honours, including the Lewis Carroll Shelf Award (1958, 1962, 1963) and the University of Southern Mississippi Silver Medallion (1970), he was awarded an OBE in 1972. He died at Midhurst, West Sussex, on 24 March 1976. His last picture was exhibited posthumously at the Royal Academy in that year.

His work is represented in the collections of the British Museum and the V&A; and the British Cartoon Archive, the University of Kent (Canterbury) and the Shepard Archive, the University of Surrey (Guildford).

Further reading:

Arthur R Chandler, *The Story of E H Shepard: the man who drew Pooh*, West Sussex: Jaydem, 2001;
Rawle Knox (ed), *The Work of E H Shepard*, London: Methuen, 1979;
C A Parker (rev), 'Shepard, Ernest Howard (1879–1976)', H C G Matthew and Brian Harrison (eds), *Oxford Dictionary of National Biography*, Oxford University Press, 2004, vol 50, pages 230-231

NIBS

Frederick Drummond Niblett, RSA (1861-1928), known as 'Nibs'

Though too little known today, Frederick Drummond Niblett produced some of the most striking caricatures of the Edwardian period in a style reminiscent of the posters and illustrations of William Nicholson and James Pryde, who worked together as the 'Beggarstaff Brothers'.

Frederick Drummond Niblett was born in Edinburgh as possibly the youngest of three children of an English father, the commission agent, Francis Burgess Niblett, and his Irish wife, Eliza (née George). His uncle was Vice-Admiral H S F Niblett, and he too was intended for the sea. Educated at Fettes College, he then studied architecture, which led him into an artistic career. In the early 1880s, he worked from 17 Drummond Place (1882) and then from Albert Studios, Shandwick Place (1884), designing posters and painting portraits in oil and watercolours of churches. Two of his views of St Giles' Cathedral were exhibited at the Royal Scottish Academy (1882 and 1884).

Niblett is likely to have moved to London in the mid 1880s to establish himself as an illustrator. His first illustrated book – Thomas Hood's *The Dream of Eugene of Aram* – was created in response to a dramatisation of the poem that was produced in London, and was issued in 1887 by a London publisher, The Leadenhall Press. Concerning a celebrated murder of the eighteenth century, *Eugene Aram* was dramatised by W G Wills, and first produced at the Lyceum Theatre in 1873, with Henry Irving in the title role. Irving had already made a party piece of reciting Hood's original poem, and became associated with the part of Aram, though he reprised it only briefly in 1879 and 1880.

Niblett dedicated his book to Irving's close friend, the actor-manager, John Lawrence Toole. Two decades later, in 1905, he would illustrate a 'Henry Irving Souvenir', as well as producing other caricatures of the actor. All this suggests an association between artist and actor or, at least, a strong theatrical interest.

In 1890, Niblett illustrated a second volume, N H Willis's *Dulcima's Doom and other Tales*, issued by the Edinburgh publisher Grant & Son. However, through the following decade, he evolved into a political cartoonist and caricaturist, contributing to a wide range of periodicals, under the pen name 'Nibs'. These included *The Crown* (1906-7), *Sketchy Bits* (1909), *Vanity Fair* (1909-13) and *The Bystander* (1916).

Niblett was living, as a lodger, at 5 Sandland Street, Holborn, in 1891; at Langham Chambers, Portland Place, in 1896; at 84 Charing Cross Road in 1911; at 7 Charles Street, Knightsbridge, in 1907; and, as a boarder, at 94 Earl's Court Road, Kensington, in 1911.

Frederick Drummond Niblett died in Margate, Kent, on 2 May 1928.

E T REED

Edward Tennyson Reed (1860-1933)

Preferring pencil to pen and ink, E T Reed developed into a superb draughtsman, using his confident line to express a rich imagination. Known equally for his political caricatures and his *Punch* series, 'Prehistoric Peeps', his range of subject and allusion was astonishingly wide.

Edward Tennyson Reed was born in Greenwich, London, on 27 March 1860. He was the third of five children, and only son, of Sir Edward James Reed, Chief Constructor of the Royal Navy and later a Liberal Member of Parliament, and his wife, Rosetta (née Barnaby). Rosetta was the sister of Sir Nathaniel Barnaby, who would succeed Sir Edward Reed as Chief Constructor. The main London home of the Reed family was 74 Gloucester Road, South Kensington, while, in 1876, Sir Edward acquired Hextable House, near Sutton at Hone, in Kent.

E T Reed was educated at Harrow School until 1877. Two years later, in 1879, he travelled with his father to Egypt and the Far East. On his return, he began to read for the Bar, but soon gave that up in favour of art. He received encouragement from Edward Burne-Jones and studied for 18 months under P H Calderon. However, he failed to get a place at the Royal Academy Schools, or to establish himself as a portrait painter, and so began work as a cartoonist and illustrator. By then, he had already illustrated his father's book, *Japan: Its History, Religion and Traditions* (1880).

Reed made his first contributions to *Punch* in June 1889, and was elected to the staff in the following year by its editor, F C Burnand. He soon became an established part of the periodical, introducing his 'Prehistoric Peeps' series into its Almanack in 1893, and following Harry Furniss as parliamentary caricaturist in 1894, a post he held till 1912. (As the son of an MP, he had long been familiar with the House of Commons.) Without obscuring his uncanny ability to capture individual likenesses, he restored to *Punch* the spirit of grotesque. Yet, despite this early association with one particular publication, he contributed some of his best political and legal cartoons elsewhere, including *The Sketch* (from 1893) and *The Bystander* (to which he moved in 1912). His work was exhibited at societies and dealers in London, including the Leicester Galleries and Fine Art Society, and also in the provinces. He was also a talented lecturer.

In 1891, Reed had married Beatrice Bullen, and they had a son and a daughter. By 1900, the family was living at 17 Fitz-George Avenue, Fulham.

E T Reed died in London on 12 July 1933.

His work is represented in the collections of the V&A.

Further reading:

E V Knox, rev Jane Newton, 'Reed, Edward Tennyson (1860-1933)', H C G Matthew and Brian Harrison (eds), *Oxford Dictionary of National Biography*, Oxford University Press, 2004, vol 46, page 302;
Shane Leslie (ed), *Edward Tennyson Reed, 1860-1933*, London: Heinemann, 1957

MAX BEERBOHM

Sir Henry Maximilian Beerbohm, IS NEAC PS (1872-1956)

Equally valued as a caricaturist and writer, Max Beerbohm sustained an elegant detachment in art and life. Though the tone of his drawings is often lightly wicked, it is also affectionate, for he hated to wound his subjects, most of whom he knew and liked. As a result, he was on safest ground in satirising artists and writers of the past, and in making many self-caricatures.

Max Beerbohm was born at 57 Palace Gardens Terrace, Kensington, London, on 24 August 1872, the youngest child of Julius Beerbohm, a prosperous corn merchant of mixed Baltic origins, and his second wife, Eliza (née Draper), the sister of his first wife. He was educated at Henry Wilkinson's preparatory school at 11 Orme Square (1881-85), Charterhouse (1885-90) and Merton College, Oxford (1890-94). Self-taught as an artist, he was an intelligent student of caricature and revered the work of Alfred Bryan and Carlo Pellegrini (Ape). On the edge of various fashionable groups, he produced lightly wicked sketches in pen and wash of many of the leading figures of the day. He contributed to *The Strand Magazine* (1892), *Pick-Me-Up* (1894) and *Vanity Fair* (1896) and published his first book of caricatures in 1896. Two years later, he began his only job, as theatre critic for the *Saturday Review*. He kept up prickly relations with his predecessor, Shaw and the editor, Frank Harris, and wrote a teasing first article, entitled 'Why I ought not to have become a theatre critic'. With the actor-manager Beerbohm Tree as a half-brother, he had actually had constant access to the theatre from an early age and was well acquainted with a number of actors, directors and playwrights. He even complemented his work as a critic with attempts at writing plays, most successfully in an adaptation of his own story, *The Happy Hypocrite* (1896), produced as a curtain raiser in 1900. A severe judge of the work of others, he believed that significant drama should combine intelligence, beauty and reality, but his theatrical taste was broad enough to encompass both music hall and the Symbolist dramas of Maeterlinck.

Soon after the appearance of his novel *Zuleika Dobson*, a decade later, in 1911, Beerbohm resigned from his position with the *Saturday Review*. He decided that, on his marriage to the American actress, Florence Kahn, in 1910, he would retire to the Villino Chiaro, Rapallo, Italy; from then he returned to England only on short visits. Nevertheless, he remained one of the country's best-known public figures. He was elected to the New English Art Club (1909), the National Portrait Society (1911) and the International Society of Sculptors, Painters and Gravers (1912). From this time, a number of exhibitions of his work were held at the Leicester Galleries, in 1911, 1913, 1921, 1923, 1925 and 1928. The Leicester Galleries mounted a retrospective in 1952, and a memorial show in 1957. He delivered the Rede Lectures at Cambridge between 1933 and 1935, and was knighted in 1939.

Following the death of his wife in 1951, Elisabeth Jungmann became his secretary and companion, and on 20 April 1956 his wife. He died in Rapallo on 20 May 1956.

His work is represented in the collections of The Courtauld Art Gallery, the National Portrait Gallery, Tate and the V&A; the Ashmolean Museum (Oxford), Charterhouse (Godalming) and Merton College Library (Oxford); and the Fine Arts Museums of San Francisco, the Harry Ransom Humanities Research Center (University of Texas at Austin), the Lilly Library (University of Indiana, Bloomington), Princeton University Library and William Andrews Clark Memorial Library (University of California at Los Angeles). His archive is held by the Houghton Library, Harvard University (Cambridge MA).

Further reading:

S N Behrman, *Portrait of Max: an intimate memoir of Sir Max Beerbohm*, New York: Random House, 1960;
Alan Bell, 'Beerbohm, Sir (Henry) Max(imilian) (*b* London, 24 Aug 1872; *d* Rapallo, 20 May 1956)', Jane Turner (ed), *The Dictionary of Art*, London: Macmillan, 1996, vol 3, pages 493;
Lord David Cecil, *Max*, London: Constable, 1964;
N John Hall, 'Beerbohm, Sir Henry Maximilian [Max] (1872-1956)', H C G Matthew and Brian Harrison (eds), *Oxford Dictionary of National Biography*, Oxford University Press, 2004, vol 4, pages 817-821;
N John Hall, *Max Beerbohm: A Kind of Life*, London: Yale University Press, 2002;
N John Hall, *Max Beerbohm. Caricatures*, New Haven: Yale University Press, 1997; Rupert Hart-Davis, *Catalogue of the Caricatures of Max Beerbohm*, London: Macmillan, 1972;
Rupert Hart-Davis (ed), *Letters of Max Beerbohm 1892-1956*, London: John Murray, 1988;
Rupert Hart-Davis (ed), Max Beerbohm, Letters to Reggie Turner, London: Rupert Hart-Davis, 1964

ADRIAN ALLINSON

Adrian Paul Allinson, RBA ROI LG PS (1890-1959)

One of the hugely talented generation of artists to emerge just before the First World War, Adrian Allinson managed to hold his own through both his personality and his work. He became best known as a painter of strongly modelled, appealingly stylised landscapes, figure compositions and flowers. However, his manifold talents encompassed sculpture, wood carving and pottery; wood engraving, poster design and set design; and, as here, distinctive caricatures.

Adrian Allinson was born Alfred Pulvermacher Allinson at 4 Spanish Place, Manchester Square, London, on 9 January 1890, the eldest of the five children of the physician and surgeon, Thomas Richard Allinson, and the Jewish German-born portrait painter, Hannah (née Pulvermacher).

Thomas Allinson was considered a radical figure and, in 1892, was both struck off the medical register for advocacy of vegetarianism and expelled from the Vegetarian Society for his views on birth control. In the same year, he founded the Natural Food Company and bought a stone grinding mill in Bethnal Green to produce wholemeal bread, which he had long argued was healthier than white bread. Wholemeal bread is still produced under the Allinson name.

From an early age, Adrian Allinson had opportunities to travel, and was encouraged by his artist mother to develop his interests in painting, music and languages. In 1901, he became a boarder at Wycliffe College, Stonehouse, Gloucestershire, the headmaster of which was a vegetarian. However, having been brought up by his father as a free thinker, he tried to convince his schoolfellows that there was no God. As a result, in 1905, he was expelled and sent to Wrekin College, Wellington, Shropshire, to complete his schooling.

While studying at Middlesex Hospital Medical School, with the intention of becoming a doctor, Allinson attended evening classes in modelling at the Regent Street Polytechnic School of Art, and so began to realise his vocation as an artist. He worked for one term at the Slade School of Fine Art under the sculptor, J Havard Thomas, and took courses at the Central School of Arts and Crafts in pottery and direct carving, the latter under John Skeaping. Then, in 1910, he started full-time studies at the Slade School, under Fred Brown, Derwent Lees, Walter Westley Russell, Philip Wilson Steer and Henry Tonks. He was there during what Tonks called a 'crisis of brilliance', alongside many equally strong students, including Mark Gertler, C R W Nevinson, Stanley Spencer and Edward Wadsworth, who, like him, became members of the 'Coster Gang', who dressed and behaved like costermongers. During his second year, he and Spencer won the two Slade Scholarships.

Allinson began to exhibit in 1911, with progressive artistic groups that included the Friday Club, the New English Art Club and the Camden Town Group (the last of which gathered around the figure of Walter Sickert). Sickert guided him in his production of scenes of the theatre, music hall and ballet, some of which he began to sell to the dance historian, bookseller and publisher, Cyril Beaumont. This would lead to his producing wooden figures of dancers to be sold in Beaumont's shop (1915-20) and illustrating Beaumont's books (1918-19).

On graduating from the Slade School in 1912, Allinson decided to study abroad. On the advice of Wadsworth, he went to Heinrich Knirr's school in Munich, later moving to Paris to study at the Grande Chaumière. Following his return to London, he helped found the London Group (1914, which subsumed the Camden Town Group) and held two joint exhibitions with Trelawney Dayrell-Reed at the Chenil Galleries in 1914 and 1915.

Though Allinson was an athletic figure, who enjoyed swimming, skiing and climbing, he suffered from a chronic gastric weakness that led to his being declared unfit for military service following the outbreak of the First World War. Nevertheless, he was a committed and outspoken pacifist, who aligned himself with the Bloomsbury Group at this time and, in 1916, registered as a conscientious objector. He continued to mix with the wide-ranging Bohemian set that frequented the Café Royal, and established close friendships with, among others, the composer, Philip Heseltine (known as Peter Warlock), and the artist, Alan Odle. He celebrated this milieu in one of his most important paintings, *The Café Royal* (private collection, 1915-16). Outside of painting, his main activities during the war were twofold. He produced caricatures for *The Bystander*, the *Daily Express*, the *Daily Graphic* and the *Weekly Dispatch*, and became the scenic designer to the Beecham Opera Company, Warlock having introduced him to Sir Thomas Beecham.

In 1919, Allinson married Adelaide Clark (née Buckland), the widow of the art teacher, Forbes Maitland Clark. It seems that she preferred to go by the Christian names 'Joan Maria Dolores', and so he followed suit, finally changing his given names by deed poll to 'Adrian Paul'. With their one son – the stage and screen actor, (John) Michael Allinson (1920-2010) – they spent much of the early stage of their marriage in a small Swiss village. However, Allinson maintained a studio at the Thackeray Studios, 35 Maple Street, Fitzroy Square, and gave that as his address when beginning to exhibit, from 1921, at the Royal Academy of Arts. The fruits of his Swiss sojourn were shown in 1922 at a solo show at the St George's Gallery.

Returning to London by the mid 1920s, the Allinsons were living at 22 Christchurch Avenue, Kilburn, by the end of the decade, and Adrian established a studio at 87a Clifton Hill, St John's Wood, by 1933 (and that later became his home). During the 1930s, he spent part of each year painting around the Mediterranean with the German artist, Heinrich Schröder. His subjects included landscapes in Greece, Italy, Tunisia, Spain and the Balearic Islands. He exhibited the results widely with leading exhibiting societies and dealers, and was elected to the Royal Society of British Artists (1933), the Royal Institute of Oil Painters (1936) and also the Pastel Society. A craftsman as well as a painter, he presented his pottery alongside his pictures in a solo show at the Redfern Gallery, in 1931, and sculpture alongside paintings at the Leicester Galleries, in 1935, and was briefly an active member of the Art Workers' Guild (1933-35, rejoining it in 1954). His forte for design was especially manifest in the posters that he produced for the Empire Marketing Board, London Transport and British Railways. Their imagery ranged from exotic figures to scenes of the Thames. A solo show at the Fine Art Society in 1939 evidenced his increasing focus on landscapes of the West Country.

During the Second World War, Allinson was selected as an official war artist by the War Artists' Advisory Committee, and produced some striking paintings of the effects of war on familiar London landmarks, including *Dig for Victory* (Westminster City Archives, 1942), which shows St James's Square in use as an allotment. His wife and son spent the war years in Minchinhampton, Gloucestershire, and she died in that county in 1943. In later years he developed a close friendship with the sculptor and potter, Mary Mitchell-Smith, and she would act as his executrix.

After the war, Allinson taught painting and drawing at Westminster Technical Institute, while continuing to work and exhibit into the late 1950s. Some months before his death, he collaborated with Bernard Tussaud on the creation of a wax sculpture of Kwame Nkrumah, then the first Prime Minister for Ghana, for Madame Tussauds.

Adrian Allinson died on 20 February 1959. A memorial exhibition was held at the gallery of the Royal Society of Painters in Water-Colours in June 1962 (the catalogue of which had an introduction by Mary Mitchell-Smith).

Allinson produced an unpublished autobiography entitled 'Painter's Pilgrimage'. The manuscript is in the collections of the McFarlin Library, University of Tulsa, Oklahoma, as part of the Dorothy Miller Richardson papers. Best known for her novel sequence, 'Pilgrimage', Richardson was the wife of Alan Odle and, through him, a friend of Allinson.

His work is represented in numerous public collections, including the London Transport Museum and the V&A; Manchester Art Gallery and The Potteries Museum & Art Gallery; and Aberystwyth University School of Art Museum and Galleries.

Further reading:

Peyton Skipwith, 'Adrian Allinson. A Restless Talent', *Connoisseur*, August 1978, pages 264-273

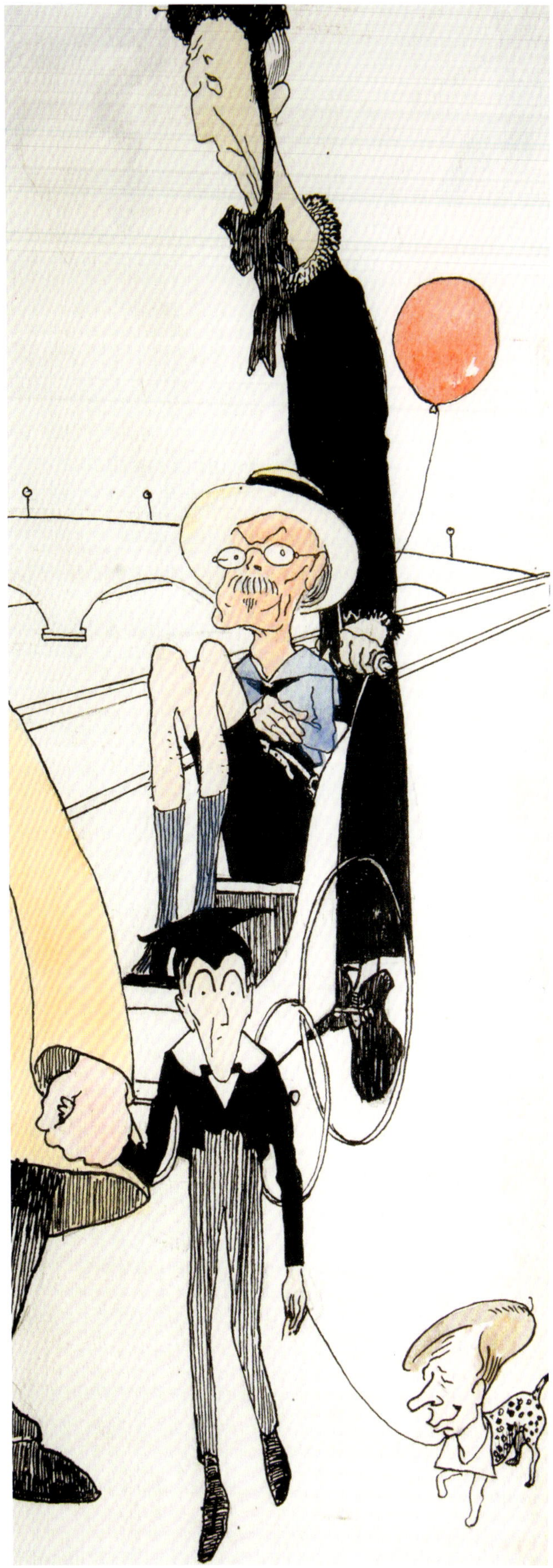

Detail of Adrian Allinson, *The Happy Family* [19]

HENRY TONKS

Professor Henry Tonks, NEAC (1862-1937)

Henry Tonks has a special place in the history of twentieth-century British art. Having established himself as a surgeon in the late 1880s, he made great use of his expert knowledge of anatomy in his progression as a draughtsman-painter (and occasional caricaturist). It informed his figure compositions, which synthesised elements of the Rococo, Impressionism and English illustration of the 1860s to distinctively satisfying ends. It also underpinned his almost legendary approach to teaching at the Slade School of Fine Art, when he became assistant to his friend and mentor, Professor Fred Brown, in 1893, and Professor himself, in 1918. He encouraged some of the most talented young artists in the country to use drawing – from the antique, from prints and from life – as the basis for individual development. At the same time, he discouraged them from visiting exhibitions of the avant-garde or engaging with the aesthetic values of its champion, Roger Fry – instead encouraging them to join the Impressionist stronghold that was the New English Art Club. His combination of qualities also made him almost uniquely placed, during the First World War, to record Harold Gillies' pioneering work in reconstructive surgery.

Henry Tonks was born in Solihull, Warwickshire, on 9 April 1862, the fifth of eleven children of Edmund Tonks, a former barrister and the owner of a well-established brass foundry in Birmingham, and his wife, Julia (née Johnson). Soon after he was born, the family moved a few miles south to Packwood Grange, a newly-built home in Knowle.

Tonks was educated at All Saints' School, Bloxham, Oxfordshire (where he was first inspired to paint), and then, from 1877, at Clifton College, Bristol ('where he declared that except chemistry he learnt little or nothing', according to *The Slade*, London: Printed by R Clay & Sons, 1907).

In 1880, Tonks began to study medicine at Sussex County Hospital, Brighton, while lodging at 16 Great College Street. During his time there, he was encouraged by a fellow student to develop his interest in art, and he even attempted to sell some of his drawings at a shop, though without success, before briefly attending the local school of art. A year later, he moved to London, to continue his studies at London Hospital Medical College, Whitechapel. In 1886, he became a member of the Royal Society of Surgeons and was appointed House Physician at London Hospital. A year later, he filled the post of House-surgeon to Sir Frederick Treves at London Hospital. Then, in 1888, he attained his Fellowship from the Royal College of Surgeons and was appointed Senior Medical Officer at the Royal Free Hospital, in Gray's Inn Road.

In his spare time, Tonks had been making frequent visits to the National Gallery, and, in 1886, had become well acquainted with the collection at Dresden's Gemäldegalerie Alte Meister, during a trip to Germany to learn the language. As a result, he decided to study painting in his spare time and, on the recommendation of a young acquaintance of a paternal uncle, took classes run by Fred Brown, the headmaster of Westminster School of Art. Brown had studied in Paris, and based his teaching on the model of the French atelier, so he introduced Tonks both to Impressionist handling and working from the life model. In 1891, Tonks exhibited for the first time – at the New English Art Club, which Brown had helped found, on progressive principles, five years earlier. Tonks would become a member of the NEAC in 1895, and continued to exhibit there regularly.

In 1892, Tonks took up the positions of Demonstrator in Anatomy and Curator of the Museum, both at London Hospital Medical School, in order to increase the time in which he could paint. Then, in 1893, he turned to art full-time, and was appointed Assistant Professor at the Slade School of Fine Art by Fred Brown, who had been appointed Slade Professor a year earlier. This demonstrated both Tonks' rapid development as an artist and the close bond of the two men. (They were joined by Wilson Steer NEAC, as a teacher of painting, and C Koe Child, from Westminster, as secretary.) It also marked the beginning of a heyday at the Slade, including what Tonks would describe as the first of two 'crises of brilliance', which saw the emergence of such star students as Harold Gilman, Spencer Gore, Gwen and Augustus John, Ambrose McEvoy and William Orpen, all of whom would be showcased at the NEAC.

In about 1894, Tonks moved from Holborn to Chelsea, and for the next two decades lived in a number of different addresses in the area, which was closely associated with artists. He also travelled widely, making sketching trips that included one to Honfleur in 1904, with the painter and critic, D S MacColl, and another to Italy in 1907 (exhibiting the resulting watercolours at the NEAC). His first solo show, held at the Carfax Gallery in 1905, helped confirm his standing as an artist, while a second 'crisis of brilliance' at the Slade, in the years 1908-14, reflected his strong influence as a teacher. That crisis was characterised by the presence and achievement of David Bomberg, Dora Carrington, Mark Gertler, Paul Nash, C R W Nevinson and Stanley Spencer. In 1910, he published, jointly with George Clausen, a report for educators entitled *Elementary Propositions in Painting and Drawing*, which proffered the fruits of his teaching. In the same year, he finally settled at 1 The Vale, Chelsea, which would remain his home for the rest of his life.

Following the outbreak of the First World War, Tonks returned to medicine. He worked first with war prisoners at a camp hospital in Dorchester, and then at the officers' hospital at Hill Hall, Essex (where he made drawings of Auguste Rodin and his wife, who were friends of the owner, and staying as refugees). By January 1915, he was in the Haut-Marne, working as an orderly, and later in the year moved to Italy to join a British ambulance unit that had been organised by the historian, G M Trevelyan. In 1916, he was commissioned as a lieutenant in the Royal Army Medical Corps, and worked with Harold Gillies, a pioneer in plastic surgery, at The Queen's Hospital, Sidcup. There he made a series of pastel drawings that compared portraits of wounded soldiers before and after surgery. These would be published in 1930, in Gillies' book, *Plastic Surgery of the Face* (and are now in the collections of the Army Dental Museum, Aldershot, Surrey).

In 1918, Tonks was appointed an official war artist, and returned to France with John Singer Sargent. As a result of the trip, he produced *Advanced Clearing Station in France: 1918* (Imperial War Museums), which was exhibited in 'The Nation's War Paintings and Other Records' held at the Royal Academy in 1919. In that year, he went to Archangel in Russia with the British expeditionary force.

When Fred Brown retired as Slade Professor in 1917, he offered the position to Tonks. Tonks suggested that Steer would be a stronger choice as the better painter, but, when Steer declined it, he accepted, and so consolidated his status as a great teacher. It might be suggested that he nurtured at least two further 'crises of brilliance', the first including Winifred Knights, Thomas Monnington, Oliver Messel and Rex Whistler in the years 1918-22, and the second, in the years 1926-29, including Tristram Hillier and William Coldstream (who would himself become Slade Professor in 1949). In 1922, he produced a mural showing the four founders of University College London, of which the Slade School is a department. In the summer of 1928, he spent five weeks in the company of A H Gerrard, head of sculpture at the Slade, travelling to countries he had not previously visited: Sweden, Denmark Holland and Belgium. Just before retiring his Professorship in 1930, he published an account of his early development, 'Notes from "Wander-Years"', in the Winter 1929 issue of *Artwork*, the quarterly edited by his friend, D S MacColl. On his retirement, he was offered a knighthood but declined. A year later, he exhibited at the Royal Academy of Arts for his one and only time; the work, *Spring Days*, was purchased under the terms of the Chantrey Bequest and entered the collection of the Tate Gallery.

Following his retirement from the Slade, Tonks continued to defend his traditional principles of observation and craftsmanship against avant-garde developments – through his own practice as a painter and his critique of others. He focussed his attacks on Roger Fry, who had curated the key Post-Impressionist exhibitions at the Grafton Gallery in 1910 and 1912, while he was Lecturer in Art History at the Slade. Between 1932 and 1934, Tonks wrote three letters to *The Times* that were critical of Fry's skills of conservation (of the Mantegna murals at Hampton Court) and connoisseurship (in attributing a portrait of Henry VIII to Hans Holbein the younger).

In 1936, a retrospective exhibition of Tonks's work was held at the Tate Gallery. He was only the second living artist to be so honoured, the first having been his friend, Wilson Steer, in 1929. Tonks died at home in Chelsea, London, on 8 January 1937. A memorial exhibition of his paintings, watercolours and pastels was held at Barbizon House in the June of the same year.

His work is represented in numerous public collections, including the British Museum, the Imperial War Museums, Tate and the UCL Art Museum; Army Dental Museum (Aldershot) and Birmingham Museums Trust; and the Art Gallery of New South Wales (Sydney).

Further reading:

Joseph Hone, *The Life of Henry Tonks*, London: Heineman, 1939;
Justine Hopkins, 'Tonks, Henry (*b* Solihull, April 9, 1862; *d* London, Jan 8, 1937)', *Grove Art Online*, 2003, https://doi.org/10.1093/gao/9781884446054.article.T085583;
Lynda Morris, 'Tonks, Henry (1862–1937)', H C G Matthew and Brian Harrison (eds), *Oxford Dictionary of National Biography*, Oxford University Press, 2004, https://doi.org/10.1093/ref:odnb/36535

POWYS EVANS

Powys Arthur Lewthall Evans (1899-1982), also known as 'Quiz'

The artistic talent of Powys Evans was nurtured in the circle of George Sheringham and by a number of teachers that included Henry Tonks at the Slade School of Fine Art. He became best known for his portrait drawings and caricatures, the latter of which he signed with the pseudonym, 'Quiz'. They were sufficiently successful in both exhibition and publication for Max Beerbohm to claim Evans as his heir.

Powys Evans was born at Cornwall Lodge, Allsop Place, Marylebone, London on 2 February 1899, the younger of the two children of a Welsh-born county court judge, William Evans, and his wife Frances (née Cheatle). Both he and sister, Gwendolyn, were encouraged to develop their artistic talents, and she also became an artist.

Evans's father patronised George Sheringham, buying his silk fans (1911) and commissioning a set of panels of *The Mabinogion* for his country house, Ilmington Hall (1912). In turn, Evans himself became part of the Sheringham circle and, a decade later, caricatured Sheringham and himself walking arm-in-arm. With precocity and rapidity, he gained an enviable training, despite time taken out to serve in the Welsh Guards on the Western Front during the First World War. He received private tuition from Robert Bevan and Spencer Gore, studied at the Slade School of Fine Art under Henry Tonks, and worked with F E Jackson, Walter Sickert and Sylvia Gosse; of the last, he said, 'to whose splendid teaching I owe what knowledge of sound drawing I possess'.

Abandoning a career as an oil painter in favour of portrait illustration, Evans made his name with a set of caricatures of Lovat Fraser's designs to *The Beggar's Opera* (1922). Exhibited at the Little Rooms and published as a portfolio, these caricatures attracted the attention of Filson Young, Assistant Editor of the *Saturday Review*, who then employed Evans as the house caricaturist under the name of 'Quiz'; a selection of these caricatures were later published as *Eighty-Eight Cartoons* (1926). In writing the preface to Evans's solo show, at the Leicester Galleries in 1924, Beerbohm claimed him as an heir, and later paid him the compliment of producing a self-caricature in Quiz's style. (That drawing, which also depicts the stage designer, Gordon Craig, later entered the collection of Ronald Searle.)

Evans had a further show at the Leicester Galleries in the following year, and regularly included work in the exhibitions of the Goupil Gallery. Contributing to a wide variety of periodicals, Evans produced a notable series of portraits in pen and ink for the *London Mercury* (some of which reappeared in *Fifty Heads*, 1928) and a number of caricatures for *G K's Weekly*; as H R Westwood noted in his study of *Modern Caricaturists* (1932), 'he is personally very much interested in Mr Chesterton's political philosophy and general outlook'. Though he exhibited a large range of works at the Cooling Gallery (1930) and had two further solo shows, at Colnaghi and Bumpus' Bookshop (both 1932), he soon ceased to exhibit or publish, retiring to Dolgellau, in Merionethshire in the late 1930s. He lived on Anglesey during the Second World War, and later in Bala, in Snowdonia, before returning to Dolgellau. It was only in 1975, when the Langton Gallery, London, mounted a retrospective, that he was fired to paint again.

Powys Evans died at The Bay Nursing Home, Tywyn, Gwynedd, on 1 December 1981.

His work is represented in the collections of the National Portrait Gallery.

Further reading:

John Jensen, 'Evans, Powys Arthur Lenthall [pseud. Quiz] (1899-1981)', H C G Matthew and Brian Harrison (eds), *Oxford Dictionary of National Biography*, Oxford University Press, 2018, https://doi.org/10.1093/odnb/9780198614128.013.109184

WILLIAM ORPEN

Major Sir William Newenham Montague Orpen, RA RWS RHA RI HROI RP PIS NEAC PNPS PS (1878-1931)

Precociously talented and greatly dedicated, the Irish artist, William Orpen, had the potential to succeed in almost any genre or medium of painting and drawing. By 1910, he had established a practice that would make him the most successful and honoured portraitist of his age. Less than a decade later, he was knighted for his significant work as an official war artist.

William Orpen was born at Oriel, Grove Avenue, Blackrock, County Dublin, Ireland, on 27 November 1878, into an Anglo-Irish family. He was the fifth and youngest child of the solicitor, Arthur Orpen, and his wife, Anne (née Caulfeild), daughter of the Rt Rev Charles Caulfeild, Bishop of Nassau. His eldest sibling, Richard Caulfeild Orpen, became an architect and watercolourist.

Orpen's father intended that he should study law and enter the family legal firm, which had been founded by his paternal grandfather, Sir Richard Orpen. However, his mother encouraged his interest in painting, and supported his wish to go to art school. She won out, and, in 1891, at the age of 13, Orpen entered the Metropolitan School of Art, Dublin, to study under its headmaster, James Brenan. During his six years there, he showed great talent and won every major prize and scholarship.

In 1897, Orpen moved to London and enrolled at the Slade School of Fine Art, where he was taught by Fred Brown, Henry Tonks and Wilson Steer. He benefitted particularly from the teaching of Tonks, following his encouragement to study the old masters and make strength of drawing the basis of one's art. As a result, he stood out as possibly the finest draughtsman among a highly talented intake of students, which included Augustus John and Ambrose McEvoy, both of whom became friends. Among other awards, he won the Slade Composition Prize for *The Play Scene from 'Hamlet'* (Houghton Hall, Norfolk), in his final year, in 1899. From that time, he began to show work at the New English Art Club, of which his Slade teachers were prominent members. Then, in 1900, he too became a member, when *The Mirror* (Tate) proved a significant early success when shown at its winter exhibition. In 1901, he held his first solo show at the Carfax Gallery.

It was also in 1901 that Orpen married Grace Knewstub, a daughter of the Pre-Raphaelite painter, Walter John Knewstub. Her sister was the actress with the stage name of 'Alice Kingsley', who in 1899 had married the painter, William Rothenstein. The Orpens soon settled at 11 & 13 Royal Hospital Road, Chelsea, and they would have three daughters. In 1903, Orpen founded Chelsea Art School at 4 & 5 Rossetti Studios, 72 Flood Street, with Augustus John and his own brother-in-law, Jack Knewstub, as secretary. Before this closed in 1907, Orpen bought the house next to Chelsea Town Hall, and set up the Chenil Gallery, which was managed by Jack Knewstub, and at which both he and John held exhibitions.

From 1902 until the outbreak of the First World War, Orpen shared his time between London and Dublin, and taught part-time at his *alma mater*, the Metropolitan School of Art. He was elected an associate of the Royal Hibernian Academy in 1904 and a full Academician in 1907. From about that time, he would rent a house at Howth Head, just north of Dublin Bay. He played a significant role in Irish cultural life, mixing with painters and collectors, and contributing to the Celtic revival. The friendships that he cultivated included those with his distant cousin, the dealer and collector, Hugh Lane, and the novelist and critic, George Moore. He also formed a strong bond with some of his students, and especially Séan Keating, who arrived at the Metropolitan School in 1909, and eventually became Orpen's studio assistant.

In 1904, Orpen accompanied Lane on a trip to France and Spain, during which Lane acquired paintings for a modern art gallery in Dublin. For Orpen, it was an opportunity to see works of the old masters that he had known only from reproductions, and especially those by Velázquez in the Prado, and it proved influential on his subsequent development. From about 1907, he and Lane shared 8 South Bolton Gardens, Chelsea, when Lane was in London, and it later became Orpen's studio (though he maintained his house in Royal Hospital Road as the family home).

In acknowledgement of his ability as a portraitist, Orpen was elected, in 1905, to the Society of Portrait Painters (which would be granted the status of a royal society in 1911). In the following year, he was asked to paint the first of a series of portraits of the wealthy American, Evelyn St George, who was married to one of his cousins. In 1908, he and Evelyn began an almost decade long affair, which would prove to be his most significant extra-marital relationship, and affect the course of his art as well of his private life, as she encouraged his ambitions. Around this time, he produced some of his boldest group portraits, including *A Bloomsbury Family* (1907, National Galleries of Scotland, showing the artist, William Nicholson, with his brood), *Homage to Manet* (1909, Manchester Art Gallery, showing key members of the NEAC sitting beneath Manet's portrait of Eva Gonzàles) and the almost caricatural, *The Selecting Jury of the New English Art Club* (1909, National Portrait Gallery).

Orpen was elected an associate of the Royal Academy of Arts in 1910, and helped to found the National Portrait Society in 1911 (later becoming its President). These were further indicators of his increased recognition as a painter and aids to his developing the most successful and remunerative portrait practice of the time, the successor to that of John Singer Sargent.

In 1916, two years into the First World War, Orpen was appointed an official war artist, and commissioned as a Major. This caused a break with his studio assistant, Séan Keating, who returned to Ireland. In April 1917, he left for France and, from then until 1921, made the war and its outcome his chief subject. In 1918, a solo show of the oils, watercolours and drawings that he had produced of the conflict was held at Thomas Agnew & Sons, under the direction of the Ministry of Information. He presented many of the contents as a gift to the nation, which was accepted by the Imperial War Museum, and this led to his being knighted in June 1918. In 1921, he published his illustrated memoirs of the war, entitled *An Onlooker in France 1917-19*.

In 1919, Orpen was appointed official artist to the British Peace Delegation, and accompanied it to the Paris Peace Conference in order to portray the delegates. The results included the traditional monumental group portrait, *The Signing of Peace in the Hall of Mirrors, Versailles, 28th June 1919* (Imperial War Museums). More controversial was *To the Unknown British Soldier in France*, which, at the time of its first being exhibited, at the RA in 1923, included two semi-nude soldiers and two cherubs surrounding a Union Jack draped coffin. He later painted out the figures and donated it to the Imperial War Museum in memory of his friend, Earl Haig.

In the years following the war, Orpen continued his reputation as a portraitist, and maintained studios at both The Boltons in London and in Paris, the home of his mistress, Yvonne Aubicq. He also became a full Royal Academician (1919), and was elected to the Académies Royales des Beaux-Arts of both Brussels and Antwerp (1919) and to a number of other exhibiting societies, including the Royal Institute of Painters in Water Colours (1919). In 1921, he began his tenure as President of the International Society of Sculptors, Painters and Gravers. Later honours include his being an honorary member of both the Royal Institute of Oil Painters (1929) and the Royal Hibernian Academy (1930).

In 1923, Orpen was the subject of a monograph by Albert Rutherston (the brother of his brother-in-law, William Rothenstein). In the same year, he became the nominal editor of the illustrated art history, *An Outline of Art*, and in the following one published his second volume of memoirs, *Stories of Old Ireland and Myself*.

William Orpen died at 2 Clareville Grove, South Kensington, London, on 29 September 1931. Memorial exhibitions were held at the Royal Academy, in London, and the Knoedler Gallery, in New York.

His work is represented in the Government Art Collection, the Royal Academy of Arts, the Royal Free Hospital and the Royal Institute of British Architects, and numerous public collections, including the Imperial War Museums, National Portrait Gallery, Tate and UCL Art Museum; Leeds Art Gallery; Aberdeen Art Gallery & Museums, Glasgow Museums and the National Galleries of Art (Edinburgh); and Mildura Arts Centre (Mildura, VI).

Further reading:

Bruce Arnold, *Orpen: Mirror to an Age*, London: Jonathan Cape, 1982;
Bruce Arnold, 'Orpen, Sir William Newenham Montague (1878–1931)', H C G Matthew and Brian Harrison (eds), *Oxford Dictionary of National Biography*, Oxford University Press, 2011, https://doi.org/10.1093/ref:odnb/35331;
Paul G Konody and Sidney Dark: *William Orpen: Artist and Man*, London: Seeley, Service & Co, 1932;
John Rothenstein, 'Orpen, Sir William (Newenham Montague), (*b* Oriel, Blackrock, Co Dublin, Nov 27, 1878; *d* London, Sept 29, 1931)', *Grove Art Online*, 2003, https://doi.org/10.1093/gao/9781884446054.article.T063956;
Robert Upstone, *William Orpen: Politics, Sex and Death*, London: Imperial War Museum/Philip Wilson, 2005

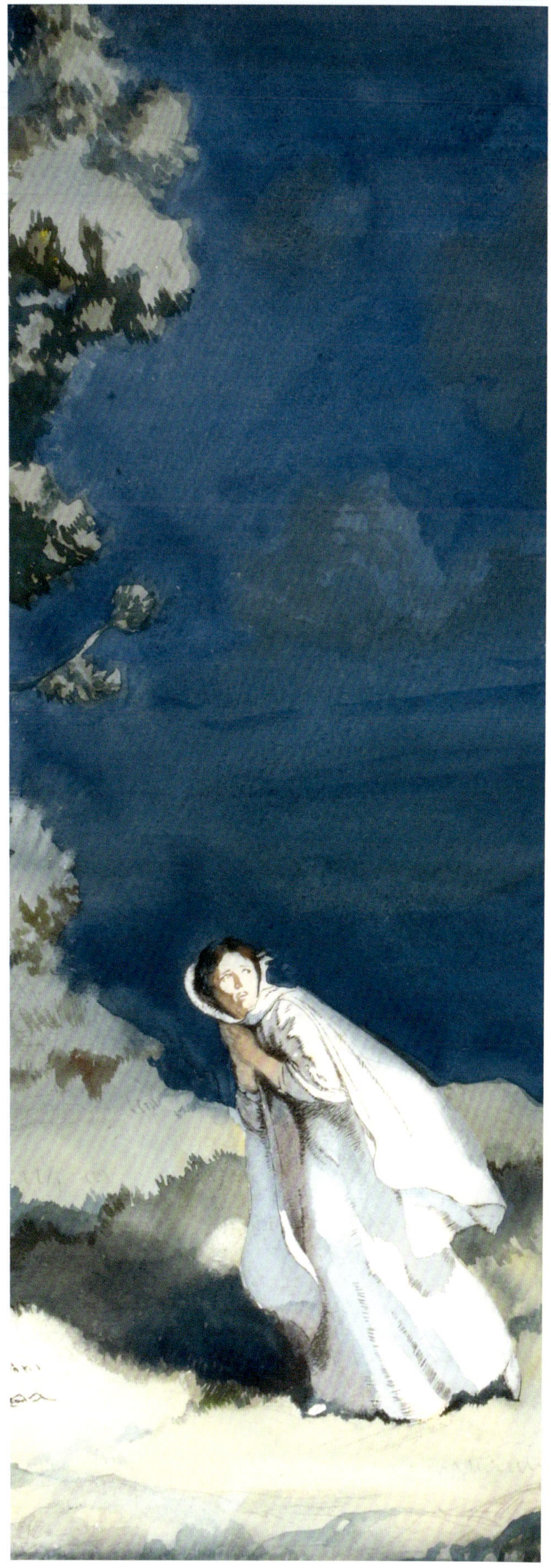

Detail of William Orpen, *The Woman in White* [27]

H M BATEMAN

Henry Mayo Bateman (1887-1970)

H M Bateman established his inimitable style before the First World War when, as he put it, he 'went mad on paper', by drawing people's mood and character. This culminated in 'The Man Who ...', his famous series of cartoons dramatising social gaffes.

Henry Mayo Bateman was born at Sutton Forest in New South Wales, Australia, on 15 February 1887, the elder of two children of English parents, the farmer turned export packager, Henry Charles Bateman, and his wife, (Amelia) Rose Mayo (formerly Brooks). A year after his birth, he returned with his family to England, and settled at Moss Vale, St Julian's Farm Road, Lambeth, South London.

Bateman was educated at Forest Hill House, South London. Given the freedom to develop his artistic leaning from an early age, he left school at the age of 16, and attended Westminster School of Art and then Goldsmiths' College. Influenced by *Comic Cuts* and *Ally Sloper's Half-Holiday*, he made contributions to *Scraps* (1903) and *The Tatler* (1904). He was encouraged by Phil May and John Hassall to spend some time in the studio of Charles van Havermaet at the New Art School, Stratford Studios, Kensington (1904-7). He also took up amateur boxing, tap-dancing, golf and fishing, hobbies that were to prove valuable as sources for cartoon material. In 1911, he was living with his family at 40 Nightingale Lane, Balham.

It was around 1911 that Bateman developed his inimitable style, when, as he put it, he 'went mad on paper' by drawing people's mood and character rather than their physical appearance. Many of his early caricatures show the influence of Sidney Sime and Henry Ospovat, and similarly depict musical and music-hall personalities and theatrical productions. He illustrated theatrical reviews in *The Bystander* (1910) and, as 'Our Untamed Artist at the Play', in *The Sketch* (1912-14). This work met with such success that he was also commissioned to produce posters for two plays by George Bernard Shaw, *Fanny's First Play* and *John Bull's Other Island* (both 1912). In the years before the First World War, he lived in South Clapham. During the war, he joined a London regiment, but was soon discharged on the grounds of ill health.

The beginning of the post-war period was marked by solo shows of Bateman's work at the Leicester Galleries (1919, 1921). It also saw the emergence of his famous series of cartoons concerning the social gaffe, 'The Man Who ...', while he also developed a sequential approach derived from Caran d'Ache and the cinema. Throughout his career he contributed to almost all the leading periodicals and illustrated a number of books. His art proved to be a breath of fresh air to the stuffy pages of *Punch*, and his vigorous, wholly visual approach was closer to continental work such as that of the German satirical magazine, *Simplicissimus*, than to anything in England. At the peak of his career in the 1930s, he was earning between four and five thousand pounds from cartoons for magazines, including *The Radio Times*, book illustrations and advertising. He drove the latest cars and, in 1925, built a house at Reigate Heath in Surrey. In 1926, he married Brenda Weir, the daughter of a country gentleman from Stratford St Mary, Suffolk. They would have two daughters.

Though Bateman continued to produce cartoons and illustrations following the Second World War, he went into something of a semi-retirement. He separated from his wife in 1947, and six years later moved to Brook Cottage, Sampford Courtenay, Devon. Despite the mounting of a retrospective of his work, at the Fine Art Society in 1962, he felt alienated from post-war Britain; so, later in the decade, he decided to move permanently to the Maltese island of Gozo, where he painted watercolour landscapes. He died on Gozo on 11 February 1970.

His work is represented in numerous public collections, including the British Museum.

Further reading:

Anthony Anderson, *The Man Who Was H M Bateman*, Exeter: Webb & Bower, 1982; John Jensen, 'Bateman, Henry Mayo (1887-1970)', H C G Matthew and Brian Harrison (eds), *Oxford Dictionary of National Biography*, Oxford University Press, 2004, vol 4, pages 299-301

SAMUEL BEGG

Samuel Begg (1854-1936)

Samuel Begg was a significant periodical illustrator, and occasional cartoonist, working initially in his adoptive home of Australasia and then, from 1886, in his native Britain. He became best known as a staff member and special artist for *The Illustrated London News*.

Samuel Begg was born at 31 Mecklenburgh Square, London, on 19 March 1854, the fourth of nine children of the Grenada-born merchant, Samuel Begg, and his Irish-born wife, Agnes (née Wilson). He was baptised at the National Scotch Church, Regent Square, on 28 May.

Early in 1860, the five-year-old Samuel Begg migrated with his family to Napier on New Zealand's North Island. His father established himself as a shipping agent and built a wooden house for the family on the hill above Napier, calling it 'Prospect'. Samuel was educated at Napier Grammar School, from which he graduated in 1868, with prizes in French and Drawing. Soon after, he left home to work as a surveyor on new settlements and the future railway line between Napier and the capital, Wellington.

In the early 1870s, Samuel Begg decided that he wanted to be an artist, and so moved to the South Island, settling in Auckland. There it was probably his brother-in-law, David McFarlane, an amateur artist, who introduced him to staff in the lithographic and printing department of the *New Zealand Herald* and *Auckland Weekly News*. In 1877, the *Herald* published a supplement containing Begg's panoramic view of Auckland surrounded by other scenes of the area (based on his own watercolour landscapes). While living in the city, he also began his own short-lived paper, the *Auckland Graphic*.

Late in the 1870s, Begg moved to Australia, and initially settled in Sydney. There he worked for the firm of printers and engravers, Gibbs, Shallard & Co, on projects that included the design of the medal awarded at the Sydney International Exhibition of 1879. He also worked on a freelance basis with his English colleague, the wood-engraver, Appleton, in order to contribute illustrations to Melbourne's *The Illustrated Australian News* (1878) and Sydney's *Town and Country Journal* (1879-80). Following Appleton's return to England, Begg helped found the *Sydney Bulletin*, in 1880, and contributed cartoons to it. However, in 1881, when the *Bulletin* seemed likely to fail financially, he moved to Melbourne, to work for *The Illustrated Australian News* and to study at the School of Design attached to the National Gallery of Victoria.

In 1883, Begg left Australia for Europe, and settled in Paris in order to further his studies at the Académie Julian. Though records indicate that he continued at Julian's until 1889, he seems to have done so while simultaneously establishing himself in London. While living at 68a Chalk Farm Road in the years 1886-87, he began to contribute to *The Illustrated London News*, and exhibited two drawings or paintings of atelier interiors at the Royal Academy of Arts. In 1891, while lodging with the Stein family at 'Roseneath', 4 Cathnor Road, Hammersmith, he exhibited a third work at the RA – a drawing showing the finish of the Melbourne Cup.

In about 1892, Begg returned to New Zealand, making some drawings en route that were later published in *The Pictorial World*, his main source of income at the time. It has been suggested that he met his future wife during the voyage. In any event, he married Ada Nelson, known as Angie, the daughter of a civil servant, in Hastings on 26 April 1893, and in the following year she gave birth to their daughter, Mary. By 1901, they were living at 23 Fairfax Road, Bedford Park. He was a member of the Savage Club, and enjoyed landscape painting as well as golf.

During the 1890s, Begg contributed to *Black and White* (1892), *Cassell's Family Magazine* (1895-96) and *The Sporting and Dramatic News* (1896), and, most importantly, joined the staff of *The Illustrated London News* in 1895. In that position, he developed as a specialist in military, sporting and theatrical subjects, and as a special artist made several trips abroad. He accompanied the Prince and Princess of Wales during their tour through India, in 1905-6, and was present at both the wedding of Queen Victoria Eugenie in Madrid, in 1906, and the funeral of King Carlos in Lisbon, in 1908. In 1912, he extended a working trip to India so that he could make a return visit to New Zealand, possibly in the company of his daughter, Mary. He retired from *The Illustrated London News* in 1919, having latterly provided images of the First World War.

In 1914, Begg's daughter, Mary, married Colin Rowntree, an architect related to the famous chocolate manufacturers. In 1925, the Rowntrees moved from Chiswick to Yorkshire, and they were soon joined by Samuel and Angie Begg. From 1927, they all lived at 17 Stonegate, York. Angie died in 1934, and Samuel two years later, on 7 January 1936.

His work is represented in the collections of the V&A.

Further reading:

Douglas Lloyd Jenkins, 'What we know about Samuel Begg', douglaslloydjenkins.wordpress.com, 2014

ROBERT TALBOT KELLY

Robert George Talbot Kelly, RBA RBC RI (1861-1934)

Robert Talbot Kelly was best known as a painter in oil and watercolour of meticulous and atmospheric Egyptian subjects. He settled in Cairo, and absorbed himself in the landscape and culture, learning Arabic and spending time with the Bedouin. As a result, his studio became a destination for foreign visitors and he was eventually awarded an Order by the Kedive of Egypt. However, he was able to broaden his range, and worked with success as far afield as Iceland and Burma.

Robert George Talbot Kelly was born in Birkenhead, Cheshire, on 18 January 1861, the fourth of the eleven children of the Dublin born artist, Robert George Kelly, and his Scottish wife, Mary (née Walker). Growing up at 'Glasnevin', 39 Balls Road, Claughton with Grange, Birkenhead, he was educated at Birkenhead School and studied art under his father. However, he worked as a clerk in a firm of cotton traders until 1882, when he then decided to take up art as a profession and go abroad. Travelling in Spain and North Africa, he settled in Cairo in 1883, and there both acquired a studio and learned Arabic. Eventually, he would receive commissions from aristocrats and dignitaries who visited his studio as one of the sights of Egypt. From the mid 1880s, he exhibited in Liverpool, at the principal London galleries, and on the Continent, and though he initially appeared as 'R G Kelly Jr', he soon inserted the family name of 'Talbot' to avoid confusion with his father.

Despite the fact that Kelly had made his name as an Orientalist, he was invited, in July 1890, by a businessman to visit and paint Iceland, in the company of eight other artists, photographers and researchers. During their fortnight's stay, they travelled to Krýsuvík, Hekla, Geysir and Þingvellir. The paintings that resulted expanded his repertoire, and, in 1893, he was elected a member of the Royal Society of British Artists. By that date, he had settled in Birkenhead, and established a studio at 24 The Temple, Dale Street, Liverpool. Then, in 1894, he married Lilias Lindsay, the daughter of Ebenezer Lindsay of Hartside Farm, Lamington and Wandel, Lanarkshire, Scotland. They would have two children, including Richard Barrett Talbot Kelly, the painter of birds and historical subjects.

In 1897, Kelly began a career as a published author and illustrator. He illustrated *Fire and Sword in the Sudan* by Baron Rudolf Carl Slatin Pasha, and wrote 'In the Desert with the Bedouin', the first of a series of articles on his Egyptian experiences that appeared in *The Century Magazine*. At the turn of the century, he began to return to Egypt, and is recorded as sailing from Liverpool to Port Said in 1899 and 1901. Then, from 1902, when he moved to Swiss Cottage, London, until 1914, he maintained a studio in Cairo as well as one at 4 Primrose Hill Studios. In 1902, he wrote and illustrated *Egypt: Painted and Described* and in both 1902 and 1904 held exhibitions of his Egyptian subjects at the Fine Art Society. At some point, he was awarded the Order of the Medjidie from the Kedive of Egypt.

In 1903-4, Kelly spent a year in Burma at the request of the Burmese Government. In 1905, he wrote and illustrated *Burma: Painted and Described* and held an exhibition of his Burmese subjects at the Leicester Galleries. He held further exhibitions with the Leicester Galleries in 1908 and 1910, and in 1908 published both *Burma* and *Egypt* in A & C Black's series, 'Peeps at Many Lands'. He was elected to the Royal Institute of Painters in Water Colours, in 1908, and the Royal British Colonial Society of Artists, in 1910, and would serve on the committee of each. He was also elected to the Royal Geographical Society and the Royal Zoological Society.

Kelly was 53 years old when the First World War broke out in 1914, and it is not known whether he undertook any war service. However, his son, Richard served in the Royal Artillery in France between 1915 and 1918 (and remained in the army until 1929). Continuing to paint and exhibit, Kelly held a solo show at the Fine Art Society in 1916 and – maintaining contact with his native Northwest – became President of the Liver Sketching Club in 1917. His wife, Lilias, died in that year.

Following the end of the war, Kelly resumed his travels, but focussed on Europe, and held a solo show of watercolours of the Côte d'Azur at the Fine Art Society in 1924. By then, he and his son, Richard, were sharing 3 St John's Wood Studios, Queen's Terrace. He died a decade later, on 30 December 1934, at the Cancer Hospital, Fulham Road, Chelsea.

His work is represented in numerous public collections, including the Williamson Art Gallery (Birkenhead).

WILLIAM ROTHENSTEIN

Sir William Rothenstein, RP IS NEAC (1872-1945)

William Rothenstein was a significant force in the British art world of the first half of the twentieth century, proving influential as an administrator, dealer, teacher and writer. As an artist, he is best remembered for his portraits and for the images that he produced at home and abroad during the First and Second World Wars.

William Rothenstein was born at 4 Spring Bank, Bradford, Yorkshire, on 29 January 1872, the fifth of six children of the prosperous German Jewish wool merchant, Moritz Rothenstein, and his wife, Bertha (née Dux). Of his two brothers, Charles became a significant collector, and Albert a painter and illustrator. Both would change their surname to Rutherston during the First World War.

Though an indifferent pupil at Bradford Grammar School, Rothenstein was a precociously talented artist, and left for London at the age of 16 in order to study at the Slade School of Fine Art. Working there under Alphonse Legros, he developed a strong enthusiasm for French art even before he went to Paris.

While a student at the Académie Julian (1889-93), he first attracted attention for his portrait drawings, and soon became a focus for anglophone artists of his generation. He also made many acquaintances among advanced French writers and painters, including Edgar Degas and Camille Pissarro, who influenced his focus on subjects of modern life.

On returning to England, Rothenstein made his name as a draughtsman and social observer, and exhibited mainly at the New English Art Club (a member from 1894). He also helped to spearhead the fashion for bravura Spanish painting, even publishing a book on *Goya* (1899) with the encouragement of John Singer Sargent. Founding the Carfax Gallery with John Fothergill in 1898, he took an important and increasingly official, even conservative, role in artistic politics.

In 1899, Rothenstein married Alice Mary Knewstub, who had appeared on stage as Alice Kingsley. In 1902, they settled in Hampstead, in north London, and there brought up two sons and two daughters. Of his two sons, John became director of the Tate Gallery, and Michael an artist best known as a printmaker.

During the 1900s, Rothenstein worked on an important series of scenes of Jewish religious life in a restrained palette. In other paintings, he made use of brighter colours, which undoubtedly reflected the influence of Post-Impressionism, despite his expressing reservations about the movement. In 1910, he took up the cause of Indian art and artists, helping to found the India Society and then visiting the country at the end of that year.

While retaining their flat in Hampstead, Rothenstein and his family moved to Gloucestershire in 1912, and settled at Iles Farm, Far Oakridge, near Stroud. With the outbreak of the First World War, he encouraged the War Office to employ official war artists, and in December 1917 was himself appointed to go to the western front, though his German name led him to be treated with some suspicion.

Through the influence of H A L Fisher, Rothenstein would take up the chair of civic art at Sheffield University (1917-26) and become the Principal of the Royal College of Art (1920-35). He also acted as a trustee of the Tate Gallery (1927-33). He was knighted in 1931 and received an honorary degree from Oxford University in 1934. His numerous books include the memoirs, *Men and Memories* (1931-32) and *Since Fifty* (1939).

During the Second World War, Rothenstein produced portrait drawings of members of the RAF on their bases in England.

He died at his home in Far Oakridge on 16 March 1945. At his memorial service, his old friend, Max Beerbohm, gave the address.

His work is represented in numerous public collections, including the Imperial War Museums, the National Portrait Gallery and Tate; Bradford Museums and Galleries, Manchester Art Gallery, Museums Sheffield, the University of Southampton and The Wilson (Cheltenham); and National Museum Wales (Cardiff).

Further reading:

Mary Lago, 'Rothenstein, Sir William (1872-1945)', H C G Matthew and Brian Harrison (eds), *Oxford Dictionary of National Biography*, Oxford University Press, 2004, vol 47, pages 896-898;
John Rothenstein, 'Rothenstein, Sir William (*b* Bradford, 29 Jan 1872; *d* Far Oakridge, nr Stroud, 14 Feb 1945)', Jane Turner (ed), *The Dictionary of Art*, London: Macmillan, 1996, vol 27, pages 218-219;
Robert Speaight, *William Rothenstein: The Portrait of an Artist in His Time*, London: Eyre & Spottiswoode, 1962

EDWARD HANDLEY-READ

Edward Harry Handley-Read, MBE RBA (1870-1935)

Establishing himself as a wide-ranging artist and illustrator during the 1890s, Edward Handley-Read produced pioneering images of the front line during the First World War.

Edward Handley-Read was born Edward Read in London. He was possibly the son of Henry Read, and his wife, Emma (née Birch), who, in 1881, were keeping an upmarket lodging house at 65 Sloane Street. He was educated at Kensington Grammar School and first studied art at the National Art Training School (more popularly known as the South Kensington Schools). He then progressed to Westminster School of Art, where he worked under Frederick Brown, and the Royal Academy Schools, where he won the Creswick Prize for landscape painting. He exhibited at the Royal Academy of Arts, the Royal Institute of Painters in Water Colours and the Royal Society of British Artists, becoming a member of the last in 1895. He also contributed illustrations to various books and magazines, including *The Graphic* and *The Illustrated London News*. During the 1890s, he gave as his addresses the Ranger's Lodge, Hyde Park (1890-94), and 1 Camden Studios, Camden Street (1893-98). By 1911, he was working at 8 Camden Studios.

In 1902, Edward Read married Sarah Elizabeth Clarke in Edmonton. However, she died a few years later and, in 1911, he married Eva Handley in Kingston upon Thames. She was a pioneering woman dental surgeon and suffragette, and in deference to her he changed his surname by deed poll to Handley-Read. They would have a son and a daughter.

During the First World War, Edward Handley-Read served in the Machine Gun Corps, first as a Sergeant-Instructor and later a Captain. In that capacity, he organised an army studio for diagrams and models for instruction on military matters, instructed on camouflage, and invented published sets of coloured diagrams for the teaching of machine-guns. He also produced several hundred watercolours of life on the front line, some of which were exhibited at the Leicester Galleries in a series of solo shows entitled 'The British Firing-Line', the first of which took place in May 1916. In the following year, the gallery published a portfolio of his colour engravings under the same title, which had a foreword by Hilaire Belloc.

By 1916, the Handley-Reads had established a home in Steyning, Sussex, where other members of Eva's family were living. It was there in that year that their son, Charles, was born. He would become a noted architectural writer and collector, with a pioneering interest in William Burges, and an inspiring teacher, at Bryanston.

After the war, Edward Handley-Read produced a variety of figure subjects and landscapes. Living at Chantry Lodge, Chantry Lane, Storrington, Sussex, until at least 1932, he died at the House of Steps, 41 High Street, Salisbury, on 6 December 1935.

His work is represented in the collections of the Imperial War Museums.

JOSEPH GRAY

Joseph Gray (1890-1963)

Joseph Gray, is now best remembered as an evocative war artist. During the First World War, he produced detailed drawings based on direct experiences in the Black Watch on the Western Front, and was subsequently sought after – by regiments and museums – as a painter of military subjects. Then, in the Second World War, he employed his expertise to develop large-scale forms of camouflage, while also creating drypoints of blitz-torn London, an indication of his broader interest in, and talent for, landscape and architectural subjects.

Joseph Gray was born in South Shields, County Durham, on 6 June 1890, the eldest of three children of the master mariner, Captain Joseph Gray, and his wife, Mary Alice (née Johnson). He and his family spent his early years at 3 Romilly Street, Westoe, South Shields, moving a short distance to 1 Lolanthe Terrace by 1901. Though he first trained as a marine engineer, he went on to study at South Shields School of Art, under its Headmaster, John Heys. He then travelled widely, making many sketches in France, Germany, Holland, Russia and Spain.

In about 1912, Gray settled in Dundee to work as an illustrator for the periodical publisher, D C Thomson, on the *Dundee Courier* and other publications. Though already partly deaf by the outbreak of the First World War, in 1914, he enlisted in the 4th (Dundee) Battalion of the Black Watch. In so doing, he joined a number of other journalists who referred to themselves as 'Fighter-Writers'. Once he reached the trenches, in August 1914, his talents as a draughtsman were quickly recognised, and he was appointed as an observer to Captain Edgar Boase, with the responsibility of delineating enemy positions and mapping trench lines for strategic use. He fought in the battles of Neuve Chapelle (March 1915), Festubert (May 1915) and Loos (September-October 1915), and sent many reports back to the *Dundee Courier*.

In March 1916, Gray was invalided off the Western Front, as the result of being wounded by sniper fire and suffering bouts of trench fever. By the time that he returned to Dundee, he was contributing to the weekly illustrated newspaper, *The Graphic*, and would become its regular 'war artist', providing articles and drawings that were based on first-hand sketches. Later the same year, he married Agnes Mary Dye (known as Nancy), the daughter of a bank clerk. They settled at 'Seacot', 14 Kerrington Crescent, Barnhill, Broughty Ferry, to the east of Dundee. They would have one daughter, Alice Maureen, born in June 1919.

Gray continued to contribute to the *Dundee Advertiser*, which, between December 1917 and January 1918, published the 31 instalments of his 'The History of the 4th Black Watch', based on his own recollections and the testimonies of other eyewitnesses. His personal experiences also led him to receive a number of commissions to paint military subjects. Having sold seven drawings to the Imperial War Museum in 1918, he then received a commission from the museum to produce the large oil painting, *A Ration Party of the 4th Black Watch at the Battle of Neuve Chapelle, 1915*. He went on to produce paintings for several regiments, including his own. Then, in April 1922, his painting, *The 4th Black Watch Bivouac on the Night of the Neuve Chapelle*, was presented to the city of Dundee. He granted the council the publication rights to the image, and copies were sold, the profits of which were donated to the Black Watch Memorial Home in Broughty Ferry.

From 1919, Gray exhibited in Edinburgh (at the Royal Scottish Academy and the dealer, Aitken Dott), London (at the Fine Art Society) and on the Continent (at international exhibitions in Florence and Stockholm). During the 1920s, he turned increasingly from military subjects to landscapes and architectural scenes, and travelled to the Low Countries and Spain in order to find new inspiration. The works that resulted were not only paintings but also etchings, and especially drypoints. Produced during a printmaking boom, these were widely exhibited and reproduced, and enthusiastically received, selling well on both sides of the Atlantic and entering such major public collections as the British Museum and the Victoria & Albert Museum. Late in the decade, Gray and his family moved across Broughty Ferry to 'Westbrook', Brook Street, which had space for both a studio and a printing room. However, by then, his print sales were beginning to fall, as the result of the international economic Depression.

In 1931, Gray moved with his family to London, in an attempt to reinvent himself as a portrait painter. He rented a studio at 33 Tite Street, Chelsea, once occupied by John Singer Sargent, and began to undertake portrait commissions, as well as painting scenes of the River Thames. In 1933, the businessman and philanthropist, Charles Nall-Cain, newly ennobled as the first Baron Brocket, commissioned a full-length portrait. However, he died before any payment was made, so that Gray was left virtually ruined and had to give up his studio.

During the 1930s, Gray became increasingly certain that there would be another war, and so considered how his experience and skills could be put to use. He developed an interest in camouflage, and specifically the ways in which Britain's cities might protect themselves from the threat of German air attack. This resulted in the treatise, 'Camouflage and Air Defence', which he completed in 1936, and submitted to the War Office. It was well received, and he was quickly recruited as a Major in the Royal Engineers and Signals Board. In that position, he travelled across Britain, visiting sites of national importance and working out how to hide them. Then, following the outbreak of the Second World War, he devised a form of steel wool camouflage, which was used to conceal factories and military bases from air attack.

Gray had a reputation among his wartime colleagues for taking nightly rambles through the bombed London streets, even during air raids. These walks inspired his portfolio of six drypoints, 'Battle of Britain' (1940). Continuing to help raise money for regimental charities, he contributed to the Fine Art Draw of May 1940, in which a hundred original signed etchings and coloured prints by celebrated artists were raffled to benefit the Camerons' Comforts Fund, organised by Gray's friend, the photographer, Andrew Paterson.

In 1938, Gray had met Mary Meade, the editor of the magazine, *The Needlewoman*, who was 15 years his junior. They began an affair, and he entered into her circle, which included the artists, Charles McCall and James Proudfoot, the novelist, Harold Freeman, and Freeman's wife, the costume designer, Elisabeth Bödecker – also Mary's brother, James, who would become a Nobel prize-winning economist. Without admitting his affair to his daughter, Maureen, Gray drew her into this circle, getting her a job at the office of *The Needlewoman*. Eventually, Gray divorced his first wife, Nancy, and, in 1943, married Mary in Chelsea. The best man was Captain John Churchill, a colleague of Gray's in the Royal Engineers and nephew of the then Prime Minister, Winston Churchill.

At the end of the war, Joseph and Mary Gray settled at a house in West Street, Marlow, Buckinghamshire. There he focussed on landscape paintings in oil, finding inspiration on his walks and in sketching trips to Dorset and Bath (both family homes to the Meades), Suffolk, Norfolk, and Kent. However, he found it increasingly difficult to part with any of them. As a result it was only after his death – in Marlow, on 1 May 1963 – that Mary was able to organise an exhibition of his work. This was held at the Grosvenor Galleries, London, in 1966, and was opened by the artist, Sir William Coldstream, who had worked with Gray during the war.

His work is represented in numerous public collections, including the British Museum, the Imperial War Museums and the V&A; and The Highlanders Museum at Fort George.

Further reading:

Mary Horlock, *Joseph Gray's Camouflage: A Memoir of Art, Love and Deception*, London: Unbound, 2018

ALGERNON TALMAGE

Algernon Mayow Talmage,
RA RBA HRE ROI RWA (1871-1939)

Talmage is principally known as a painter of *plein-air* pastorals and equestrian subjects in a restrained yet sparkling Impressionist manner. During the First World War, he applied his passion for painting animals in landscape settings to his work as an official war artist for the Canadian Government.

Algernon Talmage was born in Fifield, Oxfordshire, on 23 February 1871, the younger of the two sons of the Rev John Mayow Talmage, the Rector of Fifield and Idbury, and his second wife, Susan (née Penkivil). Both his mother and his paternal grandmother were of Cornish stock. During his childhood, he was involved in an accident with a gun, which crippled his right hand. As a result, he would paint with his left hand, and be exempted from active service in the First World War.

Little is known of Talmage's early education, though it has been variously suggested that he spent a short time at university and that he had some experience as an actor. However, he studied under Sir Hubert von Herkomer at his school of art in Bushey, Hertfordshire. Founded in 1883, the school allowed British artists to pursue an almost Continental training. The students were put to drawing heads from life and from life-casts, and every three months were allowed to try for entry into life classes, which consisted of drawing from nude models. The emphasis on studying from life, which Talmage received under Herkomer, provided him with the ability to become a versatile painter in the naturalistic tradition.

By 1888, Talmage and two of his fellow students, Arnesby Brown and William Titcomb, had discovered in St Ives, Cornwall, the familiar security of a small art colony such as that which they had known in Bushey. Along with such artists as Julius Olsson and Adrian Stokes, Talmage founded an Artists' Club, which enabled these painters of the sea to meet and discuss different techniques for capturing the essence of the wild and rugged north coast of Cornwall. The Cornish coastline, made beautiful by the ever-changing light and moods of the sea, enabled Talmage to establish his characteristic mellow palette and enchanting use of light. For the most part, he painted *plein-air* landscapes and pastorals, and especially farming scenes including horses.

In 1896, Talmage married the Cornish artist, Gertrude Rowe, and together they had two daughters, Archie and Dorothy. In 1901, they were all living with Gertrude's parents at 14 Draycott Terrace, St Ives.

By 1900, Talmage had established the Cornish School of Landscape, Figure and Sea Painting with Julius Olsson. Later, he and Gertrude ran their own school, with Olsson acting as a 'visiting' artist.

In 1907, Talmage separated from Gertrude and moved to London with his former pupil, Hilda Fearon (1878-1917), settling in Chelsea. In the following year, the critic, A G Folliott-Stokes, began to champion him in *The Studio*, and in 1909, wrote a glowing review of his first solo show, 'London from Dawn to Midnight', mounted by the Goupil Gallery.

Since 1895, Talmage had been a regular contributor to the Summer Exhibitions of the Royal Academy of Arts, and his work was included in the exhibition of 1910, which Laura Wortley describes as marking the 'highpoint of "British" Impressionism ... which hummed with "air and light"' (*British Impressionism. A Garden of Bright Images*, London: The Studio Fine Art Publications, 1988, page 280). During this period, he was elected to the Royal Society of British Artists (1903) and the Royal Institute of Painters in Oils (1908).

The influence of French painting and landscape was important to Talmage. Travelling to the country on many occasions, he was in Provence from as early as 1894, and possibly in St Tropez as late as 1932. In 1918, he worked in the country as an official war artist for the Canadian Government, attached to the Canadian Army Veterinary Corps. He exhibited successfully at the Paris Salon, winning a silver medal in 1913 and a gold medal in 1922. (He also won bronze and silver medals at the 1911 and 1920 Pittsburgh International Exhibitions of Contemporary Painting.)

Talmage was elected an associate of the Royal Academy in 1922, and a full Royal Academician seven years later. He was also elected to the Royal West of England Academy (by 1920), St Ives Society of Artists (in 1928) and – taking up etching in 1927 – the Royal Society of Painter-Etchers and Engravers (initially as an associate and later an honorary member). Later solo shows include those held at the Fine Art Society in 1920 and the Leicester Galleries in 1924.

Late in life, Talmage shared his time between 49 Elgin Crescent, London, W11, and Sherfield English, near Romsey, Hampshire. He died at the latter on 14 September 1939.

His work is represented in numerous public collections, including Bristol Museum & Art Gallery, Bushey Museum and Art Gallery, Kirklees Museums and Galleries, and the National Railway Museum (York); and the Canadian War Museum (Ottawa).

Further reading:

Ian K Barker, 'Letter to the Editor re War Artist Algernon Talmage', *Canadian Military History*, October 2013, page 76 & inside back cover;
Hugh A Halliday, 'Algernon Mayow Talmage (1871-1939)', *Canadian Military History*, Summer 2012, pages 59-63

GEORGE SOPER

George Soper, RE (1870-1942)

While beginning his career as an illustrator at the turn of the twentieth century, George Soper established a reputation as a painter and, especially, a printmaker of a wide range of rural subjects. In turn, his daughter, Eileen, was influenced by his skills and sympathies from an early age.

George Soper was born in South Hornsey, Middlesex, on 2 May 1870, the fifth of seven children of the horticultural sundriesman, George Robert Soper, and his wife, Elizabeth (née Cogan). By 1881, he was living with his family at 1 Sandford Place, Hackney, though he was educated at a boarding school in Ramsgate, Kent.

From the mid 1880s, Soper lived with his family at 300 Amherst Road, Stoke Newington, and undertook an apprenticeship with the printer and stationer, George Sydney Waterlow. His fellow apprentices included Charles Robinson, the painter-illustrator brother of William Heath Robinson. His debut as an exhibiting artist occurred in 1890, when he had a painting accepted by the Royal Academy of Arts.

After a period of two years in the 20th Middlesex Artists' Volunteers (1894-6), Soper began work as an illustrator with contributions to the children's magazine, *Golden Sunbeams*, which appeared alongside those by Charles Robinson and members of Robinson's circle. Other periodicals that published his work, and especially images of war, in the early years of the twentieth century, included *Lloyd's Weekly News*, *The Graphic*, *The Captain* and *The Boy's Own Paper*. From 1897, he also illustrated books, beginning with children's adventure and historical stories. It is possible that he was in a partnership with his brother, John, who has also served as a stationer's apprentice, but, if so, then this was dissolved in 1900.

In 1897, George Soper married Ada Lehany, the daughter of an Irish boot-maker, at St Mary's, Stoke Newington, and they settled initially at 12 Palmers Green Villas, Southgate, Enfield. Ada gave birth to their elder daughter, Eva, in 1901, and – following the family's move to Slades Hill, Enfield – to the younger prodigy, Eileen Soper, in 1905. In 1908, George moved his family out of London to Harmer Green, near Welwyn, in Hertfordshire. There he helped design a new home, at 42 Harmers Green Lane, which was originally called 'Hill Lodge', and renamed 'Wildings' by his daughters after his death. In its garden, he cultivated exotic plants.

In 1908, George Soper illustrated *The Water Babies*, the first of a number of classic gift books for Headley Brothers. His contributions to these volumes reveal his ambition to emulate a wide range of illustrators from Randolph Caldecott to Arthur Rackham.

In turning to work as a painter and printmaker, Soper continued to draw on his strengths as an illustrator in order to convey the maximum amount of information, especially that regarding the activities of the rural environment. His earliest dated prints were produced in 1911, and show views of Lanslebourg, a village in the French Alps, though most of his sketching tours would take him across England. In 1913, he exhibited his first etching, *The Wash Tub*, at the Royal Scottish Academy.

Some sources suggest that Soper took lessons in etching from Sir Frank Short as early as 1905. However, it is more likely that he first experimented alone with the medium, before studying printmaking with Short at the Royal College of Art during the years 1916-20. He worked extensively as a printmaker during the 1920s, and was elected an associate of the Royal Society of Painter-Etchers and Engravers in 1918, becoming a full member two years later.

George Soper continued to produce prints until 1940, but when the etching boom ended, he diversified his activities, and also supported his daughters in their artistic endeavours. He died on 13 August 1942.

The estate and copyright of George and Eileen Soper are in the care of the Chris Beetles Gallery through Longmores Solicitors on behalf of the AGBI. The gallery mounted a highly successful retrospective in June 1995, and followed it with a show devoted to Eileen's achievement as a printmaker.

GILBERT LEDWARD

Gilbert Ledward, OBE RA PRBS (1888-1960)

Gilbert Ledward was a highly skilled sculptor in stone and metal of portraits, figure subjects and, most notably, majestic war memorials. Trained in the conventions of the late nineteenth century, he remained loyal to academic traditions and to the representational values that were suited to public projects of commemoration. As a Royal Academician and eventually a President of the Royal British Society of Sculptors, he became involved in discussions on the roles of both sculpture and the sculptor in society.

Gilbert Ledward was born in Chelsea, London, on 23 January 1888, the third of four children of the sculptor, Richard Arthur Ledward, and his wife, Mary Jane (née Wood), who was descended from a Staffordshire family of master potters and figure makers. His father died in 1890, at the age of 33, when Gilbert was only two.

Ledward was educated at St Mark's College, Chelsea, but left in 1901, when his mother decided to take her family to live in Karlsruhe, Germany. (This family included a fifth child, Olive, who seems to have been born in 1892, and was probably the half-sister of Ledward.) He returned alone after a year, and took up a place at Chelsea Polytechnic, later transferring to Goldsmiths' College School of Art, where he obtained a London County Scholarship that enabled him, in 1905, to go to the Royal College of Art. He studied there for five years under Edouard Lantéri, the college's first Professor of Sculpture and Modelling. In 1910, he moved to the Royal Academy Schools and, while studying there, began to practise as a sculptor and became Modelling Master at South London Technical School of Art. He would exhibit more than 120 works at the Royal Academy of Arts between 1911 and 1960.

In 1911, Gilbert Ledward married Margery Beatrix Cheesman, the sister of a fellow student, and they settled at 37 Hotham Road, Putney, close to Ledward's mother. They would have two daughters and a son. In the same year, Gilbert's elder sister, (Phyllis) Hilda, married the sculptor, Newbury Abbot Trent, while in the following year his younger sister, Enid, married the painter, Percy Hague Jowett.

1913 proved a particularly important year for Ledward in the development of his career. He completed his first major commission, a stone calvary for the churchyard of St Lawrence, Bourton-on-the Water, Gloucestershire. He also won three major awards: the first Scholarship in Sculpture from the British School at Rome and both the gold medal and travelling studentship from the Royal Academy Schools. He travelled to Rome to begin his three-year scholarship, and in the summer of 1914 travelled through Italy, making sketchbook drawings (which are now in the collections of the Royal Academy). However, his travels and his residency in Rome were brought to an abrupt end by the outbreak of the First World War.

On his return to London, Ledward continued his work as a sculptor, and in 1915 took a studio at 14a Cheyne Row, and completed *Awakening*, the bronze figure of a young woman, which stands on Chelsea Embankment. However, late in 1916, he became a Second Lieutenant in the Royal Garrison Artillery, and returned to Italy to see active service, being mentioned in despatches. In April 1918, he was recalled to England and seconded to the Ministry of Information as an official war artist. In that capacity, he produced plaster reliefs of men in action that provided the foundation for his subsequent war memorials.

These memorials included collaborations with the architect, Harold Chalton Bradshaw, who had been Ledward's contemporary in Rome as the recipient of the first Rome scholarship in Architecture. Their most significant work together comprised the award-winning Guards Division Memorial on Horse Guards Parade, in London (1922-26 [see 42]), and the Ploegsteert Memorial to the Missing in Hainaut, Belgium (1926-29). Particularly impressive among Ledward's other memorials is the bronze relief at the base of Blackpool War Memorial and Cenotaph, which was designed by the Lancashire architect, Ernest Prestwich (1922-23).

Ledward was elected an associate of the Royal British Society of Sculptors in 1921, and a fellow two years later. Between those two elections, he moved to Pembroke Walk Studios, in Kensington. In 1926, he became Professor of Sculpture at the Royal College of Art, and inherited as his assistant Henry Moore, who was ten years his junior. Unfortunately, students so preferred Moore to Ledward that he had to put an ultimatum to the Principal, Sir William Rothenstein, that 'either he goes or I do' (Moriarty, 2003, page 58). As Rothenstein refused to end Moore's appointment, Ledward resigned. Nevertheless, Ledward was influenced by Moore's practice, if not his style, and during the 1930s turned away from modelling in clay to carving directly in stone. A striking example of this change of approach is *Monolith*, which was inspired by Adrian Stokes's analysis of the work of the early Renaissance sculptor, Agostino di Duccio, in *The Stones of Rimini* (1934). It was purchased by the Chantrey Bequest in 1936 for the Tate Gallery (and remains the only work by Ledward in that collection).

In 1930, Ledward was appointed a member of the Faculty of Sculpture and Council of the British School at Rome. In 1932, he joined the selection committee of the Chantrey Bequest (remaining on it until 1950) and was elected an associate of the Royal Academy (becoming a full Academician in 1937). In the same year, he revived his working partnership with Chalton Bradshaw, by contributing the coat of arms to the architect's design for the entrance to the Penmaenbach road tunnel in North Wales. He was also briefly a member of the Art Workers' Guild (1933-38), an association that probably relates to his establishing a firm, in 1934, called 'Sculptured Memorials and Headstones', which promoted the better design and craftsmanship of memorials in English churchyards. He was supported in this by Eric Gill and Sir Edwin Lutyens, among others. In 1938, he became a member of the Advisory Committee of the Royal Mint.

Through the late 1930s and into the 1940s, Ledward produced a number of statues of recent and reigning British monarchs: carved images of both King George V and Queen Mary and King George VI and Queen Elizabeth for the restored cloister of Norwich Cathedral (1938); bronze images of George V for Kampala, Uganda (1939), and Nairobi, Kenya (1940); and a bronze statue of George VI for Hong Kong (1947).

Following the end of the Second World War, Ledward again received commissions to produce memorials. These included heraldic sculptures on the entrances to shelters designed by the architect, Philip Hepworth, for the Reichswald Forest War Cemetery in Germany (opened in 1946), and the Combined Services Memorial for Westminster Abbey (unveiled by Sir Winston Churchill in 1948).

In 1949, Ledward won the competition, organised by the Royal Academy of Arts in celebration of the coronation of Queen Elizabeth II, to design a fountain for the centre of Sloane Square. The result – combining a life-size figure of Venus with a frieze of King Charles II and Nell Gwynn, who had lived near the square – was eventually installed in 1953.

Ledward also marked the accession of Queen Elizabeth by designing the Coronation Crown Piece, of which more than five million were minted. Then, in 1953, he designed the first Great Seal for Queen Elizabeth, and this was used for official purposes until 2001, when it was replaced by one designed by James Butler.

Ledward served as President of the Royal British Society of Sculptors in the years 1954-56 and as a trustee of the Royal Academy during the year 1956-57. He was awarded an OBE in 1956.

Ledward died at a nursing home at 31 Queen's Gate, South Kensington, on 21 June 1960. His final work had been *Vision and Imagination*, a Portland stone frieze produced for Barclays Bank, Broad Street, in the City of London. It was saved from destruction in 1995, by the Public Monuments and Sculpture Association, when the building was demolished.

His work is represented in the collections of the Royal Academy of Arts, and numerous public collections, including the Imperial War Museums; and The Potteries Museum & Art Gallery (Stoke-on-Trent).

Further reading:

Catherine Moriarty, 'Ledward, Gilbert (1888-1960)', H C G Matthew and Brian Harrison (eds), *Oxford Dictionary of National Biography*, Oxford University Press, 2004, https://doi.org/10.1093/ref:odnb/34463;
Catherine Moriarty, *The Sculpture of Gilbert Ledward*, Aldershot: Lund Humphries/ Leeds: Henry Moore Foundation, 2003;
Peyton Skipwith, *Gilbert Ledward: 1888-1960: drawings for sculpture: a centenary tribute*, London: Fine Art Society, 1988

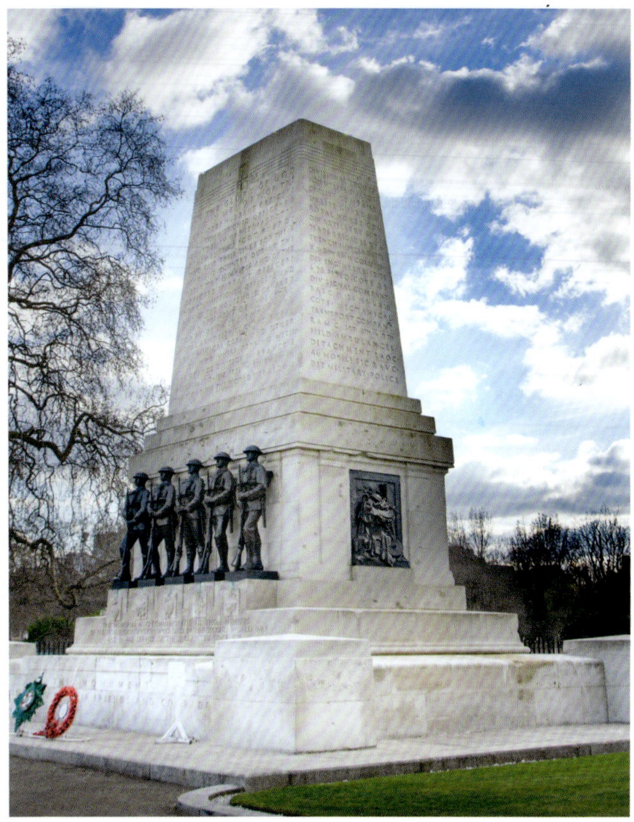

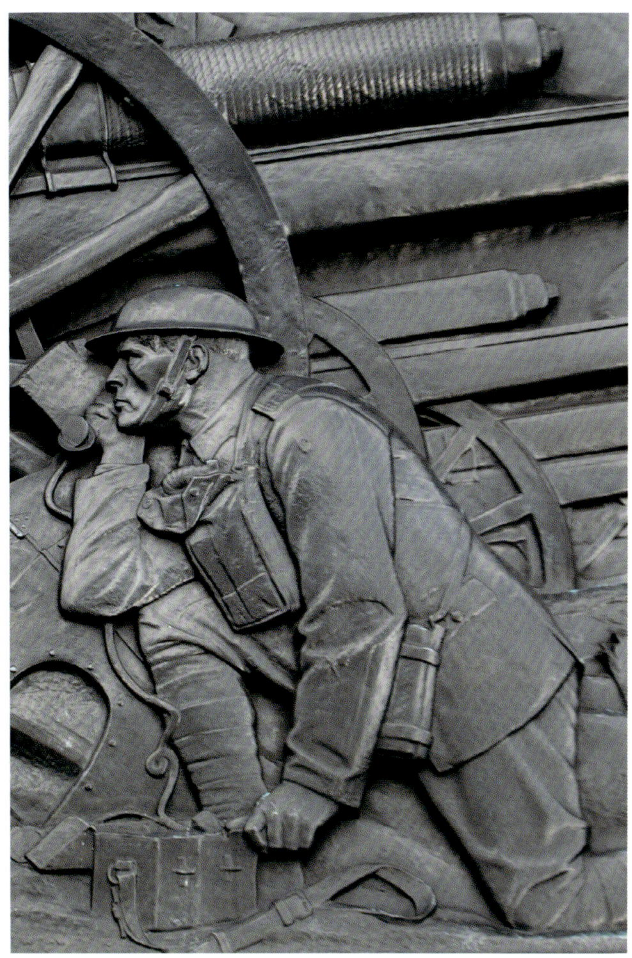

Photos of the Guard Division Memorial by Gilbert Ledward.

Study for the Guards Division Memorial, see 42

WILLIAM WALCOT

William F Walcot, RBA RE (1874-1943)

Working as a painter and printmaker, William Walcot became the most celebrated architectural artist in England during the 1920s and 30s.

William Walcot was born at Lustdorf, near Odessa, on 10 March 1874, the elder son of travelling merchant, Enoch Shannon, known as Frank Walcot, and his Russo-German wife, Catherine. During his childhood, he travelled through Europe with his parents, attending schools in Amiens and Paris in the 1880s. On returning to Russia at the age of 17, he studied architecture under Louis Benois at the Imperial Academy of Fine Arts, St Petersburg (1895-97), and also in Paris at Atelier Redon, in the Ecole des Beaux-Arts. He practised architecture in Moscow for five years, designing the city's Hotel Metropol (1898-1902) and several villas, and subsequently visiting Rome and London. While still in Moscow, he met and married an Irish governess, Margaret Ann O'Neill. However, she suffered from ill health and would die of tuberculosis on the Isle of Wight in 1904.

Settling in London in 1907, Walcot was first employed as a draughtsman to the architect Eustace Frere. He soon became a freelance draughtsman, producing presentation drawings for a number of leading architects to show their clients and to exhibit at the Royal Academy of Arts. His treatment of these drawings as works of art rather than technical exercises led to commissions from the Fine Art Society to visit Rome and Venice, and he held a total of eight solo shows with that dealer (1908-28). He also showed watercolours and etchings with leading exhibiting societies, and was elected to the membership of the Royal Society of Painter-Etchers and Engravers (ARE 1918, RE 1920) and the Royal Society of British Artists (1913). He was additionally a Fellow of the Royal Institute of British Architects (1922) and an associate of the British School at Rome. Steeped in the culture and architecture of antiquity, he designed and illustrated luxury editions of *Salammbô* (1926) and *Hérodias* (1928) by Gustave Flaubert for Les Editions d'Art Devambez.

In 1911, Walcot entered a second marriage, with Alice Maria Wheelan, and she would bear him two daughters. However, from 1926, he lived with Ada Grace Chamberlain, known as Margot; together they would have a daughter and son.

The most celebrated architectural draughtsman in England through the 1920s and 30s, Walcot worked from studios in London, Oxford and Rome at the height of his career. However, his practice collapsed on the outbreak of the Second World War, and he went into a decline. Moving with his family to the Ditchling estate of Frank Brangwyn early in the war, he entered St George's Nursing Home, Hurstpierpoint, Sussex, in 1943. While at the nursing home, on 21 May 1943, he fell from a window to his death.

His work is represented in the collections of The Cleveland Museum of Art.

Further reading:

Catherine Cooke and Polly Walcot Stewart, 'Walcot, William (1874-1943)', H C G Matthew and Brian Harrison (eds), *Oxford Dictionary of National Biography*, Oxford University Press, 2004, vol 56, pages 760-761;
J M Richards, 'Walcot, William [Valkot, V F] (b Lustdorf, near Odessa, Russia, 10 March 1874; d Hurstpierpoint, W Sussex, 21 May 1943), Jane Turner (ed), *The Dictionary of Art*, London: Macmillan, 1996, vol 32, page 773

MALCOLM OSBORNE

Malcolm Osborne, CBE RA RBC PRE (1880-1963)

Malcolm Osborne is best known as an etcher and engraver of portraits, figure subjects and townscapes. An influential teacher, he was head of the engraving school at the Royal College of Art for many years.

Malcolm Osborne was born at 2 Waterloo Place, Frome, Somerset, on 1 August 1880, the fifth of six children of Alfred Osborne, and his wife, Sarah (née Biggs), both of whom were teachers. The artistic talents of the children were encouraged by their parents and, of Malcolm's brothers, Rex would become an illustrator and Fred a designer. Malcolm was educated in Bristol at the Merchant Venturers' Technical College and then the School of Art, Queen's Road.

In 1901, Malcolm Osborne moved to London with his brother, Harold, and, as the result of a Royal Exhibition Scholarship, he studied at the Royal College of Art, taking classes in black-and-white design from Professor Charles Lethaby and etching and engraving from Sir Frank Short. While there, he won the British Institute Scholarship for etching and, in 1904, published his first etching. From 1905, he exhibited at leading galleries and societies, in London and the provinces, including the Royal Academy of Arts and the Royal Society of Painter-Etchers and Engravers. He immediately became an associate of the latter, and a full member four years later, in 1909. In this early period, he undertook a number of sketching tours, mainly in Dorset, Sussex and France.

During the First World War, Osborne served in Artists' Rifles and 60th Division in France, Salonika and Palestine. While in command of a trench mortar company outside Jerusalem in 1918, he received the news that he had been elected an associate engraver of the Royal Academy. Following his demobilisation in July 1919, and his return to London, he taught at the Central School of Arts and Crafts, while, in 1924, he succeeded Frank Short as Professor of the Engraving School at the Royal College of Art, and proved almost equally influential. He was elected to the Royal British Colonial Society of Artists in 1925 and a full Royal Academician in 1926.

In 1927, Osborne married Amy Stableford at St Luke's Church, Kensington, and they settled at 44 Redcliffe Gardens, West Brompton. Two years later, he was the subject of both an exhibition at the Rembrandt Gallery and a monograph by Malcolm Salaman (in The Studio's series 'Modern Masters of Etching').

Osborne served as President of the RE between 1938 and 1962. Until 1948, he continued to head the RCA's Engraving School, both in London and in Ambleside, when it went to the Lake District for the course of the Second World War. On his retirement from the RCA in 1948, he was created CBE. In 1956, he was elected a Senior Member of the Royal Academy.

Malcolm Osborne died at home in London on 22 September 1963.

His work is represented in numerous public collections, including the British Museum and the V&A; and the Ashmolean Museum (Oxford).

Further reading:

Hal Bishop, 'Osborne, Malcolm' (1880-1963)', H C G Matthew and Brian Harrison (eds), *Oxford Dictionary of National Biography*, Oxford University Press, 2004, https://doi.org/10.1093/ref:odnb/64828

JOB NIXON

Job Nixon, RWS RE NEAC (1891-1938)

Though a painter as well as a printmaker, Job Nixon was best known as an etcher of landscapes and figure subjects. He was the first to win the scholarship for engraving at the British School at Rome, and during his time in Italy he produced *An Italian Festa*, the large and complex plate that made his name. On his return to London, he soon became assistant to Malcolm Osborne in the engraving school of the Royal College of Art. During the later years of his short career, he worked in Cornwall and taught at the Slade School of Fine Art.

Job Nixon was born at 16 Charles Street, Stoke-on-Trent, Staffordshire, on 20 February 1891, the fourth of five children of the pottery printer, Job Nixon, and his wife, the pottery painter, Mary (née Ellerton). He grew up among pottery decorators and, on leaving school, entered the engraving department of Mintons. He was subsequently apprenticed to an engraver who supplied copper plates for transfer printing to local pottery manufacturers. In the evenings, he studied at Stoke School of Art. However, he soon changed direction, becoming a butcher's assistant, and rapidly succeeding in the trade, so that, while he was still in his teens, he employed four assistants, who helped him run two shops and a stall in Stoke Market Hall. He did not neglect his studies in art, and produced his own advertising, while also taking a position as assistant master at Burslem School of Art. By his late teens, he was living with his family at 240 London Road, Stoke-on-Trent.

In 1910, Nixon won a scholarship to the Royal College of Art, in London, and there studied etching under Sir Frank Short. In 1915, while still a student, he began to exhibit at the Royal Academy of Arts. However, following the outbreak of the First World War, he joined the 4th Eastern Company of the Army Service Corps, during which time he produced theatrical scenery for camp entertainments. On his release in 1918, he took advantage of an army scholarship to further his studies under Henry Tonks at the Slade School of Fine Art. Ever enterprising, he also painted decorations for shop windows and bazaars and worked with the theatrical designer, Hugo Rumbold, at Covent Garden Opera.

In 1920, Nixon won the first scholarship of engraving to be endowed by the British School at Rome. As a result, he spent three years in Italy (and France), and produced, among other works, the large plate, *An Italian Festa*, which brought him to the attention of the public and, in 1923, led to his election as an associate of the Royal Society of Painter-Etchers and Engravers. He was also appointed to a teaching post in the Engraving School of the Royal College of Art, as an assistant to Malcolm Obsborne, who succeeded Frank Short on his retirement in 1924. At this time, he was living at 45 Redcliffe Road, Chelsea.

In 1925, Nixon married Helen Wigan in Kensington, and they settled at Pembroke Walk Studios, later moving to Oakfield Street. However, by June 1929, he had begun an affair with Nina Berry, who was then an artist student, and this led to his wife divorcing him in 1930 on the grounds of adultery. During this period, he joined the New English Art Club, and joined and resigned from the Art Workers' Guild.

Nixon was visiting Cornwall from at least as early as 1929, when he exhibited two watercolours of Falmouth. In 1931, at the urging of his friend, Lamorna Birch, he and Nina Berry settled in the county, at Riverside Studios, Lamorna Cove, so becoming members of Birch's colony of artists. In that year, his painting, *Gypsies*, made a great impression as his first exhibit with the Newlyn Society of Artists, and won the 'position of honour'. He was elected a member of the Royal Society of Painter-Etchers and Engravers in 1933, and of the Royal Society of Painters in Water-Colours in 1934.

In 1934, Nixon and Berry moved to St Ives. They worked at St Peter's Studio and also ran a school of painting in Back Road West. However, a year later, they returned to London, and settled at 36 Danvers Street, Chelsea, so that Nixon could take up a teaching post at the Slade School of Fine Art. He also taught at Gravesend School of Art around this time.

Nixon married Nina Berry in Chelsea, in 1937, but died the following year, on 26 July 1938, while they were holidaying in their horse-drawn caravan at Mendham, Norfolk. A memorial group of his works was included later that year in the fifth annual exhibition of the Society of Staffordshire Artists, while a memorial exhibition of his paintings was held at the Colnaghi Gallery, London, in March 1939.

His work is represented in numerous public collections, including the British Museum and the V&A; the Ashmolean Museum (Oxford) and The Potteries Museum & Art Gallery (Stoke-on-Trent); and the Fine Art Museums of San Francisco (CA).

STANLEY ANDERSON

Alfred Charles Stanley Anderson, RA RE (1884-1966)

The printmaker and painter, Stanley Anderson, was a major figure in the revival of line engraving between the wars. Though a long career allowed for a diverse range of subjects, his skill was displayed particularly well in a series of prints of farm workers and rural craftsmen.

Stanley Anderson was born at 11 North Road, Bristol, on 11 May 1884, the son of the general and heraldic engraver, Alfred Ernest Anderson, and his wife, Emma Bessie (née Mitchell). He had a twin sister, Rosa, and a younger sister, Irene.

Anderson attended the Merchant Venturers' Technical College, Bristol, and, while there, determined to become an artist. Somewhat against his will, he became apprenticed to his father at the age of 15 but, as a result, learned the founding skill of his art: engraving on metal with precision. Out of the meagre earnings of an apprentice, he paid to attend a weekly evening class at Bristol Municipal School of Art, and study under its Principal, the painter-engraver, Reginald Bush. In 1907, he also joined the Bristol Savages, a club for artists, writers and musicians, that included Bush among its members.

Two years later, in 1909, Anderson won the British Institution's open etching scholarship of £50 a year, on his second attempt. This enabled him to leave Bristol for London, and study for two years at the Royal College of Art, where he received expert instruction in etching and drypoint from Frank Short. He also frequented the print rooms of the British Museum and the Victoria and Albert Museum in order to examine the work of great printmakers, from Dürer to Whistler. He exhibited the first two of 214 works at the Royal Academy of Arts in 1909, and became an associate of the Royal Society of Painter-Etchers and Engravers in 1910, when Frank Short became its President. Once his scholarship at the RCA had come to an end, in 1911, he attended evening classes in etching at Goldsmith's College School of Art, New Cross, under William Lee-Hankey.

On 10 August 1910, Anderson married Lilian Phelps, a nurse at St Thomas's Hospital, and settled with her in Brentham Garden Suburb, in Ealing. Together they would have two sons, Ivan (1911-1995) and Maxim (1914-1959), the younger of whom would become a documentary filmmaker. A combination of his own dedication and the practical support of Lilian helped Anderson to provide for his family while he attempted to establish himself as an artist. Despite financial uncertainty at this time, he made two trips to France, in 1911 and 1914.

When war broke out, Anderson was rejected as unfit for service, and instead engaged in munitions work at Woolwich, while living with his family in nearby Eltham. He felt anger about the conflict, which he expressed in a series of watercolour caricatures. At the end of the war, the family moved to Chelsea, where Anderson had lodged while he was a student. Drawing on the inspiration of Muirhead Bone, Francis Dodd and Williams Strang, he focussed mainly on views of London and portraits, and slowly began to gain a reputation as a printmaker that could be compared to that of Gerald Brockhurst, Malcolm Osborne and Henry Rushbury. Between 1919 and 1922, Henry Graves & Co published a series of 18 topographical etchings and, though he considered these to be examples of 'hack work', travel at home (and later abroad) helped him to broaden his range. The commercial success of these projects also gave him sufficient security to pursue his own preference for figure subjects, as a painter in tempera as well as a printmaker. He received official recognition in 1923 when he was elected a full member of the Royal Society of Painter-Etchers and Engravers.

In 1925, Anderson succeeded Malcolm Osborne as visiting instructor in the etching department of Goldsmiths' College School of Art, and remained on its staff until 1940, also teaching wood-engraving. In addition, he was a member of the engraving faculty of the British School at Rome between 1930 and 1952. Further recognition came when he was elected as a Royal Academician (ARA 1934, RA 1941) and chosen as the sole representative of British line engraving at the 1938 Venice Biennale.

From 1929, Anderson had turned increasingly to line engraving, and he worked exclusively in the medium from 1934, showcasing his mastery of it in a long, substantial, and now famous, series on the theme of rural crafts, labour and trade. This was founded on the rural experience that he gained from 1933, when he bought the cottage of Old Timbers in Towersey, a small village in Oxfordshire. He and his wife settled there permanently in 1941, after his London home and studio were destroyed in an air raid. He further developed his interest in rural life in the 25 watercolours of Gloucestershire and Oxfordshire that he produced for Sir Kenneth Clark's Recording Britain project, and in other paintings. Appointed a Commander of the Order of the British Empire in 1951, he ceased working two years later when he developed neuritis in his right hand.

In his last years, Anderson lived at Darobey, Church Lane, Chearsley, Buckinghamshire, dying there on 4 March 1966.

His work is represented in numerous public collections, including the British Museum and the V&A, and the Ashmolean Museum (Oxford) and The Fitzwilliam Museum (Cambridge).

Further reading:

Paul Drury, *rev* Ian Lowe, 'Anderson, (Alfred Charles) Stanley (1884-1966)', H C G Matthew and Brian Harrison (eds), *Oxford Dictionary of National Biography*, Oxford University Press, 2015, https://doi.org/10.1093/ref:odnb/30412;
Robert Meyrick and Harry Heuser, *Stanley Anderson: Prints: A Catalogue Raisonné*, London: Royal Academy of Arts, 2015

EDMUND BLAMPIED

Edmund Blampied, RBA RE (1886-1966)

Edmund Blampied is one of the most significant artists to have hailed from the Channel Islands. Greatly versatile, he worked as a painter, illustrator, and occasional sculptor, though is best remembered as a printmaker and, especially, an etcher. Having been born on a farm, he produced some particularly evocative etchings of agricultural and peasant subjects. Their fluidity of line, strong sense of humanity and Gallic humour suggest a kinship with Daumier and Gavarni.

Edmund Blampied was born on a farm in the Parish of St Martin, Jersey, on 30 March 1886, the youngest of four sons of John and Elizabeth Blampied. His father died five days before he was born, and his mother brought up the family, working as a dressmaker and shopkeeper in the Parish of Trinity. His first tongue was the Norman language of Jèrriais.

Blampied left school at the age of 14, and went to work in an architect's office in St Helier, the capital of Jersey. A year later, he exhibited some drawings at an agricultural show, and these came to the notice of Marie Josephine Klintz, who ran a private art school in the town. As a result, she gave him his first formal lessons in art. His caricatures of local politicians attracted the attention of the businessman, Saumarez James Nicolle, who offered to sponsor his art studies in England.

In January 1903, the 16-year-old Blampied left Jersey for England, and enrolled at Lambeth School of Art, in London, studying there under Philip Connard and the Principal, Thomas McKeggie. McKeggie chose him to work part-time on the staff of the *Daily Chronicle*, and his first illustrations appeared in its pages on 13 January 1905. In the September, he transferred to the LCC School of Photo-Engraving and Lithography at Bolt Court, where he studied under Walter Seymour and through him perfected the art of etching. While there, he made a number of friends, including Salomon van Abbe, whose sister, Marianne, he would marry in 1914. In 1911, he established his own studio, and worked there, mainly as a magazine illustrator, into the early years of the First World War.

Following the introduction of conscription in Britain in 1916, Blampied returned to Jersey. Though classified as not fully fit for active service in 1917, he took up guard duties in the Royal Jersey Militia, and remained on the island until 1919, when he resumed his professional life in London.

Though Blampied had been producing etchings from as early as 1909, he only now began to establish himself as a printmaker. In 1920, he became an associate of the Royal Society of Painter-Etchers and Engravers, with full membership following just a year later. Also in 1920, he held a solo show of etchings and drypoints in London at the Leicester Galleries. His first American exhibition took place at Kennedy and Company, New York, in 1922. Many other joint and solo exhibitions followed.

Experimenting with lithography from 1920, Blampied joined the Senefelder Club of lithographic artists in 1923. He took classes in the medium from Archibald Hartrick, a founder member of the Senefelder, at the Central School of Arts and Crafts in 1925, but was already sufficiently expert by that date to win a Gold Medal for lithography at the Paris International Exhibition.

During the 1920s and 30s, Blampied worked extensively as an illustrator, contributing to numerous magazines, especially *The Bystander* and *The Illustrated London News*, and illustrating a number of books, including an edition of Robert Louis Stevenson's *Travels with a Donkey in the Cevennes* (1931). His illustrations of children's books such as the 1939 edition of J M Barrie's *Peter and Wendy*, published by Hodder and Stoughton, were met with particular acclaim.

Between the wars, Blampied and his wife often travelled to France, and regularly wintered on the Riviera. In 1926, they sold their house in South London, and spent five months in southern France and Tunisia, Blampied producing a number of North African drawings and etchings.

Though he became a member of the Royal Society of British Artists in 1938, Blampied decided to return to Jersey just before the outbreak of the Second World War and stayed there, with his wife, during the German Occupation, despite the fact that she was Jewish. While he found little work as an illustrator, he received some commissions from the State of Jersey to design bank notes and postage stamps. Continuing to live on Jersey beyond the end of the war, he worked mostly in oil and watercolour during his final years. A large exhibition of his work was mounted at the John Nelson Bergstrom Art Center and Museum, Neenah, Wisconsin, in July 1954. A retrospective took place at the Societe Jersiaise, Jersey Museum, a decade later. He died on Jersey on 26 August 1966.

His work is represented in numerous public collections, including The Fitzwilliam Museum (Cambridge); Jersey Museum (St Helier); and Boston Public Library and the Cleveland Museum of Art (Ohio).

Further reading:

Jean Arnold and John Appleby, *A Catalogue Raisonné of Etchings, Drypoints and Lithographs of Edmund Blampied*, St Ouen: John Appleby Publishing, 1996;
Andrew Hall, *Edmund Blampied. An Illustrated Life*, Jersey Heritage Trust, 2010

HENRY RUSHBURY

Sir Henry George Rushbury, RA VPRWS RE HonRIBA NEAC (1889-1968)

A painter, draughtsman and printmaker, Henry Rushbury was one of the finest artists of the twentieth century to specialise in architectural and other topographical subjects. He had a great ability to capture the spirit as well as the appearance of a place through the use of light and shade and the introduction of elements of everyday life.

Henry Rushbury was born in Harborne, then a village in Staffordshire (now an area of southwest Birmingham), on 28 October 1889, the younger son of the clerk, George Norbury Rushbury, and his wife, Naomi (née Fennell). According to S C Hutchison, his father, 'when unsuccessfully job-hunting', used to take him 'on visits to churches and other old buildings, thereby … kindling … a lifelong and essential interest in immediate surroundings' (*Oxford Dictionary of National Biography*).

At the age of 13, Rushbury gained a scholarship to Birmingham School of Art, where he first studied gold and silversmithing, and later turned to stained-glass design and mural decoration. His teachers included Henry Payne, who was working on the decoration of the chapel at Madresfield Court, the Worcestershire home of William Lygon, 7th Earl Beauchamp, the results of which are considered to comprise a masterpiece of the Arts and Crafts movement. By 1906, Rushbury had become one of three student assistants to work with Payne at the chapel, alongside Joseph Sanders and Richard Stubington. And, though he left art school in 1909, he continued to work as Payne's assistant (and was living with him, at St Loe's House. Amberley, near Stroud, in Gloucestershire, at the time of the 1911 census). He and Sanders also worked for a while under Archibald John Davies at the Worcestershire stained glass workshop known as the Bromsgrove Guild.

In 1912, Rushbury settled in London, and shared a succession of Chelsea lodgings with his close friend, Gerald Brockhurst, who had been a fellow student at Birmingham School of Art. While 'working on an architectural drawing in Essex Street, off the Strand, he attracted the attention of Francis Dodd, who suggested that he try the medium of etching'. Then, when he began to gain mastery of the medium, Dodd arranged 'introductions to the dealer-publishers [Robert] Dunthorne and James Connell' (Wildman, 1989, page 5). The first work that he exhibited at the Royal Academy of Arts, in 1913, was the etching, *The Pin Mill, Gloucestershire*. By late in that year, he was sharing lodgings with the painter-etcher, James Hamilton Hay, at 18 Trafalgar Square, Chelsea (now Chelsea Square). Hamilton Hay introduced him to Florence Layzell, who, in the following year, became his wife, marrying him at Chelsea Registry Office, with the painter-etcher, Job Nixon, as best man. They would have two daughters, Janet and Julia, both of whom would become painters.

The First World War broke out a month after the wedding and, in 1915, Rushbury enlisted in the army as a draughtsman, and was stationed at Lowestoft. In 1916, he transferred to the Royal Flying Corps, serving for two years. He then became an official war artist, producing documentary drawings (that are now in the Imperial War Museums). In 1917, he was elected to the membership of the New English Art Club.

On demobilisation, Rushbury studied at the Slade School of Fine Art under Henry Tonks for a few months of 1919. He soon returned to his busy life of drawing and engraving, and worked widely in Britain and on the Continent, particularly in France and Italy (sometimes in the company of Charles Cundall and Job Nixon). In addition to his regular contributions to the Royal Academy (ARA 1927), he exhibited principally with the Royal Society of Painter-Etchers and Engravers (ARE 1921, RE 1922), the Royal Society of Painters in Water-Colours ARWS 1922, RWS 1926) and the New English Art Club. His first solo show was held at the Grosvenor Gallery in 1921. His status as an etcher was confirmed in 1923 by an article by Randolph Schwabe in *The Print Collector's Quarterly* (with a catalogue by Harold Wright), and in 1928 by Malcolm Salaman's monograph in the series, 'Modern Masters of Etching'. From 1929, the metal-window manufacturer, W F Crittall, sponsored him to produce an annual drypoint.

In 1931, Rushbury and his family settled at Lower House Farm, Stoke-by-Nayland, Suffolk, close to the border with Essex. However, he retained a studio at his London home, 8 Netherton Grove, Chelsea (and let the house to his friend, the Australian artist, Will Dyson). Unlike many of the artists who contributed to the revival of interest in etching, he continued to find a market for his prints during the Depression. Some of his best work as an etcher was produced to illustrate three books: Sidney Dark's *Paris* (1926), Sir James Rennell Rodd's *Rome of the Renaissance and Today* (1932) and Iris Wedgwood's *Fenland Rivers* (1936). However, he displayed his versatility in undertaking a series of mural decorations for Chelsmford Town Hall in 1937. His distinction as an artist was awarded in 1936 when he was elected a full Royal Academician.

During the Second World War, Rushbury again worked as an official war artist, recording the production side of the war effort. He also became a Visitor in Engraving at the Royal College of Art in 1942. From the end of the war he gained a number of further administrative roles and honorific titles. He was the Vice-President of the Royal Society of Painters in Water-Colours in the years 1945-47; Visitor in Engraving at the British School at Rome in 1948; an honorary member of the Royal Institute of British Architects in 1948; and Keeper of the Royal Academy in the years 1949-64 (so having responsibility for the RA Schools). He was created a Commander of the Victorian Order in 1955, a Commander of the British Empire in 1960, and a Knight Commander of the Victorian Order in 1964. He was a staunch member of both the Arts Club and the Chelsea Arts Club.

On retiring as Keeper of the RA in 1964, Rushbury settled at 6 Martin's Lane, Lewes, Sussex, and died there four years later on 5 July 1968. He was survived by Florence and their daughters.

His work is represented in numerous public collections, including the British Museum, Tate and the V&A; and the Ashmolean Museum (Oxford).

Further reading:

S C Hutchison (rev), 'Rushbury, Sir Henry George [Harry] (1889–1968)', H C G Matthew and Brian Harrison (eds), *Oxford Dictionary of National Biography*, Oxford University Press, 2004, https://doi.org/10.1093/ref:odnb/35873;
Tod Ramos, *Henry Rushbury, Prints: A Catalogue Raisonné*, London: Royal Academy of Arts, 2010;
Stephen Wildman, *Sir Henry Rushbury: A Centenary Exhibition of Drawings and Etchings*, Birmingham City Museum and Art Gallery, 1989

GERALD BROCKHURST

Gerald Leslie Brockhurst, RA RE RP SGA (1890-1978)

Gerald Brockhurst was a precociously gifted painter, draughtsman and printmaker, who is best known for his portraits of women, including his two wives and a number of celebrities. The work of Italian Renaissance artists informed his developing style, which at its most mature was intensely, even unnervingly, realistic.

Gerald Brockhurst was born at 106 Summer Road, Edgbaston, Birmingham, on 31 October 1890, the fourth son of the coal dealer, Arthur Brockhurst, and his wife, Amelia (née Ward). Displaying a prodigious talent for drawing at an early age, he was only 12 when he began to study at Birmingham School of Art. His fellow students included Henry Rushbury, who would become a close friend.

In 1907, at the age of 16, Brockhurst won a scholarship to the Royal Academy Schools, in London. There, he received a number of awards, including the Landseer Scholarship, the Armitage Medal, the British Institute Studentship and, in 1913, a gold medal and a travelling scholarship worth £200. This last enabled him to visit Paris, where he worked in the Louvre, copying work by such early Italian Renaissance artists as Botticelli. From there, he went on to Italy, and based himself in Milan.

In 1914, Brockhurst married Anaïs Folin, the young French woman who was employed as a governess by his artist friend, Ambrose McEvoy and his wife, Mary. An artist herself, Anaïs soon became Brockhurst's chief model. In the same year, he made his first experiments in etching, encouraged by Henry Rushbury, with whom he had shared lodgings before his marriage. However, this interest would not begin to flourish until the end of the decade.

Brockhurst began to exhibit at the Royal Academy of Arts in 1915, but in the same year moved to Ireland with Anaïs. While there, he met the poet, Oliver St John Gogarty, who provided patronage and introduced him to Augustus John. Working alongside John affected his style, and John also encouraged him to exhibit at the Chenil Gallery, in Chelsea. He held his first solo show there in 1916, and his more significant second one in 1919, the success of which led him to return to London.

From 1920, when he produced his first editioned print (a portrait of the Irish poet, Francis MacNamara), Brockhurst decided to concentrate on etching, and so meet the demand known as the modern etching boom. Developing a high degree of virtuosity, he became the most successful etcher of female figure subjects, rivalled only by William Russell Flint. In 1921, he was immediately elected a full member of the Royal Society of Painter-Etchers and Engravers, and also of the recently formed Society of Graphic Art. In addition, he soon became a member of both the Royal Society of Portrait Painters (1923) and the Art Workers' Guild (1924). Exhibiting regularly at the Royal Academy from 1923, he was elected an associate of the RA in 1928, and made a visitor of the RA Schools in the same year. At this time, he was living at 2 Fernshaw Road, Chelsea, which backed on to his studio in Gunter Grove.

It was as a visitor to the RA Schools that Brockhurst met Kathleen Woodward, a 16-year-old model, whom he dubbed 'Dorette', and with whom he soon began an affair. She inspired *Dorette and Adolescence* (both 1932), works that marked the culmination of his achievement as an etcher. The latter proved particularly popular when it was exhibited at the Royal Academy in 1933.

The slump that occurred in the etching market in the 1930s affected Brockhurst less than other artists, and he continued to produce and sell prints. Nevertheless, he had gradually returned to painting through the late 1920s, and was producing such impressive portraits as that of Henry Rushbury (1927, Carnegie Museum of Art, Pittsburgh, PA). Responding to celebrity and society commissions, he quickly established himself as one of the most fashionable portraitists of the period between the wars, and especially for female sitters. His characteristic format was inspired by the Italian Renaissance portraitists that had first excited him as student, including Leonardo and Bronzino, and set an intensely realised half-length portrayal of a subject against distant Italianate hills. Notable examples include those of the actress, Merle Oberon (exhibited at the RA in 1937, private collection), and the Duchess of Windsor (1939, National Portrait Gallery). Brockhurst was elected a full Royal Academician in 1937, though he contributed regularly at its exhibitions only until 1939. By that date, he was living at 50 Tite Street, Chelsea.

In 1939, Brockhurst left for the United States with Kathleen Woodward, and soon settled at Franklin Lakes, New Jersey, which would remain his home for the remainder of his life. He divorced Anaïs in 1940, and married Kathleen in 1947, the couple becoming American citizens two years later.

Brockhurst continued to undertake lucrative portrait commissions, and exhibited with Knoedler & Co and Portraits Inc, both of New York. However, his reputation declined in Britain, and if he was remembered at all it was more as an etcher than as a painter. He died in Franklin Lakes on 4 May 1978. The retrospective exhibition, 'A Dream of Fair Women', mounted by Sheffield Art Galleries in 1986, and touring, began the process of reviving interest in his work.

His work is represented in the collections of the Royal Academy of Arts and numerous public collections, including the National Portrait Gallery; and the Scottish National Gallery of Modern Art (Edinburgh).

Further reading:

Anne Goodchild, Marilyn F Symmes and Stephen Wildman, *A Dream of Fair Women: An exhibition of the Work of Gerald Brockhurst RA 1890-1978*, Sheffield Arts Department, 1986;
Anne L Goodchild, 'Brockhurst, Gerald Leslie (1890–1978)', H C G Matthew and Brian Harrison (eds), *Oxford Dictionary of National Biography*, Oxford University Press, 2004, https://doi.org/10.1093/ref:odnb/58743;
Anne L Goodchild, 'Brockhurst, Gerald Leslie (*b* Birmingham, Oct 31, 1890; *d* Franklin Lakes, NJ, May 4, 1978)', *Grove Art Online*, 2003, https://doi.org/10.1093/gao/9781884446054.article.T011442

A R MIDDLETON TODD

Arthur Ralph Middleton Todd, RA RWS RE RP NEAC
(1891-1966)

Middleton Todd has been described, by fellow artist, Robert Buhler, as 'by far the most sensitive and accomplished painter of his generation' (Foreword to *Works from the Studio of A R Middleton Todd*, Stow on the Wold: Fosse Gallery, 1985). His mature achievement as a portraitist was founded on a versatile *oeuvre*, in which he produced paintings, drawings and etchings of a wide range of subjects that included figures, landscapes and still life compositions. He particularly enjoyed drawing nudes in pastel, in emulation of his hero, Degas. Though modest and self-critical, he passed on many artistic insights as a successful teacher.

Arthur Todd – as he was initially known – was born at 10 Clifton Terrace, Clifton Hill, Newlyn, Cornwall, on 26 October 1891, the younger of two children of the painter, Ralph Todd, and his wife, Vasilesa (née Trahair), the daughter of a builder and carpenter. By 1901, the family had moved a short distance to 10 Carne Road. From 1907, Arthur studied under his father's friend, Stanhope Forbes, at the Newlyn School of Painting, and then in London at the Central School of Arts and Crafts, where his father sometimes taught. It was at the latter that he learned etching. By 1911, his family had moved to Mawgan-in-Meneage, southeast of Helston.

During the First World War, Todd served in the Motor Transport Company of the Royal Army Service Corps. Following demobilisation, he began to establish himself as an artist, exhibiting at the Royal Academy of Arts for the first time in 1918, while living at 226 Lauderdale Mansions, Maida Vale. However, he continued to study, taking classes at the Slade School of Fine Art under Henry Tonks during the year 1920-21. He then spent time working in France, Italy and Holland, and particularly absorbed the influence of Dutch painting.

By 1922, Todd was working from 18 Cathcart Studios, 34 Redcliffe Road, Chelsea, and identifying himself as 'A R Middleton Todd'. During his early career, he essayed a range of subjects in a variety of materials, including watercolour, pastel and etching, as well as oils. This led him to exhibit widely and, between the wars, gain election to a number of leading societies: the Royal Society of Painter-Etchers and Engravers (ARE 1923, RE 1930), the Royal Society of Painters in Water-Colours (ARWS 1929, RWS 1937) and the Royal Academy (ARA 1939, RA 1949). His dealers included Connell & Sons and the Rowley Gallery.

Todd would prove to be an inspiring teacher. He became head of drawing and painting at Leicester School of Art in 1934, and returned to London two years later to take up the position of master of the life class at Regent Street Polytechnic School of Art. During the Second World War, he received a number of commissions from the War Artists' Advisory Committee to draw and paint individuals, presaging his later career as a specialist in portraits in oils. These works included *Auxiliary Fireman Herbert Baker* (Imperial War Museums) and *Sub-Officer Henry Shaw* (Manchester Art Gallery), both exhibited at RA in 1942. By this time, he was living at 71 Campden Street, Kensington, his home for the remainder of his life.

Though Todd joined the New English Art Club in 1945, and remained a member until 1955, he developed a closer relationship with the Royal Academy. Teaching at the RA Schools between 1946 and 1949, he was elected a full Royal Academician at the end of that period, and in the same year began to sit on the Academy's Council (1949-51, and again in 1958-59). He also taught at the City and Guilds of London Art School, Kennington, from the late 1940s until 1956, his pupils there including Ann Le Bas and both Roland and Bernard Batchelor. His exhibits at the RA during this later period are dominated by portraits of such leading establishment figures as academics, clerics, politicians and soldiers, but also include pastel drawings of flowers and nudes – the last influenced by the work of one of Todd's favourite artists, Edgar Degas. Though he turned down the offer of becoming the President of the Pastel Society in 1954, he gladly accepted election to the Royal Society of Portrait Painters in 1958, an honour that confirmed his standing as a master of portraiture.

Middleton Todd died in London on 21 November 1966, and was buried alongside his parents and brother-in-law in the churchyard of the village of Devoran, Cornwall. He was survived by his sister, Charlotte.

His work is represented in numerous public collections, including the British Museum and Guildhall Art Gallery; and the Ashmolean Museum (Oxford). His papers are held in the collections of the Royal Academy.

JOHN AUSTEN

John Archibald Austen, RBA (1886-1948)

Early influenced by the work of Aubrey Beardsley, John Austen developed into an illustrator of wit and elegance by the mid 1920s, producing unusually decorative images that are associated with Art Deco. Both craftsman and auto-didact, he mastered a range of media, including etching and wood-engraving, and absorbed a variety of styles and motifs.

John Austen was born at 19 George Street, Buckland, near Dover, Kent, on 5 January 1886. He was the second child of the carpenter, Walter Austen, and his wife, Priscilla (née Hooker), the daughter of an agricultural labourer. On leaving school, he followed his father, and trained as a carpenter. However, in 1906, he moved to London, determined to become an artist, and initially took Aubrey Beardsley as his model. His studies were supplemented by life classes, and relieved by amateur dramatics. In the words of the novelist, Dorothy Richardson, he became a 'long-haired studio exquisite', entering a bohemian circle, which also contained Richardson's husband, Alan Odle, and Austin Osman Spare. Exhibiting with the Royal Society of British Artists, he became an associate in 1919 (and a full member in 1921).

In 1919, Austen married Ruby 'Tommy' Thomson, the daughter of a police pensioner, who would become his chief model. They settled in St John's Wood, and by 1926 were living at 16 Circus Road. He became a staff member of the *Penny Illustrated Paper*, and a year or more later illustrated his first book, R H Keen's *The Little Ape* (1921). Subsequent books, including an edition of *Hamlet* (1922), contributions to *The Golden Hind* (co-edited by Spare) and advertising commissions, all demonstrated a gradual stylistic independence, veering towards Art Deco decoration. With the help of the art critic, Haldane MacFall, Austen held a joint exhibition with Odle, Spare and Harry Clarke at the St George's Gallery in 1925; there he showed his illustrative artwork for the first time, including several drawings from the recently published edition of Longus' *Daphnis & Chloe*. The fame of this group was helped by the publication of Dorothy Richardson's *John Austen and the Inseparables* (1930).

At the close of the 1920s, and following an illness, Austen returned to Kent with his wife. Throwing off his aesthetic appearance, he shared his time between his artistic work and country pursuits. Living first in New Romney (circa 1928-36), he and his wife later moved to a converted oast house in Petham and then at Heart's Delight Farm, Wingham. He produced illustrations for – especially – American publishers of limited editions, and turned his hand to writing, producing most notably a study of Don Juan (1939). He also taught at the Canterbury and Thanet Schools of Art, and shared his expertise with a wider audience through the manual, *ABC of Pen and Ink Rendering* (1937). Shortly before the outbreak of the Second World War, he and his wife moved into Rose Cottage, Burmarsh Road, West Hythe. When his health began to deteriorate, he lived in straightened circumstances, though was supported by a Civil List pension. Dying at home on 27 October 1948, he was survived by his wife.

MARJORIE SHERLOCK

Alice Marjorie Sherlock, SGA WIAC (1891-1973)

A pupil of Walter Sickert, Marjorie Sherlock established herself with paintings and etchings of urban scenes, including a striking series of images of railway stations. Later, she was much inspired by trips abroad – including those to Egypt and India – which were often made in the company of, and financed by, her close friend and fellow artist, Orovida Pissarro.

Marjorie Sherlock was born at Fir Tree Cottage, George Lane, Wanstead, Essex, on 3 February 1891, the elder child of the civil engineer, Henry Sherlock, and his wife, Alice (née Platts), who was born in Benares, India. By 1901, the family was living at 'The Limes', 121 Mill Road, Cambridge, and Marjorie received an education locally. In 1918, she entered into marriage with her cousin, Major Wilfrid Barrett, though this proved unsuccessful and they later divorced (he remarrying in 1941). She then continued to live at the family home until the Second World War.

During the First World War, Marjorie Sherlock studied at Westminster Technical Institute under the Camden Town School painters, Walter Sickert and Harold Gilman. She exhibited at the Royal Academy of Arts from 1917, when she showed a powerful view of the interior of Liverpool Street Station (Government Art Collection) (to which the current etching [202] relates). In time, she would exhibit at the International Society, the New English Art Club, the Royal Society of British Artists, the Society of Graphic Art and the Women's International Art Club (becoming a member of the last two). She also showed work internationally.

Developing as a printmaker as well as a painter, Sherlock studied etching under Malcolm Osborne at the Royal College of Art in 1925. She published her etchings in four series, the titles of which indicate her love of travel: 'English Etchings, 'Egyptian Etchings' (both 1925), 'German Etchings' (1929) and 'Indian Etchings' (1932). During this period, she also visited the United States. More admiring of Continental painters than British ones, she furthered her studies, in 1938, by working in Paris under André L'Hôte and André Dunoyer de Segonzac.

During the Second World War, Sherlock moved to East Devon and settled at Oxenways, a Victorian hunting lodge, near Membury and north of Axminster. Of forceful and resourceful character, she established an independent existence on little money by keeping chickens, growing her own vegetables and making her own clothes. However, she continued to work and, in 1948, helped found Axminster Art Society. In her later years, she became a close friend of the artist, Orovida Pissarro, and Pissarro would pay for their occasional travels abroad.

Majorie Sherlock died at Angela Court, Tipton St John (to the west of Axminster), on 2 April 1973. A retrospective exhibition was held at the Maltzahn Gallery, London, in the same year.

Further reading:

Wendy Baron, 'Sickert, Walter, pupils (act 1890-1939)', H C G Matthew and Brian Harrison (eds), *Oxford Dictionary of National Biography*, Oxford University Press, 2010, https://doi.org/10.1093/ref:odnb/64748

EILEEN SOPER

Eileen Alice Soper, RMS SWLA (1905-1990)

The work of Eileen Soper – like that of her father, George – comprises some of the most popular strands of British art in the twentieth century. She placed emphasis on subjects that have diverted and delighted a large percentage of the population, and presented them directly and precisely. In working extensively as a printmaker and illustrator, she ensured wide dissemination of her images through exhibition and publication.

Eileen Soper was born at 'Reddaford', Slades Hill, Enfield, on 26 March 1905, the younger daughter of the artist, George Soper, and his wife, Ada (née Lehany). In 1908, George moved his family out of London to Harmer Green, near Welwyn, in Hertfordshire. There he helped design a new home, at 42 Harmers Green Lane, which he originally called 'Hill Lodge'.

Like her elder sister, Eva, Eileen was educated at Olive Downing's School in Knebworth and at Hitchin Girls' School. Trained in art by her father from an early age, Eileen Soper soon rivalled him in talent and surpassed him in popularity, while neatly complementing his subjects by depicting children at play. She first exhibited her etchings in 1921 at the Royal Academy of Arts and the Print Makers Society of California, and was immediately elected a member of the latter. She attracted great attention among critics, fellow artists and the general public on both sides of the Atlantic; only four years after her debut, Queen Mary purchased an impression of the print, *Flying Swings*. As she grew, Eileen moved from treating children as her subject to making them her public, so that from the time of her father's death, in August 1942, she worked primarily as an illustrator.

In a notable collaboration with Enid Blyton, comprising 35 titles, Eileen illustrated the entire series of Famous Five adventures and a vast range of other books, from *The Children's Life of Christ* to *My First Nature Book*. The 23 books that she herself both wrote and illustrated demonstrate her developing skill as a wildlife artist and her deepening response to nature from innocent anthropomorphism to empathetic observation. She was a founder member of the Society of Wildlife Artists (1964) and was elected to the membership of the Royal Society of Miniature Painters (1972). In order to encourage birds and mammals, she let much of the rare flora planted by her father return to a state of wildness and even allowed the animals of the garden into the house, which was renamed 'Wildings'. After the death of her parents, she shared this singular location with only one other human, her somewhat shadowy sister Eva. Eileen died on 18 March 1990, Eva outliving her by only six months.

The estate and copyright of George and Eileen Soper are now in the care of the Chris Beetles Gallery through Longmores Solicitors on behalf of AGBI. It mounted a highly successful major retrospective in June 1995, and followed it with a show devoted to Eileen's achievement as a printmaker.

S R BADMIN

Stanley Roy Badmin, RWS RE AIA FSIA (1906-1989)

Throughout his career, S R Badmin used his great talents – as etcher, illustrator and watercolourist – to promote a vision of the English countryside and thus of England itself. By underpinning his idealism with almost documentary precision and detail, he was able to produce images that appealed to all, and could be used for a great variety of purposes, from education through to advertising. The wellbeing suggested by each rural panorama is all the more potent, and pleasing, for the accuracy of each tree and leaf, and the plausibility of the slightest anecdotal episode.

Stanley Roy Badmin was born at 8a Niederwald Road, Sydenham, London, on 18 April 1906, the second of three sons of Charles James Badman, a teacher, and his second wife, Margaret (née Raine). He was educated at Sydenham School, where he adopted the surname 'Badmin' on the insistence of his father in the vain hope that it would divert 'jeers & insults'.

Badmin studied at Camberwell School of Arts & Crafts (1922-24), before winning a studentship to the Royal College of Art, initially to study painting, though he later transferred to the design school (1924-27). In 1925, he married Margaret Colbourn, known as 'Peggy', and soon settled with her at 'Aleroy', 45 Thorpewood Avenue, Sydenham, a house built for them by his father. Together they would have two children: Patrick (born 1936) and Joanna (born 1939).

Badmin began his career by contributing illustrations to *The Graphic* (1927) and *The Tatler* (1928), and holding his first solo show, at the Twenty-One Gallery (1930). Further solo shows would take place at the Fine Art Society (1933 & 1937). Having taken further courses at the RCA and Camberwell, he qualified as a teacher in 1928, and supplemented his income by teaching part-time at Richmond School of Art (1934) and St John's Wood School of Art (1936). However, he worked increasingly as an etcher and watercolourist, and was soon elected to the Royal Society of Painter-Etchers and Engravers (ARE 1931, RE 1935) and the Royal Society of Painters in Water-Colours (ARWS 1932, RWS 1939). He was also a member of the Artists International Association (from 1936).

In 1935, Badmin received a major commission – from the American magazine, *Fortune* – to depict various towns in the United States; the results were exhibited at M A McDonald in New York, in spring 1936. An important development in Badmin's illustrative style was marked soon after his return to England by *Highways and Byways in Essex*, a collaboration with F L M Griggs (published in 1939). Even before the Second World War, he made a mark as an educational illustrator and was particularly admired for his accurate depiction of trees. Before working in the war, for the Ministry of Information and the Royal Air Force, he made a major contribution, in 1940, to Sir Kenneth Clark's Recording Britain – a term that might well be applied to his work as a whole.

From 1945, Badmin worked increasingly as a commercial artist, designing advertisements and posters, and producing illustrations for greeting cards and calendars. Equally in demand as an illustrator of books and periodicals, he published *Trees for Town and Country* (1947) and contributed to *Radio Times*. Divorcing his first wife in

1948, he would marry the widow, Rosaline Flew (née Downey), in 1950, and bring up her daughter, Elizabeth, with his children. In 1951, Rosaline gave birth to their daughter, Galea Rosaline.

Only from the mid 1950s was Badmin able to paint two or three major pieces for each RWS exhibition, and hold a show at the Leicester Galleries (1955). Even then, he found time to embark on projects for Shell: Geoffrey Grigson's *The Shell Guide to Trees and Shrubs* (1958) and four volumes of the series of 'Shell Guides to the Counties'. In 1959, he and his family moved to Bignor, near Pulborough, West Sussex, from where he continued to paint and exhibit. He held a further solo show, at Worthing Art Gallery in 1967. His achievement was honoured by the RWS in devoting a part of its Autumn Exhibition to his work in 1984, and by the Chris Beetles Gallery, in mounting a major retrospective in 1985 and subsequent exhibitions. He died at St Richard's Hospital, Chichester, West Sussex, on 28 April 1989.

Further reading:

Chris Beetles, *S R Badmin and the English Landscape*, London: Collins, 1985;
Christopher Beetles, 'Badmin, Stanley Roy (1906-1989)', H C G Matthew and Brian Harrison (eds), *Oxford Dictionary of National Biography*, Oxford University Press, 2010, https://doi.org/10.1093/ref:odnb/64261

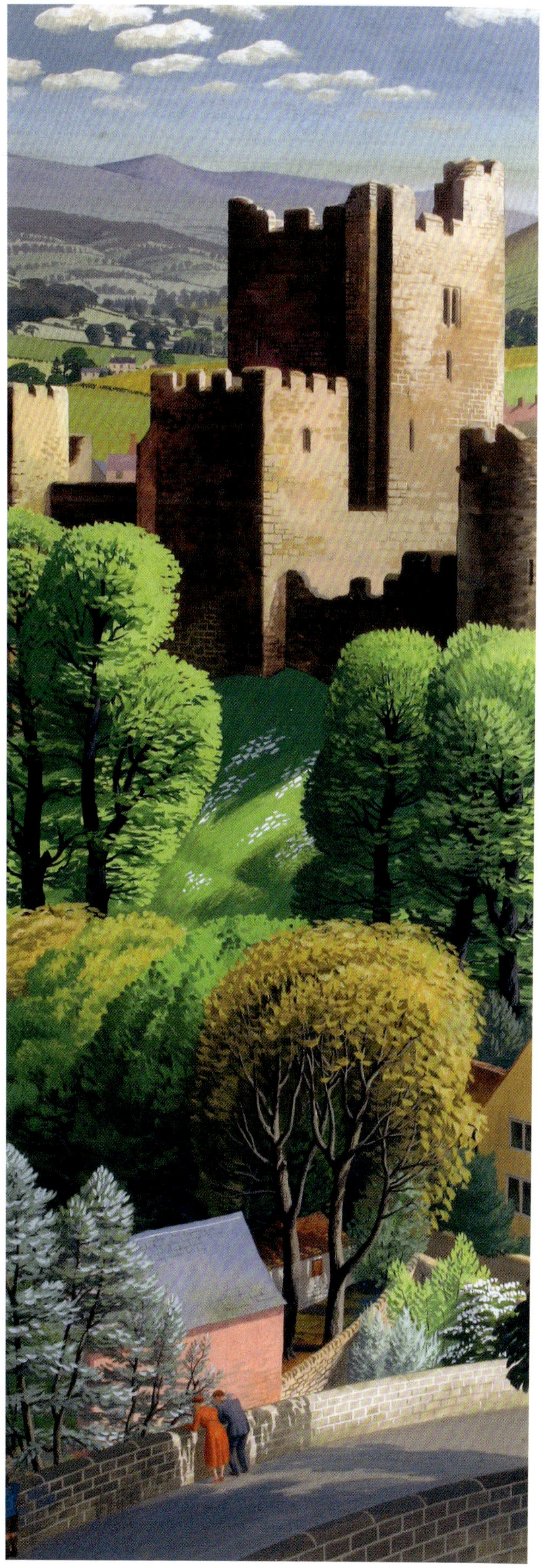

Detail of S R Badmin, *Ludlow, Shropshire* [155]

CHARLES KNIGHT

Charles Knight, VPRWS ROI (1901-1990)

The Sussex landscape painter, Charles Knight, channelled the tradition of English watercolour painting in order to produce his own original contribution. As a result, he became a pillar of the Royal Society of Painters in Water-Colours and received acclaim, from William Russell Flint, as the 'star turn' of the Recording Britain scheme.

Charles Knight was born in Hove, Sussex, on 27 August 1901, the second of three children of Charles Knight, an accountant to a publishing company, and his wife, Evelyn (née Nash). His father came from a family that had long farmed in Sussex, and remained a keen naturalist and artist, taking the young Charles on walking and sketching trips, and so initiating his love of the county. He grew up in central Brighton, first at 78 Ditchling Road and later at 61 Stanford Road, and was educated at Stanford Road Junior and Vardean School. He was also an active member of the Anglican church of St Bartholomew's, Ann Street, and sang in its choir. Its vicar, Gilbert Elliott, encouraged his gift for drawing by taking him on four trips to France, in the years 1918-25.

Studying first at Brighton School of Art (1919-23), Knight won a scholarship to the Royal Academy Schools in 1923 and, though he commuted from the South Coast, he became exposed to many new influences. His discovery of the work of John Sell Cotman was particularly seminal, for it determined his concentration on watercolour, and directed his travels, as well as affecting his early style. As a student of the RA Schools, he won the Landseer Scholarship, and the Turner Medal for his oil of the Cotmanesque subject, *Llangollen*. Shown at the Royal Academy in 1926, it was soon bought for the Tate Gallery by Sir Joseph Duveen. The publicity led to the membership of both the Royal Institute of Painters in Oils (1933) and the Royal Society of Painters in Water-Colours (ARWS 1933, RWS 1936, VPRWS 1961).

From 1925, Knight taught at Brighton School of Art, first as a full-time lecturer, and later as a visitor. Following his marriage in 1934, to Leonora Vasey, he and his wife settled at Chettles, 34 Beacon Road, in Ditchling, in the heart of the Sussex countryside. Their son, Richard, was born in 1938. The forty drawings of Sussex that he produced for Recording Britain were dubbed the 'star turn' of the project by William Russell Flint.

During the Second World War, Knight was reserved by the teaching profession, and returned to full-time teaching at the college, but also worked as a night telephone operator for the Civil Defence and a member of the Home Guard. In 1944, he was asked by the Queen Mother to give Princess Margaret lessons in watercolour painting; his appointment lasted for three years. He continued to teach at Brighton School of Art, and in 1959 became both Vice-Principal and Head of the Drawing and Painting Department. Though he retired from teaching in 1967, he continued to paint and exhibit a wide variety of confident watercolours until the end of his life. He died on 15 May 1990, his wife having died 20 years earlier.

In 1997, the Chris Beetles Gallery hosted '… More Than a Touch of Poetry', an important retrospective exhibition of the work of Charles Knight, organised in conjunction with the Towner Gallery, Eastbourne and Hove Museum and Art Gallery. It was accompanied by an illustrated catalogue.

His work is represented in the collections of the Royal Watercolour Society, and numerous public collections, including the British Museum and the V&A; and the University of Brighton.

Further reading:

Michael Brockway, *Charles Knight RWS, ROI*, Leigh-on-Sea: F Lewis, 1952

CECIL ARTHUR HUNT

Cecil Arthur Hunt, VPRWS RBA (1873-1965)

Once elected a full member of the Royal Society of Painters in Water-Colours in 1925, Cecil Arthur Hunt retired from his career as a barrister and turned his serious pastime of painting into a profession. While he had first established himself as a painter of mountains, especially the Alps and the Dolomites, he soon proved himself a master of a great variety of topographies. The impressive, often stark, effects that he achieved rival those associated with his friend and mentor, Frank Brangwyn.

Cecil Arthur Hunt was born in Torquay, Devon, on 8 March 1873, the second of three children of the highly regarded writer and geologist, Arthur Roope Hunt, and his wife, Sarah (née Gumbleton), who was born in Waterford, Ireland. He was educated at Winchester and Trinity College, Cambridge, studying Classics and Law, and being called to the Bar in 1899 (as had his father before him). He treated painting and writing as serious pastimes until 1925, when he was elected to the full membership of the Royal Society of Painters in Water-Colours. He then relinquished his legal career to become a professional painter.

Hunt had first exhibited in London in 1900, at the Alpine Club Galleries, and had held his first major show a year later, alongside E Home Bruce at the Ryder Gallery. From the first, he established himself as an atmospheric painter of mountains, especially of the Alps and Dolomites. However, he was soon accepted as a master of a great variety of topographies, for he exhibited the products of his wide travels frequently and extensively. Favourite destinations included the West Country, the West Coast of Scotland, the Rhône Valley, Northern Italy, Rome and Taormina.

In 1903, Hunt married Phyllis Lucas, and they would have two sons. From 1911, they lived at Mallord House, on the corner of Mallord Street and Old Church Street, Chelsea, which was especially designed by Ralph Knott to include a large studio on the ground floor. During the summer months, he and his family retreated to the farm estate of Foxworthy, on the edge of Dartmoor, in Devon.

During the First World War, Hunt was employed at the Home Office, first in connection with Irish prisoners interned in England following the Sinn Fein's Rebellion in 1916, and later assisting the Committee for Employment of Conscientious Objectors.

Hunt showed work regularly at the Royal Academy of Arts (from 1912), the Royal Society of British Artists (from 1914) and the Royal Society of Painters in Water-Colours (from 1918). He was elected a member of the Royal Society of British Artists in 1914, an associate of the RWS in 1919, and a full member six years later. He acted as the Vice-President of the RWS for a three-year period from 1930. His many substantial solo shows included six at the Fine Art Society (1919-34) and one at Colnaghi's (1945). Following his death on 5 August 1965, he was the subject of a large memorial show at the Royal Society of Painters in Water-Colours.

Chris Beetles has done much to revive interest in the work of Cecil Arthur Hunt. He mounted a large scale retrospective exhibition in 1996 at his London gallery, on the exact site of the artist's first substantial show in 1901. The retrospective was accompanied by a definitive catalogue.

His work is represented in the collection of the Royal Watercolour Society and numerous public collections, including the V&A.

KARL HAGEDORN

Karl Adolph Hagedorn, RBA RI RSMA NEAC NS (1889-1969)

German-born Karl Hagedorn made a consciously pioneering attempt to introduce Modernism to Manchester in the early decades of the twentieth century, through his work as a painter and designer. Later, he tempered his style so that it fitted more easily into England's naturalistic watercolour tradition.

Karl Hagedorn was born in Berlin on 11 September 1889, and brought up in Freiburg-im-Breisgau. He went to Manchester in 1905 to train in textile production at the School of Technology, and also studied under Adolph Valette at the School of Art. At the School of Art, he befriended local girl, Nelly Stiebel, who would become his wife, and Francis Sladen Smith, with whom he founded the art club, *Der Künstler Zwei*. By 1911, he was boarding with Sladen and his parents at 289 Great Western Street, Moss Side, and working as clerk.

His development into a Modernist was achieved in Paris, in the years 1912-13, when, working under Maurice Denis, he met a number of artists – notably Henri Matisse – and absorbed a range of avant-garde styles. On his return to England, he made a consciously pioneering attempt to introduce Modernism into Manchester through his work as both painter and designer. As a freelance designer, he worked in the areas of commercial art, advertising, window display and textiles, and many of the cottons that bore his patterns sold in the African market. He was the outstanding contributor to the controversial second exhibition of the Manchester Society of Modern Painters in 1913, and would continue to exhibit with the society until 1916.

Becoming a British subject at the outbreak of the First World War, in 1914, Hagedorn married Nelly in Honiton, Devon, in 1915, and she gave birth to their daughter, Elinor Anne, in Newton Abbot in 1916. In that year, he became a Lance-Corporal in the Middlesex Regiment, and during active service found time to produce some landscape studies.

In Manchester, and then in Buxton, Derbyshire, during the 1920s, Hagedorn worked in a distinctive geometric manner, which applied Cubist draughtsmanship to the tradition of the English landscape watercolour. However, on holidays in France and Italy, he began to relax the degree of abstraction and emphasised instead the element of close observation. Following his move to Belsize Park Gardens, in London, in 1927, he befriended Randolph Schwabe, who encouraged him in this direction (though it is said that the tragic death of his only child, in 1928, also had an effect on his change of style).

Hagedorn exhibited at a number of leading galleries in London, the provinces and France, and was elected to the Royal Society of British Artists, the Royal Institute of Painters in Water Colours, the Royal Society of Marine Artists, the National Society of Artists, the New English Art Club and the Salon d'Automne.

During the Second World War, Hagedorn contributed views of Derbyshire to Sir Kenneth Clark's Recording Britain project and four works to the War Artists' Advisory Committee. By the late 1940s, he and Nelly were living in a converted eighteenth-century coach house at Feltham, he was teaching part-time at Epsom School of Art. Latterly, they lived at 7, The Little Boltons, Kensington.

Karl Hagedorn died on 31 March 1969.

In 1995, the Chris Beetles Gallery hosted 'Manchester's first Modernist', an important retrospective exhibition of the work of Karl Hagedorn organised in conjunction with the Whitworth Art Gallery of the University of Manchester. It was accompanied by an illustrated biographical catalogue.

His work is represented in numerous public collections, including The Whitworth Art Gallery (Manchester).

RANDOLPH SCHWABE

Randolph Schwabe, RWS LG NEAC (1885-1948)

A clear eye and sure hand enabled Randolph Schwabe to produce drawings, etchings and lithographs of consistent clarity and strength. Trained at the Slade School of Fine Art, he would return there to become an influential Principal and Professor. He also held a significant position as an official war artist in both world wars. Though he is best remembered for his attentive, absorbing images of buildings and landscapes, his subjects included figures and still life compositions, and he also produced illustrations and designs for the theatre.

Randolph Schwabe was born at Alsbach House, 4 Cambridge Grove, Eccles, Lancashire, on 9 May 1885, the younger son of Lawrence Schwabe and Octavie Henriette (née Ermen). His paternal grandfather, a cotton merchant, had migrated from Germany to England in 1820.

Having failed in various business enterprises, Lawrence Schwabe finally settled with his family in Hemel Hempstead, Hertfordshire, and set up as a letterpress printer and stationer. Randolph was then educated privately as a day boy at the nearby Heath Brow School, Boxmoor. Revealing a prodigious talent for drawing, he contributed to the weekly school magazine, the *Heath Brow Chronicle*, which was edited by his elder brother, Eric.

At the age of 14, Schwabe left school to study at the Royal College of Art, but did not respond well to the teaching methods. So, in 1900, he transferred to the Slade School of Fine Art, and found that he much preferred its atmosphere of greater artistic freedom.

After five years, he took advantage of a Slade scholarship and, in 1906, went to Paris to study at the Académie Julian under Jean Paul Laurens. He lived at the Hôtel de la Haute Loire, Boulevard Raspail, which was popular with artists, and at some stage worked at Paul Bornet's Cercle International des Arts, which was in the same street. In 1908, Schwabe left Paris and travelled to Italy for the first time, in the company of his artist friend, Francis Unwin. They worked in Rome, and also visited Florence and Venice, among other Italian cities. On their return to London, Schwabe lived at 37 Howley Place, Maida Vale. Producing landscapes and architectural subjects in oil and watercolour, he began to exhibit at the New English Art Club. After a further extended stay in France – at Siouville, in Normandy, in 1911-12 – he settled in Chelsea, living in a flat at 43a Cheyne Walk, and moving within an artistic circle that included Francis Unwin and Gerald Summers. He also contributed to the exhibitions of the Friday Club, which had been founded by Vanessa Bell and showed at the Alpine Club Gallery, in Mill Street.

In 1913, Schwabe married Gwendolen Rosamund Jones, who had also studied at the Slade, where she acquired the nickname 'Birdie'. Honeymooning in Whitby, they then lived at the flat in Cheyne Walk. In the following year, their daughter, Alice, was born.

When war broke out in 1914, Schwabe was busily developing his career. He held his first solo show at the Carfax Gallery in April 1915, while in the November of the same year he exhibited at the London Group for the first time, and was made a member. Then, in 1917, he was elected to the New English Art Club, and added to his skills by taking lessons in lithography from C R W Nevinson, a fellow member of both the Friday Club and the London Group, who had just been appointed an official war artist.

Schwabe had attempted to enlist, in 1916, but was rejected on health grounds. However, in March 1918, he too was appointed an official war artist, and recorded members of the Women's Land Army at work at Rushden Farm, near Podington, in Northamptonshire.

Even while war continued, Schwabe began to design costumes for the theatre, drawing on a deep knowledge of historic dress. In June 1918, his designs appeared on the stage of the New Theatre, St Martin's Lane, in Leslie and Dymock's *The Loving Heart*, based on stories from Boccaccio's *The Decameron*. Then, in April 1919, his costumes were seen in a production of *Romeo and Juliet* at the Lyric Theatre, Shaftesbury Avenue. His interest in historic costume later led to collaborations with Francis Kelly, a friend from Slade student days, and together they published *Historic Costume: A Chronicle of Fashion in Western Europe, 1490–1790* (1925) and *A Short History of Costume and Armour* (1931).

In 1919, Schwabe was also employed by the writer, publisher and balletomane, Cyril Beaumont, to design wooden figures based on dancers in Diaghilev's Ballets Russes, which had become all the rage in London. This was the beginning of a close relationship, in which Schwabe and Beaumont worked on more than a dozen illustrated books, beginning with Walter de la Mare's *Crossings: A Fairy Play* (1921), and including *A Manual of the Theory and Practice of Classical Theatrical Dancing (Méthode Cecchetti)* (1922). In the same period, in 1924, Schwabe exhibited his drawings in a solo show at the Redfern Gallery.

Supplementing his income as an artist, designer and illustrator, Schwabe began to teach drawing at Camberwell and Westminster Schools of Art, in 1919, and at the Royal College of Art, in 1921. He also confirmed his scholarly reputation by regularly contributing articles and reviews of exhibitions and books to various art periodicals, including *The Burlington Magazine* and *The Studio*. Later in the decade, in 1928, and until 1945, he examined for the Ministry of Education, for the greater part as the Chief Examiner in Drawing and Painting.

In 1929, the Schwabes moved from Chelsea to Hampstead, settling into 20 Church Row, which Birdie decorated with style and maintained with care. From the following year, and until his death, Randolph kept a detailed diary, recording his artistic practice, his active public life, and his views on the arts, current affairs and the people that he met.

1930 proved a momentous year, as Schwabe replaced Henry Tonks as Principal and Professor of the Slade School of Fine Art. He gave the responsibility for painting to his friend Allan Gwynne-Jones, and concentrated on communicating the skill of drawing. His close friend, Charles Tennyson, would later describe his approach to teaching as 'enthusiastic, sympathetic and profoundly scholarly'.

These words might equally be applied to his role as Editor of *Artwork*, an international quarterly magazine of arts and crafts, which he took over from D S MacColl in 1930. However, despite his assiduousness, the magazine closed after a year, a victim of the uncertain economic climate.

Through the 1930s, Schwabe was very busy both as an artist and administrator. He held solo shows in London – at the Batsford Gallery in 1931 – and Madrid – at the Museo Nacional de Arte Moderno in 1935. He led the selection committee of the South London Group in 1931, and in subsequent years was elected as a member of the Manchester Academy of Fine Arts (1932) and the Athenaeum Club (1934). His work was grounded in the English watercolourists of the eighteenth century – despite his German origins – and so it seemed only fitting that he should be elected an associate of the Royal Society of Painters in Water-Colours in 1938, and a full member four years later. In the second half of the decade, he also worked on one of his most significant sets of illustrations, for an edition of Somerset Maugham's autobiographical novel, *Of Human Bondage*, published by Doubleday Doran in 1936. On the outbreak of the Second World War, in 1939, Schwabe supervised the evacuation of the Slade School of Fine Art to Oxford. Combined with the Ruskin School of Drawing, it was based at the Ashmolean Museum. While continuing as Principal and Professor, he also responded, in 1940, to a commission from the War Artists' Advisory Committee (WAAC) to make drawings of the bombed Coventry Cathedral and portraits of members of the Ministry of Home Security. Then, in 1941, he joined the WAAC as the art school representative, at the same time joining his fellow committee member, Sir Walter Westley Russell, as an overseas expert adviser to the Committee of the Felton Bequest on the purchase of English watercolours and drawings for the National Gallery of Victoria, Australia.

In 1942, Schwabe undertook one of the most unusual projects of his career, illustrating *Shooting to Live with the One-Hand Gun*, written by his brother, Captain 'Bill' Sykes, with Captain William E Fairbairn. (Eric had changed his surname to Sykes by deed poll in 1917 because of the German overtones of Schwabe.)

During the years of international turmoil, Schwabe had provided a strong sense of stability at the Slade School. At the end of the war, in 1945, Schwabe and his wife left Oxford in order to prepare for the school's reopening in London, which it did on 1 October. In the same month, five of his drawings were shown at the Suffolk Street Galleries in the exhibition, 'The Londoner's England', which showcased a scheme that commissioned artists to provide views of the capital. This limited sequel to the Pilgrim Trust's scheme, Recording Britain, was generated by the Central Institute of Art and Design, and funded by four leading brewers, with the intention of bringing 'the art to the pub'. From this time, Schwabe also joined Sir Kenneth Clark, a member of the selection committee for both Recording Britain and The Londoner's England, in advising the Felton Bequest on its purchases of Old Masters, French Impressionists and contemporary artists.

In 1946, as a sequel to his wartime activities, Schwabe illustrated H E Bates' *The Tinkers of Elstow*, which told the story of the Royal Ordnance Factory managed by J Lyons and Co for the Ministry of Supply during the war.

Schwabe continued as Slade Professor until his death. He died at his daughter's home at Helensburgh, Dumbartonshire, on 19 September 1948.

Three years later, the Arts Council of Great Britain mounted a memorial exhibition of his work at its gallery in St James's Square.

The Chris Beetles Gallery has had a long association with the work of Randolph Schwabe, and has recently mounted two rich and varied exhibitions devoted to his achievement. The first, in 2013, coincided with a new biography by Gill Clarke and a loan show at the St Barbe Museum, Lymington, Hampshire. The second, in 2016, coincided with the publication of Gill Clarke's edition of *The Diaries of Randolph Schwabe* and a loan show of Schwabe and his contemporaries, at the Otter Gallery, at the University of Chichester.

His work is represented in numerous public collections, including the Imperial War Museums, UCL Art Museum (University College) and the V&A; the Ashmolean Museum (Oxford) and Manchester Art Gallery; and the Art Gallery of New South Wales (Sydney).

Further reading:

Stephen Bone, *rev* Terry Anne Riggs, 'Schwabe, Randolph (1885-1948)', H C G Matthew and Brian Harrison (eds), *Oxford Dictionary of National Biography*, Oxford University Press, 2004, vol 49, pages 294-295;
Gill Clarke, *Randolph Schwabe*, Bristol: Sansom & Company, 2012

WILLIAM WILSON

William Wilson, OBE RSA RSW SAP SSA (1905-1972)

William Wilson has a reputation as the outstanding Scottish printmaker and stained glass artist of the twentieth century. Underpinning these achievements are his substantial skills as a draughtsman and painter.

Born in Edinburgh on 21 July 1905, William Wilson left school early to work as a mapmaker. Then, in 1920, at the age of 15, he began an apprenticeship in the stained glass studio of James Ballantine and Son, and also studied stained glass with Herbert Hendrie. While still an apprentice, he attended evening classes at Edinburgh College of Art and, in 1930, was elected to the Society of Scottish Artists.

In 1932, Ballantine allowed Wilson to study full time at the college, and he there discovered printmaking, becoming an outstanding student of etching and engraving under Adam Bruce Thomson, and soon winning an RSA Carnegie Travelling Scholarship. This enabled him to travel to France, Germany, Italy and Spain, and make pen and ink drawings of the places that he visited. These became the basis of many of his prints.

During the early 1930s, Wilson established himself as arguably Scotland's finest twentieth-century printmaker, producing work that initially reflected his interest in Italian primitive art, but which gradually became 'more dramatic and darkly expressive' (Frances Spalding, *20th Century Painters and Sculptors*, Woodbridge: Antique Collectors' Club, 1990, page 468). From this period, he was secretary to the Society of Artist Printmakers. A fellow member was the etcher and engraver, Ian Fleming, who shared with Wilson the skills that he had acquired from his teacher, Charles Murray, while at Glasgow School of Art.

In 1934, Wilson gained an Andrew Grant Fellowship and RSA Guthrie Award, which permitted him to study both in London, at the Royal College of Art, and in Germany, where he focussed his attention contemporary stained glass. While in London, in 1935, he met the artist, Edgar Holloway, and they travelled together in Britain and Europe. A year later, they rented a cottage for six months at Netteswell Common, Essex, where they installed a printing press.

In 1937, Wilson opened his own stained glass studio in Edinburgh, and produced glass for churches, cathedrals and secular buildings in Britain and abroad, establishing a wide reputation. Notable among buildings to include his work are the cathedrals at Canterbury, Liverpool and Brechin, Angus. His last and largest surviving set of windows, designed in about 1961, is at Craigiebuckler church, Aberdeen.

Alongside his work as a stained glass artist and printmaker, Wilson painted watercolours, including some of scenes of life in fishing ports and others of Paris. In these, he showed affinities with other members of the Edinburgh School, including William Gillies and Anne Redpath. He was elected an Associate of the Royal Scottish Academy in 1939, and a full Academician in 1949, and also a member of the Royal Scottish Society of Painters in Watercolour in 1946.

Losing his sight, as the result of diabetes, in 1961, Wilson spent the last years of his life with a sister in Bury, Lancashire. He died early in 1972.

Further reading:

Fiona Pearson, *William Wilson 1905-1972*, Edinburgh: National Galleries of Scotland, 1994

WILLIAM THOMAS WOOD

William Thomas Wood, VPRWS ROI NS (1877-1958)

A painter in both oil and watercolour, William Thomas Wood became particularly well known for atmospheric landscapes of Sussex, as well as flower still lifes. During the First World War, he served on the Balkan Front, both in the Royal Flying Corps and as an official war artist. He returned to images of aerial warfare in the Second World War, during which he served in the Home Guard.

William Thomas Wood was born in Ipswich, Suffolk, the son of the builder, Thomas Wood, and his wife, Middlesex-born, Annie (née Tighe). In *Who Was Who*, he listed his birth date as 17 June 1877; however, his birth was registered in the third quarter of 1878.

By 1891, the Wood family was living at Nos 1, 2 and 3 Green Man Cottages, Heath Lane, Putney, and Thomas was running his building and decorating business from the premises. William was the eldest of five siblings, with three brothers and a sister.

Wood studied at the Regent Street Polytechnic School of Art, in London, and then in Italy. He began to exhibit frequently at the Royal Academy of Arts in 1900, while still living with his family in Putney. After staying in various lodgings in London, he settled at The Studio, 29a Oxford Road, Putney, by 1904.

In 1909, he married Berenice Knowles, the daughter of the artist, Davidson Knowles. Ten years younger than William, she attended the Regent Street Polytechnic, possibly as his student, as he returned to the school as a teacher of painting. She would become a glass painter and decorator in cut paper, specialising in floral decorations under glass domes. By 1911, they were living together with their seven month daughter, Elise, at 35 Oakhill Court, Oakhill Road, Putney. Later that year, Berenice would give birth to their son, William.

In 1910, Wood held a solo show, 'Pictures illustrating Evening, Night and the Dawn', at the Fine Art Society. Working in both oil and watercolour, he became an associate of the Royal Society of Painters in Water-Colours in 1913.

During the First World War, Wood served as a Corporal in the Royal Flying Corps; working as an Observer of Kite Balloons in Macedonia, he was mentioned in despatches. In 1918, he became an official war artist on the Balkan Front, undertaking several commissions for the Ministry of Information. In the same year, the Leicester Galleries mounted a solo show of the resulting work. Then, he illustrated A J Mann's *The Salonika Front*, published by A & C Black, in 1920.

By the end of the First World War, Wood was living at 61 Glebe Place, Chelsea, which would remain his home for the rest of his life. In 1918, he was elected a full member of the Royal Society of Painters in Water-Colours, and between 1923 and 1926 served as Vice President. He also became a member of the Royal Institute of Oil Painters in 1927 and the National Society of Painters, Sculptors and Printmakers (which was founded in 1930). His solo shows included two devoted to oil paintings of flowers at the Leicester Galleries, in 1924 and 1927, and another, of 'English Landscape in Water Colour' at the Rembrandt Gallery, in 1936. In addition to leading London venues, he exhibited in the provinces and at the Paris Salon.

During the Second World War, Wood was a member of the Home Guard. In later years, he was involved with a number of artists' clubs, becoming Chairman of the Association of Students Sketch Clubs in 1924, and also a member of both the Arts Club and Chelsea Arts Club, and an honorary member of the Chelsea Art Society. He died in Chelsea on 2 June 1958.

His work is represented in numerous public collections, including the Imperial War Museums.

HAROLD SQUIRE

Harold Squire, LG NEAC (1881-1959)

Harold Squire was a painter of landscapes, flowers and occasional figure subjects in a refined Post-Impressionist style. Having taken lessons from Augustus John, he often employed spare landscape motifs similar to those of John Dickson Innes and Derwent Lees, artists in John's circle. However, his handling is more comparable to that of Lucien Pissarro, who exhibited with him in 1913 in a show of independence from the London Group. In addition to easel painting, he displayed an interest in interior design, and associated with a number of key artist-designers of the age, including the architect, Charles Rennie Mackintosh (who designed a studio-house for him), and members of the Bloomsbury Group.

Harold Squire was born at Quinta Esmeralda, Las Zorras, Valparaiso, Chile, and was one of the (probably five) children of Walter Squire, the director of a copper mining company, and his wife, Evelyn (née Pike). He arrived in England at the age of 10, probably to attend school at Haileybury, in Hertfordshire, as did at least one of his brothers, Geoffrey Pike Squire.

Squire studied first at the Slade School of Fine Art, in London; then – by 1901 – under Stanhope Forbes, in Newlyn, Cornwall; and latterly at the Académie Julian, in Paris. He also received lessons from Augustus John and William Orpen. In 1917, Charles Marriott and Herbert Furst (the latter writing as 'Tis') would describe Squire as one of those 'touched with [the] influence' of Augustus John (*Modern Art*, New York: Frederick Stokes Co, 1917, page 49).

By 1910, Squire was living in an apartment on the fourth floor of 30 Tite Street, Chelsea, London, and working from a studio at the Riviera Studios, on the bank of the Thames at 136a Grosvenor Road. He began to exhibit with the New English Art Club in that year, and in the following one with the Friday Club (which had been founded by Vanessa Bell in 1905). Dorset became a favourite sketching ground from this time, and he also began to show landscapes painted in France and Italy.

In 1913, Vanessa Bell's husband, the art critic, Clive Bill, bought a painting by Squire on behalf of the Contemporary Art Society. In the same year, Squire helped found the London Group (which had grown out of the Camden Town Group). However, he exhibited only in its first exhibition, held at the Goupil Gallery in March 1914 (and later in its 1928 retrospective). In the June, he, Lucien Pissarro and James Bolivar Manson marked their secession from the group by holding a show of their own – with Malcolm Milne and Diana White – at the Carfax Gallery. A notice of the show described him as a landscape painter of 'romantic scenes treated unromantically'. A contribution to an exhibition of the Friday Club in 1915, entitled *Decoration for Blue Room at 3 Sloane Court*, suggests that he was also essaying interior design.

In this period, Squire contributed to two significant surveys of contemporary art: an 'Exhibition of the Camden Town Group and Others', which was held at Brighton Art Gallery in the winter of 1913-14, and 'Twentieth Century Art: A Review of Modern Movements', at Whitechapel Art Gallery, London, in the spring of 1914. Subjects included Gummer's How (a Lake District hill) and several places in Italy: Bellagio, Venice, Capri and Vesuvius.

Nothing is known of his wartime service, but Squire was at Graylingwell War Hospital, Chichester, Sussex, in the years 1916-17. The War Office refused to release him when he was proposed as an official war artist.

Having exhibited with the New English Art Club since 1911, Squire was elected a member in 1919. In that year, he contributed pictures of Capri to a mixed exhibition at the Goupil Gallery (some of which were bought for Johannesburg Art Gallery). He also became a member of the Council of the new Arts League of Service, which was run by Ana Berry – who, like Squire, was born in Chile – and aimed, according to its motto, 'to bring the Arts into Everyday Life'. Late in the year, the League mounted 'The Exhibition of Practical Arts' at the Twenty-One Gallery, which included a number of rugs handwoven to Squire's designs, and a design by him 'for Curtains for a Travelling Theatre', no doubt for the League's own touring players. The products that he designed were also sold at the League's shop in the Adelphi (as were those by his friend, Malcolm Milne).

It was through the Arts League of Service that Squire met the architect, Charles Rennie Mackintosh. Mackintosh received a joint commission to design separate studio-houses for Squire, Francis Derwent Wood (sculptor) and Arthur Cadogan Blunt (glass artist), and a block of studio-flats for the League, all in Glebe Place, Chelsea. However, the only element of this project to be constructed was the studio-house for Squire at 49 Glebe Place, which was paid for by Squire's sister, Mrs Evelyn Claude, who had married a Chilean coal magnate. He travelled to Buenos Aires in Argentina during its construction (probably to visit his parents in Chile). On his return in 1921, he moved into Glebe Place – from nearby Church Street – with his housekeeper.
It was the only work ever to be built in London by Mackintosh (who had a studio along the street at 43 Glebe Place). Given the control that Mackintosh liked to have over his designs, it is unlikely that Squire had a great degree of creative input in the project. Nevertheless, he sustained his own interest in decoration and, at the time, was helping to revive the art of marbling (as recorded in an article in *House & Garden* in 1921).

By 1926, Squire had left Glebe Place, and was probably living at 12 Edith Grove, a little further west along King's Road. He had maintained a studio there – next to that belonging to Malcolm Milne – since the end of the First World War. In the same year, he acquired Springhead, a former mill in Fontmell Magna, a village situated south of Shaftesbury, in Dorset. There he created a garden with help from a local gardener, Harold Woolridge. However, in 1930, he lost his money on the stock exchange and had to sell the estate, Lord Ivor Spencer-Churchill being the buyer. He returned to 12 Edith Grove, in London, living there through most of the 1930s. In 1933, he travelled again to Buenos Aires (probably to visit his mother in Chile, who died in the following year).

By 1939, Squire must have recovered something of his financial stability (possibly as the result of an inheritance), for in that year he built The Hundred, a large house between Henfield and Woodmancote in Sussex, which became his home for the remainder of his life. He probably moved there to be close to Malcolm Milne, who had lived in Henfield since 1926.

In 1946, Squire was reported to have 'been ill for some time', but he lived on until 1959. He made a bequest of £1000 to the Artists' Benevolent Fund to aid 'young, needy artist painters'.

SAM HARTLEY BRAITHWAITE

Samuel Hartley Braithwaite (1883-1947)

The artist and musician, Sam Hartley Braithwaite, first established himself in London as a performer and teacher, and then gradually as a composer, mainly of short, evocative works for piano or orchestra. Following his move to Bournemouth at the end of the First World War, he developed a parallel career as a painter and printmaker, in which he produced landscape watercolours and etchings of clarity, economy and brilliance.

Sam Hartley Braithwaite was born at West Croft, Main Street, Egremont, Cumberland (now Cumbria), on 20 July 1883, the fourth of six children of the surgeon, Samuel Braithwaite, and his wife, Eleanor Elizabeth (née Hartley).

By 1901, Braithwaite had moved to London, and was living at 8 Rossiter Road, Streatham. At this stage in his development, he trained not as an artist but as a musician. He attended the Royal Academy of Music, studying clarinet, organ and piano (the last under Cuthbert Whitemore), and composition (under Frederick Corder). As a clarinettist, he was awarded an Ada Lewis Scholarship in 1902, and performed in concerts that included the Bohemian Concert of the Cumberland and Westmorland Association of London at the Holborn Restaurant in 1905, and another at the Town Hall, Egremont, in 1906. While at the RAM, he became a close friend of his fellow student, the composer, Arnold Bax, and he would later receive the dedication of Bax's piano piece, *Apple Blossom Time* (1915).

Braithwaite remained at the Royal Academy of Music as a teacher of harmony and piano, numbering among his pupils the composer, Eric Coates, who was only three years his junior. From 1910 to 1913, he also worked as the musical director of the Passmore Edwards Settlement in Tavistock Place, an educational institution for the working classes in Bloomsbury (succeeding Gustav Holst in the position). During this period, he was living close by at 37 Tavistock Place, and attempting to establish himself as a composer.

In 1914, Braithwaite was appointed to the staff of Bournemouth School of Music. However, he may not have taken up the position until 1919, following the end of the First World War. In that year, he settled in Southbourne, Bournemouth (then in Hampshire), joining his parents, who had retired there, and his brother, Henry. From that time, he began to divide his energies between music and art, and developed as an accomplished visual artist. As an indication of his shift of focus, he published an article on 'The Ethical Dominant in John Ruskin' in *Current Opinion* in 1919, and began to lecture to local institutions of adult education on 'Some aspects of the Art Teaching of John Ruskin'.

Braithwaite's career as a composer blossomed, and some of his resulting works – including the scherzo, *A Night by Dalegarth Bridge* (1920) – were performed by the Bournemouth Municipal Orchestra (now the Bournemouth Symphony Orchestra). His *Snow Picture* for orchestra (1924) and *Elegy* for orchestra (1927) both won Carnegie Trust awards and were published as part of the Carnegie Collection of British Music. In January 1927, his article, 'Modern Music', appeared in *Music Quarterly*; attempting a balanced critique of new music, it included ambivalent comments on the music of his friend, Arnold Bax.

Braithwaite took some classes at Bournemouth School of Art, and worked increasingly as a painter and printmaker, specialising in landscapes. He joined, and exhibited with, a number of local art societies, including Eric Hesketh Hubbard's The Print Society (founded in 1919) and the New Forest Group (founded in 1923). Many of his subjects were of Hampshire and Dorset, though, in 1926, he also painted in Florence. Other of his paintings were more abstract, with titles that alluded to music, such as *Foxtrot* and *Pavan*, both of which were exhibited at the Arlington Gallery, Old Bond Street, London, in 1927. By 1931, he was exhibiting regularly with both the Bournemouth Arts Club and the Bournemouth Literature and Art Association. Exhibits at the latter included the transparent oil painting, *Marigolds* (1932), an indication of a further broadening of subject and approach.

By 1933 – when he was teaching at Bournemouth Conservatoire of Music – Braithwaite had moved to 'Hillingdon', Brunstead Road, Poole. He would live there with his mother, his brother, Henry, and his sister, Jessie. During the decade, he exhibited in London at the Fine Art Society (1932-37) and the Royal Academy of Arts (1933 & 1937). His second exhibit at the RA – a watercolour of Chepstow Castle – was reproduced in *The Sphere* on 18 December 1937.

During the Second World War, Braithwaite remained in Bournemouth and had some involvement with the Wessex Philharmonic Orchestra, as both a composer and a performer. However, he then returned to the Lake District and settled at Primrose Cottage, Carr Bank, Beetham, Westmoreland. He joined the Lake Artists Society, but died soon after on 13 January 1947.

His work is represented in the collections of the Royal Academy of Music; and Aberystwyth University School of Art.

ROWLAND HILDER

Rowland Frederick Hilder, OBE PRI RSMA (1905-1993)

A highly fluent watercolourist, Rowland Hilder became synonymous with the Kent countryside that he painted for much of his life. However, he was a wide-ranging painter and illustrator, who tackled cityscapes, marines and figure subjects with equal confidence and success.

Rowland Hilder was born on 28 June 1905 at Great Neck, Long Island, New York, the son of Kentish parents, Roland Hilder, a tour organiser for Americans visiting Britain, and his wife, Kitty (née Fissenden). He was first educated in Morristown, New Jersey. Following the return of his family to England in 1915, he lived in New Cross, South London, and attended Aske's Hatcham School. In 1921, he entered the etching class of Goldsmiths' College School of Art, but soon fell under the spell of E J Sullivan, an influential teacher of illustration. He was also influenced by Muirhead Bone and Frank Brangwyn. However, he was most interested in becoming a marine painter, and so tried to follow the example of W L Wyllie, teaching himself the art of watercolour. In 1929, he married his fellow Goldsmiths student, Edith Blenkiron, the daughter of a boot and shoe buyer. They would have a son, Anthony (who worked as an artist under the name Anthony Fleming), and a daughter, Mary.

Working as an illustrator from 1925, Hilder had his status boosted a decade later, in 1935, when he took the place of Sullivan at Goldsmiths' College. In the same year, he established his reputation as a watercolour painter of British landscapes with his first solo show at the Fine Art Society. He also exhibited at the Royal Academy of Arts and other London venues and, in 1938, was elected to the membership of the Royal Institute of Painters in Water-Colours (RI). During the Second World War, he worked first as a camouflage officer and, later, as an artist in the Central Office of Information.

In the post-war period, Hilder devoted an increased amount of time to painting. He set up the Heron Press to market his prints and Christmas cards, and by 1951 'was the most popular landscape artist of the time' (Alan Horne, *The Dictionary of 20th Century British Illustrators*, Woodbridge: Antique Collectors' Club, 1994, page 247). He worked with his wife, Edith, on the *Shell Guide to the Flowers of the Countryside* (1955), and produced paintings for the *Shell Guide to Kent* (1958), the first in the series of volumes devoted to counties. In 1960 the printing and publishing company of Royle took over the stock of the Heron Press and acted as distributor, while Hilder continued to produce many paintings for reproduction.

In 1963, Royle took over the Heron Press completely, and Hilder became its consultant art adviser. His career as a commercial illustrator virtually ended and 'he devoted his time to painting for painting's sake; the fact that much of his work was reproduced [being] almost incidental' (Horne, 1994: 247). He was elected as President of the RI in 1964 and published a number of manuals, including *Starting with Watercolour* (1966) and *Painting Landscapes in Watercolour* (1983). In 1986, he was awarded the OBE. He lived at Blackheath in London for many years and died at Greenwich on 21 April 1993. His wife, Edith, had died nine months earlier.

Further reading:
John Lewis, *Rowland Hilder: Painter of the English Landscape*, Woodbridge: Antique Collectors' Club, 1988;
Denis Thomas, 'Hilder, Rowland Frederick (1905–1993)', H C G Matthew and Brian Harrison (eds), *Oxford Dictionary of National Biography*, Oxford University Press, 2004, https://doi.org/10.1093/ref:odnb/52112

AVERIL BURLEIGH

Averil Mary Burleigh (née Dell), ARWS RI SWA (1882-1949)

The versatile art of the painter and illustrator, Averil Burleigh, is distinguished by its strong sense of design. Initially influenced by the Pre-Raphaelites and drawn to Mediaeval subject matter, she became increasingly known for her luminous temperas and watercolours.

Averil Burleigh was born Averil Dell in Hassocks, Sussex, in the third quarter of 1882, the third of five children of the upholsterer, Henry Dell, and his wife Hannah (née White), the daughter of an Essex miller and agricultural labourer. By 1891, Averil had moved with her family to West House, West Street, Ditchling, and by 1901 they had all settled at 27 St Michael's Place, Brighton. By that date, her father was working as an auctioneer as well as an upholsterer. She studied at Brighton School of Art.

In 1904, Averil Dell married the artist, Charles H H Burleigh, in Brighton, and they soon settled at 7 Wilbury Crescent, Hove, a house that they designed for themselves, and which included a top floor studio. They would have a son, Duncan (1905), and a daughter, Veronica (1909), the latter becoming a painter.

Averil Burleigh was an early and prominent member of the Sussex Women's Art Club, which was founded in Brighton in 1906. However, she became more widely established as the illustrator of *The Poems of John Keats* (Chapman & Hall, 1911) and three volumes of Greening & Co's series 'Novels from Shakespeare' (1913-15). Her colour plates – with their flat, outlined figures – revealed the influence of the Pre-Raphaelites and the Arts and Crafts Movement, and chimed greatly with the aesthetic of the magazine, *The Studio*, which featured six of her drawings in April 1913. By then, she had begun to exhibit at the Royal Academy of Arts, the Royal Institute of Painters in Water Colours, the Arts and Crafts Exhibition Society and the Paris Salon.

Gaining a reputation for her temperas and watercolours, Burleigh became a member of the Arts and Crafts Exhibition Society, the Society of Mural Decorators and Painters in Tempera, the Society of Women Artists and the Royal Institute of Painters in Water Colours (1929) and later an associate of the Royal Society of Painters in Water-Colours (1939). By 1933, she was Honorary Secretary of the Sussex Women's Art Club.

Burleigh held a joint exhibition with her husband at Hove Public Library in 1923, and two solo shows at the Fine Art Society, London, in 1925 and 1934. She also showed work with the Royal Institute of Oil Painters, the International Society, the New English Art Club, and the leading provincial societies.

In 1939, the Burleighs were recorded as living in Hove with their adult children. However, they spent most the Second World War in Betws-y-Coed, in Caernarfonshire, Wales.

Averil Burleigh died in Hove on 18 March 1949, and was survived by her husband and children. A memorial exhibition of her work was held later that year at Brighton Art Gallery.

Her work is represented in the collections of Brighton and Hove Museums and Art Galleries.

ALFRED HAYWARD

Alfred Robert Hayward, ARWS RP IS NEAC (1875-1971)

Alfred Hayward was a painter of landscapes, portraits and figure subjects in oil and watercolour, and also a mural decorator. His landscapes, in particular, show a strong influence of Impressionism, and his loose application of watercolour was especially suited to his studies of such aquatic subjects as the River Thames and the city of Venice, which he worked in on several occasions. Indeed, he had a great love of Italy and of travel in general and, in the years before the First World War, went as far afield as the West Indies and Central America.

Alfred Hayward was born in Hackney, London, on 21 February 1875, the second of five children, and the eldest son, of the tax collector and farmer, Richard Hayward, and his wife, Susannah (née Blake), a former draper's assistant. Within a few months of his birth, the family settled at The Mount (also known as Quiddleswell Mount), Hooe, a village near Bexhill-on-Sea, in Sussex. He was educated privately.

Hayward studied at the National Art Training School, South Kensington, from 1891 to 1894, and at the Slade School of Fine Art, under Fred Brown, Wilson Steer and Henry Tonks, from 1895 to 1897. He began to exhibit in London from 1896, and mainly at the Royal Academy of Arts, the Royal Society of Portrait Painters and the New English Art Club (becoming a member of the last in 1910). During these years, he lived at a variety of addresses, mostly in Chelsea, including the King's Road (1901-11) and Church Street (1912-14). In 1912, he married Cicely Kettle, the daughter of a New Zealand judge, and secretary to the Impressionist painter, James Bolivar Manson, who was then Clerk to the Tate Gallery (and would later become, in the Tate's own evaluation, its 'least successful' Director). The Haywards would have one daughter.

Before the First World War, Hayward travelled not only to France and his beloved Italy (first visited in 1909) but beyond Europe, and took in the West Indies and Central America. He also showed work internationally in Paris, Rome, Venice and Pittsburgh.

From the outbreak of war, in 1914, Hayward served in the Artists' Rifles, becoming, in 1916, a Second Lieutenant in the Anti-Aircraft Unit of the Royal Garrison Artillery, and, in 1917, a Lieutenant. During the last few months of the war, in 1918-19, he worked as an official war artist, producing studies of soldiers at Charing Cross Station and more formal portraits. He also assisted William Orpen in the laying in of his official war portraits.

Hayward returned to Chelsea at the end of the war, and embarked on the most successful decade of his career, during which he often painted with his former teacher, Wilson Steer, and their friend, Ronald Gray. In 1923, he fulfilled a commission from the Bank of England to produce a decorative panel representing the First Governor for display in the Royal Exchange. Then, in the January of the following year, he held his first solo show, an exhibition of Venetian paintings and watercolours, at the Leicester Galleries. He was elected to the Royal Institute of Oil Painters in 1928 and the Royal Society of Portrait Painters in 1929.

Following the death of his father in 1931, Hayward inherited Quiddleswell Mount, Hooe, and made it his home. His income is said to have dipped sharply during the 1930s, but he continued to paint and to show work, including at a solo show at Wildenstein Galleries, in London, in 1936. He also painted the safety curtain for the stage of the De La Warr Pavilion, in nearby Bexhill-on-Sea, in 1939. By that date, he had separated from his wife, and she was living in London with her former employer, James Bolivar Manson; she later changed her name by deed poll to 'Elizabeth Manson'.

Though he was awarded a Civil List Pension in 1943, Hayward remained in financial straits and so sold Quiddleswell Mount in 1948. He then moved to Hampton-on-Thames, where he lived at various addresses, the last of which would be 14 Manor Gardens. In his later years, he taught painting and drawing from life at the City and Guilds School of Art. He retained respect within the artistic community, and was elected an Honorary Life Member of the NEAC in 1957 and an associate of the Royal Society of Painters in Water-Colours in 1960, also becoming a Freeman of the City of London. In November 1962, a dinner was held in his honour at the Chelsea Arts Club, of which he had long been an enthusiastic member. Retrospective exhibitions of his work were held at the Federation of British Artists in 1964 and 1967, and at the Edward Harvane Gallery, also in London, in 1970. He died on 2 January 1971.

His work is represented in numerous public collections, including the Imperial War Museums.

NORMAN JANES

Norman Thomas Janes, RWS RE RSMA (1892-1980)

Norman Janes was a wide-ranging painter and printmaker, who had a particular affinity with the London scene, from the busyness of railway stations and Thames embankments to the tranquil spots around his Hampstead home.

Norman Janes was born in 18 Grange Road, Egham, Surrey, on 19 May 1892, into a Methodist family, and was the younger son of the draper, Arthur T Janes, and his wife, Ada (née Croxson). He studied commercial art at the Regent Street Polytechnic School of Art, during the years 1909-14, while working as a freelance advertising designer.

Following the outbreak of the First World War in 1914, Janes served as a Corporal with the London Irish Rifles, and later as a Second Lieutenant with the Royal Irish Regiment. Experiencing action in France, he was wounded at the Battle of Cambrai in 1917. It was probably at this time that he met Dr Oliver Gotch, medical officer of the Queen Alexandra Hospital Home for disabled soldiers in Roehampton. They became good friends, and in later years went on sketching tours of Southern England and Northern France.

At the end of the war, Janes studied drawing and painting under Henry Tonks at the Slade School of Fine Art, alongside his future wife, Barbara Greg (1919-22). He then learned the skills of etching and engraving under W P Robins, in evening classes at the Central School of Arts and Crafts, (1922-23), and under Sir Frank Short and Malcolm Osborne at the Royal College of Art (1923-24). Printmaking would prove an important focus of his early career.

From 1921, Janes exhibited with many of the leading London societies, including the Royal Academy of Arts, the Royal Society of Marine Artists, the Royal Society of Painters in Water-Colours, the Society of Wood Engravers, the International Society, the New English Art Club. He also showed work in the provinces and abroad. He held a solo show at the Beaux Arts Gallery, London, in 1932. He was elected an associate of the Royal Society of Painter-Etchers and Engravers in 1922, and a full member in 1938.

In 1925, Janes married Barbara Greg at her home in Cheshire, and they settled in Hampstead, living at 2 Branch Hill from 1929 until 1961. Both working as illustrators, they sometimes collaborated, as in a series of engravings that they produced for the Aeolian Company as decorations for piano rolls. They would have one son and two daughters. He helped support the family by teaching etching and wood engraving at Hornsey School of Art (1928-60) and the Slade School (1936-50).

On the outbreak of the Second World War, Janes applied to become an official war artist, and, while he did not do so, the Imperial War Museum would purchase some of his works. He also contributed some drawings to the Recording Britain scheme, including two of Hampstead. Between 1941 and 1945, he served in the Royal Air Force, including three years in the Middle East (during which time he was mentioned in despatches).

At the end of the war, in 1945, Janes held a second solo show at the Beaux Arts Gallery, and began to serve as Honorary Secretary of the RE (until 1962). He was elected to the Society of Wood Engravers (1952) and, working increasingly as a painter, to the Royal Society of Painters in Water-Colours (ARWS 1957, RWS 1966). Further solo shows were held in Middlesborough (1962) and Clifton (1975).

Living in his later years at 70 Canonbury Park South, Norman Janes died on 23 September 1980. His wife and children survived him.

His work is represented in the collection of the Government Art Collection and numerous public collections, including the British Museum, the Imperial War Museums, the National Maritime Museum, Southwark Heritage and the V&A.

Further reading:

Elizabeth Grice, *Norman Janes: Wood Engravings and the Man*, Stonehouse: Evergreen Press, 2014

EDWARD STEEL HARPER

Edward Steel Harper, RBSA (1878-1951)

The work of the Birmingham artist, Edward Steel Harper, possesses a distinctive quality that combines late Pre-Raphaelitism with something more modern.

Though very little has been written about his life and works, Edward Steel Harper is known as a landscape painter in oil. He produced work that possesses a distinctive quality that combines late Pre-Raphaelitism with something more modern.

Edward Steel Harper was born in Handsworth, Birmingham on 11 June 1878, living much of his life at 55 Moorpool Avenue, in the Birmingham suburb of Harborne.

Harper was the eldest of three children, all of whom became professional artists following family tradition. He was the son of Edward Samuel Harper (1854-1941), a portrait, figure and genre painter, who had a significant role in the artistic life of Birmingham. He was Honorary Secretary and Professor of Anatomy at the Royal Birmingham Society of Artists (RBSA), Director of the Life Academy at Birmingham School of Art (1880-1919) and Art Critic for the *Birmingham Post*.

Harper was educated locally at King Edward VI High School and studied at Birmingham School of Art. The origins of this institution lie with the RBSA, which founded this nationally significant government school in 1843. E R Taylor, who was a notably active headmaster from 1877 to 1903, later transformed the school to form the United Kingdom's first municipal college of art. The increased freedom that municipalisation entailed permitted the school to challenge centralised strategies of teaching methods, style and content, and to construct in part an alternative Arts and Crafts movement, working with physical materials.

His landscapes in oil show that Harper experimented with the 'wet white' technique, a method established by the Pre-Raphaelite painters where white flake is spread with a palette knife onto canvas and colour subsequently applied with sable brushes. Later in his career he became a skilled craftsman in both wood and metal. Each piece of his work is signed with a delicate monogram incorporating a harp, in part to distinguish himself from his father, who shared the same initials.

Elected a member of the RBSA in 1915, Harper later became Art Master of Wolverhampton Grammar School where he remained for many years, retiring in 1942. He was known to have produced 2000 pictures during his lifetime. His principal works include *The Breath of Spring* and *Woods by the Shore*, both of which were exhibited at the RBSA and were bought directly by Birmingham Art Gallery. It is suggested that he exhibited from 1920 to 1937, at a number of leading venues, including the Royal Academy of Arts, Royal Institute of Oil Painters, Walker Art Gallery in Liverpool, as well as the RBSA.

Edward Steel Harper died on the 5 April 1951.

His work is represented in the collections of numerous public collections, including Birmingham Museum & Art Gallery.

HARRY TITTENSOR

Harry Tittensor, RI (1887-1942)

Beginning his career as a ceramic painter and designer, Harry Tittensor concentrated on oils and watercolours from 1925. He then specialised in atmospheric topographical subjects, with and without figures, seeing himself as 'a translator of objects into light and shade, tone and colour' (Cole, Heap and Lynn, *York through the Eyes of the Railways*, York: National Railway Museum, 1994, page 41).

Harry Tittensor was born in Burslem, Staffordshire, on 20 April 1887, the son of the potter, Jarvis Tittensor, and his wife Hannah (née Cliffe). He began an apprenticeship with Doulton & Co in 1900, and also received training at Burselm School of Art. Developing into one of the most versatile artists employed by Doulton, he painted figures and landscapes on vases and other ceramics and, helping to establish a new figure department with the art director, Charles Noke, he designed a number of figurines, including *The Gainsborough Hat* (1915). For many years, he was also a designer with the Chromo Transfer Co in Burslem.

On 25 May 1912, Tittensor married May Wright, daughter of the engineer, Elijah Wright, at Burslem Parish Church. By that year, he was living at Newport House, Burslem, though by 1914 he had moved to 'Kingswood', Southlands Avenue, Wolstanton.

In 1925, Tittensor left Doulton & Co in order to concentrate on his work as a painter in oil and watercolour. Though he essayed a range of subjects, including portraiture and still life, he specialised in architectural and other topographical scenes, both British and Continental. Frequent among these are places in Normandy and Brittany, which he seems to have visited from the mid 1920s. These he exhibited most frequently at the Royal Academy of Arts, the Fine Art Society and the Royal Institute of Painters in Water Colours, becoming a member of the last in 1931. He also produced artwork for carriage posters for London and North Eastern Railways. As an educator, he taught at Burslem School of Art and the Wedgwood Institute, and contributed an article on 'Water-Colour and the Picturesque' to *The Studio* in 1935.

Living at the Boat House, Barlaston, by at least 1929, he died at Cheshire Joint Sanatorium in Loggerheads on 19 July 1942, at the age of 55. A memorial exhibition was held at the Russell Gallery of Hanley Museum.

His work is represented in the collections of Stoke-on-Trent Museums.

This entry is indebted to the website www.tittensor.com, which is maintained by Paul and Eileen Tittensor.

CHARLES HOLMES

Sir Charles John Holmes, VPRWS NEAC (1868-1936)

As a painter and printmaker, Charles Holmes is best remembered for the strong forms and clear light of his landscapes and industrial scenes of the North of England. He was also central to the artistic life of Britain in the early twentieth century, as a publisher, editor, critic, historian, professor and museum director.

Charles Holmes was born in Preston, Lancashire, on 11 November 1868, the elder son of the Rev Charles Rivington Holmes, vicar of St Michael's Church, Bromley-by-Bow, and his wife, Mary (née Dickson), the daughter of a Preston solicitor. He was the nephew of Sir Richard Rivington Holmes, the artist, curator, archaeologist and librarian at Windsor Castle. He was educated at St Edmund's School, Canterbury, and then, from 1883, at Eton College. In 1887, he won a Classical Scholarship to Brasenose College, Oxford.

Mainly self-taught as an artist, Holmes produced the first of his industrial scenes in 1889. In the same year, he settled in London, and began a career in publishing. He worked with his cousin, Francis Rivington; at the Ballantyne Press; with John Cumming Nimmo; and finally, between 1896 and 1903, managing the Vale Press with the artists, Charles Ricketts and Charles Shannon. Ricketts fostered his talents for drawing and painting, while William Strang encouraged him to learn to etch. During the 1890s, he executed more than 80 plates. In 1900, he began to exhibit at the New English Art Club. (His address at the time was 22 Markham Square, Chelsea.)

At the prompting of the poet and art historian, Laurence Binyon, Holmes contributed an article on the Japanese printmaker, Hiroshige, in September 1897, to the periodical, *The Dome*. Two years later, he published his first book on another Japanese artist, Hokusai. Soon, he was sharing the task of writing art criticism for *The Athenaeum* with Roger Fry. His first major book was *Constable and his Influence on Landscape Painting* (1902).

In 1903, Holmes married his cousin, the composer and violinist, Florence Mary Hill Rivington. Initially, they lived at 58 Kensington Park Road, moving to 73 Ladbroke Grove in 1907. They would have two sons. It was also in 1903 that Homes was approached by Roger Fry to support *The Burlington Magazine*, which had recently been founded. So he became the co-editor with Robert Dell (a position he retained until 1909). A year later, in 1904, he was appointed Slade Professor of Fine Art at Oxford and elected to the New English Art Club. In 1909, he held his first solo show at the Carfax Gallery, in London. His Slade lectures formed the basis of Notes on the *Science of Picture-Making* (1909) and *Notes on the Art of Rembrandt* (1911). As both artist and writer, he was well placed to write the catalogue for the ground-breaking exhibition, 'Manet and the Post-Impressionists', which was organised by Fry and held at the Grafton Galleries in 1910.

In 1909, Holmes became Director of the National Portrait Gallery (resigning from *The Burlington Magazine* and, a year later, the Slade Professorship in order to dedicate himself to its demands). He rehung the collection and initiated a national photographic record. For a year of the First World War, from 1914-15, he served in the Anti-Aircraft Corps of the Royal Naval Volunteer Reserve. (By then, he was living at 1 Pembridge Crescent, Notting Hill.)

In 1916, Holmes moved, somewhat reluctantly, to the National Gallery to take up its Directorship. Within the constraints of working with a board of amateurs, he achieved much to increase the public's understanding of the collection. He organised the photographic and publishing departments, and raised the standard of museum publications, most notably with the *Illustrated Guide to the National Gallery* (1921) and three catalogues of the various national schools of art (1923-27). Again, as a practising artist, he was able to contribute first-hand insights to discussions of technique and approach. He was knighted in 1921 and appointed KCVO in 1928, the year in which he retired from the National Gallery.

Holmes's own work as a painter was the subject of books by Michael Sadleir (1920) and his friend and collaborator, C H Collins Baker (1924). He was elected an associate of the Royal Society of Painters in Water-Colours in 1924 and a full member in 1929, and served for a while as its Vice President.

Holmes's final publication was the autobiographical *Self and Partners (Mostly Self)*, published in 1936. He died at his home, 19 Pembridge Gardens, late the same year, on 7 December 1936.

His work is represented in numerous public collections, including the British Museum, Tate and the V&A; the Ashmolean Museum (Oxford), the Harris Museum & Art Gallery (Preston), Manchester Art Gallery and Samlesbury Hall (Blackburn); Aberdeen Art Gallery; and the National Gallery of Victoria (Melbourne).

Further reading:

C H C Baker, rev Mark Pottle, 'Holmes, Sir Charles John (1868-1936)', H C G Matthew and Brian Harrison (eds), *Oxford Dictionary of National Biography*, Oxford University Press, 2004, https://doi.org/10.1093/ref:odnb/33953;
Lee Sorensen (ed), 'Holmes, C J, Sir', *Dictionary of Art Historians*, https://arthistorians.info/holmesc

THOMAS HENNELL

Thomas Barclay Hennell, RWS NEAC (1903-1945)

Thomas Hennell expressed his love of landscape and rural life in words and images that were at once accurate and intense. Late in his short career, he became an official war artist, and presented aspects of the international conflict through his unique vision, from Iceland to Java, where he is presumed to have been killed.

Thomas Hennell was born at the rectory attached to St Peter's Church, Ridley, Kent, on 16 April 1903, the second of four children of the Rev Harold Barclay Hennell and his wife, Ethel (née Thomas), the daughter of a surgeon in the Madras Medical Establishment, India. His mother had studied at the Slade School of Fine Art.

During the first nine years of his life, Hennell developed a strong attachment to Ridley and its rural surroundings. In 1912, he and his family moved to Ash Rectory, just a mile to the west of Ridley, and he was sent to Hildersham House, a preparatory school in Broadstairs, though was later removed. Between 1916 and 1920, he attended Bradfield College, Berkshire, his schooldays ending abruptly after he and his friend, John George, protested against compulsory games.

Moving to London to study art at Regent Street Polytechnic School of Art (1921-25), Hennell became influenced by the work and personality of the artist, Archibald Standish Hartrick. He was also greatly inspired by Marion Richardson who taught him in a final pedagogical year at the London Day Training College (1925-26).

Qualifying as an art teacher, Hennell worked at Kingswood School, Bath, and, for one day a week at King's School, Bruton (1928-32). During this time, he began to make drawings of country crafts and farm implements and, from 1932, painted full time. A friend of Edward Bawden and Eric Ravilious, he visited them and their families at Great Bardfield in Essex from 1931 while preparing the first book that he both wrote and illustrated, *Change in the Farm* (1934).

Despite his apparently successful development as an artist, Hennell suffered a nervous breakdown, following the rejection by Marion Richardson of his proposal of marriage. He was confined to Claybury Mental Hospital for three years (1932-35) and, while there, drew his fellow patients and wrote poetry. Following his release, he returned to Kent, and settled at Orchard Cottage, which stood across the fields from Ridley Rectory. In 1936, he published a volume of *Poems*.

For the next seven years, Hennell painted local rural scenes, and wrote and illustrated books. He collaborated with H C Massingham on four books, including *Country Relics* (1939), and with C H Warren on two: *The Land is Yours* (1943) and *Miles from Anywhere* (1944). The most astonishing of his own prose works is *The Witnesses* (1938), an account of his experiences in hospital. He also published an essay, 'In Praise of Watercolour', in the *Old Water-Colour Society Club* volume for 1943. For, in this period, he exhibited his watercolours regularly and was elected to the Royal Society of Painters in Water-Colours (ARWS 1938, RWS 1943) and the New English Art Club (1943).

Hennell produced images of South east England for Recording Britain, and in 1941-42 was commissioned by the Ministry of Information to record aspects of toolmaking and land work in wartime. When Eric Ravilious died in 1942, Hennell replaced him as official war artist in Iceland (1943), the work he produced there being exhibited at the National Gallery (1944). He was later sent to Holland and France (1944-45, attached to Royal Navy) and India and Burma (1945, attached to RAF). In 1945, he was captured by Indonesian terrorists in Java and is presumed to have been killed. His *The Countryman at Work* appeared in 1947, with a memoir by H C Massingham. Memorial shows were mounted at Leicester Museum and Art Gallery (1955) and the Imperial War Museum (1956).

His work is represented in the collections of the Government Art Collection and Imperial College, and numerous public collections, including Bethlem Museum of the Mind, Imperial War Museums, the National Maritime Museum, the Royal Air Force Museum, Tate and the V&A; Brighton Museum and Art Gallery, Bristol Museum and Art Gallery, Cheltenham Art Gallery & Museum, Ferens Art Gallery (Hull), Graves Gallery (Sheffield), Laing Art Gallery (Newcastle upon Tyne), Manchester Art Gallery and Southampton Art Gallery; and National Museum Wales (Cardiff).

Further reading:

Jessica Kilburn, *Thomas Hennell: The Land and the Mind*, London: Pimpernel Press, 2021;
Michael Macleod, *Thomas Hennell: Countryman, Artist, Writer*, Cambridge University Press, 1988

FRANK ARCHER

Frank Joseph Archer, RWS RE (1912-1995)

As both a painter and printmaker, Frank Archer combined his talent as a draughtsman with a sensitive understanding of light. His early work was highly structured, being rooted in his experience of the British School at Rome. Later, his handling became looser and his approach more personal, as he absorbed the inspiration of historic stained glass and mosaics in order to produce vividly-coloured visual parallels to music.

Frank Archer was born in Walthamstow, Essex, on 30 June 1912, the second of three children of the dispensing chemist, Joseph Archer, and his wife, Alberta (née Blackledge), the daughter of a warehouseman. From the time of the First World War, the family lived in Eastbourne, Sussex, and Frank was educated at Eastbourne Grammar School.

Showing a talent for art from an early age, Archer received the encouragement of his parents, and his father made him some of his first paints. While studying at Eastbourne School of Art (1928-32), he painted landscapes and buildings in watercolours, and figure subjects in oil. He then trained for an Art Teacher's Diploma in Brighton (1932-33), while taking evening classes in design at the local School of Art.

In 1934, a Free Studentship enabled Archer to take up a place at the Royal College of Art. While there, he experimented with a wide variety of media, and began to etch as well as paint. The prints that he produced as a student won him the Prix de Rome in Engraving (1938), and led to his election to the Royal Society of Painter-Etchers and Engravers (ARE 1940, RE 1960).

Though his stay in Italy was cut short by the outbreak of the Second World War, Archer was still greatly influenced by the artistic tradition and appearance of the country. So in his early paintings, he employed decorative, fresco-like compositions, into which he injected an edge of menace appropriate to the times. The strategy now seems to parallel the contemporary Neo-Romantic approach of an artist like Michael Ayrton.

In 1939, Archer married Celia Cole in Hailsham, Sussex. They would have one son and one daughter. He was called up in 1940, and served in the Royal Pioneer Corps.

At the end of the war, Archer began to teach at Eastbourne School of Art. In 1949, while he was considering a post at Leicester, Wilfred Fairclough suggested that he might join him on the staff of Kingston School of Art, which later became Kingston Polytechnic. He replaced Fairclough as head of the School of Fine Art in 1962, and remained in the position until 1973. His students included Charles Bartlett, who would become President of the Royal Watercolour Society.

Though Archer continued to use some kinds of printmaking, his essential development was as a painter with a breadth of vision. He harnessed his love of the intense colour of mediaeval stained glass and Byzantine mosaics in order to create visual abstractions of favourite works of music. However, he worked concurrently in a figurative mode, depicting a range of musicians in performance, from orchestra to soloist, and sustaining an interest in landscape. Regular visits to Italy, and a trip to Ghana in 1970, provided further inspiration.

Following his retirement from teaching in 1973, Archer bought a derelict school in a valley of the Brendon Hills, within Exmoor National Park. While there, he produced a large number of watercolours. Seven years later, he returned to Sussex, and eventually settled back in Eastbourne.

The Royal Society of Painters in Water-Colours elected him as a member (ARWS 1972, RWS 1976) and mounted retrospectives of his work at the Bankside Gallery (in 1990 and 1992).

His wife, Celia, died in 1990, and he himself died in Eastbourne on 31 March 1995.

WILLIAM HEATH ROBINSON

William Heath Robinson (1872-1944)

Heath Robinson is a household name, and a byword for a design or construction that is 'ingeniously or ridiculously over-complicated' (as defined by The New Oxford Dictionary of English, 1998, page 848). Yet, he was also a highly distinctive and versatile illustrator, whose work could touch at one extreme the romantic watercolours of a Dulac or Rackham, at another the sinister grotesqueries of a Peake, and at yet another the eccentricities of an Emett.

William Heath Robinson was born in Islington, North London, on 31 May 1872, the third of seven children of Thomas Robinson, chief staff artist of the *Penny Illustrated Paper*, and his wife, Eliza (née Heath), the daughter of an innkeeper. In the hope of becoming a landscape painter, he studied at Islington School of Art and the Royal Academy Schools, but soon followed his brothers, Charles and Tom, into the more secure profession of illustration. He contributed to periodicals from 1896 and, in the following year, began to illustrate books. In 1903, he married Josephine Latey, the daughter of John Latey, the art and literary editor of the *Penny Illustrated Paper*, who had died the year before. Settling initially in the Holloway Road, they would have four sons and one daughter.

Robinson established his position in 1902, marking his individuality with illustrations to his own book, *The Adventures of Uncle Lubin*, and ensuring his financial stability by making his first drawings for advertising. In this first phase, he worked almost exclusively in black and white, fully demonstrating his mastery of monochrome in *The Works of Francis Rabelais*. This appeared in 1904, just as Grant Richards, his main patron and the book's publisher, became bankrupt. However, he was able to work with other publishers, developing his use of colour in order to produce true gift books; these began with *Twelfth Night* (Hodder, 1908), and included his own story, *Bill the Minder* (Constable, 1912), and *A Midsummer Night's Dream* (Constable, 1914). He and his family lived in Pinner, Middlessex, for the decade from 1908 to 1918, then in Cranleigh, Surrey, before returning to North London in 1929.

Though Robinson competed with others in the field of the gift book, he remained the unparalleled practitioner of the comic image. He produced an increasing number of humorous drawings for magazines and, from the First World War, was acknowledged the most original illustrator of his time. To the general public, as represented by the popular press, he was known as the 'Gadget King', that is as the inventor of perversely logical contraptions that gently mocked the products of the industrial age and so endeared society to its own rapid rate of change. He exploited this persona, by appearing on radio and television, designing a house for the *Daily Mail* Ideal Home Exhibition (1934), and parodying the self-help manual in a series of books which began with *How to Live in a Flat* (written with K R G Browne, 1936). His major set of literary illustrations in this later period further blurred the distinction between fiction and reality: Norman Hunter's *The Incredible Adventures of Professor Branestawm* (1933) concerned an amiable, eccentric inventor. The events of the Second World War, as experienced on both sides of the English Channel, enabled him to sustain his powers of invention even into his final work.

He died in Highgate, North London, on 13 September 1944.

His work is represented in the collections of the British Museum, The Cartoon Museum, the V&A and the Heath Robinson Museum.

Further reading:

Geoffrey Beare, *The Art of William Heath Robinson*, London: Dulwich Picture Gallery, 2003;
Geoffrey Beare, *Heath Robinson Advertising*, London: Bellew, 1992;
Geoffrey Beare, *The Illustrations of W Heath Robinson*, London: Werner Shaw, 1983;
Langston Day, *The Life and Art of W Heath Robinson*, London: Herbert Joseph, 1947;
James Hamilton, *William Heath Robinson*, London: Pavilion Books, 1992;
Simon Heneage, 'Robinson, William Heath (1872-1944)', H C G Matthew and Brian Harrison (eds), *Oxford Dictionary of National Biography*, Oxford University Press, 2004, vol 47, pages 428-431;
John Lewis, *Heath Robinson. Artist and Comic Genius*, London: Constable, 1973

DAVID LOW

Sir David Alexander Cecil Low (1891-1963)

David Low was considered the most outstanding British political cartoonist of his generation. Able to capture recognisable likenesses with great economy, he produced the definitive image of a number of leading figures of the day. And he did so with a subtle combination of ridicule and insight, rather than exaggeration and condemnation. A key feature of his approach was the use of such symbols as the strong but stubborn TUC carthorse and the reactionary Englishman, Colonel Blimp.

David Low was born in Dunedin, New Zealand, on 7 April 1891, the third son of four children of the businessman, David Brown Low, and his wife, Jane (née Flanagan). Educated at the Boys' High School, Christchurch, he made his debut with the Christchurch political weekly, *The Spectator*, at the age of 11 and, in 1908, became the paper's political cartoonist. Later, he moved to the *Canterbury Times* (1910) and then the *Sydney weekly, The Bulletin* (1911). At *The Bulletin*, his technique benefited from the influence of Will Dyson and Norman Lindsay, so that his lampoon of the Australian Prime Minister, William Hughes, entitled *The Billy Book* (1918), proved to be a bestseller.

The success encouraged Low to move to England, in the following year, where he began to work for the *Star*, evening stablemate of the Liberal *Daily News*. He established himself with the device of the two-headed Liberal/Tory Coalition Ass. In 1920, he married Madeline Grieve Kenning, of New Zealand. They would have two daughters.

In 1927, Low became political cartoonist for the *Evening Standard* and, though a Socialist, was given full independence on what was a very Conservative publication. This freedom led to the creation, in 1934, of his most famous character, Colonel Blimp, the epitome of British Conservativism. During the 1920s and 30s, he also produced two series of literary and political caricatures for the *New Statesman*. On leaving the *Evening Standard*, he spent a short, unhappy time at the Daily Herald (1950-53) where, however, he did produce another of his most controversial images: the TUC cart-horse. With some relief, he was taken on by the *Manchester Guardian* in 1953 and remained there until his death in London on 19 September 1963.

Low's popularity as a newspaper cartoonist created, from very early on, a market for books of caricatures; those published around the period of the Second World War are particularly impressive examples of his incisive criticism. He has total command of his medium, both artistically and intellectually, and was considered the most outstanding British political cartoonist of his generation. This position was officially acknowledged in 1962, when he was knighted.

His work is represented in numerous public collections, including the British Museum, the National Portrait Gallery and the V&A; and the British Cartoon Archive, University of Kent (Canterbury). His papers are in the Beinecke Library (Yale University).

Further reading:
Marguerite Mahood, 'Low, Sir David (Alexander Cecil) (*b* Dunedin, April 7, 1892; *d* London, Sept 20, 1963)', *Grove Art Online*, 2003, https://doi.org/10.1093/gao/9781884446054.article.T052166;
Colin Seymour-Ure, 'Low, Sir David Alexander Cecil (1891–1963)', H C G Matthew and Brian Harrison (eds), *Oxford Dictionary of National Biography*, Oxford University Press, 2008, https://doi.org/10.1093/ref:odnb/34606;
Colin Seymour-Ure and Jim Schoff, *David Low*, London: Secker & Warburg, 1985

THOMAS MONNINGTON

Sir Walter Thomas Monnington, PRA NEAC (1902-1976)

One of the outstanding draughtsmen of his generation, Thomas Monnington gained a particular reputation for his figure compositions, both easel paintings and large-scale decorations. His cool, analytical approach was honed at the Slade School – where he would return to teach – and was influenced by his encounter with artists of the Italian Quattrocento, while at the British School at Rome. That approach would later affect both his decision to turn to abstraction, and the appearance of the works that resulted. Able as an administrator as well as an artist and teacher, he became one of the most effective Presidents of the Royal Academy.

Thomas Monnington was born in Westminster, London, on 2 October 1902, the younger son of the barrister, Walter Monnington, and his wife, Catherine (née Brown), who had trained as a painter in Paris. He grew up at Seaford, Sussex, and was educated at St Peter's School, Seaford, and Brunswick School, Haywards Heath. However, at the age of 12, he developed heart trouble, and was invalided for a year, during which time he concentrated on his talent for drawing and painting, encouraged by his mother. He then spent 18 months at a farm school near Ross-on-Wye, Herefordshire.

Monnington spent a brief period of 1917 at the London School of Art before he enrolled at the Slade School of Fine Art in January 1918. Of his teachers, Henry Tonks proved especially influential on his development, and encouraged him to specialise in decorative painting.

In 1922, Monnington won the scholarship in decorative painting offered by the British School at Rome. In the following year, he arrived in Italy and spent much of his time travelling in Tuscany and Umbria, absorbing the influence of the work of artists of the Quattrocento. In 1924, he married the painter, and fellow Rome Scholar, Winifred Knights in Rome; they would have one son. They rented the top floor of a villa in Piediluco, Umbria, and he began to paint *Allegory* (Tate), the masterpiece of his early period. In April to October 1925, another of his paintings, entitled *Winter*, and its cartoon were exhibited at the International Exhibition of Modern and Decorative Industrial Art, held at the Grand Palais in Paris.

Late in 1925, the Monningtons returned to England and lived initially at 33a Oxford Road, Putney. Thomas taught part-time at the Royal College of Art, and began to work on commissions for murals for St Stephen's Hall, Westminster (1926-28), and the new Bank of England (1928-37). In 1926, he joined the Faculty of Painting of the British School at Rome.

In March 1928, the Monningtons moved into Studio A, 1 The Vale, the ground floor of Tonks's house in Chelsea. Thomas joined the NEAC in 1929, but resigned two years later, having not exhibited there. Instead, in 1931, he began to exhibit at the Royal Academy of Arts, and that became the main showcase for a range of his work (including portraits), and gradually the centre of his professional life. Immediately, he was elected an associate of the RA and was appointed first assistant teacher at the RA Schools (until 1939). In 1938, he became a full Royal Academician.

Following the death of Tonks in 1937, he and his family had moved to Leyswood, Groombridge, Tunbridge Wells, Kent. The local landscape would inspired much of his later work.

On the outbreak of the Second World War in 1939, Monnington joined the design team of the Ministry of Camouflage in Leamington Spa, and became responsible for the camouflage of aircraft production airfields. Then, from November 1943, he worked as an official war artist with the Royal Air Force. He documented the war from the air and undertook further commissions from the Ministry of Air Transport.

When the war ended, Monnington began to teach at Camberwell School of Arts and Crafts (until 1949), and became a member of the Executive Committee of the British School at Rome (until 1972), and for a period was the Chairman of its Faculty of Painting (1948-67). Between 1949 and 1967, he also taught at the Slade School. His first wife, Winifred Knights, died in 1947 and, later the same year, he married Evelyn Hunt, the daughter of a mining engineer and silver prospector. They would have one son.

By the late 1940s, Monnington had changed approach, and was producing geometric, abstract compositions, both as easel paintings and decorative schemes. It remained grounded in his love of early Italian art, but was also influenced by his wartime experiences and his scientific interests. Major projects in the later style include the ceilings of the Conference Hall in Vincent Harris's Council House, in Bristol (1954-56), and the Mary Harris Memorial Chapel, Exeter University (1956-58).

During the 1960s, Monnington was appointed to a number of administrative positions, including a Trustee of the British Museum (1963-69). They culminated in his becoming President of the Royal Academy in 1966, a role that he undertook most effectively, by helping to turn around the institution's ailing fortunes. Among other honours, he was knighted in 1967. He died in office in London on 7 January 1976. A memorial exhibition was held at the Royal Academy in 1977.

His work is represented in numerous public collections, including the Imperial War Museums, Tate and the V&A.

Further reading:

Judy Egerton, 'Monnington, Sir (Walter) Thomas (1902-1976)', H C G Matthew and Brian Harrison (eds), *Oxford Dictionary of National Biography*, Oxford University Press, 2004, https://doi.org/10.1093/ref:odnb/31455

MERVYN PEAKE

Mervyn Peake (1911-1968)

Though already developing as a painter, Mervyn Peake established himself as a writer and illustrator in 1939, with *Captain Slaughterboard Drops Anchor*, a comic fantasy intended for children. This revealed that he had an outstanding talent for the grotesque, and was ready to align himself to Romantic tendencies in British art. He applied that talent to a broad range of visual and verbal forms, central to which was his 'Gormenghast' trilogy, an extraordinary imaginative achievement detailing a parallel world.

Mervyn Peake was born on 11 July 1911 in Kuling, Central Southern China, the summer residence of his father. He was the younger son of the missionary doctor, Ernest Cromwell Peake, and his wife, Amanda (née Powell), a missionary nurse. In the calm following the Communist Revolution, the Peake family settled in Tientsin (now Tianjin), close to Peking. Apart from a sojourn in England during the First World War, Peake spent all his early years there, so that its landscape and way of life retained a strong hold on his imagination.

In 1923, the family finally settled permanently in England, and Mervyn attended Eltham College, Kent, where he excelled at drawing. He then studied at Croydon School of Art (1929) and the Royal Academy Schools (1929-32), where he won the Arthur Hacker Prize (1930). While still a student, he exhibited for his one and only time at the Royal Academy (1931). He then joined an artists' colony on the Channel Island of Sark, in order to write and paint. He exhibited with the group on the island and, in 1934, in London at the Cooling Galleries.

On his return to England in 1935, Peake spent three years as a part-time teacher at the Westminster School of Art; while there, he held his first solo show, at the Calmann Gallery (March 1937), and married a student of the art school, the painter, Maeve Gilmore (in December of the same year). Their three children – Sebastian, Fabian and Clare – would appear frequently in his drawings.

In 1939, Peake published his first book *Captain Slaughterboard Drops Anchor*, an illustrated comic fantasy. This revealed him as an illustrator with an outstanding talent for the grotesque, ready to align himself to Romantic tendencies in British art.

While serving in the army, from 1940, Peake concentrated less on painting than on writing and illustrating, and began to work on *Titus Groan*, the first novel of his famous Gormenghast trilogy. Following his discharge as an invalid, in 1943, he completed the novel and published his acclaimed illustrations to *The Rime of the Ancient Mariner* (1943). He was soon considered 'the greatest living illustrator' (John Watney, *Mervyn Peake*, London: Michael Joseph, 1976, page 121). His illustrative projects from this time include *Witchcraft in England* by Christina Hole (1945) and *Dr Jekyll and Mr Hyde* (1948) and contributions to *Radio Times* and, of his own writings, *Rhymes without Reason* (1944) and *Titus Groan* (1946). In 1945, he also visited Germany for *Leader* magazine to record the war-time devastation, and made drawings at Belsen which profoundly affected his later work.

Peake then returned to Sark, with his family, for a period of three years (1946-49), during which he wrote *Gormenghast*; published in 1950, it received both the Heinemann Award for Literature and a prize from the Royal Society of Literature in the following year. The final volume of the trilogy, *Titus Alone*, was published in 1959. Through the 1950s, he taught drawing at the Central School of Arts and Crafts. But, from the middle of the decade, he suffered from Parkinson's disease which made work increasingly difficult. He completed his illustrations to Balzac's *Droll Stories* (1961) and his own *The Rhyme of the Flying Bomb* (1962) only with his wife's help and encouragement. He died on 17 November 1968 after spending the last four years of his life in hospital.

His work is represented in numerous public collections, including the Imperial War Museum; and the Wordsworth Trust (Grasmere). The Mervyn Peake Archive, which includes original drawings, is held by the British Library.

Further reading:

John Batchelor, *Mervyn Peake. a biographical and critical exploration*, London: Duckworth, 1974;
Colin Manlove (rev Clare L Taylor), 'Peake, Mervyn Laurence (1911-1968)', in H C G Matthew and Brian Harrison (eds), *Oxford Dictionary of National Biography*, Oxford University Press, 2004, vol 43, pages 269-271;
John Watney, *Mervyn Peake*, London: Michael Joseph, 1976;
G Peter Winnington (ed), *Mervyn Peake. The Man and His Art*, London: Peter Owen Publishers, 2006;
G Peter Winnington, *Vast Alchemies. The Life and Work of Mervyn Peake*, London: Peter Owen Publishers, 2000;
Malcolm Yorke, *Mervyn Peake: My Eyes Mint Gold: A Life*, London: John Murray, 2000

FELIKS TOPOLSKI

Feliks Topolski (1907-1989)

The significance of Feliks Topolski is suggested by those projects that were closest to his heart: the regular broadsheet, *Topolski's Chronicle* (1953-82), and the sequence of murals, *Memoir of the Century* (1975-89); for his drawings and paintings comprise a uniquely comprehensive yet impartial record of the age in which he lived. He employed a swift, expressionist style for all of his projects, from illustrations to stage designs. This gave an emotional unity to his oeuvre, and even the smallest of his figures – such as a vignette for his edition of Bernard Shaw's *Pygmalion* (1941) – seems to speak volumes.

Feliks Topolski was born Felicjan Typlel-Topolski in Warsaw, Poland, on 14 August 1907, the only child of the actor-manager, Edward Topolski, and his wife, Stanislawa Drutowska (who later divorced and remarried). From an early age, he witnessed many of the country's turbulent political events, and depicted them in some of his first drawings, his artistic talent being nurtured by his mother. Educated at Mikołaj Rey School (until 1925), he studied under Tadeus Pruszkowski, first privately and then at the Warsaw Academy of Fine Art (1927-32); particularly significant to his development was the summer school that Pruszkowski ran at Kazimierz. He also served as a cadet at the Artillery Officers' School, receiving a commission as a second lieutenant in the Artillery Reserve (the influence of his mother's second marriage to an army officer). While still a student, he began to contribute cartoons to the *Cyrulik Warszawski* (The Warsaw Barber), and then gradually to other periodicals. A series of journeys across Europe, to Italy, France and other countries – that began in 1933 – informed both his political awareness and artistic skills.

In 1935, Topolski received a commission from *Waidomosć i Literackie* (Literary News) to go to Britain to record King George V's Silver Jubilee. Attracted by what he considered the country's 'exoticism', he settled in London, and associated with a group of writers that included Graham Greene. He contributed illustrations to *Night and Day*, the short-lived magazine co-edited by Greene, and the newspaper, the *News Chronicle*. Drawings made for the latter were collected in *The London Spectacle* (1935), described in the introduction by D-B Wyndham Lewis as 'his first series of English impressions'. George Bernard Shaw became a particular admirer of Topolski's work, calling him 'perhaps the greatest of all impressionists in black and white', and asking him to illustrate three of his plays: Geneva, *In Good King Charles's Golden Days* (both 1939), and *Pygmalion* (1941). His *Portrait of GBS* would be published in 1946.

Following the outbreak of the Second World War, in 1939, Topolski remained in London. While nominally serving as an officer in the Polish army, he became official war artist to the Polish government in exile and then also an official war artist for the British. In this latter capacity, he recorded bombed London streets during the Battle of Britain and the Blitz, in May 1941, receiving serious wounds and spending six weeks in hospital. His work resulted in the book, *Britain in Peace and War* (1941). In August of the same year, he received a commission from *Picture Post* to travel to Russia as a member of the first allied Arctic convoy to Russia, arriving in Moscow as the German army advanced towards the city. *Russia in War* was published in 1942. Further travels took in Egypt and the Levant, and India, Burma and China. In the final year of the war, he accompanied the Polish 2nd Corps in the advance up the Adriatic coast, and other Polish forces in the Low Countries. He was in Bergen-Belsen concentration camp two weeks after its liberation in April 1945, and later worked as an official war artist at the Nuremberg Trials. The record of these years appeared as *Three Continents 1944-45* (1946). In 1944, he had married the actress, Marian Everall. They would have a son and a daughter; the son, Daniel, became well known as the successful coach of the Oxford University boat crews.

While becoming a British subject in 1947, Topolski continued to survey and travel the world. In 1948, he attended both the Congress of Europe in The Hague (for Vogue) and the International Congress of Intellectuals for Peace in Wroclaw, Poland, and, as a result, produced *Confessions of a Congress Delegate* (1949). However, the return to his war-ravaged homeland had proved particularly painful. From 1949 into 1950, he made an extended tour that took in India, Burma, Indochina, Macao, Singapore, Japan and the United States, during which he was often treated like a foreign dignitary, so gaining access to people and places withheld from foreign journalists. Topolski's talents enabled him to develop his drawings into large-scale paintings without any loss of immediacy or passion. This is exemplified by *The Cavalcade of the Commonwealth*, a commission for the Festival of Britain of 1951, which Topolski based on drawings that he made on his recent tour. Similarly, he returned to the drawings that he made during the Coronation of Elizabeth II, on 2 June 1953, to fulfil a commission from the Duke of Edinburgh, in 1958, to produce a mural that still hangs in Buckingham Palace.

During the Festival of Britain, *The Cavalcade of the Commonwealth* was displayed in an open arch of Hungerford Bridge, on London's South Bank. Soon after, Topolski moved his studio to an arch of Hungerford Bridge, and there, in 1953, began Topolski's *Chronicle*, a fortnightly visual record of events that, printed on rough brown paper, emulated broadsheets of the eighteenth and nineteenth centuries. He considered that he gave 'to it most of my energies in the following twenty/thirty years' (*Fourteen Letters*, London; Faber and Faber, 1988, [unpaginated]). It also provided the raw material for other projects, including portraits and, ultimately, his *Memoir of the Century*, a panoramic series of murals begun in 1975 and continued until his death, also housed in the arches of Hungerford Bridge. (It now provides the setting for a bar.) In 1975, his first marriage was dissolved, and he married the architect, Caryl Jane Stanley.

As a portraitist, Topolski worked on the title sequences of the pioneering BBC television series, *Face to Face* (1959-62), providing likenesses of the 33 iconic interviewees, from Augustus John to Adam Faith. (An accompanying book, with Topolski's images, was published in 1964.) Among other commissions, he received one from The University of Texas at Austin for – what turned out to be – an astonishing set of 20 portraits of 'Britain's Twentieth-Century Literary Greats' (1961-62) that included E M Forster, Aldous Huxley and Evelyn Waugh.

However, Topolski worked with such energy and speed that he was still able to travel widely, recording key events and institutions, including Pope Paul VI's visit to the Holy Land (1964), the start of Mao's Cultural Revolution in China (1966) and the workings of the United Nations in New York, the Democratic Convention riots in Chicago and a gathering of members of the Black Panther Party in San Francisco (1968). In 1969, the American television network, CBS, commissioned him to visit Moscow to record the May Day Parade, the resulting programme, based on his drawings, being shown in the United States over the Christmas. Further films followed, the last being *South American Sketchbook*, made with his son Daniel, for BBC television, in 1982. His final book, the idiosyncratic autobiography, *Fourteen Letters*, appeared in 1988.

Honours included the Gold Medal of the International Fine Arts Council (1955), a honorary doctorate from the Jagiellonian University of Cracow (1974) and election as a Royal Academician (1989).

Painting until a few days before his death, Feliks Topolski died in St Thomas's Hospital, London, on 24 August 1989.

His work is represented in the collections of the British Museum, the Imperial War Museum, the National Portrait Gallery, Tate, Topolski (the Southbank bar) and the V&A; the Museum Narodwe w Warszawie; and the Harry Ransom Research Center (University of Texas at Austin).

Further reading:

Joseph Darracott, rev, 'Topolski, (Felician) Feliks (1907-1989)', H C G Matthew and Brian Harrison (eds), *Oxford Dictionary of National Biography*, Oxford University Press, 2016, https://doi.org/10.1093/ref:odnb/39969

INDEX OF ARTISTS

Numbers in **bold** indicate the artist's biography page

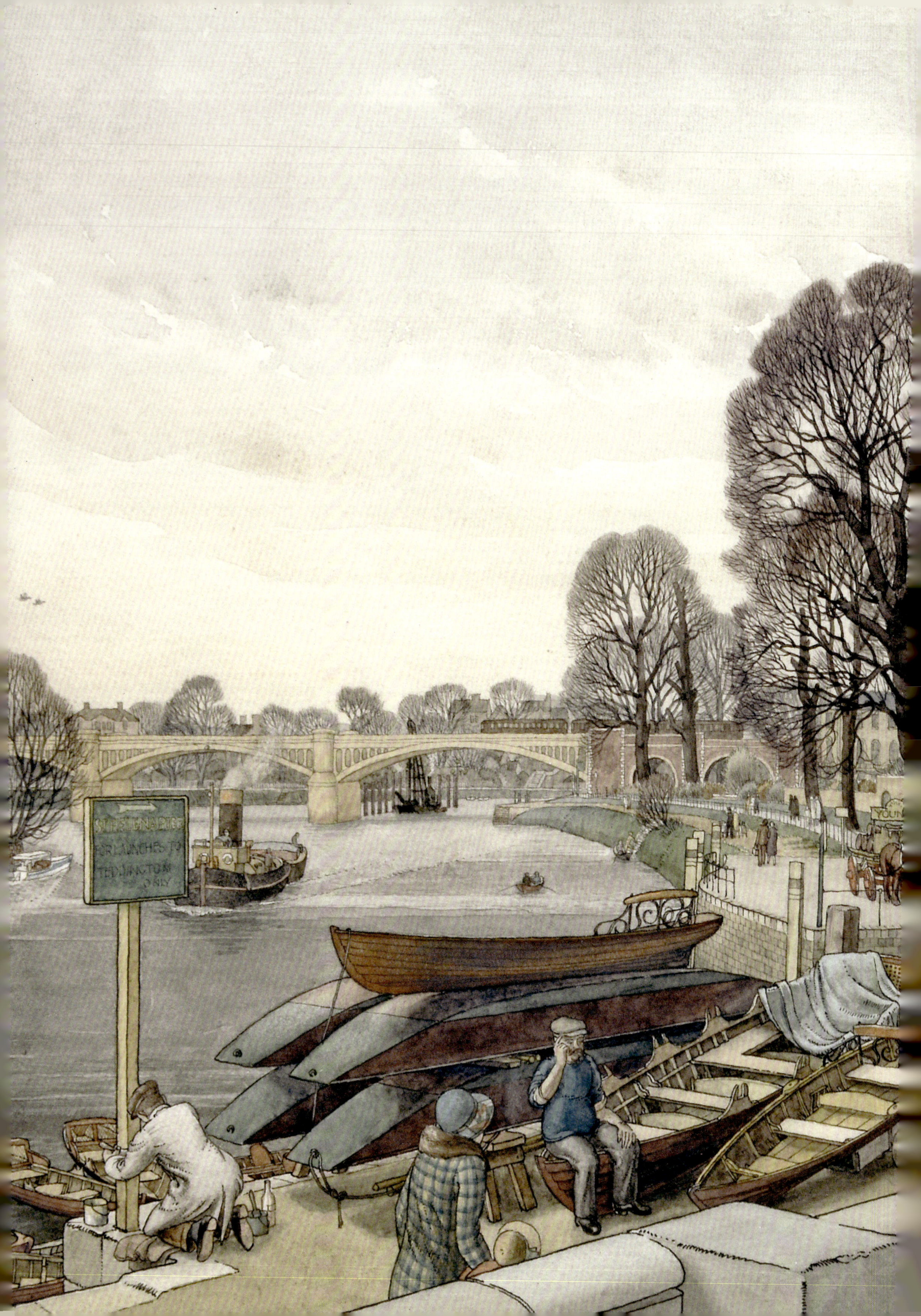